CONTEMPORARY AUDITING
REAL ISSUES AND CASES

Tenth Edition

CONTEMPORARY AUDITING
REAL ISSUES AND CASES

Tenth Edition

Michael C. Knapp
University of Oklahoma

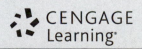

CENGAGE
Learning®

Australia • Brazil • Japan • Korea • Mexico • Singapore • Spain • United Kingdom • United States

CENGAGE Learning

Contemporary Auditing: Real Issues and Cases, Tenth Edition
Michael C. Knapp

Product Director: Rob Dewey

Product Manager: Matt Filimonov

Content Developer: Theodore Knight

Product Assistant: A. J. Smiley

Associate Marketing Manager:
Courtney Doyle-Chambers

Senior Marketing Manager:
Robin LeFevre

Senior Manufacturing Planner:
Doug Wilke

Art and Cover Direction, Production
Management, and Composition:
Integra Software Services Pvt. Ltd.

Intellectual Property

    Analyst: Christina Ciaramella

    Project Manager: Anne Sheroff

Cover Image: © iStockphoto.com/
Robert Churchill

> For product information and technology assistance, contact us at
> **Cengage Learning Customer & Sales Support, 1-800-354-9706**
>
> For permission to use material from this text or product,
> submit all requests online at **www.cengage.com/permissions**
> Further permissions questions can be emailed to
> **permissionrequest@cengage.com**

Library of Congress Control Number: 2014936225

ISBN: 978-1-285-06660-8

Cengage Learning
20 Channel Center Street
Boston, MA 02210
USA

Cengage Learning is a leading provider of customized learning solutions with office locations around the globe, including Singapore, the United Kingdom, Australia, Mexico, Brazil, and Japan. Locate your local office at:
www.cengage.com/global

Cengage Learning products are represented in Canada by Nelson Education, Ltd.

To learn more about Cengage Learning Solutions, visit
www.cengage.com

Purchase any of our products at your local college store or at our preferred online store **www.cengagebrain.com**

Printed in the United States of America
Print Number: 01   Print Year: 2014

DEDICATION

To Carol, Johnny, Lindsay, Jessi, and Emmie

BRIEF CONTENTS

CONTENTS

Arthur Edward Andersen established a simple motto that he required his subordinates and clients to invoke: "Think straight, talk straight." For decades, that motto served Arthur Andersen & Co. well. Unfortunately, the firm's association with one client, Enron Corporation, abruptly ended its long and proud history in the public accounting profession.

KEY TOPICS: history of the public accounting profession in the United States, scope of professional services provided to audit clients, auditor independence, and retention of audit workpapers.

Wall Street was stunned in September 2008 when this iconic investment banking firm filed for bankruptcy. Lehman's bankruptcy examiner charged that the company had engaged in tens of billions of dollars of "accounting-motivated" transactions to enhance its apparent financial condition.

KEY TOPICS: "accounting-motivated" transactions, materiality decisions by auditors, responsibility of auditors to investigate whistleblower allegations, auditors' legal exposure, communications with audit committee.

In the fall of 1999, just a few months after reporting a record profit for fiscal 1998, Just for FEET collapsed and filed for bankruptcy. Subsequent investigations by law enforcement authorities revealed a massive accounting fraud that had grossly misrepresented the company's reported operating results. Key features of the fraud were improper accounting for "vendor allowances" and intentional understatements of the company's inventory valuation allowance.

KEY TOPICS: applying analytical procedures, identifying inherent risk and control risk factors, need for auditors to monitor key developments within the client's industry, assessing the health of a client's industry, and receivables confirmation procedures.

The Private Securities Litigation Reform Act (PSLRA) of 1995 amended the Securities Exchange Act of 1934. This new federal statute was projected to have a major impact on auditors' legal liability under the 1934 Act. The first major test of the PSLRA was triggered by a class-action lawsuit filed against BDO Seidman for its 1995 audit of Health Management, Inc., a New York–based pharmaceuticals distributor.

KEY TOPICS: inventory audit procedures, auditor independence, content of audit workpapers, inherent risk factors, and auditors' civil liability under the federal securities laws.

Paul Polishan, the former chief financial officer of The Leslie Fay Companies, received a nine-year prison sentence for fraudulently misrepresenting Leslie Fay's financial statements in the early 1990s. Among the defendants in a large class-action lawsuit stemming from the fraud was the company's audit firm, BDO Seidman.

KEY TOPICS: applying analytical procedures, need for auditors to assess the health of a client's industry, identifying fraud risk factors, control environment issues, and auditor independence.

In January 2005, Thomas Trauger became the first partner of a major accounting firm to be sent to prison for violating the criminal provisions of the Sarbanes–Oxley Act of 2002

KEY TOPICS: identifying fraud risk factors, nature and purpose of audit workpapers, understanding a client's business model, criminal liability of auditors under the Sarbanes–Oxley Act, and collegial responsibilities of auditors.

Charles Keating's use of creative accounting methods allowed him to manufacture huge paper profits for Lincoln.

KEY TOPICS: substance-over-form concept, detection of fraud, identification of key management assertions, collegial responsibilities of auditors, assessment of control risk, and auditor independence.

"Crazy Eddie" Antar oversaw a profitable chain of consumer electronics stores on the East Coast during the 1970s and 1980s. After new owners discovered that the company's financial data had been grossly misrepresented, Antar fled the country, leaving behind thousands of angry stockholders and creditors.

KEY TOPICS: auditing inventory, inventory control activities, management integrity, the use of analytical procedures, and the hiring of former auditors by audit clients.

Barry Minkow, the "boy wonder" of Wall Street, created a $200,000,000 company that existed only on paper.

KEY TOPICS: identification of key management assertions, limitations of audit evidence, importance of candid predecessor–successor auditor communications, client confidentiality, and client-imposed audit scope limitations.

"You can't make up a story like this" observed a senior legal analyst for CBS News who tracked and reported on this outrageous financial fraud that involved a freewheeling executive who covertly used funds from the company he founded to finance his horse-racing hobby.

disarray. Drabinsky and several of his top subordinates used abusive accounting practices to conceal Livent's financial problems from their independent auditors.

KEY TOPICS: identifying audit risk factors, the role and responsibilities of an audit engagement partner, criminal and civil liability of auditors, hiring of auditors by clients, substance-over-form concept, and due diligence investigations by auditors.

The general manager of Buranello's set up a "sting" operation—with the owner's approval—to test the honesty of the employee who he believed was stealing from the business. But the plan backfired, and Buranello's eventually found itself on the wrong end of a "malicious prosecution" lawsuit.

Foamex's auditors repeatedly reported internal control problems to the company's management and audit committee. Because the company's management refused to adopt effective and timely measures to remediate those problems, Foamex became the first public company sanctioned by the SEC solely for having inadequate internal controls.

Two Boeing internal auditors disclosed information regarding alleged problems in their employer's internal controls to a newspaper reporter. After being fired, the two individuals filed lawsuits against Boeing under the whistleblowing provisions embedded in the Sarbanes–Oxley Act.

This case addresses the scandal triggered by the New York Times *article that alleged Walmart's Mexican subsidiary had routinely bribed government officials. The Pulitzer Prize–winning article focused on a wide range of internal control issues related to the alleged violations of the Foreign Corrupt Practices Act.*

Intrigue and espionage seem far removed from accounting . . . but not in this case. Creve Couer's CPA was actually a double agent. While providing accounting services to his client, the CPA also supplied incriminating evidence regarding the client to the IRS.

A financial fraud spelled the end of a company with a proud history and tested the ethics of several of its key management and accounting personnel.

Suzette Washington was a college senior majoring in accounting when she came face-to-face with an important ethical decision. Since accounting majors are entering a profession with a rigorous code of ethics, do they have a greater responsibility than other students to behave ethically?

Partners and employees of accounting firms often have access to confidential client information that they could use to gain an unfair advantage over other investors. In recent years, law enforcement authorities have filed insider trading charges against several public accountants, including a partner assigned to a professional services engagement for Freescale.

"To tell or not to tell" was the gist of an ethical dilemma faced by Wiley Jackson while completing a preemployment document for his future employer, a major accounting firm.

Should an accounting major accept an internship position with one firm when he has already decided to accept a job offer for a permanent position with another firm upon graduation?

The responsibility to maintain the confidentiality of client information obtained during a professional services engagement is at the center of a nasty disagreement that arises between two friends employed by a major accounting firm.

This case explores ethical issues raised by a pervasive earnings management scheme masterminded by Dell executives, including Michael Dell.

"Skimming" cash receipts ranks as one of the most common financial frauds. Accuhealth's chief accountant discovered that his superiors were skimming cash at certain of the company's retail outlets. What responsibility did the chief accountant have at that point?

This brief case revolves around the accounting firm that has been registered with the Texas State Board of Public Accountancy longer than any other firm. The ethical issues in this case stem from the untimely death of that firm's managing partner and the subsequent efforts of its surviving partners to liquidate his widow's equity interest in the firm.

SECTION 5   Ethical Responsibilities of Independent Auditors   369

A top executive of Cardillo pressured and manipulated three accountants, the company's controller, and two partners of public accounting firms, in an unsuccessful attempt to conceal the true nature of a fraudulent entry in the company's accounting records.

AIG is best known for receiving more federal "bailout" funds than any other company during the economic crisis that engulfed the U.S. economy beginning in the fall of 2008.

Several years earlier, AIG had been widely criticized for helping companies develop special purpose entities (SPEs) to "window dress" their financial statements. Surprisingly, Ernst & Young had partnered with AIG in developing and marketing that SPE "service."

Islamic companies are prohibited from engaging in transactions that violate Shari'a, that is, Islamic religious law. To ensure that they have complied with Shari'a, Islamic companies have their operations subjected to a Shari'a compliance audit each year. Recently, Big Four firms have begun offering Shari'a audit services.

Accountants sometimes find themselves in situations in which they must report unethical or even illegal conduct by other members of their organization. This case examines the trials and tribulations of an internal auditor who "blew the whistle" on his immediate superior for embezzling large sums of cash from their employer, the Washington, D.C., embassy of the United Arab Emirates.

"Environmental and labor practices" audits are one of many nontraditional services that major accounting firms have begun offering in recent years to generate new revenue streams. Ernst & Young provided such an audit for Nike, which had been accused of operating foreign "sweatshops." This case documents the unexpected challenges and problems that accounting firms may face when they provide services outside their traditional areas of professional expertise.

PREFACE

The past dozen years has been one of the most turbulent time periods in the history of the accounting profession and the independent audit function. Shortly after the turn of the century, the Enron and WorldCom fiascoes focused the attention of the investing public, the press, Wall Street, and, eventually, Congress on our profession. The Enron and WorldCom scandals resulted in the passage of the Sarbanes–Oxley Act of 2002 (SOX) and the creation of the Public Company Accounting Oversight Board (PCAOB). The SOX statute imposed a litany of new responsibilities and constraints on auditors of public companies, including the need to audit their clients' internal controls and prohibiting them from providing certain consulting services to their clients.

Next came the campaign to replace U.S. generally accepted accounting principles (GAAP) with International Financial Reporting Standards (IFRS). That campaign stalled when the subprime mortgage crisis in the United States caused global stock markets to implode and global credit markets to "freeze" during the fall of 2008. This economic downturn claimed many companies that had been stalwarts of the U.S. economy, the prime example being Lehman Brothers. Most of these companies, including Lehman Brothers, had received "clean" audit opinions on their financial statements one year or less before they collapsed.

As Congress and regulatory authorities struggled to revive the U.S. economy, news of the largest Ponzi scheme in world history grabbed the headlines in early 2009. Investors worldwide were shocked to learn that Bernie Madoff, an alleged "wizard of Wall Street," was a fraud. Law enforcement authorities determined that billions of dollars of client investments supposedly being held by Madoff's company, Madoff Securities, did not exist. The business press was quick to report that for decades Madoff Securities' financial statements had received unqualified audit opinions each year from a New York accounting firm. The auditing discipline absorbed another body blow in 2010 when a court-appointed bankruptcy examiner publicly singled out Lehman Brothers' former audit firm as one of the parties allegedly most responsible for the massive financial losses produced by the collapse of that Wall Street investment bank.

More recently, the aggressive regulatory stance taken by the PCAOB has resulted in public reprimands for several of the large accounting firms that dominate the auditing discipline. Additionally, the PCAOB's proposal to consider mandatory rotation for public company audit firms stirred a far-reaching controversy in the profession that ultimately prompted the U.S. Congress to weigh in on that issue.

As academics, we have a responsibility to help shepherd our profession through these turbulent times. Auditing instructors, in particular, have an obligation to help restore the credibility of the independent audit function that has been adversely impacted by recent events. To accomplish this latter goal, one strategy we can use is to embrace the reforms recommended years ago by the Accounting Education

Change Commission (AECC), many of which have been embraced by the more recent Pathways Commission, a joint project of the American Institute of Certified Public Accountants and the American Accounting Association. Among the AECC's recommendations was that accounting educators employ a broader array of instructional resources, particularly experiential resources, designed to stimulate active learning by students. In fact, the intent of my casebook is to provide auditing instructors with a source of such materials that can be used in both undergraduate and graduate auditing courses.

This casebook stresses the "people" aspect of independent audits. If you review a sample of recent "audit failures," you will find that problem audits seldom result from inadequate audit technology. Instead, deficient audits typically result from the presence of one, or both, of the following two conditions: client personnel who intentionally subvert an audit or auditors who fail to carry out the responsibilities assigned to them. Exposing students to problem audits will help them recognize the red flags that often accompany audit failures. An ability to recognize these red flags and the insight gained by discussing and dissecting problem audits will allow students to cope more effectively with the problematic situations they are certain to encounter in their own careers. In addition, this experiential approach provides students with context-specific situations that make it much easier for them to grasp the relevance of important auditing topics, concepts, and procedures.

The cases in this text also acquaint students with the work environment of auditors. After studying these cases, students will better appreciate how client pressure, peer pressure, time budgets, and related factors complicate the work roles of independent auditors. Also embedded in these cases are the ambiguity and lack of structure that auditors face each day. Aspects of the audit environment representing those two conditions that are woven into my cases include missing documents, conflicting audit evidence, auditors' dual obligation to the client and to financial statement users, and the lack of definitive professional standards for many situations.

The tenth edition of my casebook contains the following eight sections of cases: Comprehensive Cases, Audits of High-Risk Accounts, Internal Control Issues, Ethical Responsibilities of Accountants, Ethical Responsibilities of Independent Auditors, Professional Roles, Professional Issues, and International Cases. This organizational structure is intended to help adopters readily identify cases best suited for their particular needs.

My casebook can be used in several different ways. Adopters can use the casebook as a supplemental text for the undergraduate auditing course or as a primary text for a graduate-level seminar in auditing. The instructor's manual contains a syllabus for a graduate auditing course organized around this text. This casebook can also be used in the capstone professional practice course incorporated in many five-year accounting programs. Customized versions of this casebook are suitable for a wide range of accounting courses as explained later.

In preparing this edition, I retained those cases that have been among the most widely used by adopters. These cases include, among others, Enron Corporation, Golden Bear Golf, *Hopkins v. Price Waterhouse*, Lehman Brothers, Leigh Ann Walker, Madoff Securities, The Trolley Dodgers, and ZZZZ Best Company. You will find that many of the "returning" cases have been updated for relevant circumstances and events that have occurred since the publication of the previous edition.

New To This Edition This edition features 18 new cases. Three of these new cases are Comprehensive cases, including AA Capital Partners, DHB Industries, and Navistar International Corporation. The AA Capital Partners case focuses on the 2004 audits of a Chicago-based investment firm and its four private equity funds. AA Capital's auditors discovered $1.92 million of suspicious cash payments made to one of the firm's two cofounders, which was a small slice of the $24 million of funds embezzled by that individual from the firm. The SEC concluded that the auditors failed to properly investigate the suspicious cash payments they discovered, which, in turn, prevented them from uncovering the embezzlement scheme. Surprisingly, a federal judge subsequently ruled that the AA Capital audit engagement partner was not culpable because the audit manager on the engagement had failed to properly inform him of the suspicious payments discovered during the 2004 audits. After striking the sanctions that the SEC had recommended for the audit partner, the judge suspended the audit manager from practicing before the SEC for one year.

In July 2006, the founder and CEO of DHB Industries was dismissed by the company's board. Over the following year, a forensic investigation revealed that the company's impressive operating results from 2003 through 2005 had been the product of an accounting fraud. The CEO and two of his top subordinates had routinely altered DHB's accounting records to achieve earnings targets that he had established for the company. A major problem faced by the conspirators was concealing their misdeeds from the company's independent auditors. Accomplishing that objective was made easier by the fact that between 2001 and 2005 the company had four different accounting firms serve as its independent auditors. Frequent clashes between management and the company's auditors were responsible for the almost annual changes in auditors during that period.

As Navistar's 2005 audit was nearing completion, Deloitte, its audit firm, suddenly replaced the audit engagement partner. The new engagement partner effectively started the audit over, refusing to rely upon the work supervised by his predecessor. In April 2006, well after Navistar had missed its filing deadline for its annual Form 10-K with the SEC, Navistar dismissed Deloitte, which had served as its audit firm for 98 years. More than 18 months passed before the replacement audit firm, KPMG, completed the 2005 Navistar audit, which finally allowed Navistar to file its 2005 Form 10-K with the SEC. KPMG's audit was extended by a series of large accounting misstatements and internal control weaknesses discovered by the audit team. The PCAOB eventually launched an investigation of Deloitte's audits of Navistar, which was the first formal investigation of a Big Four accounting firm by that agency.

The Navistar case was apparently a key factor that prompted the PCAOB to suggest that mandatory audit firm rotation might be necessary to enhance auditor independence and the quality of independent audits.

Five of the new cases in this edition are included in two sections of my casebook that historically have been among the most popular: Audits of High-Risk Accounts and Internal Control Issues. New cases in the Audits of High-Risk Accounts section include LocatePlus Holdings Corporation, Powder River Petroleum International, and Take-Two Interactive Software. The executives of LocatePlus, a company with a New Age business model based upon a huge database containing information profiles for 98 percent of all U.S. citizens, used an Old School fraud scheme—imaginary revenues from fictitious customers—to deceive their auditors. The Powder River case highlights a Ponzi scheme involving the sale of "working interests" in oil and gas properties. Both the SEC and PCAOB chastened Powder River's independent auditors for their busted audits of the company. Take-Two produces *Grand Theft Auto*, the sixth best-selling video game "franchise" of all time and easily one of the most controversial thanks to its adult content. The Take-Two case revolves around inadequate audit tests applied to accounts receivable by the company's auditors and the father–son relationship that developed between Take-Two's audit engagement partner and the company's young founder.

The Boeing Company and Walmart de Mexico are the new cases in the Internal Control Issues section. The Boeing case examines the internal control and whistleblowing provisions of the Sarbanes–Oxley Act. Among other topics, the case questions require students to review the five components of the COSO internal control framework and to explain the difference between a "significant deficiency" and a "material weakness" in internal control. The Walmart de Mexico case raises internal control, auditing, and ethical issues stemming from Walmart's alleged violations of the Foreign Corrupt Practices Act (FCPA). Specific issues addressed by the case questions include internal control activities that may be effective in minimizing the risk of FCPA violations by public companies, the responsibility of auditors to detect and report illegal acts by clients, and the impact of differing cultural values on the ability of multinational companies to maintain proper internal control over their operations.

The two sections of my casebook that focus on ethical issues each have three new cases in this edition. The cases new to Section 4, Ethical Responsibilities of Accountants, include Accuhealth, Dell, and Wichita Falls. In Section 5, Ethical Responsibilities of Independent Auditors, I believe you will enjoy the new cases IPOC International Growth Fund; Richard Grimes, Staff Accountant; and Ryden Trucking. Accuhealth, a refurbished case that appeared in an earlier edition of my casebook, highlights an ethical dilemma faced by an accountant who stumbles upon evidence of an embezzlement ring masterminded by his new employer's top executives. The Dell case documents a pervasive earnings management scheme overseen by Michael Dell and his colleagues that involved huge "exclusivity payments" made to Dell, Inc. by its major supplier, Intel Corporation. My new Wichita Falls case examines ethical issues that the surviving partners of a Texas CPA firm faced after the death of the firm's managing partner.

The IPOC International Growth Fund case could serve as the basis for a Hollywood screenplay. That case centers on a KPMG employee who became an unwitting pawn in an international chess match of corporate espionage and murder that involved a close associate of Vladimir Putin, the Russian president at the time. Richard Grimes is an entry-level auditor who overhears a conversation between two client executives. That conversation involves a plan to withhold critical audit-relevant information from Grimes and the other members of the given company's audit team. Ryden Trucking is another refurbished case that appeared in a much earlier edition of my casebook. This case examines the thorny problems faced by an accounting firm when one of its audit staff employees embezzles cash from an audit client.

New cases in Section 7, Professional Issues, include Elizabeth Wallace, Audit Senior; Frank Coleman, Staff Accountant; and Olivia Thomas, Audit Senior. The Elizabeth Wallace case focuses on a social problem that has reached an epidemic level in our country and affects even professionals employed by major accounting firms, namely, prescription drug abuse. The Frank Coleman case addresses the huge class-action lawsuits that major accounting firms face for allegedly failing to compensate certain employees for the overtime hours that they have worked. An issue that is a taboo topic within most professional services firms—intra-office dating—is the orienting focus of the Olivia Thomas case.

The final case new to this edition is an international case, Longtop Financial Technologies Limited. In the spring of 2011, just as D & T Shanghai was completing its annual audit of Longtop, a Shanghai-based software company, allegations surfaced that company officials were fraudulently misrepresenting the company's financial data. A few days later, D & T Shanghai resigned as Longtop's auditor after determining that the allegations of fraud were true. The Longtop fraud focused attention on an issue that had been simmering in the United States for several years, namely, the refusal of the Chinese government to allow the PCAOB to inspect accounting firms, such as D & T Shanghai, that audit non-U.S. companies that have securities traded on U.S. stock exchanges. The international brouhaha stemming from the Longtop case escalated when D & T Shanghai refused to cooperate with the SEC's investigation of the Longtop fraud. D & T Shanghai officials insisted that an important Chinese federal statute precluded them from becoming involved in the SEC's investigation.

Organization of Casebook Listed next are brief descriptions of the eight groups of cases included in this text. The casebook's Table of Contents presents an annotated description of each case.

Comprehensive Cases Most of these cases deal with highly publicized problem audits performed by the major international accounting firms. Among the clients involved in these audits are Enron Corporation, Lehman Brothers, The Leslie Fay Companies, Livent, Madoff Securities, and ZZZZ Best Company. Each of these cases addresses a wide range of auditing, accounting, and ethical issues.

Audits of High-Risk Accounts In contrast to the cases in the prior section, these cases highlight contentious accounting and auditing issues posed by a single account or group of accounts. For example, the Jack Greenberg case focuses primarily on inventory audit procedures. The Take-Two Interactive Software case raises audit issues relevant to accounts receivable, while the Belot Enterprises case examines auditing issues pertinent to period-ending expense accruals.

Internal Control Issues The cases in this section introduce students to internal control topics relevant to the performance of independent audits. These topics are examined in a variety of different client contexts. For example, the Goodner Brothers case focuses on internal control issues for a wholesaler, while the Howard Street Jewelers case provides students an opportunity to discuss control issues relevant to retail businesses.

Ethical Responsibilities of Accountants Integrating ethics into an auditing course requires much more than simply discussing the AICPA's *Code of Professional Conduct*. This section presents specific scenarios in which accountants have been forced to deal with perplexing ethical dilemmas. By requiring students to study actual situations in which important ethical issues have arisen, they will be better prepared to resolve similar situations in their own professional careers. Three of the cases in this section will "strike close to home" for your students since they involve accounting majors. For example, in the Wiley Jackson case, a soon-to-graduate accounting major must decide whether to disclose in a preemployment document a minor-in-possession charge that is pending against him. Another case in this section, Freescale Semiconductor, addresses an embarrassing series of insider trading cases involving professional accountants.

Ethical Responsibilities of Independent Auditors The cases in this section highlight ethical dilemmas encountered by independent auditors. In the Cardillo Travel Systems case, two audit partners face an ethical dilemma that most audit practitioners will experience at some point during their careers. The two partners are forced to decide whether to accept implausible explanations for a suspicious client transaction given to them by client executives or, alternatively, whether to "complicate" the given engagement by insisting on fully investigating the transaction.

Professional Roles Cases in this section examine specific work roles in the auditing discipline. These cases explore the responsibilities associated with those roles and related challenges that professionals occupying them commonly encounter. The Tommy O'Connell case involves a young auditor recently promoted to audit senior. Shortly following his promotion, Tommy finds himself assigned to supervise a small but challenging audit. Tommy's sole subordinate on that engagement happens to be a young man whose integrity and work ethic have been questioned by seniors he has worked for previously. Two cases in this section spotlight the staff accountant work role, which many of your students will experience firsthand following graduation.

Professional Issues Similar to other professions, pervasive social issues such as sexual harassment, racial discrimination, and drug abuse influence the work roles and work environment of independent auditors. Cases in this section examine those sensitive but important topics in the context of independent auditing. The Elizabeth Wallace case, for example, documents how prescription drug abuse can adversely affect the personal and professional lives of independent auditors, while the Sarah Russell and *Hopkins v. Price Waterhouse* cases explore unique problems that women face in pursuing careers in public accounting. The amount of overtime worked by independent auditors, the immense legal liability of major accounting firms, and the overarching quality control issues facing those firms are among other topics addressed by cases in this section.

International Cases The purpose of these cases is to provide your students with an introduction to important issues facing the global accounting profession and auditing discipline. Several of these cases document unique challenges that must be dealt with by auditors and accountants in certain countries or regions of the world. For example, the Kaset Thai Sugar Company case vividly demonstrates that auditors and accountants may be forced to cope with hostile and sometimes dangerous working conditions in developing countries where their professional roles and responsibilities are not well understood or appreciated. Likewise, the Longtop Financial Technologies case documents how cultural differences across the globe may impact the performance of independent audits.

Customize Your Own Casebook To maximize your flexibility in using these cases, South-Western/Cengage Learning has included *Contemporary Auditing: Real Issues and Cases* in its customized publishing program, Make It Yours. Adopters have the option of creating a customized version of this casebook ideally suited for their specific needs. At the University of Oklahoma, a customized selection of my cases is used to add an ethics component to the undergraduate managerial accounting course. In fact, since the cases in this text examine ethical issues across a wide swath of different contexts, adopters can develop a customized ethics casebook to supplement almost any accounting course.

This casebook is ideally suited to be customized for the undergraduate auditing course. For example, auditing instructors who want to add a strong international component to their courses can develop a customized edition of this text that includes a series of international cases. Likewise, to enhance the coverage of ethical issues in the undergraduate auditing course, instructors could choose a series of cases from this text that highlight important ethical issues. Following are several examples of customized versions of this casebook that could be easily integrated into the undergraduate auditing course.

> *International Focus*: Longtop Financial Technologies (8.1), Kaset Thai Sugar Company (8.2), Republic of Somalia (8.3), *Shari'a* (8.5), and *Tae Kwang Vina* (8.7). This custom casebook would provide your students with insight on some of the most important issues that major accounting firms face when they enter foreign markets.

Ethics Focus (I): Suzette Washington, Accounting Major (4.3), Wiley Jackson, Accounting Major (4.5), Arvel Smart, Accounting Major (4.6), Leigh Ann Walker, Staff Accountant (6.1), Hamilton Wong, In-Charge Accountant (6.3), Avis Love, Staff Accountant (6.5). The first three cases give students an opportunity to discuss and debate ethical issues directly pertinent to them as accounting majors. The final three cases expose students to important ethical issues they may encounter shortly after graduation if they choose to enter public accounting.

Ethics Focus (II): Creve Couer Pizza (4.1), F&C International (4.2), Freescale Semiconductor (4.4), David Quinn, Tax Accountant (4.7), American International Group (5.2), Ryden Trucking (5.6). This selection of cases is suitable for auditing instructors who have a particular interest in covering a variety of ethical topics relevant to the AICPA's *Code of Professional Conduct*, several of which are not directly or exclusively related to auditing.

Applied Focus: Enron Corporation (1.1), NextCard (1.6), ZZZZ Best Company (1.9), Livent (1.15), Belot Enterprises (2.8), Cardillo Travel Systems (5.1). This series of cases will provide students with a broad-brush introduction to the *real world* of independent auditing. These cases raise a wide range of technical, professional, and ethical issues in a variety of client contexts.

Professional Roles Focus: Leigh Ann Walker, Staff Accountant (6.1), Bill DeBurger, In-Charge Accountant (6.2), Tommy O'Connell, Audit Senior (6.4), Avis Love, Staff Accountant (6.5), Charles Tollison, Audit Manager (6.6), Ligand Pharmaceuticals (7.1). This custom casebook would be useful for auditing instructors who choose to rely on a standard textbook to cover key technical topics in auditing—but who also want to expose their students to the everyday ethical and professional challenges faced by individuals occupying various levels of the employment hierarchy within auditing firms.

High-Risk Accounts Focus: Each of the cases in Section 2, Audits of High-Risk Accounts. This series of cases will provide your students with relatively intense homework assignments that focus almost exclusively on the financial statement line items that pose the greatest challenges for auditors.

Of course, realize that you are free to choose any "mix" of my cases to include in a customized casebook for an undergraduate auditing course or another accounting course that you teach. For more information on how to design your customized casebook, please contact your South-Western/Cengage Learning sales representative or visit the textbook website: www.cengage.com/custom/makeityours/knapp.

Acknowledgements I greatly appreciate the insight and suggestions provided by the following reviewers of earlier editions of this text: Alex Ampadu, University at Buffalo; Barbara Apostolou, Louisiana State University; Sandra A. Augustine, Hilbert College; Jane Baird, Mankato State University; Jason Bergner, University of Kentucky; James Bierstaker, Villanova University; Ed Blocher, University of North Carolina; Susan Cain, Southern Oregon University; Kurt Chaloupecky, Missouri State University; Ray Clay, University of North Texas; Jeffrey Cohen, Boston College; Mary Doucet, University of Georgia; Rafik Elias, California State University, Los Angeles;

Ruth Engle, Lafayette College; Diana Franz, University of Toledo; Chrislynn Freed, University of Southern California; Carolyn Galantine, Pepperdine University; Soha Ghallab, Brooklyn College; Russell Hardin, University of South Alabama; Michele C. Henney, University of Oregon; Laurence Johnson, Colorado State University; Donald McConnell, University of Texas at Arlington; Heidi Meier, Cleveland State University; Don Nichols, Texas Christian University; Marcia Niles, University of Idaho; Thomas Noland, University of South Alabama; Les Nunn, University of Southern Indiana; Robert J. Ramsay, Ph.D., CPA, University of Kentucky; John Rigsby, Mississippi State University; Mike Shapeero, Bloomsburg University of Pennsylvania; Edward F. Smith, Boston College; Dr. Gene Smith, Eastern New Mexico University; Rajendra Srivastava, University of Kansas; Richard Allen Turpen, University of Alabama at Birmingham; T. Sterling Wetzel, Oklahoma State University; and Jim Yardley, Virginia Polytechnic University. This project also benefitted greatly from the editorial assistance of my sister, Paula Kay Conatser, my wife, Carol Ann Knapp, and my son, John William Knapp. I would also like to thank Glen McLaughlin for his continuing generosity in funding the development of instructional materials that highlight important ethical issues. Finally, I would like to acknowledge the contributions of my students, who have provided invaluable comments and suggestions on the content and use of these cases.

Michael C. Knapp
McLaughlin Chair in Business
Ethics, David Ross Boyd Professor,
and Professor of Accounting
University of Oklahoma

SECTION 1

COMPREHENSIVE CASES

1

Enron Corporation

John and Mary Andersen immigrated to the United States from their native Norway in 1881. The young couple made their way to the small farming community of Plano, Illinois, some 40 miles southwest of downtown Chicago. Over the previous few decades, hundreds of Norwegian families had settled in Plano and surrounding communities. In fact, the aptly named Norway, Illinois, was located just a few miles away from the couple's new hometown. In 1885, Arthur Edward Andersen was born. From an early age, the Andersens' son had a fascination with numbers. Little did his parents realize that Arthur's interest in numbers would become the driving force in his life. Less than one century after he was born, an accounting firm bearing Arthur Andersen's name would become the world's largest professional services organization with more than 1,000 partners and operations in dozens of countries scattered across the globe.

Think Straight, Talk Straight

Discipline, honesty, and a strong work ethic were three key traits that John and Mary Andersen instilled in their son. The Andersens also constantly impressed upon him the importance of obtaining an education. Unfortunately, Arthur's parents did not survive to help him achieve that goal. Orphaned by the time he was a young teenager, Andersen was forced to take a full-time job as a mail clerk and attend night classes to work his way through high school. After graduating from high school, Andersen attended the University of Illinois while working as an accountant for Allis-Chalmers, a Chicago-based company that manufactured tractors and other farming equipment. In 1908, Andersen accepted a position with the Chicago office of Price Waterhouse. At the time, Price Waterhouse, which was organized in Great Britain during the early nineteenth century, easily qualified as the United States' most prominent public accounting firm.

At age 23, Andersen became the youngest CPA in the state of Illinois. A few years later, Andersen and a friend, Clarence Delany, established a partnership to provide accounting, auditing, and related services. The two young accountants named their firm Andersen, Delany & Company. When Delany decided to go his own way, Andersen renamed the firm Arthur Andersen & Company.

In 1915, Arthur Andersen faced a dilemma that would help shape the remainder of his professional life. One of his audit clients was a freight company that owned and operated several steam freighters that delivered various commodities to ports located on Lake Michigan. Following the close of the company's fiscal year but before Andersen had issued his audit report on its financial statements, one of the client's ships sank in Lake Michigan. At the time, there were few formal rules for companies to follow in preparing their annual financial statements and certainly no rule that required the company to report a material "subsequent event" occurring after the close of its fiscal year—such as the loss of a major asset. Nevertheless, Andersen insisted that his client disclose the loss of the ship. Andersen reasoned that third parties who would use the company's financial statements, among them the company's banker, would want to be informed of the loss. Although unhappy with Andersen's position, the client eventually acquiesced and reported the loss in the footnotes to its financial statements.

Two decades after the steamship dilemma, Arthur Andersen faced a similar situation with an audit client that was much larger, much more prominent, and much more profitable for his firm. Arthur Andersen & Co. served as the independent auditor for the giant chemical company DuPont. As the company's audit neared completion one year, members of the audit engagement team and executives of DuPont quarreled over how to define the company's operating income. DuPont's management insisted on a liberal definition of operating income that included income earned on certain investments. Arthur Andersen was brought in to arbitrate the dispute. When he sided with his subordinates, DuPont's management team dismissed the firm and hired another auditor.

Throughout his professional career, Arthur E. Andersen relied on a simple, four-word motto to serve as a guiding principle in making important personal and professional decisions: "Think straight, talk straight." Andersen insisted that his partners and other personnel in his firm invoke that simple rule when dealing with clients, potential clients, bankers, regulatory authorities, and any other parties they interacted with while representing Arthur Andersen & Co. He also insisted that audit clients "talk straight" in their financial statements. Former colleagues and associates often described Andersen as opinionated, stubborn, and, in some cases, "difficult." But even his critics readily admitted that Andersen was point-blank honest. "Arthur Andersen wouldn't put up with anything that wasn't complete, 100% integrity. If anybody did anything otherwise, he'd fire them. And if clients wanted to do something he didn't agree with, he'd either try to change them or quit."[1]

As a young professional attempting to grow his firm, Arthur Andersen quickly recognized the importance of carving out a niche in the rapidly developing accounting services industry. Andersen realized that the nation's bustling economy of the 1920s depended heavily on companies involved in the production and distribution of energy. As the economy grew, Andersen knew there would be a steadily increasing need for electricity, oil and gas, and other energy resources. So he focused his practice development efforts on obtaining clients involved in the various energy industries. Andersen was particularly successful in recruiting electric utilities as clients. By the early 1930s, Arthur Andersen & Co. had a thriving practice in the upper Midwest and was among the leading regional accounting firms in the nation.

The U.S. economy's precipitous downturn during the Great Depression of the 1930s posed huge financial problems for many of Arthur Andersen & Co.'s audit clients in the electric utilities industry. As the Depression wore on, Arthur Andersen personally worked with several of the nation's largest metropolitan banks to help his clients obtain the financing they desperately needed to continue operating. The bankers and other leading financiers who dealt with Arthur Andersen quickly learned of his commitment to honesty and proper, forthright accounting and financial reporting practices. Andersen's reputation for honesty and integrity allowed lenders to use with confidence financial data stamped with his approval. The end result was that many troubled firms received the financing they needed to survive the harrowing days of the 1930s. In turn, the respect that Arthur Andersen earned among leading financial executives nationwide resulted in Arthur Andersen & Co. receiving a growing number of referrals for potential clients located outside of the Midwest.

During the later years of his career, Arthur Andersen became a spokesperson for his discipline. He authored numerous books and presented speeches throughout the nation regarding the need for rigorous accounting, auditing, and ethical standards for the emerging public accounting profession. Andersen continually urged

---

1. R. Frammolino and J. Leeds, "Andersen's Reputation in Shreds," *Los Angeles Times* (online), 30 January 2002.

his fellow accountants to adopt the public service ideal that had long served as the underlying premise of the more mature professions such as law and medicine. He also lobbied for the adoption of a mandatory continuing professional education (CPE) requirement. Andersen realized that CPAs needed CPE to stay abreast of developments in the business world that had significant implications for accounting and financial reporting practices. In fact, Arthur Andersen & Co. made CPE mandatory for its employees long before state boards of accountancy adopted such a requirement.

By the mid-1940s, Arthur Andersen & Co. had offices scattered across the eastern one-half of the United States and employed more than 1,000 accountants. When Arthur Andersen died in 1947, many business leaders expected that the firm would disband without its founder, who had single-handedly managed its operations over the previous four decades. But, after several months of internal turmoil and dissension, the firm's remaining partners chose Andersen's most trusted associate and protégé to replace him.

Like his predecessor and close friend who had personally hired him in 1928, Leonard Spacek soon earned a reputation as a no-nonsense professional—an auditor's auditor. He passionately believed that the primary role of independent auditors was to ensure that their clients reported fully and honestly regarding their financial affairs to the investing and lending public.

Spacek continued Arthur Andersen's campaign to improve accounting and auditing practices in the United States during his long tenure as his firm's chief executive. "Spacek openly criticized the profession for tolerating what he considered a sloppy patchwork of accounting standards that left the investing public no way to compare the financial performance of different companies."[2] Such criticism compelled the accounting profession to develop a more formal and rigorous rule-making process. In the late 1950s, the profession created the Accounting Principles Board (APB) to study contentious accounting issues and develop appropriate new standards. The APB was replaced in 1973 by the Financial Accounting Standards Board (FASB).

Another legacy of Arthur Andersen that Leonard Spacek sustained was requiring the firm's professional employees to continue their education throughout their careers. During Spacek's tenure, Arthur Andersen & Co. established the world's largest private university, the Arthur Andersen & Co. Center for Professional Education located in St. Charles, Illinois, not far from Arthur Andersen's birthplace.

Leonard Spacek's strong leadership and business skills transformed Arthur Andersen & Co. into a major international accounting firm. When Spacek retired in 1973, Arthur Andersen & Co. was arguably the most respected accounting firm not only in the United States, but worldwide as well. Three decades later, shortly after the dawn of the new millennium, Arthur Andersen & Co. employed more than 80,000 professionals, had practice offices in more than 80 countries, and had annual revenues approaching $10 billion. However, in late 2001, the firm, which by that time had adopted the one-word name "Andersen," faced the most significant crisis in its history since the death of its founder. Ironically, that crisis stemmed from Andersen's audits of an energy company, a company founded in 1930 that, like many of Arthur Andersen's clients, had struggled to survive the Depression.

The World's Greatest Company

Northern Natural Gas Company was founded in Omaha, Nebraska, in 1930. The principal investors in the new venture included a Texas-based company, Lone Star Gas Corporation. During its first few years of existence, Northern wrestled with the problem

---

2. *Ibid.*

of persuading consumers to use natural gas to heat their homes. Concern produced by several unfortunate and widely publicized home "explosions" caused by natural gas leaks drove away many of Northern's potential customers. But, as the Depression wore on, the relatively cheap cost of natural gas convinced increasing numbers of cold-stricken and shallow-pocketed consumers to become Northern customers.

The availability of a virtually unlimited source of cheap manual labor during the 1930s allowed Northern to develop an extensive pipeline network to deliver natural gas to the residential and industrial markets that it served in the Great Plains states. As the company's revenues and profits grew, Northern's management launched a campaign to acquire dozens of its smaller competitors. This campaign was prompted by management's goal of making Northern the largest natural gas supplier in the United States. In 1947, the company, which was still relatively unknown outside of its geographical market, reached a major milestone when its stock was listed on the New York Stock Exchange. That listing provided the company with greater access to the nation's capital markets and the financing needed to continue its growth-through-acquisition strategy over the following two decades.

During the 1970s, Northern became a principal investor in the development of the Alaskan pipeline. When completed, that pipeline allowed Northern to tap vast natural gas reserves it had acquired in Canada. In 1980, Northern changed its name to InterNorth, Inc. Over the next few years, company management extended the scope of the company's operations by investing in ventures outside of the natural gas industry, including oil exploration, chemicals, coal mining, and fuel-trading operations. But the company's principal focus remained the natural gas industry. In 1985, InterNorth purchased Houston Natural Gas Company for $2.3 billion. That acquisition resulted in InterNorth controlling a 40,000-mile network of natural gas pipelines and allowed it to achieve its long-sought goal of becoming the largest natural gas company in the United States.

In 1986, InterNorth changed its name to Enron. Kenneth Lay, the former chairman of Houston Natural Gas, emerged as the top executive of the newly created firm that chose Houston, Texas, as its corporate headquarters. Lay quickly adopted the aggressive growth strategy that had long dominated the management policies of InterNorth and its predecessor. Lay hired Jeffrey Skilling to serve as one of his top subordinates. During the 1990s, Skilling developed and implemented a plan to transform Enron from a conventional natural gas supplier into an energy-trading company that served as an intermediary between producers of energy products, principally natural gas and electricity, and end users of those commodities. In early 2001, Skilling assumed Lay's position as Enron's chief executive officer (CEO), although Lay retained the title of chairman of the board. In the management letter to shareholders included in Enron's 2000 annual report, Lay and Skilling explained the metamorphosis that Enron had undergone over the previous 15 years:

> Enron hardly resembles the company we were in the early days. During our 15-year history, we have stretched ourselves beyond our own expectations. We have metamorphosed from an asset-based pipeline and power generating company to a marketing and logistics company whose biggest assets are its well-established business approach and its innovative people.

Enron's 2000 annual report discussed the company's four principal lines of business. Energy Wholesale Services ranked as the company's largest revenue producer. That division's 60 percent increase in transaction volume during 2000 was fueled by the rapid development of EnronOnline, a B2B (business-to-business) electronic marketplace for the energy industries created in late 1999 by Enron. During fiscal 2000 alone,

	2000	1999	1998	1997	1996
Revenues	$100,789	$40,112	$31,260	$20,273	$13,289
Net Income:					
Operating Results	1,266	957	698	515	493
Items Impacting Comparability	(287)	(64)	5	(410)	91
Total	979	893	703	105	584
Earnings Per Share:					
Operating Results	1.47	1.18	1.00	.87	.91
Items Impacting Comparability	(.35)	(.08)	.01	(.71)	.17
Total	1.12	1.10	1.01	.16	1.08
Dividends Per Share:	.50	.50	.48	.46	.43
Total Assets:	65,503	33,381	29,350	22,552	16,137
Cash from Operating Activities:	3,010	2,228	1,873	276	742
Capital Expenditures and Equity Investments:	3,314	3,085	3,564	2,092	1,483
NYSE Price Range:					
High	90.56	44.88	29.38	22.56	23.75
Low	41.38	28.75	19.06	17.50	17.31
Close, December 31	83.12	44.38	28.53	20.78	21.56

EXHIBIT 1

ENRON CORPORATION 2000 ANNUAL REPORT FINANCIAL HIGHLIGHTS TABLE (IN MILLIONS EXCEPT FOR PER SHARE AMOUNTS)

EnronOnline processed more than $335 billion of transactions, easily making Enron the largest e-commerce company in the world. Enron's three other principal lines of business included Enron Energy Services, the company's retail operating unit; Enron Transportation Services, which was responsible for the company's pipeline operations; and Enron Broadband Services, a new operating unit intended to be an intermediary between users and suppliers of broadband (Internet access) services. Exhibit 1 presents the five-year financial highlights table included in Enron's 2000 annual report.

The New Economy business model that Enron pioneered for the previously staid energy industries caused Kenneth Lay, Jeffrey Skilling, and their top subordinates to be recognized as skillful entrepreneurs and to gain superstar status in the business world. Lay's position as the chief executive of the nation's seventh-largest firm gave him direct access to key political and governmental officials. In 2001, Lay served on the "transition team" responsible for helping usher in the administration of President-elect George W. Bush. In June 2001, Skilling was singled out as "the No. 1 CEO in the entire country," while Enron was hailed as "America's most innovative company."[3] Enron's chief financial officer (CFO) Andrew Fastow was recognized for creating the

3. K. Eichenwald and D. B. Henriques, "Web of Details Did Enron In as Warnings Went Unheeded," *New York Times* (online), 10 February 2002.

financial infrastructure for one of the nation's largest and most complex companies. In 1999, *CFO Magazine* presented Fastow the Excellence Award for Capital Structure Management for his "pioneering work on unique financing techniques."[4]

Throughout their tenure with Enron, Kenneth Lay and Jeffrey Skilling continually focused on enhancing their company's operating results. In the letter to shareholders in Enron's 2000 annual report, Lay and Skilling noted that "Enron is laser-focused on earnings per share, and we expect to continue strong earnings performance." Another important goal of Enron's top executives was increasing their company's stature in the business world. During a speech in January 2001, Lay revealed that his ultimate goal was for Enron to become "the world's greatest company."[5]

As Enron's revenues and profits swelled, its top executives were often guilty of a certain degree of chutzpah. In particular, Skilling became known for making brassy, if not tacky, comments concerning his firm's competitors and critics. During the crisis that gripped California's electric utility industry during 2001, numerous elected officials and corporate executives criticized Enron for allegedly profiteering by selling electricity at inflated prices to the Golden State. Skilling brushed aside such criticism. During a speech at a major business convention, Skilling asked the crowd if they knew the difference between the state of California and the Titanic. After an appropriate pause, Skilling provided the punch line: "At least when the Titanic went down, the lights were on."[6]

Unfortunately for Lay, Skilling, Fastow, and thousands of Enron employees and stockholders, Lay failed to achieve his goal of creating the world's greatest company. In a matter of months during 2001, Enron quickly unraveled. Enron's sudden collapse panicked investors nationwide, leading to what one *Newsweek* columnist described as the "the biggest crisis investors have had since 1929."[7] Enron's dire financial problems were triggered by public revelations of questionable accounting and financial reporting decisions made by the company's accountants. Those decisions had been reviewed, analyzed, and apparently approved by Andersen, the company's independent audit firm.

Debits, Credits, and Enron

Throughout 2001, Enron's stock price drifted lower. Publicly, Enron executives blamed the company's slumping stock price on falling natural gas prices, concerns regarding the long-range potential of electronic marketplaces such as EnronOnline, and overall weakness in the national economy. By mid-October, the stock price had fallen into the mid-$30s from a high in the lower $80s earlier in the year.

On 16 October 2001, Enron issued its quarterly earnings report for the third quarter of 2001. That report revealed that the firm had suffered a huge loss during the quarter. Even more problematic to many financial analysts was a mysterious $1.2 billion reduction in Enron's owners' equity and assets that was disclosed seemingly as an afterthought in the earnings press release. This write-down resulted from the reversal of previously recorded transactions involving the swap of Enron stock for notes receivable. Enron had acquired the notes receivable from related third parties who had invested in limited partnerships organized and sponsored by the company. After studying those transactions in more depth, Enron's accounting staff and its Andersen auditors concluded

---

4. E. Thomas, "Every Man for Himself," *Newsweek*, 18 February 2002, 25.

5. Eichenwald and Henriques, "Web of Details."

6. *Ibid.*

7. N. Byrnes, "Paying for the Sins of Enron," *Newsweek*, 11 February 2002, 35.

that the notes receivable should not have been reported in the assets section of the company's balance sheet but rather as a reduction of owners' equity.

The 16 October 2001, press release sent Enron's stock price into a free fall. Three weeks later on 8 November, Enron restated its reported earnings for the previous five years, wiping out approximately $600 million of profits the company had reported over that time frame. That restatement proved to be the death knell for Enron. On 2 December 2001, intense pressure from creditors, pending and threatened litigation against the company and its officers, and investigations initiated by law enforcement authorities forced Enron to file for bankruptcy. Instead of becoming the nation's greatest company, Enron instead laid claim to being the largest corporate bankruptcy in U.S. history, imposing more than $60 billion of losses on its stockholders alone. Enron's "claim to fame" would be eclipsed the following year by the more than $100 billion of losses produced when another Andersen client, WorldCom, filed for bankruptcy.

The massive and understandable public outcry over Enron's implosion during the fall of 2001 spawned a mad frenzy on the part of the print and electronic media to determine how the nation's seventh-largest public company, a company that had posted impressive and steadily rising profits over the previous few years, could crumple into insolvency in a matter of months. From the early days of this public drama, skeptics in the financial community charged that Enron's balance sheet and earnings restatements in the fall of 2001 demonstrated that the company's exceptional financial performance during the late 1990s and 2000 had been a charade, a hoax orchestrated by the company's management with the help of a squad of creative accountants. Any doubt regarding the validity of that theory was wiped away—at least in the minds of most members of the press and the general public—when a letter that an Enron accountant sent to Kenneth Lay in August 2001 was discovered. The contents of that letter were posted on numerous websites and lengthy quotes taken from it appeared in virtually every major newspaper in the nation.

Exhibit 2 contains key excerpts from the letter that Sherron Watkins wrote to Kenneth Lay in August 2001. Watkins' job title was vice president of corporate development, but she was an accountant by training, having worked previously with Andersen, Enron's audit firm. The sudden and unexpected resignation of Jeffrey Skilling as Enron's CEO after serving in that capacity for only six months had prompted Watkins to write the letter to Lay. Before communicating her concerns to Lay, Watkins had attempted to discuss those issues with one of Lay's senior subordinates. When Watkins offered to show that individual a document that identified significant problems in accounting decisions made previously by Enron, Watkins reported that he rebuffed her. "He said he'd rather not see it."[8]

Watkins was intimately familiar with aggressive accounting decisions made for a series of large and complex transactions involving Enron and dozens of limited partnerships created by the company. These partnerships were so-called SPEs or special purpose entities that Enron executives had tagged with a variety of creative names, including Braveheart, Rawhide, Raptor, Condor, and Talon. Andrew Fastow, Enron's CFO who was involved in the creation and operation of several of the SPEs, named a series of them after his three children.

SPEs—sometimes referred to as SPVs (special purpose vehicles)—can take several legal forms but are commonly organized as limited partnerships. During the 1990s, hundreds of large corporations began establishing SPEs. In most cases, SPEs

8. T. Hamburger, "Watkins Tells of 'Arrogant' Culture; Enron Stifled Staff Whistle-Blowing," *Wall Street Journal* (online), 14 February 2002.

EXHIBIT 2

SELECTED EXCERPTS
FROM SHERRON
WATKINS' AUGUST
2001 LETTER TO
KENNETH LAY

Dear Mr. Lay,

Has Enron become a risky place to work? For those of us who didn't get rich over the last few years, can we afford to stay?

Skilling's abrupt departure will raise suspicions of accounting improprieties and valuation issues. Enron has been very aggressive in its accounting—most notably the Raptor transactions and the Condor vehicle....

We have recognized over $550 million of fair value gains on stocks via our swaps with Raptor, much of that stock has declined significantly.... The value in the swaps won't be there for Raptor, so once again Enron will issue stock to offset these losses. Raptor is an LJM entity. It sure looks to the layman on the street that we are hiding losses in a related company and will compensate that company with Enron stock in the future.

I am incredibly nervous that we will implode in a wave of scandals. My 8 years of Enron work history will be worth nothing on my resume, the business world will consider the past successes as nothing but an elaborate accounting hoax. Skilling is resigning now for "personal reasons" but I think he wasn't having fun, looked down the road and knew this stuff was unfixable and would rather abandon ship now than resign in shame in 2 years.

Is there a way our accounting gurus can unwind these deals now? I have thought and thought about how to do this, but I keep bumping into one big problem—we booked the Condor and Raptor deals in 1999 and 2000, we enjoyed a wonderfully high stock price, many executives sold stock, we then try and reverse or fix the deals in 2001 and it's a bit like robbing the bank in one year and trying to pay it back 2 years later....

I realize that we have had a lot of smart people looking at this and a lot of accountants including AA & Co. have blessed the accounting treatment. None of this will protect Enron if these transactions are ever disclosed in the bright light of day....

The overriding basic principle of accounting is that if you explain the "accounting treatment" to a man on the street, would you influence his investing decisions? Would he sell or buy the stock based on a thorough understanding of the facts?

My concern is that the footnotes don't adequately explain the transactions. If adequately explained, the investor would know that the "Entities" described in our related party footnote are thinly capitalized, the equity holders have no skin in the game, and all the value in the entities comes from the underlying value of the derivatives (unfortunately in this case, a big loss) AND Enron stock and N/P....

The related party footnote tries to explain these transactions. Don't you think that several interested companies, be they stock analysts, journalists, hedge fund managers, etc., are busy trying to discover the reason Skilling left? Don't you think their smartest people are pouring [sic] over that footnote disclosure right now? I can just hear the discussions—"It looks like they booked a $500 million gain from this related party company and I think, from all the undecipherable ½ page on Enron's contingent contributions to this related party entity, I think the related party entity is capitalized with Enron stock.".... "No, no, no, you must have it all wrong, it can't be that, that's just too bad, too fraudulent, surely AA & Co. wouldn't let them get away with that?"

were used to finance the acquisition of an asset or fund a construction project or related activity. Regardless, the underlying motivation for creating an SPE was nearly always "debt avoidance." That is, SPEs provided large companies with a mechanism to raise needed financing for various purposes without being required to report the debt in their balance sheets. *Fortune* magazine charged that corporate CFOs were using SPEs as scalpels "to perform cosmetic surgery on their balance sheets."[9] During the early 1990s, the Securities and Exchange Commission (SEC) and the FASB had wrestled with the contentious accounting and financial reporting issues posed by SPEs. Despite intense debate and discussions, the SEC and the FASB provided little in the way of formal guidance for companies to follow in accounting and reporting for SPEs.

The most important guideline that the authoritative bodies implemented for SPEs, the so-called 3 percent rule, proved to be extremely controversial. This rule allowed a company to omit an SPE's assets and liabilities from its consolidated financial statements as long as parties independent of the company provided a minimum of 3 percent of the SPE's capital. Almost immediately, the 3 percent threshold became both a technical minimum and a practical maximum. That is, large companies using the SPE structure arranged for external parties to provide exactly 3 percent of an SPE's total capital. The remaining 97 percent of an SPE's capital was typically contributed by loans from external lenders, loans arranged and generally collateralized by the company that created the SPE.

Many critics charged that the 3 percent rule undercut the fundamental principle within the accounting profession that consolidated financial statements should be prepared for entities controlled by a common ownership group. "There is a presumption that consolidated financial statements are more meaningful than separate statements and that they are usually necessary for a fair presentation when one of the companies in the group directly or indirectly has a controlling financial interest in the other companies."[10] *Business Week* chided the SEC and FASB for effectively endorsing the 3 percent rule.

> Because of a gaping loophole in accounting practice, companies can create arcane legal structures, often called special-purpose entities (SPEs). Then, the parent can bankroll up to 97 percent of the initial investment in an SPE without having to consolidate it.... The controversial exception that outsiders need invest only 3 percent of an SPE's capital for it to be independent and off the balance sheet came about through fumbles by the Securities and Exchange Commission and the Financial Accounting Standards Board.[11]

Throughout the 1990s, many companies took advantage of the minimal legal and accounting guidelines for SPEs to divert huge amounts of their liabilities to off-balance sheet entities. Among the most aggressive and innovative users of the SPE structure was Enron, which created hundreds of SPEs. Unlike most companies, Enron did not limit its SPEs to financing activities. In many cases, Enron used SPEs for the sole purpose of downloading underperforming assets from its financial statements to the financial statements of related but unconsolidated entities. For example, Enron would arrange for a third party to invest the minimum 3 percent capital required in an SPE and then sell assets to that SPE. The SPE would finance the purchase of those assets by loans collateralized by Enron common stock. In some cases, undisclosed side

9. J. Kahn, "Off Balance Sheet—and Out of Control," *Fortune*, 18 February 2002, 84.

10. *Accounting Research Bulletin No. 51*, "Consolidated Financial Statements" (New York: AICPA, 1959).

11. D. Henry, H. Timmons, S. Rosenbush, and M. Arndt, "Who Else Is Hiding Debt?" *Business Week*, 28 January 2002, 36–37.

agreements made by Enron with an SPE's nominal owners insulated those individuals from any losses on their investments and, in fact, guaranteed them a windfall profit. Even more troubling, Enron often sold assets at grossly inflated prices to their SPEs, allowing the company to manufacture large "paper" gains on those transactions.

Enron made only nominal financial statement disclosures for its SPE transactions and those disclosures were typically presented in confusing, if not cryptic, language. One accounting professor observed that the inadequate disclosures that companies such as Enron provided for their SPE transactions meant that, "the nonprofessional [investor] has no idea of the extent of the [given firm's] real liabilities."[12] The *Wall Street Journal* added to that sentiment when it suggested that Enron's brief and obscure disclosures for its off-balance sheet liabilities and related-party transactions "were so complicated as to be practically indecipherable."[13]

Just as difficult to analyze for most investors was the integrity of the hefty profits reported each successive period by Enron. As Sherron Watkins revealed in the letter she sent to Kenneth Lay in August 2001, many of Enron's SPE transactions resulted in the company's profits being inflated by unrealized gains on increases in the market value of its own common stock. In the fall of 2001, Enron's board of directors appointed a Special Investigative Committee chaired by William C. Powers, dean of the University of Texas Law School, to study the company's large SPE transactions. In February 2002, that committee issued a lengthy report of its findings, a document commonly referred to as the Powers Report by the press. This report discussed at length the "Byzantine" nature of Enron's SPE transactions and the enormous and improper gains those transactions produced for the company.

> *Accounting principles generally forbid a company from recognizing an increase in the value of its capital stock in its income statement.... The substance of the Raptors [SPE transactions] effectively allowed Enron to report gains on its income statement that were ... [attributable to] Enron stock, and contracts to receive Enron stock, held by the Raptors.*[14]

The primary motivation for Enron's extensive use of SPEs and the related accounting machinations was the company's growing need for capital during the 1990s. As Kenneth Lay and Jeffrey Skilling transformed Enron from a fairly standard natural gas supplier into a New Economy intermediary for the energy industries, the company had a constant need for additional capital to finance that transformation. Like most new business endeavors, Enron's Internet-based operations did not produce positive cash flows immediately. To convince lenders to continue pumping cash into Enron, the company's management team realized that their firm would have to maintain a high credit rating, which, in turn, required the company to release impressive financial statements each succeeding period.

A related factor that motivated Enron's executives to window dress their company's financial statements was the need to sustain Enron's stock price at a high level. Many of the SPE loan agreements negotiated by Enron included so-called price "triggers." If the market price of Enron's stock dropped below a designated level (trigger), Enron was required to provide additional stock to collateralize the given loan, to make significant cash payments to the SPE, or to restructure prior transactions with the SPE.

---

12. *Ibid.*

13. J. Emshwiller and R. Smith, "Murky Waters: A Primer on the Enron Partnerships," *Wall Street Journal* (online), 21 January 2002.

14. W. C. Powers, R. S. Troubh, and H. S. Winokur, "Report of Investigation by the Special Investigative Committee of the Board of Directors of Enron Corporation," 1 February 2002, 129–130.

In a worst-case scenario, Enron might be forced to dissolve an SPE and merge its assets and liabilities into the company's consolidated financial statements.

> What made Enron's stock price so important was the fact that some of the company's most important deals with the partnerships [SPEs] run by Mr. Fastow—deals that had allowed Enron to keep hundreds of millions of dollars of potential losses off its books—were financed, in effect, with Enron stock. Those transactions could fall apart if the stock price fell too far.[15]

As Enron's stock price drifted lower throughout 2001, the complex labyrinth of legal and accounting gimmicks underlying the company's finances became a shaky house of cards. Making matters worse were large losses suffered by many of Enron's SPEs on the assets they had purchased from Enron. Enron executives were forced to pour additional resources into many of those SPEs to keep them solvent.

Contributing to the financial problems of Enron's major SPEs was alleged self-dealing by Enron officials involved in operating those SPEs. Andrew Fastow realized $30 million in profits on his investments in Enron SPEs that he oversaw at the same time he was serving as the company's CFO. Several of his friends also reaped windfall profits on investments in those same SPEs. Some of these individuals "earned" a profit of as much as $1 million on an initial investment of $5,800. Even more startling was the fact that Fastow's friends realized these gains in as little as 60 days.

By October 2001, the falling price of Enron's stock, the weight of the losses suffered by the company's large SPEs, and concerns being raised by Andersen auditors forced company executives to act. Enron's management assumed control and ownership of several of the company's troubled SPEs and incorporated their dismal financial statement data into Enron's consolidated financial statements. This decision led to the large loss reported by Enron in the fall of 2001 and the related restatement of the company's earnings for the previous five years. On 2 December 2001, the transformed New Age company filed its bankruptcy petition in New Age fashion—via the Internet. Only six months earlier, Jeffrey Skilling had been buoyant when commenting on Enron's first quarter results for 2001. "So in conclusion, first-quarter results were great. We are very optimistic about our new businesses and are confident that our record of growth is sustainable for many years to come."[16]

As law enforcement authorities, Congressional investigative committees, and business journalists rifled through the mass of Enron documents that became publicly available during early 2002, the abusive accounting and financial reporting practices that had been used by the company surfaced. Enron's creative use of SPEs became the primary target of critics; however, the company also made extensive use of other accounting gimmicks. For example, Enron had abused the mark-to-market accounting method for its long-term contracts involving various energy commodities, primarily natural gas and electricity. Given the nature of their business, energy-trading firms regularly enter into long-term contracts to deliver energy commodities. Some of Enron's commodity contracts extended over periods of more than 20 years and involved massive quantities of the given commodity. When Enron finalized these deals, company officials often made tenuous assumptions that inflated the profits booked on the contracts.

> Energy traders must book all the projected profits from a supply contract in the quarter in which the deal is made, even if the contract spans many years. That means companies can inflate profits by using unrealistic price forecasts, as Enron has been accused of doing. If a company contracted to buy natural gas through 2010 for $3 per thousand

---

15. Eichenwald and Henriques, "Web of Details."
16. *Ibid.*

cubic feet, an energy-trading desk could aggressively assume it would be able to sup-
ply gas in each year at a cost of just $2, for a $1 profit margin.[17]

The avalanche of startling revelations regarding Enron's aggressive business, accounting, and financial reporting decisions reported by the business press during the early weeks of 2002 created a firestorm of anger and criticism directed at Enron's key executives, principally Kenneth Lay, Jeffrey Skilling, and Andrew Fastow. A common theme of the allegations leveled at the three executives was that they had created a corporate culture that fostered, if not encouraged, "rule breaking." *Fortune* magazine observed that, "If nothing else, Lay allowed a culture of rule breaking to flourish,"[18] while Sherron Watkins testified that Enron's corporate culture was "arrogant" and "intimidating" and discouraged employees from reporting and investigating ethical lapses and questionable business dealings.[19] Finally, a top executive of Dynegy, a company that briefly considered merging with Enron during late 2001, reported that "the lack of internal controls [within Enron] was mind-boggling."[20]

Both Kenneth Lay and Andrew Fastow invoked their Fifth Amendment rights against self-incrimination when asked to testify before Congress in early 2002. Jeffrey Skilling did not. While being peppered by Congressional investigators regarding Enron's questionable accounting and financial reporting decisions, Skilling replied calmly and repeatedly: "I am not an accountant."

A well-accepted premise in the financial reporting domain is that corporate executives and their accountants are ultimately responsible for the integrity of their company's financial statements. Nevertheless, frustration stemming from the lack of answers provided by Enron insiders to key accounting and financial reporting–related questions eventually caused Congressional investigators, the business press, and the public to focus their attention, their questions, and their scorn on Enron's independent audit firm, Andersen. These parties insisted that Andersen representatives explain why their audits of Enron had failed to result in more transparent, if not reliable, financial statements for the company. More pointedly, those critics demanded that Andersen explain how it was able to issue unqualified audit opinions on Enron's financial statements throughout its 15-year tenure as the company's independent audit firm.

Say It Ain't So Joe

Joseph Berardino became Andersen's chief executive shortly before the firm was swamped by the storm of criticism surrounding the collapse of its second-largest client, Enron Corporation. Berardino launched his business career with Andersen in 1972 immediately after graduating from college and just a few months before Leonard Spacek ended his long and illustrious career with the firm. Throughout its history, the Andersen firm had a policy of speaking with one voice, the voice of its chief executive. So, the unpleasant task of responding to the angry and often self-righteous accusations hurled at Andersen following Enron's demise fell to Berardino, although he had not been a party to the key decisions made during the Enron audits.

A common question directed at Berardino was whether his firm had been aware of the allegations Sherron Watkins made during August 2001 and, if so, how had Andersen responded to those allegations. Watkins testified before Congress that shortly after she communicated her concerns regarding Enron's questionable

17. P. Coy, S. A. Forest, and D. Foust, "Enron: How Good an Energy Trader?" *Business Week*, 11 February 2002, 42–43.

18. B. McLean, "Monster Mess," *Fortune*, 4 February 2002, 94.

19. Hamburger, "Watkins Tells of 'Arrogant' Culture."

20. N. Banjeree, D. Barboza, and A. Warren, "At Enron, Lavish Excess Often Came before Success," *New York Times* (online), 26 February 2002.

accounting and financial reporting decisions to Kenneth Lay, she had met with a member of the Andersen firm with whom she had worked several years earlier. In an internal Andersen memorandum, that individual relayed Watkins' concerns to several colleagues, including the Enron audit engagement partner, David Duncan. At that point, Andersen officials in the firm's Chicago headquarters began systematically reviewing previous decisions made by the Enron audit engagement team.

In fact, several months earlier, Andersen representatives had become aware of Enron's rapidly deteriorating financial condition and became deeply involved in helping the company's executives cope with that crisis. Andersen's efforts included assisting Enron officials in restructuring certain of the company's SPEs so that they could continue to qualify as unconsolidated entities. Subsequent press reports revealed that in February 2001, frustration over the aggressive nature of Enron's accounting and financial reporting decisions caused some Andersen officials to suggest dropping the company as an audit client.[21]

On 12 December 2001, Joseph Berardino testified before the Committee on Financial Services of the U.S. House of Representatives. Early in that testimony, Berardino freely admitted that members of the Enron audit engagement team had made one major error while analyzing a large SPE transaction that occurred in 1999. "We made a professional judgment about the appropriate accounting treatment that turned out to be wrong."[22] According to Berardino, when Andersen officials discovered this error in the fall of 2001, they promptly notified Enron's executives and told them to "correct it." Approximately 20 percent of the $600 million restatement of prior earnings announced by Enron on 8 November 2001, was due to this item.

The remaining 80 percent of the earnings restatement involved another SPE that Enron created in 1997. Unknown to Andersen auditors, one-half of that SPE's minimum 3 percent "external" equity had been effectively contributed by Enron. As a result, that entity did not qualify for SPE treatment, meaning that its financial data should have been included in Enron's consolidated financial statements from its inception. When Andersen auditors discovered this violation of the 3 percent rule in the fall of 2001, they immediately informed Enron's accounting staff. Andersen also informed the company's audit committee that the failure of Enron officials to reveal the source of the SPE's initial funding could possibly be construed as an illegal act under the Securities Exchange Act of 1934. Berardino implied that the client's lack of candor regarding this SPE exempted Andersen of responsibility for the resulting accounting and financial reporting errors linked to that entity.

Berardino also explained to Congress that Andersen auditors had been only minimally involved in the transactions that eventually resulted in the $1.2 billion reduction of owners' equity reported by Enron on 16 October 2001. The bulk of those transactions had occurred in early 2001. Andersen had not audited the 2001 quarterly financial statements that had been prepared following the initial recording of those transactions— public companies are not required to have their quarterly financial statements audited.

Berardino's testimony before Congress in December 2001 failed to appease Andersen's critics. Over the next several months, Berardino continually found himself defending Andersen against a growing torrent of accusations. Most of these accusations centered on three key issues. First, many critics raised the controversial and long-standing "scope of services" issue when criticizing Andersen's role in the Enron debacle. Over the final few decades of the twentieth century, the major accounting

---

21. S. Labaton, "S.E.C. Leader Sees Outside Monitors for Auditing Firms," *New York Times* (online), 18 January 2002.

22. J. Kahn and J. D. Glater, "Enron Auditor Raises Specter of Crime," *New York Times* (online), 13 December 2001.

firms had gradually extended the product line of professional services they offered to their major audit clients. A research study focusing on nearly 600 large companies that released financial statements in early 1999 revealed that for every $1 of audit fees those companies had paid their independent auditors, they had paid those firms $2.69 for nonaudit consulting services.[23] These services included a wide range of activities such as feasibility studies of various types, internal auditing, design of accounting systems, development of e-commerce initiatives, and a varied assortment of other information technology (IT) services.

In an interview with the *New York Times* in March 2002, Leonard Spacek's daughter revealed that her father had adamantly opposed accounting firms providing consulting services to their audit clients. "I remember him ranting and raving, saying Andersen couldn't consult and audit the same firms because it was a conflict of interest. Well, now I'm sure he's twirling in his grave saying, 'I told you so.'"[24] In the late 1990s, Arthur Levitt, the chairman of the SEC, led a vigorous, one-man campaign to limit the scope of consulting services that accounting firms could provide to their audit clients. In particular, Levitt wanted to restrict the ability of accounting firms to provide IT and internal audit services to their audit clients. An extensive and costly lobbying campaign that the Big Five firms carried out in the press and among elected officials allowed those firms to defeat the bulk of Levitt's proposals.

Public reports that Andersen earned approximately $52 million in fees from Enron during 2000, only $25 million of which was directly linked to the 2000 audit, caused the scope of services issue to resurface. Critics charged that the enormous consulting fees accounting firms earned from their audit clients jeopardized those firms' independence. "It's obvious that Andersen helped Enron cook the books. Andersen's Houston office was pulling in $1 million a week from Enron—their objectivity went out the window."[25] These same critics reiterated an allegation that had widely circulated a few years earlier, namely, that the large accounting firms had resorted to using the independent audit function as "a loss leader, a way of getting in the door at a company to sell more profitable consulting contracts."[26] One former partner of a Big Five accounting firm provided anecdotal evidence corroborating that allegation. This individual revealed that he had been under constant pressure from his former firm to market various professional services to his audit clients. So relentless were his efforts that at one point a frustrated client executive asked him, "Are you my auditor or a salesperson?"[27]

A second source of criticism directed at Andersen stemmed from the firm's alleged central role in Enron's aggressive accounting and financial reporting treatments for its SPE-related transactions. The Powers Report released to the public in February 2002 spawned much of this criticism. That lengthy report examined in detail several of Enron's largest and most questionable SPE transactions. The Powers Report pointedly and repeatedly documented that Andersen personnel had been deeply involved in those transactions. Exhibit 3 contains a sample of selected excerpts from the Powers Report that refers to Andersen's role in "analyzing" and "reviewing" Enron's SPE transactions.

---

23. N. Byrnes, "Accounting in Crisis," *Business Week*, 28 January 2002, 46.

24. D. Barboza, "Where Pain of Arthur Andersen Is Personal," *New York Times* (online), 13 March 2002.

25. *SmartPros.com*, "Lawsuit Seeks to Hold Andersen Accountable for Defrauding Enron Investors, Employees," 4 December 2001.

26. J. Kahn, "One Plus One Makes *What*?" *Fortune*, 7 January 2002, 89.

27. I. J. Dugan, "Before Enron, Greed Helped Sink the Respectability of Accounting," *Wall Street Journal* (online), 14 March 2002.

EXHIBIT 3

SELECTED EXCERPTS
FROM THE POWERS
REPORT REGARDING
ANDERSEN'S
INVOLVEMENT IN
KEY ACCOUNTING
AND FINANCIAL
REPORTING
DECISIONS FOR
ENRON'S SPE
TRANSACTIONS

Page 5: In virtually all of the [SPE] transactions, Enron's accounting treatment was determined with the extensive participation and structuring advice from Andersen, which Management reported to the Board.

Page 17: Various disclosures [regarding Enron's SPE transactions] were approved by one or more of Enron's outside [Andersen] auditors and its inside and outside counsel. However, these disclosures were obtuse, did not communicate the essence of the transactions completely or clearly, and failed to convey the substance of what was going on between Enron and the partnerships.

Page 24: The evidence available to us suggests that Andersen did not fulfill its professional responsibilities in connection with its audits of Enron's financial statements, or its obligation to bring to the attention of Enron's Board (or the Audit and Compliance Committee) concerns about Enron's internal controls over the related-party [SPE] transactions.

Page 24: Andersen participated in the structuring and accounting treatment of the Raptor transactions, and charged over $1 million for its services, yet it apparently failed to provide the objective accounting judgment that should have prevented these transactions from going forward.

Page 25: According to recent public disclosures, Andersen also failed to bring to the attention of Enron's Audit and Compliance Committee serious reservations Andersen partners voiced internally about the related-party transactions.

Page 25: The Board appears to have reasonably relied upon the professional judgment of Andersen concerning Enron's financial statements and the adequacy of controls for the related-party transactions. Our review indicates that Andersen failed to meet its responsibilities in both respects.

Page 100: Accountants from Andersen were closely involved in structuring the Raptors [SPE transactions].... Enron's records show that Andersen billed Enron approximately $335,000 in connection with its work on the creation of the Raptors in the first several months of 2000.

Page 107: Causey [Enron's chief accounting officer] informed the Finance Committee that Andersen "had spent considerable time analyzing the Talon structure and the governance structure of LJM2 and was comfortable with the proposed [SPE] transaction."

Page 126: At the time [September 2001], Enron accounting personnel and Andersen concluded (using qualitative analysis) that the error [in a prior SPE transaction] was not material and a restatement was not necessary.

Page 129: Proper financial accounting does not permit this result [questionable accounting treatment for certain of Enron's SPE transactions]. To reach it, the accountants at Enron and Andersen—including the local engagement team and, apparently, Andersen's national office experts in Chicago—had to surmount numerous obstacles presented by pertinent accounting rules.

Page 132: It is particularly surprising that the accountants at Andersen, who should have brought a measure of objectivity and perspective to these transactions, did not do so. Based on the recollections of those involved in the transactions and a large collection of documentary evidence, there is no question that Andersen accountants were in a position to understand all the critical features of the Raptors and offer advice on the appropriate accounting treatment. Andersen's total bill for Raptor-related work came to approximately $1.3 million. Indeed, there is abundant evidence that Andersen in fact offered Enron advice

(continued)

EXHIBIT 3—
continued

SELECTED EXCERPTS
FROM THE POWERS
REPORT REGARDING
ANDERSEN'S
INVOLVEMENT IN
KEY ACCOUNTING
AND FINANCIAL
REPORTING
DECISIONS FOR
ENRON'S SPE
TRANSACTIONS

at every step, from inception through restructuring and ultimately to terminating the Raptors. Enron followed that advice.

Page 202: While we have not had the benefit of Andersen's position on a number of these issues, the evidence we have seen suggests Andersen accountants did not function as an effective check on the disclosure approach taken by the company. Andersen was copied on drafts of the financial statement footnotes and the proxy statements, and we were told that it routinely provided comments on the related-party transaction disclosures in response. We also understand that the Andersen auditors closest to Enron Global Finance were involved in drafting of at least some of the disclosures. An internal Andersen e-mail from February 2001 released in connection with recent Congressional hearings suggests that Andersen may have had concerns about the disclosures of the related-party transactions in the financial statement footnotes. Andersen did not express such concerns to the Board. On the contrary, Andersen's engagement partner told the Audit and Compliance Committee just a week after the internal e-mail that, with respect to related-party transactions, "'[r]equired disclosure [had been] reviewed for adequacy,' and that Andersen would issue an unqualified audit opinion on the financial statements."

Source: W. C. Powers, R. S. Troubh, and H. S. Winokur, "Report of Investigation by the Special Investigative Committee of the Board of Directors of Enron Corporation," 1 February 2002.

Among the parties most critical of Andersen's extensive involvement in Enron's accounting and financial reporting decisions for SPE transactions was former SEC Chief Accountant Lynn Turner. During his tenure with the SEC in the 1990s, Turner had participated in the federal agency's investigation of Andersen's audits of Waste Management, Inc. That investigation culminated in sanctions against several Andersen auditors and in a $1.4 billion restatement of Waste Management's financial statements, the largest accounting restatement in U.S. history at that time. Andersen eventually paid a reported $75 million in settlements to resolve various civil lawsuits linked to those audits and a $7 million fine to settle charges filed against the firm by the SEC.

In an interview with the *New York Times*, Turner suggested that the charges of shoddy audit work that plagued Andersen in connection with its audits of Waste Management, Sunbeam, Enron, and other high-profile public clients was well-deserved. Turner compared Andersen's problems with those experienced several years earlier by Coopers & Lybrand, a firm for which he had been an audit partner. According to Turner, a series of "blown audits" was the source of Coopers' problems. "We got bludgeoned to death in the press. People did not even want to see us at their doorsteps. It was brutal, but we deserved it. We had gotten into this mentality in the firm of making business judgment calls."[28] Clearly, the role of independent auditors does not include "making business judgments" for their clients. Instead, auditors have a responsibility to provide an objective point of view regarding the proper accounting and financial reporting decisions for those judgments.

Easily the source of the most embarrassment for Berardino and his Andersen colleagues was the widely publicized effort of the firm's Houston office to shred a large quantity of documents pertaining to various Enron audits. In early January

28. F. Norris, "From Sunbeam to Enron, Andersen's Reputation Suffers," *New York Times* (online), 23 November 2001.

2002, Andersen officials informed federal investigators that personnel in the Houston office had "destroyed a significant but undetermined number of documents relating to the company [Enron] and its finances."[29] That large-scale effort began in September 2001 and apparently continued into November after the SEC revealed it was conducting a formal investigation of Enron's financial affairs. The report of the shredding effort immediately caused many critics to suggest that Andersen's Houston office was attempting to prevent law enforcement authorities from obtaining potentially incriminating evidence regarding Andersen's role in Enron's demise. Senator Joseph Lieberman, chairman of the U.S. Senate Governmental Affairs Committee that would be investigating the Enron debacle, warned that the effort to dispose of the Enron-related documents might be particularly problematic for Andersen.

> *It [the document-shredding] came at a time when people inside, including the executives of Arthur Andersen and Enron, knew that Enron was in real trouble and that the roof was about to collapse on them, and there was about to be a corporate scandal.... [This] raises very serious questions about whether obstruction of justice occurred here. The folks at Arthur Andersen could be on the other end of an indictment before this is over. This Enron episode may end this company's history.*[30]

The barrage of criticism directed at Andersen continued unabated during the early months of 2002. Ironically, some of that criticism was directed at Andersen by Enron's top management. On 17 January 2002, Kenneth Lay issued a press release reporting that his company had decided to discharge Andersen as its independent audit firm.[31] In the press release, Lay justified that decision by referring to the "reported destruction" of audit documents by the Enron audit team and to the fact that several Andersen partners in the firm's Houston office had faced "disciplinary actions" as a result of their conduct on Enron audits.[32]

Throughout the public relations nightmare that besieged Andersen following Enron's bankruptcy filing, a primary tactic employed by Joseph Berardino was to insist repeatedly that poor business decisions, not errors on the part of Andersen, were responsible for Enron's downfall and the massive losses that ensued for investors, creditors, and other parties. "At the end of the day, we do not cause companies to fail."[33] Such statements failed to generate sympathy for Andersen. Even the editor in chief of *Accounting Today*, one of the accounting profession's leading publications, was unmoved by Berardino's continual assertions that his firm was not responsible for the Enron fiasco. "If you accept the audit and collect the fee, then be prepared to accept the blame. Otherwise you're not part of the solution but rather, part of the problem."[34]

---

29. K. Eichenwald and F. Norris, "Enron Auditor Admits It Destroyed Documents," *New York Times* (online), 11 January 2002.

30. R. A. Oppel, "Andersen Says Lawyer Let Its Staff Destroy Files," *New York Times* (online), 14 January 2002.

31. Kenneth Lay resigned as Enron's chairman of the board and CEO on 23 January 2002, one day after a court-appointed "creditors committee" had requested him to step down.

32. M. Palmer, "Enron Board Discharges Arthur Andersen in All Capacities," *Enron.com*, 17 January 2002.

33. M. Gordon, "Labor Secretary to Address Enron Hearings," *Associated Press* (online), 6 February 2002.

34. B. Carlino, "Enron Simply Newest Player in National Auditing Crisis," *The Electronic Accountant* (online), 17 December 2001.

Ridicule and Retrospection

As 2001 came to a close, the *New York Times* reported that the year had easily been the worst ever for Andersen, "the accounting firm that once deserved the title of the conscience of the industry."[35] The following year would prove to be an even darker time for the firm. During the early months of 2002, Andersen faced scathing criticism from Congressional investigators, enormous class-action lawsuits filed by angry Enron stockholders and creditors, and a federal criminal indictment stemming from the shredding of Enron-related documents.

In late March 2002, Joseph Berardino unexpectedly resigned as Andersen's CEO after failing to negotiate a merger of Andersen with one of the other Big Five firms. During the following few weeks, dozens of Andersen clients dropped the firm as their independent auditor out of concern that the firm might not survive if it was found guilty of the pending criminal indictment. The staggering loss of clients forced Andersen to lay off more than 25 percent of its workforce in mid-April. Shortly after that layoff was announced, U.S. Justice Department officials revealed that David Duncan, the former Enron audit engagement partner, had pleaded guilty to obstruction of justice and agreed to testify against his former firm. Duncan's plea proved to be the death knell for Andersen. In June 2002, a federal jury found the firm guilty of obstruction of justice. That conviction forced the firm to terminate its relationship with its remaining public clients, effectively ending Andersen's long and proud history within the U.S. accounting profession.

Three years later, the U.S. Supreme Court unanimously overturned the felony conviction handed down against Andersen. In an opinion written by Chief Justice William Rehnquist, the high court ruled that federal prosecutors did not prove that Andersen had *intended* to interfere with a federal investigation when the firm shredded the Enron audit workpapers. The Supreme Court's decision was little consolation to the more than 20,000 Andersen partners and employees who had lost their jobs when the accounting firm was forced out of business by the felony conviction.

Numerous Enron officials faced criminal indictments for their roles in the Enron fraud, among them Andrew Fastow, Jeffrey Skilling, and Kenneth Lay. Fastow pleaded guilty to conspiracy to commit securities fraud as well as to other charges. The former CFO received a 10-year prison term, which was reduced to 6 years after he testified against Skilling and Lay. Fastow was also required to forfeit nearly $25 million of personal assets that he had accumulated during his tenure at Enron. Largely as a result of Fastow's testimony against them, Skilling and Lay were convicted on multiple counts of fraud and conspiracy in May 2006. Four months later, Skilling was sentenced to 24 years in prison but that sentence was shortened to 14 years in 2013. Kenneth Lay died of a massive heart attack in July 2006. Three months later, a federal judge overturned Lay's conviction since Lay was no longer able to pursue his appeal of that conviction.

The toll taken on the public accounting profession by the Enron debacle was not limited to Andersen, its partners, or its employees. An unending flood of jokes and ridicule directed at Andersen tainted and embarrassed practically every accountant in the nation, including both accountants in public practice and those working in the private sector. The Enron nightmare also prompted widespread soul-searching within the profession and a public outcry to strengthen the independent audit function and improve accounting and financial reporting practices. Legislative and regulatory authorities quickly responded to the public's demand for reforms.

The FASB imposed stricter accounting and financial reporting guidelines on SPEs as a direct result of the Enron case. Those new rules require most companies to include the financial data for those types of entities in their consolidated financial

---

35. Norris, "From Sunbeam to Enron."

statements. In 2002, Congress passed the Sarbanes–Oxley Act to strengthen financial reporting for public companies, principally by improving the rigor and quality of independent audits. Among other requirements, the Sarbanes–Oxley Act limits the types of consulting services that independent auditors can provide to their clients and requires public companies to prepare annual reports on the quality of their internal controls. The most sweeping change in the profession resulting from the Enron fiasco was the creation of a new federal agency, the Public Company Accounting Oversight Board, to oversee the independent audit function for SEC registrants.

Among the prominent individuals who commented on the challenges and problems facing the accounting profession was former SEC Chairman Richard Breeden when he testified before Congress in early 2002. Chairman Breeden observed that there was a simple solution to the quagmire facing the profession. He called on accountants and auditors to adopt a simple rule of thumb when analyzing, recording, and reporting on business transactions, regardless of whether those transactions involved "New Economy" or "Old Economy" business ventures. "When you're all done, the result had better fairly reflect what you see in reality."[36]

In retrospect, Commissioner Breeden's recommendation seems to be a restatement of the "Think straight, talk straight" motto of Arthur E. Andersen. Andersen and his colleagues insisted that their audit clients adhere to a high standard of integrity when preparing their financial statements. An interview with Joseph Berardino by the *New York Times* in December 2001 suggests that Mr. Berardino and his contemporaries may have had a different attitude when it came to dealing with cantankerous clients such as Enron: "In an interview yesterday, Mr. Berardino said Andersen had no power to force a company to disclose that it had hidden risks and losses in special-purpose entities. 'A client says: "There is no requirement to disclose this. You can't hold me to a higher standard."'"[37]

Berardino is certainly correct in his assertion. An audit firm cannot force a client to adhere to a higher standard. In fact, even Arthur Edward Andersen did not have that power. But Mr. Andersen did have the resolve to tell such clients to immediately begin searching for another audit firm.

Questions

1. The Enron debacle created what one public official reported was a "crisis of confidence" on the part of the public in the accounting profession. List the parties who you believe were most responsible for that crisis. Briefly justify each of your choices.

2. List three types of consulting services that audit firms are now prohibited from providing to clients that are public companies. For each item, indicate the specific threats, if any, that the provision of the given service could pose for an audit firm's independence.

3. For purposes of this question, assume that the excerpts from the Powers Report shown in Exhibit 3 provide accurate descriptions of Andersen's involvement in Enron's accounting and financial reporting decisions. Given this assumption, do you believe that Andersen's involvement in those decisions violated any professional auditing standards? If so, list those standards and briefly explain your rationale.

---

36. R. Schlank, "Former SEC Chairmen Urge Congress to Free FASB," *AccountingWeb* (online), 15 February 2002.

37. F. Norris, "The Distorted Numbers at Enron," *New York Times* (online), 14 December 2001.

4. Briefly describe the key requirements included in professional auditing standards regarding the preparation and retention of audit workpapers. Which party "owns" audit workpapers: the client or the audit firm?

5. Identify five recommendations made to strengthen the independent audit function following the Enron scandal. For each of these recommendations, indicate why you support or do not support the given measure. Also indicate which of these recommendations were eventually implemented.

6. Do you believe that there has been a significant shift or evolution over the past several decades in the concept of "professionalism" as it relates to the public accounting discipline? If so, explain how you believe that concept has changed or evolved over that time frame and identify the key factors responsible for any apparent changes.

7. As pointed out in this case, the SEC does not require public companies to have their quarterly financial statements audited. What responsibilities, if any, do audit firms have with regard to the quarterly financial statements of their clients? In your opinion, should quarterly financial statements be audited? Defend your answer.

Lehman Brothers Holdings, Inc.

Debt is a prolific mother of folly and crime.

Benjamin Disraeli

Thursday, 24 October 1929, easily ranks as the most dramatic day that Wall Street has ever seen.[1] That day witnessed the beginning of the Great Stock Market Crash that over the following few years would result in an almost 90 percent decline in the Dow Jones Industrial Average (DJIA). Although not nearly as dramatic as "Black Thursday," 15 September 2008, is a date that modern day Wall Street insiders will not soon forget. On that day, one of Wall Street's iconic investment banking firms, Lehman Brothers, filed for bankruptcy. That bankruptcy filing ended the proud history of a firm that had played a major role in shaping the nation's securities markets and economy for more than a century.

Lehman Brothers had approximately $700 billion in assets when it failed, which makes it the largest corporate bankruptcy in U.S. history, easily surpassing the previous headline-grabbing bankruptcies of Enron, General Motors, and WorldCom. By comparison, the telecommunications giant WorldCom, which temporarily held the title of the nation's largest business failure after collapsing in 2002, had less than one-sixth the total assets claimed by Lehman Brothers.

The shocking announcement that Lehman had filed for bankruptcy caused the DJIA to plunge more than 500 points within a few hours. That large loss was only a harbinger of things to come. Within six months, the DJIA had declined by more than 50 percent from its all-time high of 14,164.53 that it had reached on 9 October 2007. That market decline wiped out nearly 10 *trillion* dollars of "paper" wealth for stock market investors and plunged the U.S. and world economies into what became known as the Great Recession.

In the spring of 2010, the Lehman bankruptcy once again captured the nation's attention when the company's court-appointed bankruptcy examiner released his 2,200-page report. In preparing the highly anticipated report, the bankruptcy examiner and his staff reviewed 20 million documents and 10 million e-mails and spent $38 million. The massive report documented the circumstances and events that had contributed to Lehman's collapse and the parties that the bankruptcy examiner believed could be held civilly liable for it.

The release of the bankruptcy report prompted a public outcry because it revealed that Lehman's executives had routinely used multibillion-dollar "accounting-motivated" transactions to embellish their company's financial data. Allegedly, those transactions had been executed for the express purpose of enhancing a financial ratio that regulatory authorities, stock market analysts, and investors considered to be a key indicator of the company's overall financial condition.

As the company's financial health was rapidly deteriorating in 2007 and 2008, Lehman's executives had ramped up their use of the controversial transactions, resulting in the company's liabilities being understated by as much as $50 billion. Arguably most shocking was that Lehman never disclosed or referred to those transactions in the 10-K and 10-Q registration statements it filed periodically with the Securities and Exchange Commission (SEC).

---

1. I would like to thank Glen McLaughlin for his generous and continuing support of efforts to integrate ethics into business curricula. I would also like to thank T. J. Gillette for his excellent research that was instrumental in the development of this case.

Another revelation in the bankruptcy report that stunned the public was the fact that Lehman's audit firm had been aware of the billion-dollar transactions the company had used to window-dress its financial statements. According to the bankruptcy examiner, the Big Four audit firm had discussed those transactions on many occasions with company officials but had not insisted or, apparently, even suggested that the company disclose them in their financial statements or the accompanying notes.

The bankruptcy examiner also maintained that the audit firm had not properly informed Lehman's management and audit committee of an internal whistleblower's allegations that management was intentionally misrepresenting the company's financial statements. Because of alleged professional malpractice, Lehman's audit firm was among the parties the bankruptcy examiner suggested could be held civilly liable for the enormous losses suffered by the company's stockholders and creditors.

The Cotton Kings

Political unrest and poor economic conditions in their homeland prompted six million Germans to immigrate to the United States during the nineteenth century. Those immigrants included three brothers from Bavaria, the beautiful mountainous region of southeastern Germany. In 1844, 23-year-old Henry Lehman arrived in Montgomery, Alabama, a small city with fewer than 5,000 inhabitants in south central Alabama. Over the next few years, Henry's two brothers, Emanuel and Mayer, joined him in Montgomery.

The three brothers established a small retail store that stocked a wide range of merchandise including groceries, clothing, and hardware. Among the brothers' principal customers were cotton farmers from nearby rural areas who often paid for the merchandise they purchased with cotton bales. The brothers soon realized that there were more profits to be made in buying and selling cotton than operating a retail store so they became cotton merchants.

By 1860, "King Cotton" ruled the South. The southern states accounted for three-fourths of the cotton produced worldwide. Cotton was also the nation's largest export, accounting for 60 percent of the United States' total annual exports. In 1858, the huge demand for cotton in New England's booming textiles industry had convinced the Lehman brothers to establish an office in lower Manhattan, just a few blocks from the Wall Street financial district. But the outbreak of the Civil War in 1861 forced the Lehmans, who supported the Confederacy, to close that office.

The economic embargo imposed by President Lincoln on the South during the Civil War meant that cotton merchants such as the Lehman brothers lost their biggest market. Because the Lehmans realized that the demand for cotton would spike dramatically following the war, they bought large quantities of cotton produced during the war years and stored it in well-hidden warehouses scattered across the South. The postwar profits the brothers realized from selling that cotton helped them reestablish their firm as one of the South's largest cotton merchants following the war. By 1870, the Lehman brothers had reopened their New York City office; a short time later, they made that office the headquarters of their business.

In the latter decades of the nineteenth century, the Lehman brothers gradually expanded their business to include the trading of other commodities such as coffee, sugar, wheat, and petroleum products. The three brothers also decided to purchase a seat on the New York Stock Exchange. They realized that there was a need for financial intermediaries to funnel private investment capital to the large companies that were fueling the nation's rapid economic growth. Because of the nature of their business, the three brothers were well acquainted with the banking and credit industries and believed they could use that experience to easily segue into the emerging and lucrative investment banking industry.

By the early years of the twentieth century, the Lehman firm, which by then was being managed by the second generation of the Lehman family, had cut its ties to the cotton industry and focused its attention almost exclusively on investment banking. During that time frame, the firm served as the underwriter for several companies that would become stalwarts of the U.S. economy. These companies included B.F. Goodrich; Campbell Soup; F.W. Woolworth; R.H. Macy & Co.; and Sears, Roebuck & Co.

Investment banks facilitate the flow of investment capital in a free market economy by effectively "pricing risk." That is, investment bankers help buyers and sellers determine the appropriate relationship between the risk posed by given securities and the price at which those securities should be initially sold. This pricing process helps ensure that scarce investment capital is allocated in an efficient manner to corporations, other business organizations, and governmental agencies that need external funds to finance their operations.

Investment banking firms face a wide range of business risks. For example, investment banks sometimes absorb large losses on new client securities that they acquire during the underwriting process and are unable to sell to third parties. The most important factor contributing to the risk profile of investment banks is the degree of financial leverage they utilize. Similar to commercial banks, investment banks rely heavily on debt capital rather than invested capital. This high degree of financial leverage typically results in significant profits accruing to the firms' stockholders in a strong economic environment when the investment banking industry prospers. On the other hand, during economic downturns, investment banks often incur large losses that wipe out much of their stockholders' equity.

Throughout its history, Lehman Brothers experienced the highs and lows of the volatile business cycle common to the investment banking industry. The intensity of that cycle was magnified by a new line of investment products that Lehman and its competitors made popular on Wall Street during the 1990s.

Playing with Fire

Lehman Brothers and the other large investment banks became major players in the financial derivatives markets that emerged in the final decade of the twentieth century. Investopedia (www.investopedia.com) defines a financial "derivative" as follows:

> A security whose price is dependent upon or derived from one or more underlying assets. The derivative itself is merely a contract between two or more parties. Its value is determined by fluctuations in the underlying asset. The most common underlying assets include stocks, bonds, commodities, currencies, interest rates and market indexes. Most derivatives are characterized by high leverage.

Many types of financial derivatives have existed for decades, including the most generic, namely, put and call options on common stocks. In the mid-1990s, however, a new genre of exotic financial derivatives became increasingly prevalent. These new derivatives included collateralized debt obligations, credit default swaps, and interest rate swaps, among many others. Institutional investors accounted for the bulk of the trading volume in these new securities because they were poorly understood and thus shunned by most individual investors.

The new breed of derivatives produced large and profitable revenue streams for the investment banking industry. On the downside, the risks posed by these new securities were often difficult to assess, which, in turn, made those risks difficult, if not impossible, to manage. Some economists and Wall Street experts suggested that the risks posed by many of these derivatives were, in fact, disproportionately high compared to the rates of return they generated. Further enhancing the risk profile of these investments was the fact that they were subject to only minimal regulatory oversight.

In a 2009 retrospective overview of the securities markets, President Barack Obama observed that over the prior two decades those markets had been characterized by "wild risk-taking."[2] The president added that many of the new securities that became popular during that time frame were so complex and multifaceted that the "old regulatory schemes" developed for the securities markets in the 1930s did not provide adequate oversight for them.

Lehman flourished financially as the derivatives markets mushroomed in size and prominence during the 1990s and beyond. The firm was particularly active in the market for residential mortgage-backed securities or RMBS. By the turn of the century, government agencies, brokerage firms, and investment banks were producing a huge volume of RMBS each year. This "securitization" process involved purchasing residential mortgages from the banks, mortgage companies, and other entities that originated them, bundling or "pooling" these mortgages together, and then selling ownership interests (securities) in these pools. The purchasers of RMBS were actually purchasing a claim on the cash flows generated by the mortgages that "backed" those securities. By 2004, Lehman produced more RMBS annually than any other entity.[3]

The high yields on RMBS created a surging demand for these new hybrid securities. In turn, the increasing demand for RMBS caused mortgage originators to become increasingly aggressive in extending loans to individuals who in years past had not been able to qualify for a home mortgage because of an insufficient income, a poor credit history, or other issues. These mostly first-time home buyers were referred to as "subprime" borrowers. Mortgage originators were not concerned by the sizable default risk posed by subprime borrowers since they intended to sell their loans "downstream" and thereby transfer that risk to the purchasers of RMBS.

The critical factor that influenced the riskiness of RMBS was the underlying health of the housing market in the United States. Steadily rising housing prices during the decade from 1995 through 2005 made the default risk on residential mortgages minimal. Wall Street analysts warned, however, that a downturn in housing prices would trigger a rise in mortgage defaults that would be problematic for parties having significant investments in RMBS. On the other hand, a sudden and sharp downturn in housing prices could prove to be catastrophic for those investors. Sadly, the latter doomsday scenario took place.

Housing prices peaked in the United States in 2006. By late 2007, housing prices had begun to tumble, declining in many residential markets by 20 percent or more by mid-2008. In some of the residential markets that had seen the sharpest increases over the previous several years, such as Las Vegas and south Florida, housing prices plunged by 50 percent.

---

2. S. Labaton, "Obama Sought a Range of Views on Finance Rules," *New York Times* (online), 17 June 2009.

3. Lehman purchased a large portion of the residential mortgages that it securitized from New Century Financial Corporation, one of the nation's major subprime mortgage companies. Case 1.11 documents New Century's brief and turbulent history.

Falling housing prices caused a growing number of U.S. homeowners to be "upside down," meaning that the market values of their homes were lower than the unpaid balances of their mortgages. By early 2008, an estimated nine million Americans had a negative equity in their homes, which caused a rapid rise in mortgage defaults and foreclosures. It was only a matter of time before the sharp decline in housing prices undercut the market for RMBS.

Government agencies, large institutional investors, and investment banks having an ownership interest in RMBS suddenly found the value of those securities spiraling downward when it became obvious that housing prices would continue their free-fall. In some cases, the markets for mortgage-backed securities simply "froze," meaning that the securities could not be sold at any price. Lehman was among those entities that held a large inventory of mortgage-backed securities when the housing market crumbled. At the end of 2007, the company owned nearly $90 billion of those "toxic" assets. By comparison, Lehman's total stockholders' equity at the time was only $22.5 billion.

Prior to the collapse of the housing market, Lehman's high-risk business model had produced a string of record-breaking years. Exhibit 1 presents a financial high-lights table for Lehman for the five-year period 2003 through 2007 that is a condensed version of a similar table included in the company's 2007 annual report. Notice that during that time period the company reported record revenues and net income each successive year. Lehman's string of impressive operating results continued in early 2008. When the company posted stronger-than-expected results for the first quarter of 2008, the price of its common stock soared by nearly 50 percent in one day.

Lehman's top executives profited enormously from the consistently strong financial performance of their company. Richard Fuld served as Lehman's chief executive officer (CEO) from 1994 through 2008. Over that time, Fuld earned nearly $500 million in compensation. In addition to monetary rewards, Lehman's executives were lavished with praise and accolades. Just as Lehman's financial empire was beginning to buckle

	2007	2006	2005	2004	2003
Revenues	$ 19.3	$ 17.6	$ 14.6	$ 11.6	$ 8.7
Net Income	4.2	4.0	3.3	2.4	1.7
Total Assets	691.1	503.6	410.1	357.2	312.1
Total Stockholders' Equity	22.5	19.2	16.8	14.9	13.2
Earnings per Share	7.26	6.81	5.43	3.95	3.17
Dividends per Share	.60	.48	.40	.32	.24
Year-end Stock Price	62.63	73.67	63.00	41.89	36.11
Return on Equity	20.8%	23.4%	21.6%	17.9%	18.2%
Leverage Ratio	30.7	26.2	24.4	23.9	23.7
Net Leverage Ratio	16.1	14.5	13.6	13.9	15.3

EXHIBIT 1

LEHMAN BROTHERS FINANCIAL HIGHLIGHTS, 2003–2007*

*In billions of dollars except for per share amounts.
Source: Lehman Brothers' 2007 Annual Report.

in 2008, *Barron's* included Fuld in its list of the top 30 CEOs nationwide and tagged him with the title of "Mr. Wall Street."

Despite the glowing operating results for fiscal 2007 and the first quarter of 2008, Lehman's management recognized that the company faced daunting challenges. "Lehman was publicly presenting a rosy outlook about its future while it was privately scrambling for a solution to its deepening problems."[4] Complicating matters for Lehman's management was the fact that financial analysts and other parties closely monitoring the investment banking industry had begun raising serious questions regarding the company's financial health. Those questions stemmed primarily from two issues facing Lehman, one of which was the mayhem taking place within the housing market. The second and more important issue facing the large investment banking firm was the fact that it was "wildly overleveraged."[5] This issue was critical because by this time there was a general consensus on Wall Street that an investment bank's degree of financial leverage was the most important metric to use in evaluating its financial health.

Lehman's financial highlights table in Exhibit 1 presents two measures of financial leverage. The company's conventional leverage ratio was computed by dividing total assets by total stockholders' equity. At fiscal year-end 2007, this ratio was 30.7 for Lehman, meaning that the company had only $1 of stockholders' equity for every $30.70 of assets that it held. In the company's 2007 annual report, Lehman's management suggested that the "net leverage ratio" was a much better measure of the company's financial leverage than the conventional leverage ratio. In computing the net leverage ratio, the company excluded from total assets a large volume of "low-risk" assets. Notice that Lehman's 2007 net leverage ratio was nearly 50 percent lower than its conventional leverage ratio.

The importance being ascribed to Lehman's leverage ratios, in particular its net leverage ratio, by financial analysts in late 2007 prompted Richard Fuld to order a company-wide "deleveraging strategy." In an intercompany communication during this time frame, one of Fuld's subordinates noted that "reducing leverage is necessary to ... win back the confidence of the market, lenders, and investors."[6] Another of Fuld's subordinates subsequently testified that beginning in late 2007 "Lehman set balance sheet targets with an eye to reaching [reducing] certain leverage ratios that rating agencies used to measure and gauge Lehman's performance."

Lehman's management chose an unconventional method to reduce the company's net leverage ratio. This improvised tactic involved engaging in a large volume of "accounting-motivated" transactions, known internally as Repo 105 transactions, near the end of each quarterly reporting period. Because the Repo 105 transactions were not disclosed in Lehman's SEC filings, third-party financial statement users were unaware that the company's net leverage ratio was being intentionally sculpted by management. "Lehman never disclosed that its net leverage ratio—which Lehman publicly touted as evidence of its discipline and financial health—depended upon the Repo 105 practice."

---

4. L. Story and B. White, "The Road to Lehman's Failure Was Littered with Lost Chances," *New York Times* (online), 6 October 2008.

5. D. Leonard, "How Lehman Brothers Got Its Real Estate Fix," *New York Times* (online), 3 May 2009.

6. This and all subsequent quotes, unless indicated otherwise, were taken from the following source: *In re: Lehman Brothers Holdings, Inc., et al., Debtors*, "Report of Anton R. Valukas, Examiner," U.S. Bankruptcy Court for the Southern District of New York, Chapter 11 Case No. 08-13555, 11 March 2010.

Repo Central

In a repurchase or "repo" agreement, one party sells securities to another party while making a contractual commitment to repurchase those securities at a later date. The agreed-upon repurchase price for the given securities is nominally greater than the original selling price. In substance, the original "seller" of the securities is actually borrowing money from the original "purchaser" and using the securities transferred to the purchaser as collateral for the loan. The difference between the original selling price and the repurchase price is the interest earned on the loan by the original purchaser.

Another feature of repo transactions is what is known as the "haircut." The borrowing party (seller) transfers more than the face value of the securities involved in the transaction as collateral to the lender (purchaser). For example, if Lehman borrowed $100 million from another party under a conventional repo agreement, it would transfer more than $100 million of securities to the lender to serve as collateral for the loan. The haircut for Lehman's normal repos was typically 2 percent. So, in the example just provided, Lehman would have transferred $102 million of securities to the lender even though the actual amount of the loan was only $100 million.

Repos are a common financing tool used by large companies that need to raise a significant amount of funds for a short period of time. Repo lenders, on the other hand, view these transactions as a relatively safe way to invest excess cash at a modest rate of return without tying up those funds for an extended period of time. Similar to other investment banks, Lehman used repos as a major source of short-term financing.

For accounting purposes, repo agreements are nearly always treated as financing (borrowing) transactions by the borrower rather than as true sales of securities—Lehman recorded all of its normal repos as financing transactions. At the time, this accounting treatment was dictated by *Statement of Financial Accounting Standards (SFAS) No. 140*, "Accounting for Transfers and Servicing of Financial Assets and Extinguishment of Liabilities." When certain unusual conditions were met, however, *SFAS No. 140* provided for an exception to this general rule, meaning that repo borrowers could record the transactions as sales of securities.[7]

Lehman's executives realized that the *SFAS No. 140* exception could be used to their advantage, namely, to reduce their company's net leverage ratio. The lynchpin of this strategy was engaging in a large volume of "Repo 105s" that were repurchase agreements that the company recorded as sales rather than as financing transactions. The company's justification for treating a Repo 105 as a sale was the size of the "haircut" involved in the transaction. For Repo 105s, the amount of the haircut was 5 percent—which explained the label applied to them by the company. Lehman's accounting staff maintained that the larger haircut for the Repo 105s allowed them to be treated as sales under the exception included in *SFAS No. 140*.[8,9] Because this interpretation of *SFAS No. 140* was controversial, prior to engaging in any Repo 105s, company management decided to obtain a legal opinion confirming that the transactions could be considered "true sales" of securities.

---

7. *SFAS No. 140* has been revised in recent years, principally by *SFAS No. 166*, "Accounting for Transfers of Financial Assets."

8. Lehman Brothers' detailed justification for this accounting treatment is documented in several sources including a lengthy explanation in the bankruptcy examiner's report. For a more concise discussion of Lehman Brothers' defense of this accounting treatment, see the following source: S. K. Dutta, D. Caplan, and R. Lawson, "Poor Risk Management," *Strategic Finance*, August 2010, 23–29. Essentially, Lehman maintained that the larger haircut involved in a Repo 105 was evidence that it had surrendered control over the securities transferred to the other party, a condition required for a repo to be treated as a sale under *SFAS No. 140*.

9. Recognize that the "haircut" is not equal to the amount of interest paid by the borrower to the lender in a repo transaction. Since repos tend to be for a short period of time, the amount of interest paid by the borrower is typically a fraction of 1 percent, although the annualized interest rate might be, for example, 8 percent.

Lehman's management could not find a law firm in the United States willing to issue a legal opinion that Repo 105s were true sales. Undeterred, the company's executives began searching for a foreign law firm that would issue such an opinion. The law firm that the company eventually retained for that purpose was Linklaters, a large British firm.

> *Unable to find a United States law firm that would provide it with an opinion letter permitting the true sale accounting treatment under United States law, Lehman conducted its Repo 105 program under the aegis of an opinion letter the Linklaters law firm in London wrote for LBIE, Lehman's European broker-dealer in London, under English law.*

Because the Repo 105s had to be consummated in Great Britain, Lehman transferred securities that would be involved in those transactions from a U.S. division of the firm to a British-based division, namely, Lehman Brothers International Europe (LBIE), its London-based brokerage. Although these transactions were consummated in Great Britain, they were ultimately included in Lehman's consolidated financial statements issued in the United States.

There were actually two "legs" to each Repo 105 transaction. The first leg involved the "sale" of the securities to a third party; in the second leg of these transactions, Lehman used the proceeds from the sale to pay off a portion of its outstanding liabilities. When taken together, the two legs of Repo 105 transactions allowed Lehman to reduce its net leverage ratio and thereby strengthen its apparent financial condition.

Recognize that the impact of the first leg of a Repo 105 on net assets was zero. When securities were sold in a Repo 105, the journal entry to record the transaction included a "debit" to a cash account that was offset by an equal "credit" to the appropriate investments account.[10] However, the second leg of the transaction, that is, the use of Repo 105 cash proceeds to pay down liabilities, resulted in Lehman's total assets being reduced, which, in turn, reduced Lehman's net leverage ratio. The accounting treatment applied to conventional repos, which were simply recorded as short-term loans, did not yield this "leverage-reduction" benefit.[11]

Lehman's bankruptcy examiner documented the fact that the volume of Lehman's Repo 105s spiked dramatically at the end of each quarterly reporting period. This opportunistic timing of the transactions allowed the company to significantly reduce its net leverage ratio just days or even hours before its accounting staff closed the accounting records to prepare the company's quarterly or annual financial statements. A few days later, Lehman would reverse or unwind the Repo 105s by reacquiring the given securities with newly borrowed funds. At the end of fiscal 2007, Lehman had $39 billion of "open" Repo 105 transactions; three months later, that figure had risen to $50 billion.

Lehman's use of Repo 105s to strengthen its reported financial condition in 2007 and 2008 was the major focus of the 2,200-page report that was filed by the company's bankruptcy examiner with a federal court. Particularly appalling to the bankruptcy examiner were the efforts of Lehman's management to draw attention to the company's declining leverage while concealing the fact that Repo 105s were

---

10. This is a brief and simplified summary of the accounting treatment applied to Repo 105s by Lehman. Examples of hypothetical accounting entries used by Lehman to record its Repo 105 transactions are presented in the following article: S. K. Dutta, D. Caplan, and R. Lawson, "Poor Risk Management," *Strategic Finance*, August 2010, 23–29.

11. The conventional strategy for reducing the net leverage ratio would have been to simply sell assets and then use the proceeds to pay down liabilities. Lehman could not avail itself of that strategy since the markets for the assets (investments) that it had available for sale were highly illiquid. To sell those assets, Lehman would have been forced to absorb large losses, losses that would have reduced its stockholders' equity and thus largely negated the intended reduction of its net leverage ratio.

responsible for much of that improvement. In "earnings calls" with financial analysts tracking Lehman's stock, for example, the company's chief financial officer (CFO) stressed the fact that the company's financial leverage was being reduced, however, she "said nothing about the firm's use of Repo 105 transactions." At the same time, the CFO told those analysts that her company was committed to providing them "a great amount of transparency" regarding the company's balance sheet.

The bankruptcy examiner maintained that even if the accounting treatment applied to the Repo 105s technically complied with *SFAS No. 140*, that accounting treatment violated Generally Accepted Accounting Principles (GAAP) by causing Lehman's financial statements to be misleading. To support his position, the bankruptcy examiner referred to a ruling handed down by a federal district court in a case involving an accounting matter. "GAAP itself recognizes that technical compliance with particular GAAP rules may lead to misleading financial statements, and imposes an overall requirement that the statements taken as a whole accurately reflect the financial status of the company."

According to the bankruptcy examiner, there had been no underlying business purpose for the Repo 105s. Instead, the sole purpose of the transactions had been to make Lehman's "balance sheet appear stronger than it actually was." In sum, the transactions had been "accounting-motivated." The bankruptcy examiner referred to a prior SEC release to define that term.

> *"Accounting-motivated structured transactions" are "transactions that are structured in an attempt to achieve reporting results that are not consistent with the economics of the transaction, and thereby impair the transparency of financial reports." [Attempts] to portray the transactions differently from their substance do not operate in the interests of investors, and may be in violation of the securities laws.*

The bankruptcy examiner uncovered numerous instances of intercompany communications that suggested the Repo 105s had been accounting-driven. In responding to an inquiry regarding why Lehman was engaging in a large volume of Repo 105s at the end of each quarter, one company executive had told another, "It's basically window-dressing. We are calling repos true sales based on legal technicalities." Another company executive testified that "It was universally accepted throughout the entire institution [company] that Repo 105 was used for balance sheet relief at quarter end." A lower-level Lehman employee had referred to Repo 105s as an "accounting gimmick" and a "lazy way of managing the balance sheet." Finally, a high-ranking accounting officer admitted to the bankruptcy examiner that "there was no substance to these transactions" and that their only "purpose or motive was reduction [of assets] in the balance sheet."

Further validating the bankruptcy examiner's argument that the Repo 105s had been purely accounting-driven was the fact that they had been more expensive than Lehman's normal repo transactions. That is, the company could have secured the short-term financing provided by the several hundred billions of dollars of its Repo 105s at a lower cost by using conventional repo agreements. "Lehman could have obtained the same financing at a lower cost by engaging in ordinary repo transactions with substantially the same counterparties using the same assets involved in the Repo 105 transactions."

When considering the issue of whether the accounting treatment applied to the Repo 105s made Lehman's financial statements materially misleading, the bankruptcy examiner effectively invoked the definition of that construct found in *Statement of Financial Accounting Concepts No. 2*, "Qualitative Characteristics of Accounting Information."

The magnitude of an omission or misstatement of accounting information that, in light of the surrounding circumstances, makes it probable that the judgment of a reasonable person relying on the information would have been changed or influenced by the omission or misstatement.

The bankruptcy examiner surveyed a wide range of "reasonable" parties that had relied on Lehman's financial statements. Nearly all of these parties insisted that they would have wanted to know that the company was using the Repo 105 transactions to distort its balance sheet and key financial ratios. "Lehman's directors, the rating agencies, and government regulators—all of whom were unaware of Lehman's use of Repo 105 transactions—have advised the Examiner that Lehman's Repo 105 usage was material or significant information that they would have wanted to know." In fact, in 2008, the controller of Lehman's European operations had e-mailed a Lehman colleague in the United States and warned him that the Repo 105s "are understating what we have at risk by a material amount especially around quarter ends." The bankruptcy examiner relied on such statements in arriving at his decision that a "trier of fact," that is, a court, would likely find that the Repo 105s had resulted in Lehman's financial statements being materially misleading.

To bolster this conclusion, the bankruptcy examiner referred to a discussion of materiality included in the 2007 workpapers of Lehman's independent audit firm, Ernst & Young (E&Y). "Indeed, audit walk-through papers prepared by Lehman's outside auditor, Ernst & Young, regarding the process for reopening or adjusting a closed balance sheet stated: 'Materially is usually defined as any item individually, or in the aggregate, that moves net leverage by 0.1 or more (typically $1.8 billion). Repo 105 moved net leverage not by tenths, but by whole points.'" As shown in Exhibit 1, Lehman's reported net leverage ratio as of the end of fiscal 2007 was 16.1. According to the bankruptcy examiner, the actual ratio would have been 17.8 if the company had accounted for the Repo 105s as financing transactions.

During his investigation, the bankruptcy examiner spent considerable time reviewing the Ernst & Young audit workpapers. The prominent accounting firm ultimately became a major focus of that investigation and the target of scathing criticism by the bankruptcy examiner.

Auditors on the Firing Line

E&Y served as Lehman's independent audit firm from 1994 through 2008. For the 2007 audit, the final audit of the company prior to its collapse, Lehman paid E&Y approximately $29.5 million. That figure included the fee for the 2007 audit, fees for tax services provided to the company, and miscellaneous fees. William Schlich served as the engagement audit partner for the 2007 audit of Lehman. In July 2008, Schlich, a longtime E&Y partner, was named the head of E&Y's "Global Banking & Capital Markets" practice, the firm's largest individual industry practice.

Lehman's bankruptcy examiner interviewed Schlich extensively during his investigation. Schlich told the bankruptcy examiner that E&Y had been aware of the Repo 105 transactions and was also aware that Lehman had not disclosed the transactions in financial statements filed with the SEC. Schlich also revealed that Lehman officials had consulted with E&Y while they were developing the company's Repo 105 accounting policy, although he reported that his firm had not been directly involved in that process and had not formally approved the accounting policy.

Martin Kelly, Lehman's former financial controller, testified that he discussed the Repo 105 transactions with Schlich in late 2007. Kelly told the bankruptcy examiner that he had a certain degree of "discomfort" with the Repo 105s, ostensibly because

Lehman had been unable to obtain a legal opinion from a U.S. law firm that supported the company's decision to record those transactions as sales of securities. Kelly specifically recalled raising the latter issue with the E&Y auditors.

Surprisingly, Schlich told the examiner that he did not know whether anyone on the E&Y engagement team had actually reviewed the legal opinion on the Repo 105 transactions issued by Linklaters, the British law firm. Schlich suggested that the responsibility for reviewing that letter would have rested with his firm's British affiliate, E&Y United Kingdom, which had audited the accounting records of LBIE, the British arm of Lehman Brothers that had executed the Repo 105 transactions.

Throughout his investigation and in his report, the bankruptcy examiner repeatedly characterized the Repo 105s as "accounting-motivated" transactions without an underlying business purpose that had been intended to embellish Lehman's financial statements and its net leverage ratio. While being interviewed by the examiner, however, Schlich staunchly defended the accounting treatment that had been applied to those transactions. The E&Y partner insisted that the "off-balance sheet treatment" of the Repo 105s was purely a "consequence of the accounting rules" rather than the underlying "motive for the transactions." When the examiner asked Schlich whether "technical adherence" to *SFAS No. 140* or any other specific accounting rule could have resulted in Lehman's financial statements being misstated, "Schlich refrained from comment." On two occasions, the examiner "offered Ernst & Young the opportunity" to explain or identify the "business purpose of Lehman's Repo 105 transactions." On each occasion, the E&Y representative (apparently Schlich) "declined that invitation."

The bankruptcy examiner subsequently criticized E&Y for not addressing the possibility that Lehman's "Repo 105 transactions were accounting-motivated transactions that lacked a business purpose." According to the examiner, E&Y should have recognized, or at least considered the possibility, that the Repo 105s were simply intended to improve Lehman's apparent financial condition, in particular, its net leverage ratio. The examiner stated that there was "no question that Ernst & Young had a full understanding of the net leverage ratio" and that the auditors understood the importance of that ratio to third-party financial statement users.

The bankruptcy examiner focused considerable attention on the materiality of the Repo 105 transactions while he was interviewing Schlich. At one point, the examiner asked Schlich what volume of Repo 105 transactions would have been considered "material" by E&Y. "Schlich replied that Ernst & Young did not have a hard and fast rule defining materiality in the balance sheet context, and that, with respect to balance sheet issues, 'materiality' depends upon the facts and circumstances." In his report, the bankruptcy examiner juxtaposed this statement of Schlich with the fact that E&Y's 2007 Lehman workpapers had identified the following precise materiality threshold for the company's net leverage ratio: "Materiality is usually defined as any item individually, or in the aggregate, that moves net leverage by 0.1 or more (typically $1.8 billion)."

When questioned further regarding the materiality of the Repo 105s, Schlich told the bankruptcy examiner that E&Y's audit plan had not required the Lehman engagement team to "review the volume or timing of Repo 105 transactions." Consequently, "as part of its year-end 2007 audit, E&Y did not ask Lehman about any directional trends, such as whether its Repo 105 activity was increasing during fiscal year 2007." The bankruptcy examiner reported that Schlich was unable to "confirm or deny that Lehman's use of Repo 105 transactions was increasing in late 2007 and into mid-2008."

A final major issue raised with William Schlich by the bankruptcy examiner was E&Y's response to the whistleblower letter sent to company management in May 2008 by a senior member of Lehman's accounting staff. Lehman's management had asked E&Y to be involved in investigating the allegations in that letter.[12] Among other allegations, the whistleblower suggested that Lehman's assets and liabilities were routinely misstated by "tens of billions of dollars" in the company's periodic balance sheets. To remind his superiors of their responsibilities related to financial reporting, the whistleblower had included in his letter the following excerpt from Lehman's Code of Ethics.[13]

> *All employees ... must endeavor to ensure that information in documents that Lehman Brothers files with or submits to the SEC, or otherwise discloses to the public, is presented in a full, fair, accurate, timely and understandable manner. Additionally, each individual involved in the preparation of the Firm's financial statements must prepare those statements in accordance with Generally Accepted Accounting Principles, consistently applied, and any other applicable accounting standards and rules so that the financial statements present fairly, in all material respects, the financial position, results of operations and cash flows of the Firm.*

Approximately four weeks passed before E&Y interviewed the author of the whistleblower letter. Schlich and Hillary Hansen, another E&Y partner, conducted that interview. Hansen's handwritten notes compiled during the interview indicated that the whistleblower alleged that Lehman had used tens of billions of dollars of Repo 105 transactions to strengthen its quarter-ending balance sheets. According to the examiner, E&Y never interviewed the whistleblower a second time and never "followed up" on his allegation regarding Lehman's improper use of Repo 105s.

The day after interviewing the whistleblower, E&Y auditors met with Lehman's audit committee but, according to the bankruptcy examiner, did not inform the committee members of the whistleblower's Repo 105 allegation. Three weeks later, E&Y auditors met once more with Lehman's audit committee and again reportedly failed to mention that allegation. The bankruptcy examiner subsequently reviewed E&Y's workpapers for the 2007 audit and the 2008 quarterly reviews and "found no reference to any communication with the audit committee about Repo 105."

During his interview with the bankruptcy examiner, Schlich indicated that he did not recall the whistleblower mentioning the Repo 105 transactions when he and Hansen met with him. When informed that Hansen's handwritten notes of that meeting indicated that the whistleblower had referred to those transactions, Schlich "did not dispute the authenticity" of those notes.

In summarizing his investigation of E&Y's role as Lehman's auditor, the bankruptcy examiner reported that there was "sufficient evidence to support at least three colorable claims that could be asserted against Ernst & Young relating to Lehman's Repo 105 activities and reporting."[14] The first colorable claim involved E&Y's alleged failure to "conduct an adequate inquiry" into the whistleblower's allegations and failing "to properly inform management and the audit committee" of those allegations. Second, the bankruptcy examiner charged that E&Y had failed to "take proper action" to investigate whether Lehman's financial statements for the first two quarters

---

12. After reading the whistleblower letter, Schlich confided to two colleagues in an e-mail that the letter was "pretty ugly" and that it "will take us a significant amount of time to get through."

13. The whistleblower was dismissed approximately one month after sending his letter to Lehman's top management. He was reportedly dismissed as a result of a corporate-wide "downsizing" campaign.

14. "Colorable claim" is a legal term. A colorable claim is generally a "plausible legal claim," that is, a claim "strong enough to have a reasonable chance of being valid if the legal basis is generally correct and the facts can be proven in court." (http://topics.law.cornell.edu)

of 2008 were materially misleading due to the company's failure to disclose its Repo 105 transactions. The final colorable claim involved E&Y's alleged failure to "take proper action" to investigate whether Lehman's financial statements for fiscal 2007 were materially misleading due to the Repo 105s.[15]

The allegations that the bankruptcy examiner filed against E&Y spawned widespread discussion and debate within the accounting profession. One accounting professor defended the accounting treatment that Lehman applied to its Repo 105s and, by implication, E&Y's tacit approval of that treatment. In responding to the question of whether Lehman was entitled to account for those transactions as sales of securities, the professor responded, "Absolutely. Even if intended to influence (or deceitfully change) the numbers reported? Yes, intent doesn't matter. It [Lehman] found a rule it could utilize to its advantage and followed it."[16] The professor went on to explain that the given "rule" was a bad one that should be amended.

Three other accounting professors expressed a very different point of view. These professors noted that "a fundamental financial reporting objective that overrides the application of any specific rule is that the accounting of a transaction should not obfuscate its economic substance."[17] The professors then noted that "parties with meaningful roles in the financial reporting process" shouldn't be involved in applying "accounting rules with the intent to obfuscate the economic substance"[18] of given transactions. Finally, the professors made the following observation regarding the professional responsibilities of the accountants and auditors involved in the Lehman debacle:

External auditors, internal auditors, and management accountants all have professional standards that are aspirational in nature, and, regardless of whether Lehman's auditors and accountants met the minimum standards that might shield them from legal liability and formal professional sanction, it seems clear that they fell short of the higher standards to which all management accountants and auditors should aspire.[19]

EPILOGUE

The revelations and allegations included in the report issued by Lehman's bankruptcy examiner evoked an immediate response from the SEC. In March 2010, an SEC spokesperson reported that the federal agency had been unaware that Wall Street firms were using Repo 105-type transactions to enhance their apparent financial condition. The SEC revealed that it was contacting 20 major financial institutions to determine if they had used similar tactics to "manage" their balance sheets. To date, the SEC has not commented on the results of that survey or identified the specific firms that were contacted.

Lehman's bankruptcy report served as an "open invitation"[20] to file civil lawsuits against E&Y. And that is exactly what happened. Throughout 2010, numerous lawsuits that named E&Y as a defendant or codefendant were filed on behalf of parties that suffered losses due to Lehman's collapse. Among these lawsuits, the one with arguably the highest profile was a civil fraud lawsuit filed against E&Y in late December 2010 by Andrew Cuomo, New York's Attorney

15. The bankruptcy examiner noted that E&Y "may have valid defenses" to the colorable claims that he asserted against the firm. The examiner discussed some of these defenses including the fact that many auditing standards do not impose "bright line rules" but instead provide only "general guidance" to auditors.

16. D. Albrecht, "Repo 105 Explained with Numbers and Detail," 24 April 2010, http://profalbrecht .wordpress.com/2010/04/24.

17. S. K. Dutta, D. Caplan, and R. Lawson, "Poor Risk Management," *Strategic Finance*, August 2010, 29.

18. *Ibid.*

19. *Ibid.*

20. Texas Society of Certified Public Accountants, "Accounting Web—April 2, 2010," http://www.tscpa.org.

General and Governor-elect. In commenting on the lawsuit, Cuomo noted that Lehman had been a "house-of-cards" and that E&Y had "helped hide" this fact "from the investing public."[21]

Shortly after the release of the Lehman bankruptcy report, E&Y issued the following statement defending its unqualified opinion on Lehman's 2007 financial statements: "Our opinion stated that Lehman's financial statements for 2007 were fairly presented in accordance with U.S. GAAP, and we remain of that view."[22] E&Y's statement went on to observe that "Lehman's bankruptcy was the result of a series of unprecedented adverse events in the financial markets…. It was not caused by accounting issues or disclosures issues."[23]

E&Y's responses to Lehman-related lawsuits have typically included rebuttals of allegations initially made by the company's bankruptcy examiner. For example, E&Y has repeatedly insisted that the accounting treatment applied by Lehman to its Repo 105 transactions was GAAP compliant. In a legal document filed with a federal court, E&Y's defense counsel maintained that Lehman's Repo 105s were properly recorded as true sales of securities under *SFAS No. 140*.[24] Likewise, E&Y has maintained that at the time Lehman was not required to disclose the Repo 105 transactions in its financial statements. E&Y's attorneys have pointed out that *SFAS No. 166*, "Accounting for Transfers of Financial Assets," which was issued in June 2009, now mandates such disclosure, which, from the attorneys' perspective, reinforces their argument that such disclosure was *not* required in 2007.[25]

Considerable attention was focused by the bankruptcy examiner on the impact that Lehman's Repo 105 transactions had on the company's reported net leverage ratio. E&Y, however, has pointed out that the ratio was not included in the company's audited financial statements and thus was not a "GAAP financial measure" subject to being audited.[26] E&Y has also strongly contested the assertion that the Lehman auditors failed to properly inform the company's audit committee of the allegations included in the infamous whistleblower letter received by Lehman's management in May 2008.

The media has inaccurately reported that E&Y concealed a May 2008 whistleblower letter from Lehman's Audit Committee. The whistleblower letter, which raised significant potential concerns about Lehman's financial controls and reporting but did not mention Repo 105, was directed to Lehman's management. When we learned of the letter, our lead partner promptly called the Audit Committee Chair; we also insisted that Lehman's management inform the Securities & Exchange Commission and the Federal Reserve Bank of the letter. E&Y's lead partner discussed the whistleblower letter with the Lehman Audit Committee on at least three occasions during June and July 2008.[27,28]

---

21. P. Lattman, "Cuomo Sues Ernst & Young Over Lehman," *New York Times* (online), 21 December 2010.

22. M. Cohn, "Ernst & Young Defends Lehman Audits," *WebCPA*, 25 March 2010. (http://www.accountingtoday.com)

23. *Ibid.*

24. *In Re Lehman Brothers Equity/Debt Securities Litigation*, No. 08 Civ. 5523 (LAK), "Civil Action No. 09 MD 2017 (LAK), U.S. District Court for the Southern District of New York." E&Y's legal counsel contended that Lehman had relinquished "effective control" of the securities involved in the Repo 105 transactions and, as a result, was permitted to record those transactions as sales of securities under *SFAS No. 140*. Not surprisingly, the plaintiff attorneys disagreed with that interpretation of *SFAS No. 140*.

25. *Ibid.*

26. Texas Society of Certified Public Accountants, "Accounting Web—April 2, 2010." Recall that Lehman's net leverage ratio was included in a financial highlights table in its 2007 annual report. That ratio was also referred to in the Management's Discussion & Analysis (MD&A) section of that report.

27. Texas Society of Certified Public Accountants, "Accounting Web—April 2, 2010."

28. Notice that E&Y asserts that it discussed the whistleblower letter with Lehman's audit committee. The bankruptcy examiner, however, alleges that E&Y did not bring the Repo 105s to the attention of the audit committee members. E&Y is correct that the Repo 105s were not specifically identified in the whistleblower letter, although they were apparently alluded to in the letter and were referred to by the whistleblower during his subsequent interview with Schlich and Hansen.

Over the years to come, the gaggle of Lehman-related lawsuits that have been filed will work their way through the courts.[29] No doubt, over that time frame a clearer picture will emerge regarding the veracity of the claims and counterclaims in those lawsuits as well as the veracity of the allegations made by Lehman's bankruptcy examiner.

Similar to the Enron and WorldCom fiascoes in the past, the Lehman debacle has prompted widespread calls for accounting, auditing, and financial reporting reforms. In particular, many parties critical of Lehman's accountants and auditors have urged rule-making bodies to clarify the accounting and financial reporting rules for complex transactions, such as Repo 105-type transactions. In fact, the Financial Accounting Standards Board attempted to do just that by issuing multiple amendments to *SFAS No. 140* in the aftermath of Lehman's collapse.

The authors of an article in a practice-oriented accounting periodical, however, suggest that promulgating new, more precise accounting rules is unlikely to prevent Lehman-type accounting scandals in the future. In their view, the most effective way to prevent the recurrence of such scandals is to develop a more robust "ethical culture" within the accounting profession, a culture that encourages accountants and auditors to embrace the profession's core values such as integrity, objectivity, and commitment to public service.

Ethical behavior is not about abiding by the law. Individuals and organizations can act legally and still be acting unethically. Ethical behavior is driven by compliance with a set of values that act as the touchstone for situational decisions where rules may not exist to cover every alternative.[30]

Questions

1. When Lehman was developing its Repo 105 accounting policy, did E&Y have a responsibility to be involved in that process? In general, what role should an audit firm have when a client develops an important new accounting policy? Comment on an audit firm's responsibilities during and following that process.

2. Do you agree with the assertion that "intent doesn't matter" when applying accounting rules? That is, should reporting entities be allowed to apply accounting rules or approved exceptions to accounting rules for the express purpose of intentionally embellishing their financial statements or related financial data? Defend your answer.

3. Do auditors have a responsibility to determine whether important transactions of a client are "accounting-motivated"? Defend your answer.

4. William Schlich implied that E&Y's British affiliate had the responsibility for reviewing the legal opinion issued by a British law firm regarding the treatment of Repo 105s as sales of securities. Do you believe that Schlich or one of his subordinates should have reviewed that letter? Why or why not? In general, how should the responsibility for different facets of a multinational audit be allocated between or among the individual practice offices involved in the engagement?

29. In late 2013, Reuters announced that E&Y had reached a tentative agreement to settle a lawsuit filed against it by former Lehman stockholders. The agreement, if approved by the given federal court, would require E&Y to pay those stockholders $99 million. Prior to this announced settlement, those same plaintiffs had received more than $500 million in settlements from other named defendants in the same lawsuit, including Lehman's former executives. See, N. Brown, "Ernst & Young to Pay $99 Million to End Lehman Investor Lawsuit," www.reuters.com, 18 October 2013.

30. Dutta et al., "Poor Risk Management."

5. Lehman's net leverage ratio was not reported within the company's audited financial statements but rather in the company's financial highlights table and MD&A section of its annual report. What responsibility, if any, do auditors have to assess the material accuracy of financial data included in those two sections of a client's annual report?

6. The Repo 105 transactions reduced Lehman's net leverage ratio from 17.8 to 16.1 at the end of fiscal 2007. Do you believe that was a "material difference"? Why or why not?

7. In general, what responsibility do auditors have to investigate whistleblower allegations that relate to the material accuracy of an audit client's financial statements?

8. E&Y is a defendant in Lehman-related lawsuits filed in both state and federal courts. Identify the factors that influence E&Y's legal exposure between lawsuits filed in state courts versus those filed in federal courts.

Just For FEET, Inc.

*Life is so fragile. A single bad choice in a single moment can cause a
life to turn irrevocably 180 degrees.*

U.S. District Judge C. Lynwood Smith, Jr.

In 1971, 25-year-old Thomas Shine founded a small sporting goods company, Logo 7, that would eventually become known as Logo Athletic. Shine's company manufactured and marketed a wide range of shirts, hats, jackets, and other apparel items that boldly displayed the logos of the Miami Dolphins, Minnesota Twins, Montreal Canadiens, and dozens of other professional sports teams. In 2001, Shine sold Logo to Reebok and became that company's senior vice president of sports and entertainment marketing. In that position, Shine wined and dined major sports stars with the intent of persuading them to sign exclusive endorsement contracts with Reebok.

During his long career, Thomas Shine became one of the most well-known and respected leaders of the sporting goods industry. Shine's prominence and credibility in that industry took a severe blow in February 2004 when he pleaded guilty to a criminal indictment filed against him by the U.S. Department of Justice. The Justice Department charged that Shine had signed a false audit confirmation sent to him in early 1999 by one of Logo's largest customers. The confirmation indicated that Logo owed that customer approximately $700,000. Although Shine knew that no such debt existed, he signed the confirmation and returned it to the customer's independent audit firm, Deloitte & Touche, after being pressured to do so by an executive of the customer. As a result of his guilty plea, Shine faced a possible sentence of five years in federal prison and a fine of up to $250,000.

Out of South Africa

At approximately the same time that Thomas Shine was launching his business career in the retail industry in the United States, Harold Ruttenberg was doing the same in South Africa. Ruttenberg, a native of Johannesburg, paid for his college education by working nights and weekends as a sales clerk in an upscale men's clothing store. After graduation, he began importing Levi's jeans from the United States and selling them from his car, his eventual goal being to accumulate sufficient capital to open a retail store. Ruttenberg quickly accomplished that goal. In fact, by the time he was 30, he owned a small chain of men's apparel stores.

Mounting political and economic troubles in his home country during the early and mid-1970s convinced Ruttenberg to move his family to the United States. South Africa's strict emigration laws forced Ruttenberg to leave practically all of his net worth behind. When he arrived in California in 1976 with his spouse and three small children, Ruttenberg had less than $30,000. Despite his limited financial resources and unfamiliarity with U.S. business practices, the strong-willed South African was committed to once again establishing himself as a successful entrepreneur in the retailing industry.

Ruttenberg soon realized that the exorbitant rents for commercial retail properties in the major metropolitan areas of California were far beyond his reach. So, he moved his family once more, this time to the more affordable business environment of Birmingham, Alabama. Ruttenberg leased a vacant storefront in a Birmingham mall and a few months later opened Hang Ten Sports World, a retail store that marketed children's sportswear products. Thanks largely to his work ethic and intense desire to succeed, Ruttenberg's business prospered over the next decade.

In 1988, Ruttenberg decided to take a gamble on a new business venture. Ruttenberg had come to believe that there was an opportunity to make large profits in the retail shoe business. At the time, the market for high-priced athletic shoes—basketball shoes, in particular—was growing dramatically and becoming an ever-larger segment of the retail shoe industry. The principal retail outlets for the shoes produced by Adidas, Nike, Reebok, and other major athletic shoe manufacturers were relatively small stores located in thousands of suburban malls scattered across the country, meaning that the retail athletic shoe "subindustry" was highly fragmented. The five largest retailers in this market niche accounted for less than 10 percent of the annual sales of athletic shoes.

Ruttenberg realized that the relatively small floor space of retail shoe stores in suburban malls limited a retailer's ability to display the wide and growing array of products being produced by the major shoe manufacturers. Likewise, the high cost of floor space in malls with heavy traffic served to limit the profitability of shoe retailers. To overcome these problems, Ruttenberg decided that he would build freestanding "Just for FEET" superstores located near malls. To lure consumers away from mall-based shoe stores, Ruttenberg developed a three-pronged business strategy focusing on "selection," "service," and "entertainment."

Ruttenberg's business plan for his superstores involved a stores-within-a-store concept; that is, he intended to create several mini-stores within his large retail outlets, each of which would be devoted exclusively to the products of individual shoe manufacturers. He believed this store design would appeal to both consumers and vendors. Consumers who were committed to one particular brand would not have to search through store displays that included a wide assortment of branded products. Likewise, his proposed floor design would provide major vendors an opportunity to participate in marketing their products. Ruttenberg hoped that his planned floor design would spur the major vendors to compete with each other in providing so-called vendor allowances to his superstores to make their individual displays more appealing than those of competitors.

Customer service was the second major element of Ruttenberg's business plan for his shoe superstores. Ruttenberg planned to staff his stores so that there would be an unusually large ratio of sales associates to customers. Sales associates would be required to complete an extensive training course in "footwear technology" so that they would be well equipped to answer any questions posed by customers. When a customer chose to try on a particular shoe product, he or she would have to ask a sales associate to retrieve that item from the "back shop." Sales associates were trained to interact with customers in such a way that they would earn their trust and thus create a stronger bond with them.

Just for Feet's 1998 Form 10-K described the third feature of Harold Ruttenberg's business plan as creating an "Entertainment Shopping Experience." Rock-and-roll music and brightly colored displays greeted customers when they entered the superstores. When they tired of shopping, customers could play a game of "horse" on an enclosed basketball half-court located near the store's entrance or sit back and enjoy a multiscreen video bank in the store's customer lounge. Frequent promotional events included autograph sessions with major sports celebrities such as Bart Starr, the former Green Bay Packers quarterback who was also on the company's board of directors.

Ruttenberg would eventually include two other key features in the floor plans of his superstores. Although Just for Feet did not target price-conscious customers, Ruttenberg added a "Combat Zone" to each superstore where such customers could rummage through piles of discontinued shoe lines, "seconds," and other discounted items. For those customers who simply wanted a pair of shoes and did not have a strong preference for a given brand, Ruttenberg incorporated a "Great Wall" into his superstores that contained a wide array of shoes sorted not by brand but rather by function. In this large display, customers could quickly compare and contrast the key features of dozens of different types of running shoes, walking shoes, basketball shoes, and cross-trainers.

Quite a FEET

Just for Feet's initial superstore in Birmingham proved to be a huge financial success. That success convinced Harold Ruttenberg to open similar retail outlets in several major metropolitan areas in the southern United States and to develop a showcase superstore within the glitzy Caesar's Forum shopping mall on the Las Vegas Strip. By 1992, Just for Feet owned and operated five superstores and had sold franchise rights for several additional stores. The company's annual sales were approaching $20 million, but that total accounted for a small fraction of the retail shoe industry's estimated $15 billion of annual sales.

To become a major force in the shoe industry, Ruttenberg knew that he would have to expand his retail chain nationwide, which would require large amounts of additional capital. To acquire that capital, Ruttenberg decided to take his company public. On 9 March 1994, Just for Feet's common stock began trading on the NASDAQ exchange under the ticker symbol FEET. The stock, which sold initially for $6.22 per share, would quickly rise over the next two years to more than $37 per share.

Ruttenberg used the funds produced by Just for Feet's initial public offering (IPO) to pursue an aggressive expansion program. The company opened dozens of new superstores during the mid-1990s and acquired several smaller competitors, including Athletic Attic in March 1997 and Sneaker Stadium in July 1998. For fiscal 1996, which ended 31 January 1997, the company reported a profit of $13.9 million on sales of $250 million. Two years later, the company earned a profit of $26.7 million on sales of nearly $775 million. By the end of 1998, Just for Feet was the second largest athletic shoe retailer in the United States with 300 retail outlets.

During the mid-1990s, Just for Feet's common stock was among the most closely monitored and hyped securities on Wall Street. Analysts and investors tracking the stock marveled at the company's ability to consistently outperform its major competitors. By the late 1990s, market saturation and declining profit margins were becoming major concerns within the athletic shoe segment of the shoe industry. Despite the lackluster profits and faltering revenues of other athletic shoe retailers, Harold Ruttenberg continued to issue press releases touting his company's record profits and steadily growing sales. Most impressive was the company's 21 straight quarterly increases in same-store sales through the fourth quarter of fiscal 1998.

In November 1997, Delphi Investments released a lengthy analytical report focusing on Just for Feet's future prospects. In that report, which included a strong "buy" recommendation for the company's common stock, Delphi commented on the "Harold Ruttenberg factor." The report largely attributed the company's financial success and rosy future to "the larger-than-life founder and inventor of the Just for Feet concept."

In frequent interviews with business journalists, Harold Ruttenberg was not modest in discussing the huge challenges that he had personally overcome to establish himself as one of the leading corporate executives in the retail apparel industry. Nor was Ruttenberg reluctant to point out that he had sketched out the general frame-work of Just for Feet's successful business plan over a three-day vacation in the late 1980s. After being named one of 1996's Retail Entrepreneurs of the Year, Ruttenberg noted that Just for Feet had succeeded principally because of the unique marketing strategies he had developed for the company. "Customers love our stores because they are so unique. We are not a copycat retailer. Nobody does what we do, the way we do it. The proof is in our performance."[1] In this same interview, Ruttenberg reported that he had never been tempted to check out a competitor's stores. "I have nothing to learn from them. I'm certainly not going to copy anything they are doing."[2] Finally, Ruttenberg did not dispute, or apologize for, his reputation as a domineering, if not imposing, superior. "I can be a very demanding, difficult boss. But I know how to build teams. And I have made a lot of people very rich."[3]

Ruttenberg realized that one of his primary responsibilities was training a new management team to assume the leadership of the company following his retire-ment. "As the founder, my job is to put the right people in place for the future. I'm preparing this company for 25 years down the road when I won't be here."[4] One of the individuals who Ruttenberg handpicked to lead the company into its future was his son, Don-Allen Ruttenberg, who shared his father's single-minded determination and tenacious business temperament. In 1997, at the age of 29, Don-Allen Ruttenberg was named Just for Feet's vice president of new store development. Two years later, the younger Ruttenberg was promoted to the position of executive vice president.

Similar to most successful companies, Just for Feet's path to success was not with-out occasional pitfalls. In 1995, Wall Street's zeal for Just for Feet's common stock was tempered somewhat by an accounting controversy involving "store opening" costs. Throughout its existence, Just for Feet had accumulated such costs for each new store in an asset account and then amortized the costs over the 12-month period fol-lowing the store's grand opening. A more common practice within the retail industry was to expense such costs in the month that a new store opened. Criticism of Just for Feet's accounting for store opening costs goaded company management to adopt the industry convention, which resulted in the company recording a $2.1 million cumula-tive effect of a change in accounting principle during fiscal 1996.

In the summer of 1996, Wall Street took notice when Harold Ruttenberg; his wife, Pamela; and their son, Don-Allen, sold large blocks of their Just for Feet common stock in a secondary offering to the general public. Collectively, the three members of the Ruttenberg family received nearly $49.5 million from the sale of those securities. Major investors and financial analysts questioned why the Ruttenbergs would dispose of much of their Just for Feet stock while, at the same time, the senior Ruttenberg was issuing glowing projections regarding the company's future prospects.

Clay Feet

No one could deny the impressive revenue and profit trends that Just for Feet estab-lished during the mid- and late 1990s. Exhibit 1 and Exhibit 2, which present the company's primary financial statements for the three-year period fiscal 1996 through fiscal 1998, document those trends. However, hidden within the company's financial data for that three-year period was a red flag. Notice in the statements of cash flows

---

1. *Chain Store Age*, "Retail Entrepreneurs of the Year: Harold Ruttenberg," December 1996, 68.

2. *Ibid.*

3. *Ibid.*

4. *Ibid.*

shown in Exhibit 2 that despite the rising profits Just for Feet reported in the late 1990s, the company's operating cash flows during that period were negative. By early 1999, these negative operating cash flows posed a huge liquidity problem for the company. To address this problem, Just for Feet sold $200 million of high-yield "junk" bonds in April 1999.

A few weeks after selling the junk bonds, Just for Feet issued an earnings warning. This press release alerted investors that the company would likely post its first-ever quarterly loss during the second quarter of fiscal 1999. One month later, Just for Feet shocked its investors and creditors when it announced that it might default on its first interest payment on the $200 million of junk bonds. Investors received more disturbing news in July 1999 when Harold Ruttenberg unexpectedly resigned as Just for Feet's CEO. The company replaced Ruttenberg with a corporate turnaround

EXHIBIT 1

JUST FOR FEET, INC., 1996–1998 BALANCE SHEETS

JUST FOR FEET, INC. BALANCE SHEETS (000s omitted)			
		January 31,	
	1999	**1998**	**1997**
Current assets:			
Cash and cash equivalents	$ 12,412	$ 82,490	$138,785
Marketable securities available for sale	—	—	33,961
Accounts receivable	18,875	15,840	6,553
Inventory	399,901	206,128	133,323
Other current assets	18,302	6,709	2,121
Total current assets	449,490	311,167	314,743
Property and equipment, net	160,592	94,529	54,922
Goodwill, net	71,084	36,106	—
Other	8,230	6,550	6,169
Total assets	$689,396	$448,352	$375,834
Current liabilities:			
Short-term borrowings	$ —	$ 90,667	$100,000
Accounts payable	100,322	51,162	38,897
Accrued expenses	24,829	9,292	5,487
Income taxes payable	902	1,363	425
Current maturities of long-term debt	6,639	3,222	2,105
Total current liabilities	132,692	155,706	146,914
Long-term debt and obligations	230,998	24,562	10,364
Total liabilities	$363,690	$180,268	$157,278
Shareholders' equity:			
Common stock	3	3	3
Paid-in capital	249,590	218,616	190,492
Retained earnings	76,113	49,465	28,061
Total shareholders' equity	325,706	268,084	218,556
Total liabilities and shareholders' equity	$689,396	$448,352	$375,834

specialist, Helen Rockey. Upon resigning, Ruttenberg insisted that Just for Feet's financial problems were only temporary and that the company would likely post a profit during the third quarter of fiscal 1999.

Harold Ruttenberg's statement did not reassure investors. The company's stock price went into a freefall during the spring and summer of 1999, slipping to near $4 per share by the end of July. In September, the company announced that it had lost $25.9 million during the second quarter of fiscal 1999, a much larger loss than had been expected by Wall Street. Less than two months later, on 2 November 1999, the company shocked its investors and creditors once more when it filed for Chapter 11 bankruptcy protection in the federal courts.

Just for Feet's startling collapse over a period of a few months sparked a flurry of lawsuits against the company and its executives. Allegations of financial mismanagement and accounting irregularities triggered investigations of the company's financial affairs by state and federal law enforcement authorities, including the Alabama Securities Commission, the FBI, the Securities and Exchange Commission (SEC), and the U.S. Department of Justice. In May 2003, the Justice Department announced that a former Just for Feet executive, Adam Gilburne, had pleaded guilty to conspiracy

EXHIBIT 2

Just for Feet, Inc., 1996–1998 Income Statements and Statements of Cash Flows

JUST FOR FEET, INC. CONSOLIDATED STATEMENTS OF EARNINGS (000s omitted)			
	Year Ended January 31,		
	1999	**1998**	**1997**
Net sales	$774,863	$478,638	$256,397
Cost of sales	452,330	279,816	147,526
Gross profit	322,533	198,822	108,871
Other revenues	1,299	1,101	581
Operating expenses:			
Store operating	232,505	139,659	69,329
Store opening costs	13,669	6,728	11,240
Amortization of intangibles	2,072	1,200	180
General and administrative	24,341	18,040	7,878
Total operating expenses	272,587	165,627	88,627
Operating income	51,245	34,296	20,825
Interest expense	(8,059)	(1,446)	(832)
Interest income	143	1,370	4,750
Earnings before income taxes and cumulative effect of change in accounting principle	43,329	34,220	24,743
Provision for income taxes	16,681	12,817	8,783
Earnings before cumulative effect of a change in accounting principle	26,648	21,403	15,960
Cumulative effect on prior years of change in accounting principle	—	—	(2,041)
Net earnings	$ 26,648	$ 21,403	$ 13,919

EXHIBIT 2—
continued

JUST FOR FEET,
INC., 1996–1998
INCOME
STATEMENTS AND
STATEMENTS OF
CASH FLOWS

JUST FOR FEET, INC.
CONSOLIDATED STATEMENTS OF CASH FLOWS (000s omitted)

	Year Ended January 31,		
	1999	**1998**	**1997**
Operating activities:			
Net earnings	$ 26,648	$ 21,403	$ 13,919
Adjustments to reconcile net earnings to net cash used by operating activities:			
Cumulative effect of a change in accounting principle	—	—	2,041
Depreciation and amortization	16,129	8,783	3,971
Deferred income taxes	12,100	2,194	(744)
Deferred lease rentals	2,655	2,111	1,456
Changes in assets and liabilities providing (using) cash, net of effects of acquisitions:			
(Increase) decrease in accounts receivable	(2,795)	(8,918)	(3,143)
(Increase) decrease in inventory	(170,169)	(56,616)	(76,685)
(Increase) decrease in other assets	(8,228)	(5,643)	271
Increase (decrease) in accounts payable	34,638	7,495	16,628
Increase (decrease) in accrued expenses	7,133	2,264	2,709
Increase (decrease) in income taxes payable	(181)	543	(2,506)
Net cash used by operating activities	(82,070)	(26,384)	(42,083)
Investing activities:			
Purchases of property and equipment, net of disposals	(78,984)	(43,446)	(33,206)
Acquisitions, net of cash acquired	(199)	(25,548)	—
Purchases of marketable securities	—	(14,726)	(44,778)
Maturities and sales of marketable securities	—	51,653	63,132
Net cash used for investing activities	(79,183)	(32,067)	(14,852)
Financing activities:			
Borrowings (repayments) under credit facilities, net	(90,667)	(9,333)	45,000
Borrowings of long-term obligations	291,076	12,739	479
Principal payments on long-term obligations	(132,290)	(2,054)	(1,335)
Proceeds from issuance of common stock, net	20,000	—	52,900
Proceeds from exercise of options	3,056	804	1,822
Net cash provided by financing activities	91,175	2,156	98,866
Net increase (decrease) in cash and equivalents	(70,078)	(56,295)	41,931
Cash and equivalents, beginning of year	82,490	138,785	96,854
Cash and equivalents, end of year	$ 12,412	$ 82,490	$138,785

to commit wire and securities fraud. Gilburne, who had served in various executive positions with Just for Feet, revealed that he and other members of the company's top management had conspired to inflate the company's reported earnings from 1996 through 1999.

The information [testimony provided by Gilburne] alleges that beginning in about 1996, Just for Feet's CEO [Harold Ruttenberg] would conduct meetings at the end of every quarter in which he would lay out analysts' expectations of the company's earnings, and then draw up a list of "goods"—items which produced or added income— and "bads"—those which reduced income. The information alleges that the CEO directed Just for Feet's employees to increase the "goods" and decrease the "bads" in order to meet his own earnings expectations and those of Wall Street analysts.[5]

Approximately two years following Gilburne's guilty plea, the SEC issued a series of enforcement releases that documented the three key facets of the fraudulent scheme perpetrated by Just for Feet's management team. "Just for Feet falsified its financial statements by (1) improperly recognizing unearned and fictitious receivables from its vendors, (2) failing to properly account for excess inventory, and (3) improperly recording as income the value of display booths provided by its vendors."[6]

The stores-within-a-store floor plan developed by Harold Ruttenberg provided an opportunity for Just for Feet's vendors to become directly involved in the marketing of their products within the company's superstores. Each year, Just for Feet received millions of dollars of "vendor allowances" or "advertising co-op" from its major suppliers. These allowances were intended to subsidize Just for Feet's advertising expenditures for its superstores.

Despite the large size of the vendor allowances, in most cases there was not a written agreement that documented the conditions under which Just for Feet was entitled to an allowance or the size of a given allowance. After Just for Feet had run a series of advertisements or other promotional announcements for a vendor's product, copies of the advertising materials would be submitted to the vendor. An account manager for the vendor would then approve an allowance for Just for Feet based upon the amount of the advertised products that the company had purchased.

Generally accepted accounting principles (GAAP) dictate that vendor allowances not be offset against advertising expense until the given advertisements have been run or other promotional efforts have been completed. However, Just for Feet began routinely recording *anticipated* vendor allowances as receivables and advertising expense offsets well before the related advertising or promotional programs had been completed. Just for Feet's management team was particularly aggressive in "front-loading" vendor allowances during fiscal 1998. At the end of fiscal 1997, Just for Feet had slightly more than $400,000 of outstanding vendor allowance receivables; 12 months later, at the end of fiscal 1998, that total had soared to almost $29 million.[7]

During fiscal 1998, Just for Feet's merchandise inventory nearly doubled, rising from $206 million on 31 January 1998, to almost $400 million on 31 January 1999. Although Just for Feet had a large amount of slow-moving inventory, the company's management team refused to properly apply the lower of cost or market rule in arriving at a year-end valuation reserve for that important asset. As a result, at the end of both fiscal 1997 and fiscal 1998, the company's allowance for inventory obsolescence stood at a nominal $150,000.

The major athletic shoe vendors erected promotional displays or booths in the Just for Feet superstores. These booths were maintained by sales representatives of the vendors and were the property of those vendors. In early 1998, Don-Allen Ruttenberg concocted a fraudulent scheme to produce millions of dollars of "booth income" for

---

5. U.S. Department of Justice, "Former 'Just for Feet, Inc.' Executive Pleads Guilty to Conspiracy to Commit Wire, Securities Fraud," www.usdoj.gov, 12 May 2003.

6. U.S. Securities and Exchange Commission, "SEC Charges Deloitte & Touche and Two of Its Personnel for Failures in Their Audits of Just for Feet," www.sec.gov, 26 April 2005.

7. Although technically receivables, the vendor allowances purportedly due to Just for Feet were netted against the given vendor's accounts payable balance, which explains why these receivables do not appear explicitly in the company's balance sheets shown in Exhibit 1.

Just for Feet. Without the knowledge of its vendors, Just for Feet began recording in its accounting records monthly booth income amounts allegedly earned from those vendors. The offsets to these revenue amounts for accounting purposes were booked (debited) to a booth assets account.[8] By the end of fiscal 1998, Just for Feet had recorded $9 million of bogus assets and related revenues as a result of this scheme. More than 80 percent of these bogus transactions were recorded during the final two quarters of fiscal 1998, ostensibly to allow Just for Feet to reach its previously announced earnings targets for those two periods.

An important feature of the Just for Feet accounting fraud was Don-Allen Ruttenberg's close relationship with key executives of the major athletic shoe vendors. Since Just for Feet was among the largest customers of each of those vendors, the company had a significant amount of economic leverage on their executives. The younger Ruttenberg used this leverage to persuade those executives to return false confirmations to Just for Feet's independent audit firm, Deloitte & Touche. Those confirmations were sent to Just for Feet's vendors to confirm bogus receivables that were a product of the company's fraudulent accounting scheme. In most cases, the bogus receivables resulted from inflated or otherwise improper vendor allowances booked by Just for Feet. One of the five vendor executives who capitulated to Don-Allen Ruttenberg's demands was Thomas Shine, the senior executive of Logo Athletic. Executives of four Just for Feet vendors steadfastly refused to provide false confirmations to Deloitte. Those executives were employed by Asics-Tiger, New Balance, Reebok, and Timberland. Ironically, in 2001, Thomas Shine became an executive of Reebok when that company purchased Logo Athletic.

Footing & Cross-Footing

Deloitte & Touche served as Just for Feet's independent audit firm from 1992 through early December 1999, one month after the company filed for Chapter 11 bankruptcy. Deloitte issued unqualified audit opinions each year on Just for Feet's financial statements, including the financial statements in the S-1 registration statement the company filed with the SEC when it went public in 1994.

Steven Barry served as Just for Feet's engagement partner for the fiscal 1998 audit. Barry was initially an employee of Touche Ross & Co. and was promoted to partner with that firm in 1988. The next year, Barry became a Deloitte & Touche partner following the merger of Touche Ross with Deloitte, Haskins, & Sells. In 1996, Barry was promoted to managing partner of Deloitte's Birmingham, Alabama, office. Barry's principal subordinate on the 1998 Just for Feet audit was Karen Baker, who had been assigned to the company's audit engagement team since 1993. Initially the audit senior on that engagement team, she became the engagement audit manager after being promoted to that rank in 1995.

Deloitte assigned a "greater than normal" level of audit risk to the fiscal 1998 Just for Feet audit during the planning phase of that engagement. To help monitor high-risk audit engagements, Deloitte had established a "National Risk Management Program." In both 1997 and 1998, Just for Feet was included in that program. Each client involved in this program was assigned a "National Review Partner." This partner's duties included "discussing specific risk areas and plans to respond to them ... reviewing the audit workpapers concerning risk areas of the engagement, and reviewing the financial statements and Deloitte's audit reports with an emphasis on the identification of

---

8. This fraudulent scheme actually replaced a similar but smaller-scale scam that the younger Ruttenberg had used since December 1996 to inflate Just for Feet's operating results.

specific risk areas as well as the adequacy of the audit report and disclosures regarding these risk areas."[9]

The audit workpapers for the fiscal 1997 audit identified several specific audit risk factors. These factors included "management accepts high levels of risk," "places significant emphasis on earnings," and "has historically interpreted accounting standards aggressively." Another 1997 workpaper noted that the company's management team placed a heavy emphasis on achieving previously released earnings targets, expressed an "excessive" interest in maintaining the company's stock price at a high level, and engaged in "unique and highly complex" transactions near fiscal year-end. A summary 1997 workpaper entitled "Risk Factors Worksheet" also noted that Harold Ruttenberg exercised "one-man rule (autocrat)" over Just for Feet and that the company practiced "creative accounting."

For both the 1997 and 1998 audit engagements, Deloitte personnel prepared a "Client Risk Profile." This workpaper for those two audits identified vendor allowances and inventory valuation as key audit risk areas. In 1996, Deloitte's headquarters office had issued a firm-wide "Risk Alert" informing practice offices that vendor allowances should be considered a "high-risk area" for retail clients.

During the 1998 audit, the Deloitte engagement team identified several factors that, according to the SEC, should have caused both Barry and Baker to have "heightened professional skepticism" regarding Just for Feet's vendor allowances. The most important of these factors was the huge increase in the vendor allowance receivables between the end of fiscal 1997 and fiscal 1998. In the final few weeks of fiscal 1998, Just for Feet recorded $14.4 million of vendor allowances, accounting for almost one-half of the year-end balance of that account. Deloitte was never provided with supporting documentation for $11.3 million of those vendor allowances, although a Just for Feet executive had promised to provide that documentation. Deloitte completed its fieldwork for the fiscal 1998 audit on 23 April 1999, almost three months following the fiscal year-end. As of that date, Just for Feet had not received any payments from its suppliers for the $11.3 million of undocumented vendor allowances.

In March 1999, Deloitte mailed receivables confirmations to 13 of Just for Feet's suppliers. Collectively, those vendors accounted for $22 million of the $28.9 million of year-end vendor allowances. Again, Don-Allen Ruttenberg persuaded executives of five Just for Feet vendors to sign and return confirmations to Deloitte even though the vendor allowance receivables listed on those confirmations did not exist or were grossly inflated. The confirmations returned by the other eight vendors were generally "nonstandard," according to the SEC. That is, these confirmations included caveats, disclaimers, or other statements that should have alerted Deloitte to the possibility that the given receivable balances were unreliable. "Five vendors returned nonstandard letters that, instead of unambiguously confirming amounts owed to Just for Feet at the end of the fiscal 1998 year, as requested by the auditors, provided ambiguous information on amounts of co-op [vendor allowances] that the Company had earned, accrued, or had available during the year" [emphasis added by SEC]. Another of the returned confirmations explicitly noted that "no additional funds" were due to Just for Feet.

The eight nonstandard confirmations accounted for approximately $16 million of the $22 million of vendor allowance receivables that Deloitte attempted to confirm at year-end. "Despite these and other flaws, the Respondents [Deloitte, Barry, and

---

9. Securities and Exchange Commission, *Accounting and Auditing Enforcement Release No. 2238*, 26 May 2005. Unless noted otherwise, the remaining quotations in this case were taken from this source.

Baker] nonetheless accepted these letters as confirming approximately $16 million in receivables claimed by Just for Feet." The SEC's investigation of Deloitte's Just for Feet audits revealed that although Barry and Baker accepted these flawed confirmations, two subordinates assigned to the 1998 engagement team continued to investigate the obvious discrepancies in those confirmations well after the completion of that audit. These two individuals, who were audit seniors, twice contacted a Just for Feet executive in the months following the completion of the 1998 audit in an attempt to obtain plausible explanations for the eight nonstandard and suspicious confirmations. That executive did not respond to the audit seniors and neither Barry, nor Baker, apparently, insisted that he provide appropriate documentation and/or explanations regarding the amounts in question.

Just for Feet's large increase in inventory during fiscal 1998 raised several important issues that the Deloitte auditors had to address during the 1998 audit, the most important being whether the client's reserve for inventory obsolescence was sufficient. The primary audit procedure used by Deloitte during the 1998 audit to assess the reasonableness of the client's inventory valuation reserve was to obtain and test an inventory "reserve analysis" prepared by a company vice president. This latter document was supposed to include the following three classes of inventory items for which company policy required application of the lower of cost or market rule: (1) shoe styles for which the company had four or fewer pairs, (2) shoes and other apparel that were selling for less than cost, and (3) any inventory styles for which no items had been sold during the previous 12 months. The reserve analysis for 1998, however, excluded those inventory styles for which no sales had been made during the previous 12 months, an oversight that the Deloitte auditors never questioned or investigated. The Deloitte auditors also discovered that a large amount of inventory included in a Just for Feet warehouse had been excluded from the reserve analysis prepared by the company vice president. Again, the auditors chose not to question client personnel regarding this oversight.

After completing their inventory audit procedures, the Deloitte auditors concluded that Just for Feet's year-end reserve for inventory obsolescence was significantly understated. The SEC noted that this conclusion was reached by the Deloitte auditors despite the obvious deficiencies in audit procedures applied to Just for Feet's reserve for inventory obsolescence:

> Even using the flawed inventory analysis provided by the Vice President and the deficient inventory information that excluded the goods from the New Jersey warehouse, the Respondents concluded that Just for Feet's obsolescence reserve should have been in the range of $441,000 to over $1 million.

The Deloitte audit team proposed an audit adjustment to increase the reserve for inventory obsolescence by more than $400,000; however, the client rejected that audit adjustment, meaning that the year-end balance of that account remained at a meager $150,000.

Although not specifically identified as a "key audit risk area" during the 1998 audit, the Deloitte auditors focused considerable attention on Just for Feet's accounting decisions for the approximately $9 million of "booth income" the company recorded during that year. The Deloitte auditors discovered the monthly booth income journal entries recorded by Just for Feet during fiscal 1998 and prepared a workpaper documenting those entries. "An analysis at the end of the workpaper, which Baker reviewed, showed that the net effect of Just for Feet's booth-related journal entries was to increase assets with a corresponding increase in income. The Respondents [Deloitte, Barry, and Baker] performed no further analysis to determine the basis and propriety of these journal entries."

Instead of independently investigating these entries, the Deloitte auditors accepted the representation of a Just for Feet executive that the entries had no effect on the company's net income. According to this executive, the monthly booth income amounts were offset by preexisting "co-op" or advertising credits that had been granted to Just for Feet by its major vendors. In other words, instead of using those advertising credits to reduce reported advertising expenses, Just for Feet was allegedly converting those credits into booth income or revenue amounts.

By the end of 1998, the bogus booth income journal entries had produced $9 million of nonexistent "booth assets" in Just for Feet's accounting records. Since "neither the Company nor the auditors had internal evidence supporting the recording of $9 million of booth assets," the Deloitte engagement team decided to corroborate the existence and ownership assertions for those assets by obtaining confirmations from the relevant Just for Feet vendors. These confirmations were prepared with the assistance of certain Just for Feet executives who were aware of the fraudulent nature of the booth income/booth assets amounts. Apparently, these executives contacted the vendor representatives to whom the confirmations were mailed and told them how to respond to the confirmations. The booth assets confirmations returned by the vendors to Deloitte were replete with errors and ambiguous statements. A frustrated audit senior who reviewed the confirmations brought this matter to the attention of both Barry and Baker.

> An audit senior reviewed these confirmations and informed Barry and Baker that she was in some cases sending multiple confirmation requests to the vendors because many of their initial requests came back in forms different from that requested. The Respondents failed to discover from these indications that Just for Feet might not actually … [own]the booths as claimed.

EPILOGUE

In February 2000, after realizing that Just for Feet was no longer salvageable, Helen Rockey began the process of liquidating the company under Chapter 7 of the federal bankruptcy code. Over the next few years, settlements were announced to a number of large lawsuits linked to the Just for Feet accounting fraud and the company's subsequent bankruptcy. Just for Feet's former executives and Deloitte were among the principal defendants in those lawsuits. One of those cases, a class-action lawsuit filed by Just for Feet's former stockholders, was settled for a reported $32.4 million in 2002.

Several of Just for Feet's former executives pleaded guilty to criminal charges for their roles in the company's massive accounting fraud. Among these individuals was Don-Allen Ruttenberg. In April 2005, a federal judge sentenced Ruttenberg to 20 months in federal prison and fined him $50,000. At the same time that the younger Ruttenberg's sentence was announced, a Justice Department official reported that Harold Ruttenberg, who was gravely ill with brain cancer, would not be charged in the case. In January 2006, Harold Ruttenberg died at the age of 63.

Five executives of Just for Feet's former vendors also pleaded guilty to various criminal charges for providing false confirmations to the company's auditors. Most of these individuals, including Thomas Shine, received probationary sentences. An exception was Timothy McCool, the former director of apparel sales for Adidas, who received a four-month "noncustodial" sentence. While sentencing McCool, U.S. District Judge C. Lynwood Smith, Jr., noted, " Life is so fragile. A single bad choice in a single moment can cause a life to turn irrevocably 180 degrees. I think that is where you find yourself."[10]

Arguably, the party to the Just for Feet scandal that received the most condemnation from the courts and the business press was Deloitte. In April 2005, the SEC berated the prominent accounting firm for the poor quality of its Just for Feet audits in *Accounting and Auditing Enforcement Release No. 2238*. In that same enforcement release, the SEC fined Deloitte $375,000 and suspended Steven Barry from serving on audit engagements involving SEC registrants for two years; Karen Baker received a one-year suspension.

On the same date that the SEC announced the sanctions that it had imposed on Deloitte for its Just for Feet audits, the federal agency also revealed the sanctions that Deloitte received for its allegedly deficient audits of a large telecommunications company, Adelphia Communications. Similar to Just for Feet, the once high-flying Adelphia had suddenly collapsed in 2002 following revelations that its previously issued financial statements that had been audited by Deloitte were riddled with errors. The SEC stunned the public accounting profession by fining Deloitte $50 million for its role in the huge Adelphia scandal, which was easily the largest fine ever imposed on an accounting firm by the federal agency.

Shortly after the SEC announced the sanctions that it had levied on Deloitte for its Just for Feet and Adelphia Communications audits, James Quigley, Deloitte's CEO, issued a press release responding to those sanctions. Quigley noted in his press release that, "Among our most significant challenges is the early detection of fraud, particularly when the client, its management and others collude specifically to deceive a company's auditors."[11] This statement infuriated SEC officials. An SEC spokesperson responded to Quigley's press release by stating that, "Deloitte was not deceived in this case. The findings in the order show that the relevant information was right in front of their eyes. Deloitte just didn't do its job, plain and simple. They didn't miss red flags. They pulled the flag over their head and claimed they couldn't see."[12]

The SEC also suggested that Quigley's press release violated the terms of the agreement that the agency had reached with Deloitte in settling the Just for Feet and Adelphia cases. Under the terms of that agreement, Deloitte was not required to "admit" to the SEC's findings, nor was it allowed to "deny" those findings. Deloitte subsequently rescinded Quigley's press release and issued another that eliminated some, but not all, of the statements that had offended the SEC.

Questions

1. Prepare common-sized balance sheets and income statements for Just for Feet for the period 1996–1998. Also compute key liquidity, solvency, activity, and profitability ratios for 1997 and 1998. Given these data, comment on what you believe were the high-risk financial statement items for the 1998 Just for Feet audit.

2. Just for Feet operated large, high-volume retail stores. Identify internal control risks common to such businesses. How should these risks affect the audit planning decisions for such a client?

---

10. *The Associated Press State & Local Wire*, "Adidas America Executive Sentenced in Just for Feet Case," 22 March 2004.

11. S. Laub, "Deloitte Statement Irks SEC," *CFO.com*, 28 April 2005.

12. S. Hughes, "SEC Rebukes Deloitte over Spin of Adelphia Audit," *The Associated Press State & Local Wire*, 27 April 2005.

3. Just for Feet operated in an extremely competitive industry, or subindustry. Identify inherent risk factors common to businesses facing such competitive conditions. How should these risks affect the audit planning decisions for such a client?

4. Prepare a comprehensive list, in a bullet format, of the audit risk factors present for the 1998 Just for Feet audit. Identify the five audit risk factors that you believe were most critical to the successful completion of that audit. Rank these risk factors from least to most important and be prepared to defend your rankings. Briefly explain whether or not you believe that the Deloitte auditors responded appropriately to the five critical audit risk factors that you identified.

5. Put yourself in the position of Thomas Shine in this case. How would you have responded when Don-Allen Ruttenberg asked you to send a false confirmation to Deloitte & Touche? Before responding, identify the parties who will be affected by your decision.

Health Management, Inc.

Clifford Hotte had a problem. His company had come up short of its earnings target. For the fiscal year ended 30 April 1995, financial analysts had projected that Health Management, Inc. (HMI), a New York–based pharmaceuticals distributor, would post earnings per share of $0.74. Following the close of fiscal 1995, Drew Bergman, HMI's chief financial officer (CFO) informed Hotte, the company's founder and chief executive officer (CEO), that the actual earnings figure for fiscal 1995 would be approximately $0.54 per share. According to Bergman, Hotte refused to "take the hit," that is, the almost certain drop in HMI's stock price that would follow the announcement of the disappointing earnings.[1] Instead, Hotte wanted HMI to report 1995 earnings in line with analysts' predictions.[2]

Bergman altered HMI's accounting records to allow the company to reach its 1995 earnings target. To lower cost of sales and increase HMI's gross profit and net income, Bergman inflated the company's year-end inventory by approximately $1.8 million. Bergman also posted a few other smaller "adjustments" to HMI's accounting records. Both Bergman and Hotte realized that the company would have to take elaborate measures to conceal the accounting fraud from its audit firm. Bergman was very familiar with BDO Seidman and its audit procedures since he had been employed by that accounting firm several years earlier. In fact, Bergman had supervised BDO Seidman's 1989 and 1990 audits of HMI.

HMI's inventory fraud was not particularly innovative. Corporate executives who want to embellish their company's operating results are aware that among the easiest methods of achieving that goal is overstating year-end inventory. What was unique about HMI's inventory hoax was that it triggered one of the first major tests of an important and controversial new federal law, the 1995 Private Securities Litigation Reform Act (PSLRA). The PSLRA was the only law passed by Congress during President Clinton's first administration that overcame a presidential veto.

Among the parties most pleased by the passage of the PSLRA were the large, international accounting firms. These firms' mounting litigation losses in the latter decades of the twentieth century had prompted them to lobby Congress to reform the nation's civil litigation system. In particular, the firms argued that they were being unfairly victimized by the growing number of class-action lawsuits. The bulk of these lawsuits were being filed under the Securities Exchange Act of 1934, one of the federal statutes that created the regulatory infrastructure for the nation's securities markets in the early 1930s.

Top officials of the major accounting firms believed that the PSLRA, which amended key provisions of the 1934 Act, would make it more difficult for plaintiff attorneys to extract large legal judgments or settlements from their firms. The jury's verdict in favor of BDO Seidman in the HMI lawsuit seemed to support that conclusion. HMI's stockholders filed suit against BDO Seidman for failing to detect the

---

1. Unless indicated otherwise, the quotations in this case were drawn from court transcripts obtained for the *In Re Health Management, Inc. Securities Litigation* case that was tried in U.S. District Court (Eastern District of New York) in October 1999.

2. I would like to acknowledge a former student of mine, Amy Hollis, for her excellent research that contributed to this case. I would also like to acknowledge the kind assistance of Michael Young.

inventory fraud masterminded by Drew Bergman and Clifford Hotte. Michael Young, a prominent New York attorney who headed up BDO Seidman's legal defense team, predicted that the case would become a "watershed event" in the accounting profession's struggle to curb its litigation losses.[3]

Thinly Veiled Extortion

The federal securities laws passed by Congress in the early 1930s not only established a formal regulatory structure for the securities markets, they also strengthened an informal control mechanism that had long served to promote and preserve the integrity of the capital markets. That control mechanism was private securities litigation. The federal securities laws make it unlawful for companies registered with the SEC to issue financial statements that misrepresent their financial condition and operating results. However, the courts have also permitted those statutes to be used as the basis for civil actions. Investors and creditors can file tort actions to recover damages they suffer at the hands of parties who prepare or are otherwise associated with misrepresented financial statements of SEC registrants.

Prior to the passage of the federal securities laws and for several decades thereafter, major institutional investors and large creditors, such as metropolitan banks, filed most private securities lawsuits. Individual investors and creditors who suffered damages as a result of relying on misrepresented financial statements generally found that it was not economically feasible to use the courts to recover their losses. During the 1970s, resourceful attorneys cured this "problem" by employing the concept of a "class-action" lawsuit. In such lawsuits, the legal claims of a large number of individual plaintiffs are consolidated into one joint claim. In exchange for representing these joint plaintiffs, attorneys receive a contingent fee equal to a percentage of any collective judgment or settlement awarded to the plaintiffs.

Thanks to their newfound ability to file class-action lawsuits, attorneys specializing in private securities litigation began vigorously suing parties directly or indirectly linked to allegedly false or misleading financial statements filed with the SEC. Most of these lawsuits claimed one or more violations of Rule 10b-5 of the Securities Exchange Act of 1934. That section of the 1934 Act prohibits the "employment of manipulative and deceptive devices" in connection with the preparation and distribution of the financial statements of SEC-registered companies.[4]

By the late 1970s, class-action lawsuits predicated on Rule 10b-5 violations were commonplace. One legal scholar observed that the "low transaction cost" of filing a class-action lawsuit under the federal securities laws invited abuse of that tactic by plaintiff attorneys.[5] Former SEC Chairman Richard Breeden frequently spoke out against the epidemic of class-action securities lawsuits plaguing corporations, their executives, and related parties. Breeden characterized the securities class-action system "as a legal regime disconnected from principles of right and wrong that is riddled with abuse and that involves nothing less than thinly veiled extortion."[6]

---

3. G. Cheney, "BDO Wins Landmark Case under New Tort Reform Law," *Accounting Today*, 22 November–12 December 1999, 3.

4. Case 7.6, "*First Securities Company of Chicago*," presents the complete text of Rule 10b-5.

5. H. E. Milstein, "Recent Developments in the Private Securities Litigation Reform Act," *Securities Litigation & Regulation Reporter*, 12 January 2000, 12.

6. R. M. Phillips and G. C. Miller, "The Private Securities Litigation Reform Act of 1995: Rebalancing Litigation Risks and Rewards for Class Action Plaintiffs, Defendants, and Lawyers," *The Business Lawyer*, August 1996, 51 Bus. Law. 1009.

Class-action securities lawsuits proved to be particularly problematic for the large accounting firms that audit the financial statements of most major public companies. An unavoidable facet of these firms' primary line of business is being burdened occasionally with a client whose executives choose to use "creative" or even blatantly fraudulent accounting methods. An accounting firm that issues an unqualified opinion on financial statements later proven to contain material errors may only be guilty of accepting a client whose management is inept and/or unethical. Nevertheless, the financial resources of the large accounting firms make them inviting targets for investors and creditors who have relied to their detriment on misleading financial statements.

The executives of many large accounting firms decided that the most rational approach to dealing with class-action lawsuits filed against them was to settle those lawsuits out of court as quickly and quietly as possible. Michael Cook, former CEO of Deloitte & Touche, testified before Congress that his firm often used that strategy because of the leverage plaintiff attorneys had on his firm. That leverage stemmed from the enormous judgments Deloitte & Touche potentially faced if it allowed class-action lawsuits in which it was named as a defendant to go to trial. Most frustrating to Cook and his colleagues at other accounting firms was the need to pay large sums to settle cases in which they were convinced their firms were not at fault. According to Cook, "I am forced to settle cases in which I believe our firm did nothing wrong."[7]

Skeptics questioned the veracity of such statements by Cook and other top executives of major accounting firms. However, empirical research by Professor Zoe-Vonna Palmrose, an authority on audit-related litigation, suggested that the large accounting firms were often named as defendants in class-action lawsuits because of their "deep pockets" rather than because they were at fault.[8] The ability of plaintiff attorneys to goad defendants into settling was borne out by a study of class-action securities lawsuits filed prior to the mid-1990s. Only 2 percent of those lawsuits went to trial, while 20 percent were dismissed. In the remaining 78 percent of those cases, the plaintiffs received out-of-court settlements, often multimillion-dollar settlements, from the defendants.[9]

"Relief" Is Spelled ... PSLRA

In 1991, the Big Six accounting firms launched a costly and coordinated campaign to persuade Congress to reform the nation's private securities litigation system. Congress finally took up that cause during the mid-1990s. The resulting Congressional debate was heated, far-reaching, and drew extensive coverage by the media. The most contentious issue addressed in this debate was what "pleading standard" federal judges should invoke when deciding whether a given lawsuit should be allowed to proceed to trial. The Big Six firms wanted Congress to raise the pleading standard, making it more likely that class-action securities lawsuits would be dismissed shortly after being filed.

Congress sided with the Big Six firms when it enacted the PSLRA in December 1995 after overriding President Bill Clinton's veto of the bill. President Clinton vetoed the bill because he believed the PSLRA's tough pleading standard would make it too

---

7. *Ibid.*

8. Z-V. Palmrose, "The Joint and Several vs. Proportionate Liability Debate: An Empirical Investigation of Audit-Related Litigation," *Stanford Journal of Law, Business and Finance*, 1994 (Vol. 1), 53–72.

9. W. Hamilton, "Stock-Fraud Suits Increase Despite '95 Law," *Los Angeles Times*, 1 July 1998, D1.

difficult for plaintiffs with legitimate claims to have their day in court. Generally, the federal courts have interpreted the PSLRA to require plaintiffs to allege that a defendant was at least "reckless" for a case to proceed to trial. The law also mandates that plaintiffs identify or plead specific facts to support their allegations against defendants. Plaintiff attorneys are now barred from making general, broad-brush allegations of professional misconduct when filing class-action lawsuits against accounting firms, a tactic they commonly used prior to the PSLRA.[10]

Congress's inclusion of a proportionate liability rule in the PSLRA was also a major victory for accounting firms. Previously, the federal courts had imposed joint and several liability on defendants proven to have violated federal securities laws in a civil case. Under this standard, each such defendant was responsible for the entire judgment awarded the plaintiff. If one or more defendants could not pay their share of a judgment, their portion had to be paid by any remaining defendants that were solvent. The joint and several liability rule served to punish accounting firms since they were often the only solvent defendant in a class-action lawsuit. The PSLRA imposes joint and several liability only on defendants that knowingly participated in a fraud. A defendant guilty of no more than "recklessness" is generally responsible for only a percentage of the plaintiffs' losses. That percentage is equal to the defendant's percentage of responsibility or fault for the given series of events that produced those losses.

Another important feature of the PSLRA for the accounting profession is a clause permitting federal judges to fine plaintiff attorneys who file frivolous securities lawsuits. The PSLRA also contains several clauses that relate directly to the independent audit function, some of which were adapted from the profession's own technical standards. The statute requires audit firms to design audits to provide reasonable assurance of detecting illegal acts that have a material and direct effect on a client's financial statements. Likewise, the law mandates that auditors use appropriate procedures to identify a client's related-party transactions and to assess the client's ability to remain a going concern over the following 12 months. A new requirement that the PSLRA imposed on auditors was reporting to the SEC any illegal acts by a client that had a material effect on the client's financial statements—assuming the client refused to report such items to the SEC.

Following the passage of the PSLRA, members of the accounting profession, trial attorneys, and other interested parties waited anxiously for a major litigation case to test the new statute's key features. That test would ultimately be provided by the class-action lawsuit filed by HMI's stockholders against BDO Seidman.

Hotte Inventory

Clifford Hotte, a licensed pharmacist with a Ph.D. in nuclear pharmacology and a former president of the New York State Board of Pharmacy, founded Homecare Management in 1986. This small company sold medical supplies and equipment to the public and to individuals and firms that provided in-home medical services. Hotte's company grew rapidly and expanded into other lines of business. By the mid-1990s, Hotte had taken his company public and renamed it Health Management, Inc. (HMI). At this point, the company's principal line of business was "chronic disease management." The company specialized in marketing expensive drugs needed

---

10. Recognize that since the PSLRA served as an amendment to the Securities Exchange Act of 1934, this statute applies only to lawsuits involving the financial statements of public companies, that is, companies that file periodic financial statements with the SEC.

by individuals suffering from a wide range of chronic illnesses including AIDS, Alzheimer's, Parkinson's, and schizophrenia.

Hotte retained BDO Seidman as his company's audit firm in 1989. According to subsequent court testimony, the company's prior audit firm resigned because of concerns it had regarding HMI's inventory accounting procedures. One of the auditors assigned to the 1989 and 1990 HMI audit engagement teams was Drew Bergman. Bergman graduated from Queens College in 1979 and accepted an entry-level position with a small accounting firm that later merged with BDO Seidman's predecessor. In 1987, Bergman transferred to BDO Seidman's Long Island office. Bergman served as the senior audit manager on the 1989 and 1990 HMI audits. In court testimony, Bergman provided the following description of his responsibilities as a senior audit manager:

> In that position, I was responsible for running the engagement from the time that we started working on a particular job, making sure that the staffing was accurate [sic], that we had the appropriate levels of people to do the work that was necessary, and accumulate the work product necessary to support the conclusions that we needed to reach before reaching an opinion on the financial statements.

One of Bergman's subordinates on the 1989 and 1990 HMI audits was Mei-ya Tsai. During the three years Bergman worked for BDO Seidman's Long Island office, Tsai was assigned to approximately 20 engagements he supervised. On the 1989 and 1990 HMI audits, Tsai served as the audit senior. When Drew Bergman resigned from BDO Seidman, Tsai was promoted to audit manager and assumed Bergman's responsibilities on subsequent HMI audits. After Bergman left BDO Seidman, he and Tsai maintained the friendship they had developed while working together at the audit firm. That friendship was strengthened by a relationship between Tsai and Bergman's wife, Nancy. From 1986 through the mid-1990s, Nancy Bergman was the marketing director and administrative office manager for BDO Seidman's Long Island office. Nancy Bergman and Mei-ya Tsai became close friends during that time. The two women, their spouses, and their children frequently visited each other and occasionally spent holidays together.

Clifford Hotte hired Drew Bergman away from BDO Seidman in 1990 and appointed him HMI's CFO. Bergman testified that he was "ultimately responsible" for HMI's accounting records and for "generating financial statements which then were sent to various governmental agencies." In his role as CFO, Bergman met frequently with Hotte to discuss important accounting and financial matters for HMI. During the first week of June 1995, Bergman delivered the unpleasant news to Hotte that HMI's net income for the fiscal year ended 30 April 1995, had fallen short of the company's forecasted profit for that period.

After scouring HMI's accounting records with Bergman and confirming the earnings shortfall, Hotte told his CFO that HMI would not report an earnings figure significantly lower than the $0.74 per share financial analysts had predicted the company would earn during fiscal 1995. A flabbergasted Bergman responded, "We are already at the end of the year ... we're in June. April ended already, sales are done. Inventories have been taken." Following an awkward period of silence, Hotte made himself even more clear to Bergman when he stated that reporting disappointing earnings was "not an option." At this point, Bergman finally realized what Hotte was implying.

After "stewing over" the predicament in which he found himself, Bergman went to Hotte's office later that same day with a proposition. "I went back into Dr. Hotte, and I said, 'Dr. Hotte,' I said, 'listen, recruiting people for this, I don't want anything to do with it ... [but] if you can go out and get them [other subordinates] to go along with this, then I'd be willing to make the [accounting] adjustments.'" Over the next two weeks, Bergman and Hotte worked on their plan. Eventually, Bergman decided to increase the company's 30 April 1995, inventory by approximately $1.8 million. His justification for this increase? He had overlooked $1.8 million of inventory in transit on 30 April when compiling the results of the company's year-end physical inventory. Bergman and Hotte invented a series of bogus events and fabricated several documents to support the in-transit inventory tale. Bergman later admitted in court that these efforts were intended to "fool BDO Seidman," in other words, to conceal the inventory fraud from the auditors.

The centerpiece of the in-transit inventory hoax was a $1.3 million inventory transfer that had supposedly taken place between HMI's Pittsburgh warehouse and another HMI warehouse in New York City. An HMI truck driver had allegedly left the company's Pittsburgh facility on Friday, 28 April 1995, in a company van that contained nearly $1.3 million of drugs. (These drugs were among the most expensive marketed by HMI, which explained why such a sizable dollar value of inventory could plausibly be transported in a relatively small vehicle.) Since the driver left the Pittsburgh warehouse before the inventory counting procedures were begun at that location, the drugs in the van were not included in that site's year-end physical inventory. When the truck driver arrived at the New York warehouse on the afternoon of Monday, 1 May 1995, the inventory counting had been completed at that facility.[11] So the $1.3 million of drugs were also excluded from the year-end physical inventory of the New York warehouse.

Another bogus inventory transfer of more than $500,000 accounted for the remaining portion of the year-end in-transit inventory conjured up by Bergman. These drugs had allegedly been segregated from the other pharmaceuticals in the New York warehouse and intentionally excluded from that site's year-end physical inventory. On his return trip to Pittsburgh, the truck driver had supposedly transported this $500,000 of inventory to HMI's Pittsburgh warehouse. According to Bergman's yarn, this inventory had arrived at the Pittsburgh site too late to be included in its physical inventory.

The seven HMI employees who served as accomplices in the inventory hoax included the truck driver, pharmacists who worked at the HMI warehouses, and the company controller who reported directly to Bergman. These employees were given specific instructions on what they should tell the BDO Seidman auditors regarding the year-end inventory transfers, the objective being to ensure that each conspirator's "story" was consistent with the scam as laid out by Bergman. HMI's controller subsequently testified that Tom Boyle, the audit senior who supervised the fieldwork on the 1995 HMI audit, asked him why the $1.3 million year-end inventory transfer had been necessary. "Drew Bergman basically told me what I had to tell the auditors, and I just reiterated [to Boyle] what he [Bergman] had told me."

Bergman realized that HMI's lack of a perpetual inventory system would make it difficult for BDO Seidman's auditors to uncover the inventory scam that he and Hotte had masterminded. Nevertheless, he was very concerned that BDO Seidman would perform an "inventory rollback" to substantiate the existence assertion for the in-transit inventory. In responding to a question posed by the federal judge who presided over the HMI lawsuit, Bergman explained why he was so concerned by this possibility.

Your Honor, assuming again that I had all the information, all of the units that were sold and all of the units that were purchased for that period of time, I—you would know conclusively what the ending inventory would have been and whether this inventory in transit would have existed or did not exist.

11. The truck driver, who was a relative of Hotte, spent the weekend (supposedly) visiting his aunt in New Jersey, meaning that the $1.3 million of inventory was (supposedly) left unguarded in a residential driveway for more than two days.

"Oh, by the way..."

Mei-ya Tsai planned to begin the 1995 audit of HMI in mid-June 1995. But Drew Bergman insisted that the auditors arrive one week later than originally planned. Bergman and his confederates needed the extra week to finalize and shore up the details of the in-transit inventory ruse.

The BDO Seidman audit team finally arrived at HMI's headquarters during the latter part of June. On that first day at the client's office, Tsai received a rude shock from her old friend. During a meeting with Tsai, Bergman informed her of the $1.8 million of in-transit inventory at year-end. According to Bergman, Tsai responded to that revelation with a rhetorical question: "Inventory in transit of $1,800,000?"[12] Tsai, no doubt, was alarmed by that figure since it represented nearly 20 percent of HMI's year-end inventory of $9.8 million and approximately one-half of the year-end inventory of HMI's New York warehouse. The company typically had no, or only negligible amounts of, inventory in transit at year-end. Another unusual feature of the year-end inventory transfers was that they had been transported in an HMI vehicle. The company typically used common carriers, such as United Parcel Service (UPS), to transfer significant amounts of inventory from one location to another.

Bergman testified that he only discussed the in-transit inventory on one other occasion with members of the audit engagement team. This second discussion involved Tsai and two BDO Seidman audit partners. One of those partners was Fred Bornstein, the HMI audit engagement partner, while the other partner was Warren Fisk, who served as the concurring review partner on the engagement. During this second meeting, which took place on approximately 15 July, 10 days or so before the completion of the audit, Fred Bornstein chastised his former subordinate. "I [Bornstein] said how could you ever have let this happen? I said, you are an accountant, and you have been an accountant for 20 years, and you know that something like this never should have happened."

Warren Fisk, who was scheduled to replace Bornstein as the HMI audit partner in 1996, told Bergman that the in-transit inventory made him "uncomfortable." Fisk informed Bergman that he and his colleagues were considering various additional tests to verify the in-transit inventory and would likely require HMI officials to sign a separate management representation letter confirming that item. Bergman recalled telling Fisk that "you have to do what you have to do."

The in-transit inventory was a key focus of the month-long 1995 audit of HMI. During the engagement, several BDO Seidman auditors questioned, investigated, and fretted over that item. Those individuals included Warren Fisk, Fred Bornstein, Mei-ya Tsai, Tom Boyle, and Jill Karnick, the semi-senior who had been assigned the primary responsibility for auditing inventory. Exhibit 1 lists the principal audit procedures BDO Seidman applied to the in-transit inventory.

The BDO audit team also wrestled with several other contentious issues during the 1995 audit. Near the end of the engagement, a dispute arose between HMI management and the auditors regarding the adequacy of the allowance for doubtful accounts for the company's more than $30 million of accounts receivable. The auditors proposed an adjusting entry to increase the year-end balance of the allowance account by $1.2 million. Management insisted that an increase of only one-half of that amount was necessary. Complicating BDO Seidman's decision regarding whether to

---

12. The trial in the HMI case took place in October 1999, more than four years after the 1995 audit was completed. Not surprisingly, the witnesses in the case often had differing recollections of key events that occurred during that audit. Mei-ya Tsai testified that she first learned of the in-transit inventory from Tom Boyle, the audit senior assigned to the 1995 HMI audit. According to Tsai's testimony, early in the audit Boyle called her at BDO Seidman's Long Island office and informed her of the in-transit inventory.

EXHIBIT 1

AUDIT PROCEDURES
APPLIED BY BDO
SEIDMAN TO
HMI'S IN-TRANSIT
INVENTORY

1. Requested the usual documentation that HMI prepared for all inventory transfers.

2. Verified that the inventory transfer documents were signed by both the shipping and receiving pharmacists, identified on the documents the pharmaceuticals reportedly included in the transfers, confirmed that the quantities and per unit prices of those pharmaceuticals agreed with the information previously provided to the auditors by HMI management.

3. Interviewed the truck driver who allegedly transported the year-end inventory transfers. Compared his chronology of the relevant events with the inventory transfer documents and found no inconsistencies.

4. Examined the expense report filed by the truck driver and found it consistent with his chronology of the relevant events and the chronology of those events provided by other HMI personnel.

5. Discussed the inventory transfers with HMI's controller who provided a credible explanation for why the transfers were necessary.

6. Discussed the inventory transfers with HMI's CFO (Bergman) who indicated that he had not been able to prevent the transfers because he had not learned of them until after the fact.

7. Used various mathematical tests, including a gross profit percentage test, to challenge the reasonableness of the company's total year-end inventory; these tests suggested that the year-end inventory was reasonable.

8. Obtained a standard management representations letter and a separate representation letter from company officials focusing exclusively on the in-transit inventory; each of these letters confirmed the existence of the in-transit inventory.

Source: Trial brief prepared for BDO Seidman *In Re Health Management, Inc. Securities Litigation*, U.S. District Court, Eastern District of New York, Civil Action No. 96-CV-889 (ADS) (ARL).

accept the client's proposed adjustment was a letter of inquiry the audit firm had received from the SEC several months earlier. In that letter, the SEC had expressed concern and requested information concerning the method HMI was using to arrive at its allowance for doubtful accounts. Despite the unusual nature of that inquiry, an expert witness for the plaintiffs testified that he found no reference to it in BDO Seidman's 1995 workpapers, nor any evidence that the auditors had modified their audit procedures for the allowance account as a result of the inquiry.

After considerable discussion with HMI's officers, Fred Bornstein decided to accept the client's proposed adjustment of $600,000 for the allowance account. Bornstein provided the following justification for that decision during testimony in the HMI lawsuit:

> First of all, it is the client's financial statements. It is not our financial statements. Secondly, we may not be right all the time. The client looks at them [proposed audit adjustments] and decides which ones he agrees with and which ones he doesn't agree with. It is a give and take. And as long as we are satisfied with the client's explanation ... [we accept the client's decisions regarding those adjustments]."

Another problem the HMI audit team faced during the 1995 engagement was an earnings release issued by the company approximately one week prior to the date that the fieldwork was begun. That press release reported HMI's anticipated, postaudit net income, a figure that had been materially inflated by the fraudulent inventory scheme. This earnings release distressed Mei-ya Tsai and her superiors. Although not required to do so, client executives customarily delay such press releases until their auditors are fairly certain that the anticipated earnings figure is a "firm" number. A company that reports its earnings before the completion of the annual audit exerts subtle but significant pressure on the auditors to "pass" on proposed adjustments that would materially reduce the prematurely released earnings figure. If the auditors insist that a lower earnings figure be included in the audited financial statements, the resulting "earnings surprise" may cause a sharp drop in the client's stock price.

Even more distressing to BDO Seidman than the SEC's inquiry regarding HMI's allowance for doubtful accounts and the client's premature earnings release was an anonymous letter the audit firm received in May 1995. That letter criticized certain HMI accounting procedures and suggested the company was misleading financial analysts tracking the company's stock. The letter also charged that BDO Seidman's independence was being undermined by a close friendship involving Drew Bergman and an undisclosed member of the audit engagement team. (As discussed during the trial, Mei-ya Tsai was the auditor alluded to in the letter.) During subsequent court testimony, Fred Bornstein revealed that in his 30 years of professional audit experience he had never received such a letter. Bornstein reported that he discussed the letter's contents during a meeting with the individuals assigned to the 1995 HMI audit. But neither during that meeting nor afterwards did Bornstein directly ask individual members of the audit team whether they had a relationship with Bergman that would impair their independence.

BDO Seidman completed the 1995 HMI audit in late July. Similar to the audit opinions issued by the firm in previous years on HMI's financial statements, the 1995 audit opinion was unqualified. In December 1995, Drew Bergman was given a new title at HMI, Corporate Development Officer.[13] Paul Jurewicz, an individual with considerable accounting experience in the healthcare industry, was hired to replace Bergman as HMI's CFO. Shortly after he joined HMI, Jurewicz was having a casual conversation with the company's controller, one of Bergman and Hotte's co-conspirators. During that conversation, the controller matter-of-factly referred to the inventory fraud, believing that Jurewicz was aware of it. According to the controller, Jurewicz "turned white as a ghost" and abruptly ended the conversation. Immediately, the controller knew the "jig was up."

Jurewicz informed Clifford Hotte of the information he had accidentally obtained from the controller. Hotte denied any knowledge of the inventory fraud and refused to refer the matter to other members of HMI's board or the company's legal counsel. Jurewicz then took matters into his own hands and informed the company's legal counsel. In short order, the company's board retained the services of a former federal prosecutor to investigate the alleged inventory fraud. In February 1996, HMI issued a press release indicating that irregularities had been discovered in the company's accounting records. That press release sent HMI's stock price spiraling downward and prompted BDO Seidman to withdraw its audit opinion on the company's 1995 financial statements. Next, a flurry of lawsuits and criminal indictments swamped HMI, its corporate officers, and other parties associated with the 1995 financial statements.

Federal prosecutors filed a litany of fraud charges against Clifford Hotte and his co-conspirators. In exchange for agreeing to testify against Hotte and the other conspirators, Drew Bergman was granted immunity from prosecution.[14] Hotte's initial

---

13. Effective 1 May 1995, HMI's board of directors had more than doubled Bergman's annual salary to $200,000.

14. Drew Bergman was sanctioned by the SEC. The federal agency barred him from serving as an officer or director of a public company and fined him approximately $75,000.

trial ended in a hung jury. Throughout that first trial, Hotte insisted that Bergman had been responsible for the fraudulent inventory scheme. But, in a second trial, a jury convicted Hotte of 14 counts of conspiracy and securities fraud. The former CEO was sentenced to nine years in federal prison, ordered to pay a $250,000 fine, and required to make $9.6 million of restitution to the victims of the inventory hoax. HMI never recovered from the trauma inflicted on it by Bergman and Hotte. In October 1997, another healthcare firm acquired HMI for a nominal amount.

The class-action securities lawsuit filed against BDO Seidman by more than 4,000 HMI stockholders initially included several defendants, most of whom were Hotte and Bergman's co-conspirators. Those co-conspirators reached out-of-court settlements and were dismissed from the lawsuit. Bergman was also dismissed from the lawsuit after agreeing to testify truthfully regarding the HMI inventory fraud and other relevant events and circumstances during his tenure at HMI. The two remaining defendants were Hotte and BDO Seidman. Judge Arthur Spatt, who presided over the HMI case, ordered a "directed verdict" against Hotte, who refused to participate in the trial after invoking his Fifth Amendment rights against self-incrimination. As a result, BDO Seidman took center stage as the sole defendant in the class-action lawsuit. The attorneys for HMI's stockholders claimed that the inventory fraud had cost their clients approximately $37 million and that BDO Seidman was responsible for 75 percent of those damages.

As suggested earlier, prior to the passage of the PSLRA, large accounting firms were reluctant to "gamble" that a jury would resolve a class-action lawsuit in their favor. But the team of attorneys retained by BDO Seidman believed the PSLRA gave their client a reasonable chance of prevailing in court. BDO Seidman followed those attorneys' advice and "rolled the dice." The large accounting firm lost its first showdown when Judge Spatt ruled that the plaintiffs had made sufficiently credible and specific allegations to allow the case to proceed to trial.

Red Flags & Crooks

The skilled teams of attorneys retained by the plaintiffs and defendants in the HMI lawsuit faced many challenges in representing their clients. One of those challenges was shared by both teams of attorneys. The jury that would decide the outcome of the case was composed principally of individuals from blue-collar backgrounds who had little familiarity with the complex accounting issues, financial reporting matters, and capital market phenomena that would be discussed during the trial.

To clarify and strengthen their arguments, each team of attorneys retained prominent expert witnesses to testify during the trial. Plaintiff counsel hired a CPA specializing in forensic services to identify and explain alleged deficiencies in BDO Seidman's audit procedures. To refute much of that individual's testimony, the defense attorneys relied on a former member of the Auditing Standards Board. Each team of attorneys also hired a damages expert to estimate the losses suffered by the HMI stockholders who had filed the lawsuit. According to the trial transcripts, the two teams paid these expert witnesses approximately $600,000 in total. That amount was four times greater than the fee BDO Seidman had received for performing the 1995 HMI audit.

Each team of attorneys went into the trial with a well-rehearsed "game plan." The principal objective of the plaintiff attorneys was to convince the jury that the auditors, at a minimum, had recklessly ignored the auditing profession's technical standards during the 1995 audit and that this reckless conduct had prevented them from uncovering the inventory fraud. To paint a "reckless" image of the auditors in the minds of the jurors, the plaintiff attorneys repeatedly drew attention to the red flags the auditors had allegedly overlooked or, at least, slighted during the 1995 HMI audit.

These red flags included, among other items, the SEC's inquiry regarding HMI's allowance for doubtful accounts, the premature press release reporting the company's 1995 earnings, the allegations included in the anonymous letter that BDO Seidman received before the beginning of the 1995 audit, and the suspicious circumstances surrounding the in-transit inventory at year-end.

The plaintiff attorneys faced two major problems in presenting their case to the jury. First, they were forced to use Drew Bergman as their principal witness to attack the credibility and professionalism of the BDO Seidman auditors. Since Bergman admitted on the stand that he had been a primary architect of HMI's inventory fraud, the jury had an obvious reason to question his credibility.

A second and related challenge facing plaintiff counsel was diverting the jury's attention away from the flagrantly criminal conduct of Bergman, Hotte, and the other conspirators who had carried out the inventory fraud. Because of the PSLRA's proportionate liability rule, the plaintiff attorneys had to convince the jury that the BDO Seidman auditors had been reckless during the 1995 HMI audit *and* that they were responsible for a large proportion of the losses suffered by HMI's stockholders. A possible outcome of the trial would be the jury finding the auditors reckless but then concluding that they were responsible for only a negligible percentage of the stockholder losses. Throughout the trial, the plaintiff attorneys struggled with the awkward task of having Bergman describe the fraud that he had designed, while attempting to convince the jury that BDO Seidman was responsible for the bulk of the stockholder losses resulting from that fraud.

The team of defense attorneys led by Michael Young used a three-prong strategy during the trial to help their client prevail. First, at every opportunity, Young and his colleagues attempted to portray the auditors as victims of the inventory fraud rather than as "reckless" accomplices of Bergman and Hotte. Young and the other defense attorneys drew repeated and stark contrasts between the auditors and the HMI conspirators. In his opening statement, Michael Young introduced the jury one by one to the four BDO Seidman auditors seated in the courtroom who had been deeply involved in the 1995 audit. "Next, I would like to introduce Mei-ya Tsai … [She] lives in Bellmore with her husband and two children." This tactic was apparently meant to convey to the jury members that the auditors were similar to themselves: hard working, family-oriented individuals who lived in local communities. In contrast, when referring to the participants in the HMI fraud, the defense counsel often invoked derisive epithets such as "those crooks" or "those liars." Near the end of the trial, one of the defense attorneys told the jury members that they had to "distinguish between the liars, and those who were lied to."

A second strategy of the defense counsel was to repeatedly "thump the bible" of the auditing profession, that is, the professional auditing standards. Young and his cohorts constantly challenged the plaintiff attorneys and their witnesses to identify specific requirements in the professional standards that the auditors had violated. The defense attorneys charged that the allegations filed against the auditors were based upon abstract and largely indefensible interpretations of those standards.

The final feature of the defense counsel's trial strategy was intended to blunt the repeated allegations of the plaintiff attorneys that BDO Seidman had failed to properly investigate the $1.8 million of in-transit inventory. Throughout the trial, the defense attorneys used a phrase to characterize the auditors' consideration of that item: "But they didn't stop there." On several occasions when the plaintiff attorneys focused the jurors' attention on the bogus in-transit inventory, the defense attorneys responded by using a flip chart to sequentially and forcefully list the series of audit tests and other procedures shown in Exhibit 1 that the auditors had used to corroborate the year-end inventory transfers. After each audit test or procedure was explained, the defense attorneys would typically turn to the jury and remark, "But they didn't stop there"—before proceeding to a discussion of the next item.

The Trial: Rollbacks and Relationships

The two most contentious issues that arose during the trial centered on whether the auditors should have completed an inventory rollback during the 1995 HMI audit and whether the relationship between Drew Bergman and Mei-ya Tsai impaired BDO Seidman's independence. As noted earlier, Bergman feared that the auditors would perform an inventory rollback to test the reasonableness of the $1.8 million of in-transit inventory. The CPA who testified as an expert witness for the plaintiff attorneys insisted that had the auditors completed an inventory rollback, they would have determined that the in-transit inventory had never existed.

Mr. Fox (plaintiff attorney): *Have you seen any evidence that BDO Seidman even attempted to do any tests which resemble an inventory rollback?*

Mr. Moore (plaintiff expert witness): *Not that was included in the workpapers, no.*

Mr. Fox: *And do you have an opinion about whether BDO Seidman could have done an inventory rollback in this case?*

Mr. Moore: *Yes, I do.*

Mr. Fox: *And what is that opinion?*

Mr. Moore: *I think it would have been very easy to do. They could have done a rollback. And it was the only test that would have substantiated without a doubt whether or not the in-transit inventory existed.*

Mr. Fox: *If an inventory rollback was performed by BDO Seidman, what would it have shown?*

Mr. Moore: *It would have shown that the in-transit inventory didn't exist and couldn't have existed.*

The expert witness then used a flip-chart presentation to walk the jury through an example of how an inventory rollback is performed. Instead of completing an inventory rollback, the expert witness charged BDO Seidman with applying an "audit by conversation" approach to the in-transit inventory. That is, the expert charged that the auditors relied heavily on client representations to support the existence of that inventory.

Michael Young bluntly contested the expert witness's assertion that BDO Seidman should have performed an inventory rollback. Young began by getting the witness to agree that generally accepted auditing standards (GAAS) are the accepted benchmark for assessing the work of independent auditors. Young then produced a bound copy of those standards.

Mr. Young: *This is the bible?*

Mr. Moore: *Basically for auditors, yes.*

Mr. Young: *Okay. There is no section of this book—there is no section of generally accepted auditing standards—entitled "in-transit inventory," is there?*

Mr. Moore: *No. There is only a section entitled inventory that we have already discussed.*

Mr. Young: *Right. It doesn't tell you exactly how to go about testing in-transit inventory, does it?*

Following these exchanges, Young quoted the following section of the auditing standards: "The independent auditor must exercise his judgment in determining which auditing procedures to apply." Young maintained that this statement demonstrated that the members of the HMI engagement team were well within their rights as professional auditors to decide whether or not to perform an inventory rollback during the 1995 audit. Young was still not satisfied the jury recognized that the expert witness's opinion regarding the need for an inventory rollback during the 1995 audit was just that—one man's opinion. So, in a subsequent exchange, Young pointedly asked the witness: "Now, is it fair to say that this notion that generally accepted auditing standards required an inventory rollback is just something you made up?" The witness responded with a firm "No." Young then handed the witness a copy of the bound auditing standards and asked him to identify the phrase "inventory rollback" in the alphabetical index of those standards. Of course, Young realized that phrase was not included in the index.

Mr. Young: *Is it fair to say that the reference to rollback appears nowhere in the "bible"?*

Mr. Moore: *Yes.*

Mr. Young: *So, basically, it all boils down to your opinion that the auditors should have done more [that is, an inventory rollback]; is that correct?*

Mr. Moore: *Yes.*

Later in the trial, Jill Karnick, the BDO Seidman semi-senior who had been assigned the primary responsibility for auditing HMI's inventory account, took the witness stand. Karnick surprised the jury when she revealed that, in fact, she had attempted during the audit to perform an "inventory rollforward," which is essentially equivalent to an inventory rollback.[15] After spending three days on this task, Karnick became frustrated and decided not to continue. She testified that the volume of inventory purchases and sales was simply too large to allow her to complete the rollforward. Karnick was then asked why there was no indication in the audit workpapers that an inventory rollforward had been attempted. She replied that it was "normal practice" to discard the results of "inconclusive" audit tests.

Another surprising revelation made by Karnick during her testimony was that she never spoke directly to either Mei-ya Tsai, the audit manager on the 1995 HMI audit, or Fred Bornstein, the audit engagement partner, regarding the in-transit inventory.

Mr. Strauss (plaintiff attorney):   *Ms. Karnick, isn't it true you never spoke to your superior, Mei-ya Tsai, about the in-transit inventory?*

Ms. Karnick: *Face to face verbally, no, that's true.*

Mr. Strauss: *In fact, isn't it true that Mei-ya Tsai never even asked you to do anything concerning inventory in-transit?*

Ms. Karnick: *Not directly, no.*

Mr. Strauss: *And Mr. Bornstein never instructed you to do anything relating to inventory in-transit either, did he?*

Ms. Karnick: *Not directly, no.*

Mr. Strauss: *So, the two most senior people on the audit, the partner and the senior manager, never spoke to you about, or instructed you to do anything concerning inventory in-transit. Correct?*

Ms. Karnick: *Yes.*

---

15. Ms. Karnick attempted to roll the 30 April 1994, inventory forward to 30 April 1995, by using inventory purchases and sales data for that 12-month period.

On cross-examination, Michael Young had Karnick clarify that it was BDO Seidman's policy for semi-seniors to receive their work instructions and be supervised by their immediate superior on an audit engagement. During the 1995 HMI audit, Tom Boyle, the audit senior assigned to that engagement, had supervised Karnick. In his brief time on the witness stand, Boyle reported that he had only a "limited role" in auditing inventory during the HMI audit. "Jill [Karnick] dealt mostly directly with Mei-ya Tsai on that, as I was out in the field being Jill's supervisor.... I would provide guidance basically as to the questions she had." (The fact that this testimony seemed at odds with Karnick's assertion that she never spoke directly to Tsai regarding the in-transit inventory was apparently not addressed by either the plaintiff or defendant attorneys.)

Of all the issues raised during the trial, the one that had the most pervasive implications was the question of whether the close friendship between Drew Bergman and Mei-ya Tsai had impaired BDO Seidman's independence during the 1995 HMI audit. The auditing profession has long maintained that independence is the cornerstone of the independent audit function. If a key member of an audit team loses his or her independence, then all other issues or questions regarding the quality or integrity of the given audit become moot.

The CPA who served as an expert witness for the plaintiffs testified that he believed the social relationship between Bergman and Tsai violated the independence standard included in GAAS: "In all matters relating to the assignment, an independence of mental attitude is to be maintained by the auditor or auditors." According to the expert witness, the Bergman–Tsai friendship "made it extremely difficult to maintain a real level of professional skepticism on the part of the auditor [Ms. Tsai] in looking at the financial statements of HMI." More to the point, the expert witness believed the friendship of the two individuals would have prevented Tsai from going to Bergman after uncovering the inventory scam and telling him, "I think you are a thief, I think you are a fraud."

During her testimony, Mei-ya Tsai acknowledged that BDO Seidman's policy and procedures manual commented on independence concerns posed by social or personal relationships between auditors and officers of a client. A related issue arising during her testimony was that at some point during 1995 she had been offered the position of chief accounting officer (CAO) at HMI, an offer she eventually turned down. Tsai testified that she was unclear regarding the timing of the offer.

> **Mr. Strauss (plaintiff attorney):** *Isn't it true, Ms. Tsai, that during the 1995 audit, you were being considered for the chief accounting officer position at Health Management?*
>
> **Ms. Tsai:** *At one time. I don't remember exactly when the job offer was made to me.*
>
> **Mr. Strauss:** *And you were being considered for that job during the 1995 audit; isn't that correct?*
>
> **Ms. Tsai:** *I don't know the timing.*
>
> **Mr. Strauss:** *Isn't it—*
>
> **Ms. Tsai:** *Definitely not during the audit, no.*
>
> **Mr. Strauss:** *Isn't it true that your friend, Drew Bergman, recommended you for that job during the 1995 audit?*
>
> **Ms. Tsai:** *As I said, I don't know the timing. But it can't be during the audit.*
>
> **Mr. Strauss:** *You are sure of that?*
>
> **Ms. Tsai:** *I don't believe it's during the audit.*

Later in the trial, the plaintiff attorneys introduced evidence indicating that Drew Bergman apparently recommended that Tsai be offered the CAO position during an HMI board meeting that took place on 20 July 1995. That was one week prior to the date of the audit report issued by BDO Seidman on HMI's 1995 financial statements.

Michael Young resorted to one of his key defense strategies when tackling the contentious question of whether the Bergman–Tsai friendship impaired BDO Seidman's independence. While cross-examining Mr. Moore, the plaintiff's expert witness, Young once more handed him a bound copy of the profession's auditing standards and a copy of the *AICPA Code of Professional Conduct* and asked: "Would you please read to the jury the part where it says that an auditor may not be friends with an audit client?" Moore replied that those "specific words" were not included in either item. Young then asked Moore another question: "Isn't it possible for a representative of an audit firm to be social friends with a representative of a client company and for the audit firm to still be independent? Is that possible, Mr. Moore?" Moore grudgingly replied, "It's possible."

Once the testimony in a jury trial is complete, the presiding judge must give the jury detailed instructions for them to follow during their deliberations. Near the completion of the HMI trial, the two teams of attorneys spent three days debating before Judge Spatt—in the absence of the jury—the information that should be included in the jury instructions. The key issue facing Judge Spatt was how to define "recklessness" in the jury instructions. Both sets of attorneys realized that the outcome of the trial might hinge on Judge Spatt's definition of that critical term. Judge Spatt eventually settled on the following description of recklessness: "The plaintiff must prove that there was an egregious refusal to see the obvious or to investigate the doubtful, or that the auditing judgments made were such that no reasonable auditor would have made the same decision if confronted with the same facts."

The Verdict

During the jury's deliberations, the jury foreman sent a note to Judge Spatt asking for further clarification of the term "recklessness." Judge Spatt then brought the jury members back into the courtroom and gave them additional instructions. Judge Spatt reiterated the important distinction between negligence and recklessness. "I want to make clear that an auditor is not liable under Section 10(b) and Rule 10b-5 [of the Securities Exchange Act of 1934] merely because he or she made a mistake or was merely negligent. I repeat, recklessness is more than mere negligence. Reckless conduct represents grossly unreasonable or rash behavior."

Shortly after being sequestered once more, the jury arrived at its verdict in favor of BDO Seidman. In celebrating the victory, Michael Young commented on the PSLRA's impact on the case. "It is questionable whether an accounting firm could muster the courage to take a case like this to trial absent the innovations under the Reform Act."[16] Young went on to explain that the PSLRA's elimination of joint and several liability for auditors guilty of no more than recklessness was the principal source of BDO Seidman's "courage" to defend itself in court.

Jeffrey Zwerling, one of the plaintiff attorneys, spoke with several of the jurors following the trial.[17] Zwerling reported that the jurors had difficulty grasping the legal definition of recklessness even after asking Judge Spatt to clarify that term. Zwerling implied that confusion might have predisposed the jury to rule in favor of the

---

16. M. Riccardi, "Accounting Fraud Trial Breaks New Ground," *New York Law Journal*, 29 October 1999, 1.

17. E. L. Rosen, "Defendants Heartened by the First Trial of PSLRA Case," *The National Law Journal*, 15 November 1999, B5.

auditors. BDO Seidman's general legal counsel put a different "spin" on the outcome of the trial. He maintained that the plaintiff attorneys' strategy of relying on Drew Bergman's testimony "blew up in their faces" since Bergman admitted during the trial that he had specifically designed the fraud to deceive the auditors.[18]

Despite the favorable outcome of the HMI lawsuit for BDO Seidman, the post-PSLRA litigation trends have been mixed for the public accounting profession. Since 1995, class-action securities lawsuits have trended downward on an annual basis when expressed as a percentage of the total number of public companies.[19] However, the percentage of such lawsuits predicated on accounting irregularities has generally risen since 1995.[20] This is bad news for auditors since they are more likely to be named as defendants in a class-action securities lawsuit when a client is charged with manipulating its accounting records. More bad news for audit firms: The average settlement paid to resolve class-action lawsuits involving charges of accounting irregularities has also been rising.

Questions

1. BDO Seidman's attorneys pointed out correctly that professional standards do not prohibit auditors and client personnel from being "friends." At what point do such relationships result in violations of the auditor independence rules and guidelines? Provide hypothetical examples to strengthen your answer.

2. According to court testimony, on 20 July 1995, Drew Bergman recommended to HMI's board of directors that Mei-ya Tsai be hired as the company's chief accounting officer (CAO). One week later, BDO Seidman issued its audit report on HMI's 1995 financial statements. Under presently existing professional standards would this situation have presented an independence "problem" for BDO Seidman? Defend your answer.

3. Under what circumstances is an inventory rollback or rollforward typically performed? How valid is the evidence yielded by this audit procedure? Explain.

4. Jill Karnick abandoned her attempt to complete an inventory rollforward because of the considerable amount of work the procedure involved. Do you believe she made an appropriate decision given the circumstances she faced? How should auditors weigh the cost of an audit procedure, in terms of time and other resources, against the quantity and quality of evidence that it yields?

5. Should the results of inconclusive audit tests be included in audit workpapers? Defend your answer.

6. A major focus of the trial in this case was BDO Seidman's consideration of, and response to, the "red flags" apparent during the 1995 HMI audit. Define or describe the phrase "red flags." Explain the impact of red flags identified by auditors on each major phase of an audit.

---

18. E. MacDonald, "Federal Jury Exonerates BDO Seidman in Accounting Suit over Audit of Firm," *Wall Street Journal*, 28 October 1999, B2.

19. An exception to this trend was 2001. The bursting of the "dot-com" bubble in the stock market triggered an unusually large number of class-action securities lawsuits in that year. Likewise, there was a modest spike in such lawsuits in 2009 and 2010 as a consequence of the worldwide economic crisis linked to the subprime mortgage industry in the United States.

20. An exception to this trend was 2012 when there was a sharp drop in the number of class-action lawsuits filed against accounting firms.

7. The PSLRA requires auditors to report to the SEC illegal acts "that would have a material effect" on a client's financial statements, assuming client management refuses to do so. Briefly describe three hypothetical situations involving potential illegal acts discovered by auditors. Indicate whether the auditors involved in these situations should insist that client management report the given item to the SEC. Defend your decision for each item.

The Leslie Fay Companies

Paul Polishan graduated with an accounting degree in 1969 and immediately accepted an entry-level position in the accounting department of The Leslie Fay Companies, a women's apparel manufacturer based in New York City. Fred Pomerantz, Leslie Fay's founder, personally hired Polishan. Company insiders recall that Pomerantz saw in the young accounting graduate many of the same traits that he possessed. Both men were ambitious, hard driving, and impetuous by nature.

After joining Leslie Fay, Polishan quickly struck up a relationship with John Pomerantz, the son of the company's founder. John had joined the company in 1960 after earning an economics degree from the Wharton School at the University of Pennsylvania. In 1972, the younger Pomerantz became Leslie Fay's president and assumed responsibility for the company's day-to-day operations. Over the next few years, Polishan would become one of John Pomerantz's most trusted allies within the company. Polishan quickly rose through the ranks of Leslie Fay, eventually becoming the company's chief financial officer (CFO) and senior vice president of finance.

Leslie Fay's corporate headquarters were located in the heart of Manhattan's bustling garment district. The company's accounting offices, however, were 100 miles to the northwest in Wilkes-Barre, Pennsylvania. During Polishan's tenure as Leslie Fay's top accounting and finance officer, the Wilkes-Barre location was tagged with the nickname "Poliworld."

The strict and autocratic Polishan ruled the Wilkes-Barre site with an iron fist. When closing the books at the end of an accounting period, Polishan often required his subordinates to put in 16-hour shifts and to work through the weekend. Arriving two minutes late for work exposed Poliworld inhabitants to a scathing reprimand from the CFO. To make certain that his employees understood what he expected of them, Polishan posted a list of rules within the Wilkes-Barre offices that documented their rights and privileges in minute detail. For example, they had the right to place one, and only one, family photo on their desks. Even Leslie Fay personnel in the company's Manhattan headquarters had to cope with Polishan's domineering manner. When senior managers in the headquarters office requested financial information from Wilkes-Barre, Polishan often sent them a note demanding to know why they needed the information.

Polishan's top lieutenant at the Wilkes-Barre site was the company controller, Donald Kenia. On Polishan's frequent trips to Manhattan, Kenia assumed control of the accounting offices. Unlike his boss, Kenia was a soft-spoken individual who enjoyed following orders much more than giving them. Because of Kenia's meek personality, friends and coworkers were stunned in early February 1993 when he took full responsibility for a large accounting fraud revealed to the press by John Pomerantz. Investigators subsequently determined that Leslie Fay's earnings had been overstated by approximately $80 million from 1990 through 1992.

Following the public disclosure of the large fraud, John Pomerantz repeatedly and adamantly insisted that he and the other top executives of Leslie Fay, including Paul Polishan, had been unaware of the massive accounting irregularities perpetrated by Kenia. Nevertheless, many parties inside and outside the company expressed doubts regarding Pomerantz's indignant denials. Kenia was not a major stockholder and did not have an incentive-based compensation contract tied to the company's earnings, meaning that he had not benefited directly from the grossly inflated earnings figures he had manufactured. On the other hand, Pomerantz, Polishan, and several other Leslie Fay executives held large blocks of the company's stock and had received substantial year-end bonuses, in some cases bonuses larger than their annual salaries, as a result of Kenia's alleged scam.

Even after Kenia pleaded guilty to fraud charges, many third parties remained unconvinced that he had directed the fraud. When asked by a reporter to comment on Kenia's confession, a Leslie Fay employee and close friend of Kenia indicated that he was a "straight arrow, a real decent guy" and then went on to observe that, "something doesn't add up here."[1]

Lipstick-Red Rolls Royces and the Orient Express

Similar to many of his peers, Fred Pomerantz served his country during World War II. But instead of storming the beaches of Normandy or pursuing Rommel across North Africa, Pomerantz had served his country by making uniforms—uniforms for the Women's Army Corps. Following the war, Pomerantz decided to make use of the skills he had acquired in the military by creating a company to manufacture women's dresses. He named the company after his daughter, Leslie Fay.

Pomerantz's former subordinates and colleagues in the industry recall that he was a "character." Over the years, he reportedly developed a strong interest in gambling, enjoyed throwing extravagant parties, and reveled in shocking new friends and business associates by pulling up his shirt to reveal knife scars he had collected in encounters with ruffians in some of New York's tougher neighborhoods. Adding to Pomerantz's legend within the top rung of New York's high society was his lipstick-red Rolls Royce that he used to cruise up and down Manhattan's crowded streets.

Pomerantz's penchant for adventure and revelry did not prevent him from quickly establishing his company as a key player in the volatile and intensely competitive women's apparel industry. From the beginning, Pomerantz focused Leslie Fay on one key segment of that industry. He and his designers developed moderately priced and stylishly conservative dresses for women age 30 through 55.

Leslie Fay's principal customers were the large department store chains that flourished in major metropolitan areas in the decades following World War II. By the late 1980s, Leslie Fay was the largest supplier of women's dresses to department stores. At the time, Leslie Fay's principal competitors included Donna Karan, Oscar de la Renta, Nichole Miller, Jones New York, and Albert Nipon. But, in the minds of most industry observers, Liz Claiborne, an upstart company that had been founded in 1976 by an unknown designer and her husband, easily ranked as Leslie Fay's closest and fiercest rival. Liz Claiborne was the only publicly owned women's apparel manufacturer in the late 1980s that had larger annual sales than Leslie Fay.

Fred Pomerantz took his company public in 1952. In the early 1980s, the company went private for a period of several years via a leveraged buyout orchestrated by John Pomerantz, who became the company's CEO and chairman of the board following his father's death in 1982. The younger Pomerantz pocketed $40 million and a large bundle of Leslie Fay stock when the firm reemerged as a public company in 1986.

Like his father before him, John Pomerantz believed that the top executive of a company involved in the world of fashion should exhibit a certain amount of panache. As a result, the popular and outgoing businessman invested in several Broadway shows

---

1. S. Strom, "Accounting Scandal at Leslie Fay," *New York Times*, 2 February 1993, D1.

and became a mainstay on Manhattan's celebrity circuit. The windfall that Pomerantz realized in the mid-1980s allowed him to buy an elegant, Mediterranean-style estate in Palm Beach, Florida, where he often consorted during the winter months with New York City's rich and famous. To reward his company's best clients, he once rented the legendary Orient Express for a festive railway jaunt from Paris to Istanbul.

Despite Leslie Fay's size and prominence in the apparel industry, John Pomerantz continued operating the company much like his father had for decades. Unlike his competitors, Pomerantz shunned extensive market testing to gauge women's changing tastes in clothes. Instead, he relied on his and his designers' intuition in developing each season's new offerings. Pomerantz was also slow to integrate computers into his company's key internal functions. Long after most women apparel manufacturers had developed computer networks to monitor daily sales of their products at major customer outlets, Leslie Fay officials continued to track the progress of their sales by telephoning large customers on a weekly basis. Pomerantz's insistence on doing business the "old-fashioned way" also meant that the company's Wilkes-Barre location was slow to take advantage of the speed and efficiency of computerized data processing.

Management's aversion to modern business practices and the intense competition within the women's apparel industry did not prevent Leslie Fay from prospering after John Pomerantz succeeded his father. Thanks to the younger Pomerantz's business skills, Leslie Fay's annual revenues and earnings grew robustly under his leadership.

Fashion Becomes Unfashionable

By the late 1980s, a trend that had been developing within the women's apparel industry for several years became even more evident. During that decade, fashion gradually became unfashionable. The so-called "casualization" of America meant that millions of consumers began balking at the new designs marketed by apparel manufacturers, opting instead for denims, t-shirts, and other more comfortable attire, including well-worn, if not tattered, garments that they had purchased years earlier. Initially, this trend had a much more pronounced impact on the buying habits of younger women. But, gradually, even women in the 30-to-55-year-old age bracket, the consumers targeted by Leslie Fay, decided that casual was the way to go.

The trend toward casual clothing had the most dramatic impact on women's dress sales. Since Leslie Fay's inception, the company had concentrated its product offerings on dresses, even after pantsuits became widely recognized as suitable and stylish for women of all ages during the 1970s. In the early 1970s, annual dress sales began gradually declining. Most corporate executives in the women's apparel industry believed this trend would eventually reverse. The preference for more casual apparel that developed during the 1980s, however, resulted in declining dress sales throughout the end of the century.

The recession of the late 1980s and early 1990s compounded the problems facing the women's apparel industry. That recession caused many consumers to curtail their discretionary expenditures, including purchases of new clothes. The economy-wide decline in retail spending had particularly far-reaching implications for the nation's major department store chains, Leslie Fay's principal customers.

Even as other segments of the economy improved, continued weakness in the retail sector cut deeply into the sales and earnings of department stores. Eventually, several large chains were forced to merge with competitors or to liquidate. In late 1989, Leslie Fay incurred a substantial loss when it wrote off a receivable from Allied/ Federated Department Stores after the large retailer filed for bankruptcy. Many of the department store chains that survived wrangled financial concessions from their suppliers. These concessions included longer payment terms, more lenient return policies, and increased financial assistance to develop and maintain in-store displays, kiosks, and apparel boutiques.

The structural and economic changes affecting the women's apparel industry during the late 1980s and early 1990s had a major impact on most of its leading companies. Even Liz Claiborne, whose revenues had zoomed from $47 million in 1979 to more than $1 billion by 1987, faced slowing sales from its major product lines and was eventually forced to take large inventory write-downs. Occasionally, industry publications reported modest quarterly sales increases. But the companies that benefited the most from those increases were not the leading apparel manufacturers but rather firms that marketed their wares to discount merchandisers.

Despite the trauma being experienced by its key competitors, Leslie Fay reported impressive sales and earnings throughout the late 1980s and early 1990s. Leslie Fay's typical quarterly earnings release during that time frame indicated that the company had posted record earnings and sales for the just-completed period. For example, in October 1991, John Pomerantz announced that Leslie Fay had achieved record earnings for the third quarter of the year despite the "continued sluggishness in retail sales and consumer spending."[2]

Exhibit 1 presents Leslie Fay's consolidated balance sheets and income statements for 1987 through 1991. For comparison purposes, Exhibit 2 presents norms for key financial ratios within the women's apparel industry in 1991. These benchmark ratios are composite amounts derived from data reported by the investment services that publish financial ratios and other financial measures for major industries.

The gregarious John Pomerantz remained upbeat with the business press regarding his company's future prospects even as Leslie Fay's competitors questioned how the company was able to sustain strong sales and earnings in the face of the stubborn recession gripping the retail sector. Privately, though, Pomerantz was worried. Pomerantz realized that retailers were increasingly critical of Leslie Fay's product line. "Old-fashioned," "matronly," "drab," and "overpriced" were adjectives that the company's sales reps routinely heard as they made their sales calls.

To keep his major customers happy, Pomerantz had to approve significant markdowns in Leslie Fay's wholesale prices and grant those customers large rebates when they found themselves "stuck" with excess quantities of the company's products. To keep investors happy, Pomerantz lobbied financial analysts tracking Leslie Fay's stock. One analyst reported that an "irate" Pomerantz called her in 1992 and chastised her for issuing an earnings forecast for Leslie Fay that was too "pessimistic."[3]

"Houston, We Have a Problem"

On Friday morning, 29 January 1993, Paul Polishan called John Pomerantz who was on a business trip in Canada. Polishan told Pomerantz, "We got a problem … maybe a little more than just a problem."[4] Polishan then informed his boss of the enormous accounting hoax that Donald Kenia had secretly carried out over the past several years. According to Polishan, Kenia had admitted to masterminding the fraud, although some of his subordinates had helped him implement and conceal the various scams. Pomerantz's first reaction to the startling news? Disbelief. "I thought it was a joke."[5]

---

2. *Business Wire*, "Leslie Fay Announces Record Earnings," 17 October 1991.

3. T. Agins, "Dressmaker Leslie Fay Is an Old-Style Firm That's in a Modern Fix," *Wall Street Journal*, 23 February 1993, A8.

4. Strom, "Accounting Scandal at Leslie Fay."

5. T. Agins, "Leslie Fay Says Irregularities in Books Could Wipe Out '92 Profit; Stock Skids," *Wall Street Journal*, 2 February 1993, A5.

When revealing the fraud to the press the following Monday, Pomerantz denied having any clue as to what might have motivated Kenia to misrepresent Leslie Fay's financial data. Pomerantz also denied that he and the other top executives of Leslie Fay had suspected Kenia of any wrongdoing. He was particularly strident in defending his close friend Paul Polishan who had supervised Kenia and who was directly responsible for the integrity of Leslie Fay's accounting records. Pomerantz firmly told a reporter that Polishan "didn't know anything about this."[6]

EXHIBIT 1

THE LESLIE FAY COMPANIES 1987–1991 BALANCE SHEETS

The Leslie Fay Companies
Consolidated Balance Sheets 1987–1991
(in millions)

ASSETS	1991	1990	1989	1988	1987
Current Assets:					
Cash	$ 4.7	$ 4.7	$ 5.5	$ 5.5	$ 4.1
Receivables (net)	118.9	139.5	117.3	109.9	82.9
Inventories	126.8	147.9	121.1	107.0	83.0
Prepaid Expenses & Other Current Assets	19.7	22.5	19.5	16.4	15.9
Total Current Assets	270.1	314.6	263.4	238.8	185.9
Property, Plant, and Equipment	39.2	30.0	27.2	25.9	24.1
Goodwill	81.3	88.1	91.2	94.1	90.3
Deferred Charges and Other Assets	5.2	6.2	5.5	4.2	5.1
Total Assets	$395.8	$438.9	$387.3	$363.0	$305.4
LIABILITIES AND STOCKHOLDERS' EQUITY					
Current Liabilities:					
Notes Payable	35.0	48.0	23.0	29.0	15.5
Current Maturities of Long-term Debt	.3	.3	.3	.3	1.4
Accounts Payable	31.9	43.3	38.6	45.6	31.6
Accrued Interest Payable	3.0	3.8	4.1	3.9	3.7
Accrued Compensation	16.9	14.9	19.5	16.6	10.6
Accrued Expenses & Other	4.3	6.4	5.8	7.2	7.4
Income Taxes Payable	1.4	2.3	4.6	6.1	1.8
Total Current Liabilities	92.8	119.0	95.9	108.7	72.0
Long-term Debt	84.4	129.7	129.0	116.3	116.6
Deferred Credits & Other Noncurrent Liabilities	2.8	2.6	2.7	4.2	4.9
Stockholders' Equity:					
Common Stock	20.0	20.0	20.0	20.0	20.0
Capital in Excess of Par Value	82.2	82.2	82.1	82.2	82.2
Retained Earnings	156.9	127.6	98.5	72.8	50.5
Other	(34.3)	(31.5)	(31.9)	(32.0)	(31.7)
Treasury Stock	(9.0)	(10.7)	(9.0)	(9.1)	(9.1)
Total Stockholders' Equity	215.8	187.6	159.7	133.8	111.9
Total Liabilities and Stockholders' Equity	$395.8	$438.9	$387.3	$363.0	$305.4

(continued)

---

6. *Ibid.*

EXHIBIT 1—
continued

THE LESLIE FAY
COMPANIES
1987–1991
INCOME
STATEMENTS

	The Leslie Fay Companies Consolidated Income Statements 1987–1991 (in millions)				
	1991	**1990**	**1989**	**1988**	**1987**
Net Sales	$836.6	$858.8	$786.3	$682.7	$582.0
Cost of Sales	585.1	589.4	536.8	466.3	403.1
Gross Profit	251.5	269.4	249.5	216.4	178.9
Operating Expenses:					
Selling, Warehouse, General and					
Administrative	186.3	199.0	183.8	156.2	132.5
Amortization of Intangibles	2.7	2.9	2.6	3.3	3.8
Total Operating Expenses	189.0	201.9	186.4	159.5	136.3
Operating Income	62.5	67.5	63.1	56.9	42.6
Interest Expense	18.3	18.7	19.3	18.2	16.4
Income Before Non-recurring Charges					
(Credits)	44.2	48.8	43.8	38.7	26.2
Non-recurring Charges (Credits)	—	—	—	—	(5.0)
Income Before Taxes on Income	44.2	48.8	43.8	38.7	31.2
Income Taxes	14.8	19.7	18.0	16.4	11.5
Net Income	$ 29.4	$ 29.1	$ 25.8	$ 22.3	$ 19.7
Net Income per Share	$ 1.55	$ 1.53	$ 1.35	$ 1.17	$ 1.03

EXHIBIT 2

THE LESLIE FAY
COMPANIES 1991
INDUSTRY NORMS
FOR KEY FINANCIAL
RATIOS

Liquidity:
    Current Ratio   1.8
    Quick Ratio   .9

Solvency:
    Debt to Assets   .53
    Times Interest Earned   4.2
    Long-term Debt to Equity   .14

Activity:
    Inventory Turnover   6.7
    Age of Inventory   53.7 days
    Accounts Receivable Turnover   8.0
    Age of Accounts Receivable   45.5 days
    Total Asset Turnover   3.1

Profitability:
    Gross Margin   31.5%
    Profit Margin on Sales   2.2%
    Return on Total Assets   6.0%
    Return on Equity   14.0%

During the following weeks and months, an increasingly hostile business press hounded Pomerantz for more details of the fraud, while critics openly questioned whether he was being totally forthcoming regarding his lack of knowledge of Kenia's accounting scams. Responding to those critics, the beleaguered CEO maintained that rather than being involved in the fraud, he was its principal victim. "Do I hold myself personally responsible? No. In my heart of hearts, I feel that I'm a victim.

I know there are other victims. But I'm the biggest victim."[7] Such protestations did not prevent critics from questioning why Pomerantz had blithely accepted Leslie Fay's impressive operating results while many of the company's competitors were struggling financially.

Shortly after Pomerantz publicly disclosed Kenia's fraud, Leslie Fay's audit committee launched an intensive investigation of its impact on the company's financial statements for the previous several years. The audit committee retained Arthur Andersen & Co. to help complete that study. Pending the outcome of the investigation, Pomerantz reluctantly placed Polishan on temporary paid leave.

BDO Seidman had served as Leslie Fay's audit firm since the mid-1970s and issued unqualified opinions each year on the company's financial statements. Following Pomerantz's disclosure of the fraud, BDO Seidman withdrew its audit opinions on the company's 1990 and 1991 financial statements. In the ensuing weeks, Leslie Fay stockholders filed several large lawsuits naming the company's management team and BDO Seidman as defendants.

In April 1993, BDO Seidman officials contacted the Securities and Exchange Commission (SEC) and inquired regarding the status of their firm's independence from Leslie Fay given the pending lawsuits. The SEC informed BDO Seidman that its independence was jeopardized by those lawsuits, which forced the firm to resign as Leslie Fay's auditor in early May 1993. Company management immediately appointed Arthur Andersen as Leslie's Fay new auditor.

In September 1993, Leslie Fay's audit committee completed its eight-month investigation of the accounting fraud. The resulting 600-page report was reviewed by members of Leslie Fay's board and then submitted to the SEC and federal prosecutors. Although the report was not released publicly, several of its key findings were leaked to the press. The most startling feature of the fraud was its pervasive nature. According to a company insider who read the report, "There wasn't an entry on the cost side of the company's ledgers for those years that wasn't subject to some type of rejiggering."[8]

The key focus of the fraudulent activity was Leslie Fay's inventory. Kenia and his subordinates had inflated the number of dresses manufactured each quarterly period to reduce the per-unit cost of finished goods and increase the company's gross profit margin on sales. During period-ending physical inventories, the conspirators "manufactured" the phantom inventory they had previously entered in the company's accounting records. Forging inventory tags for nonexistent products, inflating the number of dresses of a specific style on hand, and fabricating large amounts of bogus in-transit inventory were common ruses used to overstate inventory during the period-ending counts.

Other accounting gimmicks used by Kenia included failing to accrue period-ending expenses and liabilities, "prerecording" orders received from customers as consummated sales to boost Leslie Fay's revenues near the end of an accounting period, failing to write off uncollectible receivables, and ignoring discounts on outstanding receivables granted to large customers experiencing slow sales of the company's products. Allegedly, Kenia decided each period what amount of profit Leslie Fay should report. He and his subordinates then adjusted Leslie Fay's accounts with fraudulent journal entries to achieve that profit figure. From 1990 through the end of 1992, the accounting fraud overstated the company's profits by approximately $80 million.

---

7. E. Lesly, "Who Played Dress-up with the Books?" *Business Week*, 15 March 1993, 34.

8. T. Agins, "Report Is Said to Show Pervasive Fraud at Leslie Fay," *Wall Street Journal*, 27 September 1993, B3.

Kenia and his co-conspirators molded Leslie Fay's financial statements so that key financial ratios would be consistent with historical trends. The financial ratio that the fraudsters paid particular attention to was Leslie Fay's gross profit percentage. For several years, the company's gross profit percentage had hovered near 30 percent. Leslie Fay's actual gross profit percentage was approximately 20 percent by the early 1990s, but Kenia relied on his assorted bag of accounting tricks to inflate that financial ratio to near its historical norm.

Excerpts released to the press from the audit committee's report largely exonerated John Pomerantz of responsibility for Leslie Fay's accounting irregularities. The report indicated that there was no evidence that he and other members of Leslie Fay's headquarters management team had been aware of those irregularities, but the report did criticize those executives for failing to aggressively pursue unusual and suspicious circumstances they had encountered during the course of Kenia's fraud. If those circumstances had been vigorously investigated, the audit committee concluded that the fraud might have been uncovered much earlier than January 1993. In particular, the audit committee questioned why Pomerantz had not investigated Leslie Fay's remarkably stable gross profit percentage in the early 1990s given the significant problems facing other women's dress manufacturers and the apparently poor response to many of the company's new product offerings during that period.

Following the completion of the audit committee's investigation in September 1993, Leslie Fay's board of directors allowed John Pomerantz to remain as the CEO but relieved him of all financial responsibilities related to the company's operations. The board created a committee of outside directors to oversee the company's operations while Leslie Fay dealt with the aftermath of the large-scale fraud. The board also dismissed Paul Polishan as Leslie Fay's CFO and senior vice president of finance and replaced him with an Arthur Andersen partner who had been involved in the audit committee investigation.

BDO Seidman: Odd Man Out

In April 1993, Leslie Fay filed for protection from its creditors under Chapter 11 of the federal bankruptcy code. Press reports of Kenia's fraudulent scheme had cut off the company's access to the additional debt and equity capital that it needed to continue normal operations. By early April 1993, the price of Leslie Fay's stock had dropped by nearly 85 percent since the first details of the fraud had become public two months earlier. The company's plummeting stock price and the mounting criticism of its officers in the business press triggered additional lawsuits by angry stockholders against Pomerantz, other Leslie Fay executives, and the company's longtime auditor, BDO Seidman.

The lawsuits that named BDO Seidman as a defendant charged that the firm had been at least reckless in auditing Leslie Fay's periodic financial statements during the early 1990s. Howard Schilit, an accounting professor and forensic accounting specialist, suggested in the business press that Leslie Fay's financial data had been replete with red flags. These red flags included implausible trend lines in the company's financial data, implausible relationships between key financial statement items, and unreasonably generous bonuses paid to top executives, bonuses linked directly to the record earnings Leslie Fay reported each successive period. For 1991, John Pomerantz had received total salary and bonuses of $3.6 million, three times more than the 1991 compensation of Liz Claiborne's CEO, whose company reported sales more than double those of Leslie Fay's.

BDO Seidman officials chafed at published reports criticizing their firm's Leslie Fay audits. Those officials insisted that BDO Seidman was being indicted in the press on the basis of innuendo and incomplete information. These same individuals also maintained that Leslie Fay's top management, principally John Pomerantz, should shoulder the bulk of the responsibility for the massive fraud.

During various court proceedings following the disclosure of the Leslie Fay fraud, many parties questioned the objectivity of the forensic investigation supervised by Leslie Fay's audit committee that had effectively vindicated Pomerantz. These skeptics suggested that the members of the audit committee had been reluctant to criticize Pomerantz. To squelch such criticism, the federal judge presiding over Leslie Fay's bankruptcy filing appointed an independent examiner, Charles Stillman, to prepare another report on the details of the fraud. Stillman was also charged with identifying the individuals responsible for the fraud and those responsible for failing to discover it.

In August 1994, the U.S. Bankruptcy Court released the so-called Stillman Report. This document corroborated the key findings of the audit committee investigation. Similar to the audit committee report, the Stillman Report largely exonerated Pomerantz. "The examiner's report concludes there is no evidence to suggest that viable claims exist against any members of Leslie Fay's current management or its board of directors."[9]

The Stillman Report went on to suggest that although there were likely "viable claims" against former company executives Kenia and Polishan based upon "presently available information,"[10] the limited assets of those individuals made it economically infeasible for the bankruptcy court to pursue those claims. Finally, the Stillman Report indicted the quality of BDO Seidman's audits of Leslie Fay by asserting that there may be "claims worth pursuing against . . . BDO Seidman,"[11] and that "it is likely BDO Seidman acted negligently in performing accounting services for Leslie Fay."[12]

Following the release of the Stillman Report, Leslie Fay's stockholders filed a large civil lawsuit against BDO Seidman in the federal bankruptcy courts. At approximately the same time, BDO Seidman filed a lawsuit against Leslie Fay's principal officers, including John Pomerantz. In commenting on this latter lawsuit, BDO Seidman officials laid the blame for the fraud squarely upon the shoulders of Leslie Fay's executives and insisted that they had been intentionally misled by the company.[13]

Leslie Fay's management responded immediately to the news that BDO Seidman had named John Pomerantz and his fellow officers as defendants in a large civil lawsuit. "The unsubstantiated and unfounded allegations made today by BDO Seidman are a classic example of 'revisionist history' and are clearly an attempt by the accounting firm to divert attention from its own apparent negligence by blaming others."[14]

---

9. *Business Wire*, "Independent Examiner Confirms Findings of Leslie Fay's Audit Committee Investigation," 16 August 1994.

10. *Ibid.*

11. *Ibid.*

12. *Business Wire*, "Leslie Fay Responds to Unfounded Allegations by BDO Seidman," 29 March 1995.

13. *PR Newswire*, "BDO Seidman Announces Cross-Claims and Third Party Complaints Against Key Leslie Fay Figures," 29 March 1995.

14. *Business Wire*, "Leslie Fay Responds to Unfounded Allegations."

EPILOGUE

In July 1997, a federal judge approved a $34 million settlement to the large number of lawsuits filed by Leslie Fay's stockholders and creditors against the company, its executives, and BDO Seidman. BDO Seidman contributed $8 million to the settlement pool, although the firm reported that it was agreeing to the settlement only because it was the most economical and expeditious way to "put this matter behind us."[15] In June 1997, Leslie Fay emerged from federal bankruptcy court. Over the next several years, the much smaller company returned to a profitable condition before being purchased in late 2001 by a large investment fund. A few months later, in April 2002, John Pomerantz received a lifetime achievement award at the annual American Image Awards, a glitzy event sponsored by the major companies and organizations in the fashion industries.

On 31 October 1996, federal prosecutors filed a 21-count fraud indictment against Paul Polishan. The specific charges included conspiracy, making false statements to the SEC, bank fraud, and wire fraud. Unknown to the public, three years earlier, Donald Kenia had broken down under relentless questioning by federal investigators and admitted that Polishan, his former boss, had been the architect of the Leslie Fay fraud. According to Kenia's testimony, Polishan had overseen and directed every major facet of the fraud. Because of Polishan's intimidating personality, Kenia and several of his subordinates had agreed to make the enormous number of fraudulent entries in Leslie Fay's accounting records that he had demanded. Polishan had also compelled Kenia to accept full responsibility for the accounting irregularities when it became apparent in late January 1993 that the fraud would soon be exposed.

Following a series of lengthy and fiercely contested pretrial hearings, Polishan's criminal case was finally heard in federal court in the summer of 2000. Polishan was convicted on 18 of the 21 fraud counts filed against him. His attorneys immediately appealed the guilty verdict. The attorneys' principal contention during the appeal was that there was almost no physical evidence to link their client to the fraud. Instead, they maintained that Polishan's conviction had hinged almost entirely upon the veracity of Kenia's testimony.

The federal judge who presided over Polishan's appeal did not dispute his attorneys' principal contention. Throughout the fraud, the former CFO had painstakingly avoided leaving incriminating physical evidence that linked him directly to the accounting irregularities. Despite that fact, the judge denied Polishan's appeal. The judge observed that a substantial amount of circumstantial evidence had been presented during the trial. After studying the evidence in painstaking detail, the judge ruled that it was much more consistent with Kenia's testimony than that of Polishan.

A key factor contributing to the judge's decision was the unusual relationship that had existed between Polishan and Kenia during their long tenure with Leslie Fay, a relationship that had been documented and discussed at length during the trial. The judge noted that Polishan had "dominated" Kenia through intimidation and fear. In the opinion he issued in the case, the judge referred on multiple occasions to an episode during 1992 to demonstrate how completely Polishan had controlled Kenia. In forcing Kenia to take responsibility for an accounting error that had been discovered in Leslie Fay's accounting records, Polishan insisted that Kenia tell another company executive, "I am a _____ idiot."[16]

On 21 January 2002, almost exactly nine years after the news of the Leslie Fay fraud

---

15. *The Electronic Accountant* (online), "BDO to Pay $8 Million to Settle Leslie Fay Lawsuit," 10 March 1997. As a point of information, there is no public report of any resolution to the lawsuit filed against John Pomerantz et al. by BDO Seidman. Most likely, that lawsuit was dropped by BDO Seidman following the settlement approved by the federal judge.

16. *United States of America v. Paul Polishan*, 2001 U.S. Dist. LEXIS 10662.

surfaced in the press, Paul Polishan was sentenced to serve nine years in federal prison for his role in plotting and overseeing that fraud.[17] Polishan, who filed for personal bankruptcy in 1999 claiming assets of only $17,000, was also fined $900. After losing an appeal to overturn his conviction, Polishan reported to the federal correctional facility in Schuylkill County, Pennsylvania, in early September 2003 to begin serving his nine-year sentence. In exchange for his testimony against Polishan, Donald Kenia was allowed to plead guilty to two counts of making false statements to the SEC. In 2001, Kenia was sentenced to two years in the Allenwood Federal Prison Camp in Montgomery, Pennsylvania.

Questions

1. Prepare common-sized financial statements for Leslie Fay for the period 1987–1991. For that same period, compute for Leslie Fay the ratios shown in Exhibit 2. Given these data, which financial statement items do you believe should have been of particular interest to BDO Seidman during that firm's 1991 audit of Leslie Fay? Explain.

2. In addition to the data shown in Exhibit 1 and Exhibit 2, what other financial information would you have obtained if you had been responsible for planning the 1991 Leslie Fay audit?

3. List nonfinancial variables or factors regarding a client's industry that auditors should consider when planning an audit. For each of these items, briefly describe their audit implications.

4. Paul Polishan apparently dominated Leslie Fay's accounting and financial reporting functions and the individuals who were his subordinates. What implications do such circumstances pose for a company's independent auditors? How should auditors take such circumstances into consideration when planning an audit?

5. Explain why the SEC ruled that BDO Seidman's independence was jeopardized by the lawsuits that named the accounting firm, Leslie Fay, and top executives of Leslie Fay as codefendants.

17. Polishan's attorneys asked the presiding judge to reduce their client's sentence because Polishan allegedly suffered from a narcissistic personality disorder. The judge denied that request.

CASE 1.6

NextCard, Inc.

In the late 1990s, the investing public's fascination with Internet-based companies prompted the cyberspace equivalent of the Oklahoma Land Rush, according to one prominent Wall Street analyst. "In a land rush, you suspend rules because your perception is that time is of the essence."[1] That perception caused many anxious investors who feared missing out on a once-in-a-lifetime investment opportunity to bid the prices of Internet stocks to ever-higher levels. Those investors readily discounted the fact that most Internet companies were reporting minimal revenues and sizable, if not staggering, operating losses. Over a 15-month stretch between late 1998 and March 2000, the dot-com-laced NASDAQ stock exchange rose by more than 150 percent. By comparison, over the same time frame, the largely "Old Economy" Dow Jones Industrial Average managed a much less impressive 15 percent gain.

Dot-com fever caused many investment services and publications to create new stock indices dedicated strictly to Internet companies. On 30 June 1999, *USA Today* launched the *Internet 100* to track the stock prices of 100 high-profile companies whose primary lines of business were directly or exclusively related to the Internet. Within a few months, the collective value of that index had risen by more than 60 percent. Other Internet stock indices realized similar increases. By early March 2000, the 300 companies included in the *Forbes Internet Index* had a collective market value of $1.2 trillion, which was approximately equal to the total value of all publicly traded U.S. stocks a little more than one decade earlier.

The public's feeding frenzy on Internet stocks produced numerous paper billionaires among dot-com bigwigs. Dot-com billionaires making appearances in the *Forbes 400*, a list of the 400 "richest people in America," included, among several others, Jeff Bezos (Amazon), Stephen Case (AOL), Mark Cuban (Broadcast.com), Andrew McKelvey (Monster.com), Pierre Omidyar (eBay), Jay Walker (Priceline), David Wetherell (CMGI), and Jerry Yang and David Filo (Yahoo!). As you might expect, the surging prices of Internet stocks added an even larger number of new members to the millionaires' club. By early 2000, one publication reported that in northern California's Silicon Valley alone, the Internet revolution was creating 64 new millionaires each day.[2] Among these millionaires were Jeremy and Molly Lent, a husband-and-wife team that founded the Internet-based NextCard, Inc., in 1997.

Credit on the Fly

Jeremy Lent served as the chief financial officer (CFO) of Providian Financial Corporation during the early 1990s. At the time, Providian ranked among the largest financial services companies in the United States. Experts in the financial services industry attributed Providian's success to the direct-mail marketing methods the company used to target individuals who made extensive use of credit cards. In the late 1990s, Lent decided that the marketing tactics used by Providian could be

---

1. G. Ip, S. Pulliam, S. Thurm, and R. Simon, "How the Internet Bubble Broke Records, Rules, Bank Accounts," *Wall Street Journal* (online), 14 July 2000.

2. *The Economist* (online), "The Country-Club Vote," 20 May 2000.

easily adapted to the Internet, which prompted him and his wife to create NextCard, an online company that would offer Internet users the opportunity to obtain a credit card in a matter of moments.

Because of his tenure at Providian, Lent realized that a key metric in the credit card industry is the acquisition cost of a new customer. Lent was convinced that he could use the Internet to undercut the average acquisition cost of a new customer incurred by brick-and-mortar credit card companies, such as Providian. Likewise, Lent believed that his company would have significantly lower bad debt losses than conventional credit card issuers. Marketing research had found that Internet users were generally more affluent and, thus, better credit risks, than individuals drawn from the general population of consumers.

One of Lent's first major strategic initiatives was hiring dozens of marketing researchers to analyze a large database of "clickstream data" that documented the "surfing" habits of Internet users. After analyzing these data, the company's marketing team developed Internet-based advertising campaigns targeting Internet users who made frequent use of, and maintained large balances on, their credit cards. NextCard's online ads encouraged such individuals to apply for a credit card with NextBank, a virtual bank that was NextCard's largest operating unit, and to transfer their existing credit card balances to this new card. The key inducement used by Lent to convince potential customers to apply for a NextBank credit card was a lower interest rate than that charged by conventional credit card issuers. Lent also promised those potential customers that a decision regarding their online credit card application would be made within 30 seconds of their submitting that application.

Initially, Lent's business model for NextCard appeared to be a huge success as the company quickly became recognized as one of the leaders of the Internet Revolution that made the term *e-commerce* the hottest buzzword among Wall Street analysts and individual investors. The company's website was regularly named one of the top 50 financial websites by *Money* magazine and by 2000 had more daily "hits" or visits than any other website in the financial services industry. More importantly, for several consecutive years, NextCard issued more credit cards online than any other credit card issuer, including such large and well-established firms as American Express, Bank of America, Citibank, and MBNA. Lent used NextCard's prominent position in the Internet industry to create a network of 60,000 online "affiliates" that referred potential credit card customers to NextCard. Several of these affiliates, including Amazon.com, purchased significant ownership interests in NextCard.

By early 2000, NextCard was well on its way to achieving one of Lent's primary goals for the company: obtaining one million credit card customers. During that year, NextCard extended more than $1 billion of credit to its customers. Those impressive operating statistics did not translate into immediate profits for NextCard, a fact that Lent and other company executives frequently downplayed or simply ignored in press releases and other public disclosures. In February 2000, a NextCard executive commented on the strength of his company's business model: "Our acquisition cost, credit quality, and yield—all major drivers of profitability— continue to be strong and stable, leading to continued strong revenue results."[3] This statement conveniently overlooked the fact that NextCard's New Age business

---

3. *Business Wire* (online), "NextCard Announces Significant Growth Milestones Ahead of Plan," 22 February 2000.

model had produced a large loss during the company's just-completed 1999 fiscal year, $77.2 million to be exact.

Despite the fact that NextCard was posting large losses each reporting period, Lent had taken the company public in 1999. On the first day NextCard's stock was traded, the stock's price rose from an initial selling price of $20 per share to more than $40, making Lent and several other NextCard executives instant multimillionaires. A few months later, the stock surged past $50 per share. When the "lock-up" period mandated by the Securities and Exchange Commission (SEC) following an initial public offering expired, Lent and his colleagues sold large chunks of their ownership interests in the company.

When NextCard reported an unexpectedly large loss of $81.9 million for fiscal 2000, company executives could no longer sidestep the recurring question posed by persistent Wall Street analysts, namely, "When would NextCard earn its first quarterly profit?" NextCard's management team insisted that the company had "turned the corner" and pledged that NextCard would report its first-ever quarterly profit by the fourth-quarter of fiscal 2001. At the same time, company officials predicted that NextCard would report a net income of $150 million by fiscal 2003.

In March 2000, the NASDAQ stock index crested at an all-time high of more than 5,000. Over the following 18 months, the Internet "bubble" in the stock market burst, causing the stock prices of most Internet companies, including NextCard, to spiral downward. Many of these New Age companies survived, including such firms as Amazon.com, eBay, Monster.com, and Yahoo!. NextCard would not be among those survivors.

Loose Credit = Bad Debts

The bursting of the Internet bubble in the stock market cut off NextCard's access to the debt and equity markets. Without the ability to raise additional debt or equity capital, NextCard suddenly faced the need to raise capital the "old-fashioned way," namely, via profitable operations.

Despite the promises and predictions of NextCard's executives, the company never reported a profit, principally because two of the key premises on which Jeremy Lent had predicated NextCard's business model were invalid. First, the average acquisition cost NextCard incurred to obtain new customers proved to be much higher than the figure Lent had originally projected. NextCard spent huge amounts on Internet advertising campaigns to recruit customers only to find that Internet users routinely ignored, if not treated with contempt, most efforts of online advertisers to attract their attention. The "click-through" rate for most Internet advertisements hovered at a fraction of 1 percent, considerably lower than the response rate to direct or "junk" mail advertisements used by conventional credit card issuers.

Lent's other major miscalculation had even more serious consequences for NextCard. Internet users, at least the subpopulation of Internet users who signed up for a NextBank credit card, proved to be much higher credit risks than Lent had expected. A large proportion of the Internet users who took advantage of NextCard's liberal credit policies were individuals who could not obtain credit from any other source. For these desperate and shallow-pocketed consumers, NextCard effectively served as the "lender of last resort." These individuals eventually produced the large balances that Lent had expected Internet users to carry on their credit cards but they often allowed those balances to go unpaid, resulting in large credit losses for NextCard.

In sum, instead of incurring minimal marketing expenditures to acquire "good" credit card customers, NextCard spent large amounts to acquire "bad" credit card customers. Making matters worse, many of NextCard's competitors, including American Express, "went to school" on NextCard's mistakes. These competitors learned from those mistakes and developed more cost-effective—and ultimately profitable—Internet marketing strategies to expand their market shares in the intensely competitive credit card industry.

Early in NextCard's history, the company's executives apparently realized that their business model contained serious flaws. Despite that realization, those executives continued to pursue Jeremy Lent's dream of creating one of the dominant companies in the credit card industry. To shore up the company's stock price and to maintain credibility on Wall Street and among private investors, NextCard's executives chose to conceal the extent and source of the company's financial problems. The principal means used to accomplish this goal was understating NextCard's massive credit losses by refusing to provide sufficient allowances each period for expected bad debts.

Because NextBank was subject to federal banking regulations, the Office of the Comptroller of the Currency (OCC) regularly reviewed the company's accounting records and operating policies and procedures. During 2001, OCC auditors forced NextCard to significantly increase its allowance for bad debts. When NextCard publicly reported the OCC's decision, company management denied that the larger allowance for bad debts was due to unexpectedly high credit losses. Instead, NextCard officials insisted that the increase in the allowance for bad debts was necessary because the company had suffered large losses as a result of fraudulent schemes perpetrated by hackers and other Internet outlaws. In November 2001, a skeptical Wall Street analyst questioned how such a massive problem could "pop up" so unexpectedly and without any previous warning from company officials.[4] In fact, subsequent investigations would reveal that NextCard officials had routinely and materially understated the company's allowance for credit losses.

In late 2001, angry NextCard investors filed a large class-action lawsuit against the company and its executives. Among other charges, that lawsuit alleged that NextCard's management team had intentionally concealed the extent and nature of the company's financial problems. In addition, the plaintiffs charged that the NextCard executives had engaged in insider trading by selling off large portions of their ownership interests in the company before NextCard's true financial condition became apparent. This large class-action lawsuit and widespread concerns regarding the integrity of NextCard's publicly reported financial data caused federal regulatory authorities, including the SEC, to launch investigations of the company's financial affairs.

Suspicious Audit Trails

Discovering that your largest client is the subject of a series of federal investigations for tampering with its accounting records and issuing materially misleading financial statements is, no doubt, among the life events feared most by audit partners of major accounting firms. Thirty-six-year-old Thomas Trauger found himself facing that disturbing scenario in the fall of 2001. Trauger, a partner in the San Francisco office of Ernst & Young (E&Y), had served for several years as the audit engagement partner for NextCard. In March 2001, Trauger had authorized the unqualified opinion issued on NextCard's 2000 financial statements.

After considering his options, including doing nothing and simply awaiting the outcome of the federal investigations of NextCard, Trauger decided to take matters

---

4. J. Graham, "What's the Next Move for Troubled NextCard?" *Investor's Business Daily*, 1 November 2001, 6.

into his own hands. His first decision was to contact his top subordinate on the 2000 NextCard audit, Oliver Flanagan.

Like most accounting professionals, Oliver Flanagan enjoyed challenging assignments. A native of Ireland, Flanagan accepted an entry-level position on the auditing staff of the London, England, office of E&Y in the mid-1990s. Flanagan left E&Y in late 1999 to accept a position in the banking industry but soon discovered that he missed working as an independent auditor. So, Flanagan asked E&Y for his job back. In the late 1990s, the Internet bubble had created a huge demand for the services of public accounting firms, which caused E&Y to be more than happy to rehire Flanagan. Among the locations having the greatest need for auditors at the time was the booming Silicon Valley region near San Francisco. Given his interest in the banking industry and the "adventure" of going stateside, Flanagan quickly accepted the opportunity to move to San Francisco and become a member of the NextCard audit engagement team.

Despite having only a few years of auditing experience, Flanagan was assigned to serve as the senior audit manager on the NextCard engagement, a position in which he would report directly to Thomas Trauger. Flanagan realized that Trauger was a "fast track" partner in the San Francisco office of E&Y since he was in charge of the prestigious NextCard engagement. The young Irishman hoped that Trauger would serve as his mentor and help him advance quickly within E&Y.

In early November 2001, more than six months after the 2000 NextCard audit was completed, Thomas Trauger left a message instructing Oliver Flanagan to meet him in the E&Y office the following Saturday morning. Flanagan was probably not surprised by the request since weekend work was nothing unusual with a major accounting firm. Plus, the planning phase for the 2001 audit of the financially troubled NextCard was nearing completion. If Flanagan expected Trauger to discuss the 2001 audit that Saturday morning, he was wrong. Instead, when Flanagan contacted Trauger prior to their meeting, the audit partner told him to gather all of the workpapers for the 2000 NextCard audit and "have them ready for revisions"[5] during the meeting. Flanagan knew that it was not common to revise prior-year audit workpapers once they had been archived. Almost certainly, NextCard's well-documented financial problems and the insinuations of an accounting scandal within the company caused Flanagan to wonder what types of "revisions" Trauger intended to make to the NextCard workpapers.

Before meeting with Flanagan, Trauger contacted the other audit manager on the NextCard engagement team, Michael Mullen—Mullen had not been involved in the 2000 NextCard audit since he had only been assigned to the engagement team since June 2001. Trauger instructed Mullen to determine whether it was possible to "manipulate E&Y's computer system so that he [Trauger] could alter electronically archived working papers without being discovered."[6] Trauger wanted to revise the original NextCard workpapers without leaving any evidence that they had been altered. For the conventional "hard copy" workpapers, this goal did not pose any particular challenge. But accomplishing that same goal for the electronic workpapers meant that Trauger had to change the electronic "time stamps" on those files.

Mullen complied with Trauger's request and eventually learned from another E&Y employee that it was possible to "de-archive" previously completed electronic audit workpapers and thereby change the time stamps posted on those workpapers.

---

5. Securities and Exchange Commission, *Accounting and Auditing Enforcement Release No. 1871,* 25 September 2003.

6. *Ibid.*

Mullen sent this information to both Trauger and Flanagan. During their weekend meeting, Trauger and Flanagan reviewed the 2000 NextCard audit workpapers and made numerous additions and deletions to those workpaper files. The principal items changed were the "Summary Review Memorandum" and the receivables workpapers. In a subsequent enforcement release that focused on the conduct of Oliver Flanagan, the SEC described the process used by Trauger and Flanagan to alter the NextCard workpapers. (Note: In this enforcement release, the SEC referred to Trauger as simply the "audit partner.")

> *The audit partner marked up printed versions of the documents and gave them to Flanagan for Flanagan to input using Flanagan's laptop computer. In order to ensure that the revised documents appeared to have been created as part of the original working papers, the audit partner instructed Flanagan to reset the date on his computer so that any documents bearing computer-generated dates would reflect a date in early 2001. Some documents went through more than one edit, as Flanagan input the audit partner's changes and then printed out the revised version for the audit partner's further review."[7]*

NextCard's deteriorating financial condition in late 2001 and the increasing scrutiny of the company by federal regulatory authorities prompted Trauger to ask Flanagan to meet with him once more to make additional alterations to the 2000 NextCard workpapers. Trauger also asked Michael Mullen to attend this second meeting, which took place in late November 2001. The SEC provided the following overview of what transpired during this second meeting.

> *The audit partner marked up printed versions of the memoranda he was revising and then the other audit manager [Mullen] input the changes. At the audit partner's direction, the other audit manager deleted charts, portions of tables, and discussion sections that indicated problems with NextCard's charge-off numbers and trends. The audit partner also added information and altered the tone of certain sections. One of the documents altered during this meeting was a memorandum entitled "Analysis for Loan Losses." Flanagan remained involved in the process by proofreading the other audit manager's work to ensure that all of the audit partner's changes were made.[8]*

The SEC issued multiple enforcement releases that documented the improper professional conduct of Thomas Trauger, Oliver Flanagan, and Michael Mullen. In those enforcement releases, the SEC noted on several occasions that Trauger's intent in revising the 2000 NextCard audit workpapers was to "make it appear that there was a more satisfactory basis" for the key E&Y conclusions reached during that engagement. The *New York Times* reported that "Mr. Trauger told Mr. Flanagan that he wanted to 'beef up' the workpapers to make it appear as if the auditing team had been 'right on the mark' all along."[9] During the course of the federal investigations of NextCard, the FBI retrieved e-mails that Trauger had sent to his subordinates. One of those e-mails provided a more pointed statement of Trauger's intent in modifying the NextCard workpapers. According to an FBI affidavit, in one of those e-mails Trauger stated that he did not want "some smart-ass lawyer"[10] second-guessing the decisions that he had made during the 2000 NextCard audit.

---

7. *Ibid.*

8. *Ibid.*

9. K. Eichenwald, "U.S. Charges Ernst & Young Ex-Partner in Audit Case," *New York Times*, 26 September 2003, 1.

10. J. Hoppin, "Snared by SOX," *Corporate Counsel*, December 2003, 24.

Following the two meetings in which the E&Y auditors had altered the NextCard workpapers, Trauger instructed Flanagan "to scour his hard drive and delete documents or e-mails inconsistent with the altered versions of the working papers."[11] Once more, Flanagan followed his mentor's instructions. Approximately three months later, E&Y received a subpoena from the OCC that instructed the firm to give the federal agency certain NextCard workpapers. At that time, Trauger discovered that Michael Mullen had kept a computer diskette containing some of the original NextCard workpapers that had been altered in November 2001. Trauger ordered Flanagan to obtain that diskette and destroy it. Flanagan obtained the diskette and told Trauger that he had destroyed it. In fact, Flanagan kept the diskette and subsequently gave it to federal authorities.

EPILOGUE

The computer diskette that Oliver Flanagan turned over to federal authorities investigating NextCard ultimately resulted in the FBI arresting Thomas Trauger in September 2003. The U.S. Department of Justice filed criminal charges against Trauger for obstructing the federal investigations of NextCard. Trauger was the first partner of a major accounting firm to be prosecuted for destroying audit-related documents under the criminal provisions of the Sarbanes–Oxley Act of 2002. Those provisions were included in the Sarbanes–Oxley Act as a direct consequence of the widely publicized scandal involving Enron Corporation. During an SEC investigation of Enron, Andersen, the company's audit firm, had shredded certain Enron workpapers. The subsequent felony conviction handed down against Andersen by a federal court effectively put the prominent accounting firm out of business.[12] Ironically, Trauger and his subordinates were altering the NextCard workpapers in November 2001, the same time frame during which Andersen personnel were shredding the Enron workpapers.

Shortly after being arrested in September 2003, Thomas Trauger insisted that he was innocent of the charges filed against him. When Trauger was released after posting a $1 million bail, his attorney issued the following public statement defending his client: "He's a good man, a well-respected accountant, and I'm confident he will be exonerated."[13] Despite those assertions, a little more than one year later on 28 October 2004, Thomas Trauger pleaded guilty to one count of impeding a federal investigation. As a result of that plea, Trauger faced a prison sentence of up to 25 years and a fine of $500,000. On 27 January 2005, a federal judge sentenced Trauger to one year in prison and two years of "supervised release." The judge also ordered Trauger to pay a $5,000 fine. In his plea agreement, Trauger admitted he had failed to inform federal authorities that he and his subordinates altered certain of the NextCard audit workpapers subpoenaed by those authorities.

Ernst & Young disavowed responsibility for the actions of Trauger, Flanagan, and Mullen. In a press release, an E&Y spokesperson pointed out that the actions of the three individuals were in clear violation of the firm's professional standards and internal policies. That spokesperson also noted that when E&Y discovered the nature of the individuals' conduct, firm officials cooperated fully with federal law enforcement authorities.

Not surprisingly, federal authorities were elated with the outcome of the Trauger case. In commenting on the case, a spokesperson for

---

11. Securities and Exchange Commission, *Accounting and Auditing Enforcement Release No. 1871*.

12. The U.S. Supreme Court overturned Andersen's felony conviction in May 2005; however, by that time, the firm was in the process of being disbanded.

13. E. Iwata, "Accountant Arrested under Sarbanes–Oxley," *USA Today*, 26 September 2003, 2B.

the U.S. Department of Justice observed that the proper functioning of the nation's capital markets depends, in large part, on the integrity of auditors and other professionals involved in the financial reporting process:

This is one of the first cases in the country in which an auditor has been accused of destroying key documents in an effort to obstruct an investigation. Our financial markets depend on the integrity of auditors, lawyers and other professionals to do their jobs ethically and fairly. Where they fail to do so because of negligence, markets are compromised. Where they fail to do so because of criminal intent, all of us are at risk. The U.S. Attorney's Office will bring those professionals to justice who join in criminal acts they are supposed to uncover and expose.[14]

Stephen Cutler, the SEC's Director of Enforcement, echoed these sentiments and stressed the importance of auditors' maintaining the integrity of the audit process:

Complete and accurate workpapers are critical to the integrity of the audit process and the efficacy of our investigative work. We will aggressively pursue auditors who alter or destroy workpapers or otherwise undermine the financial reporting process, and will work closely with criminal authorities to ensure that those who engage in such conduct are held accountable.[15]

Finally, an FBI spokesperson observed: "We look to certified public accountants to maintain the integrity of publicly traded companies. The criminal acts of auditors who abuse their authority, act in their own self-interest, and violate the sacred trust of shareholders will not be tolerated."[16]

In October 2004, Michael Mullen pleaded guilty to lying to an FBI agent involved in the NextCard investigation. Mullen was sentenced to one year of probation and ordered to pay a

$100 fine. As a result of his guilty plea, Mullen's right to practice before the SEC was suspended. In August 2003, Oliver Flanagan pleaded guilty to one count of criminal obstruction of justice. After cooperating with federal authorities in the prosecution of Thomas Trauger, Flanagan was allowed to return to his native Ireland. Flanagan's attorney noted that "Oliver has made peace with our [U.S.] government."[17] The attorney then added that Flanagan's only wish was that Thomas Trauger had been a "better mentor."[18]

NextCard's financial problems steadily worsened following the announcement in late 2001 that federal law enforcement authorities were investigating the company's financial affairs. In February 2002, the OCC ruled that NextBank was operating in an "unsafe and unsound" manner and placed the bank under the control of the Federal Deposit Insurance Corporation (FDIC). At the time, NextCard's stock was trading for $0.14 per share, down from its all-time high of $53.12. In the summer of 2003, a federal bankruptcy court liquidated the company. By this point, NextCard had total assets of only $20 million and liabilities of nearly $470 million.

In November 2006, the SEC announced that it had reached an agreement to settle fraud charges filed in 2004 against five former NextCard executives, including Jeremy Lent. In total, the SEC required the executives to pay $1.4 million of fines and other monetary damages. Approximately $900,000 of that amount was paid by Lent. The SEC allowed the five executives to consent to the settlement "without admitting or denying" the charges that had been filed against them.[19] One year earlier, in December 2005, the class-action lawsuit filed against NextCard and its former executives had been settled out of court. Ernst & Young contributed $23.5 million to the settlement pool, while Jeremy Lent contributed $635,000.

---

14. Securities and Exchange Commission, "Former Ernst & Young Audit Partner Arrested for Obstruction Charges and Criminal Violations of the Sarbanes–Oxley Act," *Release No. 2003-123*, 25 September 2003.

15. *Ibid.*

16. *Ibid.*

17. V. Colliver, "FBI Arrests Suspect in Fraud," *San Francisco Chronicle*, 26 September 2003, B1.

18. *Ibid.*

19. Securities and Exchange Commission, *Litigation Release No. 19903*, November 2006.

Questions

1. Should auditors evaluate the soundness of a client's business model? Defend your answer.

2. Identify and briefly describe the specific fraud risk factors present during the 2000 NextCard audit. How should these factors have affected the planning and execution of that engagement?

3. What are the primary objectives an audit team hopes to accomplish by preparing a proper set of audit workpapers?

4. Identify the key auditing principles violated by the E&Y auditors in this case. Briefly explain how each principle was violated.

5. When he became a member of the NextCard audit engagement team, Oliver Flanagan hoped that Thomas Trauger would serve as his mentor. What responsibility, if any, do senior audit personnel have to serve as mentors for their subordinates?

6. Assume the role of Oliver Flanagan in this case. What would you have done when Thomas Trauger asked you to help him alter the 2000 NextCard audit workpapers? In answering this question, identify the alternative courses of action available to you. Also identify the individuals who may be affected by your decision and briefly describe how they may be affected.

Lincoln Savings and Loan Association

Charles Keating, Jr., was a scholar-athlete at the University of Cincinnati during the mid-1940s. In 1946, Keating won an NCAA individual championship in the 200-yard butterfly, a swimming event, and two years later graduated from the University of Cincinnati Law School. Over the next 30 years, Keating established himself as the nation's leading critic of the pornography industry. In 1960, he founded the Citizens for Decency through Law, an organization dedicated to "stamping out smut." A decade later, Keating was appointed to President Nixon's Commission on Pornography. Keating became best known nationally for his successful effort to help law enforcement authorities prosecute magazine publisher Larry Flynt, another native of Cincinnati, on obscenity charges.

In 1978, Keating began focusing his time and energy on his business endeavors when he founded the real estate firm, American Continental Corporation (ACC). Six years later, ACC acquired Lincoln Savings and Loan Association, which was headquartered in Phoenix, although its principal operations were in California. In his application to purchase Lincoln, Keating pledged to regulatory authorities that he would retain the Lincoln management team, that he would not use brokered deposits to expand the size of the savings and loan, and that residential home loans would remain Lincoln's principal line of business. After gaining control of Lincoln, Keating replaced the management team; began accepting large deposits from money brokers, which allowed him to nearly triple the size of the savings and loan in two years; and shifted the focus of Lincoln's lending activity from residential mortgage loans to land development projects.

On 14 April 1989, the Federal Home Loan Bank Board (FHLBB) seized control of Lincoln Savings and Loan, alleging that Lincoln was dissipating its assets by operating in an unsafe and unsound manner. On that date, Lincoln's balance sheet reported total assets of $5.3 billion, only 2.3 percent of which were investments in residential mortgage loans. Nearly two-thirds of Lincoln's asset portfolio was invested directly or indirectly in high-risk land ventures and other commercial development projects. At the time, federal authorities estimated that the closure of Lincoln Savings and Loan would cost U.S. taxpayers at least $2.5 billion.

Congressional hearings into the collapse of Lincoln Savings and Loan initially focused on the methods Keating used to circumvent banking laws and on disclosures that five U.S. senators intervened on Keating's behalf with federal banking regulators. Eventually, the hearings centered on the failure of Lincoln's independent auditors to expose fraudulent real estate transactions that allowed the savings and loan to report millions of dollars of nonexistent profits. In summarizing the Lincoln debacle, U.S. Representative Jim Leach laid the blame for the costly savings and loan failure on a number of parties, including Lincoln's auditors and the accounting profession as a whole:

I am stunned. As I look at these transactions, I am stunned at the conclusions of an independent auditing firm. I am stunned at the result. And let me just tell you, I think that this whole circumstance of a potential $2.5 billion cost to the United States taxpayers is a scandal for the United States Congress. It is a scandal for the Texas and

California legislatures. It is a scandal for the Reagan administration regulators. And it is a scandal for the accounting profession.[1]

Creative Accounting, Influence Peddling, and Other Abuses at Lincoln Savings and Loan

Representative Henry Gonzalez, chairman of the U.S. House Committee on Banking, Finance, and Urban Affairs, charged that over the five years Charles Keating owned Lincoln, he employed accounting schemes to divert the savings and loan's federally insured deposits into ACC's treasury. Keating was aware that he would be permitted to withdraw funds from Lincoln and invest them in ACC or use them for other purposes only to the extent that Lincoln reported after-tax profits. Consequently, he and his associates wove together complex real estate transactions involving Lincoln, ACC, and related third parties to manufacture paper profits for Lincoln. Kenneth Leventhal & Company, an accounting firm retained by regulatory authorities to analyze and report on Lincoln's accounting practices, used a few simple examples to explain the saving and loan's fraudulent schemes. Exhibit 1 contains a portion of the

EXHIBIT 1

CONGRESSIONAL TESTIMONY OF KENNETH LEVENTHAL & COMPANY REGARDING LINCOLN'S REAL ESTATE TRANSACTIONS

To illustrate the accounting concepts Lincoln used, let me give you a few simple, hypothetical examples. Suppose you own a house that you paid $100,000 for, and against which you still owe $60,000. Now, suppose you could not find a buyer for your house. Therefore, you go out and find an individual who agrees to pay you the $200,000 you want for your house, but is only willing to give you one dollar in cash and a nonrecourse note for the balance of $199,999. A nonrecourse note means that you cannot get at him personally. If he defaults on the note, your only recourse is to take the house back.

So now you have one dollar in your pocket, and a note for the rest. You very likely have not parted company with your house in this situation, because your so-called buyer may be unable to pay you, or he may simply decide that he does not want to pay you. Economically, he has an option to stick to the deal if the price of the house appreciates, or he can walk away from it if it does not. That is not a sale.

Now, suppose you have the same house again. Your next-door neighbor has a different house, but it is worth the same as yours, and has the same outstanding mortgage balance. You then swap houses and mortgages with your neighbor.

You now have a house which is different, but very similar to the one that you did have. I think that you will agree, there is no profit realized on this exchange. By the accounting theory that Lincoln appears to have followed, you would be able to record a $100,000 profit: the difference between what you originally paid for your house and what you think your neighbor's house is worth.

Really, it could have been more, if you could have found an appraiser to tell you that your neighbor's house was worth $300,000. And it could have been still more if you and your neighbor had simply chosen to agree upon a stated price which was even in excess of these amounts.

As you can see, all sales of real estate are not created equal. Over the years, accountants have had to wrestle with what is economically a sale and what is not. The economic substance of a transaction should of course be the controlling consideration.

1. This and all subsequent quotations, unless indicated otherwise, were taken from the following source: U.S. Congress, House Committee on Banking, Finance, and Urban Affairs; *Investigation of Lincoln Savings and Loan Association, Part 4* (Washington, D.C.: U.S. Government Printing Office, 1990).

Leventhal firm's testimony before Representative Gonzalez's committee, which sponsored the lengthy congressional investigation of Lincoln Savings and Loan.

One of the most scrutinized of Lincoln's multimillion-dollar real estate deals was the large Hidden Valley transaction that took place in the spring of 1987. On 30 March 1987, Lincoln loaned $19.6 million to E. C. Garcia & Company. On that same day, Ernie Garcia, a close friend of Keating and the owner of the land development company bearing his name, extended a $3.5 million loan to Wescon, a mortgage real estate concern owned by Garcia's friend, Fernando Acosta. The following day, Wescon purchased 1,000 acres of unimproved desert land in central Arizona from Lincoln for $14 million, nearly twice the value established for the land by an independent appraiser one week earlier. Acosta used the loan from Garcia as the down payment on the tract of land and signed a nonrecourse note for the balance. Lincoln recorded a profit of $11.1 million on the transaction—profit that was never realized, since the savings and loan never received payment on the nonrecourse note.

In fact, Lincoln never expected to be paid the balance of the nonrecourse note. Lincoln executives arranged the loan simply to allow the savings and loan to book a large paper gain. Garcia later testified that he agreed to become involved in the deceptive Hidden Valley transaction only because he wanted the $19.6 million loan from Lincoln.[2] Recognizing a profit on the Hidden Valley transaction would have openly violated financial accounting standards if Garcia had acquired the property directly from Lincoln and used for his down payment funds loaned to him by the savings and loan.

Fernando Acosta eventually admitted that his company, Wescon, which prior to the Hidden Valley transaction had total assets of $87,000 and a net worth of $30,000, was only a "straw buyer" of the Hidden Valley property. In a *Los Angeles Times* article, Acosta reported that Wescon "was too small to buy the property and that he signed the documents without reading them to help his friend, Ernie Garcia."[3] Exhibit 2 contains a letter that a worried Acosta wrote to Garcia in 1988 regarding the Hidden Valley transaction. In that letter, Acosta encouraged Garcia to assume title to the property so that he could take it off Wescon's books.

Keating and his associates repeatedly used bogus real estate transactions, such as the Hidden Valley charade, to produce enormous gains for Lincoln. In 1986 and 1987 alone, Lincoln recognized more than $135 million of profits on such transactions. That amount represented more than one-half of the savings and loan's total reported profits for the two-year period.

The gains recorded by Lincoln on its real estate transactions allowed ACC to withdraw huge sums of cash from the savings and loan in the form of intercompany dividend payments, funds that were actually federally insured deposits. When the "purchasers" of these tracts of land defaulted on their nonrecourse notes, Lincoln was forced to recognize losses—losses that the savings and loan offset with additional "profitable" real estate transactions. This recurring cycle of events ensured that Lincoln would eventually fail. However, since the Federal Savings and Loan Insurance Corporation (FSLIC) guaranteed Lincoln's liabilities (i.e., its deposits), and since ACC had little equity capital invested in Lincoln, Keating was not overly concerned by the inevitable demise of his company's savings and loan subsidiary.

Lincoln's convoluted and contrived real estate transactions appalled members of Representative Gonzalez's congressional committee. One of the Leventhal partners

2. K. Kerwin and C. Yang, "Everything Was Fine Until I Met Charlie: The Rise and Stumble of Whiz Kid and Keating Crony Ernie Garcia," *Business Week*, 12 March 1990, 44, 46.

3. J. Granelli, "Firm Says It Was a 'Straw Man' in Lincoln Deal," *Los Angeles Times*, 3 January 1990, D1, D13.

EXHIBIT 2

LETTER FROM
WESCON TO
ERNIE GARCIA
REGARDING HIDDEN
VALLEY PROPERTY

[This letter was addressed to Mr. E.C. Garcia, E.C. Garcia and Company, Inc., and appeared on Wescon letterhead.]

Re: Hidden Valley Project/Property

Dear Ernie:

The time when we should have been out of this project is well past.

For various reasons, our discomfort with continuation in the project is growing. Particularly of late, we have been concerned with how to report this to the IRS. We are convinced that all we can do is report as if the corporation were not the true/beneficial owner, but merely the nominal title holder, which is consistent with the facts and the reality of the situation. Correspondingly, it seems you should have, and report, the real tax burdens and benefits arising from this property.

Also, we are increasingly uncomfortable with showing this property on our company's financial statements (and explaining why it is there). We absolutely need to extract this item.

In order to expedite relief for us on this matter, in line with your repeated assurances, please arrange for the transfer of this property to its rightful owner as soon as possible.

Sincerely,

FRA/Wescon

Fernando R. Acosta

who testified before the congressional committee provided the following overview of his firm's report on Lincoln's accounting schemes:

> *Seldom in our experience have we encountered a more egregious example of misapplication of generally accepted accounting principles. This association [Lincoln] was made to function as an engine, designed to funnel insured deposits to its parent in tax allocation payments and dividends. To do this, it had to generate reportable earnings. It created profits by making loans. Many of these loans were bad. Lincoln was manufacturing profits by giving money away.*

Critics chastised Charles Keating not only for employing creative accounting methods but for several other abusive practices as well. In 1979, Keating signed a consent decree with the Securities and Exchange Commission (SEC) to settle conflict-of-interest charges the agency had filed against him. In 1985, Keating handpicked his 24-year-old son, Charles Keating III, to serve as Lincoln's president. Along with the impressive job title came an annual salary of $1 million. At the time, the young man's only prior work experience was as a busperson in a country club restaurant. Years later, the younger Keating testified that he did not understand many of the transactions he signed off on as Lincoln's president.

The elder Keating's gaudy lifestyle and ostentatious spending habits were legendary. U.S. taxpayers absorbed many of the excessive expenses rung up by Keating since he pawned them off as business expenses of Lincoln. The bill for a 1987 dinner Keating hosted at an upscale Washington, D.C., restaurant came to just slightly less than $2,500. One of the guests at that dinner was a former SEC commissioner. In another incident, after inadvertently scuffing a secretary's $30 shoes, Keating wrote her a check for $5,000 to replace them—and the rest of her wardrobe as well, apparently. Other Keating excesses documented by federal and state investigators included safaris, vacations in European castles, numerous trips to the south of France, and lavish parties for relatives and government officials.

The most serious charges leveled at Keating involved allegations of influence peddling. Keating contributed heavily to the election campaigns of five prominent senators, including John Glenn of Ohio and John McCain of Arizona. These five senators, who became known as the Keating Five, met with federal banking regulators and lobbied for favorable treatment of Lincoln Savings and Loan. The key issue in these lobbying efforts was the so-called direct investment rule adopted by the FHLBB in 1985. This rule limited the amount that savings and loans could invest directly in subsidiaries, development projects, and other commercial ventures to 10 percent of their total assets. Because such investments were central to Lincoln's operations, the direct investment rule imposed severe restrictions on Keating—restrictions that he repeatedly ignored.

In 1986, a close associate of Keating's was appointed to fill an unexpired term on the FHLBB. Following his appointment, this individual proposed an amendment to the direct investment rule that would have exempted Lincoln from its requirements. The amendment failed to be seconded and thus was never adopted. Shortly before Alan Greenspan was appointed to the powerful position of chairman of the Federal Reserve Board, Keating retained him to represent Lincoln before the FHLBB. In a legal brief submitted to the FHLBB, Greenspan reported that Lincoln's management team was "seasoned and expert" and that the savings and loan was a "financially strong" institution. Congressional testimony also disclosed that Keating loaned $250,000, with very favorable payback terms, to a former SEC commissioner, who then lobbied the SEC on Lincoln's behalf.

The charges of influence peddling failed to concern or distract Keating. In responding to these charges, Keating brashly stated that he hoped that his financial support of key governmental officials had, in fact, persuaded them to support his personal agenda.[4]

Federal authorities eventually indicted Keating on various racketeering and securities fraud charges. He was also sued by the Resolution Trust Corporation, the federal agency created to manage the massive savings and loan crisis that threatened the integrity of the nation's banking system during the 1980s. That agency charged Keating with insider dealing, illegal loans, sham real estate and tax transactions, and the fraudulent sale of Lincoln securities.

Audit History of Lincoln Savings and Loan

Arthur Andersen served as Lincoln's independent auditor until 1985 when it resigned "to lessen its exposure to liability from savings and loan audits," according to a *New York Times* article.[5] That same article described the very competitive nature of the Phoenix audit market during the mid-1980s when Lincoln was seeking a replacement auditor. Because of the large size of the Lincoln audit, several audit firms pursued the engagement, including Arthur Young & Company.[6] From 1978 through 1984,

---

4. D. J. Jefferson, "Keating of American Continental Corp. Comes Out Fighting," *Wall Street Journal*, 18 April 1989, B2.

5. E. N. Berg, "The Lapses by Lincoln's Auditors," *New York Times*, 28 December 1989, D1, D6.

6. Arthur Andersen and, subsequently, Arthur Young audited both ACC and Lincoln, a wholly owned subsidiary of ACC. However, the Lincoln audit was much more complex and required much more time to complete than the ACC audit. Reportedly, the ACC/Lincoln audit accounted for one-fifth of the annual audit revenues of Arthur Young's Phoenix office during 1986 and 1987.

Arthur Young suffered a net loss of 63 clients nationwide.[7] Over the next five years, an intense marketing effort produced a net increase of more than 100 audit clients for the firm. During the 1980s, critics of the accounting profession suggested that the extremely competitive audit market induced many audit firms to accept high-risk clients, such as Lincoln, in exchange for large audit fees.

> *The savings industry crisis has revived questions repeatedly raised in the past about the profession's independence in auditing big corporate clients: whether the accounts need more controls and whether some firms are willing to sanction questionable financial statements in exchange for high fees, a practice called "bottom fishing."*[8]

Before pursuing Lincoln as an audit client, Jack Atchison, an Arthur Young partner in Phoenix, contacted the former Lincoln engagement partner at Arthur Andersen. The Arthur Andersen partner told Atchison that he had no reason to question the integrity of Lincoln's management and that no major disagreements preceded the resignation of his firm as Lincoln's auditor. At the time of Arthur Andersen's resignation, Lincoln was undergoing an intensive examination by FHLBB auditors, who were raising serious questions regarding Lincoln's financial records. Arthur Young was not informed of this investigation by Arthur Andersen. Years later, Arthur Andersen partners denied that they were aware of the examination when they resigned from the audit.

Shortly after accepting Lincoln as an audit client, Arthur Young learned of the FHLBB audit. Among the most serious charges of the FHLBB auditors was that Lincoln had provided interest-free loans to ACC—a violation of federal banking laws—and had falsified loan documents. Three years later, officials from the Office of Thrift Supervision testified before Congress that Arthur Andersen and Lincoln employees had engaged in so-called file-stuffing. These charges resulted in formal inquiries by the Federal Bureau of Investigation and the U.S. Department of Justice.[9] Arthur Andersen officials denied involvement in any illegal activities but did acknowledge that employees of their firm had worked "under the direction of client [Lincoln] personnel to assist them in organizing certain [loan] files."[10] Later, a representative of Lincoln admitted that "memorialization" had been used for certain loan files.

Congressional testimony of several Arthur Young representatives revealed that the 1986 and 1987 Lincoln audits were very complex engagements. William Gladstone, the comanaging partner of Ernst & Young (the firm formed by the 1989 merger of Ernst & Whinney and Arthur Young), testified that the 1987 audit required 30,000 hours to complete. Despite concerns being raised by regulatory authorities, Arthur Young issued an unqualified opinion on Lincoln's financial statements in both 1986 and 1987. Critics contend that these clean opinions allowed Lincoln to continue engaging in illicit activities. Of particular concern to congressional investigators was that during this time Keating and his associates sold ACC's high-yield "junk" bonds in the lobbies of Lincoln's numerous branches. The sale of these bonds, which were destined to become worthless, raised more than $250 million for ACC. The marketing campaign for the bonds targeted retired individuals, many of whom believed that the bonds were federally insured since they were being sold on the premises of a savings and loan.

---

7. L. Berton, "Spotlight on Arthur Young Is Likely to Intensify as Lincoln Hearings Resume," *Wall Street Journal*, 21 November 1989, A20.

8. N. C. Nash, "Auditors of Lincoln On the Spot," *New York Times*, 14 November 1989, D1, D19.

9. P. Thomas and B. Jackson, "Regulators Cite Delays and Phone Bugs in Examination, Seizure of Lincoln S&L," *Wall Street Journal*, 27 October 1989, A4; Berg, "The Lapses by Lincoln's Auditors."

10. Thomas and Jackson, "Regulators Cite Delays and Phone Bugs."

When called to testify before the U.S. House Committee, SEC Commissioner Richard Breeden was asked to explain why his agency did not force ACC to stop selling the junk bonds in Lincoln's branches.

Congressman Hubbard: *Didn't the SEC have not one, not two, but actually three or more opportunities to stop the sale of the ACC subordinated debt?*

Commissioner Breeden: *We did not have any opportunity—the only way in which the SEC can stop the sale of securities is if we are able to prove those securities are being distributed based on false and misleading information. And we have to prove that in court. We cannot have reasons to be concerned about it, we cannot have suspicions, we cannot just have cause to be concerned; we have to be able to prove that in court. And remember that this is a situation in which one of the Big Eight accounting firms is certifying that these accounts comply fully with generally accepted accounting principles, without caveat or limitation in any way. That is an important factor in that kind of decision.*

Following the completion of the 1987 Lincoln audit, the engagement audit partner, Jack Atchison, resigned from Arthur Young and accepted a position with ACC. Exhibit 3 contains the memorandum Atchison wrote to William Gladstone, who at the time was Arthur Young's managing partner, to inform Gladstone of his resignation. Gladstone later testified that Atchison earned approximately $225,000 annually as an Arthur Young partner before his resignation. ACC records revealed that Atchison's new position came with an annual salary of approximately $930,000.

The close relationship that Atchison developed with Keating before resigning from Arthur Young alarmed congressional investigators. Testimony before the congressional committee disclosed that Atchison, while he was serving as the engagement partner on the Lincoln audit, wrote several letters to banking regulators and U.S. senators vigorously supporting the activities of Keating and Lincoln. "Atchison seemed to drop the auditor's traditional stance of independence by repeatedly defending the practices of Lincoln and its corporate parent to Congress and federal regulators.... Since when does the outside accountant—the public watchdog—become a proponent of the client's affairs?"[11]

Congressman Gonzalez's committee also questioned Arthur Young representatives regarding Atchison's relationship with the Arthur Young audit team after he joined ACC. The committee was concerned that Atchison may have been in a position to improperly influence the auditors he had supervised just weeks earlier.

Congressman Lehman: *Did anyone at AY have any contact with Mr. Atchison after he left and went to work for Lincoln?*

Mr. Gladstone: *Yes, sir.*

Congressman Lehman: *In the course of the audit?*

Mr. Gladstone: *Yes.*

Congressman Lehman: *So he went from one side of the table to the other for $700,000 more?*

Mr. Gladstone: *That is what happened.*

Congressman Lehman: *And he—just tell me what his role was in the audits ... when he was on the other side of the table.*

---

11. Berg, "The Lapses by Lincoln's Auditors."

EXHIBIT 3

MEMORANDUM
FROM JACK
ATCHISON
TO WILLIAM
GLADSTONE

[This memorandum appeared on Arthur Young letterhead.]

TO: Office of Chairman   FROM: Phoenix Office
    William L. Gladstone   Jack D. Atchison
    Hugh Grant, West Regional Office
    Al Boos, Phoenix Office

SUBJECT:

Several weeks ago, Charles H. Keating, Jr., Chairman of American Continental Corporation, asked me to consider joining his company at a senior executive level. Because we were in the process of conducting an audit, I informed Mr. Keating that any discussions regarding future employment would have to await the conclusion of the audit. I also informed Hugh Grant of Mr. Keating's overtures to me.

Knowing Mr. Keating would raise the subject again at the conclusion of the audit, I began to seriously consider the possibility of leaving Arthur Young to join American Continental. Arthur Young has been my professional home for over 24 years, providing a comfortable source of income and rewarding professional environment. My closest personal friends are also my partners. To even consider no longer being a part of Arthur Young was difficult and traumatic, since serving as a partner in Arthur Young has been my single professional goal since 1962.

On April 8 and 11, 1988, I had discussions with Mr. Keating wherein he presented an employment offer which was very rewarding economically and very challenging professionally. His offer addressed all of my economic, job security and position description requirements and concerns. American Continental offers some unique challenges and potential rewards not presently available in Arthur Young. It also presents some risks not present in the Arthur Young environment.

Based on American Continental's offer and my perception of the future there, I have decided to accept their offer and seek to withdraw from the Arthur Young partnership at the earliest possible date. Since American Continental is an SEC client and active issuer of securities requiring registration, and Arthur Young's consent to the use of its report is needed in such filings, an expedited withdrawal arrangement would protect against any real or apparent conflicts of interest between Arthur Young and American Continental.

        Mr. Gladstone: *He was a senior vice president for American Continental when he joined them in May 1988.*

Congressman Lehman: *Did the job he had there have anything to do with interfacing with the auditors?*

        Mr. Gladstone: *To some extent, yes.*

Congressman Lehman: *What does "to some extent" mean?*

        Mr. Gladstone: *On major accounting issues that were discussed in the Form 8-K, we did have conversations with Jack Atchison.*

Congressman Lehman: *So he was the person Mr. Keating had to interface with you in major decisions?*

        Mr. Gladstone: *Him, and other officers of American Continental.*

During the summer of 1988, the relationship between Lincoln's executives and the Arthur Young audit team gradually soured. Janice Vincent, who became the Lincoln engagement partner following Atchison's resignation, testified that disagreements arose with client management that summer over the accounting treatment applied to several large real estate transactions. The most serious disagreement involved a proposed exchange of assets between Lincoln and another corporation—a transaction for which Lincoln intended to record a $50 million profit. Lincoln management insisted that the exchange involved dissimilar assets. Vincent, on the other hand, stubbornly maintained that the transaction involved the exchange of similar assets and, consequently, that the gain on the transaction could not be recognized. During the congressional hearings, Vincent described how this dispute and related disputes eventually led to the resignation of Arthur Young as Lincoln's auditor.

> These disagreements created an adversarial relationship between members of Arthur Young's audit team and American Continental officials, which resulted in Mr. Keating requesting a meeting with Bill Gladstone.... While in New York at that meeting, Mr. Keating turned to me at one point and said, "Lady, you have just lost a job." That did not happen. Rather, he had lost an accounting firm.

Following Arthur Young's resignation in October 1988, Keating retained Touche Ross to audit Lincoln's 1988 financial statements. Touche Ross became ensnared, along with Arthur Andersen and Arthur Young, in the web of litigation following Lincoln's collapse. Purchasers of the ACC bonds sold in Lincoln's branches named Touche Ross as a defendant in a large class-action lawsuit. The suit alleged that had Touche Ross not accepted Lincoln as an audit client, ACC's ability to sell the bonds would have been diminished significantly.

Criticism of Arthur Young Following Lincoln's Collapse

Both Arthur Young and its successor, Ernst & Young, were criticized for the former's role in the Lincoln Savings and Loan debacle. One of the most common criticisms was that Arthur Young readily accepted questionable documentary evidence provided by Lincoln employees to corroborate the savings and loan's real estate transactions. During the congressional hearings into the collapse of Lincoln, William Gladstone commented on the appraisals that Arthur Young obtained to support those transactions. "All appraisals of land [owned by Lincoln] were done by appraisers hired by the company, and we had to rely on them." Certainly, these appraisals were relevant evidence to be used in auditing Lincoln's real estate transactions. However, appraisals obtained by Arthur Young from independent third parties would have been just as relevant and less subject to bias.[12]

Among Arthur Young's most vocal critics during the congressional hearings was the newly appointed SEC commissioner, Richard Breeden. Commissioner Breeden berated Arthur Young for failing to cooperate with an SEC investigation into Lincoln's financial affairs.

Commissioner Breeden: *We subpoenaed the accountants [Arthur Young] to provide all of their workpapers and their backup.*

Congressman Hubbard: *Do you know if they were forthcoming and helpful in helping you resolve some of these questions, or helping the SEC resolve some of these questions?*

Commissioner Breeden: *No. I would characterize them as very unhelpful, very unforthcoming, and very resistant to cooperate in any way, shape or form.*

Earlier, Commissioner Breeden had testified that many of the subpoenaed documents that Arthur Young eventually produced were illegible or obscured: "The firm [Arthur Young] ultimately, after much discussion, produced legible copies of the documents, but not before the Commission [SEC] was forced to prepare court enforcement requests to overcome Arthur Young's uncooperative stance. Unfortunately, a

---

12. Quite possibly, Arthur Young did obtain independent appraisals in certain cases, although Gladstone's testimony suggests otherwise.

substantial amount of staff time and resources was devoted unnecessarily to overcoming this resistance to the Commission's subpoenas."

When given an opportunity to respond to Commissioner Breeden's charges, William Gladstone maintained that the delays in providing the SEC with the requested documents were not intentional: "We did not stonewall the SEC. There are Arizona state privilege statutes and ethics rules which prohibit our producing our workpapers without a client consent.... I also take issue with the allegation that we obliterated some papers.... The SEC itself requires a confidentiality stamp on all papers on which confidentiality was requested."

The most stinging criticism of Arthur Young during the congressional hearings was triggered by the report prepared by Kenneth Leventhal & Company on Lincoln's accounting decisions for its major real estate transactions. Although the Leventhal report served as the basis for much of the criticism directed at Arthur Young, the report did not mention Arthur Young or, in any way, explicitly criticize its Lincoln audits. Nevertheless, since Arthur Young had issued unqualified opinions on Lincoln's financial statements, many parties, including Ernst & Young officials, regarded the Leventhal report as an indictment of the quality of Arthur Young's audits.

The key finding of the Leventhal report was that Lincoln had repeatedly violated the substance-over-form concept by engaging in "accounting-driven" deals among related parties to manufacture illusory profits. Ernst & Young representatives contested this conclusion by pointing out that Leventhal reviewed only 15 of the hundreds of real estate transactions that Lincoln engaged in during Arthur Young's tenure. The Ernst & Young representatives were particularly upset that, based upon a review of those 15 transactions, Leventhal implied that none of Lincoln's major real estate transactions were accounted for properly. In Leventhal's defense, a congressman noted that the 15 transactions in question were all very large and, collectively, accounted for one-half of Lincoln's pretax profits during 1986 and 1987.

At times, the debate over the Leventhal report became very heated. William Gladstone maligned the report, stating that it was gratuitous; contained broad, sweeping generalizations; in certain cases was "flatly wrong"; and in his opinion, was unprofessional. In responding to these charges, Congressman Leach questioned the professionalism of Gladstone's firm.

Congressman Leach: *[addressing William Gladstone] I am going to be very frank with you, that I am not impressed with the professional ethics of your firm vis-á-vis the United States Congress. Several days ago, my office was contacted by your firm and asked if we would be interested in questions to ask of Leventhal. We said, "Surely." The questions you provided were of an offensive nature. They were to request of Leventhal how much they were paid, implying that perhaps based upon their payment from the U.S. Government that their decisions as CPAs would be biased. I consider that to be very offensive.*

Now, in addition, one of the questions that was suggested I might ask of the Leventhal firm was: Could it be that their firm is biased because a partner in their firm did not make partner in your firm?

I consider that exceedingly unprofessional. Would you care to respond to that?

Mr. Gladstone: *I do not know who contacted you, and I certainly do not know how the questions were raised.*

Later in the hearings, the individual who had submitted the questions to Congressman Leach's office was identified as an Ernst & Young employee.

Congressman Leach also took issue with the contention of Ernst & Young representatives that Leventhal's report contained angry and vengeful comments regarding their firm.

Congressman Leach: *I read that report very carefully, and I found no angry, vengeful sweeping statements. But I did find a conclusion that Arthur Young had erred rather grievously.*

In any regard, what we are looking at is an issue that is anything but an accounting kind of debate. One of the techniques of Lincoln vis-á-vis the U.S. government was to attack the opposition. You are employing the same tactics toward Leventhal.... I think that is unprofessional, unethical, and, based upon a very careful reading of their statement, irresponsible.

Now, I would like to ask you if you would care to apologize to the Leventhal firm.

Mr. Gladstone: *First, Mr. Leach, I stated in my opening remarks that I believed that their report was general and sweeping and unprofessional, because what I would call unprofessional about it is the statement that looking at 15 transactions, that therefore they would conclude that nothing Lincoln did had the substance—*

Congressman Leach: *I have carefully read their report, and they note that they have just been allowed to look at 15 transactions. They could not go into more detail, but they were saying that ACC batted 15 for 15, that all 15 transactions were unusual, perplexing, and in their judgment in each case breached ethical standards in terms of generally accepted accounting principles.*

Your firm in effect is saying, "We think that there may be some legal liabilities. Therefore, we are going to stonewall, and we are going to defend each and every one of these transactions."

I believe that you are one of the great firms in the history of accounting. But I also believe that big and great people and institutions can sometimes err. And it is better to acknowledge error than to put one's head in the sand.

I think before our committee you have rather righteously done that.

EPILOGUE

Anthony Elliot, a widower and retired accountant in his 80s, was one of thousands of elderly Californians who invested heavily in the junk bonds of Lincoln Savings and Loan's parent company, ACC. In fact, Elliot invested practically all of his life savings, approximately $200,000, in the ACC bonds. Like many of his friends who had also purchased the bonds—which they, along with Elliot, believed were federally insured—Elliot was forced to scrape by each month on his small Social Security check after ACC defaulted on the bonds. On Thanksgiving Day 1990, Elliot slashed his wrists and bled to death in his bathtub. In a suicide note, he remarked that there was "nothing left for me."[13] Elliot's story is just one of many personal tragedies resulting from the Lincoln Savings and Loan scandal.

The estimated losses linked to the demise of Lincoln Savings and Loan eventually rose to $3.4 billion, making it the most costly savings and loan failure in U.S. history at the time.

---

13. M. Connelly, "Victim of S&L Loss Kills Self," *Los Angeles Times*, 29 November 1990, B1.

In March 1991, Lincoln's remaining assets were sold to another financial institution by the Resolution Trust Corporation, which had been operating the savings and loan for more than one year. One month later, Lincoln's parent company, ACC, filed for protection from its creditors under the federal bankruptcy laws.

In late 1992, Ernst & Young paid $400 million to settle four lawsuits filed against it by the federal government. These lawsuits charged Ernst & Young with substandard audits of four savings and loans, including Lincoln Savings and Loan. In a similar settlement reported in 1993, Arthur Andersen paid $85 million to the federal government to settle lawsuits that charged the firm with shoddy audits of five savings and loans, including Lincoln. Finally, although Touche Ross served as Lincoln's auditor for only five months, that firm's successor, Deloitte & Touche, paid nearly $8 million to the federal government to settle charges filed against it for its role in the Lincoln debacle.

Ernst & Young agreed to pay the California State Board of Accountancy $1.5 million in April 1991 to settle negligence complaints that the state agency filed against the firm for Arthur Young's audits of Lincoln. An Ernst & Young spokesman noted that the accounting firm agreed to the settlement to "avoid protracted and costly litigation" and insisted that the settlement did not involve the "admission of any fault by the firm or any partner."[14] In August 1994, Arthur Andersen agreed to pay $1.7 million to the California State Board of Accountancy for its alleged negligence in auditing Lincoln. Andersen personnel were also required to perform 10,000 hours of community service. Like Ernst & Young, Andersen denied any wrongdoing when its settlement with the California State Board was announced.

In October 1990, Ernie Garcia pleaded guilty to fraud for his involvement in the Hidden Valley real estate transaction. His plea bargain agreement with federal prosecutors required him to assist them in their investigation of Charles Keating, Jr. In March 1991, the Lincoln executive who oversaw the sale of ACC's junk bonds through Lincoln's branches pleaded guilty to eight state and federal fraud charges that he had misled the investors who purchased those bonds. Two years later, Charles Keating III was sentenced to eight years in prison after being convicted of fraud and conspiracy charges.

In a California jury trial presided over by Judge Lance Ito, Charles Keating, Jr., was convicted in 1991 on 17 counts of securities fraud for his role in marketing ACC's junk bonds. While serving a 10-year prison term for that conviction, Keating was convicted of similar fraud charges in a federal court and sentenced to an additional 12 years in prison.

In April 1996, a federal appeals court overturned Keating's 1991 conviction. The appellate court ruled that Judge Lance Ito had given improper instructions to the jurors who found Keating guilty of securities fraud. Several months later, a U.S. District judge overturned Keating's federal conviction on fraud charges. The judge ruled that several jurors in the federal trial had been aware of Keating's 1991 conviction. According to the judge, that knowledge had likely prejudiced the federal jury in favor of convicting Keating. For the same reason, the judge overturned the 1993 conviction of Charles Keating III.

With both of his convictions overturned, Charles Keating was released from federal prison in December 1996 after serving four and one-half years. In January 1999, federal prosecutors announced that they would retry the 75-year-old Keating on various fraud charges. Three months later, the federal prosecutors and Keating reached an agreement, an agreement that gave both parties what they wanted most. In federal court, Keating admitted for the first time that he had committed various fraudulent acts while serving as ACC's chief executive. In return, Keating was sentenced to the time he had already served in prison. Even more important to Keating, his plea bargain arrangement required federal prosecutors to drop all charges still outstanding against his son, Charles Keating III.[15]

---

14. "E&Y Pays $1.5M in Lincoln Failure," *Accounting Today*, 13 May 1991, 1, 25.

15. In November 2000, California state prosecutors announced that they would not retry Charles Keating for his role in marketing ACC's junk bonds. This announcement effectively ended Keating's legal problems linked to the collapse of Lincoln Savings and Loan.

Questions

1. Arthur Young was criticized for not encouraging Lincoln to invoke the substance-over-form principle when accounting for its large real estate transactions. Briefly describe the substance-over-form concept and exactly what it requires. What responsibility, if any, do auditors have when a client violates this principle?

2. Explain how the acceptance of large, high-risk audit clients for relatively high audit fees may threaten an audit firm's de facto and perceived independence. Under what circumstances should such prospective clients be avoided?

3. How is an auditor's examination affected when a client has engaged in significant related-party transactions? What measures should an auditor take to determine that such transactions have been properly recorded by a client?

4. Professional standards require auditors to consider a client's "control environment." Define *control environment*. What weaknesses, if any, were evident in Lincoln's control environment?

5. What was the significance of Lincoln receiving nonrecourse notes rather than recourse notes as payment or partial payment on many of the properties it sold?

6. Professional auditing standards identify the principal "management assertions" that underlie a set of financial statements. What were the key assertions that Arthur Young should have attempted to substantiate for the Hidden Valley transaction? What procedures should Arthur Young have used for this purpose, and what types of evidence should have been collected?

7. Do you believe that Jack Atchison's close relationship with Lincoln and Charles Keating prior to his leaving Arthur Young was proper? Why or why not? After joining Lincoln's parent company, ACC, should Atchison have "interfaced" with the Arthur Young auditors assigned to the Lincoln and ACC engagements? Again, support your answer.

8. Does the *AICPA Code of Professional Conduct* discuss the collegial responsibilities of CPA firms? In your opinion, were representatives of either Ernst & Young or Kenneth Leventhal & Company unprofessional in this regard during their congressional testimony?

9. What responsibility does an auditor have to uncover fraud perpetrated by client management? Discuss factors that mitigate this responsibility and factors that compound it. Relate this discussion to Arthur Young's audits of Lincoln.

Crazy Eddie, Inc.

In 1969, Eddie Antar, a 21-year-old high school dropout from Brooklyn, opened a consumer electronics store with 150 square feet of floor space in New York City.[1] Despite this modest beginning, Antar would eventually dominate the retail consumer electronics market in the New York City metropolitan area. By 1987, Antar's firm, Crazy Eddie, Inc., had 43 retail outlets, sales exceeding $350 million, and outstanding stock with a collective market value of $600 million. Antar personally realized more than $70 million from the sale of Crazy Eddie stock during his tenure as the company's chief executive.

A classic rags-to-riches story became a spectacular business failure in the late 1980s when Crazy Eddie collapsed following allegations of extensive financial wrongdoing by Antar and his associates. Shortly after a hostile takeover of the company in November 1987, the firm's new owners discovered that Crazy Eddie's inventory was overstated by more than $65 million. This inventory shortage had been concealed from the public in registration statements filed with the Securities and Exchange Commission (SEC). Subsequent investigations by regulatory authorities revealed that Eddie Antar and his subordinates had grossly overstated Crazy Eddie's reported profits throughout its existence.[2]

Eddie Antar: The Man Behind the Legend

Eddie Antar was born into a large, closely knit Syrian family in 1947. After dropping out of high school at the age of 16, Antar began peddling television sets in his Brooklyn neighborhood. Within a few years, Antar and one of his cousins scraped together enough cash to open an electronics store near Coney Island. It was at this tiny store that Antar acquired the nickname "Crazy Eddie." When a customer attempted to leave the store empty-handed, Antar would block the store's exit, sometimes locking the door until the individual agreed to buy something—anything. To entice a reluctant customer to make a purchase, Antar first determined which product the customer was considering and then lowered the price until the customer finally capitulated.

Antar became well known in his neighborhood not only for his unusual sales tactics but also for his unconventional, if not asocial, behavior. A bodybuilder and fitness fanatic, he typically came to work in his exercise togs, accompanied by a menacing German shepherd. His quick temper caused repeated problems with vendors, competitors, and subordinates. Antar's most distinctive trait was his inability to trust anyone outside of his large extended family. In later years, when he needed someone to serve in an executive capacity in his company, Antar nearly always tapped a family

---

member, although the individual seldom had the appropriate training or experience for the position. Eventually, Antar's father, sister, two brothers, uncle, brother-in-law, and several cousins would assume leadership positions with Crazy Eddie, while more than one dozen other relatives would hold minor positions with the firm.

Crazy Eddie's Formula for Success

In the early 1980s, sales in the consumer electronics industry exploded, doubling in the four-year period from 1981 to 1984 alone. As the public's demand for electronic products grew at an ever-increasing pace, Antar converted his Crazy Eddie stores into consumer electronics supermarkets. Antar stocked the shelves of Crazy Eddie's retail outlets with every electronic gadget he could find and with as many different brands of those products as possible. By 1987, the company featured seven product lines. Following are those product lines and their percentage contributions to Crazy Eddie's 1987 sales.

Televisions	53%
Audio products and systems	15
Portable and personal electronics	10
Car stereos	5
Accessories and tapes	4
Computers and games	3
Miscellaneous items—including microwaves, air conditioners, and small appliances	10
Total	100%

Antar encouraged his salespeople to supplement each store's profits by pressuring customers to buy extended product warranties. Many, if not most, of the repair costs that Crazy Eddie paid under these warranties were recovered by the company from manufacturers that had issued factory warranties on the products. As a result, the company realized a 100 percent profit margin on much of its warranty revenue.

As his firm grew rapidly during the late 1970s and early 1980s, Antar began extracting large price concessions from his suppliers. His ability to purchase electronic products in large quantities and at cut-rate prices enabled him to become a "transhipper," or secondary supplier, of these goods to smaller consumer electronics retailers in the New York City area. Although manufacturers frowned on this practice and often threatened to stop selling to him, Antar continually increased the scale of his transhipping operation.

The most important ingredient in Antar's marketing strategy was large-scale advertising. Antar created an advertising "umbrella" over his company's principal retail market that included the densely populated area within a 150-mile radius of New York City. Antar blanketed this region with raucous, sometimes annoying, but always memorable radio and television commercials.

In 1972, Antar hired a local radio personality and part-time actor known as Doctor Jerry to serve as Crazy Eddie's advertising spokesperson. Over the 15 years that the bug-eyed Doctor Jerry hawked products for Crazy Eddie, he achieved a higher "recognition quotient" among the public than Ed Koch, the longtime mayor of New York City. Doctor Jerry's series of ear-piercing television commercials that featured him screaming "Crazy Eddie—His prices are insane!" brought the company national notoriety when they were parodied by Dan Akroyd on *Saturday Night Live*.

Crazy Eddie's discounting policy served as the focal theme of the company's advertising campaigns. The company promised to refund the difference between the selling price of a product and any lower price for that same item that a customer found within 30 days of the purchase date. Despite the advertising barrage intended to convince the public that Crazy Eddie was a deep-discounter, the company's prices on most products were in line with those of its major competitors. Customers drawn to Crazy Eddie outlets by "advertised specials" were routinely diverted by sales staff to higher-priced merchandise.

Crazy Eddie Goes Public

In 1983, Antar decided to sell stock in Crazy Eddie to raise capital to finance his aggressive expansion program. The underwriting firm retained by Antar delayed Crazy Eddie's initial public offering (IPO) for more than one year after discovering that the company's financial records were in disarray. Among other problems uncovered by the underwriter were extensive related-party transactions, interest-free loans to employees, and speculative investments unrelated to the company's principal line of business. The underwriting firm was also disturbed to find that nearly all of the company's key executives were members of the Antar family. Certain of these individuals, including Antar's wife and mother, were receiving salaries approaching $100,000 for little or no work.

To prepare for the IPO, the underwriter encouraged Antar, Crazy Eddie's chairman of the board and president, to clean up the company's accounting records and financial affairs. The underwriter also urged Antar to hire a chief financial officer (CFO) who had experience with a public company and who was not a member of the Antar family. The underwriter warned Antar that investors would question the competence of Crazy Eddie's executives who were his relatives. Despite the underwriter's concern, Antar hired his first cousin, Sam E. Antar, to serve as Crazy Eddie's CFO.

The sale of Crazy Eddie's stock to the public was a tremendous success. Because the IPO was oversubscribed, the company's underwriter obtained permission from the SEC to sell 200,000 more shares than originally planned. Following the public offering, Antar worked hard to convince the investment community, particularly financial analysts, that his firm was financially strong and well managed. At every opportunity, Antar painted a picture of continued growth and increased market share for Crazy Eddie.

One tactic Antar used to convince financial analysts that the company had a rosy future was to invite them to a store and demonstrate in person his uncanny ability to "close" sales. Such tactics worked to perfection as analysts from prominent investment firms released glowing reports regarding Crazy Eddie's management team and the company's bright prospects. One analyst wrote, "Crazy Eddie is a disciplined, competently organized firm with a sophisticated management and a well-trained, dedicated staff."[3] Another analyst wrote that Antar is a "brilliant merchant surrounded by a deeply dedicated organization eager to create an important retail business."[4] Because of such reports and continued strong operating results (as reflected by the company's 1984–1987 financial statements shown in Exhibit 1 and Exhibit 2), the price of Crazy Eddie's stock skyrocketed. Many investors who purchased the company's stock in the IPO realized a 1,000 percent increase in the value of their investments.

---

3. J. E. Tannenbaum, "How Mounting Woes at Crazy Eddie Sank Turnaround Effort," *Wall Street Journal*, 10 July 1989, A1, A4.

4. G. Belsky and P. Furman, "Calculated Madness: The Rise and Fall of Crazy Eddie Antar," *Crain's New York Business*, 5 June 1989, 26.

EXHIBIT 1

1984–1987
BALANCE SHEETS
OF CRAZY EDDIE

CRAZY EDDIE, INC.
BALANCE SHEETS (000s omitted)

	March 1, 1987	March 2, 1986	March 3, 1985	May 31, 1984
Current assets:				
Cash	$ 9,347	$ 13,296	$22,273	$ 1,375
Short-term investments	121,957	26,840	—	—
Receivables	10,846	2,246	2,740	2,604
Merchandise inventories	109,072	59,864	26,543	23,343
Prepaid expenses	10,639	2,363	645	514
Total current assets	261,861	104,609	52,201	27,836
Restricted cash	—	3,356	7,058	—
Due from affiliates	—	—	—	5,739
Property, plant and equipment	26,401	7,172	3,696	1,845
Construction in process	—	6,253	1,154	—
Other assets	6,596	5,560	1,419	1,149
Total assets	$294,858	$126,950	$65,528	$36,569
Current liabilities:				
Accounts payable	$ 50,022	$ 51,723	$23,078	$20,106
Notes payable	—	—	—	2,900
Short-term debt	49,571	2,254	423	124
Unearned revenue	3,641	3,696	1,173	764
Accrued expenses	5,593	17,126	8,733	6,078
Total current liabilities	108,827	74,799	33,407	29,972
Long-term debt	8,459	7,701	7,625	46
Convertible subordinated debentures	80,975	—	—	—
Unearned revenue	3,337	1,829	635	327
Stockholders' equity:				
Common stock	313	280	134	50
Additional paid-in capital	57,678	17,668	12,298	574
Retained earnings	35,269	24,673	11,429	5,600
Total stockholders' equity	93,260	42,621	23,861	6,224
Total liabilities and stockholders' equity	$294,858	$126,950	$65,528	$36,569

Crazy Eddie Goes ...Bust

Despite Crazy Eddie's impressive operating results during the mid-1980s and the fact
that the company's stock was one of the hottest investments on Wall Street, all was
not well within the firm. By 1986, the company was in deep trouble. By the latter
part of that year, the boom days had ended for the consumer electronics industry.
Although sales of consumer electronics were still increasing, the rate of growth had
tapered off considerably as compared with the dramatic growth rates realized by
the industry during the early 1980s. Additionally, the industry had become saturated
with retailers, particularly in major metropolitan areas such as New York City, Crazy

EXHIBIT 2

1984–1987 INCOME
STATEMENTS OF
CRAZY EDDIE

CRAZY EDDIE, INC. INCOME STATEMENTS (000s omitted)				
	Year Ended March 1, 1987	Year Ended March 2, 1986	Nine Months Ended March 3, 1985	Year Ended May 31, 1984
Net sales	$352,523	$262,268	$136,319	$137,285
Cost of goods sold	(272,255)	(194,371)	(103,421)	(106,934)
Gross profit	80,268	67,897	32,898	30,351
Selling, general and administrative expense	(61,341)	(42,975)	(20,508)	(22,560)
Interest and other income	7,403	3,210	1,211	706
Interest expense	(5,233)	(820)	(438)	(522)
Income before taxes	21,097	27,312	13,163	7,975
Pension contribution	(500)	(800)	(600)	—
Income taxes	(10,001)	(13,268)	(6,734)	(4,202)
Net income	$ 10,596	$ 13,244	$ 5,829	$ 3,773
Net income per share	$.34	$.48	$.24	$.18

Eddie's home base. Increased competition meant smaller profit margins for Crazy Eddie and diminished Antar's ability to extract sweetheart deals from his suppliers.

Besides the problems posed by the increasingly competitive consumer electronics industry, Crazy Eddie faced a corporate meltdown in the late 1980s. The tripling of the company's annual sales volume between 1984 and 1987 and the more complex responsibilities associated with managing a public company imposed an enormous administrative burden on Crazy Eddie's executives. Complicating matters was the disintegration of Antar's inner circle of relatives, who had served as his principal advisors during the first 15 years of his company's existence. Antar forced many of his relatives to leave the firm after they sided with his former wife in a bitter divorce. Even as Crazy Eddie's internal affairs spiraled into chaos and the firm lurched toward financial disaster, Wall Street continued to tout the company's stock as a "can't miss" investment.

In late 1986, Eddie Antar resigned as company president, although he retained the title of chairman of the board. A few weeks later, he simply dropped out of sight. In the absence of Antar, Crazy Eddie's financial condition worsened rapidly. Poor operating results that the company reported for the fourth quarter of fiscal 1987—which ended 1 March 1987—sent Crazy Eddie's stock price into a tailspin from which it never recovered. In November 1987, a takeover group headed by two well-known financiers gained control of the company. A company-wide physical inventory taken by the new owners uncovered the $65 million shortage of inventory alluded to earlier. That inventory shortage, which was larger than the cumulative profits the company had reported since it went public in 1984, would eventually plunge Crazy Eddie into bankruptcy and send regulatory authorities in pursuit of Eddie Antar for an explanation.

Charges of Accounting Irregularities

Extensive investigations of Crazy Eddie's financial records by the new owners and regulatory authorities culminated in fraud charges being filed against Eddie Antar and his former associates. The SEC alleged that after Crazy Eddie went public in 1984, Antar became preoccupied with the price of his company's stock. Antar realized that Crazy Eddie had to keep posting impressive operating results to maintain the upward trend in the stock's price. An SEC investigation revealed that within the first six months after the company went public, Antar ordered a subordinate to overstate inventory by $2 million, resulting in the firm's gross profit being overstated by the same amount. The following year Antar ordered year-end inventory to be overstated by $9 million and accounts payable to be understated by $3 million. Court records documented that Crazy Eddie employees overstated year-end inventory by preparing inventory count sheets for items that did not exist. To understate accounts payable, employees prepared bogus debit memos from vendors and entered them in the company's accounting records.

As the economic fortunes of Crazy Eddie began to fade in the late 1980s, Antar became more desperate in his efforts to enhance the company's reported revenues and profits. He ordered company employees to include in inventory consigned merchandise and goods being returned to suppliers. Another fraudulent tactic Antar used to overstate inventory involved transhipping transactions, the large-volume transactions between Crazy Eddie and many of its smaller competitors.

Antar knew that financial analysts closely monitor the annual percentage change in "same-store" sales for retailers. A decline in this percentage is seen as a negative indicator of a retailer's future financial performance. As the consumer electronics industry became increasingly crowded, the revenues of Crazy Eddie's individual stores began to fall, although the firm's total revenues continued to climb due to new stores being opened each year. To remedy the drop in same-store sales, Antar instructed his employees to record selected transhipping transactions as retail sales of individual stores. For instance, suppose that Crazy Eddie sold 100 microwaves costing $180 each to another retailer at a per unit price of $200. The $20,000 in sales would be recorded as retail sales with a normal gross profit margin of 30 to 50 percent—meaning that inventory would not be credited for the total number of microwaves actually sold. This practice killed two birds with the proverbial one stone. Same-store sales were inflated for selected operating units, and inventory was overstated with a corresponding increase in gross profit from sales.

Where Were the Auditors?

"Where were the auditors?" was a question posed repeatedly by investors, creditors, and other interested parties when the public learned of the Crazy Eddie fraud. Four different accounting firms audited Crazy Eddie's financial statements over its turbulent history. Antar dismissed Crazy Eddie's first accounting firm, a local firm, before he took the company public. The underwriter that managed Crazy Eddie's IPO urged Antar to retain a more prestigious accounting firm to increase the public's confidence in the company's financial statements. As a result, Antar retained Main Hurdman to serve as Crazy Eddie's audit firm. Main Hurdman had a nationwide accounting practice with several prominent clients in the consumer electronics industry. In the mid-1980s, Peat Marwick became Crazy Eddie's audit firm when it merged with Main Hurdman. Following the corporate takeover of Crazy Eddie in 1987, the new owners replaced Peat Marwick with Touche Ross.

Much of the criticism triggered by the Crazy Eddie scandal centered on Main Hurdman and its successor, Peat Marwick. Main Hurdman charged Crazy Eddie comparatively modest fees for the company's annual audits.[5] A leading critic of major accounting firms alleged that Main Hurdman had done so because it realized that it could make up for any lost revenue by selling consulting services to the company.[6]

This same individual challenged Main Hurdman's ability to objectively audit an inventory system that it had effectively developed. Main Hurdman's independence was also questioned because many of Crazy Eddie's accountants were former members of that accounting firm. Critics charge that a company that hires one or more of its former auditors can more easily conceal fraudulent activities during the course of subsequent audits. That is, a former auditor may help his or her new employer undermine subsequent audits. In fact, Crazy Eddie's practice of hiring its former auditors is not unusual. Many accounting firms actually arrange such "placements" with audit clients.

> You would think that if an auditor wanted to leave a public accounting firm, he or she would be discouraged from going to work for clients they had audited. Instead, just the opposite is true with big accounting firms encouraging their personnel to work for clients in the apparent belief that it helps cement the accountant–client relationship.[7]

Most of the criticism directed at Crazy Eddie's auditors stemmed from their failure to uncover the huge overstatement of the company's inventory and the material understatement of accounts payable. Third parties who filed suit against the auditors accused them of "aiding and abetting" the fraud by failing to thoroughly investigate numerous suspicious circumstances they discovered. Of particular concern were several reported instances in which the auditors requested client documents, only to be told that those documents had been lost or inadvertently destroyed.

In Peat Marwick and Main Hurdman's defense, Antar and his associates engaged in a large-scale plan to deceive the auditors. For example, after determining which inventory sites the auditors would be visiting at year-end, Antar shipped sufficient inventory to those stores or warehouses to conceal any shortages. Likewise, Crazy Eddie personnel systematically destroyed incriminating documents to conceal inventory shortages from the auditors. Antar also ordered his employees to "junk" the sophisticated, computer-based inventory system designed by Main Hurdman and to return to the outdated manual inventory system previously used by the company. The absence of a computer-based inventory system made it much more difficult for the auditors to determine exactly how much inventory the firm had at any point in time.

A particularly disturbing aspect of the Crazy Eddie scandal was the involvement of several key accounting employees in the various fraudulent schemes. These parties included the director of the internal audit staff, the acting controller, and the director of accounts payable. Past audit failures demonstrate that a fraud involving the collusion of key accounting personnel is difficult for auditors to uncover.

---

5. This practice is commonly known as "lowballing."

6. M. I. Weiss, "Auditors: Be Watchdogs, Not Just Bean Counters," *Accounting Today*, 15 November 1993, 41.

7. *Ibid.*, 42.

EPILOGUE

In June 1989, Crazy Eddie filed a Chapter 11 bankruptcy petition after losing its line of credit. Later that year, the company closed its remaining stores and liquidated its assets. Meanwhile, Eddie Antar was named as a defendant in several lawsuits, including a large civil suit filed by the SEC and a criminal indictment filed by a U.S. district attorney. In January 1990, a federal judge ordered Antar to repatriate $52 million that he had transferred to foreign bank accounts in 1987.

The following month, federal marshals began searching for Antar after he failed to appear in federal court. A judge had scheduled a hearing to force Antar to account for the funds he had transferred to overseas bank accounts. After Antar surrendered to federal marshals, the judge found him in contempt and released him on his own recognizance. Following this court appearance, Antar became a fugitive. For the next two years, Antar eluded federal authorities despite reported sightings of him in Brooklyn, Jerusalem, and South America.

On 25 June 1992, Israeli police arrested Eddie Antar. At the time, he was living in a small town outside Tel Aviv and posing as an Israeli citizen, David Jacob Levi Cohen. On 31 December 1992, Antar's attorney announced that an extradition agreement had been reached with the U.S. Department of Justice and Israeli authorities. After being extradited, Antar was convicted in July 1993 on 17 counts of financial fraud including racketeering, conspiracy, and mail fraud. In May 1994, a federal judge sentenced Antar to 12 1/2 years in federal prison and ordered him to pay restitution of $121 million to former stockholders and creditors.

A federal appeals court overturned Antar's fraud conviction in April 1995. The appeals court ruled that the judge who had presided over Antar's trial had been biased against him and ordered that a new trial be held under a different judge. In May 1996, Antar's attorneys and federal prosecutors arranged a plea bargain agreement to settle the charges outstanding against him. Under the terms of this agreement, Antar pleaded guilty to one federal charge of racketeering and publicly admitted, for the first time, that he had defrauded investors by manipulating his company's accounting records. Following his admission of guilt, one of the prosecuting attorneys commented that "Crazy Eddie wasn't crazy, he was crooked."[8]

In early 1997, Eddie Antar was sentenced to seven years in federal prison. Antar, who had remained in custody since being extradited to the United States in 1993, received credit for the time he had already spent in prison. As a result, he was required to serve only two years of his seven-year sentence.

Several of Antar's former cohorts have also been convicted or have pleaded guilty to fraud charges, including Sam E. Antar, Crazy Eddie's former CFO. After being released from prison, Sam E. Antar openly described and discussed his role in the fraud masterminded by his cousin. He revealed that Eddie had financed his college degree in accounting because the family needed an expert accountant to help design, manage, and conceal the company's fraudulent schemes. Sam graduated magna cum laude in accounting and passed the CPA exam on his first attempt. Upon joining Crazy Eddie, Sam confessed that he became a "thug" and a willing participant in the massive fraud:

Crazy Eddie was an empire built on deceit. The company was rotten to its core. Eddie Antar, his father, brothers, brother-in-law, me and others formed the nucleus of this massive criminal enterprise. In our day, we considered the humanity of others as weaknesses to be exploited in our efforts to commit our crimes. We simply gave investors, creditors, and many customers a raw deal.... We were nothing but cold-hearted and soulless criminals. We were two-bit thugs.[9]

---

8. F. A. McMorris, "Crazy Eddie Inc.'s Antar Admits Guilt in Racketeering Conspiracy," *Wall Street Journal*, 9 May 1996, B7.

9. Sam E. Antar, "Crazy Eddie Speaks, Cousin Sam E. Antar Responds," *White Collar Fraud* (http://whitecollarfraud.blogspot.com), 25 June 2007.

In March 1993, an agreement was reached to settle dozens of pending civil lawsuits spawned by the Crazy Eddie fraud. The contributions of the various defendants to the $42 million settlement pool were not disclosed; however, the defendants contributing to that pool included Peat Marwick and the local accounting firm used by Crazy Eddie before the company went public. Law enforcement authorities recovered more than $150 million from the parties that profited from the fraud. Those funds included more than $40 million that a federal judge ordered Sam Antar, Eddie Antar's father, to surrender in August 2002.

In the late 1990s, Eddie Antar's mother purchased the Crazy Eddie logo and the company's former advertising catch phrase, "Crazy Eddie—His prices are insane!" which had been sold in bankruptcy proceedings years earlier. In 1998, two nephews of Eddie Antar revived their uncle's business. The "new" Crazy Eddie operated principally as a mail-order and Internet-based retailer of consumer electronics. In June 2001, a New York business publication reported that the company had hired a former executive in the consumer electronics industry to serve as the "creative force" behind its marketing efforts.[10] That individual was none other than Crazy Eddie Antar.[11]

Questions

1. Compute key ratios and other financial measures for Crazy Eddie during the period 1984–1987. Identify and briefly explain the red flags in Crazy Eddie's financial statements that suggested the firm posed a higher-than-normal level of audit risk.

2. Identify specific audit procedures that might have led to the detection of the following accounting irregularities perpetrated by Crazy Eddie personnel: (a) the falsification of inventory count sheets, (b) the bogus debit memos for accounts payable, (c) the recording of transhipping transactions as retail sales, and (d) the inclusion of consigned merchandise in year-end inventory.

3. The retail consumer electronics industry was undergoing rapid and dramatic changes during the 1980s. Discuss how changes in an audit client's industry should affect audit planning decisions. Relate this discussion to Crazy Eddie.

4. Explain what is implied by the term lowballing in an audit context. How can this practice potentially affect the quality of independent audit services?

5. Assume that you were a member of the Crazy Eddie audit team in 1986. You were assigned to test the client's year-end inventory cutoff procedures. You selected 30 purchase invoices entered in the accounting records near year-end: 15 in the few days prior to the client's fiscal year-end and 15 in the first few days of the new year. Assume that client personnel were unable to locate 10 of these invoices. How should you and your superiors have responded to this situation? Explain.

6. Should companies be allowed to hire individuals who formerly served as their independent auditors? Discuss the pros and cons of this practice.

---

10. *Crain's New York Business*, "Week in Review," 11 June 2001, 34.

11. In 2004, the "new" Crazy Eddie failed. The company's trademarks were subsequently purchased by a Texas-based firm, which then sold them to an entrepreneur in Eddie Antar's hometown of Brooklyn, New York. This latter individual's attempt to revive the Crazy Eddie franchise ended in 2012 when he closed the website for the venture.

ZZZZ Best Company, Inc.

On 19 May 1987, a short article in the *Wall Street Journal* reported that ZZZZ Best Company, Inc., of Reseda, California, had signed a contract for a $13.8 million insurance restoration project. This project was just the most recent of a series of large restoration jobs obtained by ZZZZ Best (pronounced "zee best"). Located in the San Fernando Valley of southern California, ZZZZ Best had begun operations in the fall of 1982 as a small, door-to-door carpet cleaning business. Under the direction of Barry Minkow, the extroverted 16-year-old who founded the company and initially operated it out of his parents' garage, ZZZZ Best experienced explosive growth in both revenues and profits during the first several years of its existence. In the three-year period from 1984 to 1987, the company's net income surged from less than $200,000 to more than $5 million on revenues of $50 million.

When ZZZZ Best went public in 1986, Minkow and several of his close associates became multimillionaires overnight. By the late spring of 1987, the market value of Minkow's stock in the company exceeded $100 million, while the total market value of ZZZZ Best surpassed $200 million. The youngest chief executive officer in the nation enjoyed the "good life," which included an elegant home in an exclusive suburb of Los Angeles and a fire-engine red Ferrari. Minkow's charm and entrepreneurial genius made him a sought-after commodity on the television talk show circuit and caused the print and visual media to tout him as an example of what America's youth could attain if they would only apply themselves. During an appearance on *The Oprah Winfrey Show* in April 1987, Minkow exhorted his peers with evangelistic zeal to "Think big, be big" and encouraged them to adopt his personal motto, "The sky is the limit."

Less than two years after appearing on *Oprah*, Barry Minkow began serving a 25-year prison sentence. Tried and convicted on 57 counts of securities fraud, Minkow had been exposed as a fast-talking con artist who swindled his closest friends and Wall Street out of millions of dollars. Federal prosecutors estimate that, at a minimum, Minkow cost investors and creditors $100 million. The company that Minkow founded was, in fact, an elaborate Ponzi scheme. The reported profits of the firm were nonexistent and the large restoration contracts, imaginary. As one journalist reported, rather than building a corporation, Minkow created a hologram of a corporation. In July 1987, just three months after the company's stock reached a market value of $220 million, an auction of its assets netted only $62,000.

Unlike most financial frauds, the ZZZZ Best scam was perpetrated under the watchful eye of the Securities and Exchange Commission (SEC). The SEC, a large and reputable West Coast law firm that served as the company's general counsel, a prominent Wall Street brokerage firm, and an international public accounting firm all failed to uncover Minkow's daring scheme. Ultimately, the persistence of an indignant homemaker who had been bilked out of a few hundred dollars by ZZZZ Best resulted in Minkow being exposed as a fraud.

How a teenage flimflam artist could make a mockery of the complex regulatory structure that oversees the U.S. securities markets was the central question posed by a congressional subcommittee that investigated the ZZZZ Best debacle. That subcommittee was headed by Representative John D. Dingell, chairman of the U.S. House Committee on Energy and Commerce. Throughout the investigation, Representative

Dingell and his colleagues focused on the role the company's independent auditors played in the ZZZZ Best scandal.

> The ZZZZ Best prospectus told the public that revenues and earnings from insurance restoration contracts were skyrocketing but did not reveal that the contracts were completely fictitious. Where were the independent auditors and the others that are paid to alert the public to fraud and deceit?[1]

Like many other daring financial frauds, the ZZZZ Best scandal caused Congress to reexamine the maze of rules that regulate financial reporting and serve as the foundation of the U.S. system of corporate oversight. However, Daniel Akst, a reporter for the *Wall Street Journal* who documented the rise and fall of Barry Minkow, suggested that another ZZZZ Best was inevitable. "Changing the accounting rules and securities laws will help, but every now and then a Barry Minkow will come along, and ZZZZ Best will happen again. Such frauds are in the natural order of things, I suspect, as old and enduring as human needs."[2]

The Early History of ZZZZ Best Company

Barry Minkow was introduced to the carpet cleaning industry at the age of 12 by his mother, who helped make ends meet by working as a telephone solicitor for a small carpet cleaning firm. Although the great majority of companies in the carpet cleaning industry are legitimate, the nature of the business attracts a disproportionate number of shady characters. There are essentially no barriers to entry: no licensing requirements, no apprenticeships to be served, and only a minimal amount of start-up capital is needed. A 16-year-old youth with a driver's license can easily become what industry insiders refer to as a "rug sucker," which is exactly what Minkow did when he founded ZZZZ Best Company.

Minkow quickly learned that carpet cleaning was a difficult way to earn a livelihood. Customer complaints, ruthless competition, bad checks, and nagging vendors demanding payment complicated the young entrepreneur's life. Within months of striking out on his own, Minkow faced the ultimate nemesis of the small businessperson: a shortage of working capital. Because of his age and the fact that ZZZZ Best was only marginally profitable, local banks refused to loan him money. Ever resourceful, the brassy teenager came up with his own innovative ways to finance his business: check kiting, credit card forgeries, and the staging of thefts to fleece his insurance company.

Minkow's age and personal charm allowed him to escape unscathed from his early brushes with the law that resulted from his creative financing methods. The ease with which the "system" could be beaten encouraged him to exploit it on a broader scale.

Throughout his tenure with ZZZZ Best, Minkow recognized the benefits of having an extensive social network of friends and acquaintances. Many of these relationships he developed and cultivated at a Los Angeles health club. After becoming a friend of Tom Padgett, an insurance claims adjuster, Minkow devised a scheme to exploit that friendship. Minkow promised to pay Padgett $100 per week if he would simply confirm over the telephone to banks and any other interested third parties

---

1. This and all subsequent quotations, unless indicated otherwise, and each of the exhibits appearing in this case were taken from the following source: U.S. Congress, House Subcommittee on Oversight and Investigations of the Committee on Energy and Commerce, *Failure of ZZZZ Best Co.* (Washington, D.C.: U.S. Government Printing Office, 1988).

2. D. Akst, *Wonder Boy, Barry Minkow—The Kid Who Swindled Wall Street* (New York: Scribner, 1990), 271.

that ZZZZ Best was the recipient of occasional insurance restoration contracts. Ostensibly, Minkow had obtained these contracts to clean and do minor remodeling work on properties damaged by fire, storms, or other catastrophes. Minkow convinced the gullible Padgett that the sole purpose of the confirmations was to allow ZZZZ Best to circumvent much of the bureaucratic red tape in the insurance industry.

From this modest beginning, the ZZZZ Best fraud blossomed. Initially, Minkow used the phony insurance restoration contracts to generate the paper profits and revenues he needed to convince bankers to loan him money. Minkow's phony financial statements served their purpose, and he expanded his operations by opening several carpet cleaning outlets across the San Fernando Valley. Minkow soon realized that there was no need to tie his future to the cutthroat carpet cleaning industry when he could literally dictate the size and profitability of his insurance restoration "business." Within a short period of time, insurance restoration, rather than carpet cleaning, became the major source of revenue appearing on ZZZZ Best's income statements.

Minkow's "the sky is the limit" philosophy drove him to be even more innovative. The charming young entrepreneur began using his bogus financial statements to entice wealthy individuals in his ever-expanding social network to invest in ZZZZ Best. Eventually, Minkow recognized that the ultimate scam would be to take his company public, a move that would allow him to tap the bank accounts of unsuspecting investors nationwide.

Going Public with ZZZZ Best

Minkow's decision to take ZZZZ Best public meant that he could no longer control his firm's financial disclosures. Registering with the SEC required auditors, investment bankers, and outside attorneys to peruse ZZZZ Best's periodic financial statements.

ZZZZ Best was first subjected to a full-scope independent audit for the 12 months ended 30 April 1986. George Greenspan, the sole practitioner who performed that audit, confirmed the existence of ZZZZ Best's major insurance restoration contracts by contacting Tom Padgett. Padgett served as the principal officer of Interstate Appraisal Services, which reportedly contracted the jobs out to ZZZZ Best. By this time, Padgett was an active and willing participant in Minkow's fraudulent schemes. Minkow established Interstate Appraisal Services and Assured Property Management for the sole purpose of generating fake insurance restoration contracts for ZZZZ Best.

In testimony before the congressional subcommittee that investigated the ZZZZ Best scandal, Greenspan insisted that he had properly audited Minkow's company. Greenspan testified that while planning the 1986 audit he had performed various analytical procedures to identify unusual relationships in ZZZZ Best's financial data. These procedures allegedly included comparing ZZZZ Best's key financial ratios with industry norms. Regarding the insurance contracts, Greenspan testified that he had obtained and reviewed copies of all key documents pertaining to those jobs. However, Greenspan admitted that he had not inspected any of the insurance restoration sites.

Congressman Lent: *Mr. Greenspan, I am interested in the SEC Form S-1 that ZZZZ Best Company filed with the SEC…. You say in that report that you made your examination in accordance with generally accepted auditing standards and accordingly included such tests of the accounting records and other auditing procedures as we consider necessary in the circumstances…. You don't say in that statement that you made any personal on-site inspections.*

Mr. Greenspan: *It's not required. Sometimes you do; sometimes you don't. I was satisfied that these jobs existed and I was satisfied from at least six different sources, including payment for the job. What could you want better than that?*

Congressman Lent: *Your position is that you are an honest and reputable accountant.*

Mr. Greenspan: *Yes, sir.*

Congressman Lent: *You were as much a victim as some of the investors in this company?*

Mr. Greenspan: *I was a victim all right…. I am as much aghast as anyone. And every night I sit down and say, why didn't I detect this damned fraud.*

Retention of Ernst & Whinney by ZZZZ Best

Shortly after Greenspan completed his audit of ZZZZ Best's financial statements for fiscal 1986, which ended 30 April 1986, Minkow dismissed him and retained Ernst & Whinney to perform the following year's audit. Apparently, ZZZZ Best's investment banker insisted that Minkow obtain a major accounting firm to enhance the credibility of the company's financial statements. At approximately the same time, and for the same reason, Minkow retained a high-profile Los Angeles law firm to represent ZZZZ Best as its legal counsel.

The congressional subcommittee asked Greenspan what information he provided to Ernst & Whinney regarding his former client. In particular, the subcommittee wanted to know whether Greenspan discussed the insurance restoration contracts with the new auditors.

Congressman Wyden: *Mr. Greenspan, in September 1986, Ernst & Whinney came on as the new independent accountant for ZZZZ Best. What did you communicate to Ernst & Whinney with respect to the restoration contracts?*

Mr. Greenspan: *Nothing. I did—there was nothing because they never got in touch with me. It's protocol for the new accountant to get in touch with the old accountant. They never got in touch with me, and it's still a mystery to me.*

Representatives of Ernst & Whinney later testified that they did, in fact, communicate with Greenspan prior to accepting ZZZZ Best as an audit client. However, Ernst & Whinney did not comment on the nature or content of that communication. (Greenspan was not recalled to rebut Ernst & Whinney's testimony on this issue.)[3]

Exhibit 1 contains the engagement letter signed by Ernst & Whinney and Barry Minkow in September 1986. The engagement letter outlined four services that the audit firm intended to provide ZZZZ Best: a review of the company's financial statements for the three-month period ending 31 July 1986; assistance in the preparation of a registration statement to be filed with the SEC; a comfort letter to be submitted to ZZZZ Best's underwriters; and a full-scope audit for the fiscal year ending 30 April 1987. Ernst & Whinney completed the review, provided the comfort letter to ZZZZ Best's underwriters, and apparently assisted the company in preparing the registration statement for the SEC; however, Ernst & Whinney never completed the 1987 audit.

---

3. After a lengthy investigation, the American Institute of Certified Public Accountants ruled in 1998 that there was no "prima facie evidence" that Greenspan had violated the organization's *Code of Professional Conduct* during the time that ZZZZ Best was his client. A similar conclusion was reached by two state boards of accountancy with which Greenspan was registered to practice public accounting.

EXHIBIT 1

ERNST &
WHINNEY'S ZZZZ
BEST ENGAGEMENT
LETTER

September 12, 1986

Mr. Barry Minkow
Chairman of the Board
ZZZZ Best Co., Inc.
7040 Darby Avenue
Reseda, California

Dear Mr. Minkow:

This letter is to confirm our understanding regarding our engagement as independent accountants of ZZZZ BEST CO., INC. (the Company) and the nature and limitations of the services we will provide.

We will perform the following services:

1. We will review the balance sheet of the Company as of July 31, 1986, and the related statements of income, retained earnings, and changes in financial position for the three months then ended, in accordance with standards established by the American Institute of Certified Public Accountants. We will not perform an audit of such financial statements, the objective of which is the expressing of an opinion regarding the financial statements taken as a whole, and, accordingly, we will not express an opinion on them. Our report on the financial statements is presently expected to read as follows:

> "We have made a review of the condensed consolidated balance sheet of ZZZZ BEST CO., INC. and subsidiaries as of July 31, 1986, and the related condensed consolidated statements of income and changes in financial position for the three-month period ended July 31, 1986, in accordance with standards established by the American Institute of Certified Public Accountants. A review of the condensed consolidated financial statements for the comparative period of the prior year was not made.
>
> A review of financial information consists principally of obtaining an understanding of the system for the preparation of interim financial information, applying analytical review procedures to financial data, and making inquiries of persons responsible for financial and accounting matters. It is substantially less in scope than an examination in accordance with generally accepted auditing standards, which will be performed for the full year with the objective of expressing an opinion regarding the financial statements taken as a whole. Accordingly, we do not express such an opinion. Based on our review, we are not aware of any material modifications that should be made to the condensed consolidated interim financial statements referred to above for them to be in conformity with generally accepted accounting principles."

Our engagement cannot be relied upon to disclose errors, irregularities, or illegal acts, including fraud or defalcations, that may exist. However, we will inform you of any such matters that come to our attention.

2. We will assist in the preparation of a Registration Statement (Form S-1) under the Securities Act of 1933 including advice and counsel in conforming the financial statements and related information to Regulation S-X.

3. We will assist in resolving the accounting and financial reporting questions which will arise as a part of the preparation of the Registration Statement referred to above.

4. We will prepare a letter for the underwriters, if required (i.e., a Comfort Letter), bearing in mind the limited nature of the work we have done with respect to the financial data.

(continued)

EXHIBIT 1—
continued

ERNST &
WHINNEY'S ZZZZ
BEST ENGAGEMENT
LETTER

5. We will examine the consolidated financial statements of the Company as of April 30, 1987, and for the year then ended and issue our report in accordance with generally accepted auditing standards approved by the American Institute of Certified Public Accountants. These standards contemplate, among other things, that (1) we will study and evaluate the Company's internal control system as a basis for reliance on the accounting records and for determining the extent of our audit tests; and (2) that we will be able to obtain sufficient evidential matter to afford a reasonable basis for our opinion on the financial statements. However, it should be understood that our reports will necessarily be governed by the findings developed in the course of our examination and that we could be required, depending upon the circumstances, to modify our reporting from the typical unqualified opinion. We will advise you, as our examination progresses, if any developments indicate that we will be unable to express an unqualified opinion. Because our examination will be performed generally on a test basis, it will not necessarily disclose irregularities, if any, that may exist. However, we will promptly report to you any irregularities which our examination does disclose.

Our fees will be derived from our customary rates for the various personnel involved plus out-of-pocket expenses. Certain factors can have an effect on the time incurred in the conduct of our work. Among these are the general condition of the accounting records, the amount of assistance received from your personnel in the accumulation of data, the size and transaction volume of business, any significant financial reporting issues that arise in connection with the SEC's review of the S-1, as well as unforeseen circumstances. Based upon our current understanding of the situation, the amount of our proposed billing for the various services which we will be providing are estimated to be:

Review of the July 31, 1986 financial statements	$ 5,000-$7,500
Assistance in the preparation of the Registration Statement	8,000-30,000
Comfort Letter	4,000-6,000
Audit of financial statements as of April 30, 1987	24,000-29,000

We will invoice you each month for the time charges and expenses incurred in the previous month and such invoices are due and payable upon presentation.

Larry D. Gray, Partner, is the Client Service Executive assigned to the engagement. Peter Griffith, Audit Manager, and Michael McCormick, Tax Manager, have also been assigned.

We greatly appreciate your engagement of our firm; if you have any questions, we shall be pleased to discuss them with you. Please indicate your acceptance of the above arrangements by signing and returning the enclosed copy. This letter constitutes the full understanding of the terms of our engagement.

Very truly yours,
Ernst & Whinney
By Larry D. Gray, Partner
ACCEPTED:
ZZZZ BEST CO., INC.
Barry J. Minkow, Chairman of the Board (signed)
9/16/86

The audit firm resigned on 2 June 1987, amid growing concerns that ZZZZ Best's financial statements were grossly misstated.

The congressional subcommittee investigating the ZZZZ Best fraud questioned Ernst & Whinney representatives at length regarding the bogus insurance restoration contracts—contracts that accounted for 90 percent of ZZZZ Best's reported profits.

Congressional testimony disclosed that Ernst & Whinney repeatedly insisted on visiting several of the largest of these contract sites and that Minkow and his associates attempted to discourage such visits. Eventually, Minkow realized that the auditors would not relent and agreed to allow them to visit certain of the restoration sites, knowing full well that none of the sites actually existed.

To convince Ernst & Whinney that the insurance restoration contracts were authentic, Minkow plotted and carried out a series of sting operations that collectively cost millions of dollars. In the late fall of 1986, Larry Gray, the engagement audit partner for ZZZZ Best, told client personnel that he wanted to inspect a restoration site in Sacramento on which ZZZZ Best had reported obtaining a multimillion-dollar contract. Minkow sent two of his subordinates to Sacramento to find a large building under construction or renovation that would provide a plausible site for a restoration contract. Gray had visited Sacramento a few weeks earlier to search for the site that Minkow had refused to divulge. As chance would have it, the building chosen by the ZZZZ Best conspirators was the same one Gray had identified as the most likely site of the insurance restoration job.

Minkow's two confederates posed as leasing agents of a property management firm and convinced the supervisor of the construction site to provide the keys to the building one weekend on the pretext that a large, prospective tenant wished to tour the facility. Prior to the arrival of Larry Gray and an attorney representing ZZZZ Best's law firm, Minkow's subordinates visited the site and placed placards on the walls at conspicuous locations indicating that ZZZZ Best was the contractor for the building renovation. No details were overlooked by the two co-conspirators. They even paid the building's security officer to greet the visitors and demonstrate that he was aware in advance of their tour of the site and its purpose. Although the building had not been damaged and instead was simply in the process of being completed, the sting operation went off as planned. Exhibit 2 presents the memorandum Gray wrote describing his tour of the building—a memorandum included in Ernst & Whinney's ZZZZ Best workpapers.

Congressional investigators quizzed Gray regarding the measures he took to confirm that ZZZZ Best actually had a restoration contract on the Sacramento building. They were particularly concerned that he never discovered the building had not suffered several million dollars in damages a few months earlier, as claimed by ZZZZ Best personnel.

> Congressman Lent: …*Did you check the building permit or construction permit?*
>
> Mr. Gray: *No, sir. That wouldn't be necessary to accomplish what I was setting out to accomplish.*
>
> Congressman Lent: *And you did not check with the building's owners to see if an insurance claim had been filed?*
>
> Mr. Gray: *Same answer. It wasn't necessary. I had seen the paperwork internally of our client, the support for a great amount of detail. So, I had no need to ask—to pursue that.*
>
> Congressman Lent: *You understand that what you saw was not anything that was real in any sense of the word? …You are saying you were duped, are you not?*
>
> Mr. Gray: *Absolutely.*

Before allowing Ernst & Whinney auditors to visit a bogus restoration project, Minkow insisted that the firm sign a confidentiality agreement. Exhibit 3 presents a copy of that agreement. Members of the congressional subcommittee were troubled by the following stipulation of the confidentiality agreement: "We will not make

EXHIBIT 2

ERNST & WHINNEY
INTERNAL MEMO
REGARDING VISIT
TO ZZZZ BEST
RESTORATION
PROJECT

TO: ZZZZ Best Co., Inc. File

FROM: Larry D. Gray

RE: Visit to Sacramento Job

At our request, the Company arranged for a tour of the job site in Sacramento on November 23rd [1986]. The site (not previously identified for us because of the confidentiality agreement with their customer) had been informally visited by me on October 27. I knew approximately where the job was, and was able to identify it through the construction activity going on.

On November 23, Mark Morse accompanied Mark Moskowitz of Hughes Hubbard & Reed and myself to Sacramento. We visited first the offices of the Building Manager, Mark Roddy of Assured Property Management, Inc. Roddy was hired by the insurance company (at Tom Padgett's suggestion according to Morse) to oversee the renovation activities and the leasing of the space. Roddy accompanied us to the building site.

We were informed that the damage occurred from the water storage on the roof of the building. The storage was for the sprinkler systems, but the water was somehow released in total, causing construction damage to floors 17 and 18, primarily in bathrooms which were directly under the water holding tower, then the water spread out and flooded floors 16 down through about 5 or 6, where it started to spread out even further and be held in pools.

We toured floor 17 briefly (it is currently occupied by a law firm) then visited floor 12 (which had a considerable amount of unoccupied space) and floor 7. Morse pointed out to us the carpet, painting and clean-up work which had been ZZZZ Best's responsibility. We noted some work not done in some other areas (and in unoccupied tenant space). But per Mark, this was not ZZZZ Best's responsibility, rather was work being undertaken by tenants for their own purposes.

Per Morse (and Roddy) ZZZZ Best's work is substantially complete and has passed final inspection. Final sign-off is expected shortly, with final payment due to ZZZZ Best in early December.

Morse was well versed in the building history and in the work scope for ZZZZ Best. The tour was beneficial in gaining insight as to the scope of the damage that had occurred and the type of work that the Company can do.

any follow-up telephone calls to any contractors, insurance companies, the building owner, or other individuals involved in the restoration contract." This restriction effectively precluded the auditors from corroborating the insurance restoration contracts with independent third parties.

Resignation of Ernst & Whinney

Ernst & Whinney resigned as ZZZZ Best's auditor on 2 June 1987, following a series of disturbing events that caused the firm to question Barry Minkow's integrity. First, Ernst & Whinney was alarmed by a *Los Angeles Times* article in mid-May 1987 that revealed Minkow had been involved in a string of credit card forgeries as a teenager. Second, on 28 May 1987, ZZZZ Best issued a press release, without consulting or notifying Ernst & Whinney, that reported record profits and

Mr. Barry Minkow, President
ZZZZ Best Co., Inc.
7040 Darby Avenue
Reseda, California

Dear Barry,

In connection with the proposed public offering (the Offering) of units consisting of common stock and warrants of ZZZZ Best Co., Inc. (the Company), we have requested a tour of the site of the Company's insurance restoration project in Sacramento, California, Contract No. 18886. Subject to the representations and warranties below, the Company has agreed to arrange such a tour, which will be conducted by a representative of Assured Property Management Inc. (the Representative), which company is unaffiliated with Interstate Appraisal Services. The undersigned, personally and on behalf of Ernst & Whinney, hereby represents and warrants that:

1. We will not disclose the location of such building, or any other information with respect to the project or the building, to any third parties or to any other members or employees of our firm;

2. We will not make any follow-up telephone calls to any contractors, insurance companies, the building owner, or other individuals involved in the restoration project;

3. We will obey all on-site safety and other rules and regulations established by the Company, Interstate Appraisal Services, and the Representative;

4. The undersigned will be the only representative of this Firm present on the tour.

This Confidentiality Letter is also being furnished for the benefit of Interstate Appraisal Services, to the same extent as if it were furnished directly to such company.

EXHIBIT 3

ERNST & WHINNEY'S CONFIDENTIALITY AGREEMENT WITH ZZZZ BEST REGARDING VISITS TO RESTORATION PROJECTS

revenues. Minkow intended this press release to restore investors' confidence in the company—confidence that had been shaken by the damaging *Los Angeles Times* story. Third, and most important, on 29 May, Ernst & Whinney auditors discovered evidence supporting allegations made several weeks earlier by a third-party informant that ZZZZ Best's insurance restoration business was fictitious.

The informant had contacted Ernst & Whinney in April 1987 and asked for $25,000 in exchange for information proving that one of the firm's clients was engaging in a massive fraud. Ernst & Whinney refused to pay the sum, and the individual recanted shortly thereafter, but not until the firm determined that the allegation involved ZZZZ Best. (Congressional testimony disclosed that the individual recanted because of a bribe paid to him by Minkow.) Despite the retraction, Ernst & Whinney questioned Minkow and ZZZZ Best's board of directors regarding the matter. Minkow insisted that he did not know the individual who had made the allegation. On 29 May 1987, however, Ernst & Whinney auditors discovered several cancelled checks that Minkow had personally written to the informant several months earlier.

Because ZZZZ Best was a public company, the resignation of its independent auditor had to be reported to the SEC in an 8-K filing. This requirement alerts investors and creditors of circumstances that may have led to the change in auditors. At the time, SEC registrants were allowed 15 days to file an 8-K auditor change announcement. After waiting the maximum permissible time, ZZZZ Best reported the change in auditors but, despite Ernst & Whinney's insistence, made no mention in the 8-K of the fraud allegation that had been subsequently recanted.

The SEC requires a former audit firm to prepare a letter to be filed as an exhibit to its former client's 8-K auditor change announcement. That exhibit letter must comment on the 8-K's accuracy and completeness. In 1987, former audit firms had 30 days to file an exhibit letter, which was the length of time Ernst & Whinney waited before submitting its exhibit letter to the SEC. In that letter, Ernst & Whinney revealed that ZZZZ Best's insurance contracts might be fraudulent.

The congressional subcommittee was alarmed that 45 days passed before the charges of fraudulent misrepresentations in ZZZZ Best's financial statements were disclosed to the public. By the time the SEC released Ernst & Whinney's exhibit letter to the public, ZZZZ Best had filed for protection from its creditors under Chapter 11 of the federal bankruptcy code. During the period that elapsed between Ernst & Whinney's resignation and the public release of its 8-K exhibit letter, ZZZZ Best obtained significant financing from several parties, including $1 million from one of Minkow's close friends. These parties never recovered the funds invested in, or loaned to, ZZZZ Best. As a direct result of the ZZZZ Best debacle, the SEC shortened the length of time that registrants and their former auditors may wait before filing auditor change documents.

The congressional subcommittee also quizzed Ernst & Whinney representatives regarding the information they disclosed to Price Waterhouse, the audit firm Minkow retained to replace Ernst & Whinney.[4] Congressman Wyden wanted to know whether Ernst & Whinney had candidly discussed its concerns regarding Minkow's integrity with Price Waterhouse.

> Congressman Wyden: *I am going to insert into the record at this point a memo entitled "Discussion with successor auditor," written by Mr. Gray and dated June 9, 1987. Regarding a June 4 meeting, Mr. Gray, with Dan Lyle of Price Waterhouse concerning the integrity of ZZZZ Best's management, you stated that you had no reportable disagreements and no reservations about management integrity pending the results of a board of directors' investigation. Then you went on to say that you resigned because, and I quote here: "We came to a conclusion that we didn't want to become associated with the financial statements." Is that correct?*

> Mr. Gray: *That is correct.*

> Mr. Wyden: *…Mr. Gray, you told the committee staff on May 29, 1987, that when you uncovered evidence to support allegations of fraud that you decided to pack up your workpapers and leave the ZZZZ Best audit site. How did your leaving without telling anybody except the ZZZZ Best management and board of directors the reasons for leaving help the public and investors?*

A final twist to the ZZZZ Best scandal was an anonymous letter Ernst & Whinney received one week after the firm resigned as ZZZZ Best's auditor. At that time, no one other than Ernst & Whinney and ZZZZ Best's officers was aware of the firm's resignation. The letter, shown in Exhibit 4, contained several allegations suggesting that ZZZZ Best's financial statements were fraudulent. According to the congressional testimony, Ernst & Whinney forwarded this letter to the SEC on 17 June 1987.

---

4. Price Waterhouse never issued an audit report on ZZZZ Best's financial statements. ZZZZ Best was liquidated less than two months after Price Waterhouse was retained.

June 9, 1987

Mr. Guy Wilson
Ernst & Whinney
515 South Flower
Los Angeles, California 90021

Dear Mr. Wilson:

I am an individual having certain confidential information regarding the financial condition of ZZZZ Best Co., Inc. I have read the prospectus and your Review Report dated October 3, 1986, and recognize you have not done an examination in accordance with generally accepted auditing standards, but that such audit will be forthcoming by you.

I wish to make you aware of the following material facts which require you to confirm or disaffirm:

1. The electric generators which appear on the balance sheet under Note 6 as being purchased for $1,970,000 were purchased for scrap for less than $100,000 thru intermediaries of ZZZZ Best and resold to ZZZZ Best at the inflated value. The sole purpose was to boost the assets on the balance sheet. These generators have never been used and have no utility to the company.

2. Note 5 of the balance sheet discusses joint ventures and two restoration contracts. These contracts are fictitious as are the bookkeeping entries to support their validity. Interstate Appraisal Service [sic] did not let such contracts although they confirm their existence. The same is true for the alleged $7,000,000 Sacramento contract and the $40–100 million contracts with Interstate.

3. Further, checks made and passed between ZZZZ Best, its joint venturers and some of its vendors are no more than transactions among conspirators to support the validity of these restoration contracts.

4. Earnings reported by ZZZZ Best are being reported as Billings in excess of costs and estimated earnings on restoration contracts. These contracts do not exist nor do the earnings. This can be confirmed directly by contacting the alleged insurance carriers as well as physical inspections as to the existence and extent of the contracts.

5. Billings and Earnings for 1985 and 1986 were fabricated by the company before being presented to other accountants for certification.

Confirmation of these allegations can be accomplished by a careful due diligence. Such due diligence on your behalf is imperative for your protection.

Very truly yours,

B. Cautious
(Signed)

Collapse of ZZZZ Best

The *Los Angeles Times* article published in mid-May 1987 that disparaged Barry Minkow ultimately doomed the young entrepreneur and his company. Several years earlier, a homemaker had fallen victim to Minkow's credit card forgeries. Minkow had added a fraudulent charge to a credit charge slip the woman had used to make a payment on her account. Despite her persistence, Minkow avoided repaying the small amount. The woman never forgot the insult and tracked down, and kept a record of, individuals who had been similarly harmed by Minkow. At the urging of this woman, a reporter for the *Los Angeles Times* investigated her allegations. The woman's diary eventually became the basis for the *Los Angeles Times* article that, for the first time, cast doubt on the integrity of the "boy wonder" who was the talk of Wall Street.

The newspaper article triggered a chain of events that caused ZZZZ Best to collapse and disappear less than three months later. First, a small brokerage firm specializing in newly registered companies with suspicious earnings histories began short-selling ZZZZ Best stock, forcing the stock's price into a tailspin. Second, Ernst & Whinney, ZZZZ Best's law firm, and ZZZZ Best's investment banker began giving more credence to the allegations and rumors of financial wrongdoing by Minkow and his associates. Third, and most important, the article panicked Minkow and compelled him to make several daring moves that cost him even more credibility. The most critical mistake was his issuance of the 28 May 1987 press release that boldly reported record profits and revenues for his firm.

EPILOGUE

Among the parties most vilified for their role in the ZZZZ Best scandal was Ernst & Whinney. The transcripts of the congressional testimony focusing on the ZZZZ Best fraud included a list of 10 "red flags" that the audit firm had allegedly overlooked while examining ZZZZ Best's financial statements (see Exhibit 5). Ernst & Whinney officials flatly rejected assertions that their firm was even partially to blame for the ZZZZ Best fiasco. In his congressional testimony, Leroy Gardner, the West Coast director of accounting and auditing for Ernst & Whinney, maintained that when all the facts were revealed, his firm would be totally vindicated:

> The ZZZZ Best situation proves at least one thing: a well-orchestrated fraud will often succeed even against careful, honest, hardworking people.... The facts that have begun to emerge establish that Minkow along with confederates both inside and outside ZZZZ Best went to extraordinary lengths to deceive Ernst & Whinney. For example, Thomas Padgett, an alleged conspirator, revealed in a recent televised interview that Minkow spent $4 million to deceive Ernst & Whinney during a visit to one of ZZZZ Best's job sites.... Ernst & Whinney never misled investors about the reliability of ZZZZ Best's financial statements.

> Ernst & Whinney never even issued an audit opinion for ZZZZ Best.... We are not part of the problem in this case. We were part of the solution.

In one of the largest civil suits stemming from the ZZZZ Best fraud, a court ruled that Ernst & Whinney was not liable to a large California bank that had extended ZZZZ Best a multimillion-dollar loan in 1986. The bank alleged that in granting the loan, it had relied upon the review report issued by Ernst & Whinney on ZZZZ Best's financial statements for the three-month period ending 31 July 1986. However, an appellate judge ruled that the bank was not justified in relying on the review report since Ernst & Whinney had expressly stated in the report that it was not issuing an opinion on the ZZZZ Best financial statements. "Ernst, because it issued only a review report, specifically declined to express an opinion on ZZZZ Best's financial statements. The report expressly disclaimed any right to rely on its content."[5]

In the late 1980s, ZZZZ Best's former stockholders filed a class-action lawsuit against Ernst & Whinney, ZZZZ Best's former law firm, and ZZZZ Best's former investment banker. An Internet publication reported in March 1996

---

5. "Ernst & Young Not Liable in ZZZZ Best Case," *Journal of Accountancy*, July 1991, 22.

EXHIBIT 5

TEN RED FLAGS
THAT ZZZZ
BEST'S AUDITORS
ALLEGEDLY
OVERLOOKED

1. The amounts called for by the insurance restoration contracts were unrealistically large.

2. The number of multimillion-dollar insurance restoration contracts reportedly obtained by ZZZZ Best exceeded the total number available nationwide during the relevant time period.

3. The purported contracts failed to identify the insured parties, the insurance companies, or the locations of the jobs.

4. The contracts consisted of a single page which failed to contain details and specifications of the work to be done, such as the square yardage of carpet to be replaced, which were usual and customary in the restoration business.

5. Virtually all of the insurance restoration contracts were with the same party.

6. A large proportion of the ZZZZ Best insurance restoration contracts occurred immediately, and opportunistically, prior to a planned offering of stock.

7. The purported contracts provided for payments to ZZZZ Best or Minkow alone rather than to the insured or jointly with ZZZZ Best and the insured, contrary to the practice of the industry.

8. The purported contracts provided for payments by the insurance adjustor contrary to normal practice in the industry under which payments are customarily made by the insurance company directly to its insured or jointly to its insured and the restorer.

9. ZZZZ Best's purported gross profit margins for its restoration business were greatly in excess of the normal profit margins for the restoration industry.

10. The internal controls at ZZZZ Best were grossly inadequate.

that this lawsuit had been settled privately. The defendants reportedly paid the former ZZZZ Best stockholders $35 million. However, the contribution of each defendant to the settlement pool was not disclosed.[6]

Barry Minkow was released from prison in late 1994. Minkow secured the reduction in his 25-year prison sentence for "good behavior and efforts to improve himself."[7] These efforts included earning by correspondence bachelor's and master's degrees in religion from Liberty University. Shortly after being paroled, Minkow married a young woman introduced to him by a fellow inmate. That inmate was a former subordinate of Charles Keating, the principal architect of the massive Lincoln Savings and Loan fraud.

In early 1995, Minkow began serving as the associate pastor of an evangelical church in a community near his hometown of Reseda. Two years later, Minkow was appointed the senior pastor of a large nondenominational church in San Diego. Besides his pastoral duties, Minkow served as the spokesperson for an Internet company, the Fraud Discovery Institute, which marketed various fraud prevention and detection services.

For more than a decade, Minkow regularly presented lectures and seminars across the United States that focused on his "experience" with corporate fraud. He spoke to groups of CPAs, educational institutions, and, most notably, the FBI Academy at Quantico, Virginia. Minkow often chastised the accountants and auditors in his audience. During one presentation, Minkow noted that, "CPAs are creatures of habit. You're interested in making tick marks and footnotes, not in thinking outside of the

6. C. Byron, "$26 Million in the Hole," *Worth Online*, March 1996.

7. M. Matzer, "Barry Minkow," *Forbes*, 15 August 1994, 134.

box."[8] Minkow also chided auditors for being overly willing to accept weak forms of audit evidence, such as client representations. He warned auditors, "Don't give up objectivity for convenience."[9]

Unfortunately, the redemptive phase of Barry Minkow's life ended abruptly in 2011. In May of that year, Minkow pleaded guilty to conspiracy to commit securities fraud. Law enforcement authorities established that Minkow had participated in a scheme during January 2009 to drive down the stock price of Lennar Corporation and to extort money from the company's executives. At the time, Minkow wrongfully accused Lennar of fraudulently misrepresenting its publicly released financial statements.

On 21 July 2011, Barry Minkow appeared before Judge Patricia Seitz in a federal courtroom in Miami, Florida. Judge Seitz denied Minkow's request for leniency and sentenced him to five years in federal prison, the maximum sentence requested by federal prosecutors.

Questions

1. Ernst & Whinney never issued an audit opinion on financial statements of ZZZZ Best but did issue a review report on the company's quarterly statements for the three months ended 31 July 1986. How does a review differ from an audit, particularly in terms of the level of assurance implied by the auditor's report?

2. Professional auditing standards identify the principal "management assertions" that underlie a set of financial statements. The occurrence assertion was particularly critical for ZZZZ Best's insurance restoration contracts. ZZZZ Best's auditors obtained third-party confirmations to support the contracts, reviewed available documentation, performed analytical procedures to evaluate the reasonableness of the revenues recorded on the contracts, and visited selected restoration sites. Comment on the limitations of the evidence that these procedures provide with regard to the management assertion of occurrence.

3. In testimony before Congress, George Greenspan reported that one means he used to audit the insurance restoration contracts was to verify that his client actually received payment on those jobs. How can such apparently reliable evidence lead an auditor to an improper conclusion?

4. What is the purpose of predecessor–successor auditor communications? Which party, the predecessor or successor auditor, has the responsibility for initiating these communications? Briefly summarize the information that a successor auditor should obtain from the predecessor auditor.

5. Did the confidentiality agreement that Minkow required Ernst & Whinney to sign improperly limit the scope of the ZZZZ Best audit? Why or why not? Discuss general circumstances under which confidentiality concerns on the part of a client may properly affect audit planning decisions. At what point do client-imposed audit scope limitations affect the type of audit opinion issued?

6. What procedures, if any, do professional standards require auditors to perform when reviewing—prior to the completion of the audit—a client's post-year-end earnings press release?

---

8. T. Sickinger, "Ex-Con Artist Helps Find Fraud," *The Kansas City Star*, 18 October 1995, B1.

9. *Ibid.*

CASE 1.10

DHB Industries, Inc.

You can't make up a story like this.

Andrew Cohen, Senior Legal Analyst, CBS News

As a small child, Brooklyn native David Brooks loved horses.[1] In 1969, when he was 14 years old, Brooks went to work at a local racetrack as a groom to help support his family. Brooks loved the tough job that involved arriving at the racetrack in the wee hours of the morning, wiping down sweaty horses, wrestling large bales of hay, and "mucking" (cleaning out) horse stalls. Although he wanted to spend his life working in the horse-racing industry, Brooks' family encouraged him to pursue a more stable and pragmatic career after he graduated from high school. Because he was intrigued by the stock market, David Brooks eventually decided to major in business at one of New York City's prominent universities. The young extrovert relied on a variety of part-time jobs to finance an undergraduate business degree with a concentration in accounting at New York University.

Ironically, Brooks' successful business career provided the path for him to return to his first love. More than three decades after having worked at one of the lowest ranking jobs in horse racing, David Brooks quickly rose to the pinnacle of that sport by spending tens of millions of dollars to establish his own stable, Bulletproof Enterprises. At its height, Brooks' stable included more than 400 racehorses. In 2004, one of Brooks' horses, Timesareachanging, won the Little Brown Jug, which is the equivalent of the Kentucky Derby for standardbred horses that specialize in pacing.[2]

The Brooks Brothers Tangle with the SEC

In the mid-1980s, Jeffrey Brooks, David Brooks' brother and best friend, founded a small brokerage firm, Jeffrey Brooks Securities. Jeffrey recruited David to join the firm and become his right-hand man. Several years later, in 1992, the two brothers ran afoul of the Securities and Exchange Commission (SEC) when one of their subordinates was charged with insider trading. The SEC alleged that the Brooks brothers had failed to establish proper control procedures to prevent their subordinates from improperly using material nonpublic information obtained from their clients.

In addition to a $405,000 fine, the SEC filed separate injunctions against the brothers. The SEC banned David Brooks from serving as a director, officer, or employee of a brokerage firm or an investment company for five years. The injunction did not prohibit him from serving as an executive of an SEC registrant that was other than a brokerage or investment company.

A few months before the SEC sanctioned the Brooks brothers, David, with the financial backing of his brother, organized a small company based in Westbury, New

---

1. This case was originally published by the American Accounting Association in *Issues in Accounting Education*, Vol. 28 (February 2013), 131–152. The case was coauthored by Carol A. Knapp. I would like to thank Tracey Sutherland, Executive Director of the American Accounting Association, for granting permission to include this case in this edition of *Contemporary Auditing: Real Issues and Cases*. I would like to thank Glen McLaughlin for his generous and continuing support of efforts to integrate ethics into business curricula.

2. Standardbred is a breed of horses developed in North America that dominates harness racing. There are two types of harness races: trotting and pacing races.

York, a Long Island suburb of New York City. That company, DHB Capital Group, Inc., which was subsequently renamed DHB Industries, Inc. (DHB is David Brooks' initials), was intended to serve as the umbrella organization for a corporate conglomerate that Brooks hoped to build. Brooks' goal was to identify and then purchase small, underperforming companies and convert them into profitable operations by retooling their business models.

In 1994, Brooks attempted to register DHB on the NASDAQ stock exchange to provide it greater access to the nation's capital markets. The NASDAQ denied Brooks' application because of the sanctions that had been levied against him by the SEC. In defending that decision, the NASDAQ observed that "given the extremely serious nature of the SEC allegations made against Brooks, and the fact that he was only recently enjoined" it was necessary to exclude his company from the NASDAQ "to protect investors and the public interest and to maintain public confidence"[3] in that market. Brooks appealed the NASDAQ's decision to the SEC. After reviewing the matter, the SEC ruled in favor of the NASDAQ.

> *The facts remain that Brooks has a history of serious securities law violations and a significant ownership interest in DHB, and proposes to retain his position as a DHB director. We do not find it unreasonable that the NASD,[4] reviewing both Brooks' past conduct and his proposed level of involvement in DHB, remains uneasy about the potential for illicit conduct in connection with the operation of DHB or the market for its securities, and unwilling to expose public investors to that possibility.[5]*

Despite being rejected by the NASDAQ, the strong-willed Brooks persevered in his effort to have DHB's securities listed on a national stock exchange. A few years later, he finally accomplished that goal when those securities were registered on the American Stock Exchange.

Timing Is Everything

Brooks used the initial financing provided to him by his brother and the capital that DHB raised through a public stock offering to acquire five small firms during the 1990s. DHB's principal operating unit would become Point Blank Body Armor, a Florida-based firm purchased out of bankruptcy for a cash payment of $2 million. Throughout the existence of DHB, the Point Blank subsidiary accounted for upwards of 95 percent of its annual consolidated revenues. Point Blank's primary product was the Interceptor Vest, a bullet-resistant vest used by all branches of the U.S. military and by law enforcement agencies.

Brooks' acquisition of Point Blank was a timely decision. The small company had struggled for decades, but three circumstances ultimately triggered a surge in the demand for bullet-resistant vests after Point Blank was acquired by DHB. First, the 11 September 2001, terrorist attacks convinced law enforcement agencies throughout the nation to increase their budgets for weaponry and protective equipment for their personnel. Second, in early 2003, President George W. Bush's launching of Operation Iraqi Freedom, commonly referred to by the press as the Second Gulf War, prompted the U.S. Army and U.S. Marine Corps to purchase large quantities of bullet-resistant vests. Finally, one of Point Blank's primary competitors, Second Chance Body Armor,

---

3. Securities and Exchange Commission, "Release No. 34-37069," www.sec.gov, 5 April 1996.

4. At the time, the National Association of Securities Dealers (NASD) oversaw the operations of the NASDAQ.

5. Securities and Exchange Commission, "Release No. 34-37069."

was forced into bankruptcy in 2004 after being sued repeatedly by law enforcement agencies for allegedly manufacturing a large number of defective protective vests.

Brooks relied on his outgoing personality, persistent manner, and, most importantly, three Washington, D.C.–based political lobbyists to outmaneuver his competitors when vying for protective vest contracts put up for competitive bids by the U.S. military. Between 2001 and 2005, the U.S. military purchased nearly one million protective vests from DHB, accounting for the majority of the company's revenues during that time frame. In a period of only six months in 2004, Brooks landed three large contracts for body armor from the Pentagon totaling nearly $500 million. By comparison, DHB's total revenues in 2000 had been only $70 million, while the company's total stockholders' equity at the end of that year had been a negative $5 million due to a retained earnings deficit of more than $29 million.

The rapid expansion of DHB's Point Blank subsidiary caused the company's revenues and profits to soar. By 2004, DHB's annual revenues were approaching $350 million and the company's net income had topped $30 million. Despite those impressive figures, some analysts were concerned by the company's weak operating cash flows. In 2004, for example, the company had a negative net operating cash flow of $10 million despite reporting the $30 million profit. Exhibit 1 presents the audited income statements and balance sheets included in DHB's 2004 Form 10-K filed with the SEC in early 2005.

Patriot or Profiteer?

DHB's sudden financial success focused considerable attention on David Brooks, the company's chairman of the board and chief executive officer (CEO). The Industrial College of the Armed Forces, a military agency administered by the Joint Chiefs of Staff, lauded Brooks for developing lifesaving body armor technology for hundreds of thousands of U.S. soldiers. Military officials also praised Brooks for establishing a charitable foundation that provided financial assistance for wounded veterans.

Not all of the attention focused on Brooks and his company was favorable. In 2003, a group of DHB employees maintained that the company's protective vests suffered from flaws similar to those evident in the products of Second Chance Body Armor. In November 2004, Brooks and his two top subordinates, Sandra Hatfield, DHB's chief operating officer (COO), and Dawn Schlegel, DHB's chief financial officer (CFO), were disparaged by the press when they received financial windfalls upon selling most of their DHB stock. Brooks alone received more than $180 million from the sale of the majority of his DHB stock, an amount that was six times greater than DHB's net income for 2004. News reports of Brooks' huge stock market gain caused one organization to label him a "body armor profiteer."[6] A DHB spokesperson responded by defending Brooks' sale of his stock. "The American economic system rewards those who take great risks with commensurate benefits. The compensation Mr. Brooks received is directly attributable to the risk he undertook in aiding the capitalization of DHB and achieving extraordinary results for the company."[7]

The large stock sales by Brooks, Hatfield, and Schlegel were followed by a sharp decline in DHB's stock price. More bad news was soon to follow for the company. Within a few months, additional allegations surfaced that a large number of Point Blank vests being used by military personnel in Iraq had "critical, life-threatening

---

6. T. O'Brien, "All's Not Quiet on the Military Supply Front," *New York Times* (online), 22 January 2006.
7. *Ibid.*

EXHIBIT 1

DHB INDUSTRIES,
INC.'S 2003–2004
BALANCE SHEETS
AND INCOME
STATEMENTS

DHB Industries, Inc.
Balance Sheets 2003–2004 (000s omitted)

| | December 31, | |
	2004	2003
Current assets:		
Cash and cash equivalents	$ 447	$ 441
Accounts receivables (net)	47,560	33,707
Accounts receivable (related party)	6,583	--
Inventories	85,973	54,753
Deferred income tax assets	483	372
Prepaid expenses and other current assets	1,220	1,518
Total current assets	142,266	90,791
Property and equipment, net	2,632	1,819
Other assets:		
Deferred income tax assets	593	437
Deposits and other assets	366	381
Total assets	$145,857	$93,428
Current liabilities:		
Accounts payable	$ 8,014	$ 9,465
Accrued expenses and other current liabilities	8,350	5,635
Notes payable – bank	4,000	2,000
Income taxes payable	14,816	6,869
Total current liabilities	35,180	23,969
Long-term liabilities:		
Notes payable – bank	25,634	22,012
Term loan payable	6,500	--
Other liabilities	1,086	502
Total long-term liabilities	33,220	22,514
Total liabilities	$ 68,400	$46,483
Minority interest in consolidated subsidiary	431	207
Stockholders' equity:		
Preferred stock	1	1
Common stock	45	41
Additional paid-in capital	35,540	35,384
Accumulated other comprehensive loss	--	(53)
Retained earnings	41,440	11,365
Total stockholders' equity	77,026	46,738
Total liabilities and stockholders' equity	$145,857	$93,428

Source: DHB Industries, Inc., 2004 Form 10-K.

flaws."[8] Those allegations were followed by the U.S. military recalling more than 20,000 Point Blank vests. Then, in April 2005, DHB's audit firm resigned citing "deficiencies"[9] in the method used by the company to value its inventory. The announcement was particularly unsettling to investors because it was the third time

8. *Ibid.*

9. J. Bernstein, "DHB Accountant Resigns," *Newsday* (online), 16 April 2005.

EXHIBIT 1—
continued

DHB INDUSTRIES,
INC.'S 2003–2004
BALANCE SHEETS
AND INCOME
STATEMENTS

DHB Industries, Inc.
Income Statements 2003-2004 (000s omitted)

	Years Ended December 31,	
	2004	**2003**
Net sales*	$340,075	$230,011
Cost of goods sold**	245,940	166,670
Gross profit	94,135	63,341
Selling, general and administrative expenses	44,564	37,325
Income before other income (expense)	49,571	26,016
Other income		
Interest expense	(1,374)	(1,344)
Write-down of other investment	--	(904)
Gain on sale of subsidiary stock	--	1,450
Miscellaneous income	35	1,059
Total other income	(1,339)	261
Income before income tax	48,232	26,277
Income tax expense	17,573	11,098
Income before minority interest of subsidiary	30,659	15,179
Less minority interest of subsidiary	(224)	(7)
Net income	$ 30,435	15,172
Dividend – preferred stock (related party)	(360)	(360)
Net income available to common stockholders	$ 30,075	$ 14,812
Basic earnings per common share	$ 0.73	$ 0.36
Diluted earnings per common share	$ 0.67	$ 0.34

*Includes related-party sales of $6,559 for 2004 and $15,109 for 2003, respectively.
**Includes related-party purchases of $17,627 for 2004 and $29,243 for 2003, respectively.
Source: DHB Industries, Inc., 2004 Form 10-K.

since 2001 that a DHB audit firm had resigned after commenting on major problems involving the company's internal controls.

David Brooks' public image was sullied even more in November 2005 when several major publications reported that he had spent more than $10 million on a bat mitzvah party for his 13-year-old daughter in the elegant Rainbow Room in midtown Manhattan. Brooks used DHB's corporate jet to fly several famous musicians to the party to serenade invited guests, including 50 Cent, Aerosmith, Kenny G, Stevie Nicks, and Tom Petty. Brooks, who was decked out in a hot pink suede bodysuit during the affair, also handed out party bags to the bat mitzvah guests that contained a wide range of merchandise, including a digital camera and an Apple iPod, allegedly purchased with DHB corporate funds.

"Hurricane Brooks"

In July 2006, amid growing concerns regarding the reliability of DHB's accounting records, the company's board dismissed David Brooks and hired a team of forensic accountants to investigate those records. That investigation revealed that Brooks and his two top subordinates, Sandra Hatfield and Dawn Schlegel, had orchestrated a large-scale accounting fraud that had grossly inflated DHB's reported operating results and financial condition.[10] In addition to uncovering the massive fraud, the year-long forensic investigation yielded disturbing insights into the company's corporate culture during David Brooks' reign.

> Brooks exercised absolute control over every aspect of DHB's business, using the company's weak corporate governance and almost nonexistent internal controls to facilitate and hide the financial fraud he directed through Schlegel and Hatfield.... Brooks' control extended to DHB's board of directors, which consisted of Brooks' friends and neighbors and Schlegel. At all times relevant to this action, Brooks had a chokehold over DHB's board which exercised no real oversight.... Brooks also controlled the flow of communication with DHB's outside auditors, who regarded Brooks as the key decision-maker.[11]

Brooks used threats of physical harm to enforce his policies and directives. "When anyone questioned the accounting and financial reporting practices underlying the fraud at DHB, Brooks became furious and threatening." During one board meeting, Brooks told a board member who questioned one of his decisions, "You know what we do to outsiders …you know what we do to people that aren't on the team."

A primary target of Brooks' anger and threats was the company's independent auditors. When DHB's audit engagement partner questioned the authenticity of certain journal entries, Brooks told another company official that "if she [the audit partner] were not careful, she would be wearing cement blocks on her feet in the Atlantic Ocean." Later during that same audit, the audit engagement partner questioned Brooks directly regarding circumstances that took place during the company's prior audit that was performed by a different accounting firm. During this conversation, Brooks stated that "someone should …put a bullet" in the brain of the previous year's audit engagement partner.

Brooks also routinely withheld critical information from DHB's auditors, including information regarding significant related-party transactions. DHB purchased many of the components used to manufacture its protective vests from Tactical Armor Products (TAP), a privately owned company based in Florida. In early 2003, after discovering that Brooks' wife was TAP's CEO, DHB's auditors insisted that the company issue an amended Form 10-K for fiscal 2002 to disclose that fact. In truth, Brooks exercised total control over TAP's operations, a fact that was not divulged to the auditors nor disclosed in the amended Form 10-K.[12]

In addition to repeatedly failing to disclose that TAP was a related-party entity, Brooks also failed to disclose in DHB's SEC registration statements that he had been sanctioned by the federal agency in 1992. This information was allegedly a material fact that would have been of significant interest to DHB's stockholders, prospective investors, and a wide range of other parties involved with the company.

According to a federal prosecutor, a principal goal of Brooks' accounting fraud "was to ensure that DHB consistently reported gross profit margins of 27 percent or more and increased earnings, to correspond to the expectations of professional

---

10. Hatfield had worked for Brooks in several capacities after he organized the company in 1992. Brooks eventually appointed her as DHB's COO in December 2000. Schlegel's first connection with DHB was as an independent auditor. In late 1999, Brooks hired her to serve as DHB's CFO. Schlegel, who was a CPA, also served on the company's board of directors.

11. Unless indicated otherwise, the remaining quotes were taken from the following source: Securities and Exchange Commission v. David H. Brooks, U.S. District Court, Southern District of Florida, Case No. 07-61526, 15 October 2007.

12. Brooks used his control of both companies to funnel millions of dollars from DHB to himself via TAP.

stock analysts."[13] One facet of the fraud was a series of bogus journal entries. From 2003 through 2005, Dawn Schlegel instructed her subordinates on DHB's accounting staff to record multimillion-dollar entries that reclassified components of cost of goods sold as operating expenses. Although these reclassification entries did not improve the company's "bottom line" profits, they did serve the purpose of significantly inflating DHB's gross profit ratio each period.

The major focus of the DHB fraud was the company's inventory accounts. From 2003 through 2005, DHB's period-ending inventories were consistently and materially inflated. Throughout that three-year period, "Hatfield was responsible for assigning values to inventory and Schlegel was responsible for reviewing and approving the inventory valuation before incorporating it into the company's consolidated financial statements." Brooks "directly supervised Schlegel and Hatfield in performing all their duties, and demanded to review all financial statements and disclosures DHB included in its [SEC] filings."

Near the end of fiscal 2004, Hatfield realized that DHB would fall well short of the 27 percent gross profit margin that Brooks believed was necessary to satisfy financial analysts tracking the company's stock. To solve this problem, Hatfield, increased the already overstated value of the company's year-end inventory by several million dollars through various "pricing manipulations." The offsetting reduction of cost of goods sold allowed DHB to reach the 27 percent threshold for gross profit margin and to inflate its reported net income.

When DHB's controller reviewed the company's year-end inventory values for 2004, he immediately realized that they were overstated. After preparing schedules documenting the inventory overstatements, the controller went to Hatfield and Schlegel who "acknowledged that the inventory was overstated." Despite that acknowledgment, the two executives refused to correct the inventory values. "Troubled by concerns over the company's inflated inventory values, the controller turned in his resignation."

Before leaving DHB, the controller informed the company's independent auditors that he believed the year-end inventory values were overstated. The auditors then raised this matter directly with Brooks. "Brooks and Hatfield told the auditors that the controller's inventory analysis was incorrect and that there were 'no real problems in the inventory.'"

After meeting with the auditors, Brooks stormed into the controller's office. During Brooks' subsequent trial, the controller testified that an "enraged" Brooks called him a "____ snake" and "flung …water all over me."[14] While an unidentified man blocked the door to the controller's office, Brooks shouted "I'm going to kick your ___."[15] Brooks then "confiscated the controller's inventory analysis and violently ejected him from the premises." When DHB's auditors subsequently questioned Brooks regarding the controller's ejection from the company's headquarters, Brooks responded that the controller "had violated …internal policies and procedures" when he had told them of his concerns regarding the valuation of inventory.

The circumstances surrounding the resignation of DHB's controller served to heighten the auditors' concern regarding the valuation of year-end inventory. Making matters worse, Brooks instructed his subordinates to file the company's 2004 Form 10-K with the SEC before the auditors had concluded their investigation of DHB's

---

13. *Broward Bulldog*, "Update: Former Pompano Beach Body Armor Tycoon Convicted in Huge Fraud Trial," www.browardbulldog.org, 14 September 2010.

14. R. Kessler, "Ex-controller: Brooks Threatened Me," *Newsday* (online), 10 February 2010.

15. *Ibid.*

EXHIBIT 2

EXCERPTS FROM
AUDITORS' REPORT
ON INTERNAL
CONTROL
INCLUDED IN
DHB INDUSTRIES'
AMENDED 2004
FORM 10-K

A material weakness is a control deficiency, or combination of control deficiencies, that results in more than a remote likelihood that a material misstatement of the annual or interim financial statements will not be prevented or detected. We have identified the following two material weaknesses that have not been identified as material weaknesses in management's assessment:

- The company transmitted its annual report on Form 10-K for the year ended December 31, 2004, for filing via EDGAR with the Securities and Exchange Commission having been informed by representatives of Weiser LLP, its auditors, that it had not completed its final review of the last revisions to the Form 10-K and accordingly had not yet released its audit report for filing. Despite Weiser's call, the 2004 Form 10-K was forwarded to the SEC for filing...
- The conduct of the audit committee did not demonstrate its understanding of its oversight role of the Company's financial reporting and internal control over financial reporting processes.

Source: DHB Industries, Inc., Amended 2004 Form 10-K.

inventory, a decision that deeply troubled the auditors. To placate the auditors, Brooks amended the company's 2004 Form 10-K. This amendment disclosed a material weakness in DHB's inventory valuation process.[16]

DHB's "Management Report on Internal Control over Financial Reporting" in the amended 2004 Form 10-K noted that "there existed certain significant deficiencies in the Company's systems of inventory valuation rendering it inadequate to accurately capture cost of materials and labor components of certain work in progress and finished goods inventory."[17] The report went on to observe, however, that the material weakness "did not affect the Company's financial statements or require any adjustment to the valuation of its inventory or any other item in its financial statements."[18]

DHB's auditors insisted on including an updated version of their report on the company's internal controls in the amended Form 10-K. This updated report identified two additional material weaknesses in internal controls that were not documented in DHB's management report on internal controls. Exhibit 2 contains excerpts from the auditors' updated internal control report that described these two items. The first item involved DHB's decision to file its original 2004 Form 10-K prior to the auditors completing their final review of key financial statement amounts in that document. The second of the two additional material weaknesses indicated that DHB's audit committee did not have a proper understanding of its important oversight role for the company's financial reporting process.

To mitigate the damage caused by the reporting of these two additional material weaknesses, Brooks took the unusual step of including an insert in the amended 2004 Form 10-K that challenged the auditors' updated internal control report. In this insert, DHB maintained that the two additional material weaknesses identified by the auditors were not, in fact, true material weaknesses (see Exhibit 3). DHB's auditors resigned shortly after this contentious disagreement was aired in the company's SEC filings.

---

16. The amended Form 10-K was filed with the SEC prior to the date that the original 2004 Form 10-K was released to the public.

17. DHB Industries, Inc., "Form 10-K/A (Amendment No. 2)," Securities and Exchange Commission, 2 May 2005.

18. *Ibid.*

EXHIBIT 3

RESPONSE OF
MANAGEMENT TO
AUDITORS' REPORT
ON INTERNAL
CONTROL INCLUDED
IN DHB INDUSTRIES'
AMENDED 2004
FORM 10-K

Difference of Opinion on Management's Assessment of Internal Controls:

The Attestation report of Weiser LLP identifies what that firm considers to be two additional material weaknesses in internal controls: (1) failure of the Company to complete consultation with Weiser LLP prior to filing Form 10-K for the year ended December 31, 2004 (an amended Form 10-K was promptly filed thereafter to include certain changes to the financial statements as set forth in Form 8-K filed by the Company dated April 14, 2005); and (2) a need to enhance and strengthen the Audit Committee to improve the Committee's effectiveness. The Company believes that, to a significant degree, an evaluation of these two issues involves subjective judgment and the Company does not agree that either of these matters constitutes a material weakness in internal control over financial reporting. The Company promptly took action to amend the 2004 Form 10-K when it learned that Weiser LLP identified issues that required correction in connection with its final review of the Form 10-K, and the Form 10-K/A was filed before the Form 10-K was disclosed to the public. Furthermore, the Company believes that the members of its Audit Committee have consistently fulfilled their duties and obligations responsibly and appropriately. Although the Company does not believe that Weiser LLP has a proper basis for its conclusions, the Company takes Weiser LLP's views seriously and intends to explore opportunities to improve the process of preparing its filings with the Securities and Exchange Commission and the effectiveness of its Audit Committee.

Source: DHB Industries, Inc., Amended 2004 Form 10-K.

DHB's Form 10-Q for the first quarter of fiscal 2005 reported a net income of $7.6 million—the company's net operating cash flow for that period was a negative $5.0 million. The company's gross profit margin for that quarter was 27.4 percent, a figure that was almost identical to the gross profit margins realized by the company for fiscal 2003 and 2004. DHB surpassed the "magic" 27 percent gross profit threshold for the first quarter of 2005 because Hatfield and Schlegel had inflated the quarter-ending inventory by adding 63,000 nonexistent vest components to the company's inventory accounting records.

The decision to add fictitious items to DHB's inventory posed a vexing problem for the co-conspirators that they had not anticipated, namely, how to conceal that fact from the company's new auditors, the company's fourth audit firm in four years. (In prior periods, the three executives had overstated DHB's inventory values by increasing the cost-per-unit assigned to individual inventory items rather than by adding fictitious items to the accounting records.) Near the end of 2005, Brooks came up with a plan for solving the problem posed by the fictitious inventory. Brooks told Schlegel to include the cost of the $7 million of bogus vest components in a large write-off entry that was necessary for a line of business that DHB was discontinuing.[19]

A few months later, during the fiscal 2005 audit, DHB's auditors questioned Brooks regarding the inventory included in the loss from discontinued operations. Brooks told the auditors that the $7 million of vest components had to be written off because the U.S. military had changed its color requirements for the vests in which those components were to be incorporated. When asked where the obsolete vest components

19. In August 2005, a government agency "decertified" the bullet-resistant material being used in the manufacture of a certain product line of DHB's vests, which caused DHB to discontinue that product line.

were, the quick-thinking Brooks replied that they no longer existed because the warehouse in which they had been stored had been destroyed by a hurricane a few months earlier. Brooks later relayed this bogus explanation to Schlegel so that she would be prepared to corroborate it with the auditors. "In exasperation, Schlegel asked Brooks why he had told that story, since they had nothing to support it, and the auditors would want support and details." Despite her concern, Schlegel did as she was instructed and confirmed the story when DHB's auditors queried her regarding the $7 million inventory item.

When the auditors continued to press for additional details regarding the written-off inventory, a flummoxed Brooks altered his story. He told the auditors that the "hurricane" explanation was a lie made up by his subordinates, which he had not known when he passed that information to the auditors. This troubling about-face and the inability of Brooks or his subordinates to account for the mysterious $7 million of inventory caused DHB's auditors to begin seriously questioning whether they could issue an opinion on the company's 2005 financial statements.

In early March 2006, the auditors told Brooks that they would not be able to release their audit report on DHB's 2005 financial statements in time for the company to meet the SEC filing deadline for its 2005 Form 10-K. Law enforcement authorities subsequently discovered that Brooks attempted to "shop for a favorable audit opinion" by replacing those auditors with another audit firm that he had secretly contacted. That effort proved unsuccessful. A few months later in July 2006, Brooks' turbulent tenure as DHB's founder and top executive came to an end when he was dismissed by the company's board.

The following month, DHB recalled its audited financial statements for 2003 and 2004 and warned third parties that they should no longer rely on them. DHB issued restated financial statements for those two years that radically altered the company's previously reported operating results. DHB's restated income statement for 2004, for example, reported a $9.5 million net loss compared to the $30 million net income the company had originally reported for that year. Exhibit 4 presents DHB's restated income statements and balances sheets for 2003 and 2004.

The SEC filed a civil complaint against Hatfield and Schlegel on August 18, 2006. The SEC alleged that the two individuals had participated in an accounting fraud that had grossly inflated DHB's reported operating results and financial condition. Law enforcement authorities subsequently filed criminal fraud charges against both Hatfield and Schlegel.

On 25 October 2007, the SEC filed a civil complaint against David Brooks that alleged he was the master architect of the DHB fraud. Later that morning, federal law enforcement authorities arrested Brooks in his lavish home on Long Island, and then filed more than one dozen criminal charges against him during his arraignment. Two days prior to Brooks' arrest, his former close friend and confidante, Dawn Schlegel, had pleaded guilty to two criminal charges, conspiracy to defraud the government and conspiracy to conceal tax information. In exchange for sentencing considerations, Schlegel agreed to serve as the government's "star witness"[20] during the criminal trial of Brooks and Hatfield.

---

20. S. Gardiner and P. Hurtado, "DHB Industries Ex-Chief David Brooks Looted Company, Jury Told," www.bloomberg.com, 26 January 2010.

EXHIBIT 4

DHB INDUSTRIES,
INC.'S 2003–2004
RESTATED BALANCE
SHEETS AND INCOME
STATEMENTS

DHB Industries, Inc.
Balance Sheets 2003–2004 (000s omitted)

	December 31,	
	2004	**2003**
Current assets:		
Cash and cash equivalents	$ 498	$ 441
Accounts receivables (net)	47,425	33,565
Inventories	38,231	30,001
Deferred income tax assets	19,094	1,424
Prepaid expenses and other current assets	1,219	1,597
Total current assets	106,467	67,028
Property and equipment, net	2,371	1,771
Other assets:		
Deferred income tax assets	--	124
Deposits and other assets	366	381
Total assets	$109,204	$ 69,304
Current liabilities:		
Note payable – current portion	$ 10,500	$ 2,000
Accounts payable	8,004	9,642
Accrued expenses and other current liabilities	9,015	5,776
Income taxes payable	4,931	118
Employment tax withholding obligation	29,718	737
Total current liabilities	62,168	18,273
Long-term liabilities:		
Note payable – bank	25,644	22,022
Other liabilities	674	527
Total long-term liabilities	26,318	22,549
Total liabilities	$ 88,486	$ 40,822
Minority interest in consolidated subsidiary	49	(1)
Stockholders' equity:		
Convertible preferred stock	3,000	3,000
Common stock	45	41
Additional paid-in capital	63,776	62,089
Retained deficit	(46,152)	(36,647)
Total stockholders' equity	20,669	28,483
Total liabilities and stockholders' equity	$109,204	$ 69,304

Source: DHB Industries, Inc., 2006 Form 10-K.

(*continued*)

Circus Trial

The criminal trial of David Brooks and his codefendant Sandra Hatfield commenced
in late January 2010. Brooks faced a 17-count federal indictment that included allegations of corporate fraud, insider trading, conspiracy, and obstruction of justice.
Hatfield faced similar charges in the 16-count federal indictment filed against her.

EXHIBIT 4—
continued

DHB INDUSTRIES,
INC.'S 2003–2004
RESTATED BALANCE
SHEETS AND INCOME
STATEMENTS

DHB Industries, Inc.
Income Statements 2003-2004 (000s omitted)

	Years Ended December 31,	
	2004	2003
Net sales	$322,276	$206,375
Cost of goods sold	265,607	177,066
Gross profit	56,669	29,309
Selling, general and administrative expenses	37,461	29,478
Litigation and cost of investigations	943	--
Employment tax withholding charge	28,981	737
Total operating costs	67,385	30,215
Operating loss	(10,716)	(906)
Interest expense	1,371	1,410
Other (income) expense	(190)	(1,925)
Total other (income) expense	1,181	(515)
Loss before income tax (benefit) expense	(11,897)	(391)
Current taxes	14,726	413
Deferred income tax (benefit) expense	(17,526)	3,172
Total income tax (benefit) expense	(2,800)	3,585
Loss before minority interest in subsidiary	(9,097)	(3,976)
Less minority interest in subsidiary	48	(1)
Net loss	(9,145)	(3,975)
Dividends – preferred stock (related party)	360	360
Loss available to common stockholders	$ (9,505)	$ (4,335)
Basic loss per common share	$ (0.23)	$ (0.11)
Diluted loss per common share	$ (0.23)	$ (0.11)

Source: DHB Industries, Inc., 2006 Form 10-K.

Throughout the trial, jurors were pelted with an unrelenting stream of evidence that documented how Brooks had used "DHB as his personal piggy bank." Personal expenditures paid with corporate funds included purchases of luxury automobiles, expensive art, jewelry, designer clothing, and real estate. Court testimony revealed that the largest benefactor of Brooks' embezzlement scheme was his beloved harness racing operation. Brooks reportedly diverted nearly $15 million of DHB funds through TAP to help finance his expensive hobby.

Other testimony during the long criminal trial documented how Brooks had repeatedly lied to DHB's independent auditors to conceal his fraudulent scams. Schlegel's testimony laid out in minute detail the extreme lengths to which she, Brooks, and Hatfield had gone to mislead the auditors. The most elaborate hoaxes were required to conceal the large overstatements of inventory from the curious and persistent teams of auditors.

Throughout the eight-month trial, the presiding federal magistrate, Judge Joanna Seybert, faced the daunting task of maintaining a sense of civility and decorum in her Long Island courtroom. The first drama involved the revocation of David Brooks' bail. In January 2008, three months after his initial arrest, Brooks' attorneys secured his release on bail. Because Judge Seybert believed that Brooks posed a significant flight risk, she required him to post a $400 million bail bond that included cash and other collateral of nearly $50 million. The bail terms also required Brooks to retain a security firm at an estimated cost of $3,500 per day to monitor him around the clock. *ABC News*[21] reported that Brooks' bail terms were more stringent than those imposed years earlier by a federal judge on the infamous mobster John Gotti.

Just as Brooks' trial was beginning, Judge Seybert revoked his bail and remanded him to jail because of two reports given to her by the FBI. An undercover video forwarded to the FBI by Scotland Yard detectives allegedly showed Jeffrey Brooks and one of his subordinates transferring millions of euros to a large safety deposit box in a London bank. The FBI was convinced that the funds belonged to David Brooks. The FBI also informed Judge Seybert that they had discovered evidence suggesting that Brooks had secretly transferred tens of millions of dollars to bank accounts in the tiny European nation of San Marino. Judge Seybert revoked Brooks' bail because the two incidents violated the conditions of his bail agreement that mandated that all of his financial assets be "frozen."

Midway through the trial, Judge Seybert threatened to have David Brooks removed from the courtroom after he was discovered attempting to smuggle anxiety suppression medication into his jail cell. The antianxiety pills were hidden in a ballpoint pen that had been placed at Brooks' desk during a break in the courtroom proceedings. Following this incident, Judge Seybert barred Jeffrey Brooks and one of David Brooks' close friends from the courtroom. Brooks' personal psychiatrist subsequently testified that the psychiatrist at the correctional facility where Brooks was being held had prescribed him an insufficient dosage of the antianxiety medication. Brooks reportedly needed larger-than-normal dosages of that medication to ward off the panic attacks that he frequently experienced.

Later in the trial, federal prosecutors revealed that several months earlier David Brooks had allegedly asked a veterinarian who worked in his harness racing operation to obtain a medication administered to horses. If taken by a human, this medication would supposedly wipe out his or her memory. According to the veterinarian, Brooks hoped to somehow administer the medication to Dawn Schlegel, the prosecution's principal witness, prior to the beginning of his criminal trial. This revelation and Brooks' other antics during the trial caused *Comedy Central*'s Stephen Colbert to name Brooks his "Alpha Dog of the Week" during the August 2, 2010, airing of the popular television program *The Colbert Report*.

Andrew Cohen, a senior legal analyst for *CBS News* who monitored Brooks' trial, observed that many of its details were so salacious that major publications, such as the *New York Times*, would not report them.[22] One veteran reporter summarized some of the more outrageous events and testimony that took place during the trial.

> It's not an everyday federal trial in which …the defense asserts that the payment of company money to prostitutes might be an acceptable technique to motivate employees. Or in which a defendant says he is entitled to have his company pay for the grave of his mother, camp tuition for his children, [and] family trips to St. Barts and St. Tropez.[23]

After spending two months studying the massive amount of evidence that prosecutors had presented to prove their allegations, a federal jury convicted Brooks on all 17 counts filed against him. Sandra Hatfield, Brooks' former colleague and codefendant, was found guilty on 14 of the 16 counts included in her federal indictment.

---

21. *ABC News*, "'War Profiteer' Gets 'Bulletproof' Bail Terms: Released on $400 Million Bond," http://blogs.abcnews.com, 4 January 2008.

22. A. Cohen, "Hurricane Brooks: The Trial of the Century (Finally) Ends," www.theatlantic.com, 15 September 2010.

23. *Ibid.*

EPILOGUE

In April 2010, near the midpoint of David Brooks' criminal trial, Point Blank Solutions, the successor to DHB Industries, Inc., filed for protection from its creditors in U.S. Bankruptcy Court. The following year, a federal judge approved the sale of the company's remaining assets to Sun Capital Partners, Inc., a private investment company, for approximately $37 million.

Following the completion of Brooks' criminal trial, his attorneys immediately appealed his conviction. Among other arguments, the attorneys maintained that Brooks was incompetent and unable to contribute to his defense during much of the trial because of the antianxiety medication that he was taking. In August 2013,

after losing his appeal, Brooks was sentenced to 17 years in federal prison by Judge Joanna Seybert.

In February 2011, the SEC filed a civil complaint against three former members of DHB's audit committee. The federal agency charged the three individuals with being "willfully blind to numerous red flags signaling accounting fraud, reporting violations, and misappropriation at DHB."[24] The civil complaint went on to allege that the three former audit committee members "merely rubber-stamped the decisions of DHB's senior management while making substantial sums from sales of DHB's securities."[25]

Questions

1. Exhibits 1 and 4 present DHB's original 2003–2004 balance sheets and income statements and the restated balance sheets and income statements for those two years, respectively. Review the original and restated financial statements for 2004 and identify the "material" differences between them. (Note: You are not required to identify the sources of these differences.) Defend your choices.

2. Identify the fraud risk factors posed by DHB for its independent auditors. Which of these factors, in your opinion, should have been of primary concern to those auditors?

3. During the 2004 DHB audit, the company's independent auditors had considerable difficulty obtaining reliable audit evidence regarding the $7 million of obsolete vest components that allegedly had been destroyed by a hurricane. What responsibility do auditors have when the client cannot provide the evidence they need to complete one or more audit tests or procedures?

4. What responsibility, if any, do auditors have to search for related-party transactions? If auditors discover that a client has engaged in related-party transactions, what audit procedures should be applied to them?

5. Compare and contrast the internal control reporting responsibilities of the management and independent auditors of public companies.

6. What potential consequences do frequent changes in auditors have for the quality of a given entity's independent audits? Identify professional standards or other rules and regulations that are intended to discourage auditor changes or provide disclosure of the circumstances surrounding them.

24. Securities and Exchange Commission v. Jerome Krantz, Cary Chasin, and Gary Nadelman, U.S. District Court, Southern District of Florida, Case No. 0:11-cv-60432, 28 February 2011.
25. *Ibid.*

7. David Brooks apparently made threatening remarks to certain of his company's independent auditors. What actions should auditors take when they are the target of hostile statements or actions by client executives or employees?

8. Does the SEC have a responsibility to protect the investing public from self-interested corporate executives? Do professional auditing standards or other rules or regulations impose such a responsibility on independent auditors?

9. The audit committee of DHB Industries was criticized for failing to carry out its oversight responsibilities. What are the primary responsibilities of a public company's audit committee?

New Century Financial Corporation

It is well enough that people of the nation do not understand our banking and monetary system, for if they did, I believe there would be a revolution before tomorrow morning.

Henry Ford

From 1962 to 1992, Ed McMahon served as the quintessential sidekick and straight man to Johnny Carson on the long-running and popular television program *The Tonight Show*. After leaving that program, McMahon stayed in the television spotlight for 12 years by serving as the host of *Star Search*, a syndicated talent show. McMahon's résumé also included long stints as cohost of *TV Bloopers and Practical Jokes*, the annual Macy's Thanksgiving Day Parade, and the Jerry Lewis Labor Day Telethon and as commercial spokesperson for such companies as Budweiser and American Family Publishing.

McMahon's 50-year-plus career in television made him one of the most recognized celebrities in that medium. Understandably then, the American public was shocked when press reports in June 2007 revealed that McMahon was more than $600,000 past due on his home mortgage payments. The $5 million mortgage on McMahon's Beverly Hills mansion was held by Countrywide Financial Corporation.

Unfortunately, millions of everyday Americans with mortgage balances only a fraction of Ed McMahon's also faced the unhappy prospect of losing their homes due to the worst financial crisis to strike the United States economy since the Great Depression. As that crisis quickly worsened and spread to the global economy, the search began for the parties responsible for it. Among the potential culprits identified by the press was the accounting profession, in particular, independent auditors.

Mortgage Mess

Nearly one-half of recent mortgage foreclosure victims obtained their loans from so-called subprime lenders that became dominant forces within the mortgage industry during the past two decades. The largest of those lenders were Countrywide, HSBC, New Century Financial Corporation (New Century), and Wells Fargo, but more than a dozen other large companies provided loans to borrowers with suspect credit histories. The implosion of the lucrative but high-risk subprime sector of the mortgage industry in 2007 and 2008 ignited the financial panic in the United States that quickly engulfed the global economy.

The origins of the subprime mortgage debacle in the United States can be traced to the collapse of New Century, the nation's second largest subprime lender. New Century was founded in 1995 by three friends who had previously worked together at a mortgage banking company. New Century, which was based in Irvine, California, grew dramatically over its brief existence. In 1996, New Century reported total revenues of $14.5 million and total assets of $4.4 million. Nine years later, the company reported total revenues of $2.4 billion and total assets of $26 billion.

During the heyday of subprime mortgage lending in 2005 and 2006, New Century funded $200 million of new mortgage loans on a typical business day. In early February 2007, just a few months after company executives insisted that New Century

Tremendous growth

was financially strong, those same executives unsettled Wall Street when they revealed that the company would be restating previously released financial statements as a result of the misapplication of generally accepted accounting principles (GAAP).

Two months later, New Century declared bankruptcy. A court-appointed bankruptcy examiner summarized the far-reaching implications that New Century's downfall had for the global economy:

> The increasingly risky nature of New Century's loan originations created a ticking time bomb that detonated in 2007.... The demise of New Century was an early contributor to the subprime market meltdown. The fallout from this market catastrophe has been massive and unprecedented. Global equity markets were rocked, credit markets tightened, recession fears spread, and losses are in the hundreds of billions of dollars and growing.[1]

In fact, New Century would be just the first of many high-profile companies brought down by the turmoil in the mortgage industry. Other longtime stalwarts of the nation's financial services industries that fell victim to that turmoil included Bear Stearns, Lehman Brothers, and Merrill Lynch.

All three firms failed

In September 2008, the federal government assumed control of the Federal National Mortgage Association and the Federal Home Loan Mortgage Company, two "government-sponsored" but publicly owned companies better known as Fannie Mae and Freddie Mac, respectively. At the time, the two organizations owned or guaranteed nearly one-half of the approximately $12 trillion of home mortgages in the United States. For decades, the federal government had used Fannie Mae and Freddie Mac to create an orderly and liquid market for homeowner mortgages, but the enormous losses each suffered in 2007 and 2008 undercut that role and forced the U.S. Department of the Treasury to take over their operations.

Angry investors lashed out at a wide range of parties who they believed bore some measure of responsibility for the massive financial crisis. Those parties included the major subprime mortgage lenders in the United States, such as New Century, and the politicians, regulatory authorities, ratings agencies, and independent auditors who had failed to prevent or rein in the imprudent business practices of those lending institutions.

Only a few years removed from the sweeping reforms prompted by the Enron and WorldCom scandals, the accounting profession was once again forced to defend itself from a wide range of angry and often self-righteous critics. Among these critics was the *New York Times*. The prominent newspaper castigated the auditors of subprime lenders for stamping those institutions' financial statements with the accounting profession's equivalent of the Good Housekeeping Seal of Approval. "While accounting firms don't exert legal or regulatory authority over their clients, they do bestow seals of approval, the way rating agencies do. People in the financial industry, as well as investors, have reason to believe that a green light from an auditor means that a company's accounting practices have passed muster."[2]

The following section of this case provides a historical overview of subprime mortgage lending in the United States. Next, the history and operations of New Century Financial Corporation are reviewed with a particular focus on the company's major role in the subprime mortgage fiasco. The case then examines the criticism of KPMG,

---

1. "Final Report of Michael J. Missal, Bankruptcy Court Examiner," In re New Century TRS Holdings, Inc., a Delaware corporation, et al., U.S. Bankruptcy Court for the District Delaware, Case No. 07-10416 (KJC), 29 February 2008. Unless indicated otherwise, the quotations appearing in this case were taken from this source.

2. V. Bajaj and J. Creswell, "A Lender Failed. Did Its Auditor?" *New York Times* (online), 13 April 2008.

New Century's longtime independent audit firm, by the federal bankruptcy examiner appointed to investigate the company's sudden collapse in early 2007.

Subprime Lending: A Historical Perspective

Like all businesses, mortgage companies struggle to achieve a proper balance between "risk" and "return" in their operations. The principal risk historically faced by mortgage lenders is the possibility that their clients will be unable or unwilling to pay the principal and interest on their mortgage loans.

Prior to the 1980s, individuals who were poor credit risks effectively had only two choices for obtaining a mortgage to purchase a home. Those alternatives were obtaining a home loan insured by either the Federal Housing Administration (FHA) or the Department of Veteran Affairs (VA). Borrowers with good credit histories, so-called prime borrowers, would typically seek financing for a new loan directly from a bank, savings and loan, or other financial institutions.

The deregulation of the lending industry beginning in the 1980s made it much easier for subprime borrowers to obtain mortgage loans to finance the purchase of a new home. The Depository Institutions Deregulation and Monetary Control Act of 1980 did away with restrictions that imposed a ceiling on the interest rates lending institutions could charge on new mortgage loans. Subsequent legislation allowed mortgage lenders to create a wide array of financing alternatives to compete with the standard 30-year, fixed interest rate mortgage loan that had long been the industry's principal product. Most notably, these nontraditional mortgage loans included ARMs, or adjustable rate mortgages, that would become particularly popular with mortgage borrowers who had impaired or "subprime" credit histories or profiles.

Despite the deregulatory legislation of the 1980s, the subprime sector of the mortgage industry did not experience explosive growth until the "securitization" of mortgage loans became increasingly common following the turn of the century. Wikipedia defines securitization as "a structured finance process in which assets, receivables, or financial instruments [such as mortgage loans] are acquired, classified into pools, and offered as collateral for third-party investment."

The securitization option caused many mortgage lenders to adopt an "originate to distribute" business model. This new business model meant that the credit risk posed by new mortgages was no longer exclusively absorbed by lending institutions but rather was shared with investors worldwide who purchased so-called mortgage-backed securities or MBS. By 2006, nearly one-fourth of all new residential mortgage loans in the United States were made to subprime borrowers; three-fourths of those mortgages were securitized and sold to investors in the United States and around the world.

The insatiable demand for high-yield MBS among investors, particularly institutional investors such as large banks and hedge funds, caused subprime lenders to ratchet up their marketing efforts. To persuade individuals who were high credit risks to obtain mortgage loans, the subprime lenders developed new products designed specifically for that sector of the mortgage market.

Among the most popular mortgage products developed for the subprime lending market were "stated-income" and "interest-only" mortgages. An applicant for a stated-income loan was simply asked to report his or her annual income during the application process for the loan. The applicant's self-reported income was used by the lender to determine the size of the loan that the individual could afford. Not surprisingly, many applicants for stated-income loans, commonly known as "liars' loans" in the mortgage industry, grossly overstated their annual incomes so that they could purchase a larger home than was economically feasible given their actual annual incomes.

A borrower who obtained an interest-only or IO mortgage loan was required to pay only interest on his or her loan balance for a fixed period of the mortgage term. The IO feature of these loans typically extended over either the first 5 or the first 10 years of the mortgage term. Similar to other mortgage loans, the most common term of an IO loan was 30 years.

Housing prices in those regions of the country where subprime lending was particularly prevalent—such as Arizona; California; south Florida; and Las Vegas, Nevada—rose steeply during the late 1990s and into the early years of the new century. Many subprime borrowers in those housing markets purchased a home with the express intention of reaping a short-term windfall profit. An individual who obtained a 100 percent loan to acquire a $2 million home could realize a more than $400,000 "profit" on that home in two years if housing prices rose 10 percent each year. After two years, the borrower could extract that profit by refinancing his or her mortgage. That profit could then be used to make the monthly payments on the new mortgage. Or, that individual could sell the home and use the resulting profit to purchase a much larger home—with a much larger mortgage—that he or she could also "flip" in a few years.

Housing prices generally reached their peak in the United States in mid-2006, although they had been declining in some regions of the country over the previous 12 months. By late 2007, prices in several major regional housing markets had declined by 10 percent from their peak levels. By mid-2008, housing prices in those same markets had declined by 20 percent, or more, from their high water marks.

As housing prices steadily fell, a growing number of subprime borrowers began defaulting on their monthly mortgage payments. In fact, many of those individuals quickly became "upside down in their homes," that is, the unpaid balances of their mortgages exceeded the market values of their homes. By early 2008, an estimated nine million U.S. homeowners had a negative equity in their homes.

The sharp downturn in the housing market had an immediate and drastic impact on mortgage lenders, particularly subprime mortgage lenders such as New Century. Many of the subprime loans originated and packaged for sale by New Century included repurchase clauses. If the default rate on those packages of loans exceeded a certain rate, New Century could be forced to repurchase those loans. As the housing market weakened, New Century and other subprime lenders were flooded with loan repurchase requests.

The financial problems facing the mortgage industry soon spread to other sectors of the economy because of the securitization of subprime mortgage loans. Many high-profile companies in the financial services industry, such as Merrill Lynch, that had no direct connection to the large subprime lenders, suffered huge losses as the market value of MBS plunged. Making matters worse, a large proportion of MBS that originated in the United States was sold worldwide. As one observer of the mortgage market noted, the securitization process effectively "spread the cancer of subprime mortgages to investors throughout the U.S. and the rest of the world."[3]

New Century: Poster Child for Subprime Mortgage Lending

Bob Cole, Ed Gotschall, and Brad Morrice found themselves without jobs in 1995 when the company for which they had worked for several years, Plaza Home Mortgage, was purchased by a much larger competitor. The three friends decided to pool their resources and establish their own mortgage company, a company that

---

3. K. Amadeo, "Understanding the Subprime Mortgage Crisis," *About.com* (online), 9 October 2008.

would focus on the "low-end" or subprime sector of the mortgage market. Cole served as New Century Financial Corporation's chief executive officer (CEO), Gotschall was the company's chief financial officer (CFO), and Morrice oversaw New Century's lending operations as the company's chief operating officer (COO). Morrice would eventually replace Cole as New Century's CEO. In June 1997, the company went public by listing its stock on the NASDAQ—New Century's stock would be switched to the New York Stock Exchange in late 2004.

Cole, Gotschall, and Morrice earned relatively modest annual salaries throughout their tenure with the company. For example, in 2005, each of them received a salary of $569,250. However, New Century's incentive compensation plan rewarded the three cofounders handsomely with significant bonuses and stock option grants when the company met or exceeded its financial goals. During 2005, the three executives received total compensation of approximately $15 million each. In addition, the *New York Times* reported that, collectively, they realized more than $40 million in trading profits on the sale of New Century stock between 2004 and 2006.[4]

New Century thrived from its inception thanks largely to three key factors. First, mortgage interest rates, which had spiked during the mid-1990s, stabilized and then generally trended downward for more than a decade—lower mortgage rates serve to fuel the housing and mortgage industries. Second, the economic and regulatory environment at the time made subprime lending the most lucrative sector of the mortgage industry. Finally, the booming housing market in Orange County, California, where the company was located, provided New Century a large and easily accessible market to tap.

Once New Century was well established in Orange County, the company's ruling troika of Cole, Gotschall, and Morrice began pursuing expansion opportunities for their company in other "hot" real estate markets in the United States. At its zenith, New Century operated more than 200 retail mortgage offices in the United States from which company employees originated new mortgage loans. The company's wholesale division, which produced the bulk of its loan originations, operated through a far-flung network of more than 35,000 independent mortgage brokers.

New Century's 2003 Form 10-K filed with the Securities and Exchange Commission (SEC) provided a concise summary of the company's business model:

> We offer mortgage products designed for borrowers who generally do not satisfy the credit, documentation or other underwriting standards prescribed by conventional mortgage lenders and loan buyers, such as Fannie Mae and Freddie Mac. We originate and purchase loans on the basis of the borrower's ability to repay the mortgage loan, the borrower's historical pattern of debt repayment and the amount of equity in the borrower's property (as measured by the borrower's loan-to-value ratio, or LTV). We have been originating and purchasing these types of loans since 1996 and believe we have developed a comprehensive and sophisticated process of credit evaluation and risk-based pricing that allows us to effectively manage the potentially higher risks associated with this segment of the mortgage industry.

In 2004, New Century's management reorganized the company as a real estate investment trust (REIT) so that it would qualify for favorable tax treatment under the Internal Revenue Code. This organizational change had little impact on the company's operations or the underlying nature of its principal line of business, that is, originating subprime mortgage loans.

---

4. V. Bajaj, "Report Assails Auditor for Work at Failed Home Lender," *New York Times* (online), 26 March 2008.

New Century experienced impressive growth from its founding in 1996 through 2001, however, a significant increase in subprime lending activity quadrupled New Century's revenues from fiscal 2002 to fiscal 2005. In the latter year, New Century originated or purchased more than $56 billion of mortgage loans and securitized $17 billion of those loans, resulting in net earnings of $411 million for the company.

The decision by New Century's management to focus the company's marketing efforts principally on stated-income and IO loans contributed significantly to its remarkable growth in revenues beginning in 2002. By 2005, approximately three-fourths of the company's loan originations involved one of those two products.

Throughout the period that New Century's revenues were increasing dramatically, company spokespeople repeatedly insisted in press releases and public filings with the SEC that the company had a strong and sophisticated system of internal controls. That contention was subsequently questioned by the bankruptcy examiner appointed to investigate the collapse of New Century.

Several interviewees told the Examiner that they thought New Century's information technology and data entry and processing systems were not "state of the art" and were not sufficient for a business of the size and nature of New Century's. In particular, New Century's loan production processes were apparently manual and people-intensive through the fall of 2005. Up until that time, New Century apparently used an outdated DOS-based loan underwriting and appraising operating system, which, according to one Management interviewee, allowed users to "finagle anything."

The bankruptcy examiner's report went on to note that the company's accounting system was particularly lax with regard to tracking "loan repurchase claims." According to the examiner, New Century did not develop an "automated system or protocol" for tracking such claims until late 2006. By that time, the company was being swamped by loan repurchase requests due to the weakening housing markets in the principal geographical areas that it served. Besides failing to properly track loan repurchase requests throughout most of its history, New Century "did not have a formal policy spelling out exactly how to calculate reserves"[5] for loans that it would be required to repurchase.

By late 2005, several members of New Century's board of directors were openly challenging top management's high-risk business strategies as well as questionable accounting and financial reporting decisions made by the company. The most vocal of these critics was Richard Zona, an outside director who also served on the company's audit committee.

Earlier in his long and distinguished career, Zona had been a senior partner with Ernst & Young (E&Y) and had served for a time as E&Y's National Director of Financial Services, a position in which he oversaw the firm's audit, tax, and management consulting services. In the late 1990s, Zona had also served on an advisory council to the Federal Reserve Board.

In late 2005, Zona drafted a resignation letter, which he addressed to New Century's board of directors. In that letter, Zona suggested that company management was manipulating reported earnings, employing "aggressive" revenue recognition methods, and failing to provide an adequate allowance for loan losses.[6] Excerpts from Zona's letter are included in Exhibit 1.

---

5. Bajaj and Creswell, "A Lender Failed."

6. Zona eventually rescinded the 2005 resignation letter and remained on the company's board until September 2007.

EXHIBIT 1

EXCERPTS FROM
DRAFT OF 2005
RESIGNATION
LETTER SUBMITTED
BY RICHARD ZONA
TO NEW CENTURY'S
BOARD

At the October 25th and 26th [2005] Board meeting, Management informed the Board that its current forecast and analyst consensus for third quarter EPS of $2.24 per share could not be achieved unless Management reversed $.26 per share of loan loss reserves ... Obviously, Management's desire to reverse reserves in the third quarter smacked of earnings manipulation.

Management use of off-balance sheet gain on sale accounting substantially overstates earnings when compared to cash flows, thus generating extremely aggressive income recognition.

Our largest shareholder has questioned the appropriateness of our accounting for loan losses.

As to accounting for loan losses, it is a long-standing accounting maxim that accounting should be designed and applied to match revenues with expenses. Management's methodology to provide for loan losses based upon their estimate of charge-offs over the next 18 months does not accomplish that objective ...Management's methodology does not result in a proper matching of revenues with costs, (loan loss provisions), because charge-offs are back ended.

Source: "Final Report of Michael J. Missal, Bankruptcy Court Examiner," In re: New Century TRS Holdings, Inc., a Delaware corporation, et al., U.S. Bankruptcy Court for the District Delaware, Case No. 07-10416 (KJC), 29 February 2008.

Throughout 2006, New Century's financial condition and operating results deteriorated rapidly. To quell concerns regarding the company's health, New Century management repeatedly assured Wall Street that the company was financially sound. In August 2006, New Century reported a significant increase in its earnings for the second quarter of the year compared with that for the same period of the prior year. A company spokesperson noted that those operating results were "evidence of the strength and stability of our franchise." New Century's third quarter earnings press release for 2006 admitted that subprime lenders faced "challenging" market conditions because of increasing loan delinquencies. Nevertheless, the press release assured the investing public that New Century was "adequately reserved for the expected higher level of loan losses."

On 31 January 2007, New Century's management team met with the company's board of directors and audit committee. At that meeting, management told the board and audit committee that New Century had understated its reserve for loan repurchase losses for each of the first three quarterly reporting periods of 2006. New Century's controller, David Kenneally, attributed those understatements to an "inadvertent oversight" in the method used to compute the reserve. Members of New Century's board and audit committee testified that they were "shocked" by this revelation and described the 31 January meeting as "ugly" and "very emotional."

On 7 February 2007, New Century filed a Form 8-K with the SEC, which publicly disclosed the prior understatements of the loan repurchase loss reserve. The 8-K indicated that the understatements were due to the company failing "to account for expected discounts upon the disposition of repurchased loans" and due to its failure to "properly consider the growing volume of repurchase claims outstanding that resulted from the increasing pace of repurchase requests." The 8-K filing did not disclose to what extent the loan repurchase loss reserve had been understated but instead simply indicated that the previously reported earnings for the first three quarters of 2006 "should no longer be relied upon."

EXHIBIT 2

FICTITIOUS LETTER
SUPPOSEDLY
WRITTEN BY
FORMER NEW
CENTURY CEO
FOLLOWING
THE COMPANY'S
BANKRUPTCY FILING

Dear BankNet360 Readers:

Hi, my name is Brad Morrice and I've just bailed out of my sinking ship, the SS New Century Financial.

But don't feel bad for me; I'll be doing just fine. I may have bankrupt the company, treated mortgage underwriting like a bad cold, and helped cause more layoffs than a recession, but I should still bank about $25 million. To the creditors I say, "nanee-nanee billy goat."

Regrets? Sure, I've got some. I should have cashed in more of my options when the NEW stock was on a rocket ship fueled by option ARMs and I.O. loans from heaven. Ah, those were the days, when loans fell from the sky—and into the laps of subprime borrowers who can more easily discern Britney from J-Lo than understand all the conditions of their upcoming loan repricings.

You know, I wonder also how I can walk away from New Century with so much dough. This Chief Restructuring Officer, Holly Etlin, I don't know what planet she is from, but she can come over to my palace, er, place, anytime.

Oh, look at the time. That money's going to hit my account any moment now, and I've got shopping to do. Well, my regards to the subprime mortgage industry. All you Wall Street guys—hope you can handle the risk.

Sincerely yours,

Brad A. Morrice
Founder (ret.)
New Century Financial Corp. (bankrupt)

Source: BankNet360.com (www.banknet360.com/viewpoints/Discussion.do?discussion_id=191), 13 June 2007.

On March 2, 2007, New Century informed the SEC that its 2006 Form 10-K would be delayed and that it would eventually report a loss for the entire year. At the same time, New Century disclosed that KPMG was considering issuing a going-concern opinion on the company's 2006 financial statements—KPMG resigned as New Century's auditor a few weeks later without having issued an opinion on those financial statements. On 2 April 2007, New Century filed for bankruptcy in a U.S. federal court. At the time, New Century was the ninth largest company to file for bankruptcy in U.S. history.[7] In May 2008, company management announced that New Century's audited financial statements for 2005 should no longer be relied upon.

Within a few days of New Century's bankruptcy filing, the company's stock price fell to less than $1 per share, down from more than $30 per share two months earlier—the stock had reached its all-time high of $66 per share in 2004. Not surprisingly, stockholders and other parties were enraged by the company's sudden collapse that mimicked the downfall of Enron and WorldCom a few years earlier. Exhibit 2 presents a sarcastic commentary on New Century's collapse by one of the company's many critics. This commentary was in the form of a fictitious letter addressed to the readers of an online banking forum.

---

7. The five largest companies to file for bankruptcy in 2007 were mortgage lenders. Four of those five companies were subprime lenders.

"Go-To Auditor"

The *New York Times* characterized KPMG as the "go-to auditor" for the subprime sector of the mortgage industry.[8] KPMG's audit clients in that sector included the largest subprime lenders, namely, Countrywide, HSBC, New Century, and Wells Fargo. KPMG served as New Century's auditor from the company's inception in 1995 until its resignation in April 2007.

New Century's bankruptcy filing resulted in heated criticism of KPMG. The *New York Times* drew a parallel between Arthur Andersen's audits of Enron Corporation that had failed to expose the huge energy company's aggressive accounting treatments and KPMG's audits of New Century. According to the newspaper, KPMG had failed to warn investors that New Century's "mortgage freight train was about to run off the rails."[9]

> *New Century's accounting methods let it prop up profits, charming investors and allowing the company to continue to tap a rich vein of Wall Street cash that it used to underwrite more mortgages. Without the appearance of a strong bottom line, New Century's financial lifeline could have been cut earlier than it was.*[10]

The federal bankruptcy examiner appointed for New Century carried out an exhaustive investigation of the large subprime lender's sudden failure. A major focus of that investigation was KPMG's 2005 audit of New Century and the accounting firm's reviews of the financial statements included in the company's Form 10-Qs for the first three quarters of 2006. KPMG was required to provide the bankruptcy examiner with nearly 2 million pages of documents relating to those engagements. Exhibit 3 presents KPMG's audit report on New Century's 2005 financial statements.

In his 560-page report, the bankruptcy examiner alleged that KPMG had failed to perform its New Century engagements "in accordance with professional standards." The examiner's specific allegations included charges that the 2005 New Century audit was improperly staffed and that the independence of certain KPMG auditors may have been impaired. The examiner also maintained that KPMG failed to adequately consider serious internal control problems evident in New Century's accounting and financial reporting system and failed to properly audit the company's critically important loan repurchase loss reserve.

Staffing Issues on the New Century Engagement

In the spring of 2005, shortly after KPMG completed the 2004 audit of New Century, an almost entirely new team of auditors, approximately 15 KPMG employees in total, was assigned to that client. The only two members of the 2004 audit engagement team "held over" for the 2005 audit were two first-year associates. The two key members of the 2005 audit team, the audit engagement partner and the senior manager, had just joined the Los Angeles office of KPMG, the practice office responsible for servicing New Century.

John Donovan, the engagement partner for the 2005 New Century audit, had served for 17 years as an audit partner with Arthur Andersen prior to that firm being forced to disband in 2002. After Andersen's demise, Donovan became an audit partner with E&Y, which he left in early 2005 to take a similar position with KPMG.

New Century's audit committee was unhappy with KPMG's decision to appoint Donovan as the audit engagement partner for the 2005 audit. Members of the audit

---

8. Bajaj and Creswell, "A Lender Failed."

9. *Ibid.*

10. *Ibid.*

EXHIBIT 3

KPMG's 2005
Audit Report on
New Century's
Financial
Statements

New Century Financial Corporation and Subsidiaries

Report of Independent Registered Certified Public Accounting Firm

The Board of Directors

New Century Financial Corporation

We have audited the accompanying consolidated balance sheets of New Century Financial Corporation and subsidiaries as of December 31, 2005, and 2004, and the related consolidated statements of income, comprehensive income, changes in stockholders' equity, and cash flows for each of the years in the three-year period ended December 31, 2005. These consolidated financial statements are the responsibility of Company's Management. Our responsibility is to express an opinion on these consolidated financial statements based on our audits.

We conducted our audit in accordance with the standards of the Public Company Accounting Oversight Board (United States). Those standards require that we plan the audit to obtain reasonable assurance about whether the financial statements are free of material misstatement. An audit includes examining, on a test basis, evidence supporting the amounts and disclosures in the financial statements. An audit also includes assessing the accounting principles used and significant estimates made by management, as well as evaluating the overall financial statement presentation. We believe that our audits provide a reasonable basis for our opinion.

In our opinion, the consolidated financial statements referred to above present fairly, in all material respects, the financial position of New Century Financial Corporation and subsidiaries as of December 31, 2005 and 2004, and the results of their operations and their cash flows for each of the years in the three-year period ended December 31, 2005, in conformity with U.S. generally accepted accounting principles.

We have also audited, in accordance with the standards of the Public Company Accounting Oversight Board (United States), the effectiveness of the Company's internal control over financial reporting as of December 31, 2005, based on criteria established in Internal Control—Integrated Framework issued by the Committee of Sponsoring Organizations of the Treadway Commission (COSO), and our report dated March 15, 2006 expressed an unqualified opinion on management's assessment of, and the effective operation of, internal control over financial reporting.

KPMG LLP
Los Angeles, California
March 15, 2006

Source: New Century's 2005 10-K.

committee believed that Donovan's lack of experience with the mortgage industry made him a poor choice to supervise that audit and asked KPMG to appoint another partner to oversee the engagement. When KPMG refused, the audit committee considered dismissing KPMG and retaining a different audit firm. "Ultimately, the Audit Committee determined that a switch to a new accounting firm would be tremendously disruptive and would send a bad signal to its lenders."

Mark Kim accepted a position with KPMG in May 2005, shortly before being assigned to serve as the senior manager on the 2005 New Century audit engagement.

Kim had several years of prior experience as an auditor and had served for three years as the assistant controller of a small mortgage lending company.

During his tenure on the New Century audit team, Mark Kim complained to John Donovan that it was difficult to recruit a "good team" of auditors to work on the engagement. In an e-mail to Donovan, an exasperated Kim remarked, "We will never get a good team out here because of the reputation that the engagement has." Another e-mail sent by a New Century accountant to the company's controller, David Kenneally, seemed to corroborate Kim's opinion. This latter e-mail noted that KPMG had not assigned the "A team" to the New Century audit.

In fact, Kenneally, a former KPMG employee, was apparently the key reason that the New Century engagement had a negative reputation within KPMG's Los Angeles office. Evidence collected by the New Century bankruptcy examiner suggested that the company's accounting function was "weak" and was overseen by Kenneally who was "domineering" and "difficult, condescending, and quick-tempered." One KPMG subordinate on the New Century audit team testified that Kenneally often berated Donovan and Kim. In another e-mail sent by Kim to Donovan, the KPMG senior manager indicated that "Dave [Kenneally] seems to know the answers for everything and anything and the rest of the accounting department is on almost the same boat as the audit team is—little knowledge of what's going on. This intimidates everyone on the engagement team."

The tense relationship between the KPMG audit engagement team and New Century's management, particularly Kenneally, worsened as the 2005 audit neared completion. Two individuals with KPMG's FDR (Financial Derivatives Resource) Group were brought in to review New Century's accounting for certain hedges and other financial derivatives during the final phase of the audit. They requested various documents from New Century that were needed to complete their review of the aforementioned items. When New Century failed to provide that documentation, the two specialists refused to "sign off" on the company's relevant accounting decisions. This refusal prevented Donovan from releasing the opinion on New Century's financial statements that were to be included in the company's 2005 Form 10-K.

Hours before the SEC filing deadline for New Century's 2005 10-K, an angry Donovan e-mailed one of the FDR specialists. "I am very disappointed we are still discussing this. As far as I am concerned, we are done. The client thinks we are done. All we are going to do is p___ everybody off." Later that same day, a high-ranking KPMG partner in the firm's New York headquarters office told Donovan to release the unqualified opinion on New Century's 2005 financial statements. Donovan was instructed to release the opinion even though the two FDR specialists had not approved the company's accounting decisions for its financial derivatives.[11]

The following day, New Century's audit committee called a meeting with Donovan and Kim. In that meeting, members of the audit committee reportedly "yelled" and "screamed" at the two KPMG auditors. Later, Kenneally told the New Century bankruptcy examiner that he had been "furious" over the "near-disaster"—that is, the fact that New Century's filing of its 2005 10-K with the SEC had almost been delayed.

---

11. The FDR specialists were allowed to dissociate themselves from the decision to issue the audit opinion on New Century's 2005 financial statements in a "disagreement memorandum" included in the 2005 workpapers. The following month, New Century finally provided the documentation that had been requested by those specialists. A review of that documentation revealed that New Century had improperly accounted for certain of its derivatives, resulting in "a misstatement of several million dollars." However, KPMG ruled that those errors were immaterial, meaning that it was not necessary to restate the 2005 financial statements.

KPMG ruled them to be immaterial

Because of the incident, New Century's audit committee deferred the decision of whether to reappoint KPMG as the company's auditor for the 2006 fiscal year. Donovan later testified that he had been concerned that the audit committee would dismiss KPMG.

Over the following two months, Donovan assured New Century's audit committee that "a situation like this will never happen again." After receiving that assurance, the audit committee reappointed KPMG as New Century's audit firm.

The bankruptcy examiner speculated that the 2005 10-K incident impaired KPMG's independence during the remainder of the firm's tenure with New Century. "In particular, it is possible that Donovan and Kim were not as skeptical as they might otherwise have been with regard to critical assumptions [underlying New Century's accounting decisions]." The examiner went on to suggest that "Donovan and Kim may have looked for ways to add unique value in order to salvage KPMG's reputation, such as by providing proactive (though erroneous) advice in connection with the repurchase reserve calculation methodology."

In a subsequent interview with the *New York Times*, the bankruptcy examiner further questioned KPMG's independence when he maintained that the New Century auditors had been eager to please the company's management team. "They acquiesced overly to the client, which in the post-Enron era seems mind-boggling."[12] In another interview with the Reuters news agency, the examiner expressed a similar point of view. "In the post-Enron era, one of the lessons should have been that accountants need to be skeptical, strong, and independent. You didn't have any of those attributes here."[13]

Inadequate Consideration of Internal Control Problems

Section 404 of the Sarbanes–Oxley Act requires auditors of public companies to audit the effectiveness of their clients' internal controls over financial reporting.[14] In both 2004 and 2005, KPMG concluded that New Century maintained effective internal control over its financial reporting function.

During the 2004 internal control audit, the KPMG auditors identified five "significant deficiencies" in internal controls that they reported to New Century's audit committee. Since the KPMG auditors concluded that those deficiencies did not qualify as "material weaknesses," the audit firm was able to issue an unqualified opinion on New Century's internal controls for 2004. No significant deficiencies or material weaknesses in internal controls were identified by KPMG during the 2005 internal control audit.

New Century's bankruptcy examiner challenged KPMG's conclusion that the company's internal controls over financial reporting were effective during 2004 and 2005. The examiner pointed out that throughout its existence New Century did not have an "effective mechanism for tracking, processing and handling [loan] repurchase claims." This internal control weakness prevented the company from determining the magnitude of loan repurchase requests at any point in time, which, in turn, prevented the company from properly considering those requests in arriving at the period-ending balances of the loan repurchase loss reserve.

---

12. Bajaj, "Report Assails Auditor."

13. A. Beck, "KPMG Allowed Fraud at New Century, Report Says," *Reuters.com*, 27 March 2008.

14. KPMG's 2004 and 2005 audits of New Century were completed while PCAOB *Auditing Standard No. 2*, "An Audit of Internal Control Over Financial Reporting Performed in Conjunction with an Audit of Financial Statements" was in effect. That standard was subsequently replaced by PCAOB *Auditing Standard No. 5*, "An Audit of Internal Control Over Financial Reporting That Is Integrated with an Audit of Financial Statements." The two standards are very similar.

A related internal control weakness was New Century's failure to adopt "formal policies and procedures" for calculating the loan repurchase loss reserve at the end of each accounting period. The lower-level accountants who were assigned the task of computing the reserve balance each reporting period testified that they simply followed the instructions passed down to them by the individual who had previously been responsible for the reserve computation.

During both the 2004 and 2005 audits, the KPMG auditors discovered the internal control weaknesses related to New Century's loan repurchase loss reserve. The bankruptcy examiner noted that those control weaknesses had particularly critical implications for New Century in 2005 when the volume of loan repurchase requests was increasing rapidly. Despite those implications, KPMG characterized those weaknesses as "inconsequential" during the 2005 audit. Since the internal control problems were not deemed significant deficiencies or material weaknesses, KPMG did not communicate them to New Century's audit committee.

The bankruptcy examiner insisted that for at least the 2005 audit, the inadequate accounting procedures for loan repurchase requests qualified as a material weakness in internal control that should have caused KPMG to issue an adverse opinion on New Century's internal controls. In fact, New Century's management reached a similar conclusion in early 2007.

> The material weaknesses identified [by New Century's management in early 2007] were: (1) the failure to maintain effective controls over the interpretation and application of the accounting literature relating to the Company's critical accounting policies (specifically as to the calculation of repurchase reserves); and (2) the failure to maintain effective controls to provide reasonable assurances that the Company collected, analyzed, and used information relating to outstanding purchase claims when establishing the allowance for repurchase losses.

[handwritten margin note: NCF did not have adequate controls]

Debbie Biddle was the KPMG audit senior principally responsible for the 2005 internal control audit. Similar to John Donovan and Mark Kim, Biddle had joined KPMG's Los Angeles office shortly before the 2005 New Century audit began. Biddle had transferred to the Los Angeles office from a KPMG affiliate in the United Kingdom. Prior to being assigned responsibility for the 2005 New Century internal control audit, Biddle had "virtually no experience auditing U.S. clients and no prior SOX experience."

The bankruptcy examiner reported that Biddle and her colleagues failed to thoroughly review the 2004 audit workpapers for New Century. As a result, they may have been unaware of the internal control problems discovered by KPMG auditors the prior year and thus failed to properly consider those problems in planning and carrying out the 2005 audit.

[handwritten margin note: Biddle had no SOX experience]

> The Examiner found no evidence that the KPMG [2005] engagement team engaged in a formal process to compare year over year deficiency findings in connection with the 2005 SOX 404 audit. Conducting this analysis would have been prudent given the wholesale turnover in the KPMG engagement team. This failure is significant, as it impacted the planning for the 404 audit in 2005, the evaluation of findings in 2005, and the planning for the year-end audits.

Failure to Properly Audit New Century's Loan Repurchase Loss Reserve

In early 2005, the quality of New Century's loan portfolio, as measured by such objective criteria as delinquency and default rates, began declining rapidly. Internal data collected by New Century revealed that the delinquency rate on loans originated during 2005 was approximately double that of loans originated during the previous year. The delinquency rate continued to rise throughout 2006 as conditions within the housing market deteriorated.

The increasing delinquency and default rates on loans originated by New Century caused a large increase in the number of loan repurchase claims filed by investors that had purchased large blocks of those loans. Because of the inadequate accounting procedures and internal controls for loan repurchase claims, New Century's accounting staff failed to record the needed increases in the loan repurchase loss reserve throughout 2005 and beyond. For example, despite the large increase in loan repurchase requests in 2005, New Century's loan repurchase loss reserve actually declined from the end of 2004 to the end of 2005.

New Century's bankruptcy examiner estimated that the understatement of the loan repurchase loss reserve and errors in related accounts inflated New Century's reported pretax earnings for fiscal 2005 by 14.3 percent or approximately $64 million. The examiner determined that errors in those same accounts overstated New Century's reported pretax earnings for the first three quarters of 2006 by approximately $200 million or 59 percent.

New Century's accountants used a 90-day "look-back" period in determining the adequacy of the loan repurchase loss reserve each financial reporting period. That is, only repurchase requests for loans sold in the 90 days immediately preceding the balance sheet date were considered in arriving at the reserve balance. In fact, the company often received repurchase requests for loans sold more than three months earlier.

The bankruptcy examiner criticized KPMG for not insisting that New Century use a longer than 90-day "window" in computing the loan repurchase loss reserve. In fact, a KPMG workpaper suggested that policy was reasonable. "Based on the review of the Company's repurchase log and discussions with management, it appears reasonable that the most recent three months sales are at risk for repurchase." The bankruptcy examiner contested the assertion that KPMG had reviewed the log of loan repurchase requests since that accounting record indicated that loans were being reacquired by New Century as long as three years after the date they were sold. The examiner also uncovered evidence suggesting that a New Century executive had informed a KPMG auditor that a significant number of loans older than 90 days were being repurchased by the company.

KPMG's audit workpapers documented the ominous increase in loan repurchase requests received by New Century beginning in late 2004. In 2005, New Century repurchased $332 million of loans, compared with $135 million the prior year. Despite this large increase, the bankruptcy examiner reported that KPMG "failed to perform any increased procedures or testing of New Century's repurchase reserves" during the 2005 audit.

A secondary factor that contributed to the understatement of New Century's loan repurchase loss reserve was the company's failure to consider an "interest recapture" element in computing that reserve each reporting period. The bankruptcy examiner found this obvious oversight by the company's accountants "perplexing."

> The failure to include Interest Recapture in the repurchase reserve calculation from the outset is perplexing because the Examiner understands that it was a longtime requirement under loan repurchase agreements for New Century to pay investors the amount of interest that the borrower had failed to pay.

A workpaper memorandum that summarized the audit tests KPMG applied during the 2005 audit to the loan repurchase loss reserve indicated that interest recapture was a component of the reserve.

A KPMG workpaper from January 2006 notes that estimated losses on future repur-chases "include accrued interest the investor [loan purchaser] would have collected from the borrower, if the loan had performed, that New Century must pay to the inves-tor at the time of repurchase."

The evidence that KPMG relied on to reach that erroneous conclusion was a state-ment made by David Kenneally. The bankruptcy examiner criticized the KPMG auditors for not corroborating Kenneally's assertion with other audit evidence. "If KPMG had performed adequate tests and calculations, it would have determined that Interest Recapture was omitted from the repurchase reserve calculation."

During early 2006, New Century changed the method used to compute the period-ending balance of the loan repurchase loss reserve.[15] This change resulted in large increases in the understatements of that account at the end of each subsequent quar-terly reporting period—by the third quarter of 2006, the reserve was understated by approximately 1000 percent.

Kenneally testified that the change in accounting for the reserve account was rec-ommended by Mark Kim, the KPMG senior audit manager. Kim would later testify that he did not explicitly remember making that recommendation. Nevertheless, evidence collected by the bankruptcy examiner caused him to conclude that a KPMG auditor "almost certainly" recommended the change in accounting for the reserve account.

At a time when KPMG was aware, as evidenced by its own workpapers, that market conditions were worsening and repurchases were increasing, KPMG made a recom-mendation to New Century to remove a component of the repurchase reserve that had the effect of decreasing the reserve …and then failed to inform the Audit Committee of the change in this critical accounting policy.

In November 2006, New Century hired a new chief financial officer (CFO) who had 30 years of prior experience in the mortgage industry. The CFO immediately questioned the adequacy of the company's loan repurchase loss reserve and asked KPMG to provide him with a written statement that the reserve was properly stated. KPMG refused to provide that written assurance.

As a result of the new CFO's persistent inquiries, New Century's accounting staff eventually recognized that the accounting change made in early 2006 for the loan repurchase loss reserve had been improper and had materially understated the reserve for each of the first three quarterly reporting periods of 2006. That realization led to the 7 February 2007, 8-K filing in which New Century reported those under-statements. That 8-K disclosure triggered the series of events that resulted in New Century filing for bankruptcy less than two months later.

In Defense of KPMG

Representatives of KPMG responded forcefully to the allegations against their firm in the report prepared by New Century's bankruptcy examiner. Particularly galling to the large accounting firm was the suggestion that KPMG auditors had "deferred excessively"[16] to client executives during the course of the New Century

---

15. The change in the method of computing the loss reserve involved deleting the "inventory severity" component of that reserve. That component involved those losses expected to be incurred by New Century on loans that had already been reacquired as of the given balance sheet date. Kim allegedly suggested dropping this component because he believed that it was considered by New Century in arriving at the balance of a related valuation account for the company's portfolio of outstanding loans. In fact, that was not the case.

16. Bajaj, "Report Assails Auditor."

engagements. In response to that allegation, a KPMG spokesperson told a reporter with the *New York Times*, "There is absolutely no evidence to support that contention."[17] In a subsequent interview with the *Times*, that same individual suggested that the bankruptcy examiner's report was unfair and "one-sided."

> *The examiner was appointed by the court to identify potential lawsuits in a bankruptcy case. Consistent with that charge, he has prepared an advocacy piece, which has many one-sided statements and significant omissions. In the end, the examiner concluded that the bankruptcy estate may be able to file a lawsuit against KPMG for negligence—a claim we strongly dispute—and a claim even the examiner notes in his report for which KPMG has strong defenses.[18]*

Several other parties also came to KPMG's defense. An accounting professor at the University of Chicago maintained that KPMG was not at fault in the New Century case and instead attributed the company's bankruptcy to its high-risk business model. "The business model of New Century depended on real estate values that would continue to go up and certainly not go down. The economic model here is what is at fault. It's the cause of what happened, not anything that KPMG did."[19]

At a minimum, the New Century bankruptcy report served to sustain a string of embarrassing public relations incidents for KPMG. In 2005, KPMG had faced potential criminal charges for a series of questionable tax shelters that it had marketed to well-heeled tax clients. In that same year, KPMG had agreed to pay the SEC $22.5 million to settle charges that audits of one of its largest clients, Xerox, were flawed. Subsequent to that announcement, KPMG paid $80 million to settle civil litigation stemming from its Xerox audits.

Even before the New Century bankruptcy report was released, KPMG had been linked to the ongoing crises and scandals in the mortgage industry. Charges of large-scale earnings manipulation by Fannie Mae called into the question the quality of KPMG's audits of that organization, which for decades had played such a large role in the mortgage industry. Finally, in early January 2008, KPMG was named a codefendant in a large class-action lawsuit that charged Countrywide, another KPMG audit client, with perpetrating an accounting fraud.

EPILOGUE

In August 2008, Ed McMahon revealed that he had finally found a buyer for his Beverly Hills mansion that would allow him to pay off his large mortgage.[20] Most individuals snared by the financial crisis that overwhelmed the mortgage industry and housing market in the United States did not share McMahon's good fortune. By the end of 2008, more than 1.5 million Americans would face foreclosure proceedings on their homes, easily the largest number of residential foreclosures in U.S. history.

In an effort to thwart the nationwide financial panic caused by the meltdowns in the mortgage and housing industries, the U.S. Congress passed a massive bailout plan in October 2008. The price tag for that plan was measured in hundreds of billions of dollars. Despite that massive effort to shore up the nation's crumbling financial infrastructure, most experts expected that the U.S. economy, as well as the global economy, would suffer adverse lingering effects for years, if not decades, to come.

---

17. *Ibid.*

18. Bajaj and Creswell, "A Lender Failed."

19. *Ibid.*

20. Mr. McMahon passed away in June 2009.

New Century's collapse resulted in numerous criminal investigations by regulatory and law enforcement authorities as well as a barrage of civil litigation. In July 2010, the SEC announced that it had reached a settlement to resolve fraud charges that it had filed against three former New Century officers including Brad Morrice and David Kenneally. In addition to monetary sanctions of approximately $750,000 for Morrice and $160,000 for Kenneally each was barred from serving as an officer of a public company for five years. Among the civil lawsuits decided to date, KPMG reportedly agreed to contribute $45 million to a settlement pool in late 2010 to resolve a class-action lawsuit filed by New Century's former stockholders.

Questions

1. KPMG served as the independent audit firm of several of the largest subprime mortgage lenders. Identify the advantages and disadvantages of a heavy concentration of audit clients in one industry or subindustry.

2. As noted in the case, there was an almost complete turnover of the staff assigned to the New Century audit engagement team from 2004 to 2005. What quality control mechanisms should accounting firms have in such circumstances to ensure that a high-quality audit is performed?

3. Section 404 of the Sarbanes–Oxley Act requires auditors of a public company to analyze and report on the effectiveness of the client's internal controls over financial reporting. Describe the responsibilities that auditors of public companies have to discover and report (a) *significant deficiencies* in internal controls and (b) *material weaknesses* in internal controls. Include a definition of each item in your answer. Under what condition or conditions can auditors issue an unqualified or clean opinion on the effectiveness of a client's internal controls over financial reporting?

4. One of New Century's most important accounts was its loan repurchase loss reserve. Each accounting period, New Century was required to estimate the ending balance of that account. What general principles or procedures should auditors follow when auditing important "accounting estimates"?

5. New Century's bankruptcy examiner charged that KPMG did not comply with applicable "professional standards" while auditing the company. List specific auditing standards or principles that you believe KPMG may have violated on its New Century engagements. Briefly defend each item you list.

6. Mortgage-backed securities (MBS) produced by New Century and other major subprime lenders were a focal point of attention during the recent financial crisis. Many parties maintain that the mark-to-market rule for investments in securities such as MBS contributed significantly to that crisis and that the rule should be modified, suspended, or even eliminated. Briefly summarize the principal arguments of those parties opposed to the mark-to-market rule. Do you believe that those arguments are legitimate? Why or why not?

7. Identify what you consider to be the three most important "take-aways" or learning points in this case. Rank these items in order of importance (highest to lowest). Justify or defend each of your choices.

Madoff Securities

Bernie wanted to be rich; he dedicated his life to it.

John Maccabee, longtime friend of Bernie Madoff

Bernard Lawrence Madoff was born on 29 April 1938, in New York City. Madoff spent his childhood in a lower middle-class neighborhood in the borough of Queens. After graduating from high school, Madoff enrolled in the University of Alabama but transferred to Hofstra College on Long Island, now known as Hofstra University, at the beginning of his sophomore year. Three years later in 1960, he graduated with a political science degree from Hofstra.

According to a longtime friend, the driving force in Madoff's life since childhood was becoming wealthy. "Bernie wanted to be rich; he dedicated his life to it."[1] That compelling force no doubt accounted for Madoff's lifelong fascination with the stock market. As a teenager, Madoff frequently visited Wall Street and dreamed of becoming a "major player" in the world of high finance. Because he did not have the educational training or personal connections to land a prime job on Wall Street after he graduated from college, Madoff decided that he would set up his own one-man brokerage firm.

While in college, Madoff had accumulated a $5,000 nest egg by installing sprinkler systems during the summer months for wealthy New Yorkers living in the city's affluent suburbs. In the summer of 1960, Madoff used those funds to establish Bernard L. Madoff Investment Securities LLC, which was typically referred to as Madoff Securities. Madoff operated the new business from office space that was provided to him by his father-in-law, who was a partner in a small accounting firm. For nearly five decades, Madoff served as the senior executive of Madoff Securities. During that time, the shy New Yorker who had an occasional stammer and several nervous tics would accumulate a fortune estimated at more than one billion dollars.

Taking on Wall Street

Madoff's brokerage firm initially traded only securities of small over-the-counter companies, securities commonly referred to as "penny stocks." At the time, the securities of most large companies were traded on the New York Stock Exchange (NYSE). The rules of that exchange made it extremely difficult for small brokerage firms such as Madoff's to compete with the cartel of large brokerage firms that effectively controlled Wall Street. Madoff and many other small brokers insisted that the NYSE's rules were anticompetitive and inconsistent with a free market economy. Madoff was also convinced that the major brokerage firms kept securities transaction costs artificially high to produce windfall profits for themselves to the detriment of investors, particularly small investors.

Because of Madoff's resentment of the major Wall Street brokerage firms, he made it his mission to "democratize" the securities markets in the United States while at the same time reducing the transaction costs of trading securities. "Bernie was the king of democratization. He was messianic about this. He pushed to automate the [securities trading] system, listing buyers and sellers on a computer that anyone could access."[2]

---

1. J. Maccabee, "Mom and Dad and Ruth and Bernie," *New York Magazine* (nymag.com), 22 February 2009.
2. S. Fishman, "The Monster Mensch," *New York Magazine* (nymag.com), 22 February 2009.

In fact, Madoff Securities was one of the first brokerage firms to utilize computers to expedite the processing of securities transactions. Bernie Madoff is also credited as one of the founders of the NASDAQ stock exchange that was organized in 1971. The NASDAQ was destined to become the world's largest electronic stock exchange and the largest global stock exchange in terms of trading volume. In the late 1980s and early 1990s, Madoff served three one-year terms as the chairman of the NASDAQ.

Madoff's leadership role in the development of electronic securities trading contributed significantly to his firm's impressive growth throughout the latter decades of the twentieth century. By the early years of the twenty-first century, Madoff Securities was the largest "market maker" on the NASDAQ, meaning that the firm accounted for more daily transaction volume on that exchange than any other brokerage.[3] By that time, the firm was also among the largest market makers for the New York Stock Exchange, accounting for as much as 5 percent of its daily transaction volume. This market-making service was lucrative with low risk for Madoff Securities and reportedly earned the firm, which was privately owned throughout its existence, annual profits measured in the tens of millions of dollars.

In 1962, Madoff had expanded his firm to include investment advisory services. For several years, most of the individuals who set up investment accounts with Madoff Securities were referred to him by his father-in-law. Although the firm was a pioneer in electronic trading and made sizable profits from its brokerage operations, investment advisory services would prove to be its most important line of business. By late 2008, the total value of customer accounts managed by Madoff Securities reached $65 billion.

The key factor that accounted for the incredible growth in the amount of money entrusted to Madoff's firm by investors worldwide was the impressive rates of return that the firm earned annually on the funds that it managed. For decades, those funds earned an average annual rate of return generally ranging from 10 to 15 percent. Although impressive, those rates of return were not spectacular. What *was* spectacular was the consistency of the returns. In 2001, *Barron's* reported that some of the Madoff firm's largest investment funds had never experienced a losing year despite significant stock market declines in several individual years.[4] Even when the stock market collapsed in late 2008, individual Madoff funds continued to report net gains for the year-to-date period.

Although Madoff would eventually serve as an investment advisor to dozens of celebrities, professional athletes, and other wealthy individuals, most of the money he managed came from so-called "feeder firms," which were large hedge funds, banks, and other investment companies. The individuals who had committed their funds to these feeder firms were typically unaware that those funds had been turned over to Madoff.

The reclusive Madoff and his subordinates disclosed as little as possible about the investment strategy responsible for their firm's success in the stock market. On one occasion, Madoff told an executive of a feeder firm, "It's no one's business what goes on here."[5] The *Wall Street Journal* reported that Madoff commonly "brushed

---

3. *Investopedia,* an online encyclopedia of business terms, provides the following description of a "market maker": "Broker-dealer firm that accepts the risk of holding a certain number of shares of a particular security in order to facilitate trading in that security. Each market maker competes for customer order flow by displaying buy and sell quotations for a guaranteed number of shares. Once an order is received, the market maker immediately sells from its own inventory or seeks an offsetting order."

4. *Barron's* (online), "What We Wrote About Madoff," 12 December 2008.

5. *Ibid.*

off" skeptics who questioned his firm's investment results by pointing out that those results had been audited and by insisting that his investment strategy "was too complicated for outsiders to understand."[6]

The only substantive information Madoff Securities provided regarding its investment policies was that it employed a "split-strike conversion" investment model. In simple terms, this strategy involved purchasing several dozen blue-chip stocks and then simultaneously selling both put options and call options on those securities. Supposedly, this strategy ensured a positive rate of return on those investments whether the stock market went up or went down.

Competitors, financial analysts, and academics repeatedly attempted to replicate the success of Madoff Securities' investment strategy. None of those attempts were successful, which only added to Bernie Madoff's stature and mystique on Wall Street. As one industry insider noted in 2001, "Even knowledgeable people can't really tell you what he's doing."[7] A CNN reporter observed that by the turn of the century Madoff was widely regarded as a stock market wizard and that "everyone" on Wall Street, including his closest competitors, was "in awe of him."[8]

The Bubble Bursts

On 10 December 2008, Bernie Madoff asked his two sons, Andrew and Mark, who worked at Madoff Securities, to meet him at his apartment that evening. In this meeting, Madoff told his sons that the impressive returns earned for clients of his firm's investment advisory division over the previous several decades had been fraudulent. Those returns had been produced by an elaborate Ponzi scheme engineered and overseen by Madoff without the knowledge of any of his employees or family members.[9] The following day, an attorney representing Madoff's sons notified the SEC of their father's confession. That evening, FBI agents came to Madoff's apartment. One of the agents asked Madoff "if there was an innocent explanation"[10] for the information relayed to the SEC from his sons. Madoff replied, "There is no innocent explanation."[11] The agents then placed Madoff under arrest and within hours filed securities fraud charges against him.

The public announcement of Madoff's fraudulent scheme in December 2008 stunned investors worldwide. That announcement further undercut the stability of global stock markets that were already reeling from the subprime mortgage crisis in the United States, which had "frozen" the world's credit markets, caused stock prices to drop precipitously, and threatened to plunge the global economy into a deep depression. Politicians, journalists, and everyday citizens were shocked to learn that a massive investment fraud, apparently the largest in history, could go undetected for decades within the capital markets of the world's largest economic power. Even more disconcerting was the fact that the Madoff fraud went undetected for several

---

6. G. Zuckerman, "Fees, Even Returns and Auditor All Raised Flags," *Wall Street Journal* (online), 13 December 2008.

7. *Ibid.*

8. A. Chernoff, "What Drove Bernie Madoff," *CNNMoney.com*, 5 January 2009.

9. *Investopedia* provides the following description of a "Ponzi scheme": "A fraudulent investing scam promising high rates of return with little risk to investors. The Ponzi scheme generates returns for older investors by acquiring new investors. This scam actually yields the promised returns to earlier investors, as long as there are more new investors. These schemes usually collapse on themselves when the new investments stop."

10. Fishman, "The Monster Mensch."

11. *Ibid.*

years after the implementation of the far-reaching regulatory reforms mandated by the U.S. Congress in the wake of the Enron and WorldCom debacles.

News of the Madoff fraud caused a wide range of parties to angrily demand that the federal government and law enforcement authorities determine why the nation's "watchdog" system for the capital markets had failed once again. The accounting profession was among the first targets of the public's anger. On the day that Madoff's fraud was publicly reported, Floyd Norris, a *New York Times* reporter acquainted with Madoff, asked a simple question that was on the minds of many people, namely, "Who were the auditors?"[12]

"Rubber-Stamped" Financial Statements

Business journalists quickly determined that the auditor of Madoff Securities was Friehling & Horowitz, an accounting firm located in the small New York City suburb of New City. Friehling & Horowitz had issued unqualified opinions on the financial statements of Madoff Securities since at least the early 1990s, audits for which the small firm was paid as much as $200,000.

Further investigation revealed that Friehling & Horowitz had only one active accountant, one nonprofessional employee (a secretary), and operated from a tiny office occupying approximately two hundred square feet. The active accountant was David Friehling who had performed the annual audits of Madoff's firm and signed off on the firm's unqualified audit opinions. Accounting and auditing experts interviewed by the Associated Press insisted that it was "preposterous" to conceive that any one individual could complete an audit of a company the size of Madoff Securities by himself.[13]

Friehling and his firm were members of the American Institute of Certified Public Accountants (AICPA). A spokesperson for that organization revealed that Friehling had reported to the AICPA each year that he did not perform any audits. As a result, Friehling's firm was not required to submit to the AICPA's peer review program for CPA firms. Friehling's firm was also not required to have a periodic peer review at the state level. At the time, New York was one of six states that did not have a mandatory peer review program for accounting firms.

In March 2009, the *New York Times* reported that Friehling had maintained dozens of investment accounts with Madoff Securities, according to documents obtained by the court-appointed trustee for that firm. Those same documents indicated that Friehling & Horowitz had another 17 investment accounts with Madoff's firm. In total, Friehling, his accounting firm, and his family members had nearly $15 million invested in funds managed by Madoff. Federal prosecutors noted that these investments had "flouted" the accounting profession's auditor independence rules and "disqualified" Friehling from serving as the auditor of Madoff Securities.[14]

David Friehling would be the second person arrested by federal law enforcement authorities investigating Madoff's fraud. Among other charges, federal prosecutors indicted Friehling for securities fraud, aiding and abetting an investment fraud, and obstructing the IRS. The prosecutors did not allege that Friehling was aware of Madoff's fraudulent scheme but rather that he had conducted "sham audits" of

---

12. F. Norris, "Bernie Madoff," *New York Times* (online), 12 December 2008.

13. *Associated Press* (online), "Questions Surround Madoff Auditor," 17 December 2008.

14. New York State Society of Certified Public Accountants, "Madoff Auditor Charged for Role in Massive Fraud," 19 March 2009 (www.nysscpa.org/ezine/ETPArticles/ML31909a.htm).

Madoff Securities that "helped foster the illusion that Mr. Madoff legitimately invested his clients' money."[15]

News reports of Friehling's alleged sham audits caused him to be berated in the business press. A top FBI official observed that Friehling's "job was not to merely rubber-stamp statements that he didn't verify" and that Friehling had betrayed his "fiduciary duty to investors and his legal obligation to regulators."[16] An SEC official maintained that Friehling had "essentially sold his [CPA] license for more than 17 years while Madoff's Ponzi scheme went undetected."[17] Many parties found this and other denigrating remarks made by SEC officials concerning Friehling ironic since the federal agency was itself the target of scornful criticism for its role in the Madoff fiasco.

Sir Galahad and the SEC

On at least eight occasions, the SEC investigated alleged violations of securities laws by Madoff Securities during the two decades prior to Bernie Madoff's startling confession. In each case, however, the investigation concluded without the SEC charging Madoff with any serious infractions of those laws. Most of these investigations resulted from a series of complaints filed with the SEC by one individual, Harry Markopolos.

On the 1 March 2009, edition of the CBS news program *60 Minutes*, investigative reporter Steve Croft observed that until a few months earlier Harry Markopolos had been an "obscure financial analyst and mildly eccentric fraud investigator from Boston." Beginning in 1999, Markopolos had repeatedly told the SEC that Bernie Madoff was operating what he referred to as the "world's largest Ponzi scheme." Between May 2000 and April 2008, Markopolos mailed or hand delivered documents and other evidence to the SEC that purportedly proved that assertion. Although SEC officials politely listened to Markopolos's accusations, they failed to vigorously investigate them.

One lengthy report that Markopolos sent to the SEC in 2005 identified 29 specific "red flags" suggesting that Madoff was perpetrating a massive fraud on his clients. Among these red flags was Madoff's alleged refusal to allow the Big Four auditor of an investment syndicate to review his financial records. Another red flag was the fact that Madoff Securities was audited by a one-man accounting firm, namely, Friehling & Horowitz. Also suspicious was the fact that Madoff, despite his firm's leadership role in electronic securities trading, refused to provide his clients with online access to their accounts, providing them instead with monthly account statements by mail.

Among the most credible and impressive evidence Markopolos gave to the SEC were mathematical analyses and simulations allegedly proving that Madoff's split-strike conversion investment strategy could not consistently produce the investment results that his firm reported. Markopolos noted that if such an investment strategy existed, it would be the "Holy Grail" of investing and eventually be replicated by other Wall Street investment advisors. Even if Madoff had discovered this "Holy Grail" of investing, Markopolos demonstrated there was not sufficient transaction volume in the options market to account for the huge number

15. L. Neumeister, "Federal Appeals Court to Hear Madoff Jail Argument," *Associated Press* (online), 19 March 2009.

16. W. K. Rashbaum and D. B. Henriques, "Accountant for Madoff Is Arrested and Charged with Securities Fraud," *New York Times* (online), 18 March 2009.

17. *Ibid.*

of options that his investment model would have required him to buy and sell for his customers' accounts.

In the months following the public disclosure of Madoff's fraud, Harry Markopolos reached cult hero status within the business press. Markopolos was repeatedly asked to comment on and explain the scope and nature of Madoff's scheme. Markopolos's dissection of Madoff's fraud suggested that three key factors accounted for it continuing unchecked for decades. First, Madoff targeted investors who were unlikely to question his investment strategy. According to Markopolos, a large number of "smart" investors had refused to invest with Madoff despite his sterling record. "Smart investors would stick to their investment discipline and walk away, refusing to invest in a black-box strategy they did not understand. Greedy investors would fall over themselves to hand Madoff money."[18]

The second factor that allowed Madoff's fraud to continue for decades was his impeccable credentials. Even if his impressive investment results were ignored, Madoff easily qualified as a Wall Street icon. He was a pioneer of electronic securities trading and throughout his career held numerous leadership positions within the securities industry, including his three stints as NASDAQ chairman. Madoff's stature on Wall Street was also enhanced by his well-publicized philanthropy. He regularly contributed large sums to several charities.

The final and most important factor that allowed Madoff to sustain his fraudulent scheme was the failure of the regulatory oversight function for the stock market. In testimony before Congress and media interviews, Harry Markopolos insisted that the Madoff debacle could have been avoided or at least mitigated significantly if federal regulators, particularly the SEC, had been more diligent in fulfilling their responsibilities. According to Markopolos, Madoff knew that the SEC's accountants, attorneys, and stock market specialists were "incapable of understanding a derivatives-based Ponzi scheme"[19] such as the one he masterminded. That knowledge apparently emboldened Madoff and encouraged him to continually expand the scope of his fraud.

Even after Markopolos explained the nature of Madoff's fraud to SEC officials, they apparently did not understand it. "I gift wrapped and delivered the largest Ponzi scheme in history to them ... [but the SEC] did not understand the 29 red flags that I handed them."[20] The outspoken SEC critic went on to predict that "If the SEC does not improve soon, they risk being merged out of existence in the upcoming rewrite of the nation's regulatory scheme."[21]

Markopolos's pointed criticism of the SEC and additional harsh criticism by several other parties forced the agency's top officials to respond. An embarrassed SEC Chairman Christopher Cox admitted that he was "gravely concerned"[22] by the SEC's failure to uncover the fraud.

> In an extraordinary admission that the SEC was aware of numerous red flags raised about Bernard L. Madoff Investment Securities LLC, but failed to take them seriously enough, SEC Chairman Christopher Cox ordered a review of the agency's oversight of the New York securities-trading and investment-management firm.[23]

18. D. Carozza, "Chasing Madoff," *Fraud Magazine*, May/June 2009, 39.

19. *Ibid*, 57.

20. J. Chung and B. Masters, "SEC 'Illiteracy' to Blame for Madoff Affair," *Financial Times* (online), 4 February 2009.

21. Carozza, "Chasing Madoff," 58.

22. A. Lucchetti, K. Scannell, and A. Efrati, "SEC to Probe Its Ties to Madoffs," *Wall Street Journal* (online), 17 December 2008.

23. *Ibid*.

EPILOGUE

On March 12, 2009, Bernie Madoff appeared before Judge Denny Chin in a federal courthouse in New York City. After Judge Chin read the 11 counts of fraud, money laundering, perjury and theft pending against Madoff, he asked the well-dressed defendant how he pled. "Guilty," was Madoff's barely audible one-word reply. Judge Chin then told Madoff to explain what he had done. "Your Honor, for many years up until my arrest on December 11, 2008, I operated a Ponzi scheme through the investment advisory side of my business."[24] Madoff then added, "I knew what I did was wrong, indeed criminal. When I began the Ponzi scheme, I believed it would end shortly and I would be able to extricate myself and my clients …[but] as the years went by I realized this day, and my arrest, would inevitably come."[25]

Despite allegations that his two sons, his brother, and his wife were at least knowledgeable of his fraud and possibly complicit in it, Madoff refused to implicate any of them or any of his other subordinates. Madoff claimed that he alone had been responsible for the fraud and that the brokerage arm of his business, which had been overseen by his brother and his two sons, had not been affected by his Ponzi scheme. On 29 June 2009, Madoff appeared once more in federal court. After reprimanding Madoff for his actions, Judge Chin sentenced him to 150 years in federal prison, meaning that the 71-year-old felon would spend the rest of his life incarcerated.[26]

David Friehling, Madoff's longtime auditor, pleaded guilty in November 2009 to the nine-count indictment filed against him by federal prosecutors. Through late 2013, Friehling's sentencing hearing had been delayed six times while he cooperated with the ongoing investigations of the Madoff fraud. In 2009, the AICPA announced that it had expelled Friehling for not cooperating with its investigation of his audits of Madoff Securities; one year earlier, Friehling had been stripped of his CPA license by the state of New York. The controversy over the failure of Friehling's firm to undergo any peer reviews persuaded the New York state legislature to pass a law in December 2008 requiring New York accounting firms that provide attest services to be peer reviewed every three years.[27, 28]

Although none of the Big Four accounting firms were directly linked to Madoff Securities, legal experts speculated that those firms would face civil lawsuits in the wake of Madoff's fraud. That potential liability stemmed from the Big Four's audits of the large "feeder firms" that entrusted billions of dollars to Madoff. Lynn Turner, a former chief accountant of the SEC, contended that the auditors of the feeder firms had a responsibility to check out Madoff's auditor. "If they didn't, then investors will have to hold the auditors [of the feeder firms] accountable."[29]

In February 2009, KPMG became the first of the Big Four firms to be named as a defendant in a civil lawsuit triggered by the Madoff

24. D. B. Henriques and J. Healy, "Madoff Goes to Jail After Guilty Plea," *New York Times* (online), 13 March 2009.

25. *Ibid.*

26. In August 2009, Frank DiPascali, Madoff Securities' former chief financial officer, pleaded guilty to complicity in Madoff's fraudulent scheme. During an appearance in federal court, DiPascali testified that, "It was all fake; it was all fictitious. It was wrong and I knew it at the time" (C. Bray and T. Lauricella, "'All Fake': Key Madoff Executive Admits Guilt," *Wall Street Journal* (online), 11 August 2009).

27. Ironically, the New York law exempts accounting firms that have fewer than three professional accountants, meaning that Friehling & Horowitz would not have been required to undergo a peer review if the law had been in place during the time span covered by Madoff's fraud.

28. In November 2012, David Friehling's 23-year-old son, Jeremy, a medical student at Ohio State University, committed suicide.

29. I. J. Dugan and D. Crawford, "Accounting Firms That Missed Fraud at Madoff May Be Liable," *Wall Street Journal* (online), 18 February 2009.

fraud. A California charity sued the prominent accounting firm to recover the millions of dollars it lost due to Madoff's scheme. KPMG had served as the independent auditor of a large hedge fund that had hired Madoff to invest the charity's funds. Among the critical risk factors allegedly overlooked by the KPMG auditors was the fact that Madoff's huge organization was serviced by a tiny accounting firm operating out of a strip mall in a New York City suburb.[30]

Over the following years, several other major international accounting firms would be named as defendants in civil lawsuits prompted by the Madoff fraud. Those firms included BDO Seidman, Ernst & Young, and PricewaterhouseCoopers.

In early 2009, President Obama appointed Mary Schapiro to replace Christopher Cox as the chairperson of the SEC. In the aftermath of the Madoff fraud, Schapiro reported that her agency would revamp its oversight policies and procedures for investment advisors having physical custody of customer assets. Among the proposals announced by Schapiro were annual "surprise audits" of such firms to ensure that customer funds were being properly safeguarded. Schapiro also recommended that those firms be required to have internal control audits by independent accounting firms to determine whether they have "the proper controls in place."[31] Finally, Schapiro pledged that the SEC would implement specific measures to ensure that credible whistleblowing allegations, such as those made by Harry Markopolos

regarding Madoff's firm, would be investigated on a thorough and timely basis.

Bernie Madoff's victims included a wide range of prominent organizations and individuals. The large asset management firm Fairfield Greenwich Advisors alone had more than one-half of its investment portfolio of $14 billion invested with Madoff. Other companies and organizations that had significant funds in the custody of Madoff Securities include the large Dutch bank Fortis Bank, the large British bank HSBC, the International Olympic Committee, Massachusetts Mutual Life Insurance Company, New York University, Oppenheimer Funds, and Yeshiva University.

One media outlet reported that the list of individuals who had investments with Madoff reads like a lineup from *Lifestyles of the Rich and Famous*, a popular television program of the 1980s. Those individuals include award-winning actors and actresses, Hollywood directors and screenwriters, media executives, journalists, professional athletes, a Nobel Prize winner, and high-profile politicians. Among these individuals are Kevin Bacon, Zsa Zsa Gabor, Jeffrey Katzenberg, Henry Kaufman, Larry King, Ed Koch, Sandy Koufax, Senator Frank Lautenberg, John Malkovich, Stephen Spielberg, Elie Wiesel, and Mort Zuckerman.[32]

By late 2013, Irving Picard, the court-appointed trustee charged with recovering the billions of dollars stolen or misused by Madoff, had filed more than 1,000 civil lawsuits against a wide range of defendants. To date, he has recouped nearly $10 billion of the losses suffered by Madoff's victims.

---

30. USLaw.com, "The Madoff Saga Continues as Pomerantz Files the First Derivative Suit Against an Auditor," 11 February 2009.

31. S. N. Lynch, "SEC to Consider Surprise Audits of Advisers," *Wall Street Journal* (online), 14 May 2009.

32. To date, several suicides have been attributed to Madoff's massive fraud. One of those victims was Mark Madoff. Bernie Madoff's oldest son took his life on 11 December 2010, two years to the date that his father admitted that he had masterminded a huge investment fraud.

Questions

1. Research recent developments involving this case. Summarize these developments in a bullet format.

2. Suppose that a large investment firm had approximately 10 percent of its total assets invested in funds managed by Madoff Securities. What audit procedures should the investment firm's independent auditors have applied to those assets?

3. Describe the nature and purpose of a "peer review." Would peer reviews of Friehling & Horowitz have likely resulted in the discovery of the Madoff fraud? Why or why not?

4. Professional auditing standards discuss the three key "conditions" that are typically present when a financial fraud occurs and identify a lengthy list of "fraud risk factors." Briefly explain the difference between a fraud "condition" and a "fraud risk factor" and provide examples of each. What fraud conditions and fraud risk factors were apparently present in the Madoff case?

5. In addition to the reforms mentioned in this case, recommend other financial reporting and auditing-related reforms that would likely be effective in preventing or detecting frauds similar to that perpetrated by Madoff.

CASE 1.13

AA Capital Partners, Inc.

A desire to be their "own bosses" and a burning entrepreneurial spirit compelled John Orecchio and Paul Oliver to leave the ranks of well-paid, white-collar employees and strike out on their own. In February 2002, the two friends established a new investment advisory firm, AA Capital Partners, Inc. (AA Capital), on historic LaSalle Street in downtown Chicago. The two men realized that the investment advisory field was extremely competitive but planned to rely on their large network of friends and business associates and their impressive credentials to get their firm off to a fast start. Orecchio was particularly well known in Chicago and was a much sought-after speaker on the banquet circuit within the Windy City's business community. For several years, he had managed a $5 billion private equity fund for Bank of America, the nation's second largest bank holding company. During the same time frame, Paul Oliver served as the chief financial officer (CFO) of ABN AMRO, a large Dutch bank that has a major presence in the United States.

Getting Started

Orecchio and Oliver agreed to be equal partners in AA Capital. Orecchio assumed the titles of president and secretary for the new firm, while Oliver took the titles of chairman and treasurer. Because of Orecchio's extensive experience in investment management, the two partners agreed that he would oversee the firm's day-to-day operations. Orecchio's key responsibilities would be recruiting clients and managing AA Capital's investments. Initially, Orecchio intended to focus his recruiting efforts on key officials of local labor unions. He hoped that he could quickly establish a customer base by convincing several of those individuals to entrust the management of their unions' pension funds to AA Capital.

Orecchio's plan was successful. By the end of 2004, he had persuaded six labor unions to transfer the assets in their pension funds to AA Capital. The collective value of those funds was approximately $200 million. Orecchio allocated the $200 million to four private equity funds organized under the corporate umbrella of AA Capital. The largest of these funds was the AA Capital Equity Fund, which was commonly referred to as the Equity Fund.

AA Capital's accounting function was the responsibility of one person, Mary Beth Stevens. Stevens, who was not a CPA but had several years of accounting experience, was eventually given the title of CFO and chief compliance officer, as well. In the latter role, Stevens had the responsibility for complying with the complicated maze of governmental rules and regulations imposed on AA Capital by various federal and state statutes, principal among them the Investment Advisers Act of 1940. Stevens also served as AA Capital's liaison to the company's independent auditors. The Investment Advisers Act requires investment advisory firms that manage more than $25 million of assets to register with the Securities and Exchange Commission (SEC) and file annual audited financial statements with that federal agency.

Earnest Auditors

The Chicago office of Ernst & Young audited AA Capital and its four private equity funds. In 2004, Gerard Oprins, an Ernst & Young partner since 1995, was asked to oversee the AA Capital audits. Oprins, who had just returned to Ernst & Young's Chicago office after spending nearly three years in the firm's Luxembourg office, was unfamiliar with AA Capital. Before agreeing to serve as the firm's audit engagement partner, Oprins spoke with several colleagues and business associates who were acquainted with AA Capital and its owners. Based upon his research, Oprins' determined that AA Capital would be a "legitimate, respectable client."[1]

Wendy McNeeley, an audit manager, served as Oprins' principal subordinate on the 2004 AA Capital engagement. Similar to Oprins, McNeeley was unfamiliar with AA Capital. To prepare for her assignment, McNeeley reviewed prior-year workpapers and gained an understanding of the "basic client structure, the nature of the entity, and its industry." The independent review or concurring partner for the AA Capital engagement was John Kavanaugh. The remaining members of the audit team consisted of two seniors and two staff accountants.

A subsequent report prepared by the SEC provided the following descriptions of the roles and responsibilities of Oprins, McNeeley, and Kavanaugh on the AA Capital engagement.

> Oprins was the engagement partner. His role was to set the tone for the audit, staff the audit team adequately, and focus on high-risk areas. His responsibility was to oversee the audit manager and sign the audit report. As engagement partner, Oprins used discretion in reviewing the detailed audit workpapers, but typically reviewed workpapers that involved planning and audit strategy, as well as the GAAP Disclosure Checklist[2].... [His principal] responsibility was to review and analyze significant auditing issues brought to his attention by McNeeley or the audit team.

> McNeeley was the audit manager. She was responsible for the day-to-day oversight of audit planning and execution of the audit strategy. She also supervised the audit staff and reviewed audit workpapers in significant risk areas.

> Kavanaugh provided quality control. This required him to read the financial statements, to understand the audit approach, and to ensure that the financial statements were stated in accordance with GAAP or any other basis of presentation used.

After an initial planning meeting of the audit engagement team, Oprins and McNeeley met with Orecchio and Stevens in AA Capital's downtown Chicago office in late April 2005. During this meeting, the four individuals discussed various accounting matters and the procedures that the firm had in place to prevent and detect fraud.

Next, McNeeley outlined the "planning and audit strategy" for the AA Capital engagement in a standard Ernst & Young audit document referred to as the Audit Strategies Memorandum (ASM). In this document, McNeeley noted that she and her subordinates would not "rely on AA Capital's internal controls." Instead, the audit team would perform "substantive testing on all account balances." McNeeley also oversaw the preparation of another standard Ernst & Young audit document for the AA Capital engagement, Internal Control and Fraud Considerations (ICFC). The purpose of this document is to identify "potential risks of material misstatement due to fraud."

---

1. Securities and Exchange Commission, *In the Matter of Gerard A.M. Oprins, CPA, and Wendy McNeeley, CPA, Initial Decision Release No. 411,* 28 December 2010. Unless indicated otherwise, the quotations in this case were taken from this source.

2. This document is used by Ernst & Young auditors to determine whether an audit client has properly applied generally accepted accounting principles (GAAP), including making all appropriate disclosures in its audited financial statements.

The team of auditors spent nearly 800 hours on the 2004 AA Capital engagement, 200 hours more than budgeted. At the conclusion of the engagement, Ernst & Young issued unqualified audit opinions on the financial statements of AA Capital, the Equity Fund, and the three smaller private equity funds established and controlled by AA Capital. According to the SEC, Ernst & Young's audit procedures focused primarily on three key items within the series of financial statements: investments, partners' capital, and management fees paid to AA Capital.

The only major problem that McNeeley and her four subordinates encountered during the audit fieldwork involved the partners' capital accounts with AA Capital. While testing a client-prepared schedule that detailed the activity in those accounts during 2004, the auditors identified four unusual cash transfers to Orecchio. Those transfers totaled $1.92 million and were described in the client-prepared schedule as "tax payments or tax distributions" to Orecchio. (In other documents and correspondence, these transactions were sometimes referred to as "tax advances," "tax loans," or "tax transfers.") In each case, the cash had been transferred from the Equity Fund to AA Capital and ultimately disbursed to John Orecchio. As a result of these transactions, the year-end accounting records of the Equity Fund included a $1.92 million receivable from AA Capital. Likewise, AA Capital's year-end accounting records included a $1.92 million receivable from John Orecchio and an offsetting $1.92 million payable to the Equity Fund.

A Taxing Problem

A staff accountant assigned to the AA Capital audit team questioned Mary Beth Stevens regarding the nature of the $1.92 million of cash transfers made to John Orecchio from the Equity Fund. The auditor noted on a workpaper that, "The $1,921,150 is essentially a loan made to John Orecchio." The loan to Orecchio had been necessary, allegedly, because the IRS had levied a $1.92 million tax assessment on Orecchio in error. Stevens told the auditor that the amount would either be repaid to AA Capital by the IRS or Orecchio.

After reviewing the information collected by her subordinate regarding the $1.92 million of cash payments made to Orecchio, McNeeley "initiated a series of e-mails with Stevens in which she attempted to solidify her understanding of the transfers." McNeeley initially thought that the $1.92 million in cash transfers involved payments made for disputed tax liabilities of AA Capital rather than John Orecchio, despite the workpaper notation made by her subordinate. "Contrary to McNeeley's assumption that the payments were for corporate taxes, Stevens replied that the tax accruals were, in fact, related to Orecchio and that 'John was dinged by the IRS and incurred multiple fees and tax payments.'" Stevens went on to explain to McNeeley that the IRS had mistakenly assessed Orecchio with the taxes and that the matter would not be resolved until after the 2004 audit was completed. After the series of e-mail exchanges with Stevens, McNeeley made the following notation in the Ernst & Young audit workpapers:

> Note: Per the last page of N2 [workpaper reference], the Equity Fund made approximately $1,921,304 of tax payments for John Orecchio during 2004. The Equity Fund has set up a receivable from AA Capital Partners for reimbursement of this amount. E&Y verified that AA Capital Partners has a reciprocal payable balance to Equity. E&Y also noted that AA Capital has an offsetting receivable balance from John Orecchio. Appears proper.

Despite the conclusion by McNeeley that the $1.92 million of cash payments to Orecchio appeared "proper," Stevens' explanations did not fully satisfy her. The audit manager subsequently asked the CFO to provide her with "any and all documentation that she had regarding the tax advances." Stevens never responded to that request.

McNeeley eventually decided that sufficient evidence had been collected for her to sign off on the $1.92 million of tax transfers to Orecchio that she recognized as being "quantitatively material." This evidence included the information in the client-prepared schedule that reported the amount and timing of each of the four cash transfers, the related entries in the client's accounting records for those transactions, and the 2004 management representations letters signed by Orecchio and Stevens in which they "represented to E&Y that the accounting records were complete and accurately reflected all of the company's transactions."

Years later, McNeeley testified that she had also reviewed the partnership agreement of AA Capital at the beginning of the 2004 audit and "understood" as a result of that review that it "permitted tax distributions and tax advances" to Orecchio and Oliver. She could not recall, however, whether she had specifically reviewed the partnership agreement "in connection with her analysis of the transfers." McNeeley also testified that she "did not recall any member of the audit team speaking with Orecchio or Oliver about the Transfers." An audit checklist item mandated that the audit team "gain an understanding of the business rationale" for significant transactions "outside the normal course of business" that may have been linked to an effort to conceal the "misappropriation of assets." For that checklist item, McNeeley made the following entry: "None noted."

Near the end of the 2004 audits of AA Capital and its private equity funds, McNeeley performed the mandatory "subsequent period" audit tests. These tests include reviewing significant events and transactions that occur following the date of the given client's year-end balance sheet but prior to the issuance of the audit report. McNeeley performed this subsequent period review for the time frame 1 January–31 March 2005. Ernst & Young's workpapers "indicated that disbursements during the period ... were reviewed for significant unusual items." McNeeley noted in the workpapers that "no unusual items" were found during the review of those disbursements despite the fact that an additional $482,000 of "tax distributions" were made to John Orecchio during the first three months of 2005.

Ernst & Young auditors prepare a Summary Review Memorandum (SRM) near the completion of an audit. The SEC described the SRM as a "document completed by the audit team near the end of the audit that summarizes key accounting and auditing matters that arose during the audit and the core team's ultimate conclusions regarding the audit and the opinion(s) to be issued." The SRM is reviewed at the conclusion of an audit by both the audit engagement partner and the independent review partner. Neither McNeeley nor her subordinates commented in the SRM on the tax payments made on behalf of John Orecchio during 2004 or the first three months of 2005.

The 2004 year-end audited balance sheet of the Equity Fund reported the $1.92 million of cash transfers made to John Orecchio, by way of AA Capital, on a line item entitled "Accounts Receivable from AA Capital Partners, Inc." According to the SEC, "There was no disclosure in the 'Notes to Financial Statements' regarding the fact that money from the Equity Fund ultimately went to Orecchio for a 'tax loan' or 'tax distribution.'" In AA Capital's 2004 balance sheet, the $1.92 million receivable from John Orecchio was embedded in a $2.3 million line item labeled "Accounts Receivable from Affiliates," while the $1.92 million payable to the Equity Fund was embedded in a $2.5 million line item labeled "Fees and Accounts Payable." AA Capital's financial statement footnotes included a "Related-party Note," but that note did not mention the $1.92 million of transactions involving Orecchio and the Equity Fund.

With one exception, the key members of the 2004 AA Capital engagement team returned to work on the 2005 engagement. Because Wendy McNeeley was on maternity leave, she was replaced on the 2005 audit team by another audit manager, Jennifer Aquino. The $1.92 million of tax distributions or loans made to John Orecchio during 2004 had not been repaid by the end of 2005. In fact, by the end of 2005, the amount owed to the Equity Fund by AA Capital on behalf of Orecchio had swelled to $5.7 million because Orecchio had received an additional $3.8 million in "tax loans" from the Equity Fund during 2005.

During the 2005 audit, Jennifer Aquino asked Mary Beth Stevens for "documentation supporting the [$5.7 million of] Transfers, but never received anything." Aquino noted that "other than the inquiry of Stevens and sending an e-mail to Orecchio, there were no other audit procedures to perform on the Transfers 'because the audit team didn't have anything to audit.'" The members of the AA Capital audit team held several "internal discussions" regarding the tax loans to Orecchio during the 2005 audit. During one of these meetings, "the audit team determined that it would not proceed with the 2005 audit until Orecchio paid back the 'tax loan' and they received sufficient documentation" to audit the transactions related to that loan. On 30 June 2006, Gerard Oprins informed Mary Beth Stevens and John Orecchio of that decision.

In early August 2006, the SEC launched an investigation of the financial affairs of AA Capital after receiving an anonymous tip that members of the firm were involved in "improprieties." Six weeks later, a federal judge appointed a receiver to take control of AA Capital. The latter decision prompted Ernst & Young to recall its audit opinions on the 2004 financial statements of AA Capital and its four private equity funds.

Oh, Orecchio!

In February 2010, John Orecchio pleaded guilty to embezzling approximately $24 million from AA Capital's Equity Fund. That amount included the $5.7 million that had been labeled as "tax loans." Instead of using the funds transferred to him from the Equity Fund for tax payments and other allegedly legitimate purposes, Orecchio had used the stolen money to finance a "high roller" lifestyle.

Law enforcement authorities revealed that Orecchio spent millions of dollars to establish and sustain a romantic relationship with a young exotic dancer that he met at a Detroit nightclub. Orecchio reportedly purchased $1.4 million of jewelry for his mistress, bought her a boat and several luxury automobiles, paid for $180,000 in renovations at the club where she worked so that the owner would promote her to a management position, and once rented a small Caribbean island to throw a party for her and her friends. In late 2005, Orecchio convinced his partner, Paul Oliver, that AA Capital should invest $8.7 million of their customers' funds in a real estate development project. In fact, Orecchio invested only $1.3 million of that amount in the real estate project and used the bulk of the other $7.4 million to renovate a Michigan horse farm that he had purchased to impress his girlfriend.

Las Vegas was a prime destination for Orecchio while he was embezzling from his clients' pension funds that were intended to finance the retirements of thousands of carpenters, millwrights, and other skilled tradesmen. Court records revealed that Orecchio spent more than $300,000 in Las Vegas nightclubs, including a one-night extravaganza costing $4,900 at MGM's Studio 54 and a blow-out party costing $14,000 at Wynn's Tryst. He also spent $500,000 of his clients' funds to purchase a Las Vegas condominium.

Orecchio spent large sums attempting to purchase favors from politicians and government officials who could influence the investment decisions made by labor union pension funds. One of the politicians he attempted to bribe unsuccessfully was Detroit Mayor Kwame Kilpatrick. Orecchio had hoped that he could convince Kilpatrick to steer the large pension funds of the Detroit police and fire departments to AA Capital.

In addition to the $24 million that he embezzled, Orecchio admitted that he was responsible for more than $30 million in additional losses suffered by his labor union clients. The largest of those losses stemmed from an investment that he had made on behalf of those clients in a sports drink company organized by several of his Las Vegas acquaintances. The venture eventually failed and AA Capital recovered only a small fraction of the large investment.

Auditors Front and Center

Once the SEC determined that Orecchio had used AA Capital's Equity Fund as his personal piggy bank, the federal agency turned its attention to the Ernst & Young auditors who had issued unqualified opinions on the financial statements of that fund and AA Capital. In March 2010, the SEC issued an *Accounting and Auditing Enforcement Release* in which it maligned Ernst & Young's audits of those entities. That document included the following statement that summarized the SEC's principal criticism of Ernst & Young, Gerard Oprins, and Wendy McNeeley.

> During the [2004] audits, Oprins, the engagement partner, and McNeeley, the manager, learned that … John Orecchio purportedly had borrowed $1.92 million in funds belonging to AA Capital's clients … to pay a personal tax liability arising from his ownership interest in AA Capital's private equity funds. In fact, Orecchio had invented the story about the so-called "tax loan" to conceal his ongoing misappropriation of client assets for his personal use. Despite learning about the [bogus] "tax loan" during the [2004] audits, Oprins and McNeeley failed to review the transaction in accordance with GAAS. Instead of properly evaluating the "tax loan" as a related party transaction, Oprins and McNeeley relied solely upon dubious and unsubstantiated information obtained from AA Capital's chief financial officer, Mary Beth Stevens. As a result, Oprins and McNeeley caused Ernst & Young to issue unqualified audit reports for AA Capital's and the Equity Fund's 2004 financial statements even though Orecchio's purported "tax loan" was not adequately disclosed in conformity with GAAP and Ernst & Young's audits were not conducted in accordance with GAAS.[3]

The *Accounting and Auditing Enforcement Release* also identified other oversights made by the Ernst & Young auditors.

> The audit team did not obtain any documentation reflecting Orecchio's tax liability or the terms of the 'tax loan.'

> They did not discuss the 'tax loan' with Orecchio.

> They did not take steps to assess the collectability of the 'tax loan.'

> They also failed to discuss Orecchio's tax liability with their colleagues in Ernst & Young's tax department who prepared the tax filings for AA Capital and its affiliated private equity funds.

The SEC's Enforcement Division recommended that Oprins and McNeeley be suspended from practicing before the SEC for three years as a result of their alleged "improper professional conduct" during the 2004 audits of AA Capital and its Equity

---

3. Securities and Exchange Commission, *Accounting and Auditing Enforcement Release No. 3116A*, 1 March 2010.

Fund. The two auditors quickly appealed that decision. A federal judge, Judge Robert Mahony, presided over their appeals in a hearing that extended over two weeks from late July through early August 2010.

Ernst & Young retained two high-profile expert witnesses to testify on behalf of Oprins and McNeeley during the hearing. One of those experts was John Ellingsen who had served for 25 years as an audit partner with Deloitte & Touche, including 6 years in which he was the firm's senior technical audit partner. Ellingsen had also served for four years on the Auditing Standards Board. The SEC also retained a high-profile expert witness John Barron, who, like Ellingsen, was a former longtime audit partner with Deloitte & Touche.

In a 41-page opinion that he wrote following the conclusion of the hearing for Oprins and McNeeley, Judge Mahony confirmed that the SEC has the authority to sanction accountants and auditors for "improper professional conduct." The applicable federal regulations identify two gradients of improper professional conduct: "reckless conduct" and "negligent conduct."

To find that an auditor was reckless, the SEC's Enforcement Division must establish that "the audit amounted to no audit at all, or an egregious refusal to see the obvious, or to investigate the doubtful." To find that an auditor was negligent, which is the less severe form of improper professional conduct, the SEC must establish that the individual was guilty of at least one instance of "highly unreasonable conduct." This misconduct involves a violation of the relevant professional standards "in circumstances in which an accountant [auditor] knows that heightened scrutiny is warranted." Judge Mahony noted that the key benchmark to use in making a determination of whether an auditor is guilty of highly unreasonable conduct is to compare the given individual's conduct with "the actions a reasonable accountant [auditor] should have taken" in identical circumstances.

In his opinion, Judge Mahony ruled in favor of Gerard Oprins by finding that the audit partner had not engaged in either reckless or highly unreasonable (negligent) conduct. A key factor that influenced Judge Mahony's decision was the testimony of John Ellingsen that an audit engagement partner is not "responsible for all decisions made in the course of an engagement." In siding with that argument, Judge Mahony concluded that it was improper for the SEC to hold Oprins responsible for the deficient audit procedures applied to the alleged tax transfers to John Orecchio because Wendy McNeeley had failed to adequately inform him of those transactions. "As the engagement partner, Oprins reasonably relied on McNeeley, a highly regarded auditor, to perform the audit in accordance with professional standards and escalate issues, such as the Transfers, to his attention." The judge maintained that because McNeeley had failed to highlight the transfers in the SRM or discuss those transfers directly with the audit partner, Oprins never realized that they were "outside the normal course of business."

Judge Mahony did rule that Oprins had sufficient information to determine that the tax transfers qualified as related-party transactions and should have been disclosed as such in the 2004 financial statements of the Equity Fund and AA Capital. However, the judge found that this one oversight did not rise to the level of reckless or highly unreasonable conduct.

Wendy McNeeley, not Gerard Oprins, was the individual "primarily responsible for ensuring that the 2004 audit complied with GAAS," according to Judge Mahony. The judge ruled that McNeeley had not obtained "sufficient competent evidential matter" to corroborate the alleged tax transfers to John Orecchio during 2004. After characterizing McNeeley's "failures" as "significant," Judge Mahony summarized the specific errors in judgment that she had made during the 2004 engagement.

She missed significant warning signs throughout the audit, not the least of which was the increase in the Transfers balance that should have been discovered during the subsequent review testing and investigated. She failed to follow up on her request of Stevens to provide documentary support for the Transfers. And she failed to ensure that the Transfers were disclosed in the financial statements in accordance with GAAP.

Despite his finding that McNeeley had made several significant mistakes during the AA Capital audits, Judge Mahony concluded that a three-year ban from practicing before the SEC was too severe of a punishment for her. He based this decision, in part, on the fact that she "has had a distinguished career and no disciplinary history." McNeeley subsequently appealed the one-year suspension that Judge Mahony imposed on her, however, that appeal was apparently unsuccessful.

EPILOGUE

John Orecchio faced a prison sentence of up to 25 years for the fraud and embezzlement charges filed against him. To reduce his sentence, Orecchio agreed to participate in a "sting operation" organized by federal law enforcement authorities. While wearing a "wire" to record his conversations, Orecchio met with 20 different union representatives. The union reps who accepted the bribes offered to them by Orecchio found themselves facing a felony indictment as well. Following his cooperation with the "feds," Orecchio received a prison term of nine years and four months after pleading guilty to one count of fraud and one count of theft in early 2010. In a largely symbolic move, the federal judge who sentenced Orecchio also ordered him to repay the more than $50 million of losses suffered by AA Capital's pension fund clients as a result of his theft and mismanagement. When he was formally sentenced, Orecchio had already been stripped of any remaining assets that he had accumulated during his crime spree.

The loss of material possessions was not the most significant price that John Orecchio paid for his indiscretions. At the height of his embezzlement scheme, while he was still married and clandestinely living a dual existence, Orecchio had asked his mistress to marry him, but that relationship dissolved when his embezzlement scheme surfaced. Then, his wife left him, taking with her their three children. After both relationships had ended, a despondent Orecchio attempted suicide in 2009. Before being sentenced in June 2010, Orecchio was living with his mother in New Jersey. His only request at his sentencing was that he be incarcerated in New Jersey so that his three children could visit him in prison during trips to see their grandmother. Orecchio pledged to the judge that, "I'll do what I can do make it up to them the rest of my days."[4,5]

Gerard Oprins left Ernst & Young in April 2009 and at last report was self-employed as a private consultant. Wendy McNeeley left Ernst & Young in July 2006. At last report she was employed by another major accounting firm.

---

4. *Daily Herald* (online), "Ex-Arlington Heights Man Gets 9 Years in Prison in Pension Fraud," 18 June, 2010.

5. Mary Beth Stevens did not face criminal charges as a result of her role in John Orecchio's fraud. However, the SEC barred Stevens from being associated with a registered investment advisory firm and levied monetary penalties of approximately $150,000 on her. The federal agency barred Paul Oliver, Orecchio's partner, from being associated with an investment advisory firm for 12 months and levied fines and other civil sanctions on him totaling $130,000.

Questions

1. What factors likely contributed to the oversights made by the Ernst & Young auditors during the 2004 AA Capital engagement? Identify measures that audit firms can implement to minimize the likelihood of such oversights on audit engagements.

2. Was it appropriate for Ernst & Young to decide not to rely on AA Capital's internal controls during the 2004 audits? Under what circumstances can auditors choose not to rely on a client's internal controls?

3. What audit procedures do professional auditing standards require that auditors apply to related-party transactions? Would any of these procedures have resulted in Ernst & Young discovering the true nature of the cash transfers made to John Orecchio?

4. What objectives do auditors hope to accomplish in performing "subsequent period" audit tests?

5. Do you agree with the assertion of John Ellingsen that an audit engagement partner is not "responsible for all decisions made in the course of an engagement?" Defend your answer. What quality control implications does that assertion, if true, have for audit firms?

Navistar International Corporation

Cyrus McCormick revolutionized American agriculture in the mid-nineteenth century when he invented a mechanical reaper. His horse-drawn harvester would become the primary product marketed by McCormick Harvesting Machine Company. Decades later, Cyrus McCormick II merged his father's company with three competing firms to create International Harvester Company, the nation's largest manufacturer of agricultural equipment.

In addition to being successful businessmen, the McCormicks were pioneers in the field of management science. Each of them realized that modern management techniques were critical to a large company's success. As an example, to help him maintain control over his rapidly growing company, Cyrus McCormick II retained an independent accounting firm to audit its financial records long before independent audits were mandated for public companies. That accounting firm was the predecessor of Deloitte, one of the Big Four firms that now dominate the public accounting profession.

By the late 1980s, International Harvester had been renamed Navistar International Corporation because the company's principal line of business had migrated away from farming equipment and into the manufacture of trucks, school buses, and automotive engines. As the company evolved and changed over the decades, one of its most enduring relationships was with the accounting firm that Cyrus McCormick II retained in 1908. The business community was shocked in 2006 when, after 98 years, Navistar dismissed Deloitte as its independent audit firm. Even more shocking was a $500 million lawsuit subsequently filed by the company against Deloitte. Among other allegations, the lawsuit alleged that Navistar management had been duped into believing that Deloitte provided professional quality accounting and auditing services.[1] The dramatic end to Deloitte's relationship with Navistar caught the attention of the Public Company Accounting Oversight Board (PCAOB), resulting in that agency's first formal investigation of a Big Four accounting firm.

New Partner ... New Audit

In late 2005, Deloitte's Navistar audit for the fiscal year ending 31 October 2005, was nearing completion when the audit engagement partner took a "mysterious medical leave"[2] and was replaced. Navistar's new audit engagement partner was a former Arthur Andersen partner who had joined Deloitte after a felony conviction in 2002 drove Andersen out of business.[3] The new engagement partner was apparently shocked at the condition of Navistar's accounting records and the work that had been done to that point on the 2005 audit. "The new lead engagement partner ... began questioning almost everything that had been done or approved previously

---

1. J. Stempel, "Navistar Sues Ex-Auditor Deloitte for $500 million," 26 April 2011, www.reuters.com.

2. F. McKenna, "Navistar Sues Deloitte Proving No Statute of Limitations on Idiocy," 31 May 2011, www.forbes.com.

3. Arthur Andersen's felony conviction was overturned in 2005 by the U.S. Supreme Court but it was not practical for the firm to resume operations at that point.

… [and] refused to accept any of the work … the [audit] team had already done and basically, according to Navistar, started the audit over." [4]

Navistar's management team was less than happy with the sudden turn of events. The company's executives were even more dismayed when the delay in the 2005 audit prevented Navistar from meeting the filing deadline for its annual Form 10-K with the Securities and Exchange Commission (SEC). In February 2006, Deloitte advised Navistar management that it could no longer rely on representations made by the company's controller, which caused Navistar to replace that individual. Deloitte also asked Navistar to reassign a top executive of its large finance subsidiary, Navistar Financial Corporation, which the company did. The tense relationship between Deloitte and Navistar ended in April 2006 when the company's audit committee dismissed Deloitte and retained KPMG as the company's independent auditor.

Over the following 20 months, "Navistar spent more than $200 million to reconduct their 2002–2004 audits, redo and complete their 2005 audit, and reevaluate a never-ending list of material weaknesses and significant deficiencies in internal controls over financial reporting." [5] Navistar hired PricewaterhouseCoopers, Ernst & Young, and two large consulting firms to overhaul its accounting and financial reporting functions. In the meantime, the New York Stock Exchange delisted Navistar's common stock, which complicated the company's efforts to raise needed capital. In late 2007, Navistar finally filed its 2005 Form 10-K and restated financial statements for fiscal 2003, fiscal 2004, and the first three quarters of 2005 with the SEC. The restatements reduced Navistar's previously reported profits by nearly $680 million.

Navistar's 2005 Form 10-K reported 15 material weaknesses in the company's internal controls over financial reporting. Exhibit 1 provides brief summaries of those material weaknesses that were excerpted from that Form 10-K.

SEC Weighs In

The long delay in the filing of Navistar's 2005 Form 10-K caused the SEC to investigate the company's financial affairs. In 2010, the federal agency issued a series of enforcement and litigation releases focusing on the company and members of its management team. Despite uncovering circumstances in which financial statement amounts had been intentionally misstated, the SEC concluded that Navistar's management did not engage in a "coordinated scheme" to misrepresent the company's financial statements. Instead, the SEC reported that the Navistar case primarily involved a "deficient system of internal controls."

> These findings do not reflect a coordinated scheme by senior management to manipulate the Company's reported results or conduct committed with the intent of personal gain. Instead, these findings reflect misconduct that resulted in large part from a deficient system of internal controls, evidenced in part by insufficient numbers of employees with accounting training, a lack of written accounting policies and procedures, and flaws in the Company's organizational structure. [6]

The SEC identified several "improper accounting practices" that materially overstated Navistar's profits in the early 2000s. The fiscal year most affected by the restatements was 2003. Navistar originally reported a net loss of $18 million for 2003; after restatement, the company reported a net loss for that year of

---

4. McKenna, "Navistar Sues Deloitte."

5. *Ibid.*

6. Securities and Exchange Commission, *Accounting and Auditing Enforcement Release No. 3165,* 5 August 2010.

EXHIBIT 1

MATERIAL
WEAKNESSES IN
INTERNAL CONTROL
REPORTED BY
NAVISTAR IN ITS
2005 FORM 10-K

1. *Control Environment:* As of October 31, 2005, management was unsuccessful in establishing an adequately strong consciousness regarding the consistent application of ethics across all areas of the company and the importance of internal controls over financial reporting, including adherence to GAAP.

2. *Accounting Personnel:* We did not have a sufficient number of accounting personnel with an appropriate level of accounting knowledge, experience and training in the application of GAAP.

3. *Accounting Policies:* We did not have a formalized process for monitoring, updating, disseminating, and implementing GAAP-compliant accounting policies and procedures.

4. *Internal Audit:* Our internal audit department was not an effective monitoring control over financial reporting.

5. *Segregation of Duties:* We did not maintain effective controls to ensure adequate segregation of duties.

6. *Information Technology ("IT"):* Our IT general controls over computer program development, computer program changes, computer operations and system user access to programs and data were ineffectively designed.

7. *Journal Entries:* We did not maintain effective controls over the preparation, support, review and approval of journal entries.

8. *Account Reconciliations:* We did not maintain effective controls over account reconciliations and financial analysis and review.

9. *Period End Close:* We did not maintain effective controls over the period end close process.

10. *Pension Accounting:* We did not maintain effective controls to accurately estimate our pension and OPEB obligations.

11. *Warranty Accounting:* We did not have appropriate warranty cost accounting models and methodologies in place to adequately estimate warranty accruals and we did not perform appropriate financial analyses of the warranty cost estimates on a periodic basis.

12. *Income Tax Accounting:* We did not have sufficient modeling tools in place or a process to validate the positive and negative evidence necessary to determine whether valuation allowances were required to reduce the carrying values of deferred tax assets.

13. *Inventory Accounting:* We did not maintain effective controls over our inventory accounting process.

14. *Revenue Accounting:* We did not maintain effective controls over the revenue accounting process.

15. *Contracts and Agreements:* We did not perform effective reviews of contracts and agreements, including customer agreements, supplier agreements, agreements related to variable interest entities, derivatives, debt, and leases to assess the accounting implications related to the contracts and agreements.

Source: Navistar International Corporation's 2005 Form 10-K.

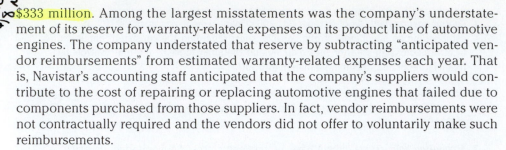

instead of $8 Mil.

$333 million. Among the largest misstatements was the company's understatement of its reserve for warranty-related expenses on its product line of automotive engines. The company understated that reserve by subtracting "anticipated vendor reimbursements" from estimated warranty-related expenses each year. That is, Navistar's accounting staff anticipated that the company's suppliers would contribute to the cost of repairing or replacing automotive engines that failed due to components purchased from those suppliers. In fact, vendor reimbursements were not contractually required and the vendors did not offer to voluntarily make such reimbursements.

Navistar also improperly accounted for vendor rebates that were dictated by the volume of purchases the company made in a given period. Instead of recording rebates strictly when they were earned, Navistar's accountants began recording "anticipated" rebates to be received from the company's vendors based upon the volume of purchases expected to be made from them in the future.

> *Under GAAP, a company could recognize rebates only when they were actually earned, i.e., when the entity had substantially accomplished what was necessary to be entitled to such rebates. Accordingly, Navistar could record the full rebate as income in the then-current period only if no contingencies existed on its right to receive the rebate. Conversely, the Company was prohibited from booking rebates as income in the then-current period if they were based on future business.[7]*

Navistar also improperly deferred "start-up costs" related to a long-term contract being negotiated with one of its major customers. In anticipation of that contract being signed, Navistar spent nearly $60 million, including expenditures to construct a production facility where the engines to be supplied under the contract would be manufactured. When the other party cancelled the contract negotiations, Navistar was forced to absorb those costs. According to the SEC, Navistar was entitled to defer the start-up costs only "if there existed an objectively verified and measured contractual guarantee of reimbursement."[8]

The SEC sanctioned several of Navistar's top executives despite ruling that the company's misrepresented financial statements were not due to a coordinated scheme. Those executives included Daniel Ustian, Navistar's chairman of the board and chief executive officer (CEO), and Robert Lannert, the company's chief financial officer (CFO). In addition to agreeing to "cease and desist" from future violations of federal securities laws, Ustian and Lannert forfeited more than $1 million in bonuses they had each received due to Navistar's inflated earnings. The SEC did not fine Navistar because the firm had implemented a wide range of measures to remedy its serious accounting and internal control problems. Those measures included hiring 50 additional accountants, a new chief accounting officer, a new vice president of internal audit, and a new chief information officer.

Navistar's sloppy accounting practices triggered the filing of a class-action lawsuit against the company by investors who had purchased the company's common stock during the time periods when its financial statements were misrepresented. Navistar settled that lawsuit in 2011 by agreeing to pay the plaintiffs $13 million. Deloitte had previously been dismissed as a defendant in that case by a federal judge who ruled that there was an insufficient basis for the allegations filed against the accounting firm by the plaintiffs' attorneys. Deloitte would not be so fortunate when it came to the PCAOB's investigation of its Navistar audits.

---

7. *Ibid.*
8. *Ibid.*

Deloitte vs. The Feds

In June 2005, the SEC, which oversees the PCAOB's operations, inadvertently revealed that the PCAOB was investigating Deloitte's 2003 audit of Navistar. The PCAOB had notified the SEC of that investigation the prior month in a document that was not intended to be released to the public. An SEC spokesperson admitted his agency had accidentally included that document with other documents routinely made available to the public. The spokesperson apologized for the error and indicated that steps were being taken to improve the SEC's administrative procedures. The release of the PCAOB document was newsworthy because it signaled the PCAOB's first formal investigation of a Big Four accounting firm.

Prior to the SEC's inadvertent disclosure of the PCAOB's Deloitte investigation, there was already considerable tension between the SEC and Deloitte. In April 2005, the SEC had fined Deloitte $50 million for its audits of the fraudulent financial statements of Adelphia Communications, a large telecommunications company that collapsed into bankruptcy in 2002. That fine was easily the largest ever levied against a Big Four firm by the SEC.

Shortly after the SEC announced the $50 million fine, James Quigley, Deloitte's CEO, issued a press release that infuriated SEC officials. In the press release, Quigley noted that, "Among our most significant challenges is the early detection of fraud, particularly when the client, its management and others collude specifically to deceive a company's auditors."[9] An SEC spokesperson responded harshly to Quigley's statement. "Deloitte was not deceived in this case. The findings in the order show that the relevant information was right in front of their eyes. Deloitte just didn't do its job, plain and simple. They didn't miss red flags. They pulled the flag over their head and claimed they couldn't see."[10]

The SEC also suggested that Quigley's press release violated the terms of the agreement the agency had reached with Deloitte in settling the Adelphia case. Under the terms of that agreement, Deloitte was not required to "admit" to the SEC's findings, nor was it allowed to "deny" those findings. Deloitte subsequently rescinded Quigley's press release and issued another that eliminated some, but not all, of the statements that had offended the SEC.[11]

A few weeks after the brouhaha involving Deloitte and the SEC, the PCAOB began investigating the accounting firm's 2003 audit of Navistar. The PCAOB's investigation of that audit was in addition to the agency's mandated annual inspections of Deloitte. The Sarbanes–Oxley Act of 2002 requires accounting firms that audit companies with securities traded on U.S. stock exchanges to register with the PCAOB. Accounting firms that audit more than 100 SEC registrants are inspected annually by the PCAOB; accounting firms that audit fewer than 100 SEC registrants are inspected every three years.

PCAOB inspections are intended to "identify and address weaknesses and deficiencies related to how a firm conducts audits."[12] The PCAOB identifies two types

---

9. S. Laub, "Deloitte Statement Irks SEC," *CFO.com*, 28 April 2005.

10. S. Hughes, "SEC Rebukes Deloitte over Spin of Adelphia Audit," *The Associated Press State & Local Wire*, 27 April 2005.

11. In late 2007, a Deloitte audit partner would become the first individual barred by the PCAOB from being associated with an accounting firm approved by the agency to audit SEC registrants. That individual, James Lazio, had supervised an audit of the San Diego–based Ligand Pharmaceuticals. The joint SEC–PCAOB investigation of Deloitte's Ligand audit also resulted in Deloitte being publicly censured and fined $1 million. See Case 7.1, "Ligand Pharmaceuticals."

12. Public Company Accounting Oversight Board, *PCAOB Release No. 104-2008-070A*, "Report on 2007 Inspection of Deloitte & Touche LLP," 19 May 2008.

of such weaknesses and deficiencies: those on specific audits reviewed by PCAOB inspectors and those that involve more pervasive "matters related to the firm's quality control system."[13] Deficiencies on specific audit engagements are included in the publicly available inspection reports issued by the PCAOB for individual accounting firms, although the disclosures do not reveal the identities of the given audit clients. The more critical quality control deficiencies are excluded, at least initially, from PCAOB inspection reports released to the public. If a firm does not properly resolve or remediate quality control deficiencies observed by PCAOB inspectors within 12 months of the date that an inspection report is released, the PCAOB may subsequently disclose those quality control matters to the public.

In May 2008, the PCAOB released its 2007 inspection report for Deloitte. In that report, the PCAOB revealed that the inspection team had visited Deloitte's national headquarters and 18 of the firm's approximately 70 practice offices in the United States. The inspection team identified audit deficiencies on nine of the 61 Deloitte audits that it reviewed. It was widely believed that one of those clients was Navistar given the SEC's inadvertent disclosure that the PCAOB was investigating the 2003 Navistar audit.

As dictated by the PCAOB's policies, the 2007 inspection report did not reference any quality control deficiencies or defects in Deloitte's audit process. The inspection report included the following statement regarding any such items: "Any defects in, or criticisms of, the Firm's quality control system are discussed in the nonpublic portion of this report and will remain nonpublic unless the Firm fails to address them to the Board's satisfaction within 12 months of the date of this report."[14]

Navistar Audit Partners Sanctioned by PCAOB

In November 2008, the PCAOB released its first public statement regarding the ongoing investigation of the 2003 Navistar audit. The agency reported that it had fined Christopher Anderson, an audit partner in Deloitte's Chicago office, $25,000 and suspended him from being associated with a PCAOB-registered accounting firm for one year. This was the first fine ever imposed on an individual by the PCAOB. Anderson had supervised the 2003 audit of Navistar Financial Corporation (NFC), Navistar's finance subsidiary. NFC's 2003 financial statements were included in Navistar's consolidated financial statements for that year.[15]

Among other charges, the PCAOB reported that Anderson had accepted a decision made by a member of the Navistar audit engagement team, presumably the Navistar audit engagement partner, to increase the planning materiality threshold for NFC by 50 percent during the final few days of the 2003 Navistar and NFC audits. According to the PCAOB, Anderson "believed that the original threshold remained appropriate and understood that the increased threshold would make it easier to treat known misstatements as immaterial."[16] The "known misstatements" referred to by the PCAOB involved errors discovered in NFC's accounting records shortly before the completion of the 2003 audit.

---

13. *Ibid.*

14. *Ibid.*

15. Because NFC issued debt securities that were publicly traded, it filed an annual Form 10-K with the SEC in addition to the annual Form 10-K filed by its parent, Navistar.

16. Public Company Accounting Oversight Board, *PCAOB Release No. 105-2008-003*, "Order Instituting Disciplinary Proceedings, Making Findings and Imposing Sanctions, In the Matter of Christopher E. Anderson, CPA, Respondent," 31 October 2008.

Following the announcement of the PCAOB sanctions, a Deloitte spokesperson reported that Anderson was still with the firm "with responsibilities consistent with the settlement [with the PCAOB]."[17] A PCAOB official refused to comment on why Deloitte was not sanctioned at the same time that the penalties were handed down against Anderson. "We do not comment on considerations involved in whether to charge firms or persons other than named respondents. The Board's order only finds violations relating to Mr. Anderson."[18] When asked to comment on the same issue, a former PCAOB official provided a more elaborate response. "The firm tends to be the subject of disciplinary action when there is a failure of oversight or supervision. Where a particular partner simply makes an error but the firm was not negligent, only the party may get named in the proceeding."[19]

Less than one year after sanctioning Anderson, the PCAOB issued a second enforcement release focusing on Deloitte's 2003 Navistar and NFC audits. This second release centered on Thomas Linden, the Deloitte partner who had supervised the 1997–2003 Navistar audits. In that role, Linden effectively served as Anderson's supervisor during the 2003 audit. Linden was fined $75,000 by the PCAOB and received a two-year suspension. Published reports indicated that at the time the PCAOB sanctioned Linden in August 2009 he was no longer associated with Deloitte.

On 1 December 2003, Linden participated in a meeting with Navistar's audit committee in which the company's 2003 operating results were discussed. The audit committee was reviewing those results in anticipation of releasing them the next day in a telephone conference call to securities analysts who tracked the company's common stock. During the 1 December meeting, Linden "informed the Audit Committee at that time that Deloitte had substantially completed its audit and expected to issue an unqualified report."[20] The following day, the preaudit operating results, which were "on the top side" of the previous earnings guidance provided by Navistar's management, were communicated to the company's securities analysts.

Linden expected Navistar to file its 2003 Form 10-K, including Deloitte's audit report, with the SEC on 18 December, one week before Christmas, which was the company's standard practice. Two days prior to that date, on the evening of 16 December, Christopher Anderson told Linden of $20 million of errors in NFC's accounts that his subordinates had uncovered, errors that had materially overstated NFC's assets, revenues, and earnings. That figure was also material to the consolidated operating results of Navistar.[21]

---

17. T. Whitehouse, "PCAOB Suspends Second Deloitte Engagement Partner," 3 November 2008, www.complianceweek.com.

18. *Ibid.*

19. *Ibid.*

20. This quote and the remaining quotes in this case, unless indicated otherwise, were taken from the following source: Public Company Accounting Oversight Board, *PCAOB Release No. 105-2009-004*, "Order Making Findings and Imposing Sanctions, In the Matter of Thomas J. Linden, CPA, Respondent," 11 August 2009.

21. For fiscal 2003, Navistar reported a net loss of $18 million. However, the company reported a $77 million profit for the fourth quarter of 2003. For the previous three quarters of 2003, the company had reported a net income (loss) of ($99 million), ($14 million), and $18 million, respectively. Apparently, company management was intent on not reducing the impressive preaudit earnings for the fourth quarter in order to signal to investors that the company was in the midst of a significant turnaround. For fiscal 2002, the company had reported a net loss of $536 million. Although the $20 million in errors were material to NFC's financial statements, the PCAOB was most concerned by how the treatment of the NFC errors impacted Navistar's consolidated financial statements.

Executives of both Navistar and NFC were informed of the $20 million of errors. "Because NFC's financial results were consolidated into NIC's [Navistar's] financial statements, correction of the overstatement created the prospect that NIC would have to revise its previously announced earnings." According to the PCAOB, Linden was aware that Navistar's executives had a "certain level of anxiety" concerning the errors and that they "would prefer not to revise its [Navistar's] announced earnings."

Over the following two days, NFC made a series of accounting adjustments to "neutralize" most of the errors discovered by the NFC audit team. For example, the company recomputed the gains that it had previously recorded on certain securitization transactions during 2003. The increased gain on those transactions, which were recorded with Linden's knowledge, "canceled out" approximately $7.2 million of the $20 million in errors discovered by the NFC auditors.

After the "neutralizing" adjustments were made, only $4.5 million in overstatements due to the discovered errors remained. NFC's accounting staff chose to defer the write-off of that amount until the first quarter of 2004. Linden was aware that NFC made the decision to postpone that write-off "without identifying a sufficient basis under GAAP to do so."

On the morning of 17 December, Linden "initiated, and the NFC engagement partner [Anderson] adopted" a 50 percent increase in the "planning materiality threshold" for the 2003 NFC audit. Anderson had used a planning materiality threshold of 5 percent of NFC's pretax income during each of the four years that he had supervised the NFC audit. Linden increased that threshold to 7.5 percent of NFC's pretax income. The increase in the materiality threshold allowed the Deloitte auditors to accept NFC's decision not to record a year-end adjustment for the postponed $4.5 million write-off. That is, the increase in the materiality threshold made the $4.5 million error "presumptively immaterial" under Deloitte's policies and procedures. Absent the increase in the materiality threshold, the $4.5 million error would have been "presumptively material."[22]

In addition to increasing NFC's materiality threshold, Linden prepared an audit workpaper justifying that change. "[Linden] authored, with the assistance of the NFC engagement team, an NFC audit workpaper that inaccurately characterized the reasons for and circumstances surrounding the increase."

More Pushback from the PCAOB

In October 2011, the PCAOB surprised the public accounting profession by releasing "Part II" of its 2007 inspection report for Deloitte. Part II of that report included the discussion of quality control deficiencies the PCAOB had identified during its 2007 inspection of Deloitte but not included in the version of that report made available to the public. This was the first instance in which the PCAOB had released information from Part II of an inspection report for a Big Four accounting firm. The decision to release that information was made because Deloitte allegedly had not properly addressed the issues raised in that section of the report in the 12 months following its release. Exhibit 2 includes statements excerpted from Part II of the 2007 inspection report.

The most pervasive cause for concern that the PCAOB raised in Part II of the 2007 inspection report revolved around Deloitte's internal "culture." In particular, the PCAOB questioned whether the rank-and-file employees of that firm had "embraced" the need to change how they performed audits.

---

22. The original planning materiality threshold was approximately $4.1 million; the revised threshold was approximately $6.1 million.

EXHIBIT 2

EXCERPTS
FROM PART II,
"ISSUES RELATED
TO QUALITY
CONTROLS,"
PCAOB's 2007
INSPECTION REPORT
FOR DELOITTE &
TOUCHE

1. The engagement reviews provide cause for concern that the Firm's system of quality control may not do enough to assure that the Firm performs appropriate procedures to audit significant accounting estimates, including evaluating management's assumptions and testing the data supporting the estimates.

2. The engagement reviews provide cause for concern about the effectiveness of the Firm's quality controls with respect to the audit procedures performed on income tax balances.

3. The engagement reviews provide cause for concern about the effectiveness of the Firm's quality controls with respect to the use of specialists.

4. The inspection results provide cause for concern that the Firm's system of quality control may not do enough to assure that accounting and auditing issues are evaluated with the objectivity that is contemplated in the auditing standards.

5. The Firm's apparent failure to appropriately challenge management's representations occurred in numerous areas, including when the Firm evaluated management's estimates, considered the valuation of investment securities, performed alternative procedures in connection with confirmations, and tested income tax accounts and disclosures.

6. The engagement reviews provide cause for concern that the Firm's quality controls may not result in appropriate and effective consultations when necessary. Further, the Firm's policy on consultations ... appears to be deficient in that it lacks a mechanism reasonably designed to provide that significant, complex matters are raised to the appropriate level in the hierarchy in order to ensure a sufficient level of rigor in the analysis.

7. Deloitte Touche Tohmatsu (DTT) uses its global internal inspection program to assess and monitor the quality of the audit work of its member firms. However, the specific results of the inspections of member firms or practice offices are not disseminated to the Firm's partners.... Accordingly, the global inspection program does not routinely provide a U.S. engagement partner with a basis for assessing a foreign office's qualifications and familiarity with U.S. GAAP, PCAOB standards, and SEC reporting requirements.

Source: Public Company Accounting Oversight Board, "Report on 2007 Inspection of Deloitte & Touche LLP."

These deficiencies may result, in part, from a Firm culture that allows, or tolerates, audit approaches that do not consistently emphasize the need for an appropriate level of critical analysis and collection of objective evidence, and that rely largely on management representations. While it appears that the Firm has instituted positive changes to its audit practice over the years of PCAOB inspections, and that the Firm's senior leadership has accepted the need to do so, some questions remain about whether the Firm's audit personnel have embraced the concept that change in audit performance is necessary in order to achieve compliance with PCAOB standards.[23]

Before the 2007 inspection report was released in May 2008 to the public, Deloitte was given an opportunity to respond to a draft of that report. Deloitte wrote two letters to the PCAOB in response to the report: one letter addressing the audit deficiencies identified by the PCAOB on specific engagements that were reviewed (Part I) and a second letter responding to the observed defects in Deloitte's quality controls (Part II). Deloitte was aware that the letter written in response to Part II of the report

23. Public Company Accounting Oversight Board, *PCAOB Release No. 104-2008-070A*, "Report on 2007 Inspection of Deloitte & Touche LLP," 19 May 2008.

would not be made publicly available unless the PCAOB subsequently released that section to the public.

In its letter addressing Part II of the inspection report, Deloitte strenuously objected to the PCAOB's suggestion that the firm's culture needed to change. "We believe that such a broad statement by the Board mischaracterizes our audit approach and our practices. Further, we strongly take exception to the observation that our culture or system of quality control allows or tolerates such audit approaches.... We do not believe that the inspection results support such a broad statement by the Board and such statement should not be included in the final report."[24]

Deloitte also objected to many of the issues identified in Exhibit 2. Deloitte's most ardent complaints revolved around the broad-brush statements made by the PCAOB that were based on "limited instances" observed by the inspection team. Deloitte also suggested that the PCAOB was improperly "second-guessing" the judgments of highly skilled professionals. "Professional judgments of reasonable and highly competent people may differ as to the nature and extent of necessary auditing procedures, conclusions reached and required documentation. We believe that reasonable judgments should not be second guessed."[25]

Following the PCAOB's release of Part II of the 2007 Deloitte inspection report, Deloitte's CEO once again defended his firm's audit practices. At the same time, though, he admitted that his firm was aware of the need to continually improve the quality of its professional services. "We have complete confidence in our professionals and the quality of our audits, and agree that there were and always will be areas where we can improve."[26]

Navistar Sues Deloitte

In August 2011, two months prior to the PCAOB's release of Part II of Deloitte's 2007 inspection report, Navistar filed a $500 million lawsuit against its former audit firm.[27] Among the company's harshest allegations against Deloitte was that the auditing services were seriously flawed due to the inadequate training of its professional staff.[28] In the 134-page complaint filed against Deloitte, Navistar's attorneys also suggested that Deloitte had been much more than Navistar's independent audit firm. In fact, the attorneys alleged that Deloitte had been so deeply involved in the company's accounting and financial reporting function that the firm was a "de facto adjunct to Navistar's accounting department."

> *Deloitte provided Navistar with much more than audit services. Deloitte also acted as Navistar's business consultant and accountant. For example, Navistar retained Deloitte to advise it on how to structure its business transactions to obtain accounting treatment under Generally Accepted Accounting Principles (GAAP) ... Deloitte advised and directed Navistar in the accounting treatments Navistar employed for numerous complex accounting issues apart from its audits of Navistar's financial statements, functioning as a de facto adjunct to Navistar's accounting department.... Deloitte even had a role in selecting Navistar's most senior accounting personnel by directly interviewing applicants.*[29]

---

24. *Ibid.*

25. *Ibid.*

26. S. Johnson, "PCAOB: Deloitte Trusted Management Too Much," 17 October 2011, www3.cfo.com.

27. The specific civil charges filed against Deloitte in the complaint included fraud, fraudulent concealment, negligent misrepresentation, professional malpractice, breach of contract, and breach of fiduciary duty.

28. Stempel, "Navistar Sues Ex-Auditor."

29. McKenna, "Navistar Sues Deloitte."

Many parties within the profession came to the defense of Deloitte when the Navistar lawsuit was reported. One widely quoted observer of the profession pointed out that Navistar's lawsuit against Deloitte ignored two important features of the auditor–client relationship: (1) a company's financial statements are ultimately the responsibility of senior management; (2) a public company's audit committee has a "responsibility to certify the independence of the auditor every year and to change or reduce the services they perform, or fire them, if their independence and objectivity becomes compromised."[30]

The most visceral reaction to the lawsuit within the profession was, not surprisingly, from Deloitte itself. Deloitte representatives vigorously defended their firm in the business press. A Deloitte spokesperson told *Accounting Today* that Navistar's lawsuit was a "cynical and baseless attempt to shift responsibility for the wrongdoing of Navistar's own management."[31] The spokesperson added that, "Several members of Navistar's past or present management team were sanctioned by the SEC for the very matters alleged in the complaint. This claim is without merit and we will defend ourselves vigorously."[32]

EPILOGUE

In June 2008, Navistar's common stock regained its listing on the New York Stock Exchange, signaling to many observers that the company had recovered from the embarrassing accounting scandal that had tarnished its reputation. Over the next several years, the company posted impressive profits, culminating in a record net income of $1.7 billion for fiscal 2011. Bad news returned in August 2012 when the SEC launched another investigation of the company's accounting records. The announcement of that investigation caused the company's stock price to drop sharply. Less than four weeks later, Navistar's board of directors fired Daniel Ustian as the company's CEO and chairman of the board. In December 2012, the company reported a massive $3 billion loss. Over the next several months, unhappy investors filed several class-action lawsuits against Navistar charging the company and its management team with issuing misleading financial reports.

As Navistar's troubles mounted, the company quietly announced in its Form 10-Q for the first quarter of 2013 that it had settled the lawsuit filed against Deloitte in 2011. Neither Navistar nor Deloitte publicly commented on the financial aspects, if any, of that settlement.

In October 2013, the PCAOB announced that it was fining Deloitte $2 million for permitting Christopher Anderson to perform audit services during the time that he was serving his one-year suspension. According to published reports, in anticipation of his suspension, Anderson had resigned as a Deloitte partner and accepted a salaried position as a director with the firm. In that role, Anderson had interacted with, and provided advice on auditing matters to, three different Deloitte audit engagement teams.[33]

The PCAOB has continued to vigorously pursue its legislative mandate to strengthen the independent audit function for SEC registrants. The agency made mandatory audit firm rotation the hottest topic within the public accounting profession when it issued a concept release in August 2011 to solicit input from the public on ways to strengthen auditor independence. One of the measures mentioned prominently by the PCAOB was limiting the tenure of public

---

30. *Ibid.*

31. M. Cohn, "Navistar Sues Deloitte Over Audits," 28 April 2011, www.accountingtoday.com.

32. *Ibid.*

33. S. Strahler, "Deloitte Fined $2 Million for Letting Suspended Exec Work on Audit," www.chicagobusiness.com, 23 October 2013.

company auditors to a discrete number of years. James Doty, the chairman of the PCAOB, raised this possibility while discussing the problems posed by long-term auditor–client relationships.

> The PCAOB's efforts to address these problems through inspections and enforcement are ongoing. But considering the disturbing lack of skepticism we continue to see, and because of the fundamental importance of independence to the performance of quality audit work, the Board is prepared to consider all possible methods of addressing the problem of audit quality—including whether mandatory audit firm rotation would help address the inherent conflict created because the auditor is paid by the client.[34]

Although PCAOB officials never referred to Deloitte's 98-year tenure as Navistar's auditor or the allegedly "cozy" relationship that developed between the two organizations over that time, many parties believed that relationship was a key factor that prompted the agency's interest in mandatory audit firm rotation.[35]

In March 2012, Chairman Doty was asked to testify before the U.S. House Subcommittee on Capital Markets and Government Sponsored Enterprises. The principal topic that the subcommittee wanted to pursue with Doty was the issue of mandatory audit firm rotation. The opening remarks made by U.S. Representative Scott Garrett set the tone for the hearing. "I do think it is important to remind the PCAOB that it is not a policy-making entity; Congress and this committee are the policy makers. The PCAOB's job is to regulate and oversee the accounting profession. I am very concerned about some of the recent activist proposals put forth by the PCAOB."[36]

Representative Garrett and other members of the subcommittee then grilled Doty on why mandatory audit firm rotation was the major agenda item being pursued by his agency. At one point, Representative Garrett challenged Doty to provide "data" other than "anecdotal" circumstances to demonstrate that lengthy tenure between auditors and clients impairs auditors' independence. Doty could not provide such data but noted that the lack of auditor skepticism in such situations "recurs in our findings over the years. It is not an isolated issue."[37]

Instead of mandatory audit firm rotation, members of the congressional subcommittee suggested that other strategies for strengthening auditor independence might be less costly and more fruitful to consider. One such recommendation was limiting the percentage of revenue that a PCAOB-registered accounting firm could receive from any one client.

In 2013, the U.S. Congress once more took up the topic of mandatory audit firm rotation. On 19 June 2013, the U.S. House Financial Services Committee voted unanimously to approve a bill that would prohibit mandatory audit firm rotation for SEC registrants. In commenting on that bill, U.S. Representative Jeb Hensarling, the chairman of the congressional committee, observed that, "It is boards of directors, management and shareholders who should ultimately make the decision about which accounting firms should audit a company's financial statements—not the PCAOB."[38] Three weeks later, on 8 July 2013, the U.S. House of Representatives voted 321 to 62 in favor of the bill and sent it to the U.S. Senate for its consideration.

---

34. F. McKenna, "Two Wildly Different Stories About Deloitte: Or Are They?" 8 June 2011, http://retheauditors.com.

35. The record for the longest auditor–client relationship involving a Big Four accounting firm and a public company belongs to Deloitte and Procter & Gamble. That relationship began in 1890.

36. J. Hamilton, "'Mission Creep' Replaced 'Increased Skepticism' as the Word of the Day," 30 March 2012, Accounting News Report (http://accountingnewsreport.com).

37. Ibid.

38. S. Lynch, "House Panel OKs Bill to Prohibit Mandatory Auditor Rotation," 19 June 2013, Reuters (www.reuters.com).

Questions

1. Identify the advantages and disadvantages of mandatory audit firm rotation. What, if any, auditor rotation rules are in effect in the United States?

2. What is the formal definition of a "material weakness" in internal control? How do material weaknesses in internal control differ from "significant deficiencies" in internal control? Identify the three material weaknesses in Exhibit 1 that you believe were most critical. Defend your choices. Can an organization's internal controls be so inadequate that it is not possible for the entity to be audited? Defend your answer.

3. Is it appropriate for an audit firm "to function as a *de facto* adjunct" to a client's accounting department? Why or why not? Which party or parties were primarily responsible for Deloitte being dismissed as Navistar's independent auditor in April 2006? Defend your answer.

4. Define what is meant by the phrase "planning materiality threshold"? What factors should be considered in establishing such thresholds? Are there any conditions under which it is appropriate for auditors to change a planning materiality threshold after the given audit has begun?

5. This case includes the following quote from a former PCAOB official: "The [audit] firm tends to be the subject of disciplinary action when there is a failure of oversight or supervision. Where a particular partner simply makes an error but the firm was not negligent, only the party may get named in the proceeding." Do you believe that Deloitte, in addition to Linden and Anderson, should have been sanctioned by the PCAOB in connection with the 2003 Navistar audit? Justify your answer.

6. What professional standards require accounting firms to develop quality controls for their audit practices? What key issues should such quality controls address? In commenting on Deloitte's quality controls, the PCAOB referred to the "culture" of that firm. What are the key factors or conditions that influence the "culture" within an accounting firm's audit practice?

7. Do you believe that the PCAOB overstepped its regulatory role and responsibilities by beginning a dialogue regarding the possible need for mandatory audit firm rotation? Why or why not? Do you agree with U.S. Representative Garrett that the PCAOB is not a policy-making body? Explain.

8. Deloitte maintained that it was not appropriate for PCAOB inspection teams to "second-guess" the "reasonable judgments" of skilled professionals. Do you agree? Defend your answer.

Livent, Inc.

The structure of a play is always the story of how the birds came home to roost.

Arthur Miller

In 1995, Canadian native Maria Messina achieved one of the most sought-after career goals in the public accounting profession when she was promoted to partner with Deloitte & Touche, Chartered Accountants, the Canadian affiliate of the U.S.-based Deloitte & Touche LLP. In an interview she granted to an accounting trade publication shortly after receiving that promotion, Ms. Messina noted that "Becoming a partner is exciting because you are a part of everything." [1] Messina's promotion earned her the respect and admiration of her family, her friends, and her colleagues and catapulted her to a much higher tax bracket and a more comfortable standard of living. But another opportunity soon arose, an opportunity that promised even more intrinsic and extrinsic rewards for Messina.

Throughout the 1990s, Livent, Inc., was the only publicly owned company whose primary line of business was live theatrical productions. Livent's cofounder and the individual recognized as the creative genius responsible for the company's impressive string of Tony Award–winning shows was Garth Drabinsky. Livent's audit firm was Deloitte & Touche, Chartered Accountants. Maria Messina served as the engagement partner for the 1996 audit, after having been the audit manager on several prior audits of the company. Following the completion of the 1996 Livent audit, Drabinsky asked Messina to leave Deloitte & Touche and become Livent's chief financial officer (CFO). After carefully weighing the challenges, opportunities, and potential drawbacks of making the job change, Messina gave up the partnership position with Deloitte & Touche that she had coveted for years in exchange for a "back office" but high-paying and high-profile position in the glitzy and glamorous world of show business.

Within a few weeks of signing on with Livent, Maria Messina was questioning the wisdom of her decision. Time budgets, out-of-town travel, inexperienced subordinates, and an array of other common "stressors" faced by partners of major accounting firms had complicated Messina's professional and personal life when she was at Deloitte. But, at Livent, the pressures she faced were much more intense, much more difficult to manage and control, even physically debilitating at times. Each passing month imposed a heavier emotional burden on Messina. By the late summer of 1998, Messina's life was in complete disarray. A few months later, in January 1999, Messina pleaded guilty to a felony for her role in a massive financial fraud. Following that plea, the single mother of a 10-year-old daughter faced up to 5 years in prison and a $250,000 fine.

There Is No Business Like Show Business

The entertainment industry had fascinated Garth Drabinsky from an early age. Unlike many of his colleagues in the industry, Drabinsky did not benefit from a network of

---

1. T. Frank, "Opportunity Knocks," *CA Magazine*, March 1997, 27.

family members and friends in show business. Instead, Drabinsky relied on his own drive, inspiration, and indomitable work ethic to claw his way to the top of the volatile and fickle entertainment industry. Born in Toronto in 1947, Drabinsky was struck down by polio at age three, leaving him with a severe limp for the remainder of his life. The young Canadian refused to allow his physical limitations to prevent him from reaching his goals. In fact, Drabinsky freely admits that his physical problems and his modest upbringing—his father sold air conditioners—were key factors that motivated him to "aim for the stars."

During his college years, Drabinsky made his first foray into show business by publishing a free magazine that provided critiques of movies appearing in local theaters. After graduating from law school, where he concentrated his studies on the entertainment industry, Drabinsky became involved in real estate development. The young attorney hoped to accumulate a nest egg that he could use to begin producing movies and live plays. A successful condominium project provided him with the funds he needed to begin dabbling in motion pictures and Broadway productions. By age 30, Drabinsky had produced three feature-length movies and one Broadway musical, none of which were particularly well received by critics or the ticket-buying public.

In 1979, Drabinsky and a close friend, Myron Gottlieb, decided to enter the show business world via the "back door." The two young entrepreneurs persuaded a prominent Toronto businessman to invest nearly $1 million in a "cinema complex" project they had conceived.[2] This project involved converting the basement of a large shopping mall into a multiscreen theater. The design for the "cineplex" included plush interiors for each theater, luxurious seats, and cappuccino bars in the lobby. Drabinsky intended to make a trip to the local movie theater the captivating experience that it had been several decades earlier in the halcyon days of Hollywood.

Most industry insiders predicted that Drabinsky's blueprint for his cineplex concept would fail, principally because the large overhead for his theaters forced his company to charge much higher ticket prices than competitors. But the critics were wrong. Toronto's moviegoers were more than willing to pay a few extra dollars to watch a film in Drabinsky's upscale theaters. Over the next several years, Drabinsky and Gottlieb expanded their company with the help of well-heeled investors whom they convinced to pony up large sums to finance the development of multiscreen theater complexes throughout Canada and the United States. By the mid-1980s, their company, Cineplex Odeon, controlled nearly 2,000 theaters, making it the second-largest theater chain in North America.

Several major investors in Cineplex Odeon eventually began complaining of Drabinsky's unrestrained spending practices. The company's rapid expansion and the increasingly sumptuous designs Drabinsky developed for new theaters required Cineplex Odeon to borrow enormous amounts from banks and other lenders. An internal investigation in 1989 uncovered irregularities in the company's accounting records that wiped out a large profit for the year and resulted in Cineplex Odeon reporting a significant loss instead. The controversy sparked by the discovery of the accounting irregularities gave Cineplex Odeon's major investors the leverage they needed to force Drabinsky and Gottlieb to resign. During the negotiations that led to their departure from the company, Drabinsky and Gottlieb acquired the Pantages Theatre, a large live production theater in Toronto, as well as the Canadian rights to certain Broadway plays.

Within a few weeks after severing their ties with Cineplex Odeon, Drabinsky and Gottlieb had organized Live Entertainment Corporation to produce Broadway-type

---

2. The key financial amounts reported in this case are expressed in Canadian dollars.

shows in their hometown of Toronto. Drabinsky's concept for this new company, which he coaxed several large investors and lenders to bankroll, was to bring "corporate management" to the notoriously freewheeling and undisciplined show business industry. Following a series of widely acclaimed productions, the company—renamed Livent, Inc.—went public in 1993.[3] In May 1995, Livent filed an application with the Securities and Exchange Commission (SEC) to sell its stock in the United States. The SEC approved that application, and Livent's stock began trading on the NASDAQ stock exchange. Within two years, U.S. investors controlled the majority of Livent's outstanding stock.

By early 1998, Livent owned five live production theaters in Canada and the United States, including a major Broadway theater in New York. The company's productions, among them *Fosse, Kiss of the Spider Woman, Ragtime, Show Boat,* and *The Phantom of the Opera*, had garnered a total of more than 20 Tony Awards. Show business insiders attributed Livent's rapid rise to prominence to Garth Drabinsky. After organizing Livent, Drabinsky quickly developed a keen sense of the types of shows that would appeal to the public. Even more important, he was able to identify and recruit talented directors, actors, set designers, and the array of other skilled artisans needed to produce successful Broadway shows. The domineering Drabinsky micromanaged not only the creative realm of Livent's operations but every other major facet of the company's operations as well, although he relied heavily on his friend and confidant, Myron Gottlieb—who had an accounting background—to help him oversee the company's accounting and financial reporting functions.

Despite the artistic success enjoyed by several Livent productions and the company's increasing stature in the entertainment industry, Garth Drabinsky was dogged by critics throughout the 1990s. The enigmatic Drabinsky had a well-deserved reputation as flamboyant and charming with Wall Street analysts, metropolitan bankers, and fellow corporate executives. But critics were prone to point out that Drabinsky also had a darker side to his personality. "He is—by his own admission—complex and difficult, cranky and litigious, breathtakingly ambitious, singled-minded and self-centered."[4] According to company insiders, Drabinsky could be "tyrannical and abusive"[5] to his subordinates, berating them when they failed to live up to his perfectionist standards or when they questioned his decisions. Maria Messina subsequently revealed that Livent's accountants were common targets of verbal abuse by Drabinsky and other Livent executives. "They [Livent's accountants] were told on a very regular basis that they are paid to keep their [expletive] mouths shut and do as they are [expletive] told. They are not paid to think."[6]

Critics also charged that Drabinsky failed to live up to his pledge of bringing a disciplined style of corporate management to Broadway. In reality, Drabinsky was anything but disciplined in managing Livent's finances. Because he demanded that the company's live productions be "motion-picture perfect," most of Livent's shows, particularly those that were box-office successes, incurred huge cost overruns. By 1998, Livent was

---

3. Drabinsky and Gottlieb's company was not affiliated with the California-based Live Entertainment, Inc. Jose Menendez organized the latter company in 1988 but was murdered along with his wife, Kitty, in August 1989. In one of the many "trials of the century," the Menendez's sons, Lyle and Erik, were subsequently convicted of murdering their parents.

4. K. Noble, "The Comeback King: Garth Drabinsky Is Back, and Creating a Lot of Showbiz Buzz," *MacLean's* (online), 4 June 2001.

5. M. Potter and T. Van Alphen, "Livent Charges $7.5 Million Kickback Scam," *Toronto Star* (online), 19 November 1998.

6. *Profit*, "Backstage at Livent," May 1999, 29.

buckling under the huge load of debt Drabinsky had incurred to finance the company's lavish productions. In early 1998, Roy Furman, a Wall Street investment banker and close friend, persuaded Drabinsky to accept a $20 million investment from former Disney executive Michael Ovitz to alleviate Livent's financial problems. A condition of Ovitz's investment was that he be granted sufficient common stock voting rights to allow him to control the company's board of directors.

During the 1980s, Ovitz had reigned as Hollywood's top talent agent. When he became chairman of the Creative Artists Agency, show business periodicals tagged him with the title of "Hollywood's most powerful man." In late 1995, Disney chief executive officer (CEO) Michael Eisner chose Ovitz to serve as his top lieutenant and gave him the title of company president. A little more than one year later, repeated personality clashes between the two Hollywood heavyweights resulted in Eisner dismissing Ovitz. No doubt, Ovitz hoped that Livent would provide him with an opportunity to refurbish his reputation in the entertainment industry, a reputation that had been tarnished during his brief and turbulent stint with Disney. Just as important, taking control of Livent would allow Ovitz to compete head-to-head with his former boss. At the time, Disney's *The Lion King* was a colossal hit on Broadway.

Before agreeing to invest in Livent, the cautious Ovitz retained the Big Five accounting firm KPMG to scrutinize the company's accounting records. After KPMG's "due diligence" investigation yielded a clean bill of health for Livent, Ovitz became the company's largest stockholder in early June of 1998 and took over effective control of the company. Ovitz took a seat on the company's board and became chairman of the board's executive committee, while Furman assumed Drabinsky's former titles of chairman of the board and CEO. Drabinsky was given the titles of vice chairman and chief creative director. In the latter role, Drabinsky continued to oversee the all-important creative facets of Livent's operations. To provide a second opinion on artistic matters, Ovitz appointed the noted producer and songwriter Quincy Jones to Livent's board.

Ovitz also demoted Myron Gottlieb to a vice president position. A former Disney executive who left that company along with Ovitz assumed Gottlieb's former position as Livent's president. Among other changes that Ovitz made in Livent's corporate management structure was the hiring of former KPMG audit partner Robert Webster to serve as an executive vice president of the company. Webster, who had supervised KPMG's due diligence investigation of Livent's accounting records, was given a broad range of responsibilities, but his principal role was to monitor Livent's accounting and finance functions for Ovitz's new management team.

Webster's Summer of Discontent

Like Maria Messina, Robert Webster quickly discovered that the work environment within Livent was much less than ideal. After joining Livent in the early summer of 1998, Webster found that the accounting staff, including Messina, who remained Livent's CFO, was reluctant to discuss accounting matters with him. Webster later testified that some of the Livent accountants "told him that Mr. Drabinsky had warned them not to provide certain financial information until [Drabinsky] had reviewed and approved it."[7] Even more troubling to Webster was Drabinsky's management style. Webster testified that, "I had never before experienced anyone with Drabinsky's

---

7. M. Petersen, "The Roar of the Accountants: The Strange Last Days of a Theater Impresario's Reign," *New York Times* (online), 10 October 1998.

abusive and profane management style."[8] He was shocked to find that Livent's executives often screamed and swore at the company's accountants. Webster reported that after meeting with Drabinsky, Livent's accountants were often in tears or even nauseated. Following one such meeting, Webster recalled Messina "shaking like a leaf."[9]

When Webster demanded that Livent's accountants provide him with unrestricted access to the company's accounting records, the former KPMG partner became the target of Drabinsky's wrath. Drabinsky accused Webster of attempting to "tear the company" apart with his persistent inquiries and told him that he was there to "service his [Drabinsky's] requirements."[10] Webster refused to be deterred by Drabinsky's bullying tactics. In early August 1998, after Webster began asking questions regarding a suspicious transaction he had uncovered, Messina and four of her subordinates secretly met with him. The five accountants admitted to Webster that Livent's accounting records had been distorted by a series of fraudulent schemes initiated and coordinated by Drabinsky and other top Livent executives.

Webster relayed the disturbing revelations to Livent's board. On 11 August 1998, Roy Furman issued a press release announcing that "significant financial irregularities" adversely affecting Livent's financial statements for the past three years had been discovered. The press release also indicated that Drabinsky and Gottlieb had been indefinitely suspended pending the outcome of a forensic investigation by KPMG. During the fall of 1998, company officials issued successive press releases suggesting that the impact of the accounting irregularities would be more severe than initially thought. Adding to Livent's problems was the suspension of all trading in the company's stock and a series of large class-action lawsuits filed against the company and its officers. In August 1998 alone, 12 such lawsuits were filed.

On 18 November 1998, Livent's board announced that KPMG's forensic investigation had revealed "massive, systematic, accounting irregularities that permeated the company."[11] The press release issued by Livent's board also disclosed that Deloitte & Touche had withdrawn its audit opinions on the company's 1995–1997 financial statements. Finally, the press release reported that Drabinsky and Gottlieb had been dismissed and that Livent had simultaneously filed for bankruptcy in Canada and the United States. A few weeks later, a federal grand jury in New York issued a 16-count fraud indictment against Drabinsky and Gottlieb. When the former Livent executives failed to appear for a preliminary court hearing, a U.S. federal judge issued arrest warrants for the two Canadian citizens and initiated extradition proceedings.

A "Pervasive and Multifaceted" Fraud

Details of the fraud allegedly conceived by Garth Drabinsky and Myron Gottlieb were eventually revealed to the public by the SEC, the Ontario Securities Commission—a Canadian agency comparable to the SEC, and publicly available records of various court proceedings in civil lawsuits. In numerous enforcement and litigation releases, SEC officials repeatedly used the descriptive phrase "pervasive and multifaceted" when referring to the Livent fraud. One of the earliest elements of the fraud was a large kickback scheme.

---

8. A. Clark, "An Epic from Livent: Executive Accuses Drabinsky of Bullying Tactics," *MacLean's* (online), 1 March 1999.

9. *Ibid.*

10. *Ibid.*

11. *In re Livent, Inc. Noteholders Securities Litigation*, 151 F. Supp. 2d 371 (2001).

"As early as 1990, and continuing through 1994, Drabinsky and Gottlieb operated a kickback scheme with two Livent vendors designed to siphon millions of dollars from the company directly into their own pockets."[12] Gottlieb reportedly instructed the two vendors to include in the invoices that they submitted to Livent charges for services that they had not provided to the company. After Livent paid the inflated invoice amounts, Drabinsky and Gottlieb received kickbacks equal to the payments for the bogus services. According to the SEC, over a four-year period in the 1990s, Drabinsky and Gottlieb received approximately $7 million in kickbacks from the two Livent vendors. The fake charges billed to Livent by the vendors were capitalized in "preproduction" cost accounts for the various shows being developed by the company. Legitimate costs charged to those accounts included expenditures to produce sets and costumes for new shows, costs that were amortized over a maximum period of five years.

By the mid-1990s, the kickback scheme and large losses being registered by several of Livent's plays made it increasingly difficult for the company to achieve quarterly earnings targets that Drabinsky and Gottlieb had relayed to Wall Street analysts. The two conspirators realized that if Livent failed to reach those earnings targets, the company's credit rating and stock price would fall, jeopardizing the company's ability to raise the additional capital needed to sustain its operations. Faced with these circumstances, the SEC reported that beginning in 1994 Drabinsky and Gottlieb directed Livent's accounting staff to engage in an array of "accounting manipulations" to obscure the company's financial problems.

These manipulations included such blatant subterfuges as simply erasing from the accounting records previously recorded expenses and liabilities at the end of each quarter. A particularly popular accounting scam within Livent involved the transfer of preproduction costs from a show that was running to a show still in production. Such transfers allowed the company to defer, sometimes indefinitely, the amortization of those major cost items. To further reduce the periodic amortization charges for preproduction costs, Livent's accountants began charging such costs to various fixed asset accounts. These assets were typically depreciated over 40 years, compared with the five-year amortization period for preproduction costs. Eventually, the company's accountants began debiting salary expenses and other common operating expenses to long-term fixed asset accounts.

The SEC estimated that the accounting manipulations understated Livent's expenses by more than $30 million in the mid-1990s. Despite the resulting favorable impact on Livent's financial statements, Drabinsky and Gottlieb eventually realized that additional efforts were needed to embellish the company's financial data. So, beginning in 1996, Drabinsky and Gottlieb organized and carried out what the SEC referred to as a "fraudulent revenue-generating" scheme.

This new scam involved several multimillion-dollar transactions arranged by Drabinsky and Gottlieb. The specific details of these transactions varied somewhat, but most of them involved the sale of production rights owned by Livent to third parties. For example, Livent sold the rights to produce *Ragtime* and *Show Boat* in various U.S. theaters to a Texas-based company. The contract for this transaction indicated that the $11.2 million fee paid to Livent by the Texas company was not refundable under any circumstances. However, a secret side agreement arranged by Livent's executives shielded the Texas company from any loss on this deal and, in fact, guaranteed it a reasonable rate of return on its large investment. Despite the considerable

---

12. Securities and Exchange Commission, *Accounting and Auditing Enforcement Release No. 1095*, 19 May 1999.

uncertainty regarding the actual profit, if any, that would ultimately be earned on this and similar transactions, Livent's accounting staff included at least $34 million of revenues on those transactions in the company's 1996 and 1997 income statements.

A final Livent scam documented by the SEC involved inflating reported box-office results for key productions. In late 1997, Livent opened *Ragtime* in a Los Angeles theater. The agreement with that theater allowed it to close the show if weekly ticket sales fell below $500,000. Livent's executives planned to open *Ragtime* on Broadway in January 1998. Those executives realized that if the show fared poorly in Los Angeles, its Broadway opening could be jeopardized. To inflate *Ragtime*'s ticket sales during its Los Angeles run, Livent executives arranged to have two of the company's vendors—the same individuals involved in the fraudulent kickback scheme alluded to previously—purchase several hundred thousand dollars of tickets to the show. Livent reimbursed the vendors for these ticket purchases and charged the payments to various fixed asset accounts.

The fraudulent schemes engineered by Livent's executives caused the company's periodic financial statements to be grossly misrepresented. For example, in 1992, the company reported a pretax profit of $2.9 million when the actual figure was approximately $100,000. Four years later, Livent reported a pretax profit of $14.2 million, when it actually incurred a loss of more than $20 million. By 1997, the company's total fixed assets of $200.8 million were overstated by nearly $24 million due to the various accounting schemes.

SEC officials found two features of the Livent fraud particularly disturbing. As the scope of the fraud steadily grew throughout the 1990s, the company's accounting staff found it increasingly difficult to provide meaningful financial data to top management. "Because of the sheer magnitude and dollar amount of the manipulations, it became necessary for senior management to be able to track both the real and the phony numbers."[13] Gordon Eckstein, the company's senior vice president of finance and administration and Maria Messina's immediate superior, allegedly instructed a subordinate to develop computer software that would solve this problem. This software could be used to filter the bogus data out of the company's accounting records. The secret software also served a second purpose, namely, allowing Livent's accountants to record fraudulent transactions "without leaving a paper trail that Livent's outside auditors might stumble across."[14] The accountants processed in a batch mode the fraudulent changes in the accounting records demanded by Livent's executives. When these so-called "adjustments" were processed, they replaced the initial journal entries for the given transactions, making the adjustments appear as if they were the original transactions, thus duping the company's Deloitte auditors.

The second extremely troubling feature of the Livent fraud, according to the SEC, was the matter-of-fact manner in which the company's management team organized and carried out the fraud. Reportedly, Drabinsky, Gottlieb, and Robert Topol, Livent's chief operating officer (COO), regularly met with Eckstein, Messina, and other members of the company's accounting staff to discuss the details of the fraud. At these meetings, the three top executives reviewed preliminary financial reports prepared by the accounting staff and instructed the accountants on the "adjustments" needed to improve or embellish those reports. As suggested earlier, Livent's top executives relied on coercion and intimidation to browbeat their accountants, including Messina, into accepting these illicit changes. Once the adjustments were processed,

---

13. *Ibid.*

14. M. A. Hiltzik and J. Bates, "U.S. Indicts Stage Producer Drabinsky," *Los Angeles Times* (online), 14 January 1999.

"the bogus numbers were presented to Livent's audit committee, the auditors, investors, and eventually filed with the Commission [SEC]."[15]

Keeping the Auditors in the Dark

Press reports of a large accounting fraud involving a public company often prompt scathing criticism of the company's independent audit firm. The disclosure of the Livent fraud in the late summer and fall of 1998 caused Deloitte & Touche to become a target of such criticism. A Canadian financial analyst observed that investors depend on auditors to clamp down on their clients and force them to prepare reliable financial reports. "They [auditors] are the only ones in a position to question the policies, to question the numbers, to make sure they're right."[16]

Critics could readily point to several red flags or fraud risk factors during Deloitte's tenure with Livent that should have placed the accounting firm on high alert regarding the possible existence of financial statement misrepresentations. Among those factors were an extremely aggressive, growth-oriented management team; a history of prior financial reporting indiscretions by Drabinsky and Gottlieb; a constant and growing need for additional capital; and the existence of related-party transactions. Regarding the latter factor, several of Livent's fraudulent "revenue-generating transactions" that were documented by the SEC involved companies or corporate executives affiliated with Livent or its management team.

In Deloitte's defense, a massive collusive fraud that involves a client's top executives and the active participation of its accountants is difficult to detect. Making matters worse for Deloitte was the contemptuous attitude that Livent's executives had toward independent auditors. At one point, a top Livent officer told a subordinate that independent auditors were a "necessary evil and that it was no one's business how they [Livent's executives] ran their company."[17] Also complicating the Livent audits for Deloitte was the fact Maria Messina and Christopher Craib, two former members of the Livent audit engagement team, had accepted key accounting positions with the company. The personal relationships the auditors had with Messina and Craib may have impaired their objectivity during the Livent engagements.

Christopher Craib replaced Maria Messina as the audit manager assigned to the Livent audit engagement team following Messina's promotion to partner in 1995. After the 1996 audit was completed, Drabinsky hired Craib to serve as Livent's senior controller for budgeting. Not long after joining Livent, Craib, a chartered accountant, became involved in the ongoing effort to segregate Livent's "real" accounting data from its bogus data. In subsequent testimony, Craib recalled meeting with Gordon Eckstein to discuss Livent's schizoid accounting system. Eckstein explained to Craib why it was imperative to track both the real and bogus accounting data: "I have to keep all the lies straight. I have to know what lies I'm telling these people [outside auditors]. I've told so many lies to different people I have to make sure they all make sense."[18]

Like Craib, Maria Messina realized that concealing the Livent fraud from the Deloitte auditors was among her primary responsibilities. During a meeting shortly after Messina joined Livent, she became aware of the adversarial attitude that Livent's top executives had toward the company's independent auditors. During this meeting,

15. Securities and Exchange Commission, *Accounting and Auditing Enforcement Release No. 1095.*

16. J. McCarten, "Auditors Taking the Heat after Financial Scandals," *Toronto Star* (online), 18 August 1998.

17. Securities and Exchange Commission, *Accounting and Auditing Enforcement Release No. 1096,* 19 May 1999.

18. *Ibid.*

Topol became angry when Messina raised an issue involving what documents to turn over to Deloitte. Topol responded with an angry outburst. "[Expletive] you and your auditors…. I don't care what they see or don't see."[19]

Despite the efforts of Livent officials to sabotage their independent audits, the company's Deloitte auditors focused considerable attention on several suspicious transactions that they uncovered. The Deloitte auditors became increasingly skeptical of Livent's accounting records in 1996 and 1997 when Drabinsky and his colleagues were scrambling to conceal the deteriorating financial condition of their company while, at the same time, attempting to raise much needed debt and equity capital.

Near the end of the 1996 audit, Deloitte & Touche LLP, the U.S.-based branch of the firm, initially refused to allow its Canadian affiliate to issue an unqualified audit opinion on Livent's financial statements that were to be filed with the SEC. Deloitte's top technical partners in the United States believed that Livent had been much too aggressive in recognizing revenue on a few large transactions—transactions that, unknown to partners of both the firm's Canadian and U.S. affiliates, included fraudulent elements. After a series of meetings between Livent officials and representatives of Deloitte & Touche LLP, a compromise was reached. Livent agreed to defer the recognition of revenue on one of the two large transactions in question until 1997. In return, Deloitte allowed the company to record the full amount of the revenue for the other disputed transaction.

During 1997, a major transaction with a real estate firm triggered another conflict between Deloitte and Livent management. In the second quarter of that year, the real estate firm purchased for $7.4 million the development rights to a valuable parcel of land owned by Livent. The contract between the two companies included a stipulation or "put agreement" allowing the real estate firm to cancel the transaction prior to the date that it began developing the property. When the Deloitte audit engagement partner learned of the put agreement, he insisted that no revenue could be recorded for the transaction. Complicating matters was the fact that the transaction involved a related party since Myron Gottlieb served on the board of directors of the real estate firm's parent company.

To quell the audit partner's concern, Gottlieb arranged to have an executive of the real estate firm send the partner a letter indicating that the put agreement had been cancelled—which it had not. After receiving the letter, the Deloitte partner told Gottlieb that the revenue resulting from the transaction could be recorded during Livent's third quarter when the put agreement had allegedly been cancelled. At this point, a frustrated Gottlieb ignored the partner's decision and included the disputed revenue in Livent's earnings press release for the second quarter of 1997.

When Deloitte officials learned of the press release, they demanded a meeting with Livent's board of directors. At this meeting, Deloitte threatened to resign. After considerable discussion, Livent's board and the Deloitte representatives reached a compromise. According to a subsequent legal transcript, the board agreed to reverse the journal entry for the $7.4 million transaction in the second quarter, recording it instead during the third quarter. The board also agreed to issue an amended earnings release for the second quarter. In exchange for these concessions, Deloitte officials purportedly agreed to allow Livent to reverse certain accrued liabilities that had been recorded at the end of the second quarter. The reversal of those accrued liabilities and the corresponding expenses reduced by approximately 20 percent the profit

19. Securities and Exchange Commission, *Accounting and Auditing Enforcement Release No. 1097*, 19 May 1999.

"correction" reported by Livent in the amended earnings press release for the second quarter.[20]

Another serious disagreement arose between Livent executives and Deloitte auditors shortly after the dispute just described was resolved. During the third quarter of 1997, Livent's management arranged to sell for $12.5 million the naming rights for one of its existing theaters and a new theater that the company was planning to build. Neither Maria Messina nor the Deloitte auditors assigned to the Livent engagement believed that the $12.5 million payment should be recorded immediately as revenue since the contract between Livent and the other party, AT&T, was strictly an oral agreement at the time and since one of the theaters was yet to be built. Gottlieb retained Ernst & Young (E&Y) to review the matter.

The report E&Y submitted to Gottlieb did not take a firm position on the revenue recognition issue. Instead, E&Y's report simply suggested that the $12.5 million payment for the naming rights could be "considered" for recording during the third quarter. After receiving a copy of E&Y's report, Deloitte hired Price Waterhouse to review the transaction. When Price Waterhouse reached the same conclusion as E&Y, Deloitte allowed Livent to book the $12.5 million as revenue during the third quarter.

Don't Blame Me, Blame...

Resolving the legal implications of a major accounting and financial reporting fraud can require years. However, one Canadian journalist suggested that in the Livent case the legal wrangling could continue even longer, possibly for decades.[21] From its inception, a key factor complicating the resolution of this case was its "cross-border" nature.

Beginning in late 1998, officials from several federal agencies in Canada and the United States became embroiled in a tedious and often contentious struggle to determine which agency would be the first to prosecute the key parties involved in the Livent fraud. Those agencies included the Royal Canadian Mounted Police, the Ontario Securities Commission, the SEC, and the U.S. Department of Justice, among others. Law enforcement authorities in the United States failed to win the cooperation of their Canadian counterparts in attempting to extradite Garth Drabinsky and Myron Gottlieb to face a series of federal fraud charges filed against them in U.S. courts. Even more frustrating to U.S. authorities was the snail's pace at which Canadian authorities moved in pursuing legal action against the two alleged fraudsters.

While Canadian and U.S. law enforcement authorities tangled over jurisdictional matters, the leading actors in the final Livent "production" waged a public relations war against each other in major metropolitan newspapers and in the courts. Drabinsky and Gottlieb were the most vocal of these individuals. They repeatedly insisted that they were not responsible for the various fraudulent schemes that had been uncovered within Livent. At a press conference held in early 1999, Drabinsky suggested that he had been too busy overseeing Livent's creative operations to become involved in any creative bookkeeping.[22] In his typical Shakespearean manner, Drabinsky declared: "The final act of this tragedy has yet to be played out

20. *In re Livent, Inc. Noteholders Securities Litigation*. As a point of information, this legal transcript did not include any commentary from Deloitte's perspective regarding the nature and outcome of these negotiations.

21. Noble, "The Comeback King."

22. M. Lewyckyj, "Livent's Accounting Designed to Deceive," *Toronto Sun* (online), 15 January 1999.

and, when it is, Myron Gottlieb and I have complete confidence that we will be vindicated."[23]

In January 1999, Myron Gottlieb filed a civil lawsuit against Maria Messina, Christopher Craib, Gordon Eckstein, and three other former Livent accountants; the lawsuit charged those six individuals with responsibility for the Livent accounting fraud. In court documents filed with this lawsuit, Gottlieb alleged that he was not "an expert on accounting practices" and that he had relied on Livent's accounting staff to ensure that the company's financial statements were accurate.[24] In responding to that lawsuit, the six named defendants, with the exception of Eckstein, claimed that they had been coerced into participating in the fraud by its principal architects.[25] These defendants also rejected Gottlieb's assertion that he was unfamiliar with accounting practices. "Gottlieb was and remains an experienced businessman with a sophisticated and comprehensive grasp of accounting and auditing issues and intimate knowledge of the details of Livent's accounting practices."[26]

When Eckstein eventually responded to Gottlieb's lawsuit, he charged the Livent cofounder with being a key architect of the accounting fraud.[27] Eckstein also insisted that Maria Messina had played a key role in the fraudulent scheme. In particular, Eckstein claimed that Messina had used her relationship with the Deloitte auditors to ensure that they approved Livent's fraudulent financial statements.[28]

Messina answered Eckstein and other critics by maintaining that she had attempted to dissuade Livent's executives from using accounting gimmicks to boost the company's revenues and profits. She insisted that she had "begged" her former colleagues at Deloitte to crack down on the aggressive revenue recognition policies being used by Livent's management.[29] To support her claim that she had not been a willing member of the Livent conspiracy, Messina pointed out that she had refused to sign the letters of representations for the 1996 and 1997 audits, each of which indicated that there were no material inaccuracies in Livent's financial statements. In fact, near the end of the 1997 audit, Messina had redrafted Deloitte's preformatted letter of representations to remove her name from it.[30]

After firing Drabinsky and Gottlieb, Michael Ovitz and the members of the new management team he installed at Livent in June 1998 sued the company's cofounders for $325 million for their alleged role in the fraudulent accounting schemes. That lawsuit prompted Drabinsky and Gottlieb to file a $200 million defamation-of-character lawsuit against Ovitz and his colleagues.

In September 1998, Drabinsky sued KPMG, the accounting firm that Ovitz had retained to perform a due diligence investigation earlier in the year and the firm retained by Livent's board of directors in August 1998 to investigate the charges of

---

23. C. Brodesser and M. Peers, "U.S. Indicts Duo in Liventgate," *Variety*, 18 January 1999, 137.

24. *The Gazette* (online), "Livent Co-Founder Sues 6 Employees," 19 February 1999.

25. V. Menon, "Livent Whistle-Blowers File Defence," *Toronto Star* (online), 1 April 1999.

26. B. Bouw, "Livent Employees Fight Back: 'Gottlieb to Blame,'" *National Post* (online), 1 April 1999.

27. B. Shecter, "Drabinsky's Assertions Refuted," *National Post* (online), 26 June 1999.

28. *Ibid.*

29. *Profit*, "Backstage at Livent." In a deposition filed in one of the many lawsuits triggered by the Livent fraud, Messina described Deloitte's audits of the company as "inadequate." See D. Francis, "Livent: A Bean Counter Scandal," *National Post* (online), 10 May 2001.

30. In a court document, Messina reported that she did not reveal the various Livent fraudulent schemes prior to August 1998 because she feared Drabinsky and Gottlieb and because she believed that she would be "implicated by association." See B. Bouw, "Livent Employees Fight Back: 'Gottlieb to Blame,'" *National Post* (online), 1 April 1999.

accounting irregularities revealed by Maria Messina and her subordinates. That law-suit, which requested damages of more than $26 million, was predicated on the fact that Drabinsky had been a client of KPMG over the past two decades. Drabinsky charged that by agreeing to perform the forensic audit requested by Livent's board in August 1998, KPMG had placed itself in a conflict of interest between two clients.[31]

Deloitte & Touche was a primary target of the various plaintiffs attempting to hold someone responsible for the Livent debacle and the resulting financial losses. In December 1999, a U.S. federal judge dismissed Deloitte as a defendant in one of those lawsuits filed by Livent's former stockholders. The judge concluded that the plaintiffs had not made a reasonable argument that Deloitte was at least "reckless" in auditing Livent. For lawsuits filed under the Securities and Exchange Act of 1934, as amended by the Private Securities Litigation Reform Act (PSLRA) of 1995, plaintiffs must allege or "plead" that the given defendant was at least "reckless."

In another class-action lawsuit filed by Livent creditors, a federal judge ruled in June 2001 that the plaintiffs had met the pleading standard of recklessness, mean-ing that the lawsuit could proceed. This judge observed that Livent's "accounting manipulations" were so flagrant that there was a reasonable likelihood Deloitte was reckless in failing to discover them. "Deloitte & Touche's actions and omissions in connection with Livent's manipulations of its books and records display acqui-escence and passivity that, in this Court's reading of the pleadings, cross over the boundary of ordinary breaches of reasonable care into the zone of recklessness."[32] Published reports indicate that Deloitte & Touche was dropped as a defendant in this case after it agreed to pay $5.5 million to a restitution fund established for Livent's former creditors.

EPILOGUE

As predicted, Canadian law enforcement authorities were extremely methodical in pursuing their investigation and prosecution of Garth Drabinsky, Myron Gottlieb, and the other key individuals involved in the Livent scandal. In late 2002, the Royal Mounted Canadian Police finally filed a fraud indict-ment against Drabinsky and Gottlieb that contained 19 individual charges. Five years later, Gordon Eckstein pleaded guilty to one count of fraud and agreed to testify against Drabinsky and Gottlieb. Eckstein's testimony and the testimony of Maria Messina would prove to be pivotal evidence in the 11-month long criminal trial of Drabinsky and Gottlieb. That trial ended in late March 2009 with both Drabinsky and Gottlieb being convicted of fraud and forgery.

The Canadian judge who presided over the lengthy trial rejected Drabinsky and Gottlieb's principal argument that they had been unaware of the massive accounting fraud and that it had been orchestrated by their subordinates. In handing down her verdict, the judge con-cluded that the two executives "had initiated the improper accounting system" that had "systemically manipulated" Livent's reported operating results and financial condition.[33,34]

---

31. Drabinsky and KPMG ultimately settled this lawsuit out of court. Although the settlement's financial terms were not disclosed, KPMG acknowledged that it had breached its "fiduciary duty" to Drabinsky by agreeing to perform the forensic audit requested by Livent's board.

32. *In re Livent, Inc. Noteholders Securities Litigation.*

33. *Reuters* (online), "Former Broadway Impresario Drabinsky Found Guilty," 25 March 2009.

34. Robert Topol, Livent's former COO, had faced charges similar to those for which Drabinsky and Gottlieb were prosecuted. However, those charges were dismissed in 2008 when his attorneys con-vinced the judge that he had been denied his right to a speedy trial.

In August 2009, the judge sentenced Drabinsky and Gottlieb to prison sentences of seven years and six years, respectively.

Drabinsky and Gottlieb lost the appeals of their convictions, but the appellate court reduced their prison sentences to five years and four years, respectively. The two men began serving their sentences in 2011. After serving approximately one-third of his sentence, Gottlieb was paroled in early 2013. After serving 17 months of his sentence, Drabinsky received a "day parole" in February 2013, meaning that he would be free to leave the halfway house where he was serving his sentence during daytime hours but would be required to return to that facility each night. Drabinsky was expected to receive a full parole in early 2014. The double jeopardy provisions in Canada's criminal statutes prevented the two men from being extradited to the United States where they would be subject to prosecution for the same crimes for which they had been convicted in Canada.

In July 1999, SFX Entertainment purchased the remaining assets of Livent, ending the company's dramatic and turbulent existence after only 10 years. In June 2000, the disciplinary committee of the Institute of Chartered Accountants of Ontario (ICAO) sanctioned the former Livent accountants who had publicly admitted some degree of involvement in the Livent fraud. Maria Messina, who pleaded guilty to three charges of professional misconduct, was fined $7,500 and suspended from practicing as a chartered accountant for two years. Christopher Craib received a six-month suspension and a $1,000 fine.

In 2007, the ICAO found three of the Deloitte auditors who had been assigned to the 1997 Livent audit engagement team guilty of professional misconduct, publicly reprimanded them, and levied fines against them and Deloitte totaling $1.55 million. In early 2010, a Canadian appellate court overturned those sanctions. The court ruled that the ICAO had failed to prove that the Deloitte auditors were guilty of a "significant departure" from professional standards during the 1997 Livent audit.

The SEC sanctioned Craib and three other Livent accountants who had confessed to some role in the Livent accounting fraud. Craib received a three-year suspension from practicing before the SEC. During the criminal trial of Drabinsky and Gottlieb, their defense attorneys revealed that Maria Messina was being paid $325,000 annually by Livent's bankruptcy receiver to testify in the various Livent-related lawsuits. Those attorneys also reported that law enforcement authorities in the United States had privately agreed to drop all charges against Messina if Drabinsky and Gottlieb were ultimately sent to prison. Subsequent to the imprisonment of Drabinsky and Gottlieb, neither the SEC nor the U.S. Justice Department has publicly commented on Messina's status. In 1999, after pleading guilty to violating U.S. federal securities laws, Messina's sentencing had been delayed pending the resolution of the criminal charges filed against Drabinsky and Gottlieb.

The criminal convictions and subsequent imprisonment of Drabinsky and Gottlieb did not end the long-running Livent legal ordeal. As of late 2013, a $450 million civil lawsuit against Deloitte stemming from the firm's Livent audits was still in process in a Toronto court.

Questions

1. Identify common inherent risk factors that companies involved in the entertainment industry pose for their independent auditors. List and briefly describe specific audit procedures that would not be used on "typical" audit engagements but would be required for audits of companies involved in live theatrical productions, such as Livent.

2. Compare and contrast the responsibilities of an audit partner of a major accounting firm with those of a large public company's CFO. Which work role do you believe is more important? Which is more stressful? Which role would you prefer and why?

3. Explain why some corporate executives may perceive that their independent auditors are a "necessary evil." How can auditors combat or change that attitude?

4. When auditor–client disputes arise during an audit engagement, another accounting firm is sometimes retained by the client and/or the existing auditor to provide an objective report on the issue at the center of the dispute—as happened during Deloitte's 1997 audit of Livent. Discuss an accounting firm's responsibilities when it is retained to issue such a report.

5. Do you believe Deloitte & Touche should have approved Livent's decision to record the $12.5 million "naming rights" payment as revenue during the third quarter of 1997? Defend your answer. What broad accounting concepts should be considered in determining the proper accounting treatment for such transactions?

6. Maria Messina testified that when she learned of the accounting irregularities at Livent shortly after becoming the company's CFO she felt "guilty by association," which prevented her from revealing the fraud to regulatory or law enforcement authorities. Explain what you believe she meant by that statement. Place yourself in Messina's position. What would you have done after discovering the fraudulent schemes affecting Livent's accounting records?

7. What professional standards apply to "due diligence" investigations performed by accounting firms?

SECTION 2

AUDITS OF HIGH-RISK ACCOUNTS

Jack Greenberg, Inc.

Auditors commonly find themselves facing situations in which they must persuade client executives to do something they absolutely and resolutely do not want to do. When all else fails, auditors may be forced to use a tactic that clinical psychologists, marriage counselors, parents of toddlers, and other interpersonal experts typically frown upon; namely, the old-fashioned "if you don't cooperate, I will punish you" threat. In the mid-1990s, an exasperated team of Grant Thornton auditors resorted to threatening a stubborn client executive to goad him into turning over key documents that had significant audit implications. The executive eventually capitulated and turned over the documents—which resulted in even more problems for the auditors.

The Brothers Greenberg

For decades, Jack Greenberg oversaw a successful wholesale meat company, a company that he eventually incorporated and named after himself.[1] Jack Greenberg, Inc., marketed a variety of meat, cheese, and other food products along the Eastern Seaboard of the United States from its Philadelphia headquarters. Jack Greenberg's failing health in the early 1980s prompted him to place his two sons in charge of the company's day-to-day operations. After their father's death, the two brothers, Emanuel and Fred, became equal partners in the business. Emanuel assumed the title of company president, while Fred became the company's vice president. The two brothers and their mother made up the company's three-person board of directors. Several other members of the Greenberg family also worked in the business.

Similar to many family-owned and -operated businesses, Jack Greenberg, Inc. (JGI), did not place a heavy emphasis on internal control. Like their father, the two Greenberg brothers relied primarily upon their own intuition and the competence and integrity of their key subordinates to manage and control their company's operations. By the mid-1980s, when the privately owned business had annual sales measured in the tens of millions of dollars, Emanuel realized that JGI needed to develop a more formal accounting and control system. That realization convinced him to begin searching for a new company controller who had the expertise necessary to revamp JGI's outdated accounting function and to develop an appropriate network of internal controls for the growing company. In 1987, Emanuel hired Steve Cohn, a CPA and former auditor with Coopers & Lybrand, as JGI's controller. Cohn, who had extensive experience working with a variety of different inventory systems, immediately tackled the challenging assignment of creating a modern accounting and control system for JGI.

Among other changes, Cohn implemented new policies and procedures that provided for segregation of key responsibilities within JGI's transaction cycles. Cohn also integrated computer processing throughout most of JGI's operations, including the payroll, receivables, and payables modules of the company's accounting function. One of the more important changes that Cohn implemented was developing an internal reporting system that produced monthly financial statements the Greenbergs

---

1. The facts of this case and the quotations included in it were taken from the following court opinion: *Larry Waslow, Trustee for Jack Greenberg, Inc., v. Grant Thornton LLP*; United States Bankruptcy Court for the Eastern District of Pennsylvania, 240 B.R. 486; 1999 Bankr. LEXIS 1308.

could use to make more timely and informed decisions for their business. Cohn's new financial reporting system also allowed JGI to file more timely financial statements with the three banks that provided the bulk of the company's external financing. By the early 1990s, JGI typically had a minimum of $10 million in outstanding loans from those banks.

One area of JGI's operations that Cohn failed to modernize was the company's accounting and control procedures for prepaid inventory. Since the company's early days, imported meat products had accounted for a significant portion of JGI's annual sales. Because foreign suppliers required JGI to prepay for frozen meat items, the company maintained two inventory accounts: Prepaid Inventory and Merchandise Inventory. Prepayments for imported meat products were debited to the Prepaid Inventory account, while all other merchandise acquired by the company for resale was debited to the Merchandise Inventory account. Prepaid inventory typically accounted for 60 percent of JGI's total inventory and 40 percent of the company's total assets.

Long before Cohn became JGI's controller, Jack Greenberg had given his son Fred complete responsibility for the purchasing, accounting, control, and other decisions affecting the company's prepaid inventory. Following their father's death, the two brothers agreed that Fred would continue overseeing JGI's prepaid inventory. When Cohn attempted to restructure and computerize the accounting and control procedures for prepaid inventory, Fred refused to cooperate. Despite frequent and adamant pleas from Cohn over a period of several years, Emanuel refused to order his younger brother to cooperate with Cohn's modernization plan for JGI's accounting system.

Accounting for Prepaid Inventory

Fred Greenberg processed the purchase orders for meat products that JGI bought from foreign vendors. The items purchased were inspected by the appropriate authority in the given country and then loaded into refrigerated lockers to be transported by boat to the United States. When a vendor provided documentation to JGI that a shipment was in transit, Fred Greenberg approved payment of the vendor's invoice. Again, these payments were debited to JGI's Prepaid Inventory account. Fred Greenberg maintained a handwritten accounting record known as the prepaid inventory log to keep track of the items included in the Prepaid Inventory account at any point in time.

When a shipment of imported meat products arrived at a U.S. port, a customs broker retained by JGI arranged for the individual items to be inspected and approved for entry into the United States by customs officials. After a shipment had cleared customs, the customs broker sent a notification form to that effect to Fred Greenberg. When the product arrived by truck at JGI's warehouse, a U.S. Department of Agriculture (USDA) official opened and inspected the items included in the order. The USDA official completed a document known as Form 9540-1 to indicate that the items had passed inspection. Each Form 9540-1 also indicated the date that the given products had arrived at JGI's warehouse.

Upon completion of the USDA inspection process, the prepaid inventory items were turned over to the manager of JGI's warehouse. The warehouse manager stamped the items to indicate that they had passed the USDA inspection and then completed a document known as a delivery receipt that listed the date of arrival, the vendor, the type of product, and the quantity of the product. The warehouse manager sent the delivery receipt form to Fred Greenberg, who matched the form with the appropriate vendor invoice. Fred then deleted the given inventory items from the prepaid inventory log and forwarded the matched invoice and delivery receipt to Steve Cohn, who processed an accounting entry that transferred the product from the Prepaid Inventory account to the Merchandise Inventory account. At the end of each year, JGI took a physical inventory of the company's warehouse and adjusted the balance of the Merchandise Inventory account to agree with the results of the physical inventory.

Because of the accounting procedures used for JGI's two inventory accounts, there was some risk that certain inventory items would be "double-counted" at year-end. That is, certain inventory items might be included in both the Prepaid Inventory and Merchandise Inventory accounts if there was any delay in processing the delivery receipt forms. For example, suppose that a shipment of imported meat products arrived at JGI's warehouse on 29 December, two days before the close of the company's fiscal year. If Fred Greenberg failed to delete the items in the shipment from the prepaid inventory log and failed to forward the delivery receipt and invoice for the shipment to Steve Cohn on a timely basis, the items in the shipment would be included in both inventory accounts at the end of the year.[2] To reduce the risk of such errors, Cohn reconciled the prepaid inventory log maintained by Fred to the year-end balance of the Prepaid Inventory account. Cohn also asked Fred to allow him to review any delivery receipts that arrived during the last few days of the fiscal year.

Fred's Fraud

Steve Cohn realized that the accounting procedures for prepaid inventory increased the risk that JGI's year-end inventory would be misstated. In early 1992, Cohn, who by this time had been given the title of chief financial officer, designed a computerized accounting system for JGI's prepaid inventory. Cohn then called a meeting with the two Greenberg brothers to illustrate the system and demonstrate the important information and control advantages that it would provide over the "sloppy" manual system that Fred had used for years to account for prepaid inventory. Several years later, Cohn would recount how the Greenberg brothers reacted to his proposal.

> I told Fred how this was a great idea and how I believed that this would be a big step forward in being able to monitor the [prepaid] inventory and determine what was open.... And I showed it to Fred, looked at it and said, "Isn't this great? We can do this." And I said, "Don't you want to do this?" And he looked at me and said, "No."

> I was flabbergasted. I looked over to Manny [Emanuel]. He just sat there. And I was furious. I didn't talk to Fred for weeks. I was—I was having a hard time dealing with it. I couldn't imagine why he wouldn't want me to do this. It was such a good thing for the company. And he didn't want to do it.

Later in 1992, the persistent Cohn decided to personally collect the information needed to maintain a computerized accounting system for JGI's prepaid inventory. Cohn would watch for delivery trucks arriving at JGI's warehouse, which was adjacent to the company's administrative offices. When a truck arrived, either he or a subordinate would go to the shipping dock and make copies of the delivery receipt and other documents for each shipment of imported meat products. "We used to run back and forth trying to get these receivings [delivery receipts] that [the warehouse manager] was preparing and it became a game. I became a laughingstock because it was a joke that I was trying to get this information." After several weeks, an exasperated Cohn gave up his futile effort.

---

2. Because such items would be present during the year-end physical inventory of JGI's warehouse, the book-to-physical inventory adjustment would cause them to be included in the 31 December balance of the Merchandise Inventory account.

Fred Greenberg had reason not to cooperate with Cohn's repeated attempts to overhaul the accounting and control procedures for JGI's prepaid inventory. Since the mid-1980s, Fred had been intentionally overstating the company's prepaid inventory. Those overstatements had materially understated JGI's annual cost of goods sold as well as overstated the company's gross profit and net income each year. In subsequent court testimony, Fred reported that his father's failing health had compelled him to begin manipulating JGI's reported operating results. "To avoid aggravating his illness, I started the practice [inflating prepaid inventory] so he would feel better about his business."

Fred also testified that following his father's death "significant changes occurring in the market which adversely affected us" caused him to continue his fraudulent scheme. During the late 1980s and early 1990s, Fred and his brother found it increasingly difficult to compete with larger wholesalers that were encroaching on their company's market. To compete with these larger companies, JGI was forced to reduce the gross margins on the products that it sold. To mitigate the impact of this competitive pressure on JGI's operating results, Fred routinely overstated prepaid inventory to produce gross margins that approximated those historically realized by the company.

> Fred manipulated the dates upon which the prepaid inventory was received in order to make it appear that the company's operations generated the same general financial performance from period to period. He did this by determining how much inventory needed to be prepaid inventory so that the percentages of gross profit and net income would remain consistent.

To overstate prepaid inventory, Fred destroyed delivery receipts forwarded to him by JGI's warehouse manager and neglected to update the prepaid inventory log for the given shipments. Weeks or even months later, he would prepare new delivery receipts for those shipments, delete the items in the shipments from the prepaid inventory log, and then forward the receipts along with the corresponding vendor invoices to Cohn. This practice resulted in inventory items being included in the Prepaid Inventory account well after they had arrived at JGI's warehouse.

Auditing Prepaid Inventory

Grant Thornton served as JGI's independent audit firm from 1986 through 1994. Because prepaid inventory was JGI's largest asset and because it posed significant audit risks, the engagement audit team allocated a disproportionate amount of audit resources to that item. Several weeks before the end of each fiscal year, Grant Thornton provided Steve Cohn with an "Engagement Compliance Checklist" that identified the documents and other information needed by the audit engagement team to complete the audit. Many of these requested items involved JGI's prepaid inventory, including "government forms, bills of lading, insurance information, and the delivery receipts prepared by the warehouse personnel evidencing the date upon which the [prepaid] inventory was received at the warehouse." Each year, Grant Thornton also requested a copy of Fred Greenberg's prepaid inventory log and Cohn's reconciliation of the information in that record to JGI's general ledger controlling account for prepaid inventory.

One key item that Grant Thornton did not request from Cohn was the Form 9540-1 prepared for each shipment of imported meat products delivered to JGI's warehouse. Grant Thornton auditors later testified that they became aware in 1988 that a Form 9540-1 was prepared for each prepaid inventory shipment received by JGI. However, the audit team did not learn until 1993 that the USDA official who completed the 9540-1 gave a copy of that document to a JGI warehouse clerk.

Each year, Cohn diligently collected the information requested by Grant Thornton and gave it to the accounting firm well before the date the audit was to begin, with one exception. Because Fred Greenberg failed to give the prepaid inventory log, delivery receipts, and other information he maintained for JGI's prepaid inventory to Cohn on a timely basis, Grant Thornton received that information well after the audit had begun each year.

Grant Thornton audited all of JGI's prepaid inventory transactions each year. "Grant Thornton tested 100 percent of the prepaid inventory transactions which meant that Grant Thornton examined every invoice for prepaid inventory and reviewed the delivery receipts to confirm if and when a delivery had been made." By examining the invoices and delivery receipts, the auditors could determine which prepaid inventory purchases were apparently "still open" at year-end, that is, the prepaid inventory shipments that were properly included in JGI's year-end Prepaid Inventory account.

Because Fred Greenberg had destroyed many of the delivery receipts prepared by the warehouse manager, the Grant Thornton auditors failed to discover that much of JGI's year-end prepaid inventory was "double-counted." A critical issue in subsequent litigation stemming from this case was whether Grant Thornton was justified in relying on the delivery receipts to audit JGI's year-end prepaid inventory. Members of the audit engagement team maintained that because JGI's warehouse manager prepared the delivery receipts independently of the company's accounting function for prepaid inventory, those documents provided sufficient competent evidence to corroborate prepaid inventory. "Grant Thornton believed it was acceptable to rely on the Delivery Receipt to verify the date of delivery because JGI's internal control procedures for inventory were based on a system of 'segregation of duties.'" A Grant Thornton representative provided the following explanation of exactly what was implied by the phrase "segregation of duties."

Question: *You speak of segregation of duties. What do you mean by that?*

Answer: *Somebody is separate—you know, the purchasing function is separate from the receiving function and the approval function is different from the person who executes the transactions.*

Question: *Does that mean that there are separate people that do these different functions?*

Answer: *Yes. Separate people or departments.*

1993 and 1994 JGI Audits

During the 1992 JGI audit, members of the Grant Thornton audit team told Steve Cohn and Emanuel Greenberg they were concerned by the large increase in prepaid inventory over the previous three years.[3] The auditors also expressed concern regarding the haphazard accounting procedures applied to prepaid inventory. These concerns caused the auditors to include the following comments in a report entitled "Internal Control Structure Reportable Conditions and Advisory Comments" that was submitted to Emanuel Greenberg at the conclusion of the 1992 audit. "Prepaid inventory should be set up on a personal computer and updated daily from purchases. This would identify a problem much sooner and reduce the risk of loss should such a problem occur." Cohn later testified that he had encouraged Grant Thornton to include this recommendation in the report filed with Emanuel Greenberg. Despite this recommendation, Emanuel would not

---

3. The dollar value of JGI's prepaid inventory increased by 303 percent from the end of 1989 to the end of 1992.

pressure his brother to cooperate with Cohn's effort to strengthen the accounting procedures for prepaid inventory.

Grant Thornton auditors had access to the notification forms JGI's customs broker sent to Fred Greenberg when a prepaid inventory shipment arrived in a U.S. port. During the 1993 audit, a Grant Thornton auditor noticed that for several prepaid inventory shipments an abnormally long period of time had elapsed between the date the customs broker inspected the merchandise and the date that merchandise arrived at JGI's warehouse. When asked about this issue, Fred Greenberg explained that "floods in the Midwest" had slowed down many shipments en route to the East Coast from ports on the West Coast. A Grant Thornton auditor contacted JGI's customs broker regarding Fred's explanation. The customs broker told the auditor that Fred's explanation was valid.

Near the end of the 1993 audit, a Grant Thornton auditor stumbled across a large stack of Form 9540-1 documents in the receiving office of JGI's warehouse. Following this discovery, the Grant Thornton audit team attempted to match individual delivery receipts with the corresponding Form 9540-1 documents to verify the dates reported on the delivery receipts. Because the latter documents were in no particular alphabetical, chronological, or numerical order, the "task proved insurmountable and was abandoned." In explaining why the auditors did not insist on JGI providing those forms in a usable condition, a Grant Thornton representative noted that the 1993 audit program did not require the delivery receipts to be matched with the Form 9540-1 documents. "However, Grant Thornton decided that since JGI had access to the forms, it wanted them produced for the 1994 audit so that it could use them to verify the date recorded on the delivery receipts."

Following the completion of the 1993 audit, Grant Thornton once again submitted a report entitled "Internal Control Structure Reportable Conditions and Advisory Comments" to Emanuel Goldberg. In this report, Grant Thornton included several specific recommendations regarding improvements needed in the accounting procedures applied to prepaid inventory. One of these recommendations was to maintain an orderly file of the Form 9540-1 documents that could be used for internal control purposes and during the annual independent audit. A second recommendation called for JGI to begin using a specific set of computer-based accounting and internal control procedures and documents for prepaid inventory. These latter items were the same procedures and documents that Steve Cohn had developed and presented to the Greenberg brothers in 1992.

Throughout 1994, Fred Greenberg continued to refuse to adopt Grant Thornton's recommendations for improving the accounting for, and control over, prepaid inventory. In the fall of 1994, Cohn contacted Grant Thornton and told members of the audit engagement team that Fred had not complied with their recommendations. A Grant Thornton representative then met with Fred and told him that, at a minimum, JGI would have to provide the Form 9540-1 documents to Grant Thornton if the accounting firm was to complete the 1994 audit. Still, Fred refused to comply.

Shortly after Grant Thornton began the 1994 audit, a senior member of the audit engagement team advised Fred that unless the Form 9540-1 documents were provided, the accounting firm would likely resign as JGI's independent auditor. Within a few days, Fred turned over the documents to Grant Thornton. "However, before he did so, he altered the dates on them. Apparently, the alterations were so obvious that after reviewing the forms for only 10 seconds, Grant Thornton knew there was a problem. Grant Thornton informed Emanuel and Cohn that the dates were falsified and terminated the audit." When Emanuel confronted his brother regarding the altered documents, the suddenly remorseful Fred "admitted everything."

Following Fred's confession, JGI retained Grant Thornton to determine the impact of the fraudulent scheme on the company's prior financial statements and to develop a set of current financial statements that were reliable. The Greenbergs provided this information to their company's three banks. Within six months, JGI filed for bankruptcy and ceased operations.

EPILOGUE

JGI's sudden collapse sparked a spate of lawsuits. In February 1997, JGI's court-appointed bankruptcy trustee filed a civil action that contained eight specific charges against Grant Thornton. These charges included, among others, breach of contract, negligence, and fraud. A primary defense Grant Thornton used in attempting to rebut those allegations was contributory negligence on the part of JGI and its management.

Grant Thornton argued that JGI had a responsibility to implement internal controls that would have been effective in uncovering Fred Greenberg's fraudulent scheme. In particular, Grant Thornton contended that Emanuel Greenberg should have required his brother to adopt the computer-based accounting and control procedures initially proposed by Steve Cohn in 1992. The accounting firm also maintained that Emanuel Greenberg had been negligent in failing to discover Fred's subterfuge since he had never taken any steps to check or verify his brother's work for the all-important Prepaid Inventory account.

The federal judge who presided over the lawsuit filed against Grant Thornton by JGI's bankruptcy trustee responded to the firm's contributory negligence defense by first suggesting that the accounting firm, rather than JGI's management, had more "leverage" to force Fred Greenberg to adopt Cohn's recommendations. "Cohn could not insist that Fred implement tighter controls over the prepaid inventory, but Grant Thornton, as JGI's auditor, could. Indeed, that is how the fraud was finally discovered in 1994." Additionally, the judge pointed out that Grant Thornton had failed to present any

compelling evidence that Emanuel Greenberg had suspected his brother was misrepresenting JGI's prepaid inventory. "Accordingly, Emanuel had no reason to check or verify his brother's work in matching up the delivery receipts with the other prepaid inventory documentation." The judge went even further in absolving Emanuel of responsibility for his brother's misconduct by suggesting that independent auditors are the parties primarily responsible for discovering such schemes.

> Given Fred's equal ownership in the company and his apparent control, not only is there no evidence that Emanuel was "slipshod," there is no evidence that he could have prevented Fred's wrongful acts. Rather, in the unique circumstances where a corporation is owned and operated by family members, the goal of deterring wrongdoing is best served by subjecting the auditors to potential liability, thereby encouraging greater diligence by them in such situations in the future.

After responding to Grant Thornton's arguments, the federal judge criticized several aspects of the firm's JGI audits. Although Grant Thornton identified the large increase in prepaid inventory during the late 1980s and early 1990s as an audit risk factor, the judge suggested that the accounting firm did not thoroughly investigate the underlying cause of that dramatic increase. Likewise, the judge maintained that during the 1993 audit Grant Thornton did not adequately investigate the abnormally long time lag between the date that certain imported meat shipments arrived at a U.S. port and the date they were delivered to JGI's warehouse.[4] The judge also referred to

---

4. Recall that JGI's customs broker had confirmed Fred Greenberg's assertion that floods in the Midwestern states during 1993 were responsible for this time lag. Apparently, that assertion was not valid.

criticism of Grant Thornton that was included in a report prepared by an expert witness retained by JGI's bankruptcy trustee. Among other issues, this report criticized Grant Thornton for not discovering until 1993 that JGI had copies of the Form 9540-1 documents. According to the expert witness, if the auditors had performed a routine "walk-through" audit procedure to document their understanding of JGI's important accounting and control procedures, they would have immediately discovered that "third-party documentation [Form 9540-1] existed to verify the arrival dates of the inventory."

The federal judge was most critical of Grant Thornton's decision near the end of the 1993 audit to continue relying on the internally generated delivery receipts when the firm had access to externally generated documentation to vouch the prepaid inventory transactions and year-end balance. In the judge's opinion, that decision could be construed as "reckless."

According to Grant Thornton, although it now knew that third-party verification of the delivery dates existed, it considered it unnecessary to have the USDA forms for the 1993 audit because of its reliance on JGI's segregation of duties. Yet, Grant Thornton refused to rely upon JGI's segregation of duties for its 1994 audit. Rather, it demanded that JGI produce the USDA forms for the 1994 audit.... If Grant would not issue an unqualified opinion in 1994 relying solely upon JGI's segregation of duties, then why did it do so in 1993?

In October 1999, the federal judge issued a 36-page opinion weighing the merits of the allegations filed by JGI's trustee against Grant Thornton and the validity of the accounting firm's rebuttals of those allegations. After striking down one of the charges filed against Grant Thornton, the judge ruled that the other charges would be addressed in a subsequent trial. Since no further mention of this case can be found in public records, Grant Thornton and JGI's bankruptcy trustee apparently settled the case privately.

Questions

1. Identify important audit risk factors common to family-owned businesses. How should auditors address these risk factors?

2. In your opinion, what primary audit objectives should Grant Thornton have established for JGI's (a) Prepaid Inventory account and (b) Merchandise Inventory account?

3. Assess Grant Thornton's decision to rely heavily on JGI's delivery receipts when auditing the company's prepaid inventory. More generally, compare and contrast the validity of audit evidence yielded by internally prepared versus externally prepared client documents.

4. Describe the general nature and purpose of a "walk-through" audit procedure. Are such tests required by professional auditing standards?

5. Identify audit procedures, other than a walk-through test, that might have resulted in Grant Thornton discovering that Fred Greenberg was tampering with JGI's delivery receipts.

6. Once an audit firm has informed client management of important internal control weaknesses, what further responsibility, if any, does the audit firm have regarding those items? For example, does the audit firm have a responsibility to insist that client management correct the deficiencies or address them in some other way?

Golden Bear Golf, Inc.

Jack Nicklaus electrified sports fans worldwide in 1986 when he won the prestigious Masters golf tournament at the ripe old age of 46. Over the previous several years, the "Golden Bear" had been struggling to remain competitive with the scores of talented young players who had earned the right to play in the dozens of golf tournaments sponsored each year by the Professional Golfers' Association (PGA).

Regaining his golden touch on the golf course was not the only challenge that Nicklaus faced during the mid-1980s. In 1985, Richard Bellinger, an accountant employed by Golden Bear International, Inc. (GBI), the private company that oversaw the famous golfer's many business interests, mustered the courage to approach his employer. Bellinger told Nicklaus that his company was on the verge of bankruptcy. Nicklaus, who had allowed subordinates to manage his company's operations, was startled by the revelation. In a subsequent interview with the *Wall Street Journal*, Nicklaus admitted that after a brief investigation he realized that he had allowed his company to become a tangled knot of dozens of unrelated businesses. "We were an accounting nightmare … I didn't know what any of them did and neither did anyone else."[1]

Nicklaus immediately committed himself to revitalizing his company. The first step that he took to turn around his company was naming himself as its chief executive officer (CEO). Nicklaus then placed Bellinger in charge of GBI's day-to-day operations. Within a few years, the two men had returned GBI to a profitable condition by focusing its resources on lines of business that Nicklaus knew best, such as golf course design, golf schools, and the licensing of golf equipment.

In the late 1990s, Jack Nicklaus, however, once again found himself coping with an "accounting nightmare." This time, Nicklaus could not blame himself for the predicament he faced. Instead, the responsibility for the new crisis rested squarely on the shoulders of two of Nicklaus's key subordinates who had orchestrated a fraudulent accounting scheme that jeopardized their employer's corporate empire.

Player of the Century

Jack Nicklaus began playing golf as a young boy and had mastered the game by his mid-teens. After graduating from high school, the golf prodigy accepted a scholarship to play collegiately for Ohio State University in his hometown of Columbus. At the age of 21, Nicklaus joined the professional golf tour and was an instant success, racking up more than one dozen victories within a few years.

Shortly after joining the professional golf tour, the business-minded Nicklaus realized that winning golf tournaments was not the most lucrative way to profit from his enormous skills. At the time, the undisputed "king" of golf was Arnold Palmer, who endeared himself to the golfing public with his easy smile and affable manner on the golf course. Adoring legions of fans known as "Arnie's Army" tracked Palmer's every move during a tournament. Palmer's popularity with the public translated into a

---

1. R. Lowenstein, "A Golfer Becomes an Executive: Jack Nicklaus's Business Education," *Wall Street Journal*, 27 January 1987, 34.

series of high-profile and profitable endorsement deals. On the other hand, golf fans generally resented Nicklaus's no-nonsense approach on the golf course. Those same fans resented Nicklaus even more when it became evident that the burly Ohioan with the trademark crew cut would likely replace Palmer as the world's best golfer, which he did. Nicklaus would ultimately win a record 18 major golf championships and edge out Palmer for the "Player of the Century" award in the golfing world.

With the help of a professional sports agent, Nicklaus worked hard to develop a softer, more appealing public image. By the mid-1970s, Nicklaus's makeover was complete and his popularity rivaled that of Palmer. As his popularity with the public grew, Nicklaus was able to cash in on endorsement deals and other business opportunities. Eventually, Nicklaus founded GBI to serve as the corporate umbrella for his business interests.

In 1996, Nicklaus decided to expand his business operations by spinning off a subsidiary from GBI via an initial public offering (IPO). Nicklaus named the new public company Golden Bear Golf, Inc. (Golden Bear). One of Golden Bear's principal lines of business would be the construction of golf courses. GBI would remain a privately owned company that would continue to manage Nicklaus's other business ventures. Because Nicklaus planned to retain more than 50 percent of Golden Bear's common stock, he and his subordinates would be able to completely control the new company's operations.

Nicklaus chose his trusted associate Richard Bellinger to serve as Golden Bear's CEO. Bellinger then appointed John Boyd and Christopher Curbello as the two top executives of Paragon International, Golden Bear's wholly owned subsidiary that would be responsible for the company's golf course construction business. Boyd became Paragon's president and principal operating officer, while Curbello assumed the title of Paragon's vice president of operations. On 1 August 1996, Golden Bear went public. The company's stock traded on the NASDAQ exchange under the ticker symbol JACK.

Triple Bogey for Golden Bear

Shortly after Golden Bear's successful IPO, Paragon International's management team was inundated with requests to build Jack Nicklaus–designed golf courses. In a few months, the company had entered into contracts to build more than one dozen golf courses. Wall Street analysts, portfolio managers, and individual investors expected these contracts to translate into sizable profits for Golden Bear. Unfortunately, those profits never materialized.

Less than one year after Golden Bear's IPO, Boyd and Curbello realized that they had been much too optimistic in forecasting the gross profit margins Paragon would earn on its construction projects. Instead of earning substantial profits on those projects, Paragon would incur large losses on many of them. To avoid the embarrassment of publicly revealing that they had committed Paragon to a string of unprofitable construction projects, the two executives instructed Paragon's accounting staff to embellish the subsidiary's reported operating results.

A key factor that may have contributed to Boyd and Curbello's decision to conceal Paragon's financial problems was the incentive compensation package each had received when they signed on with the company. The two executives could earn sizable bonuses if Paragon met certain operating benchmarks. In addition, Boyd had been granted a large number of Golden Bear stock options.

Because Paragon's construction projects required considerably more than one year to complete, the company used percentage-of-completion accounting to recognize the revenues associated with those projects. Initially, Paragon applied the widely used "cost-to-cost" percentage-of-completion method that requires a company to determine the percentage of a project's total estimated construction costs incurred in a given accounting period. Then, the same percentage of the total revenue (and gross profit) to be earned on the project is booked that period.

During the second quarter of fiscal 1997, Boyd and Curbello determined that Paragon would have a large operating loss if the cost-to-cost method was used to recognize revenue on the golf course construction projects. At that point, the two executives instructed Paragon's controller to switch to what they referred to as the "earned value" percentage-of-completion accounting method. "In developing its percentage-of-completion estimates under the earned value method, Paragon relied not on objective criteria, such as costs incurred, but instead relied on management's subjective estimates as to its [a project's] progress."[2]

Throughout the remainder of fiscal 1997 and into fiscal 1998, Paragon's management routinely overstated the percentage-of-completion estimates for the company's golf course construction projects each quarter. To further enhance Paragon's operating results, the company's accounting staff inflated the contractual revenue amounts for most of the company's construction projects. These increased revenue amounts were allegedly attributable to "change orders" that amended the original construction contracts between Paragon and the company's clients. A final window-dressing scheme used by Paragon was recording revenue for *potential* construction projects.

> *In some cases, Paragon recognized revenue in connection with potential projects that Paragon had identified while looking for new work, even though Paragon had no agreements in connection with these projects. In other cases, Paragon recognized revenue in connection with projects where the project's owners were either entertaining bids from Paragon and other contractors or were negotiating with Paragon regarding a project yet to be awarded.[3]*

During the spring of 1998, John Boyd and several of his top subordinates, including Christopher Curbello, attempted to purchase Paragon International from Golden Bear. When that effort failed, Boyd and Curbello resigned their positions with Paragon. After their departure, Paragon's new management team quickly discovered that the subsidiary's operating results had been grossly misrepresented.

A subsequent investigation carried out jointly by Arthur Andersen & Co. (Paragon's audit firm), PricewaterhouseCoopers, and Golden Bear's external legal firm resulted in Golden Bear issuing restated financial statements in October 1998 for fiscal 1997 and for the first quarter of fiscal 1998. For fiscal 1997, Golden Bear had initially reported a $2.9 million net loss and golf course construction revenues of $39.7 million; the restated amounts included a $24.7 million net loss for fiscal 1997 and golf course construction revenues of only $21.8 million. For the first quarter of fiscal 1998, Golden Bear had reported an $800,000 net loss and golf course construction revenues of $16.0 million. Those amounts were restated to a $7.2 million net loss and golf course construction revenues of $8.3 million.

"Audit Failures"

The Securities and Exchange Commission (SEC) launched its own investigation of Golden Bear shortly after the company issued the restated financial statements. A primary target of the SEC investigation was Michael Sullivan, the Arthur Andersen

---

2. Securities and Exchange Commission, *Accounting and Auditing Enforcement Release No. 1604*, 1 August 2002.

3. Securities and Exchange Commission, *Accounting and Auditing Enforcement Release No. 1603*, 1 August 2002.

audit partner who served as the Golden Bear engagement partner. Sullivan had been employed by Andersen since 1970 and had been a partner in the firm since 1984.

The SEC enforcement release that disclosed the results of its investigation of Andersen's Golden Bear audits included a section entitled "Sullivan's Audit Failures." According to the SEC, Sullivan was well aware that the decision to use the earned value method "accelerated revenue recognition by material amounts" for Paragon.[4] In fact, Sullivan was very concerned when Paragon decided to switch from the cost-to-cost method to the "new and untested" earned value method. This concern prompted him to warn Paragon's management, at the time the switch was made, that the earned value method should produce operating results approximately in line with those that would have resulted from the continued application of the cost-to-cost method. To monitor the impact of the earned value method on Paragon's operating results, Sullivan required the client's accounting staff to "provide detailed schedules showing Paragon's project-by-project results under both methods for each reporting period from the second quarter of 1997 through the first quarter of 1998."

By the end of fiscal 1997, the comparative schedules prepared by Paragon's accountants clearly revealed that the earned value method was allowing Paragon to book much larger amounts of revenue and gross profit on its construction projects than it would have under the cost-to-cost method. When Sullivan questioned Paragon's executives regarding this issue, those executives maintained that "uninvoiced" construction costs had caused the cost-to-cost method to significantly understate the stages of completion of the construction projects. To quell Sullivan's concern, in early fiscal 1998 Paragon's management recorded $4 million of uninvoiced construction costs in a year-end adjusting entry for fiscal 1997. These costs caused the revenue that would have been recorded under the cost-to-cost method to approximate the revenue that Paragon actually recorded by applying the earned value method. Unknown to Sullivan, the $4 million of uninvoiced construction costs booked by Paragon were fictitious.[5]

The SEC criticized Sullivan and his subordinates for failing to adequately investigate the $4 million of uninvoiced construction costs that materialized at the end of fiscal 1997. According to the SEC, Sullivan relied almost exclusively on management's oral representations to corroborate those costs.

> Sullivan knew that Paragon booked costs for which no invoices had been received and which were not reflected in the company's accounts payable system, and that recording these uninvoiced costs would have substantially reduced the gap between the results produced by the two estimation methods.... While procedures with respect to invoiced and paid costs were performed, Sullivan did not employ any procedures to determine whether the uninvoiced costs had actually been incurred as of year-end.

Paragon's scheme to overstate its reported revenues and profits by applying the earned value method resulted in a dramatic increase in unbilled revenues by the end of 1997. Approximately 30 percent of the revenues reported in Golden Bear's 1997 income statement had not been billed to its customers. When Paragon's executives switched to the earned value method, they had assured Sullivan that they would bill their customers on that basis. Despite that commitment, Paragon continued to bill

---

4. The remaining quotations in this case were taken from Securities and Exchange Commission, *Accounting and Auditing Enforcement Release No. 1676*, 26 November 2002.

5. Recognize that the $4 million of uninvoiced construction costs that were accrued in the adjusting entry did not reduce Golden Bear's gross profit that it had recognized for fiscal 1997 under the earned value method. The $4 million of construction costs simply replaced an equal amount of expenses that had been recorded to produce the "proper" amount of gross profit under the earned value method.

their customers effectively on a cost-to-cost basis. (Paragon could not bill customers for the full amount of revenue that it was recording on the construction projects since those customers were generally aware of the *actual* stages of completion of those projects.)

The SEC maintained that Sullivan and his subordinates should have rigorously tested Paragon's large amount of unbilled revenues at the end of 1997. "A significant unbilled revenue balance requires adequate testing to determine the reason that the company is not billing for the work it reports as complete and whether unbilled amounts are properly recognized as revenue." Instead, the SEC charged that Sullivan relied "excessively" on oral representations from Paragon management to confirm the unbilled revenues and corresponding receivables.

In at least one case, the SEC reported that members of the Golden Bear audit team asked the owner of a Paragon project under construction to comment on the reasonableness of the $2 million unbilled receivable that Paragon had recorded for that project at the end of 1997. The owner contested that amount, alleging that Paragon had overestimated the project's stage of completion. "Despite this significant evidence that a third party with knowledge of the project's status disputed Paragon's estimated percentage-of-completion under the contract, the audit team did not properly investigate this project or otherwise expand Andersen's scope of testing of Paragon's unbilled revenue balances." According to the SEC, Sullivan did not believe the unbilled revenue posed major audit issues but instead was a "business issue" that Paragon had to resolve with its clients.

A second tactic Paragon used to inflate its reported profits was to overstate the total revenues to be earned on individual construction projects. During the 1997 audit, Andersen personnel selected 13 of Paragon's construction projects to corroborate the total revenue figures the company was using in applying the earned value percentage-of-completion accounting method to its unfinished projects. For 11 of the 13 projects selected, the Andersen auditors discovered that the total revenue being used in the percentage-of-completion computations by Paragon exceeded the revenue figure documented in the construction contract. Paragon's management attributed these differences to unsigned change orders that had been processed for the given projects "but could not produce any documents supporting these oral representations." Sullivan accepted the client's representations that the given revenue amounts were valid. "In each instance, Sullivan failed to properly follow up on a single undocumented amount; instead, Sullivan relied solely on Paragon management's oral representations that the estimated revenue amounts accurately reflected the economic status of the jobs."

Another scam used by Paragon to inflate its revenues and profits was to record revenue for nonexistent projects. In the enforcement release that focused on Sullivan's role in the Paragon scandal, SEC officials pointed out that the publication *AICPA Audit and Accounting Guide—Construction Contracts* is clearly relevant to the audits of construction companies such as Paragon. This publication recommends that auditors visit construction sites and discuss the given projects with project managers, architects, and other appropriate personnel. The purpose of these procedures is to assess "the representations of management (for example, representations about the stage of completion and estimated costs to complete)." Despite this guidance, the Andersen auditors did not visit any project sites during the 1997 audit.[6] Such visits may have resulted in Andersen discovering that some of Paragon's projects were purely

---

6. As a point of information, most of Paragon's golf construction projects were outside of the United States. During 1996, auditors employed by foreign affiliates of Andersen visited some of these sites.

imaginary. In addition, Andersen would likely have determined that Paragon was overstating the stages of completion of most of its existing projects.

The SEC reprimanded Andersen for not visiting any of Paragon's jobsites or discussing those projects with knowledgeable parties. "Failing to discuss project status, including percentage-of-completion estimates, with project managers and other on-site operating personnel was, under the circumstances, a reckless departure from GAAS."

The SEC also criticized Sullivan for not insisting that Golden Bear disclose in its 1997 financial statements the change from the cost-to-cost to the earned value method of applying percentage-of-completion accounting. Likewise, the SEC contended that Sullivan should have required Golden Bear to disclose material related-party transactions involving Paragon and Jack Nicklaus, Golden Bear's majority stockholder.

Finally, the SEC noted that Sullivan failed to heed his own concerns while planning the 1997 Golden Bear audit. During the initial planning phase of that audit, Sullivan had identified several factors that prompted him to designate the 1997 Golden Bear audit a "high-risk" engagement. These factors included the subjective nature of the earned value method, Paragon's large unbilled revenues, the aggressive revenue recognition practices advocated by Golden Bear management, and severe weaknesses in Paragon's cost accounting system. Because of these factors, the SEC maintained that Sullivan and his subordinates should have been particularly cautious during the 1997 Golden Bear audit and employed a rigorous and thorough set of substantive audit procedures.

EPILOGUE

In August 1998, angry Golden Bear stockholders filed a class-action lawsuit against the company, its major officers, and its principal owner, Jack Nicklaus. That same month, the NASDAQ delisted the company's common stock, which was trading for less than $1 per share, dramatically below its all-time high of $20. Richard Bellinger resigned as Golden Bear's CEO two months later to "pursue other interests." In December 1999, Golden Bear announced that it had reached an agreement to settle the class-action lawsuit. That settlement required the company to pay its stockholders $3.5 million in total and to purchase their shares at a price of $0.75. In 2000, Golden Bear, by then a private company, was folded into Nicklaus Companies, a new corporate entity that Jack Nicklaus created to manage his business interests.

In November 2002, Michael Sullivan was suspended from practicing before the SEC for one year. Sullivan's employer, Andersen, had effectively been put out of business a few months earlier when a federal jury found it guilty of obstruction of justice for destroying audit documents pertaining to its bankrupt client Enron Corporation.[7] In August 2002, Paragon's former controller received a two-year suspension from practicing before the SEC. At the same time, the SEC sanctioned three former Golden Bear executives by ordering them to "cease and desist" from any future violations of the federal securities laws. One of those executives was Richard Bellinger. The SEC maintained that Bellinger approved Paragon's change from the cost-to-cost to the earned value method. Additionally, the SEC charged that Bellinger knew the change would materially increase Golden Bear's reported revenues and gross profit but failed to require that the change be disclosed in the company's financial statements.

---

7. As discussed in Case 1.1, Andersen's conviction was subsequently overturned by the U.S. Supreme Court.

Finally, in March 2003, a federal grand jury indicted John Boyd and Christopher Curbello on charges of securities fraud and conspiracy to commit securities fraud. Curbello was arrested in San Antonio, Texas, on 14 March 2003, while Boyd was apprehended in Bogota, Colombia, a few days later by Secret Service and FBI agents who immediately flew him to the United States. In June 2003, Curbello pleaded guilty to conspiracy to commit securities fraud and was sentenced to three and one-half years in prison. A few months later, Boyd pleaded guilty to similar charges and was given a five-year prison sentence.

Questions

1. Professional auditing standards identify the "management assertions" that commonly underlie a set of financial statements. Which of these assertions were relevant to Paragon's construction projects? For each of the assertions that you listed, describe an audit procedure that Arthur Andersen could have employed to corroborate that assertion.

2. The SEC referred to several "audit failures" that were allegedly the responsibility of Michael Sullivan. Define what you believe the SEC meant by the phrase "audit failure." Do you believe that Sullivan, alone, was responsible for the deficiencies that the SEC noted in Andersen's 1997 audit of Golden Bear? Defend your answer.

3. Sullivan identified the 1997 Golden Bear audit as a "high-risk" engagement. How do an audit engagement team's responsibilities differ, if at all, on a high-risk engagement compared with a "normal" engagement? Explain.

4. The AICPA has issued several *Audit and Accounting Guides* for specialized industries. Do auditors have a responsibility to refer to these guides when auditing clients in those industries? Do these guides override or replace the authoritative guidance included in the professional auditing standards?

5. Was the change that Paragon made in applying the percentage-of-completion accounting method a "change in accounting principle" or a "change in accounting estimate"? Briefly describe the accounting and financial reporting treatment that must be applied to each type of change.

Take-Two Interactive Software, Inc.

Grand Theft Auto ranks among the best-selling video games of all time as well as one of the most controversial.[1] By the time *Grand Theft Auto V* was released in 2013, over 125 million copies of the video game had been sold worldwide since the original version of the game was introduced in 1997. *Wikipedia* provides the following general description of the game.

> *Game play focuses on an open world where the player can choose missions to progress an overall story, as well as engaging in side activities, all consisting of action-adventure, driving, occasional role-playing, stealth, and racing elements. The subject of the game is usually a comedic satire of American culture, but the series has gained controversy for its adult nature and violent themes.*

Prominent public officials, major media outlets, and public service organizations have condemned *Grand Theft Auto*. Senator Hillary Clinton urged the Federal Trade Commission (FTC) to assign a rating of "Adults Only" to the game because of its "pornographic and violent content," which includes one setting that "encourages them [game players] to have sex with prostitutes and then murder them."[2] Senator Joseph Lieberman denounced the game as "gruesome, and grotesque."[3] The mayor of New York City, Michael Bloomberg, bluntly noted that the game "Teaches children to kill."[4]

In fact, law enforcement authorities have linked the commission of serious crimes to *Grand Theft Auto*. A teenager killed three police officers in Alabama in June 2003 in a set of circumstances similar to a scene in the game. The teenager, who played the game "day and night" and had no previous criminal record, calmly told his captors that, "Life is like a video game. Everybody's got to die sometime."[5] In referring to that case, a CNN commentator branded *Grand Theft Auto* a "cop killing simulator."[6]

Mothers Against Drunk Driving (MADD) have criticized the game for encouraging drunk driving. "Drunk driving is not a game, and it is not a joke."[7] A spokesperson for Take-Two Interactive Software, Inc., the producer of the game, responded by maintaining that MADD's criticism was unfair since the given version of *Grand Theft Auto* involved only one drunk driving scene. "For the same reason that you can't judge an entire film or television program by a single scene, you can't judge *Grand Theft Auto IV* by a small aspect of the game."[8]

---

1. *Wikipedia* reports that *Grand Theft Auto* ranks as the sixth best-selling video game franchise of all time. The best-selling video game franchise is *Mario* followed by *Super Mario*, *Pokemon*, *Wii*, and *The Sims*.

2. *USA Today* (online) "Clinton Seeks '*Grand Theft Auto*' Probe," 14 July 2005.

3. B. McLean, "Sex, Lies, and Videogames," *Fortune* (*money.cnn.com*), 22 August 2005.

4. *PC World*, "Rants Begin Against *Grand Theft Auto IV*," www.pcworld.com, 3 May 2008.

5. R. Leung, "Can A Video Game Lead To Murder?" www.cbsnews.com, 11 February 2009.

6. *CNN Headline News*, 8 May 2008.

7. D. Lang, "MADD Attacks '*Grand Theft Auto IV*'," www.nbcnews.com, 1 May 2008.

8. *Ibid.*

Take-Two's executives have been the target of most of the emotionally charged criticism of *Grand Theft Auto*. A Wall Street analyst who tracked Take-Two's stock for years suggested that, "You'd be hard-pressed to find a worse set of guys."[9] Despite repeated challenges to the suitability of *Grand Theft Auto* filed with the FTC by various parties, the federal agency that eventually posed the most significant challenge for the company's management team was the Securities and Exchange Commission (SEC). The SEC sanctioned several of Take-Two's top executives for issuing a series of financial statements that contained fraudulent misrepresentations. Those sanctions resulted in Take-Two restating its financial statements three separate times between 2001 and 2004.

Striking Out on His Own

In 1992, Ryan Brant graduated from the University of Pennsylvania's Wharton School of Business with a degree in economics. The 20-year-old Brant began his business career by working for a company owned by his father, Peter Brant, a billionaire businessman. Eighteen months later, Brant decided to leave that company and establish his own business. After raising $1.5 million from family members and "angel" investors, Brant organized Take-Two Interactive Software, Inc., in late 1993.

Robert Fish, a partner with Price Waterhouse, Take-Two's audit firm, served as one of Brant's principal business advisors from the inception of his company. Following the merger of Price Waterhouse with Coopers & Lybrand in 1998 to form PricewaterhouseCoopers (PwC), Fish became the Senior Managing Partner of the Venture Capital Practice of PwC's New York City office. That unit provided a wide range of professional services to developmental stage companies.

In addition to serving as a general business advisor to the much younger Brant, Fish supervised the annual audits of Take-Two's financial statements from 1994 through 2001. In a 1998 interview with *Crain's New York Business*, Fish suggested that he and Brant had a father–son type relationship. In discussing PwC's relationship with Take-Two, Fish noted that, "We [PwC] make an investment of our time in growth-oriented companies."[10] He went on to observe that, "Most start-ups coming to larger accounting firms know they don't just want the accountants to handle debits and credits, but to focus on the structure of the enterprise."[11]

PwC's "investment" in Take-Two included initially discounting the fees that it charged the company for its professional services. According to Brant, PwC billed Take-Two "a mere $20,000" for the services provided annually to the newly formed company, a figure that was "roughly one-third what the firm would have charged had it applied its standard hourly rate."[12]

For the first few years of Take-Two's existence, the company realized modest success with several video games including *Ripper* and *Hell: A Cyberpunk Thriller*. To survive in the ultra-competitive video gaming industry, Brant realized that his company had to grow, and quickly. Brant decided that the best strategy for achieving that goal was to acquire other video game companies, which would require a considerable amount of external financing. To raise those funds, Brant took his company public in 1997 with an initial public offering (IPO). Brant relied heavily on Fish for professional advice regarding accounting and financial reporting issues related to the IPO and the subsequent series of acquisitions made by the company.

---

9. McLean, "Sex, Lies, and Videogames."

10. L. Aron, "Fatherly Advice on Facts of Financial Life," *Crain's New York Business*, 12 October 1998, 34.

11. *Ibid.*

12. *Ibid.*

Among the nearly 20 acquisitions that Take-Two made in the late 1990s was a small operating unit of Bertelsmann, a large German mass media company. The video games owned by that entity included the game that would become *Grand Theft Auto*, which would prove to be Take-Two's first major gaming "franchise." Every few years, Take-Two releases a new version of the game. On 29 April 2008, the date that *Grand Theft Auto IV* was released, the game established the single-day sales record for the video gaming industry, selling 3.6 million units with a total revenue of $180 million.[13]

Grand Theft Auto resulted in Take-Two becoming one of the leading worldwide developers and distributors of video games. The successful game also allowed Take-Two to survive the "tech crash" that began in early 2000 with the bursting of the "dot-com bubble" in the stock market. That financial crisis proved to be the death knell for many of Take-Two's competitors. Despite the challenging circumstances faced by Take-Two during that time frame, the company continued to post surprisingly strong operating results.

Exhibit 1 presents key financial data for Take-Two that document the company's rapid growth from 1998 through 2000, the first three full fiscal years that it was a public company. A footnote to that exhibit includes selected amounts included in Take-Two's 1997 financial statements.

"Parking" Violations

In 2000 and 2001, a stock analyst who tracked Take-Two's financial statements and public earnings releases noted apparent discrepancies between the company's reported sales and data reported by the NDP Group, a market research company that monitors video game sales. That analyst's concerns prompted an SEC investigation of Take-Two's 2000 and 2001 financial statements. The federal agency's investigation revealed that Take-Two executives had recorded millions of dollars of sham sales transactions to inflate their company's reported operating results, transactions that involved Take-Two temporarily "parking" large amounts of inventory with its customers.

On October 31, 2000, the final day of Take-Two's fiscal year 2000, the company's chief operating officer (COO) and chief financial officer (CFO) arranged a bogus sale of $5.4 million of video games to Capitol Distributing, a video game distributor based in Virginia. The transaction was the largest individual sale ever recorded by Take-Two. To make the sale appear legitimate to the company's PwC auditors, Take-Two shipped 230,000 video games to Capitol. Both parties agreed prior to the shipment that the games would be returned by Capitol to Take-Two over the following few months. When the video games were returned to Take-Two in fiscal 2001, the two parties forged various documents to make the returns appear as if they were purchases of new product inventory by Take-Two from another company—this latter company was an affiliate of Capitol.

In 2001, Take-Two recorded three additional fictitious sales of video games to Capitol that totaled more than $9 million. Similar to the $5.4 million transaction, the merchandise shipped to Capitol as a result of these "sales" was returned to Take-Two under the guise of inventory purchases.

During fiscal 2000 and 2001, Take-Two recorded dozens of smaller bogus sale transactions to four other video game distributors. Nearly all of this merchandise was subsequently reacquired by Take-Two—some of these transactions were camouflaged as purchases of new inventory, while others were processed and recorded as normal sales returns. Take-Two also recorded sales during 2000 and 2001 for video games

---

13. C. Feldman, "*Grand Theft Auto IV* Steals Sales Records," www.cnn.com, 8 May 2008.

EXHIBIT 1

TAKE-TWO
INTERACTIVE
SOFTWARE, INC.
FINANCIAL
HIGHLIGHTS
1998–2000
(000S OMITTED)

	2000	1999	1998
Sales	$387,006	$305,932	$194,052
Gross Profit	139,210	90,810	46,496
Operating Income	45,061	27,381	10,690
Net Income	24,963	16,332	7,181
Accounts Receivable	134,877	107,799	49,139
Inventories	44,922	41,300	26,093
Total Current Assets	214,908	187,970	95,302
Total Assets	351,641	231,712	109,385
Current Liabilities	152,023	146,531	73,505
Total Liabilities	164,639	146,609	73,820
Net Operating Cash Flows	(55,259)	(16,748)	(8,022)
Net Investing Cash Flows	(12,906)	(21,540)	(727)
Net Financing Cash Flows	71,564	46,780	9,017

Note: The following financial statement amounts for 1997 were included in Take-Two's 1999 Form 10-K.

Sales	$97,341
Gross Profit	15,862
Operating Income	(895)
Net Income	(2,904)
Accounts Receivable	36,369
Inventories	20,784
Total Assets	56,395
Total Stockholders' Equity	11,935
Net Operating Cash Flows	(14,460)
Net Investing Cash Flows	(2,583)
Net Financing Cash Flows	18,809

Source: Form 10-K's filed with the Securities and Exchange Commission by Take-Two Interactive Software, Inc.

that were still in production and that would not be delivered to the given customers until a subsequent quarterly reporting period.[14]

Take-Two's fraudulent accounting during 2000 allowed the company to meet or surpass its consensus quarterly earnings forecasts for that year. For the fourth quarter of 2000, for example, Take-Two reported earnings of $.42 per share, slightly higher than the company's consensus earnings forecast of $.41 per share and considerably higher than the company's actual earnings per share of $.27. The accounting fraud also allowed Take-Two to report a net income for that quarter that was higher than the figure reported for the prior quarter. This fact was significant to Take-Two's CFO since his bonus each quarterly reporting period was contingent on the company increasing its net income over the previous quarter.

In February 2002, Take-Two issued restated financial statements for fiscal 2000 and for the first three quarters of fiscal 2001 to eliminate the fraudulent sales transactions recorded during those periods and to correct other instances of improper accounting treatments. Two years later, in February 2004, Take-Two issued restated financial statements for fiscal years 1999 through 2003 after additional improper accounting

---

14. Take-Two also improperly accounted for acquisitions that it made of other companies and failed to record a proper reserve for "price protection guarantees" that it made to its customers.

decisions were discovered for those years. The two restatements materially reduced Take-Two's revenues and earnings from 1999 through 2003, but the company's reported operating results for 2000 bore the brunt of those restatements. Take-Two's 2000 sales were reduced from $387 million to $358 million, while its net income for that year was lowered from $25 million to $4.6 million.

PwC's 2000 Audit of Take-Two

Despite the fact that Take-Two actively concealed its fraudulent schemes from PwC, the SEC alleged that PwC failed to comply with generally accepted auditing standards (GAAS) while auditing the company's financial statements. The SEC's allegations centered on the role that Robert Fish had played in supervising PwC's 2000 audit of Take-Two.

In preparing for the 2000 engagement, Fish identified "revenue recognition" and "accounts receivable reserves" as "areas of higher risk" that would be given "special attention" during that audit.[15] Following its investigation of the 2000 audit, the SEC concluded that, "Fish did not properly respond to those risks as he failed to exercise due professional care and professional skepticism, and failed to obtain sufficient competent evidential matter."[16] The SEC ruled that as a result of Fish's poor decisions, PwC improperly issued an unqualified opinion on Take-Two's 2000 financial statements.

A major focus of the 2000 audit was the $104 million of "domestic" accounts receivable that represented the majority of Take-Two's total receivables at the end of fiscal 2000.[17] The principal audit test applied to the domestic receivables was the mailing of positive confirmation requests to 15 of Take-Two's customers that accounted for approximately 70 percent of those receivables. The PwC auditors received only one confirmation from that sample of customers, a confirmation that represented less than 2 percent of the company's domestic receivables.[18] Capitol Distributing was among the 14 customers that failed to respond to PwC's confirmation requests.

Because of the poor response rate to the confirmation requests, Fish decided that PwC would apply alternative audit procedures to Take-Two's domestic receivables. The principal alternative audit procedure employed by Fish and his subordinates was reviewing payments that Take-Two received in the new fiscal year from the 14 customers who had failed to return a confirmation.

The PwC auditors identified $18 million of cash payments received by Take-Two from those 14 customers over the first 6 weeks of the new fiscal year. During its investigation, the SEC determined that the auditors had failed to track many of those payments to specific invoiced sales transactions because Take-Two's accounting records often reflected only "aggregate" cash collections for individual customers.

> As a result, Fish knew, or should have known, that he could not be certain whether the cash he examined from November 1 through December 8, 2000, related to the accounts receivable balances that existed as of October 31, 2000, or to sales recorded after that date.... The fact that Take-Two's records often showed only aggregate cash collected was a red flag to Fish that any subsequent cash receipts testing relying on this data would prove ineffective.[19]

15. Securities and Exchange Commission, *Accounting and Auditing Enforcement Release No. 2783*, 11 February 2008.

16. *Ibid.*

17. The SEC enforcement releases that focused on the Take-Two fraud did not discuss the company's more than $30 million of receivables from nondomestic customers as of fiscal year-end 2000, or PwC's audit of those receivables. Presumably, those receivables were not affected by the fraud.

18. The SEC reported that the one returned confirmation was "false" but did not elaborate on how or why the confirmation was not authentic.

19. Securities and Exchange Commission, *Accounting and Auditing Enforcement Release No. 2783*.

The SEC also harshly criticized the audit procedures PwC used to test the sufficiency of the client's reserve for sales returns. One of these tests involved examining five sales returns received by Take-Two during the first few days of fiscal 2001. Because Fish and his subordinates did not track these returns to the original sales invoices, they failed to discover evidence suggesting that Take-Two was grossly underestimating its year-end reserve for sales returns.

> *Of the five specific returns tested, Fish did not compare the returns with the original sales invoices. Had he done so, he would have discovered that in four of the five instances, much more than 75% of the games purportedly purchased had been returned ... when Take-Two only reserved for returns at the rate of 5%. Fish determined, nonetheless, that Take-Two's reserves were adequate without, for instance, examining other returns from fiscal year 2000, or inquiring of the customers regarding these particular sales.*[20]

The SEC went on to point out that the four sales returns in question involved "parking transactions" that Take-Two had used to inflate its 2000 sales and earnings.[21]

EPILOGUE

In June 2005, the SEC sanctioned Take-Two's vice president of sales and three of its former executives for their role in the company's accounting fraud. These latter individuals included Ryan Brant, Take-Two's former chief executive officer, as well as the company's former COO, and former CFO. Take-Two was fined $7.5 million, while the four executives paid fines ranging from $50,000 for the vice president of sales to $500,000 for Brant. Brant was also ordered to forfeit $3.1 million of stock market gains he had earned on Take-Two's common stock. The company's former CFO, who was a CPA, was also suspended from practicing before the SEC for 10 years.

In February 2008, the SEC issued an *Accounting and Auditing Enforcement Release* focusing on Robert Fish's role as Take-Two's audit engagement partner. The federal agency imposed a one-year suspension on Fish, who had previously resigned from PwC.

In 2007, the SEC filed dozens of civil cases against companies and individual executives involved in the "backdating" of stock option grants. Over the previous two decades, these defendants had identified specific dates on which a given company's stock price was at a relatively low level and then retrospectively issued stock option grants on those dates. This retrospective dating of stock option grants allowed the grantees to receive "in the money" stock options that they subsequently exercised, resulting in large stock market gains. Take-Two and Ryan Brant were among the parties that the SEC filed charges against in the huge options backdating scandal.

The SEC alleged that Brant was the mastermind of Take-Two's options backdating scheme. "From 1997 to September 2003, Brant awarded himself 10 backdated option grants, representing a total of approximately 2.1 million shares of Take-Two common stock."[22] Brant exercised all of those options before he left the company during the midst of the SEC's investigation of Take-Two's stock option grants. The SEC fined Brant $1 million for his role in

---

20. *Ibid.*

21. Recall that when some of the merchandise involved in "parking" transactions was returned to Take-Two it was disguised as purchases of new inventory. The other merchandise involved in parking transactions was processed as normal sales returns when it was subsequently shipped back to Take-Two.

22. Securities and Exchange Commission, *Litigation Release No. 20003*, 14 February 2007.

the scheme and required him to forfeit more than $5 million in stock market gains that he realized as a result of it. In a related criminal case, Brant pleaded guilty to a felony charge filed by a New York state prosecutor and paid a $1 million fine.

In April 2009, Take-Two reached an agreement with the SEC to settle the charges filed against it for the backdating of options by paying a $3 million fine. Prior to reaching that settlement, the company had restated its financial statements for the third time in five years to correct the misrepresentations linked to the improper stock option grants.

Take-Two weathered the fraudulent financial reporting and options backdating scandals and retained its prominent position in the video gaming industry. In 2008, Electronic Arts, the largest video gaming company in the U.S., launched a $2 billion hostile takeover bid for Take-Two. Electronic Arts dropped that takeover bid in late 2008 after it met with fierce resistance from the management team that had replaced Ryan Brant and his former colleagues.

Questions

1. Analyze Take-Two's 1998-2000 financial data included in Exhibit 1. Compute the following financial ratios for each of those years: age of accounts receivable, age of inventory, gross profit percentage, profit margin percentage, return on assets, return on equity, current ratio, debt-to-equity ratio, and the quality-of-earnings ratio. What major "red flags," if any, were present in Take-Two's financial statements given these ratios? Explain.

2. Identify the primary audit objectives that auditors hope to accomplish by confirming a client's year-end accounts receivable. Explain the difference between "positive" and "negative" confirmation requests and discuss the quality of audit evidence yielded by each.

3. Identify audit tests that may be used as alternative audit procedures when a response is not received for a positive confirmation request. Compare and contrast the quality of audit evidence yielded by these procedures with that produced by audit confirmation procedures.

4. In your opinion, did the apparent mistakes made by the PwC auditors in auditing Take-Two's receivables and reserve for sales returns involve "negligence" on their part? Would you characterize the mistakes or errors as "reckless" or "fraudulent"? Justify your answers.

5. Is it appropriate for audit firms to sharply discount their professional fees for developmental stage companies? Why or why not? What problems, if any, may this practice pose for audit firms?

6. Do you believe that the relationship between Robert Fish and Ryan Brant was inappropriate? Explain.

7. Should audit firms accept "ethically challenged" companies and organizations as audit clients? Defend your answer.

General Motors Company

As long as the unwritten rule stands that the best way to achieve success at GM is to be a good finance man, the bad habit of juggling numbers in order to present the picture people want to see cannot be broken.

> Maryann Keller,
> analyst for the automotive industry,
> September 1990

The Great Depression dealt a devastating blow to Billy Durant. During the depths of the Depression in 1936, Durant, a high school dropout who was born a few months after the outbreak of the Civil War in 1861, was forced to declare bankruptcy. Like millions of Americans, the tough-minded and resilient Durant survived the Depression by becoming a jack-of-all-trades, a "job" that he had mastered as a young man. During his early 20s, the free-spirited Durant had worked as an itinerant salesman traveling from town to town peddling patent medicines. During the latter days of the Depression, Durant, who was in his late 70s by this time, made ends meet by managing a bowling alley. After suffering a stroke in 1942, he and his wife subsisted on a pension provided to him by a company that he had once managed. Durant died a few years later in 1947.

If one considered only the early and later years of Durant's life, his life story would not be particularly compelling. However, in the 50-year span between working as a traveling medicine man and managing a bowling alley, William C. "Billy" Durant created an organization that would become the United States' biggest corporation and have the largest workforce of any company worldwide.

Durant made a fortune in the late 1880s and 1890s manufacturing horse-drawn carriages, a business that he had launched in 1886 on $3,000 of borrowed money. In the early days of the twentieth century, Durant realized that the horseless carriage would soon supplant his company's product. Over the next few years, Durant invested much of his personal wealth in several automobile manufacturers, most notably the Buick Motor Company. In 1908, Durant merged those companies to create General Motors Corporation (GM).

For 77 years, from 1931 through 2008, GM reigned as the number one automobile manufacturer worldwide. Only a few months after that long run ended, GM, just like Billy Durant some seven decades earlier, filed for bankruptcy.[1] GM's bankruptcy filing in June 2009 had been foreshadowed by the going-concern audit opinion issued on its 2008 financial statements a few months earlier by Deloitte & Touche, its long-time audit firm.

Pensions & Panic

Similar to many companies, GM was victimized by the economic crisis triggered in late 2008 by collapsing housing prices and the implosion of the subprime sector of the mortgage industry. That crisis quickly spread to other sectors of the U.S.

---

1. After losing control of General Motors in the early 1920s, Billy Durant became preoccupied with "playing" the stock market. The stock market crash of 1929 wiped out Durant's massive wealth and eventually forced him to file for bankruptcy.

economy, including the large automotive industry. Panic and fear caused millions of distraught U.S. consumers to delay or cancel "big-ticket" discretionary expenditures, such as purchases of new automobiles.

Well before the economic crisis that gripped the country in 2008 and 2009, GM's financial condition had been deteriorating. The generous pensions that the company historically paid to its former workers and executives, such as Billy Durant, were a key factor that contributed to GM's declining health. Wage freezes implemented during World War II by the federal government had prompted many companies, including GM, to establish an employee pension plan—or expand an existing one—to give their employees a legal pay "raise." The retirement benefits provided by those pension plans became increasingly lucrative during the latter half of the twentieth century due largely to the effective negotiation skills of such labor unions as the United Auto Workers (UAW).

The large expenses stemming from GM's pension plan and other postretirement benefit plans added significantly to the company's cost of producing automobiles. Because foreign competitors such as Toyota paid more modest wages and provided their employees with less liberal pension and other postretirement benefits, they could produce automobiles more cheaply than GM. Over time, this economic disadvantage caused the annual sales of GM to shrink as car buyers gravitated to foreign models. In 2009, Toyota finally overtook GM as the world's largest automobile producer.

Easily one of the most controversial issues surrounding GM's financial problems in early 2009 was what would happen to the company's huge and significantly underfunded pension plan if the company failed. Nearly 500,000 GM retirees or surviving spouses received monthly pension payments financed by the company. The majority of those individuals relied on their GM pension as the principal source of their retirement income. Likewise, the approximately 250,000 active GM employees had built their retirement plans around the pension benefits promised to them by their employer. What frightened GM's retirees and employees was that the present value of the liabilities associated with GM's pension plan were estimated to exceed $100 billion while the pension plan had total assets of only $85 billion. As the company tottered on the verge of bankruptcy, it was unclear how, or whether, the pension plan would be salvaged if the company filed for bankruptcy.

Pension Accounting: A Brief History

GM's impending bankruptcy in early 2009 refocused attention on long-standing allegations that top management manipulated the company's financial data to conceal its deteriorating financial condition and operating results. The company's critics included Maryann Keller, a longtime analyst of the automotive industry who two decades earlier had published a book entitled *Rude Awakening: The Rise, Fall, and Struggle for Recovery of General Motors* (HarperCollins, 1990). Keller suggested that GM management routinely "juggled" the company's accounting numbers to conceal its serious financial problems. Among the financial statement items that GM management allegedly distorted were the expenses and liabilities associated with the company's enormous pension plan.

In fairness to GM, a large number of companies have faced similar allegations, that is, charges that they "manage" their reported earnings and apparent financial condition by improperly accounting for their employee pension plans. In fact, accounting for pension-related financial statement items has long been one of the most complex and controversial issues facing the accounting profession.

Prior to the mid-1960s, most companies accounted for their pension plan expenses on a pay-as-you-go or cash basis. In addition to simply ignoring the long-term liabilities associated with pension plans, a major drawback to this accounting method was that it allowed companies to readily and legally manipulate their reported earnings by varying the amounts they contributed each year to their pension plans. For example, if a company was having a poor year profit-wise, it could simply reduce its pension plan contribution and thus reduce its pension expense for the year.

Accounting for pension plan–related expenses and liabilities did not change dramatically until 1985 when the Financial Accounting Standards Board (FASB) adopted a new accounting standard that moved the profession toward accrual basis accounting for those items. However, this new standard, *Statement on Financial Accounting Standards No. 87 (SFAS No. 87)*, "Employers' Accounting for Pensions," still provided opportunities for companies to window-dress their financial statements.

SFAS No. 87 required companies for the first time to make several key assumptions in accounting for financial statement items associated with a defined-benefit pension plan, similar to the one that GM provided to its employees.[2] Critics of the new standard argued that since these assumptions were "discretionary," they could be easily "manipulated" by corporate executives hoping to make their company's financial statements more impressive.[3] Among the most important of these assumptions was the discount rate used to determine the present value of a company's pension liability. This choice had important financial statement implications, particularly for labor-intensive companies with huge pension plans, such as GM. For example, a company could raise or lower—most likely the latter—the present value of its pension liability by varying the discount rate it applied to those liabilities.[4]

Rate Debates

In late 2002, GM faced an unpleasant predicament. Falling stock market prices were driving down the value of the assets held by its pension plan, while falling interest rates were increasing the present value of its pension liability. These two conditions were causing the unfunded portion of GM's pension liability and the company's projected pension expense under *SFAS No. 87* to increase dramatically.

During the final few months of 2002, several GM executives, including the company's chief financial officer (CFO), chief accounting officer (CAO), and controller, agonized over the decision of which discount rate to apply to the company's pension liability. Those executives recognized that the choice of that discount rate would have a material impact on GM's reported operating results and financial condition. *SFAS No. 87* obligated GM to choose the most reasonable discount rate to apply in computing the present value of its pension liability but did not specify how that discount rate was to be chosen. The mathematical method historically used by the company produced a discount rate of 6.0 percent. As in years past, the company also asked its actuarial firm to develop an independent estimate of the appropriate discount rate to apply to its pension liability. GM's actuarial firm reported that its mathematical modeling suggested that a 6.18 percent discount rate was appropriate.

---

2. Recognize that a company's pension plan is nearly always a legal entity independent of the company that created it. The issue in this context is not the actual accounting for a pension plan but rather the accounting for pension plan–related financial statement amounts of the given employer or "sponsor" of that plan.

3. Audit Integrity (www.auditintegrity.com), "Pension Liabilities: The Elephant in the Room," March 2009.

4. Addressing the specific features and requirements of pension accounting is beyond the scope of this case. Refer to any intermediate accounting text for a comprehensive treatment of that topic. In 2006, the FASB replaced *SFAS No. 87* with *SFAS No. 158*, "Employers' Accounting for Defined Benefit Pension and Other Postretirement Plans." Following the issuance of *SFAS No. 158*, the FASB has continued to debate and consider additional modifications to its pension accounting guidelines and rules.

Instead of using either a 6.0 percent or 6.18 percent discount rate, GM's executives chose a discount rate of 6.75 percent to apply to the company's pension liability. This latter discount rate was not produced by a rigorous mathematical model but rather by simply averaging the interest rates on a relatively small sample of high-quality corporate bonds tracked by the Moody's investment service. In fact, the actual average interest rate of the sample used by the executives to arrive at the 6.75 percent discount rate was 6.63 percent. (When choosing a discount rate, GM "rounded" the given estimate of that rate to the nearest quarter of a percent.)

By the first week of January 2003, Deloitte's audit of GM's 2002 financial statements was well under way. On 7 January 2003, Deloitte auditors met with representatives of the GM department responsible for developing the discount rate to apply to the company's pension liability. At that meeting, the GM representatives presented the three point estimates of the discount rate that had been considered and the source of each of those estimates. Their principal justification for choosing the 6.75 percent point estimate was that "most companies"[5] were relying on the Moody's database of interest rates to choose the discount rate to apply to their pension liability. The Securities and Exchange Commission (SEC) subsequently challenged that assertion. The federal agency also maintained that GM officials had made no effort to determine whether the companies actually using the Moody's data were "demographically similar to GM" and thus a valid sample to use in supporting the company's decision to rely on that source.

Following the 7 January 2003, meeting, the Deloitte auditors informed client personnel that they would begin their review of the company's decision to apply the 6.75 percent discount rate. The auditors also informed the client that a second meeting to discuss the issue would be necessary. Finally, the auditors noted that their initial impression was that the 6.75 percent discount rate was too high.

A few days later, the Deloitte auditors asked to meet again with the client to discuss the 6.75 percent discount rate. Deloitte insisted that representatives of GM's actuarial firm attend this second meeting. GM's controller also attended this meeting. Following this second meeting, the controller told GM's CFO and CAO that the Deloitte auditors were "now resigned to our use of 6.75%."

GM personnel at this second meeting apparently convinced the Deloitte auditors to accept the 6.75 percent rate by pledging to include a "sensitivity analysis in the company's 2002 Form 10-K." This supplemental disclosure would supposedly illustrate the impact of an array of discount rates on GM's pension-related financial statement items. In an intercompany communication, GM's controller told the CFO and CAO that a Deloitte audit partner accepted this compromise as a "reasonable although imperfect solution or compromise to his concerns." Despite agreeing to the compromise solution proposed by GM, the Deloitte partner believed that a 6.50 percent discount rate would have been a "better choice." Deloitte subsequently issued an unqualified audit opinion on GM's 2002 financial statements.

GM filed its 2002 Form 10-K with the SEC on 13 March 2003. As the company had pledged to Deloitte, it included a sensitivity analysis in the 10-K relevant to its choice of the 6.75 percent discount rate. That analysis disclosed what GM's pension expense and total pension liabilities would have been for both a 6.5 percent and 7.0 percent discount rate. If the 6.5 percent discount rate had been applied, the company's pension expense for 2002 would have increased by $120 million, which would have lowered its pretax earnings by approximately 6 percent. Likewise, the choice of a 6.5 percent

---

5. The remaining quotes in this case were taken from the following source: *Securities and Exchange Commission v. General Motors Corporation*, Case 1:09-cv-00119, U.S. District Court for the District of Columbia, 22 January 2009.

discount rate would have increased GM's total pension liability reported on its balance sheet by approximately 10 percent or $1.8 billion and would have reduced the company's stockholders' equity by approximately 16 percent or $1.1 billion.[6]

In a subsequent complaint filed against GM by the SEC in January 2009, the federal agency maintained that the pension-related amounts and disclosures within the company's 2002 financial statements were "materially misleading." The SEC was particularly concerned by GM's lack of candor in the sensitivity analysis that it presented for its selected pension discount rate. Since that analysis disclosed the financial statement impacts of using 6.5 and 7.0 percent discount rates, it implied that the selected discount rate of 6.75 percent was near the midpoint of the discount rates that had been considered by the company, which was not the case. The SEC also criticized GM for failing to disclose that an unconventional method had been used to select the 2002 discount rate.

EPILOGUE

In late January 2009, the SEC issued *Accounting and Auditing Enforcement Release No. 3033* that disclosed a litany of accounting and financial reporting abuses by GM over the previous several years. The principal focus of that document was the improper decisions that the company had made in accounting for its pension-related expenses and liabilities. Without admitting or denying the charges, GM agreed to a consent decree under which the SEC enjoined the company from any future violations of federal securities laws. The SEC did not sanction Deloitte for its role in GM's pension accounting debacle.

Six months after being sanctioned by the SEC, GM emerged from bankruptcy as the "new" General Motors or "General Motors Company." Following GM's reorganization, the federal government was its largest stockholder as a result of investing nearly $60 billion in the company through the Troubled Asset Relief Program (TARP).[7] Fortunately for GM's retirees and workforce, the bankruptcy reorganization plan left the company's huge pension plan intact. In 2012, GM announced a series of measures to reduce its pension plan liabilities. Those measures included offering a lump sum settlement to certain former employees to liquidate GM's pension obligation to them and purchasing a group annuity from Prudential Insurance Company to cover the future pension payments to a group of existing and former employees. These two measures alone reduced GM's outstanding pension obligations by approximately 25 percent.

Questions

1. Auditing standards don't specifically discuss the audit procedures that should be applied to a client's pension-related financial statement amounts. Identify five audit procedures that would be relevant to those items. For each audit procedure that you list, identify the related audit objective.

---

6. In its 2002 Form 10-K, GM reported total assets of $370.8 billion, total liabilities of $364 billion, and total stockholders' equity of $6.8 billion.

7. On 17 November 2010, General Motors Company went public. On that day, trading in GM's stock accounted for nearly 10 percent of the trading volume on the New York Stock Exchange. The federal government eventually recovered the majority of the funds invested in GM by selling its ownership interest in the company.

2. Under what general circumstances should auditors retain outside experts to assist them in completing an audit? How could an expert be useful in auditing a client's pension-related financial statement items?

3. Do you believe that Deloitte behaved properly by accepting GM's decision to apply a 6.75 percent discount rate to its pension liabilities? What, if any, other steps or measures should Deloitte have taken under the circumstances?

4. Did the choice of the 6.75 percent discount rate in 2002 have a material impact on GM's financial statements? Defend your answer.

Lipper Holdings, LLC

Over the past few decades, hedge funds have become among the most controversial and largest investment vehicles on Wall Street. Critics of hedge funds argue that their high-risk investment strategies contributed significantly to the economic crisis that gripped the world's capital markets beginning in late 2008. Prior to that crisis, the total market value of investments held by hedge funds was estimated to be a staggering $2.5 trillion.

In fact, pegging the total value of hedge funds at any point in time is a difficult task since there is a lack of consensus among even Wall Street experts on exactly which investment funds qualify as "hedge funds." Hedge funds are generally thought of by lay investors as investment funds that use sophisticated risk management techniques to limit the downside risk of the investments that they hold. Many hedge funds, however, do just the reverse. These latter funds employ investment strategies, such as buying and selling a wide range of exotic financial derivatives, that serve to increase, rather than decrease, the overall risk of their investment portfolios.

The two traits that most commonly cause an investment fund to be labeled a "hedge fund" are minimal regulatory oversight and the payment of "performance fees" to the fund managers. Many hedge funds are domiciled in offshore tax havens, such as the Cayman Islands, that impose little regulatory oversight on investment companies, banks, and related entities. Hedge funds headquartered in the United States typically have a legal structure that allows them to avoid intense scrutiny by the Securities and Exchange Commission (SEC) and other federal and state regulatory authorities.

In addition to the annual management fees that most investment fund managers are paid, the managers of hedge funds collect performance fees equal to a certain percentage of their fund's profit each year. These performance fees vary considerably from fund to fund but range as high as 20 percent. Critics of hedge funds, such as renowned investor Warren Buffett, maintain that performance fees encourage fund managers to adopt high-risk, if not reckless, investment strategies, which would explain why many hedge funds specialize in "junk bonds" and "distressed" corporate securities.[1]

Hedge Funds and Hollywood

During the 1990s, Kenneth Lipper emerged as a leader of the rapidly growing hedge fund "industry" in the United States. Born in 1941, Lipper, the son of a shoe salesman, spent his childhood in a modest working-class neighborhood in New York City's South Bronx. As an adolescent, he enjoyed a wide range of interests, including sports, movies, and the stock market. Unlike his childhood friend, Alfredo "Sonny" Pacino, Lipper decided as a young adult to pursue a career on Wall Street rather than in Hollywood—at least initially.

Lipper was a brilliant student who relied on academic scholarships to finance an undergraduate degree at Columbia, a law degree at Harvard, and a master's degree from the New York University School of Law before pursuing postgraduate studies

---

1. Increasing the risk preference of hedge fund managers is the fact that they do not absorb any portion of a net loss suffered in a given year by a fund that they manage.

at the University of Paris. The charismatic Lipper developed an impressive list of wealthy and well-connected friends and acquaintances during his college years.

In 1966, when he was 25 years old, Lipper married the daughter of one of New York's richest philanthropists. That marriage placed Lipper's Wall Street career on the "fast track, according to *Business Week*."[2] Shortly thereafter, he joined the prestigious Wall Street firm of Lehman Brothers; by the age of 32, Lipper was among that firm's youngest partners.

Lipper left Lehman in 1975 to become a partner and managing director of a competing firm, Salomon Brothers. His bright career was briefly derailed when the SEC accused him of aiding and abetting violations of the federal securities laws in a covert attempt to take over a large public company. Lipper settled those charges without admitting or denying any wrongdoing and escaped with only mild sanctions being imposed on him by the federal agency.

In 1983, one year after settling the SEC charges, Lipper took a sabbatical from the world of high finance to serve as deputy mayor of New York City. After three years in New York City's rough-and-tumble political arena, Lipper became involved in a Hollywood film project being developed by Oliver Stone. The famous movie director tapped Lipper to serve as a technical advisor for the film *Wall Street* starring Michael Douglas and Charlie Sheen. Following the release of the Academy Award–winning movie, Lipper wrote a novel of the same name based upon the film's screenplay.

Over the next two decades, Lipper lived a high-profile, bicoastal lifestyle in which he was a mainstay in both the West Coast's glitzy movie industry and Wall Street's economic powerhouse some 3,000 miles away. In Hollywood, Lipper enjoyed a successful career as a screenwriter and film producer and even collaborated with his old friend Al Pacino on a major film project.[3] At the same time, Lipper oversaw a burgeoning financial empire on the East Coast through his investment firm, Lipper Holdings, LLC, that he organized in the late 1980s. Lipper's firm, for which he served as both president and chief executive officer (CEO), would eventually manage investments having a total market value exceeding $4 billion dollars.

Lipper's network of influential friends on both coasts served as a pipeline of clients to his Wall Street firm. Julia Roberts, Sylvester Stallone, and Disney CEO Michael Eisner were among the many Hollywood luminaries for whom Lipper served as a financial advisor. One-time presidential candidate U.S. Senator Fritz Hollings, former Federal Reserve Chairman Paul Volcker, and Lipper's former boss Ed Koch, the longtime and very popular mayor of New York City, were among the political heavyweights that entrusted much of their wealth to Lipper's firm. As *Business Week* reported, "The flashy pitchman [Kenneth Lipper] with his fancy connections and wealth was a magnet for investors who never questioned his ability to manage their money.... These were... people who were wowed by his blue-chip Wall Street credentials."[4]

Lipper delegated the day-to-day responsibility of managing his firm's investment funds to subordinates. One of his principal subordinates was Edward Strafaci, an executive vice president of Lipper Holdings. Strafaci served as the portfolio manager for three large hedge funds within the family of Lipper investment funds. Those three hedge funds were Lipper Convertibles, Lipper Convertibles Series II, and Lipper

---

2. M. Vickers, "The Fallen Financier," *Business Week* (online), 9 December 2002.

3. In 1999, Lipper received an Oscar for his role as the producer of *The Last Days*, a documentary film focusing on the Holocaust. Al Pacino played the lead role in *City Hall*, a 1996 feature film produced by Lipper.

4. Vickers, "The Fallen Financier."

Fixed Income Fund. Each of the funds had been legally structured so that they were not required to register with the SEC as investment companies under the Investment Company Act of 1940. Because Lipper Convertibles and Lipper Convertibles Series II were legally "broker-dealers," however, they were required to file annual audited financial statements with the SEC pursuant to the requirements of the Securities Exchange Act of 1934.

Strafaci used financial leverage to enhance the rates of return earned by the investors in the three hedge funds, that is, he arranged for the funds to borrow large amounts of cash that were then invested along with the equity capital of the investors. This financial leverage caused the rates of return earned by investors to be considerably higher than the returns earned on the funds' investment portfolios. Of course, the use of financial leverage also meant that when the funds suffered losses in a given year, the corresponding losses of the funds' investors were magnified.

The marketing materials Lipper's firm used to promote his hedge funds reported that 70 percent of their holdings were high quality, "investment grade" securities. In fact, the actual percentage of investment grade securities held by the three hedge funds was considerably lower than that figure. To ensure that the funds continued to attract new investors, Strafaci believed it was imperative for them to earn impressive rates of return. Because investment grade securities didn't yield such returns, he invested an increasingly large percentage of the hedge funds' assets in high-risk, high-return securities. These securities were typically convertible bonds and convertible preferred stocks issued by companies experiencing financial problems.

"Recipe for Fraud"

When the volatile securities that Strafaci purchased for Lipper's hedge funds failed to produce the rates of return that he wanted, he began intentionally overstating their reported market values to achieve those desired returns. In January 2002, Strafaci resigned his lucrative position with Lipper Holdings. His unexpected resignation prompted an internal investigation over the following several weeks that led to the discovery of his fraudulent scheme.

In late February 2002, Lipper Holdings publicly reported that the market values of the investments held by the three hedge funds formerly managed by Strafaci had been overstated. When those investments were reflected at their true market values, the investors in the largest of the three funds, Lipper Convertibles, realized a nearly 50 percent reduction in their equity capital. More modest but still significant losses were suffered by the investors in Lipper's two other hedge funds.

Subsequent investigations by regulatory and law enforcement authorities revealed that Strafaci had personally supervised the "marking to market" of the investments held by the three hedge funds that he managed.[5] This revelation caused a prominent Wall Street money manager to point out that most hedge fund managers use an independent third party to value their investment portfolios and that allowing "insiders" to do so was a "recipe for fraud."[6]

When the overstatements of the Lipper hedge funds' investments were initially reported, Edward Strafaci vehemently denied any involvement in, or knowledge of, them. Instead, Strafaci laid the blame for the misstatements squarely on the shoulders

---

5. Many of these securities were "thinly traded" securities for which readily determinable market values were not available.

6. Vickers, "The Fallen Financier."

of his former boss, Kenneth Lipper. "We [Strafaci and his subordinates] don't bear any responsibility at all. Clients have to go to Ken Lipper if they're mad—he was the CEO."[7]

In August 2004, Strafaci did a sudden about-face. Strafaci pleaded guilty to fraudulently overstating the collective value of the investments he had managed for Lipper's hedge funds and subsequently received a six-year prison sentence. He was also ordered by a federal judge to pay restitution of nearly $90 million. Despite Strafaci's guilty plea, many parties, including former Lipper investors, maintained that Kenneth Lipper was ultimately responsible for the huge losses suffered by the Lipper hedge funds.

> *Lipper most likely knew these traders were mispricing the portfolio and juicing the returns all along. But he was so concerned with his reputation and impressing his celebrity clients that he allowed it, until they just got too deep to recover. It was pure hubris.*[8]

Auditors Miss the "Mark"

While federal prosecutors dogged Edward Strafaci and Kenneth Lipper, PricewaterhouseCoopers (PwC), Lipper's longtime audit firm, was being investigated by the SEC for failing to uncover the grossly overstated values of the investments held by the Lipper hedge funds. Particularly galling to the hedge fund investors was the allegation that those overstatements should have been readily apparent to the auditors. Making the situation even less palatable for the investors was the fact that Lipper Holdings had chosen PwC to audit its three hedge funds in part because of that firm's "touted expertise with respect to hedge funds and valuation of hard-to-price securities."[9,10]

The principal focus of the SEC's investigation of PwC was the firm's 2000 audits of the three Lipper hedge funds, the final audits completed by PwC prior to the discovery of the accounting fraud. The primary individual targeted by the federal agency during that investigation was Larry Stoler. Stoler became a partner with PwC's predecessor firm, Price Waterhouse, in 1980 and retired from the firm in 2002, shortly after the Lipper scandal surfaced. With the exception of two years in the mid-1990s, Stoler served as the audit engagement partner for each of the three Lipper hedge funds from 1989 through the collapse of those funds in early 2002. During the two years that he was not the audit engagement partner, Stoler had served as the concurring partner on the audits of those funds.

During its investigation of PwC's 2000 audits, the SEC discovered that Stoler had for several years been aware of internal control weaknesses that should have "heightened [PwC's] scrutiny of the valuation of their [the hedge funds'] investments." Most importantly, Stoler had been aware that Edward Strafaci personally supervised the marking to market of the hedge funds' investments each year and that there was no "formal review" of that process by another credible party.

The most important audit procedures applied by PwC during its 2000 audit of the Lipper hedge funds were the audit tests intended to determine whether the funds' major investments were appropriately valued at year-end.[11] According to the SEC,

---

7. *Ibid.*

8. *Ibid.*

9. Lipper actually retained the predecessor firm of PwC, Price Waterhouse, as the auditor of the three hedge funds. In 1998, Price Waterhouse merged with Coopers & Lybrand to create PwC.

10. This and all subsequent quotations, unless indicated otherwise, were taken from the following source: Securities and Exchange Commission, *Accounting and Auditing Enforcement Release No. 2470*, 31 July 2006.

11. These audit procedures were applied to the investments held by the Lipper Convertibles hedge fund, the largest of the three Lipper hedge funds. The investment portfolios of the other two hedge funds consisted of subsets of the securities held by Lipper Convertibles.

the basis for the values assigned to those investments by Strafaci was allegedly 31 December 2000, price quotes that he had received directly from a sample of the brokers that executed securities trades for the three hedge funds. PwC's audit workpapers, however, did not include copies of the documents containing those alleged price quotes or any evidence that the auditors had reviewed those documents.

The initial audit procedure applied to the year-end securities prices of the hedge funds' investments involved a review of the 31 December 2000, statements obtained by the auditors from the brokers actually holding those investments on that date on behalf of the funds. These prices were inconsistent with the market prices that had been applied to the investments by Strafaci. According to the SEC, Stoler did not discuss these inconsistencies "with anyone at Lipper Holdings," nor did the PwC workpapers indicate how these inconsistencies were resolved.

PwC's workpapers documented the fact that the year-end market values of the hedge funds' investments appeared to be overstated given the results of the initial audit test. For Lipper Convertibles the apparent overstatement was approximately 13 percent. However, this amount "ignored the impact of leverage on the portfolio" of that fund. If the auditors had considered the impact of that leverage, they would have determined that the apparent errors made by Strafaci in marking to market Lipper Convertibles' investments had overstated the equity capital of the fund's investors "by approximately 48%."

The PwC auditors also used year-end market prices reported by the Bloomberg investment service "to obtain an independent price for 65% of the total market value positions held at 12/31/00" by the Lipper hedge funds. This audit procedure resulted in the auditors once again discovering apparent overstatements in the year-end market values of the hedge funds' investments. PwC's audit program called for the investigation of any "significant variances" between the year-end Bloomberg prices and the prices applied by Strafaci to those investments.

> Any Bloomberg prices that were "greater than 2% of what Lipper Convertibles has recorded" were to be "independently confirmed" by "directly contacting" the brokers with whom Convertibles traded and from whom Strafaci purportedly obtained the quotes on which he based his values for the securities "so that they may confirm the price of the positions."

This follow-up audit procedure involved a junior auditor assigned to the PwC audit team sending faxes to salespersons at five broker-dealers used by the Lipper hedge funds. These faxes included a schedule of all the securities prices used by Strafaci to mark the hedge funds' investments to market at 31 December 2000. The faxes asked the recipients to "Please verify the attached schedule of broker quotes as of 12/31/00 were [sic] provided by you to Lipper Convertibles." The faxes also instructed the recipients to sign the schedules and fax them back to the auditor.

Representatives of four of the five brokers signed the schedules and faxed them back to the junior auditor "without any notation or comments." PwC considered these four returned faxes to be "clean confirmations" of the year-end market prices applied by Strafaci. The fifth returned fax was unsigned and included notations indicating that several of the market prices were significantly higher than the actual year-end prices of the given securities.

The SEC charged that PwC's confirmation audit procedure was "flawed in several significant respects." For example, the faxed confirmations did not specifically instruct the recipients to "provide quotes for the specified securities or ask them to attest to the reasonableness of the values listed on the schedules." As a result, with the exception of the one broker-dealer representative who questioned several of the market prices included in the confirmation, there was no evidence "that the salespeople who returned signed confirmations had actually ascertained the broker-dealer's quote or valued the security." In fact, in some cases, the given broker-dealers did not make a market in certain securities listed on the confirmation and thus had no basis for attesting to the year-end market prices of those securities.

EPILOGUE

In a July 2006 enforcement release, the SEC reported that "most" of the relevant audit evidence collected by PwC during its 2000 audit of Lipper's hedge funds "indicated that Strafaci's valuation of the Funds' assets were substantially overstated." For that reason, the federal agency ruled that the unqualified audit reports on the funds' financial statements, reports signed by Larry Stoler, were unjustified.

Stoler ignored, discounted, or failed to apprise himself of, the evidence produced by the audit tests. . . . Thus, he ailed to obtain sufficient competent evidential matter concerning the valuation of the Funds' assets, and failed to adequately supervise the assistants working on the audit.

Accompanying the 2000 audited financial statements filed with the SEC by the Lipper Convertibles and Lipper Convertibles Series II hedge funds were supplemental reports on their internal controls prepared by PwC, reports mandated at the time for broker-dealers registered with the federal agency. The reports, signed by Stoler, indicated that PwC had uncovered no material weaknesses in the two hedge funds' internal controls. In its 2006 enforcement release, the SEC ruled that the latter conclusion was "inaccurate."

The SEC sanctioned Larry Stoler for failing to comply with generally accepted auditing standards (GAAS) during the 2000 audits of Lipper Holdings' three hedge funds.[12] According to the SEC, Stoler was "a cause" of the funds' violations of the federal securities laws.

The Funds' audited financial statements for the year ended December 31, 2000, were disseminated to investors/clients and prospective investors/clients, along with PwC's unqualified audit reports on those statements. PwC's unqualified audit reports on those statements gave comfort to investors/clients, among others, that the Funds were being properly valued. Investors/clients who received those audited financial statements were solicited to make, and in some cases made, investments or additional investments in the Funds.

The three Lipper hedge funds audited by Stoler and his subordinates were liquidated by Lipper Holdings beginning in 2002. Those forced liquidations resulted in hundreds of millions of dollars of losses for the funds' investors. Numerous civil lawsuits stemming from the Lipper scandal were filed by the investors or their representatives. One of the largest of those lawsuits was filed against PwC by a court-appointed bankruptcy trustee. According to published reports, that lawsuit was settled in 2010 when PwC agreed to pay $29.9 million to the former Lipper investors.[13,14]

In 2011, the SEC adopted measures to make hedge funds "a bit less mysterious."[15] The new measures required many hedge funds to disclose "potential conflicts of interest," "general information about their size and ownership," and the identity of their independent auditors.[16]

---

12. Although Stoler had retired in 2002, in its 2006 enforcement release the SEC suspended his right to practice before it for one year.

13. Kirby McInerney LLP, "Lipper Convertibles, L.P.," http://kmslaw.us/news.asp?type=cases&id=32.

14. Kenneth Lipper was not sanctioned by the SEC following its investigation of Edward Strafaci's fraudulent scheme nor was he criminally indicted for any role in that scheme.

15. *SmartPros* (online), "SEC Votes to Force Public Disclosures from Hedge Funds," 23 June 2011, http://accounting.smartpros.com/x72218.xml.

16. *Ibid.*

Questions

1. Identify specific fraud risk factors present during PwC's audits of the Lipper hedge funds. Explain how PwC should have responded to the fraud risk factors that you identified.

2. Provide examples of important audit objectives for complex financial instruments and transactions. For each audit objective that you identify, list one or more audit procedures that could be used to accomplish that objective.

3. Identify the factors that may have contributed to the alleged flaws in the audit procedures that PwC applied in testing the year-end market values of the Lipper hedge funds' investments. Discuss specific measures that audit firms can employ to reduce the likelihood that such factors will undercut the quality of their audits.

CBI Holding Company, Inc.

During the 1980s, CBI Holding Company, Inc., a New York–based firm, served as the parent company for several wholly owned subsidiaries, principal among them Common Brothers, Inc. CBI's subsidiaries marketed an extensive line of pharmaceutical products. The subsidiaries purchased these products from drug manufacturers, warehoused them in storage facilities, and then resold them to retail pharmacies, hospitals, long-term care facilities, and related entities. CBI's principal market area stretched from the northeastern United States into the upper Midwest.

In 1991, Robert Castello, CBI's president and chairman of the board, sold a 48 percent ownership interest in his company to Trust Company of the West (TCW), a diversified investment firm. The purchase agreement between the two parties gave TCW the right to appoint two members of CBI's board; Castello retained the right to appoint the three remaining board members. The purchase agreement also identified several so-called "control-triggering events." If any one of these events occurred, TCW would have the right to take control of CBI. Examples of control-triggering events included CBI's failure to maintain certain financial ratios at a specified level and unauthorized loans to Castello and other CBI executives.

Castello engaged Ernst & Young (E&Y) as CBI's independent audit firm several months before he closed the TCW deal. During this same time frame, Castello was named "Entrepreneur of the Year" in an annual nationwide promotion cosponsored by E&Y. From 1990 through 1993, E&Y issued unqualified opinions on CBI's annual financial statements.

Accounting Gimmicks

Castello instructed several of his subordinates to misrepresent CBI's reported operating results and financial condition for the fiscal years ended 30 April 1992, and 1993.[1] Those misrepresentations allowed Castello to receive large, year-end bonuses to which he was not entitled. CBI actively concealed the fraudulent activities from TCW's management, from TCW's appointees to CBI's board, and from the company's E&Y auditors because Castello realized that the scheme, if discovered, would qualify as a control-triggering event under the terms of the 1991 purchase agreement with TCW. Several years later in a lawsuit prompted by Castello's fraud, TCW executives testified that they would have immediately seized control of CBI if they had become aware of that scheme.

Understating CBI's year-end accounts payable was one of the methods Castello and his confederates used to distort CBI's 1992 and 1993 financial statements. At any point in time, CBI had large outstanding payables to its suppliers, which included major pharmaceutical manufacturers such as Burroughs-Wellcome, Schering, and FoxMeyer. At the end of fiscal 1992 and fiscal 1993, CBI understated payables due to its large vendors by millions of dollars. Judge Burton Lifland, the federal magistrate who presided over the lawsuit stemming from Castello's fraudulent scheme, ruled that the intentional understatements of CBI's year-end payables were very material to the company's 1992 and 1993 financial statements.

---

1. Due to a change in CBI's fiscal year, the company's 1992 fiscal year was only 11 months.

E&Y's 1992 and 1993 CBI Audits

In both 1992 and 1993, E&Y identified the CBI audit as a "close monitoring engagement." The accounting firm's audit manual defined a close monitoring engagement as "one in which the company being audited presents significant risk to E&Y . . . there is a significant chance that E&Y will suffer damage to its reputation, monetarily, or both."[2] E&Y's workpapers for the 1992 and 1993 audits also documented several "red flags" suggesting that the engagements posed a higher-than-normal audit risk.

Control risk factors identified for the CBI audits by E&Y included the dominance of the company by Robert Castello,[3] the absence of an internal audit function, the lack of proper segregation of duties within the company's accounting department, and aggressive positions taken by management personnel regarding key accounting estimates. These apparent control risks caused E&Y to describe CBI's control environment as "ineffective." Other risk factors identified in the CBI audit workpapers included the possible occurrence of a control-triggering event, an "undue" emphasis by top management on achieving periodic earnings goals, and the fact that Castello's annual bonus was tied directly to CBI's reported earnings.

For both the 1992 and 1993 CBI audits, the E&Y engagement team prepared a document entitled "Audit Approach Plan Update and Approval Form." This document described the general strategy E&Y planned to follow in completing those audits. In 1992 and 1993, this document identified accounts payable as a "high risk" audit area. The audit program for the 1992 audit included two key audit procedures for accounts payable:

a. Perform a search for unrecorded liabilities at 30 April 1992, through the end of fieldwork.

b. Obtain copies of the 30 April 1992, vendor statements for CBI's five largest vendors, and examine reconciliations to the accounts payable balances for such vendors as shown on the books of CBI.

The 1993 audit program included these same items, although that program required audit procedure "b" to be applied to CBI's 10 largest vendors.

During the 1992 audit, the E&Y auditors discovered numerous disbursements made by CBI in the first few weeks of fiscal 1993 that were potential unrecorded liabilities as of 30 April 1992. The bulk of these disbursements included payments to the company's vendors that had been labeled as "advances" in the company's accounting records. CBI personnel provided the following explanation for these advances when questioned by the auditors: "When CBI is at its credit limit with a large vendor, the vendor may hold an order until they receive an 'advance.' CBI then applies the advance to the existing A/P balance."

In truth, the so-called advances, which totaled nearly $2 million, were simply payments CBI made to its vendors for inventory purchases consummated on, or prior to, 30 April 1992. Castello and his confederates had chosen not to record these transactions—their purpose being to strengthen key financial ratios of CBI at the end of fiscal 1992 and otherwise embellish the company's apparent financial condition. The conspirators developed the advances ruse because they feared that E&Y would discover the material understatements of accounts payable at year-end.

Subsequent court testimony revealed that after reviewing internal documents supporting the advances explanation—documents that had been prepared to deceive

---

2. This and all subsequent quotes were taken from the following court opinion: *In re CBI Holding Company, Inc., et al., Debtors; Bankruptcy Services, Inc., Plaintiff—against—Ernst & Young, Ernst & Young, LLP, Defendants;* 247 B.R. 341; 2000 Bankr. LEXIS 425.

3. The CBI audit engagement partner noted during the 1993 audit that the company's CFO appeared to be "afraid of his boss, Castello." When questioned by an auditor regarding an important issue, the CFO typically responded by telling the individual to "ask Castello." In the audit partner's view, this raised an "integrity red flag."

E&Y—the E&Y auditors readily accepted that explanation and chose not to treat the items as unrecorded liabilities. This decision prompted severe criticism of the audit firm by Judge Lifland.

The federal judge pointed out that the auditors had failed to rigorously investigate the alleged advances and consider the veracity of the client's explanation for them. For example, the auditors did not investigate the "credit limit" feature of that explanation. The E&Y auditors neglected to determine the credit limit that the given vendors had established for CBI or whether CBI had "maxed out" that credit limit in each case as maintained by client personnel. Nor did the auditors attempt to analyze the given vendors' payable accounts or contact those vendors directly to determine if the alleged advances applied to specific invoice amounts, particularly invoice amounts for purchases made on or before 30 April 1992. Instead, the auditors simply chose to record in their workpapers the client's feeble explanation for the advances, an explanation that failed to address or resolve a critical issue. "The advance explanation recorded in E&Y's workpapers, even if it were true, did not tell the E&Y auditor the essential fact as to whether the merchandise being paid for by the advance had been received before or after April 30, 1992."

Because of the lack of any substantive investigation of the advances, the E&Y auditors failed to determine "whether a liability should have been recorded for each such payment as of fiscal year-end, and whether, in fact, a liability was recorded for such payment as of fiscal year-end." This finding caused Judge Lifland to conclude that E&Y had not properly completed the search for unrecorded liabilities. The judge reached a similar conclusion regarding the second major audit procedure for accounts payable included in the 1992 audit program for CBI.

The 1992 audit program required the E&Y auditors to obtain the year-end statements sent to CBI by the company's five largest vendors and to reconcile the balances in each of those statements to the corresponding balances reported in CBI's accounting records. E&Y obtained year-end statements mailed to CBI by five of the company's several hundred vendors and completed the reconciliation audit procedure. However, the vendors involved in this audit test were not the company's five largest suppliers. In fact, E&Y never identified CBI's five largest vendors during the 1992 audit. The federal judge scolded E&Y for this oversight and maintained that the "minimal" amount of testing applied by E&Y to the small sample of year-end vendor statements was "not adequate."

The audit procedures that E&Y applied to CBI's year-end accounts payable for fiscal 1993 suffered from the same flaws evident during the firm's 1992 audit. Similar to the previous year, CBI's management attempted to conceal unrecorded liabilities at year-end by labeling subsequent payments of those amounts as "advances" to the given vendors. Once more, Judge Lifland noted that the "gullible" auditors readily accepted the explanation for these advances that was relayed to them by CBI personnel. As a result, the auditors failed to require CBI to prepare appropriate adjusting entries for approximately $7.5 million of year-end payables that the client's management team had intentionally ignored.

The 1993 audit program mandated that E&Y obtain the year-end statements for CBI's 10 largest vendors and reconcile the balances in those statements to the corresponding accounts payable balances in CBI's accounting records. Again, E&Y failed to identify CBI's largest vendors and simply applied the reconciliation procedure to a sample of 10 CBI vendors.[4]

---

4. The court opinion that provided the background information for this case did not indicate what criteria E&Y used to select the vendor accounts to which the reconciliation procedure was applied in the 1992 and 1993 audits.

One of CBI's 10 largest vendors was Burroughs-Wellcome. If the E&Y auditors had reconciled the balance due Burroughs-Wellcome in its year-end statement with the corresponding account payable balance in CBI's accounting records, the auditors would have discovered that a $1 million "advance" payment made to that vendor in May 1993 was actually for an inventory purchase two weeks prior to 30 April 1993. This discovery would have clearly established that the $1 million amount was an unrecorded liability at year-end.

E&Y Held Responsible for CBI's Bankruptcy

In March 1994, E&Y withdrew its opinions on CBI's 1992 and 1993 financial statements after learning of the material distortions in those statements that were due to Castello's fraudulent scheme. Almost immediately, CBI began encountering difficulty obtaining trade credit from its principal vendors. A few months later in August 1994, the company filed for bankruptcy. In early 2000, Judge Lifland presided over a 17-day trial in federal bankruptcy court to determine whether E&Y would be held responsible for the large losses that CBI's collapse inflicted on TCW and CBI's former creditors. Near the conclusion of that trial, Judge Lifland ruled that E&Y's conduct during the 1992 and 1993 CBI audits was the "proximate cause" of those losses.

> *The demise of CBI was a foreseeable consequence of E&Y's failure to conduct its audits in fiscal 1992 and 1993 in accordance with GAAS, which was the cause of its failure to detect the unrecorded liabilities, which in turn foreseeably caused it to withdraw its opinions in March 1994. As direct and reasonably foreseeable consequences thereof, CBI's vendors restricted the amount of credit available, CBI's inventory and sales declined, its revenues declined, its value as a going concern diminished, and ultimately it filed for bankruptcy and was liquidated.*

Judge Lifland characterized E&Y's conduct as either "reckless and/or grossly negligent" and identified several generally accepted auditing standards that the accounting firm violated while performing the 1992 and 1993 CBI audits. Although the bulk of the judge's opinion dealt with the audit procedures E&Y applied to CBI's accounts payable, his harshest criticism focused on the firm's alleged failure to retain its independence during the CBI engagements.

Several circumstances that arose during E&Y's tenure as CBI's audit firm called into question its independence. For example, Judge Lifland referred to an incident in 1993 when Robert Castello demanded that E&Y remove the audit manager assigned to the CBI engagement. Apparently, Castello found the audit manager's inquisitive and probing nature disturbing. The CBI audit engagement partner "submissively acquiesced" to Castello's request and replaced the audit manager.

Shortly after the completion of the 1993 audit, Castello hired a new chief financial officer (CFO). This individual resigned eight days later. The CFO told members of the E&Y audit team he was resigning because of several million dollars of "grey accounting" he had discovered in CBI's accounting records. Judge Lifland chided E&Y for being slow to pursue this allegation. Nearly five months passed before the CBI audit engagement partner contacted the former CFO. By that point, E&Y had already discovered Castello's fraudulent scheme and withdrawn its 1992 and 1993 audit opinions.

In February 1994, the audit engagement partner met with Castello to discuss several matters. E&Y's unpaid bill for prior services provided to CBI was the first of those matters, while the second issue discussed was E&Y's fee for the upcoming audit. The last topic on the agenda was the allegation by CBI's former CFO regarding the company's questionable accounting decisions. According to Judge Lifland, the audit partner "wanted to speak to [the former CFO] in order to ask him whether his leaving the post of chief financial officer and his allegations of 'grey accounting' had anything to do with the financial statements that E&Y had just certified; however, [the audit partner] obligingly allowed himself to be put off." In Judge Lifland's opinion, the E&Y audit partner was "more concerned about insuring E&Y's fees than he was about speaking to [the former CFO]."

The final matter Judge Lifland discussed in impugning E&Y's independence was the accounting firm's effort to retain CBI as an audit client after discovering that the 1992 and 1993 audits had been deficient. Judge Lifland charged that E&Y officials realized, when they withdrew the audit opinions on CBI's 1992 and 1993 financial statements, that the CBI audits had been flawed. In the days prior to withdrawing those opinions, two individuals, a former CBI accountant and CBI's controller at the time, informed E&Y that the "advances" discovered during the 1992 and 1993 audits had been for payment of unrecorded liabilities that existed at the end of CBI's 1992 and 1993 fiscal years. After investigating these admissions, E&Y determined that they were true. E&Y also determined that the CBI auditors "had failed to detect the unrecorded liabilities because they had failed to properly perform the search [for unrecorded liabilities]."

E&Y failed to notify CBI's board of directors of the flaws in the 1992 and 1993 audits.[5] According to Judge Lifland, E&Y did not inform the board members of those flaws because the accounting firm realized that doing so would lower, if not eliminate, its chance of landing the "reaudit" engagement for CBI's 1992 and 1993 financial statements. "E&Y's egocentric desire to get the reaudit work is illustrated by the fact that it prepared an audit program for the reaudit two days before E&Y met with the CBI board of directors and one day before they withdrew their opinion."

CBI's board ultimately selected E&Y to reaudit the company's 1992 and 1993 financial statements. Given the circumstances under which E&Y obtained that engagement, Judge Lifland concluded that the accounting firm's independence was likely impaired. "Thus, E&Y knew prior to agreeing to perform the reaudit work that it had not complied with GAAS. E&Y also knew that CBI's board of directors did not know of E&Y's failure to comply with GAAS. It is reasonable to infer that if CBI's board of directors knew of such failure, E&Y and CBI would be in adversarial positions."[6]

Questions

1. Most of Judge Lifland's criticism of E&Y focused on the firm's audit procedures for CBI's accounts payable. Generally, what is the primary audit objective for accounts payable? Do you believe that E&Y's two principal audit tests for CBI's accounts payable would have accomplished that objective if those tests had been properly applied? Why or why not?

2. Do you believe that the E&Y auditors should have used confirmations in auditing CBI's year-end accounts payable? Defend your answer. Briefly explain the differing audit objectives related to accounts receivable and accounts payable confirmation procedures and the key differences in how these procedures are applied.

---

5. At this point, the TCW representatives on CBI's board were apparently the company's principal decision-makers.

6. The plaintiffs in this case were initially awarded a judgment of approximately $70 million. E&Y appealed that judgment, an appeal that prompted what one legal expert referred to as a decade-long "epic battle" in the appellate courts. In late 2010, Judge Lifland brokered a settlement to end that court battle. The amount paid by E&Y to the plaintiffs to settle the case was apparently never reported publicly.

3. In early 1994, E&Y officials discovered that the CBI auditors had failed to determine the true nature of the "advances" they had uncovered during the 1992 and 1993 audits. In your view, did E&Y have an obligation to inform CBI management of this oversight prior to seeking the "reaudit" engagement? More generally, does an auditor have a responsibility to inform client management of mistakes or oversights made on earlier audits?

4. Under what circumstances, if any, should an audit engagement partner acquiesce to a client's request to remove a member of the audit engagement team?

5. E&Y officials believed that the CBI audits were high-risk engagements. Under what general circumstances should an audit firm choose not to accept a high-risk engagement?

Geo Securities, Inc.

In 1980, Frank Sinopoli, a 27-year-old accountant, accepted a job offer from a CPA firm based in Dallas, Texas. Four years later, Sinopoli became a partner with the firm. Perkins, Dexter, Sinopoli & Hamm (PDSH) provided accounting and accounting-related services to small and medium-sized businesses located principally in the Dallas-Fort Worth metroplex. During his long tenure with PDSH, Sinopoli supervised a wide range of engagements. Those engagements included the 2000 through 2005 audits of a small brokerage firm, Geo Securities, Inc.

Geo Companies of North America (GCNA), a Dallas-based oil and gas exploration company, organized Geo Securities as a wholly owned subsidiary in June 1996. The sole business purpose of Geo Securities was to market interests in oil and gas properties owned or controlled by GCNA. Similar to GCNA, Geo Securities was not a public company. However, because Geo Securities was a registered broker-dealer with the Securities and Exchange Commission (SEC), its annual financial statements had to be audited by an independent accounting firm.

Throughout the six-year period that Sinopoli supervised the annual audits of Geo Securities, the company was entangled in two civil lawsuits filed in a federal district court in Georgia. The two principal defendants in these lawsuits were GCNA and Geo Securities. The primary allegation filed against the defendants was that they had "fraudulently offered and sold"[1] joint partnership interests in oil and gas properties.

In 2004, the Georgia federal court ordered the defendants to pay a nominal amount of damages, approximately $217,000, to the plaintiffs to settle the two civil lawsuits. The court also appointed an arbitrator to determine whether the plaintiffs would be entitled to recover some or all of their sizable attorneys' fees from the defendants. In April 2005, three months before Geo Securities' 2005 fiscal year-end of 31 July 2005, the arbitrator ruled that GCNA, Geo Securities, and the other defendants in the civil lawsuits—who were individuals affiliated with the two companies—would be required to reimburse the plaintiffs for $949,688 of legal fees they had incurred in pursuing the case. The defendants were jointly and severally liable for those legal fees. GCNA had informed Geo Securities and the other defendants that it would pay the $217,000 settlement but did not make such a commitment regarding the much larger arbitration award.

GCNA, Geo Securities, and the other defendants appealed the 2004 court-ordered settlement and filed a challenge to the 2005 arbitration decision. Because Geo Securities' management believed that GCNA would pay the full amount of the arbitration award—if it was not overturned—the company did not record a contingent liability or loss related to that award in its accounting records. Instead, the company disclosed the arbitration award in a financial statement footnote accompanying its 2005 financial statements (see Exhibit 1).

---

1. This and all subsequent quotes were taken from the following source: Securities and Exchange Commission, *Accounting and Auditing Enforcement Release No. 2979*, 27 May 2009.

EXHIBIT 1

LOSS
CONTINGENCIES
FOOTNOTE
ACCOMPANYING
GEO SECURITIES'
2005 FINANCIAL
STATEMENTS

NOTE EIGHT—LOSS CONTINGENCIES

During 2000 and 2002, two separate lawsuits were filed against the Company (Geo Securities), GCNA, and other related parties by individuals in Georgia. The suits allege that the Company violated applicable security laws. During the fiscal year ended July 31, 2005, the trial judge granted a motion to enforce a contested settlement and ordered the issue of the plaintiffs' attorney fees to be resolved at arbitration. The arbitrator determined that $949,688 in attorney fees should be paid by the Company, GCNA, and the other related parties. The judge construed that a settlement agreement had been reached. This settlement agreement is currently being appealed. Additionally, the Company, GCNA, and other related parties have sued the plaintiffs and their attorneys for unrelated claims not related to the Georgia lawsuits. Management believes that the original suits are without merit and are vigorously defending its position in both lawsuits. The Company, GCNA, and the other related parties feel the original claims have no merit.

Geo Securities reported total assets of $155,183, total liabilities of $12,441, and total stockholder's equity of $142,742 in its 31 July 2005, balance sheet. The company's income statement for the year ended 31 July 2005, reflected total revenues of $551,131 and a net loss of $100,167. The unqualified opinion that PDSH issued on Geo Securities' 2005 financial statements is shown in Exhibit 2.

EXHIBIT 2

AUDIT REPORT
ISSUED BY PDSH ON
GEO SECURITIES'
2005 FINANCIAL
STATEMENTS

To the Board of Directors

GEO SECURITIES, INC.

Dallas, Texas

Independent Auditors' Report

We have audited the accompanying statement of financial condition of GEO SECURITIES, INC. as of July 31, 2005, and the related statements of income, changes in stockholder's equity, and cash flows for the year then ended that you are filing pursuant to Rule 17a-5 under the Securities Exchange Act of 1934. These financial statements are the responsibility of the Company's management. Our responsibility is to express an opinion on these financial statements based on our audit.

We conducted our audit in accordance with auditing standards generally accepted in the United States of America. Those standards require that we plan and perform the audit to obtain reasonable assurance about whether the financial statements are free of material misstatement. An audit includes examining, on a test basis, evidence supporting the amounts and disclosures in the financial statements. An audit also includes assessing the accounting principles used and significant estimates made by management, as well as evaluating the overall financial statement presentation. We believe that our audit provides a reasonable basis for our opinion.

In our opinion, the financial statements referred to above present fairly, in all material respects, the financial position of GEO SECURITIES, INC. at July 31, 2005, and the results of its operations and its cash flows for the year then ended in conformity with accounting principles generally accepted in the United States of America.

Our audit was conducted for the purpose of forming an opinion on the basic financial statements taken as a whole. The supplemental information presented in Schedule

EXHIBIT 2–
continued

AUDIT REPORT
ISSUED BY PDSH ON
GEO SECURITIES'
2005 FINANCIAL
STATEMENTS

1 – Computation of Net Capital Pursuant to Rule 15c3-1 and Schedule 2 – Exemptive Provision of Rule 15c3-3 is presented for the purposes of additional analysis and is not a required part of the basic financial statements, but is supplementary information required by Rule 17a-5 under the Securities Exchange Act of 1934. Such information has been subjected to the audit procedures applied in the examination of the basic financial statements, and, in our opinion, is fairly stated in all material respects in relation to the basic financial statements taken as a whole.

Perkins, Dexter, Sinopoli & Hamm, PC [signed]

Richardson, Texas

September 30, 2005

In May 2009, the SEC ruled that Geo Securities' 2005 financial statements were materially misstated because they "failed to include a material liability for the Arbitrator's award." The SEC pointed out that generally accepted accounting principles (GAAP) require companies to record a loss and a liability in their accounting records for a loss contingency that is both probable and subject to reasonable estimation. Since the arbitration award met both criteria and since the defendants in the lawsuit were jointly and severally liable, the SEC deemed that Geo Securities should have reported a loss and corresponding liability of $949,688 in its 2005 financial statements.

Compounding this error was Geo Securities' failure to consider the arbitration award when computing its "net capital." Registered broker-dealers must include a "computation of net capital" schedule with their audited financial statements that they file each year with the SEC. The purpose of this schedule is to demonstrate that a broker-dealer has sufficient equity to sustain its operations. In this schedule, broker-dealers must make certain adjustments to the stockholders' equity reported in their audited balance sheets to arrive at a more conservative (lower) net capital figure.[2] In computing its net capital, Geo Securities did not consider the large contingent loss stemming from the arbitration award, which was not surprising given the accounting treatment it applied to that award.[3]

The SEC also sanctioned Frank Sinopoli for failing to properly audit Geo Securities' 2005 financial statements and the net capital schedule that accompanied those statements. According to the SEC, Sinopoli was fully aware of the arbitration award when he planned and performed the 2005 Geo Securities audit. In fact, Sinopoli "assisted" Geo Securities management when it was deciding whether to record the award as a loss and liability in the company's 2005 financial statements or simply disclose the arbitration award in the accompanying financial statement footnotes.

Despite Sinopoli's awareness of Geo Securities' litigation problems, he did not identify "litigation, claims, and assessments as an area of significant risk" while planning the 2005 audit. Sinopoli also did not identify the attorneys representing Geo Securities in those legal matters, nor did he request that Geo Securities "send an audit inquiry letter" to those attorneys.

The SEC also criticized Sinopoli for relying on a representation made by Geo Securities' president that GCNA, Geo Securities' parent company, would ultimately pay the arbitration award in full if the effort to overturn that award proved unsuccessful.

---

2. Among many other items, these adjustments include reductions for "non-allowable" or illiquid assets.

3. Geo Securities did include a supplementary disclosure in its net capital schedule that referred to "contingent indebtedness" equal to the full amount of the arbitration award.

That representation was particularly relevant to Geo Securities' status as a going concern. In fact, the SEC reported that during the 2005 audit Sinopoli did not explicitly consider whether Geo Securities was a going concern. Sinopoli "failed to evaluate GSI's ability to continue as a going concern, failed to obtain additional information about the conditions raising the concerns and failed to evaluate management's plans for dealing with the adverse effects of the conditions raising the concerns, as required by GAAS."

The SEC maintained that, at a minimum, Sinopoli should have corresponded with GCNA to determine whether it intended to pay the arbitration award, as claimed by Geo Securities' president. Since GCNA was also a client of PDSH, Sinopoli could have easily contacted the company regarding that matter. The SEC noted that when Geo Securities subsequently disclosed its net capital deficiency in January 2006, GCNA failed to intervene, resulting in Geo Securities being forced out of business.

A final complaint lodged against Sinopoli by the SEC was his failure to identify the impact of the arbitration award on Geo Securities' net capital computation in the supplemental schedule accompanying its 2005 financial statements. As reflected in Exhibit 2, Sinopoli's 2005 audit opinion indicated that the information in that schedule was "fairly stated in all material respects in relation to the basic financial statements taken as a whole." In contrast to Sinopoli's conclusion, the SEC ruled that Geo Securities' net capital computation was "materially misstated" since it ignored the large contingent loss due to the arbitration award.

In a May 2009 *Accounting and Auditing Enforcement Release*, the SEC summarized its overall conclusions regarding Sinopoli's 2005 audit of Geo Securities.

> *Sinopoli failed to conduct the 2005 GSI [Geo Securities] audit in accordance with GAAS. Among other things, he failed to exercise professional skepticism and failed to obtain sufficient evidential matter to evaluate adequately and report properly the Arbitrator's award in GSI's financial statements. Furthermore, Sinopoli's work papers fail to evaluate GSI's ability to continue as a going concern. Nonetheless, Sinopoli signed, on behalf of PDSH, an audit report dated September 30, 2005, containing an unqualified opinion incorrectly claiming that PDSH's audit of GSI's July 31, 2005, financial statements had been conducted in accordance with GAAS. The opinion also incorrectly claims that GSI's audited financial statements present fairly, in all material respects, the financial position of GSI in conformity with GAAP.*

The sanctions imposed on Sinopoli included a cease and desist order prohibiting him from any future violations of the federal securities laws and a one-year suspension from practicing before the SEC.

EPILOGUE

The Dodd–Frank Act that was passed by Congress in 2010 required the Public Company Accounting Oversight Board (PCAOB) to oversee the audits of SEC-registered broker-dealers. Congress included this provision in the Dodd–Frank Act as a direct consequence of the Madoff Securities[4] scandal that contributed to the financial crisis that paralyzed the U.S. and global economies beginning in late 2008. In April 2012, the PCAOB released a report on its initial review of brokerage audits. The agency reported finding "deficiencies" in each of the 23 brokerage audits that it reviewed. A PCAOB spokesperson noted that the auditors of the brokerage firms

---

4. See Case 1.12, Madoff Securities.

"were not properly fulfilling their responsibilities to provide an independent check on brokers' and dealers' financial reporting and compliance with SEC rules."[5] Lynn Turner, former chief accountant of the SEC, characterized the PCAOB report as "mind-boggling."[6]

Questions

1. When auditing contingent liabilities, which of the management assertions discussed in professional auditing standards are of primary concern to an auditor? Explain.

2. The SEC criticized Frank Sinopoli for not sending an "audit inquiry letter" to Geo Securities' external legal counsel. Describe the nature and purpose of such a letter. Do you agree with the SEC that Sinopoli should have contacted Geo Securities' external legal counsel?

3. Under what circumstances must audit procedures be applied to supplemental information accompanying a client's financial statements? Describe the responsibilities auditors have when auditing such information.

4. Under what circumstances, if any, are auditors required to assess the going-concern status of an audit client? What procedures should auditors apply when performing such an assessment?

---

5. F. Norris, "Regulator Says Broker Audits Fail to Include Required Work," *New York Times* (online), 20 August 2012.

6. *Ibid.*

CASE 2.8

Belot Enterprises

As David Robinson works his way through the large, festive crowd, he keeps bumping into people he knows. All the while, Robinson is hoping that he will avoid the one person he doesn't want to meet face to face.[1]

Belot Enterprises' several hundred employees and their family members are celebrating the Fourth of July with a corporate picnic. For the occasion, the company reserved a municipal park perched on the bank of the Mississippi River in a Minneapolis suburb. The corporate picnic actually serves two purposes. In addition to celebrating the Fourth of July, Belot's employees are marking the end of the successful corporate-wide "Nail the Number" campaign.

The campaign was the brainchild of Kyle Allen, Belot's chief operating officer (COO) who joined the company six months ago. Allen was handpicked for the COO position by the top management of Helterbrand Associates, Belot's parent company. Helterbrand is a large, publicly owned conglomerate with five wholly owned subsidiaries that operate in five diverse industries.

Belot, a consumer products company, accounts for approximately one-third of Helterbrand's annual revenues and consolidated assets. During the previous several years, however, Belot has never accounted for more than 10 percent of Helterbrand's consolidated operating income. Two decades ago, Belot was the flagship of the Helterbrand corporate family. Declining profit margins in Belot's mature and intensely competitive industry have caused the company's profitability to gradually erode despite low but persistent growth in its annual revenues.

Allen, a 38-year-old Harvard MBA who established himself as a corporate turn-around specialist in the automotive supplies industry, was hired to reinvigorate Belot. After spending several weeks studying all facets of Belot's operations, Allen organized the Nail the Number campaign for the company's second quarter—1 April through 30 June. The goal of the campaign was to increase Belot's year-over-year quarterly operating income by 100 percent. Although that goal seemed impressive, it was not earthshaking since the company had earned a very modest, even by recent historical standards, operating income during the previous year's second quarter.

The tactics employed by Allen during the three-month campaign were also not earthshaking. They included focusing Belot's marketing efforts on products with relatively high profit margins, incentive-based compensation programs for the company's sales staff, and a variety of corporate-wide cost-cutting initiatives.

When David Robinson learned of the details of the Nail the Number campaign, he was not impressed. In his mind, the company should have implemented each of those strategic measures long ago. Then again, as a member of Belot's audit engagement team, Robinson recognized that his responsibilities did not include openly critiquing corporate management or its policies.

---

1. This case was developed from an actual series of events. Certain background information has been changed to conceal the identities of the individuals involved in the case.

Detox and Grizz

In two months, David Robinson will mark his fourth anniversary with the Big Four accounting firm that serves as the independent auditor of Helterbrand Associates and each of its five subsidiaries, including Belot Enterprises. During the past spring, Robinson completed his fourth busy season assigned to the Belot engagement. Since joining the firm after graduating with bachelor's and master's degrees in accounting from the University of Minnesota, 60 percent of Robinson's chargeable hours have been spent working at Belot.

Robinson has spent so much time at Belot's headquarters office on the northern edge of Minneapolis that he often feels as if he is an employee rather than an independent auditor of the firm. As he surveys the large throng of people attending the company's Fourth of July picnic, Robinson isn't sure that it is appropriate for him to be there. But the Belot audit engagement partner, R. B. Hansen, insisted that he attend the event.

The person that Robinson is hoping to avoid at the picnic is Belot's accounting general manager, Zachariah Crabtree. As the current in-charge senior on the audit team, Robinson interacts with Crabtree on an almost daily basis. The two men have an excellent relationship. In fact, over the previous few years, Robinson and Crabtree have become good friends, so much so that they regularly refer to each other using the nicknames—Detox and Grizz, respectively, that each was tagged with at the University of Minnesota.

Crabtree is a huge man, six-feet five-inches tall with a sturdy frame and girth. In his early 40s, he wears old-fashioned, black plastic-framed glasses that have lenses as thick as the bottom of a Coke bottle and sports an unruly head of bushy, prematurely gray hair. Making Grizz—short for "grizzly bear"—stand out even more in a crowd is his Johnny Cash–like insistence on wearing black. His standard workday attire is a pair of black cowboy boots, black denim jeans, a black button-down shirt, and a garish tie—the maroon and gold colors of the University of Minnesota's Golden Gophers are his favorite hues when it comes to ties.

Topping off Grizz's imposing persona is a dour expression that seems to convey that he is perpetually unhappy, if not chronically sociopathic. In truth, Crabtree is a kind and likable person with a dry sense of humor, who despite his unconventional appearance is well respected by both his superiors and subordinates.

Unlike Crabtree, Robinson could easily be mistaken for a Ralph Lauren model. The audit senior is a tall, handsome, athletically built 27-year-old who wears a stylish suit to work each day along with a starched, white button-down Polo shirt that is accessorized with a matching Polo tie. Robinson has a gregarious, outgoing personality. As for as his nickname, "Detox" is not a reference to any personal shortcomings but simply a jazzed-up version of the initials of his first and middle names given to him by his fraternity brothers.

Despite being so different in appearance and temperament, Robinson and Crabtree share one interest that binds them together. Both are certified sports fanatics. Each is a long-suffering fan of the various athletic teams fielded by the Golden Gophers and the local professional sports franchises, most notably the purple-clad Minnesota Vikings. The two sports aficionados typically start each conversation with the latest sports controversy being fueled by ESPN.

Nailing the Number the Easy Way

During his time at Belot, there have been few disputes between Robinson and Crabtree over accounting matters. Sit-down discussions involving the two accountants have centered on topics such as dollar-value LIFO, foreign currency translations, and impairment of long-lived assets. Robinson is grateful to Crabtree for his patience and willingness to explain the finer points of complex accounting issues despite his busy work schedule.

Robinson and Crabtree recently experienced their first truly unpleasant confrontation over an accounting issue, which explains why Robinson is hoping that he doesn't encounter Crabtree at the picnic. The dispute stemmed from Kyle Allen's Nail the Number campaign.

Crabtree is extremely loyal to Belot. He is concerned that if Belot's operating results don't improve soon, Helterbrand's top management may decide to sell the company outright or, even worse, split it up and sell it on a piecemeal basis. Crabtree once confided in Robinson that if the company is jettisoned by Helterbrand, he will probably lose his job and have difficulty finding a comparable position in the area. Like Robinson, Crabtree has strong family and emotional ties to the state of Minnesota and to the Minneapolis–St. Paul metroplex.

Over the past three months, Crabtree wore one of the promotional stickers for the Nail the Number campaign on his shirt pocket each day. The stickers, which feature a cartoonish icon of a large hammer posed over a dollar sign, were distributed to all of Belot's employees but few actually wore them.

Crabtree came up with his own personal contribution to the Nail the Number campaign by deciding to tighten the company's major discretionary accruals as of June 30. Those accruals include the allowances for bad debts, coupon redemptions, employee vacations, inventory obsolescence, and product warranties. Crabtree defends his decision by pointing out that in the past Belot's controller, Travis Logan, instructed him to err on the side of conservatism in establishing the accruals, meaning that each of them have been routinely overstated by a modest amount. Crabtree maintains that he is simply reducing the accruals to their appropriate levels.

Robinson rarely speaks with Logan who, like Crabtree, has spent his entire professional career with Belot. Only a few years away from retirement, Logan is a straitlaced, no-nonsense accountant who can quote specific passages from key accounting standards. Robinson particularly admires Logan because of his exemplary personal life. Logan spends hundreds of hours each year working as a volunteer and fund-raiser for a local charity that operates a private school for disabled children.

Crabtree's decision to record relatively modest 30th June balances for the five discretionary accruals has created a rift between himself and Logan. When he made that decision, Crabtree did something very uncharacteristic for him, namely, bypassing Logan, his immediate superior, and discussing the matter directly with Kyle Allen. Allen responded enthusiastically to Crabtree's proposal and agreed that all of the "fat" should be cut out of the accruals. He then sent an e-mail to Logan telling him that he approved Crabtree's decision.

After receiving the e-mail, Logan immediately met with Allen and voiced his disapproval. At that point, Allen reportedly told Logan point-blank that the accruals would be reduced whether he liked it or not. When Logan continued to object, Allen told him that Crabtree would have complete authority for establishing the period-ending balances of the accruals for the foreseeable future. Not surprisingly, Allen's decision made Logan livid. Robinson had heard rumors that Logan is considering submitting his resignation as a result of the incident.

Allen's actions have confirmed Robinson's perception that Belot's new COO is its de facto chief executive officer (CEO). Allen apparently has *carte blanche* authority from the top management of Helterbrand Associates to do whatever is necessary to improve Belot's operating results.

The controversy over the period-ending accruals has cast a tense pall over Belot's corporate accounting staff. Each member of that staff has effectively been forced to side with either Logan or Crabtree who are barely speaking to each other. Robinson feels as if he is being forced to make the same choice. Although he seldom interacts with Logan, he does sit down with him during each audit and quarterly review to discuss the major "hot spots" in Belot's financial statements.

Robinson realizes that if Logan resigns, Crabtree will likely be chosen to replace him. He is also convinced that Crabtree's decision to reduce the accruals was not motivated by his desire to replace Logan. Robinson believes that Crabtree is a man of honesty and integrity and that his actions were motivated strictly by his desire to help save Belot.

The most troubling aspect of the accrual controversy for Robinson is its impact on Belot's second-quarter operating results. Kyle Allen's Nail the Number campaign was successful. In fact, just yesterday, the day before the corporate picnic, Allen circulated an e-mail to all Belot employees thanking them for making the campaign an "unmitigated, flabbergasting success"—his exact words. Belot's operating income for the just-completed quarter is 140 percent higher than the corresponding figure for the prior year's second quarter. Granted, Allen included a brief caveat in the e-mail indicating that the second-quarter numbers are not yet "official," meaning that the auditors have not yet signed off on them.

Robinson has determined that the reductions in the five discretionary accruals at the end of the second quarter account for approximately 70 percent of the improvement in Belot's year-over-year operating results. If Travis Logan's "conservative" strategy was used in establishing those accruals, Robinson estimates that Belot would post a modest 40 percent increase in its second-quarter operating income, considerably less than the 100 percent goal targeted by Allen for the Nail the Number campaign.

[handwritten margin note: Accruals were 70% of improvement, + no real improvement]

Conservatism vs. Precision

Robinson reviewed Belot's major discretionary accruals while performing analytical procedures on the company's preliminary second-quarter financial statements. It was then that he found that each of the accruals was smaller than expected given the relevant benchmark amount. For example, the allowance for bad debts is a smaller-than-normal percentage of the period-ending balance of accounts receivable. Robinson immediately went to Crabtree's office to ask him about the unexpectedly modest discretionary accruals. In response to Robinson's inquiry, Crabtree told him of a new "precise point estimate" method that he had used to establish those accruals.

"'Precise point estimate'? What's that?" Robinson had asked.

"Just what it implies. We're using the best available information we have to arrive at a precise point estimate of each of those accruals."

"So, Grizz, you're saying that the method you used the previous 419 quarters was wrong?" Robinson had used his normal lighthearted style in posing the question to Crabtree. He was surprised when Crabtree seemed offended.

"Yeah, they were wrong. Just like the rest of the numbers we feed you high and mighty and holier-than-thou auditors constantly," Crabtree had snapped.

"Well, hey, Grizz, there's no reason to bite my head off. You know, I have a job to do."

"Detox, I know what your *job* is. Your job is to scan the second-quarter numbers during a coffee break, rack up a few hours of chargeable time, and then call your bosses and tell them that everything looks okay. Right?"

"Well, I think a quarterly review is a little more involved than that." Before Robinson could continue, Crabtree had cut him off.

"There you are. Key word 'review.' All you have to do is 'review' those numbers. You don't have to rip them apart or *audit* them. Right?"

Crabtree's impertinence had caused Robinson to adopt a more professional demeanor. Over the following 10 to 15 minutes, the two men had an evenhanded, frank discussion of the method Belot had used in the past to compute the discretionary accruals, the method that had been used to compute them at the end of the just-completed second quarter, and the reason for the change.

During their discussion, Crabtree had repeatedly defied Robinson to prove that the "precise point estimate" method he had used to determine the accruals was improper in any way or resulted in a violation of generally accepted accounting principles. Crabtree insisted that all he had done was eliminate what Travis Logan had always referred to as the "add-ons" to "fudge" those numbers a little higher than they should be. The tone of the discussion became tense when Robinson asked Crabtree about the connection between Kyle Allen's Nail the Number campaign and the more modest accrual balances.

"Allen didn't have anything to do with this. This didn't start with him. This was my idea. Everyone around here has been busting their behind over the past three months to keep this ship from sinking. I thought I should do my part too."

Near the end of his meeting with Crabtree, Robinson had mentioned matter-of-factly that he would have to discuss the accruals with Anna Bledsoe, the audit manager for the Belot engagement, and, ultimately, with R. B. Hansen, both of whom were out of town but would be returning on 5th July. Crabtree had grimaced at that point and shook his head in disgust.

"Come on, Detox. There's no reason to try to score some points for yourself by bringing this up with either of them. Why make trouble for yourself, for them, and for me? This is a nonissue. We haven't done anything wrong. The numbers are okay." When Robinson didn't reply immediately, Crabtree had continued. "Hey, if you pass on these accruals, no one will ever be the wiser. There is no way you can argue that any of them are individually 'wrong' or 'materially inaccurate' or whatever. So, just drop it and go play golf this afternoon." Ironically, the more desperate Crabtree had become in defending the accruals, the more worried Robinson had become that the accruals were a problem.

Crabtree was unaware that his comment regarding "scoring points" had struck close to home for Robinson. Over the past four years, Robinson seldom gave much thought to any career planning initiatives. Instead, he simply plodded along, completing each assignment given to him. Robinson reserved most of his energy and enthusiasm for his principal "outside" interest, namely, sports. When he wasn't rooting for the Golden Gophers or the Vikings, he was playing golf or tennis or managing one of his many fantasy sports teams.

Two recent incidents, however, have made Robinson dwell at length for the first time on his future in the accounting profession. First, he realized that as his four-year anniversary with his employer approached, he was one of the few members of his "start class" still with the firm. Nearly all of his former colleagues have moved on to other jobs, most of them higher-paying positions with clients. The second and more important event that caused him to think of his future was a lunch meeting a few weeks ago with R. B. Hansen.

During that lunch, Hansen encouraged Robinson to become more focused on his career and to devote himself more fully to his job. According to Hansen, Robinson's strong interpersonal skills are just what the firm is looking for in partner candidates. Hansen told Robinson he could use those skills to recruit new clients to the firm, a talent that is highly valued by existing partners, many of whom are not "natural communicators" or "marketing types."

Hansen's pep talk caused Robinson to seriously consider for the first time that he may be partner "material." Robinson has always possessed a remarkable degree of self-confidence. When he commits himself to accomplishing a goal, he always rises to the occasion. In his mind, there is no reason why he cannot become a partner with his firm if he adopts that objective as a personal and career goal.

Prior to his meeting with Hansen, Robinson would very likely have just "gone along" with Zachariah Crabtree's suggestion that he "pass" on the 30th June discretionary accruals. But now that he realizes he is potential partner material, his outlook on his job has changed suddenly and dramatically.

Robinson doesn't want to do anything that would cause R. B. Hansen to perceive that he is "coasting" along as usual. In fact, standing up to Grizz, who Hansen knows he is very close to, would provide Robinson an opportunity to demonstrate to the partner that he has adopted a more professional mindset to his job and responsibilities.

Grizzly Sighting

Prior to the Belot company picnic, Robinson spent much of the two previous days stewing over his dilemma. He eventually settled on a compromise plan that would possibly appease Crabtree while at the same time allowing him to impress R. B. Hansen. His compromise, which he intends to discuss with Hansen before relaying it to Crabtree, involves requiring Belot to increase the 30th June balances of the allowances for bad debts and inventory obsolescence to more normal levels, while allowing the company to use the "precise point estimates" for the other three discretionary accruals. Robinson realizes that Hansen is most concerned with the bad debts and inventory obsolescence accruals since they have a "higher profile" in Belot's financial statements than the other accruals.

Robinson's compromise plan would reduce the year-over-year increase in Belot's operating income for the just-completed quarter from 140 percent to approximately 103 percent—slightly above the target figure that Allen established for the Nail the Number campaign. Although Robinson believes his compromise is reasonable, he is worried that Crabtree will react negatively to it.

Because he wants to avoid discussing the accruals issue with Crabtree at the picnic, Robinson has been scanning the clusters of people in front of him trying to spy Grizz's hulking figure as he works his way across the large park. Suddenly, Robinson feels a large hand clamp down on his shoulder from behind. As he turns around, he finds himself standing face to face with Zachariah Crabtree. Plastered across Grizz's chest are three creased and crinkled Nail the Number stickers.

Questions

1. Is David Robinson's suggested compromise appropriate? Why or why not?

2. Do you believe that Zachariah Crabtree is a person of integrity? What about David Robinson? Defend both of your answers. Does Robinson have an inappropriate relationship with Crabtree? Explain.

3. Identify the primary audit objectives for a client's year-end discretionary expense accruals. Is it permissible for companies to overstate period-ending expense accruals to make their financial statements more "conservative"?

4. Discuss the scope and nature of an auditor's responsibilities during a review of a client's quarterly financial statements.

Powder River Petroleum International, Inc.

In 1999, a group of private investors founded Celebrity Sports Network, Inc., a company that retained professional athletes and former professional athletes to sponsor "fringe" sporting events such as professional wrestling, competitive dancing, and roller derby. When that business plan proved less than successful, the company was reorganized in 2001. The business model of the new company, Powder River Basin Corporation, ultimately evolved into purchasing and developing oil and gas properties. In 2007, the company was renamed Powder River Petroleum International, Inc.

Brian Fox, a Canadian citizen, became the principal stockholder of Powder River in 2003 when he acquired 40 percent of its outstanding common stock. Fox assumed the titles of chief executive officer (CEO) and chief financial officer (CFO) for the small company that had only eight full-time employees, two of whom were his daughters. Although initially incorporated in Colorado and later reincorporated in Oklahoma, Powder River's de facto headquarters were in Calgary, Alberta, the home of the Fox family.

In 2002, prior to Fox's arrival, Powder River reported total revenues of only $15,000 and a net loss of $1.3 million. Because Fox had considerable experience in Canada's oil and gas industry, the company's other stockholders hoped that he could transform it into a profitable operation. But Fox also came with a certain amount of undesirable "baggage." In 2000, the Alberta Securities Commission, a Canadian regulatory agency, had barred him from serving as a corporate officer or director for 18 months. The agency alleged that Fox had sold unregistered securities of a company for which he served as a senior executive.

Marketing Miracle

Brian Fox quickly "turned around" Powder River. In 2006, the company reported a net income of $5.7 million on revenues of $13.2 million. The company's balance sheet for that year reported nearly $25 million of assets, the bulk of which consisted of investments in oil and gas properties. Thanks to the company's profitable operations in 2006, Fox's compensation for the following year approached $1.5 million.

Powder River's rapid turnaround was due to a new business strategy that Fox implemented for the company. In 2004, Fox began marketing minority "working interests"[1] in oil and gas properties owned by Powder River to foreign investors through a business associate that he had worked with in the past. Fox arranged for the company to purchase oil and gas properties in several southern states, including Louisiana, Oklahoma, and Texas, and then, with the help of his business associate, sold working interests in those properties to Asian investors, principally well-heeled citizens

---

1. The online dictionary, *Investopedia*, defines a working interest as follows: "a form of investment in oil and gas drilling operations in which the investor is directly liable for a portion of the ongoing costs associated with exploration, drilling and production. In a similar fashion, working interest owners also fully participate in the profits of any successful wells. This stands in contrast to royalty interests, in which an investor's cost is usually limited to their initial investment, also resulting in a lower potential for large profits."

of Singapore. The company reported that it intended to use the proceeds from the sale of the working interests to develop its oil and gas properties and to purchase additional properties.

A key factor in the initial success of this strategy was the huge difference between the amounts paid for the oil and gas properties by Powder River and the prices at which the company sold working interests in those properties to the Asian investors. For example, Powder River's 2006 federal tax return reported $17.7 million of taxable revenue from the sale of working interests in oil and gas properties that it had purchased over the previous 12 months. The cost basis of those working interests for Powder River was less than $150,000.

During the time frame that the company was selling the working interests, Brian Fox repeatedly maintained that the company's "primary focus" was "oil and gas exploration and development," while its "secondary focus" was the marketing of minority working interests in those properties.[2] In fact, the $13.2 million of revenue reported in the company's 2006 income statement consisted of $12.6 million of revenue from "Property and Working Interest Sales" and only $554,000 of revenue from "Oil and Gas Sales."[3] Following is the description of Powder River's revenue recognition policy for the sales of working interests that was included in the company's 2006 financial statement footnotes.

As the Company finds and purchases new properties, it makes arrangements to sell partial working interests to various individuals referred to by [sic] the Singapore Group. The revenues are recorded as operating revenues, net of any commission or other costs associated with earning the revenues. The related percentage of capitalized cost of the property sold is also removed from the oil and gas property account and offset against the proceeds to calculate the net revenue recorded in the operating revenues.

Powder River's common stock traded over the counter on what was known at the time as the "Pink Sheets" network, a nationwide network of stock brokers that shared bid and ask prices for small publicly owned companies. Because Powder River's securities were registered with the SEC, the company filed audited financial statements annually with that federal agency.

Bountiful Audit Firm

Throughout its history, Powder River was audited by Chisholm, Bierwolf & Nilson[4] (CBN), an accounting firm based in Bountiful, Utah, a suburb of Salt Lake City. In 2003, CBN registered with the Public Company Accounting Oversight Board (PCAOB) to enable it to audit financial statements of publicly owned companies. From 2003 through 2007, CBN had two audit partners, Todd Chisholm and Troy Nilson, and five to nine other auditors on its professional audit staff. Chisholm also served as CBN's managing partner.

CBN's audit clientele included dozens of small public companies whose securities were traded on over-the-counter networks such as the Pink Sheets network. In 2006 and 2007, CBN issued 52 and 49 audit reports, respectively. Chisholm and Nilson swapped roles on CBN's audit engagements. For those clients that Chisholm served as the audit engagement partner, Nilson was the concurring partner, and vice versa.

---

2. *Securities and Exchange Commission v. Brian D. Fox*, U.S. District Court, Northern District of Oklahoma, Civil Action No. 11-CV-211-CVE-PJC, 8 April 2011.

3. Not surprisingly, the total revenues reported in Powder River's GAAP-based income statement differed from the total revenues reported in its federal tax return.

4. The accounting firm's name changed over time but it was known by this name in both 2006 and 2007.

Chisholm served as Powder River's audit engagement partner through 2006, while Nilson assumed that role beginning in 2007.

Powder River paid CBN $39,712 for the 2006 audit and $38,251 for the 2007 audit, according to the company's 2007 Form 10-K filed with the SEC. The accounting firm also prepared Powder River's 2006 and 2007 tax returns, charging the company less than $2,000 for that service each year. In neither year did Powder River pay CBN any "audit related" fees for professional services.

SEC Investigation

A footnote to Powder River's 2007 financial statements reported a previously undisclosed stipulation of the contracts with the Asian investors who had purchased working interests in oil and gas properties owned by the company.

> Powder River's contracts with Asian investors provided that they would receive guaranteed payments yielding an annual minimum of 9%, and in some cases more, beginning approximately six months after the date of investment until investors reached the "break-even" point, i.e., when their principal had been repaid (the "guaranteed payments"). Thereafter, investors received lease production payments based on their respective [percentage] working interests.[5]

The disclosure of this feature of the working interest contracts prompted a comprehensive investigation of Powder River's accounting records and prior financial statements by the SEC.

In April 2011, the SEC filed a civil complaint against Brian Fox in a federal district court in Oklahoma. The central feature of the complaint was that from 2004 through early 2008, Fox had fraudulently misrepresented the nature of Powder River's operating results in its periodic filings with the SEC. The SEC charged that the company's alleged sales of working interests to Asian investors were, in substance, loans to Powder River since the company "guaranteed" to pay back those investments over a period of approximately 11 years.

Beginning in early 2007, Powder River had been forced to use the proceeds from new "sales" of working interests to "fulfill its ongoing guaranteed minimum payment obligations to prior investors," which created a "Ponzi-style" fraud.[6] "Although Fox was aware of the Ponzi-style payments, he nonetheless caused the company to continue to represent in Commission filings that Asian investor proceeds would be used to purchase and develop oil and gas properties."[7]

The SEC's investigation of Powder River uncovered a laundry list of other alleged accounting and financial reporting abuses by the company. From 2005 through 2007, the company included as assets in its balance sheets oil and gas properties that it did not own. While negotiating to purchase a $5 million leasehold in New Mexico during 2005, Powder River made a nonrefundable $500,000 down payment on that property. In August 2005, the negotiations ended and Powder River forfeited the down payment. Despite not completing the purchase, the company included the $5 million leasehold in "Oil and Gas Properties" reported on its 2005 through 2007 balance sheets. Similarly, in 2006, Powder River made a $1.5 million nonrefundable down payment on a $6.5 million oil and gas lease in Texas. Because the transaction

5. Securities and Exchange Commission, *Accounting and Auditing Enforcement Release No. 3266*, 8 April 2011.

6. *Securities and Exchange Commission v. Brian D. Fox*, U.S. District Court, Northern District of Oklahoma.

7. *Ibid.*

was never consummated, Powder River forfeited the down payment. Nevertheless, in 2006 and 2007, the $6.5 million leasehold was included in the company's reported oil and gas properties.

In 2006 and 2007, oil and gas properties accounted for 67 percent and 82 percent, respectively, of Powder River's total assets on its annual balance sheets. In a footnote appended to the company's 2006 and 2007 financial statements, Powder River reported that the "proved reserves" related to those properties could have a value as high as $382 million.[8] The SEC subsequently determined that the company's reserve estimates were unreliable and did not meet its definition of "proved reserves."

> *Fox obtained reserve reports for Powder River and oversaw its reserve-reporting process. At least some of the company's reserve reports were prepared by a Texas engineer, an individual Fox knew, or was severely reckless in not knowing, was a convicted felon and securities fraud recidivist. Powder River, however, represented in its annual and quarterly reports from 2004 to 2007 that the company's proved reserves were based on evaluations prepared by a certain Oklahoma petroleum engineer. In fact, the Oklahoma engineer performed no services for Powder River after 2005, and his earlier reports were not intended for use in SEC filings.... By 2007, Powder River had still not obtained bona fide historical or updated reserve reports, despite the fact that oil and gas properties represented approximately 82% of its total reported assets.[9]*

These items and other misstatements in Powder River's annual and quarterly financial statements caused those financial statements to grossly misrepresent the company's financial condition and operating results. For 2006, the SEC ruled that Powder River's assets, revenues, and net income were overstated by 40 percent, 638 percent, and 324 percent, respectively. The corresponding overstatements for 2007 were 45 percent, 301 percent, and 114 percent. Despite these huge misstatements, Powder River received unqualified opinions for both 2006 and 2007 from its independent audit firm, CBN. Exhibit 1 presents the 2006 audit opinion.

EXHIBIT 1

AUDIT OPINION ON POWDER RIVER'S 2006 FINANCIAL STATEMENTS

REPORT OF INDEPENDENT REGISTERED PUBLIC ACCOUNTING FIRM

To the Board of Directors and Shareholders of
Powder River Basin Corp.

We have audited the accompanying balance sheet of Powder River Basin Corp. as of December 31, 2006, and the related statement of operations, stockholders' equity, and cash flows for the year then ended. These financial statements are the responsibility of the Company's management. Our responsibility is to express an opinion on these financial statements based on our audit.

We conducted our audit in accordance with the standards of the PCAOB (United States). Those standards require that we plan and perform the audit to obtain reasonable assurance about whether the financial statements are free of material misstatement. The Company is not required to have, nor were we engaged to perform, an audit of its internal control over financial reporting. Our audit included consideration of internal control over financial

---

8. *Ibid.*
9. *Ibid.*

reporting as a basis for designing audit procedures that are appropriate in the circumstances, but not for the purpose of expressing an opinion on the effectiveness of the Company's internal control over financial reporting. Accordingly, we express no such opinion. An audit includes examining, on a test basis, evidence supporting the amounts and disclosures in the financial statements. An audit also includes assessing the accounting principles used and significant estimates made by management, as well as evaluating the overall financial statement presentation. We believe that our audit provides a reasonable basis for our opinion.

In our opinion, the financial statements referred to above present fairly, in all material respects, the financial position of Powder River Basin Gas Corp. at December 31, 2006, and the results of its operations and cash flows for the year then ended in conformity with U.S. generally accepted accounting principles.

/s/Chisholm, Bierwolf & Nilson
Chisholm, Bierwolf & Nilson, LLC
Bountiful, UT
March 7, 2007

Source: Powder River's 2006 Form 10-K.

Calling Out the Auditors

During CBN's 2006 audit of Powder River, Todd Chisholm, the audit engagement partner, learned for the first time of the 9 percent repayment clause in Powder River's working interest contracts with the Asian investors. In a subsequent *Accounting and Auditing Enforcement Release*, the SEC reported that Chisholm "failed to inquire further about them [guaranteed payments] or consider how those payments might affect Powder River's revenue recognition or whether the company should disclose its payment obligation in its 2006 financial statements."[10] Instead, Chisholm simply relied on Brian Fox's characterization of the amounts paid to Powder River by the Asian investors as "sales."

During both the 2005 and 2006 Powder River audits, the CBN audit team failed to discover that Powder River had included in its reported assets oil and gas properties that it did not own. The SEC held Chisholm responsible for this oversight because he "failed to review the oil-and-gas lease purchase documents" for those alleged assets.[11] The SEC also criticized Chisholm's review of the oil and gas reserve reports that Powder River supplied him to corroborate the impressive proved reserves reported in the company's financial statement footnotes.

> In auditing Powder River's 2005 and 2006 financial statements, Respondent [CBN] and Chisholm obtained and relied upon brief excerpts from oil-and-gas reserve reports. He did little, if anything, to: a) evaluate the qualifications of the petroleum engineer who prepared the oil-and-gas reserve reports; b) understand the nature of the work performed in preparing the oil-and-gas reserve reports; and c) evaluate the petroleum engineer's relationship to Powder River.[12]

10. Securities and Exchange Commission, *Accounting and Auditing Enforcement Release No. 3266.*

11. Securities and Exchange Commission, *Accounting and Auditing Enforcement Release No. 3267*, 8 April 2011.

12. *Ibid.*

According to the SEC, Chisholm should have been alerted to the possibility that Powder River's reserve estimates were suspect because in 2005 the federal agency had questioned the qualifications of the engineer who had prepared the 2004 estimate and the method used to arrive at that estimate. In fact, during the 2005 audit of Powder River, Chisholm had participated in a conference call with the SEC in which a company representative had responded to those concerns.

Todd Nilson assumed the role of audit engagement partner for Powder River in 2007. During early 2007, Powder River had begun charging (debiting) the guaranteed payments made to the Asian investors to an asset account, "Prepaid Production Payments."[13] After reviewing the working interest contracts, Nilson determined that this accounting treatment was improper. As a result of that decision, Powder River issued restated financial statements for the first three quarters of 2007 that eliminated that accounting treatment for the guaranteed payments. In addition, apparently because of concern expressed by Nilson, Powder River disclosed for the first time in the footnotes to its 2007 financial statements that the guaranteed payments were being made to the Asian investors.[14]

Despite investigating the working interest contracts and questioning the accounting treatment applied to the guaranteed payments, Nilson failed to consider whether the cash received from the Asian investors "should have been reported as borrowings rather than sales"[15] in Powder River's 2007 financial statements. "As a result, the company continued to improperly report the proceeds from its working interest conveyances as revenues."[16] The SEC also criticized Nilson for failing to include a "going concern" paragraph in the unqualified audit opinion issued on Powder River's 2007 financial statements. Because the guaranteed payments due to the Asian investors in 2008 would almost certainly exceed the company's oil and gas revenues by a wide margin, the SEC maintained that there was "substantial doubt" that Powder River would remain a going concern.

Similar to Todd Chisholm during the 2005 and 2006 Powder River audits, Nilson, during the 2007 audit, failed to discover that the company was including in its reported assets large oil and gas properties that it did not own. The SEC reported that CBN did not perform any audit procedures to verify the existence and ownership of the $5 million New Mexico and $6.5 million Texas leaseholds during the 2007 audit "despite the size of the assets and the fact that the company had not paid any significant development costs or taxes on the properties in 2007."[17]

The SEC also reported that, similar to Chisholm, Nilson failed to properly investigate Powder River's reserve reports that the company used to corroborate its proved reserves disclosures in its 2007 financial statements. In fact, during

---

13. Prior to 2007, the company had recorded these payments as a contra revenue item to "Oil and Gas Sales." For income statement purposes, Powder River reported only net "Oil and Gas Sales," that is, the guaranteed payments were not reported separately.

14. The company characterized the obligation to make these guaranteed payments as a "future commitment," a characterization disputed by the SEC which maintained that the guaranteed payments should have been reported as a "current and ongoing—not future—commitment." After the restatement, Powder River returned to netting the guaranteed payments to the Asian investors against its revenues. However, rather than netting them directly against oil and gas revenues, the company reported a separate contra revenue line item for these payments in the subsequent comparative income statements for 2006 and 2007 included in its 2007 Form 10-K. That line item was entitled "Production Payment to Working Interest Owners."

15. Securities and Exchange Commission, *Accounting and Auditing Enforcement Release No. 3267.*

16. *Ibid.*

17. *Ibid.*

2007, the company failed to update those reports and instead simply relied on the inadequate prior year reserve reports for financial statement disclosure purposes.

The SEC's investigation of the Powder River fraud and the deficient audits of the company prompted a parallel investigation of CBN by the PCAOB. In addition to investigating CBN's Powder River audits, the PCAOB reviewed audits performed by the firm during the same time frame for three other companies.

In reviewing CBN's Powder River audits, the PCAOB reiterated and, in some instances, expanded on the SEC's criticisms of those engagements. The PCAOB also addressed firm-wide deficiencies in CBN's audit practice.

> *The large number of [CBN audit] clients severely limited the amount of time and attention that Chisholm and Nilson, the Firm's only audit partners, could spend providing supervision to audit assistants. As a result, planning for many audits consisted of little more than referring audit assistants to standardized audit programs and checklists, which failed to take into account, among other things, specific audit risks for each engagement.*

> *The Firm's typical practice with respect to staffing audit engagements entailed one audit assistant teaming up with either Chisholm or Nilson.... The large number of issuer audit engagements prevented Chisholm or Nilson from providing appropriate supervision of audit procedures. Audit assistants with limited experience were often left to decide for themselves what audit procedures should be performed in an audit. Further, Chisholm and Nilson failed to properly evaluate whether the audit reports issued by the Firm were supported by sufficient competent evidential matter.*[18]

The PCAOB also reprimanded Chisholm for failing to establish a proper "tone at the top" of his firm. "Chisholm was the managing partner of the Firm during the relevant time period and was principally responsible for setting the tone at the top. As the managing partner, Chisholm was responsible for designing, implementing and monitoring the Firm's system of quality control. Accordingly, Chisholm had overall responsibility for ensuring that the Firm complied with PCAOB rules and standards."[19]

Some of PCAOB's harshest criticism of Chisholm and Nilson was reserved for their decision to make undocumented changes in the audit workpapers for engagements that were subject to inspection by the agency, including the workpaper files for the 2006 Powder River audit. During the summer of 2007, the PCAOB notified CBN that it would be inspecting the firm's audit practice. "In preparation for the Board's inspection, Chisholm and Nilson, and at their instruction, Firm assistants, created and added audit documentation to the audit files [to be inspected]."[20] The alterations included several instances in which information was added to the given workpaper files "to create the appearance that Firm auditors had performed certain audit procedures that had not, in fact, been performed during the audits."[21] According to the PCAOB, "hundreds of hours" were spent revising the given workpaper files.

---

18. Public Company Accounting Oversight Board, *PCAOB Release No. 105-2011-003*, 8 April 2011.

19. *Ibid.*

20. *Ibid.*

21. *Ibid.*

EPILOGUE

Powder River filed for Chapter 11 bankruptcy reorganization in a federal district court in December 2008. Court records in the case revealed that the company had sold working interests in its oil and gas properties to more than 2,000 individual investors; collectively, the investors had paid more than $43 million for those working interests. An independent appraisal of Powder River's oil and gas properties obtained by the company's court-appointed bankruptcy receiver in late 2008 assigned them a value of approximately $1.2 million. Just a few months earlier, the company's 2007 balance sheet had reported a value of $23 million for those properties. In November 2010, Powder River's Chapter 11 bankruptcy petition was converted to a Chapter 7 bankruptcy filing, meaning that the company's assets would be involuntarily liquidated and the proceeds distributed to the company's creditors.

In April 2011, the SEC filed a civil complaint against Brian Fox. Among other charges, the complaint alleged that Fox had used various accounting and financial reporting schemes to defraud purchasers and sellers of Powder River's common stock. Fox responded to the SEC charges filed against him in an interview with a representative of an online investment news service. In that interview, Fox insisted that the transactions involving Powder River and its Asian investors had been bona fide sales transactions and not loans. He also claimed that Powder River had been a "viable operating entity"[22] when a federal judge appointed a bankruptcy receiver to take over the company's operations in 2008. According to Fox, the bankruptcy receiver had destroyed the company by curtailing its business operations. Fox also criticized his former business associate who had been involved in arranging the working interest transactions. He claimed that individual improperly withheld some of the proceeds from those transactions from Powder River.

In November 2012, a federal judge issued an order banning Fox from serving as an officer or director of an SEC registrant. Three months later, the SEC issued an enforcement order in which it ruled that Fox "had misled the investing public by fraudulently inflating the revenues and assets of Power River Petroleum International, Inc … and by making other false and misleading public disclosures."[23] The order suspended Fox's right to "appear or practice" before the SEC.

Todd Chisholm and Troy Nilson were suspended from practicing before the SEC for five years beginning in April 2011. The federal agency also indefinitely suspended CBN. At the same time, the PCAOB permanently revoked CBN's registration, meaning that the firm was prohibited from providing audit services to public companies. The PCAOB also permanently banned Chisholm from being associated with a PCAOB-registered accounting firm. Nilson was barred from being associated with such a firm for five years.

Questions

1.   Identify the primary audit risk factors that were evident within Powder River's operations. Briefly explain the significance of each.

2.   How should Powder River have recorded the sales of the working interests and the guaranteed payments made to the purchasers of those working interests in its accounting records?

---

22.   M. Caswell, "SEC Target Fox Denies Inflating Revenue," *Stockwatch.com* (online), 7 July 2011.

23.   Securities and Exchange Commission, *Accounting and Auditing Enforcement Release No. 3469*, 28 June 2013.

3. U.S. auditing standards identify the principal "management assertions" that underlie a set of financial statements. What management assertions were particularly relevant to (a) the "sales" of working interests and (b) the guaranteed payments made annually by Powder River to the purchasers of those working interests?

4. The SEC and PCAOB criticized CBN for failing to discover that Powder River did not own certain assets included in its reported oil and gas properties. How would you characterize that oversight? That is, did this oversight constitute negligence, recklessness, or fraud on the part of those auditors or none of these? Defend your answer.

5. Powder River relied on the expertise of a "specialist" in arriving at the estimates of its proved reserves. What responsibilities, if any, do U.S. auditing standards impose on auditors when a client has used the services of a "specialist" for accounting or financial reporting purposes?

6. The PCAOB criticized Todd Chisholm for failing to establish a proper "quality control" system for CBN. What are the primary issues that should be addressed by the quality control system of an audit firm that has public company clients? Provide examples of circumstances in which Chisholm and/or CBN violated the PCAOB's quality control standards for audit firms.

LocatePlus Holdings Corporation

In August 2004, an Internet-based investment advisory service included the common stock of LocatePlus Holdings Corporation in its "Stocks to Watch"[1] alert. The advisory service touted the New Age business model of LocatePlus, a company whose headquarters were in a Boston suburb. That business model included providing government agencies, business entities, and individuals access to a massive online database that LocatePlus had collected and organized, a database that included information profiles on 98 percent of all U.S. citizens. Customers of LocatePlus purchased access to the company's database for a wide array of investigative uses, including antiterrorism initiatives by law enforcement agencies, criminal background checks by prospective employers, and identity theft investigations by private individuals.

Ironically, LocatePlus, a company that developed an important tool to combat fraud and other criminal activities in the Internet Age, found itself the focus of a fraud investigation in late 2010. That investigation, which involved the Federal Bureau of Investigation (FBI), the Internal Revenue Service (IRS), and the Securities and Exchange Commission (SEC), resulted in the downfall of the company, criminal prosecutions of its top executives, and harsh regulatory sanctions for the company's independent audit firm.

Channeling Fraud

LocatePlus had two principal revenue streams. Slightly more than one-half of the company's annual revenue was generated by selling direct, one-time access to its large database. The company's other major revenue source involved so-called "channel partner" arrangements. A channel partner paid LocatePlus a fixed monthly royalty in exchange for unlimited access to its database. Channel partners were typically large government agencies or corporations.

To enhance their company's disappointing operating results, two LocatePlus executives created a bogus channel partner in 2005. Those two executives were James Fields, the company's chief financial officer (CFO), and Jon Latorella, the company's chief executive officer (CEO). The fictitious company, Omni Data Services, allegedly paid several hundred thousand dollars in monthly royalties to LocatePlus. These royalties accounted for $3.6 million of LocatePlus's 2005 revenues of $11.6 million and $2.7 million of the company's 2006 revenues of $12.2 million. Despite these bogus revenues, LocatePlus continued to post large losses each year. In 2004, the company had reported a net loss of $7.5 million. In 2005 and 2006, the company reported net losses of $5.6 million and $5.9 million, respectively.

LocatePlus used a series of sham transactions, including fraudulent cash transfers, to make it appear that the Omni Data revenues were genuine. The principal purpose of these sham transactions and the corresponding fraudulent journal entries was to

---

1. Wall Street Capital Funding LLC, "Wall Street Alert's U.S. Hot Stock Highlights," *GlobeNewswire* (online), 24 August 2004.

deceive LocatePlus's independent auditors. Because LocatePlus was a public company, it had to file audited financial statements annually with the SEC.

Predecessor–Successor Auditor Communications

In early 2005, LocatePlus contacted Livingston & Haynes (L & H), a Massachusetts-based accounting firm. LocatePlus needed a new independent auditor because its previous one had abruptly resigned. The Form 8-K that LocatePlus filed with the SEC to disclose that resignation included the resignation letter. In that letter, the former audit firm noted that it had "concerns about the timeliness of information we received and about the reliability of certain representations of your company's management."[2]

Before making a decision to accept or reject LocatePlus as an audit client, two L & H audit partners met with the individual who had served as the company's previous audit engagement partner. These two L & H partners were William Wood and Kevin Howley. Wood was the senior technical partner on L & H's audit staff.

In his meeting with Wood and Howley, LocatePlus's former audit engagement partner identified several factors that had contributed to his firm's decision to resign as the company's independent auditor: "difficulty getting information from management, management providing contradictory information, management providing unsigned contracts as audit evidence, and difficulty getting management to accept its proposed audit adjustments." The former audit engagement partner also provided Wood and Howley access to his firm's audit workpapers for LocatePlus. Included in these workpapers was a letter that the former audit firm had received from an individual who had previously served as a member of LocatePlus's management team. This letter alleged that a LocatePlus business partner with whom it had engaged in a multimillion-dollar transaction was "not a legitimate entity." Despite the information obtained from LocatePlus's former audit engagement partner, L & H accepted LocatePlus as an audit client.

After accepting LocatePlus as an audit client, L & H designated the company a "high-risk audit client." The planning workpapers for the engagement required the audit team to "use extensive care" in auditing the company. Howley was appointed to serve as the audit engagement partner, while Wood served as the concurring partner on the engagement.

Red Flags Discovered During 2005

During their 2005 reviews of LocatePlus's quarterly financial statements, L & H auditors "became aware of multiple red flags concerning the revenue recognized from Omni Data and the resulting receivable on LocatePlus's balance sheet." In June 2005, Howley noted in an e-mail that he sent to James Fields that Omni Data was not included on a government website that supposedly listed all corporations domiciled in its home state. More troubling was the fact that the L & H auditors could not find a website for that company "despite the fact that Omni Data was purportedly a business doing data sales over the Internet." Fields subsequently told Howley that Omni Data did not have a website because the company was "trying to keep a low profile."

In August 2005, a former member of LocatePlus's board of directors contacted Howley and made disturbing allegations regarding the reliability of the company's accounting records. Over the next several months, this individual contacted Howley on "numerous occasions" and made similar statements to him. The individual's most

---

2. Securities and Exchange Commission, *Accounting and Auditing Enforcement Release No. 3288*, 6 June 2011. The remaining quotations in this case were taken from this source.

serious allegation was that Omni Data did not exist. Among other evidence to support this claim, he pointed out that the alleged President of Omni Data knew "nothing" about the company and that she was a ballet teacher who had previously been Latorella's girlfriend. Howley informed Wood of each of the successive communications he received from the former board member.

Wood discussed the allegations of LocatePlus's former board member with L & H's president and forwarded them to the chairman of the company's audit committee. Wood recommended that the audit committee chairman arrange a meeting of the audit committee with the former board member and Howley to address the allegations. Such a meeting never took place.

During the fraud "brainstorming session" for the 2005 LocatePlus audit, the L & H audit team identified "overstated and/or fictitious revenues/accounts receivable" related to Omni Data as a fraud risk factor. For the revenues LocatePlus received from its channel partners other than Omni Data, the L & H auditors compared the "amounts billed and recognized as revenue to LocatePlus's data usage logs to ensure that the customer had agreed to purchase the product and had actually used it." This critical audit test was not applied to the Omni Data revenues despite those revenues accounting for nearly one-third of LocatePlus's 2005 revenues. If the auditors had applied this test to the Omni Data revenues, they would have discovered that Omni Data never accessed the company's online database in 2005.

In auditing the Omni Data revenues, L & H "relied on the executed agreement between LocatePlus and Omni Data and a confirmation received from Omni Data regarding the monies earned and owed." In fact, both the executed agreement (contract) between the two parties as well as the confirmation received from Omni Data were fraudulent.

As of 31 December 2005, LocatePlus's accounting records included a $3.3 million receivable from Omni Data that accounted for 75 percent of the company's net receivables and represented nearly 40 percent of its total assets. The confirmation for this large receivable was sent to the alleged president of Omni Data. That initial confirmation was returned as "undeliverable" by the U.S. Postal Service. After being provided with a new address for Omni Data's president, L & H mailed a second confirmation that was signed and returned without any exceptions being noted.

The L & H auditors documented the allegations made by the former board member of LocatePlus in their 2005 workpapers but failed to rigorously investigate those allegations. For example, the SEC discovered that the "Fraud Risk Assessment Form" included in the 2005 LocatePlus workpapers was left blank by the L & H auditors. In fact, according to the SEC, the auditors failed to reach "any conclusion about the merits" of the former board member's disturbing allegations.

Lingering concern about the validity of the Omni Data revenues and receivable prompted the L & H auditors to include specific statements regarding those items in the 2005 letter of representations that was signed by Fields and Latorella. In the letter of representations, Fields and Latorella maintained that they had "no knowledge of any fraud or suspected fraud" and that they were unaware of any "allegations of fraud or suspected fraud" related to the Omni Data transactions.

2006 Audit

By 31 December 2006, the receivable from Omni Data totaled $5.1 million. In late 2006, LocatePlus had supposedly amended Omni Data's payment terms. These amended terms resulted in most of the large receivable being reclassified from current assets to long-term assets on LocatePlus's 31 December 2006, balance sheet. The company also reduced the gross amount of the long-term portion of the receivable to its net present value and recorded an allowance of nearly $600,000 against the receivable. After these adjustments, the net reported value of the Omni Data receivable was approximately $3 million, an amount that represented slightly more than one-half of LocatePlus's total assets as of 31 December 2006.

The principal evidence collected by L & H to support the Omni Data receivable during the 2006 audit was once again a confirmation. As in the prior year, the initial mailing of the confirmation resulted in it being returned as "undeliverable." After informing LocatePlus that the original confirmation had not been delivered, Howley was told that Omni Data was operating under a new name and had a new president. L & H mailed the confirmation a second time with the corrected address information, which resulted in the confirmation being returned signed without any reported exceptions.

While investigating the 2006 LocatePlus audit, the SEC obtained a document from Howley that was entitled "LocatePlus Memorandum—Gallagher Allegations." This memo summarized the fraud allegations made by the former LocatePlus board member. In the memo, Howley reported that he had discussed the allegations with the chairman of LocatePlus's audit committee who had "indicated that he did not believe there was any basis" for them. The memo also noted that Howley had discussed the allegations with LocatePlus's outside legal counsel who also "found no basis for them." The outside legal counsel suggested that the former board member had made the allegations out of vengeance because he and Latorella were no longer on good terms. Although the memo included evidence pertinent to the Omni Data receivable, it was not included in the LocatePlus workpapers, nor was it dated.

The 2006 workpapers did include a document that referenced an investigation carried out in September 2006 by the Massachusetts Securities Division, an investigation that involved LocatePlus. The state agency's report on that investigation indicated that "even the most cursory review of LocatePlus's business would reveal that many aspects of its business were either highly exaggerated or fictitious." This report was readily available on the state agency's website, however, Howley apparently never accessed the report.

In the 2006 letter of representations, Fields and Latorella once again indicated that they were unaware of any suspected fraud or fraudulent allegations involving Omni Data. Near the conclusion of the 2006 audit, William Wood approved Kevin Howley's decision to issue an unqualified opinion on LocatePlus's 2006 financial statements. Wood, who had been involved in the planning for both the 2005 and 2006 audits, had also approved the unqualified opinion issued on the company's 2005 financial statements.

Both the 2005 and 2006 audit opinions on LocatePlus's financial statements included a fourth explanatory paragraph. In that paragraph, L & H reported that there was substantial doubt that LocatePlus would remain a going concern. Exhibit 1 includes the 2006 audit opinion.

"Highly Unreasonable Conduct"

In June 2011, the SEC issued an *Accounting and Auditing Enforcement Release* summarizing its investigation of L & H's 2005 and 2006 audits of LocatePlus. The SEC accused Howley and Wood of engaging in "highly unreasonable conduct."

> In light of the specific allegations that the [Omni Data revenue and receivable] … were fictitious…. The failure of L & H and Howley to properly plan the audits, adequately test the Omni Data revenue, obtain sufficient competent evidence to serve as a basis for L & H's audit reports, exercise due professional care, apply skepticism,

EXHIBIT 1

AUDIT OPINION
ISSUED BY L & H ON
LOCATEPLUS'S
2006 FINANCIAL
STATEMENTS

INDEPENDENT AUDITORS' REPORT

To the Stockholders and Board of Directors of
LocatePlus Holdings Corporation
Beverly, Massachusetts

We have audited the accompanying consolidated balance sheet of LocatePlus Holdings
Corporation as of December 31, 2006, and the related consolidated statements of operations,
stockholders' equity (deficit) and cash flows for the year ended December 31, 2006, and
December 31, 2005. These financial statements are the responsibility of the Company's
management. Our responsibility is to express an opinion on these financial statements based
on our audit.

We conducted our audit in accordance with the standards of the Public Company Accounting
Oversight Board (United States). Those standards require that we plan and perform the audit
to obtain reasonable assurance about whether the financial statements are free of material
misstatement. An audit includes examining, on a test basis, evidence supporting the amounts
and disclosures in the financial statements. An audit also includes assessing the accounting
principles used and significant estimates made by management, as well as evaluating the
overall financial statement presentation. We believe that our audit provides a reasonable
basis for our opinion.

In our opinion, the financial statements referred to above present fairly, in all material
respects, the consolidated financial position of LocatePlus Holdings Corporation and its
subsidiaries as of December 31, 2006, and the results of its consolidated operations and its
consolidated cash flows for the years ended December 31, 2006, and December 31, 2005, in
conformity with accounting principles generally accepted in the United States of America.

The accompanying financial statements have been prepared assuming that the Company will
continue as a going concern. As disclosed in the financial statements, the Company has an
accumulated deficit at December 31, 2006, and has suffered substantial net losses in each of
the last two years, which raise substantial doubt about the Company's ability to continue as
a going concern. Management's plans in regard to these matters are disclosed in Note 1. The
consolidated financial statements do not include any adjustments that might result from the
outcome of this uncertainty.

/s/LIVINGSTON & HAYNES, P.C.
Livingston & Haynes, P.C.
Wellesley, Massachusetts
May 1, 2007

Source: LocatePlus's 2006 Form 10-K.

---

*and properly assess the risks of material misstatement due to fraud, and the failure of
Wood to address these deficiencies … constituted highly unreasonable conduct that
resulted in a violation of applicable professional standards in circumstances in which
each knew, or should have known, that heightened scrutiny was warranted.*

Both Howley and Wood were suspended from practicing before the SEC for three
years. L & H was fined $130,000, prohibited from accepting any new SEC clients for
one year, and required to undergo an extensive quality control review. Each professional staff member of L & H who served public clients was also required to undergo
24 hours of training involving audit documentation standards, fraud detection, assessing the risk of material misstatements, and obtaining and evaluating audit evidence.

EPILOGUE

In November 2010, the SEC announced that James Fields and Jon Latorella were being charged with criminal violations of the federal securities laws. In March 2012, Latorella pleaded guilty to conspiring to commit securities fraud and related charges, including making false statements to his former company's independent auditors. Three months later, Latorella was sentenced to five years in prison. In November 2012, a federal jury found James Fields guilty of 29 criminal charges, including securities fraud, money laundering, and making false statements to his former company's independent auditors. A federal judge sentenced Fields to five years in prison in February 2013.

LocatePlus filed for bankruptcy in June 2011. The company's assets, including its name and website, were sold to a private investment firm in November 2011.

Questions

1. The PCAOB's Interim Standards identify auditors' responsibilities when addressing the possibility that fraud has materially impacted a public company's financial statements. Identify in a bullet format the key instances in which the L & H auditors apparently failed to comply with these responsibilities during the 2005 and 2006 LocatePlus audits.

2. What is the purpose of predecessor–successor auditor communications? Which party, the predecessor or successor auditor, has the responsibility for initiating those communications? Briefly summarize the information that a successor auditor should obtain from the predecessor auditor.

3. What are the primary responsibilities of a "concurring partner" under current U.S. auditing standards?

4. What is the nature and purpose of a "letter of representations"? Comment on the quality or strength of the audit evidence yielded by a letter of representations.

SECTION 3

INTERNAL CONTROL ISSUES

3

The Trolley Dodgers

In 1890, the Brooklyn Trolley Dodgers professional baseball team joined the National League. Over the following years, the Dodgers would have considerable difficulty competing with the other baseball teams in the New York City area. Those teams, principal among them the New York Yankees, were much better financed and generally stocked with players of higher caliber.

After nearly seven decades of mostly frustration on and off the baseball field, the Dodgers shocked the sports world by moving to Los Angeles in 1958. Walter O'Malley, the flamboyant owner of the Dodgers, saw an opportunity to introduce professional baseball to the rapidly growing population of the West Coast. More important, O'Malley saw an opportunity to make his team more profitable. As an inducement to the Dodgers, Los Angeles County purchased a goat farm located in Chavez Ravine, an area two miles northwest of downtown Los Angeles, and gave the property to O'Malley for the site of his new baseball stadium.

Since moving to Los Angeles, the Dodgers have been the envy of the baseball world: "In everything from profit to stadium maintenance . . . the Dodgers are the prototype of how a franchise should be run."[1] During the 1980s and 1990s, the Dodgers reigned as the most profitable franchise in baseball with a pretax profit margin approaching 25 percent in many years. In late 1997, Peter O'Malley, Walter O'Malley's son and the Dodgers' principal owner, sold the franchise for $350 million to media mogul Rupert Murdoch. A spokesman for Murdoch complimented the O'Malley family for the long-standing success of the Dodgers organization: "The O'Malleys have set a gold standard for franchise ownership."[2]

During an interview before he sold the Dodgers, Peter O'Malley attributed the success of his organization to the experts he had retained in all functional areas: "I don't have to be an expert on taxes, split-fingered fastballs, or labor relations with our ushers. That talent is all available."[3] Edward Campos, a longtime accountant for the Dodgers, was a seemingly perfect example of one of those experts in the Dodgers organization. Campos accepted an entry-level position with the Dodgers as a young man. By 1986, after almost two decades with the club, he had worked his way up the employment hierarchy to become the operations payroll chief.

After taking charge of the Dodgers' payroll department, Campos designed and implemented a new payroll system, a system that only he fully understood. In fact, Campos controlled the system so completely that he personally filled out the weekly payroll cards for each of the 400 employees of the Dodgers. Campos was known not only for his work ethic but also for his loyalty to the club and its owners: "The Dodgers trusted him, and when he was on vacation, he even came back and did the payroll."[4]

Unfortunately, the Dodgers' trust in Campos was misplaced. Over a period of several years, Campos embezzled several hundred thousand dollars from his employer. According to court records, Campos padded the Dodgers' payroll by adding fictitious

---

1. R. J. Harris, "Forkball for Dodgers: Costs Up, Gate Off," *Wall Street Journal*, 31 August 1990, B1, B4.

2. R. Newhan, "Dodger Sale Heads for Home," *Los Angeles Times*, 5 September 1997, C1, C12.

3. Harris, "Forkball for Dodgers," B1.

4. P. Feldman, "7 Accused of Embezzling $332,583 from Dodgers," *Los Angeles Times*, 17 September 1986, Sec. 2, 1, 6.

employees to various departments in the organization. In addition, Campos routinely inflated the number of hours worked by several employees and then split the resulting overpayments 50-50 with those individuals.

The fraudulent scheme came unraveled when appendicitis struck down Campos, forcing the Dodgers' controller to temporarily assume his responsibilities. While completing the payroll one week, the controller noticed that several employees, including ushers, security guards, and ticket salespeople, were being paid unusually large amounts. In some cases, employees earning $7 an hour received weekly paychecks approaching $2,000. Following a criminal investigation and the filing of charges against Campos and his cohorts, all the individuals involved in the payroll fraud confessed.

A state court sentenced Campos to eight years in prison and required him to make restitution of approximately $132,000 to the Dodgers. Another of the conspirators also received a prison sentence. The remaining individuals involved in the payroll scheme made restitution and were placed on probation.

EPILOGUE

The San Francisco Giants are easily the most heated, if not hated, rival of the Dodgers. In March 2012, a federal judge sentenced the Giants' former payroll manager to 21 months in prison after she pleaded guilty to embezzling $2.2 million from the Giants organization. An attorney for the Giants testified that the payroll manager "wreaked havoc" on the Giants' players, executives, and employees. The attorney said that the embezzlement "included more than 40 separate illegal transactions, including changing payroll records and stealing employees' identities and diverting their tax payments."[5] A federal prosecutor reported that the payroll manager used the embezzled funds to buy a luxury car, to purchase a second home in San Diego, and to travel.

When initially confronted about her embezzlement scheme, the payroll manager had "denied it completely."[6] She confessed when she was shown the proof that prosecutors had collected. During her sentencing hearing, the payroll manager pleaded with the federal judge to sentence her to five years probation but no jail term. She told the judge, "I cannot say how sorry that I am … that I did this, because it's not who I am. I have no excuse for it. There is no excuse in the world for taking something that doesn't belong to you."[7]

Questions

1. Identify the key audit objectives for a client's payroll function. Comment on objectives related to tests of controls and substantive audit procedures.

2. What internal control weaknesses were evident in the Dodgers' payroll system?

3. Identify audit procedures that might have led to the discovery of the fraudulent scheme masterminded by Campos.

5. A. Burack, "Former Giants' Payroll Manager Sentenced to 21 Months in Prison for Embezzlement," *San Francisco Examiner* (online), 26 March 2012.

6. *Ibid.*

7. *Ibid.*

Howard Street Jewelers, Inc.

Lore Levi was worried as she scanned the most recent monthly bank statement for the Howard Street Jewelers.[1] For decades, she and her husband, Julius, had owned and operated the small business that they had opened after fleeing Nazi Germany during World War II. Certainly the business had experienced ups and downs before, but now it seemed to be in a downward spiral from which it could not recover. In previous times when sales had slackened, the Levis had survived by cutting costs here and there. But now, despite several measures the Levis had taken to control costs, the business's cash position continued to steadily worsen. If a turnaround did not occur soon, Lore feared that she and her husband might be forced to close their store.

Lore had a theory regarding the financial problems of Howard Street Jewelers. On more than one occasion, she had wondered whether Betty the cashier, a trusted and reliable employee for nearly 20 years, might be stealing from the cash register. To Lore, it was a logical assumption. Besides working as a part-time sales clerk, Betty handled all of the cash that came into the business and maintained the cash receipts and sales records. If anybody had an opportunity to steal from the business, it was Betty.

Reluctantly, Lore approached her husband about her theory. Lore pointed out to Julius that Betty had unrestricted access to the cash receipts of the business. Additionally, over the previous few years, Betty had developed a taste for more expensive clothes and more frequent and costly vacations. Julius quickly dismissed his wife's speculation. To him, it was preposterous to even briefly consider the possibility that Betty could be stealing from the business. A frustrated Lore then raised the subject with her son, Alvin, who worked side by side with his parents in the family business. Alvin responded similarly to his father and warned his mother that she was becoming paranoid.

Near the end of each year, the Levis met with their accountant to discuss various matters, principally taxation issues. The Levis placed considerable trust in their CPA because for years he had given them solid, professional advice on a wide range of accounting and business matters. So, it was only natural for Lore to confide in him about her suspicions regarding Betty the cashier. The accountant listened intently to Lore and then commented that he had noticed occasional shortages in the cash receipts records that seemed larger than normal for a small retail business. Despite Julius's protestations that Betty could not be responsible for any cash shortages, the accountant encouraged the Levis to closely monitor her work.

Embezzlements are often discovered by luck rather than by design. So it was with the Howard Street Jewelers. Nearly two years after Lore Levi had suggested that Betty might be stealing from the business, a customer approached the cash register and told Alvin Levi that she wanted to make a payment on a layaway item. Alvin, who was working the cash register because it was Betty's day off, searched the file of layaway sales tickets and the daily sales records but found no trace of the customer's layaway purchase. Finally, he apologized and asked the customer to return the next day when Betty would be back at work.

---

1. Most of the facts of this case were reconstructed from information included in several legal opinions. The following two articles served as additional sources for this case: *Securities Regulation and Law Report*, "Accounting & Disclosure: Accounting Briefs," Vol. 23, No. 21 (24 May 1991), 814; *Securities Regulation and Law Report*, "Accounting & Disclosure: Accounting Briefs," Vol. 24, No. 19 (8 May 1992), 708.

The following day, Alvin told Betty that he was unable to find the layaway sales ticket. Betty expressed surprise and said she would search for the ticket herself. Within a few minutes, Betty approached Alvin, waving the sales ticket in her hand. Alvin was stumped. He had searched the layaway sales file several times and simply could not accept Betty's explanation that the missing ticket had been there all along. Suspicious, as well, was the fact that the sale had not been recorded in the sales records—a simple oversight, Betty had explained.

As Alvin returned to his work, a troubling and sickening sensation settled into the pit of his stomach. Over the next several weeks, Alvin studied the daily sales and cash receipts records. He soon realized that his mother had been right all along. Betty, the trusted, reliable, longtime cashier of the Howard Street Jewelers, was stealing from the business. The estimated embezzlement loss suffered by Howard Street Jewelers over the term of Betty's employment approached $350,000.

Questions

1. Identify the internal control concepts that the Levis overlooked or ignored.

2. When Lore Levi informed the CPA of her suspicions regarding Betty, what responsibilities, if any, did the CPA have to pursue this matter? Alternately, assume that, in addition to preparing tax returns for Howard Street Jewelers, the CPA (a) *audited* the business's annual financial statements, (b) *reviewed* the annual financial statements, and (c) *compiled* the annual financial statements.

3. Assume that you have a small CPA firm and have been contacted by a husband and wife, Chris and Brooke Arbeitman, who are in the final stages of negotiating to purchase a local jewelry store. Chris will prepare jewelry settings, size jewelry for customers, and perform related tasks, while Brooke will be the head salesclerk. The Arbeitmans intend to retain four of the current employees of the jewelry store—two salesclerks, a cashier, and a college student who cleans the store, runs errands, and does various other odd jobs. They inform you that the average inventory of the jewelry store is $300,000 and that annual sales average $1,400,000, 30 percent of which occur in the six weeks prior to Christmas.

    The Arbeitmans are interested in retaining you as their accountant should they purchase the store. They know little about accounting and have no prior experience as business owners. They would require assistance in establishing an accounting system, monthly financial statements for internal use, annual financial statements to be submitted to their banker, and all necessary tax returns. Chris and Brooke are particularly concerned about control issues—given the dollar value of inventory that will be on hand in the store and the significant amount of cash receipts that will be processed daily.

    You see this as an excellent opportunity to acquire a good client. However, you have not had a chance to prepare for your meeting with the Arbeitmans because they came in without an appointment. You do not want to ask them to come back later since that may encourage them to check out your competitor across the street.

    Required: Provide the Arbeitmans with an overview of the key internal control issues they will face in operating a jewelry store. In your overview, identify at least five control activities you believe they should implement if they acquire the store. You have never had a jewelry store as a client but you have several small retail clients. Attempt to impress the Arbeitmans with your understanding of internal control issues for small retail businesses.

United Way of America

In 1887, several of Denver's community and religious leaders established the Charity Organization Society. During its first year of operation, the organization raised a little more than $20,000, which it then distributed to several local charities. The charity-of-charities fundraising concept spread across the United States over the following decades. After several name changes, the original Denver-based organization adopted the name United Way in 1963.

United Way grew rapidly during the latter decades of the twentieth century, eventually becoming the nation's largest charitable organization. In 2006, United Way raised four billion dollars, more than double the charitable donations received that year by the Salvation Army, the nation's second largest charitable organization. Each year, approximately 40,000 charities across the United States receive cash distributions from United Way.

Football & Fraud

For more than two decades beginning in the early 1970s, William Aramony served as the president of United Way of America. The Virginia-based United Way of America serves as the umbrella organization for the almost 1,400 local United Way chapters scattered across the United States. An alliance that Aramony negotiated with the National Football League (NFL) resulted in huge nationwide exposure for the United Way during every Sunday afternoon and Monday night NFL game. That exposure was largely responsible for the explosive growth that United Way realized during Aramony's tenure as president.

In recent years, United Way has faced two major challenges that threaten its leadership position in the charitable sector. Over the past several decades, the number of charitable and other not-for-profit organizations in the United States has skyrocketed. Currently, there are nearly two million registered tax-exempt organizations in the United States, the majority of which are charities. Collectively, these organizations employ one of every ten working Americans. Registered charities alone raise more than $300 billion each year in donations from the public and private sector. The intense and growing competition for Americans' charitable donations has made it increasingly difficult for United Way to sustain the impressive growth that it realized under William Aramony's leadership.

The second major challenge facing United Way is a loss of credibility suffered by the organization due to a series of embarrassing and highly publicized embezzlement schemes. In the early 1990s, federal prosecutors indicted William Aramony for embezzling millions of dollars of United Way funds. In 1995, a federal jury found Aramony guilty of more than two dozen of the individual fraud charges that had been filed against him. Aramony was later sentenced to serve seven years in federal prison. Testimony during his trial revealed that he had squandered United Way funds on lavish trips to Las Vegas, Europe, Africa, and other destinations. The 68-year-old Aramony reportedly used United Way funds to finance multiple romantic relationships as well.

Shortly before Aramony went to trial, another United Way executive in Westchester, New York, admitted to embezzling several hundred thousand dollars of her chapter's funds. This individual, Evol Sealy, who oversaw the Westchester chapter's accounting and finance functions, was later sentenced to a three-year prison term. In 2003, Jacquelyn Allen-MacGregor, the former vice president of finance of a United Way chapter in East Lansing, Michigan, pleaded guilty to stealing $1.9 million from the organization. Allen-MacGregor revealed that she had used the stolen funds to support her hobby, namely, horses—over the course of her embezzlement scheme she purchased more than 70 quarter horses. In June 2004, Allen-MacGregor was sentenced to four years in prison to be followed by three years of supervised probation.

In 2004, Aramony's friend and former associate, Oral Suer, who served for almost three decades as the president of a large United Way chapter in Washington, D.C., pleaded guilty to embezzling $1.5 million of United Way funds. The evidence collected by federal prosecutors against Suer included testimony documenting that Suer and Aramony had spent time together at a local racetrack. That evidence also documented that Suer used cash taken from his chapter to make good on the generous and well-publicized personal contribution pledges that he made during annual United Way fundraising campaigns. At his sentencing hearing, a contrite Suer told the presiding judge, "This is a very sad day for me, for the community and for the United Way. What I feel is embarrassment, shame and guilt."[1] The judge then handed Suer a three-year prison sentence, the maximum permissible under federal sentencing guidelines.

United Way's reported theft losses have had a chilling effect on the organization's fundraising efforts nationwide in recent years. Individual chapters impacted directly by the embezzlement losses have experienced the most dramatic declines in their annual receipts. For example, adverse publicity resulting from the embezzlement loss at the United Way chapter in the Washington, D.C., area caused that chapter's annual donations to plummet from $45 million to $18 million.

Other major charities have also been victimized by organizational insiders. In 1989, former television evangelist Jim Bakker was sentenced to 18 years in federal prison. Bakker was convicted of diverting millions of dollars for his personal use from the PTL Club, a religious broadcasting network that he and his wife, Tammy Faye, founded in the 1970s. The Bakkers had used passionate and persistent televised fundraising campaigns to convince the faithful and mostly shallow-pocketed viewers of their network to send them donations.

In 1997, John G. Bennett, the founder of the New Era Philanthropy Foundation, was sentenced to 12 years in prison after embezzling an estimated $8 million from that charitable organization. In California, seven employees of Goodwill Industries, all of whom were related, operated a large-scale "fencing" operation from the early 1970s through 1998 in which they sold furniture, clothing, and other goods donated to that charity. Law enforcement authorities estimate that the seven relatives stole more than $25 million from that organization over the course of the fraudulent scheme.

To date, the largest fraud impacting a charity was a Ponzi scheme involving the Baptist Foundation of Arizona. In 2006, William Crotts, the chief executive of that charitable religious organization, received an eight-year prison sentence for defrauding an estimated 10,000 individuals of nearly $160 million. Making matters worse, most of the victims of Crotts' fraud were elderly individuals, many of whom lost a sizable portion of their retirement nest eggs as a result of the fraud.

Empirical research has confirmed that fraud is a major problem plaguing the charitable sector. A recent study by four accounting professors suggests that approximately one of every eight dollars contributed to charitable organizations in the United States

---

1. J. Markon, "Ex-Chief of Local United Way Sentenced," *Washington Post* (online), 15 May 2004.

is stolen each year, resulting in annual losses to those organizations of $40 billion.[2] That study found that 95 percent of the losses suffered by charities result from the theft of cash and that the culprits are typically involved in the charity's financial functions. "They're usually done by someone in the financial area—the treasurer, the bookkeeper, the signer of checks—who knows how to avoid getting caught."[3]

Recipe for Theft: Weak Controls and Ineffective Regulatory Oversight

A common theme of the frauds that have plagued charities in recent years has been inadequate or nonexistent internal controls. Understandably, charitable organizations make every effort to minimize their administrative expenses, including their accounting and control-related expenditures. For example, an internal study by United Way of America in 2002 found that fewer than 15 percent of the organization's local chapters had invested the time and other resources to develop written policies to address fundamental accounting and control issues.[4] No doubt, the porous nature of charities' internal control systems not only encourages opportunistic individuals to take advantage of those organizations but also makes it difficult to detect ongoing frauds.

In 2004, PricewaterhouseCoopers released a 200-page report that detailed the results of a seven-month investigative audit of the embezzlement loss suffered by the East Lansing, Michigan, chapter of United Way. That report castigated United Way for failing to implement some of the most rudimentary control procedures intended to prevent thefts by organizational insiders. "The audit, more than seven months in the making, gives a scathing review, depicting the charity as a place where top managers were permitted to dip into the millions of dollars in public donations with little or no oversight."[5]

According to the *New York Times*, the individual who embezzled the funds from the East Lansing chapter "did not need to be a criminal mastermind to succeed in the theft."[6] Instead, that individual took advantage of the chapter's lack of proper internal controls and stole the funds at will. "She simply wrote checks to herself, forging the signatures of the required cosigners and destroying the canceled checks when the bank mailed them back. No one noticed this because she also kept the organization's books."[7]

Similar to the other United Way fraudsters, the executive who embezzled several hundred thousand dollars from the Westchester, New York, United Way chapter used a simple scam to "rip off" her organization. The executive endorsed checks made payable to United Way from local donors and then deposited those checks in her personal bank account. The fraud was uncovered when a bank teller reported her to local authorities. In commenting on the embezzlement scheme, the local district attorney noted, "There was most certainly a total lack of supervision which permitted this to occur."[8] The president of that chapter expressed a different point of view:

---

2. S. Strom, "Report Sketches Crime Costing Billions: Theft From Charities," *New York Times* (online), 29 March 2008.

3. *Ibid.*

4. S. Strom, "Questions Arise on Accounting at United Way," *New York Times* (online), 19 November 2002.

5. J. Salmon and P. Whoriskey, "Audit Excoriates United Way Leadership," *Washington Post* (online), 25 June 2004.

6. S. Strom, "Guilty Plea Due Today in Big United Way Theft," *New York Times* (online), 6 February 2003.

7. *Ibid.*

8. J. Steinberg, "United Way Accountant Admits $282,500 Theft," *New York Times* (online), 19 May 1992.

"As in the case of virtually any organization, our system of internal control procedures, no matter how strong, is based on trust."[9]

Compounding the weakness of the internal control systems of charities such as
United Way is the absence of strong regulatory oversight for the charitable sector.
The regulatory infrastructure for charities is weak and enforcement is inconsistent. Unlike public companies that are overseen by the Securities and Exchange
Commission (SEC), charitable organizations are not subject to direct oversight by a
federal agency. Federal oversight of charities involves principally an annual information filing with the Internal Revenue Service (IRS).

Similar to other tax-exempt organizations, most charities are required to submit a
Form 990 to the IRS each year. Among many other required disclosures in Form 990,
charities must report their total annual revenues and the principal sources of those
revenues, fundraising expenses, the salaries of highly paid executives, and losses
due to theft, embezzlement, and other fraudulent activities. The latter disclosure was
added to Form 990 beginning in 2008 as a direct consequence of the mounting theft
losses being incurred by charities. A searchable database of the approximately two
million Form 990's filed each year with the IRS is available at www.guidestar.org.

Although there is no federal agency with a direct responsibility to regulate charities, many states have established such an agency. Nevertheless, these state agencies tend to be underfunded and are ineffectual as a result. "While most states have
agencies [overseeing charitable organizations], most are inactive, ineffective or
significantly understaffed."[10]

Bring in the Auditors?

Following the passage of the Sarbanes–Oxley Act in 2002, some charities adopted internal control reforms and other provisions included in that federal statute. Not satisfied,
prominent members of the philanthropic community have lobbied state and federal
legislators to pass legislation that would require charities to implement a comprehensive reform agenda similar to that mandated by Sarbanes–Oxley. "The American government can no longer make a plausible argument that charities don't deserve the type
of scrutiny that the for-profit sector warrants. Quite simply, the charitable sector is much
too large to warrant the continued disinterest our government has shown it."[11]

One proponent of regulatory reform has suggested that charities be required to
obtain a "seal of approval" of some type to reassure donors that their contributions
are not being misused.[12] In fact, a common measure included in proposed regulatory
reforms for charities is a requirement that they be subject to an annual independent
audit by an accounting firm.

> Only a few states currently require annual financial audits of nonprofit corporations.
> … Independent financial audits have become such a fundamental and essential test
> of the financial soundness of any corporate enterprise that all best practice codes of
> nonprofit governance require that every nonprofit corporation with substantial assets
> or annual revenue should be audited annually by an independent auditing firm.[13]

---

9. *Ibid.*

10. A. Rothschild, "Public Scrutiny of Exempt Organizations," www.abanet.org/rppt/publications/
estate/2004/2/Rothschild-PublicScr.pdf.

11. T. Stamp, "Why Does Our Government Ignore Charities?" *Charity Navigator* (online), 14 October 2002.

12. W. Muller, "Charities and Anti-Money Laundering: Is a 'Seal of Approval' the Answer?" *Trusts and
Trustees*, 14 (May 2008): 259–271.

13. T. Silk, "Good Governance Practices for 501 (c)(3) Organizations: Should the IRS Become Further
Involved?" *International Journal of Not-for-Profit Law*, 2007 (Vol. 10), 40.

California and Massachusetts are examples of states that have passed legislation in recent years to require certain charities to be audited annually. California's Nonprofit Integrity Act of 2004 requires charities with annual gross revenues exceeding $2 million to be audited. The comparable state statute in Massachusetts requires charities with annual revenues exceeding $500,000 or total assets greater than $5 million to be audited. These same charities are also required by the Massachusetts law to establish an audit committee.

Not all charity reform advocates believe that mandatory independent audits would remedy the problems facing the charitable sector. These parties point out that several of the charities that suffered large losses due to embezzlement and other fraudulent schemes had been audited by accounting firms. One such charity was United Way of America, which was audited by Arthur Andersen during the time frame that Aramony was embezzling from the organization. Andersen was widely criticized for failing to detect Aramony's fraud. The managing partner of the Andersen office that audited the organization responded to that criticism by insisting that United Way officials had intentionally concealed the fraudulent activities from the auditors.[14]

The auditors of the East Lansing, Michigan, United Way chapter that suffered an embezzlement loss of $1.9 million were also criticized for failing to uncover that fraud. The audit partner who supervised the annual audits of that chapter staunchly defended himself and his subordinates. "This [embezzlement scheme] went on prior to our being engaged in 1999, and when you have fraud going on a long time, it's hard to find because it has become the norm [within the organization]."[15]

Questions

1. Identify and briefly describe fundamental and cost-effective internal controls that charitable organizations could implement to reduce their exposure to theft losses.

2. Do CPA firms have a responsibility to perform audits of charitable organizations for reduced or lower-than-normal audit fees? Defend your answer. Other than audit fees, what other benefits do accounting firms accrue by auditing a charity?

3. Identify unique or uncommon audit risk factors posed by a charity. How should accounting firms modify their audits to address these risk factors?

14. J. Garnatz, "United Way Cleaning House Nationally, Doing Well Locally," *St. Petersburg Times*, 17 April 1992, 11.

15. Strom, "Guilty Plea Due Today."

First Keystone Bank

A Japanese bank introduced the concept of around-the-clock access to cash in the 1960s when it installed the world's first cash-dispensing machine. In 1968, the first networked ATM appeared in Dallas, Texas.[1] Two generations later, there are more than two million "cashpoints," "bancomats," and "holes-in-the-wall" worldwide, including one in Antarctica.

Not surprisingly, ATMs have been a magnet for thieves since their inception. In 2009, an international gang of racketeers used a large stash of counterfeit ATM cards to steal $9 million from hundreds of ATMs scattered around the globe in a well-planned and coordinated 30-minute crime spree. Several high-tech thieves have hacked into the computer networks of banks and modified their ATM software. One such miscreant reprogrammed a network of ATMs to change the denomination of bills recognized by the brainless machines—the ATMs treated $20 bills as if they were $5 bills. High-powered video cameras and miniature electronic devices attached to ATMs have been used to steal personal identification numbers (PINs) from a countless number of unsuspecting bank customers.

A variety of low-tech schemes have also been used to rip off banks and their customers via ATMs, including forced withdrawals and post-withdrawal armed robberies. "Ram-raiding" involves using heavy-duty equipment to rip an ATM from its shorings. The ram-raiders then haul the ATM to a remote location and blast it open with explosives. The most common and lowest-tech type of ATM pilfering involves the aptly named tactic of "shoulder-surfing."

Many banks have suffered losses from their ATM operations due to embezzlement schemes perpetrated by employees. One such bank was the Swarthmore, Pennsylvania, branch of First Keystone Bank. Swarthmore, a quiet suburb of Philadelphia, is best known for being home to one of the nation's most prestigious liberal arts colleges. In 2013, *Forbes Magazine* ranked Swarthmore College as the sixth best institution of higher learning in the United States—two slots below Yale, but two slots higher than Harvard.

In January 2010, three tellers of First Keystone's Swarthmore branch were arrested and charged with stealing more than $100,000 from its ATM over the previous two years. The alleged ringleader was Jean Moronese, who had worked at the branch since 2002 and served as its head teller since 2006. According to media reports, Moronese told law enforcement authorities that she initially began taking money from the branch's ATM in 2008 to pay her credit card bills, rent, and day care expenses.

No doubt emboldened by the ease with which she could steal the money, Moronese reportedly began taking cash from the ATM "just to spend" because she "got greedy."[2] Prior to taking a vacation in the fall of 2008, a tearful Moronese approached one of her subordinates and fellow tellers, Kelly Barksdale, and confessed that she had been stealing from the ATM. Moronese "begged" Barksdale to help her conceal her

---

1. In the United States, "ATM" generally refers to an "automated teller machine" or "automated transaction machine." In some English-speaking countries, however, "ATM" refers to "all-time-money."

2. C. Scharr, "Bank Employees Charged in Embezzlement Scheme," *Delaware County Daily Times* (online), 12 January 2010.

thefts "because she didn't want her children to see her go to jail."[3] Barksdale was apparently persuaded by Moronese's tearful plea and agreed to help her cover up the embezzlement scheme.

In fact, the cover-up was easily accomplished. According to the local police, Moronese and Barksdale simply changed the ledger control sheets that were supposed to report the amount of cash stored in the ATM and in the locked vault within the ATM. First Keystone's internal control procedures mandated that two employees be involved in resupplying the ATM and its locked vault and in maintaining the ATM ledger control sheets. However, either Moronese or Barksdale completed those tasks by themselves.

In early 2009, a third teller, Tyneesha Richardson, overheard Moronese and Barksdale discussing the embezzlement scheme. Richardson then reportedly asked Moronese for money to pay off her car loan. Moronese agreed to give Richardson the money and told her that she shouldn't worry because "the bank had a lot of money and they would never miss it."[4,5] After telling Barksdale that she had given money to Richardson, Moronese told Barksdale that if she ever needed any money "to let her know."[6] Not long thereafter, Barksdale allegedly asked Moronese for $600 to pay her rent.

An internal audit eventually uncovered the embezzlement scheme at First Keystone's Swarthmore branch. That internal audit revealed that $40,590 was missing from the branch's ATM, while another $60,000 was missing from the locked vault within the ATM's interior.

While being interrogated by law enforcement authorities, Barksdale reportedly confessed that she and her colleagues had also stolen money from the local municipality. City employees periodically dropped off at the First Keystone branch large bags of coins collected from Swarthmore's parking meters. Tellers at the branch were supposed to feed the coins into a coin-counting machine and then deposit the receipts printed by the machine into the city's parking account. According to Barksdale, she and her two fellow conspirators diverted money from Swarthmore's parking funds and split it among themselves. The police estimated that the three tellers stole approximately $24,000 of the parking funds.

In January 2010, when the three tellers were arrested, they did not have far to go since the Swarthmore police station was across the street from the First Keystone branch where they worked. In commenting on the case, the local district attorney observed that Barksdale and Richardson had a choice to make when they learned of Moronese's embezzlement scheme and that each had made the wrong choice. "So, the lesson is you can either be a witness or you can be a defendant. These two chose to be defendants."[7]

The district attorney also commented on the branch's failure to require employees to comply with internal control procedures. "The case is yet another example of the importance of not only implementing internal accounting safeguards, but ensuring that those safeguards are being followed by all employees at all levels of the business."[8,9]

---

3. M. Schaefer, "Ex-tellers at Swarthmore Bank Charged in Theft," www.philly.com, 12 January 2010.

4. Scharr, "Bank Employees Charged."

5. While at work, the three coworkers reportedly used the code word "Todd" to refer to "their friend" when they needed or wanted to take money from the ATM.

6. Scharr, "Bank Employees Charged."

7. Schaefer, "Ex-tellers at Swarthmore Bank."

8. Press release issued 11 January 2010, by G. Michael Green, District Attorney, Delaware County, Media, Pennsylvania (http://www.delcoda.com/documents/FirstKeystoneStatement byMikeGreen.pdf).

9. In March 2010, an employee of First Keystone's branch in Berwick, Pennsylvania, pleaded guilty to embezzling $750,000 over the 17 years that she had worked for that branch. According to published reports, the employee routinely "skimmed" money received by the bank and deposited the stolen funds into bank accounts that she controlled.

Questions

1. Prepare a list of internal control procedures that banks and other financial institutions have implemented, or should implement, for their ATM operations.

2. What general conditions or factors influence the audit approach or strategy applied to a bank client's ATM operations by its independent auditors?

3. Identify specific audit procedures that may be applied to ATM operations. Which, if any, of these procedures might have resulted in the discovery of the embezzlement scheme at First Keystone's Swarthmore branch? Explain.

Goodner Brothers, Inc.

"Woody, that's $2,400 you owe me. Okay? We're straight on that?"

"Yeah, yeah. I got you."

"And you'll pay me back by next Friday?"

"Al, I said I'd pay you back by Friday, didn't I?"

"Just checkin'."

Borrowing money from a friend can strain even the strongest relationship. When the borrowed money will soon be plunked down on a blackjack table, the impact on the friendship can be devastating.

Woody Robinson and Al Hunt were sitting side by side at a blackjack table in Tunica, Mississippi. The two longtime friends and their wives were spending their summer vacations together as they had several times. After three days of loitering in the casinos that line the banks of the Mississippi River 20 miles south of Memphis, Woody found himself hitting up his friend for loans. By the end of the vacation, Woody owed Al nearly $5,000. The question facing Woody was how he would repay his friend.[1]

Two Pals Named Woody and Al

Woodrow Wilson Robinson and Albert Leroy Hunt lived and worked in Huntington, West Virginia, a city of 60,000 tucked in the westernmost corner of the state. The blue-collar city sits on the south bank of the Ohio River. Ohio is less than one mile away across the river, while Kentucky can be reached by making a 10-minute drive westward on Interstate 64. Woody and Al were born six days apart in a small hospital in eastern Kentucky, were best friends throughout grade school and high school, and roomed together for four years at college. A few months after they graduated with business management degrees, each served as the other's best man at their respective weddings.

Following graduation, Al went to work for Curcio's Auto Supply on the western outskirts of Huntington, a business owned by his future father-in-law. Curcio's sold lawnmowers, bicycles, and automotive parts and supplies, including tires and batteries, the business's two largest revenue producers. Curcio's also installed the automotive parts it sold, provided oil and lube service, and performed small engine repairs.

Within weeks of going to work for Curcio's, Al helped Woody land a job with a large tire wholesaler that was Curcio's largest supplier. Goodner Brothers, Inc., sold tires of all types and sizes from 14 locations scattered from southern New York to northwestern South Carolina and from central Ohio to the Delaware shore. Goodner concentrated its operations in midsized cities such as Huntington, West Virginia; Lynchburg, Virginia; Harrisburg, Pennsylvania; and Youngstown, Ohio, home to the company's headquarters.

Founded in 1979 by two brothers, T. J. and Ross Goodner, nearly three decades later Goodner Brothers' annual sales approached $40 million. The Goodner family dominated the company's operations. T. J. served as the company's chairman of the

---

1. The central facts of this case were drawn from a legal opinion. The names of the actual parties involved in the case and the relevant locations and dates have been changed. Additionally, certain of the factual circumstances reported in this case are fictionalized accounts of background material disclosed in the legal opinion.

board and chief executive officer (CEO), while Ross was the chief operating officer (COO). Four second-generation Goodners also held key positions in the company.

Goodner purchased tires from several large manufacturers and then sold those tires at wholesale prices to auto supply stores and other retailers that had auto supply departments. Goodner's customers included Sears, Walmart, Kmart, and dozens of smaller retail chains. The company also purchased discontinued tires from manufacturers, large retailers, and other wholesalers and then resold those tires at cut-rate prices to school districts, municipalities, and to companies with small fleets of automobiles.

Goodner Brothers hired Woody to work as a sales rep for its Huntington location. Woody sold tires to more than 80 customers in his sales region that stretched from the west side of Huntington into eastern Kentucky and north into Ohio. Woody, who worked strictly on a commission basis, was an effective and successful salesman. Unfortunately, a bad habit that he acquired during his college days gradually developed into a severe problem. A gambling compulsion threatened to wreck the young salesman's career and personal life.

Woody bet on any and all types of sporting events, including baseball and football games, horse races, and boxing matches. He also spent hundreds of dollars each month buying lottery tickets and lost increasingly large sums on frequent gambling excursions with his friend Al. By the summer of 2006 when Woody, Al, and their wives visited Tunica, Mississippi, Woody's financial condition was desperate. He owed more than $50,000 to the various bookies with whom he placed bets, was falling behind on his mortgage payments, and had "maxed out" several credit cards. Worst of all, two bookies to whom Woody owed several thousand dollars were demanding payment and had begun making menacing remarks that alluded to his wife, Rachelle.

Woody Finds a Solution

Upon returning to Huntington in early July 2006, Woody struck upon an idea to bail him out of his financial problems: he decided to begin stealing from his employer, Goodner Brothers. Other than a few traffic tickets, Woody had never been in trouble with law enforcement authorities. Yet, in Woody's mind, he had no other reasonable alternatives. At this point, resorting to stealing seemed the lesser of two evils.

One reason Woody decided to steal from his employer was the ease with which it could be done. After several years with Goodner, Woody was very familiar with the company's sloppy accounting practices and lax control over its inventory and other assets. Goodner's executives preached one dominant theme to their sales staff: "Volume, volume, volume." Goodner achieved its ambitious sales goals by undercutting competitors' prices. The company's dominant market share in the geographical region it served came at a high price. Goodner's gross profit margin averaged 17.4 percent, considerably below the mean gross profit margin of 24.1 percent for comparable tire wholesalers. To compensate for its low gross profit margin, Goodner scrimped on operating expenses, including expenditures on internal control measures.

The company staffed its 14 sales outlets with skeletal crews of 10 to 12 employees. A sales manager supervised the other employees at each outlet and also worked a sales district. The remaining staff typically included two sales reps, a receptionist who doubled as a secretary, a bookkeeper, and five to seven employees who delivered tires and worked in the unit's inventory warehouse. Goodner's Huntington location had two storage areas: a small warehouse adjacent to the sales office and a larger storage area two miles away that had previously housed a discount grocery store. Other than padlocks, Goodner provided little security for its tire inventory, which typically ranged from $300,000 to $700,000 for each sales outlet.

Instead of an extensive system of internal controls, T. J. and Ross Goodner relied heavily on the honesty and integrity of the employees they hired. Central to the company's employment policy was never to hire someone unless that individual could provide three strong references, preferably from reputable individuals with some connection to Goodner Brothers. Besides following up on employment references, Goodner Brothers obtained thorough background checks on prospective employees from local detective agencies.

For almost three decades, Goodner's employment strategy had served the company well. Fewer than 10 of several hundred individuals employed by the company had been terminated for stealing or other misuse of company assets or facilities.

Each Goodner sales outlet maintained a computerized accounting system. These systems typically consisted of an "off-the-shelf" general ledger package intended for a small retail business and a hodgepodge of assorted accounting documents. Besides the Huntington facility's bookkeeper, the unit's sales manager and two sales reps had unrestricted access to the accounting system.

Because the large volume of sales and purchase transactions often swamped the bookkeeper, sales reps frequently entered transactions directly into the system. The sales reps routinely accessed, reviewed, and updated their customers' accounts. Rather than completing purchase orders, sales orders, credit memos, and other accounting documents on a timely basis, the sales reps often jotted the details of a transaction on a piece of scrap paper. The sales reps eventually passed these "source documents" on to the bookkeeper or used them to enter transaction data directly into the accounting system.

Sales reps and the sales manager jointly executed the credit function for each Goodner sales outlet. Initial sales to new customers required the approval of the sales manager, while the creditworthiness of existing clients was monitored by the appropriate sales rep. Sales reps had direct access to the inventory storage areas. During heavy sales periods, sales reps often loaded and delivered customer orders themselves.

Each sales office took a year-end physical inventory to bring its perpetual inventory records into agreement with the amount of inventory actually on hand. One concession that T. J. and Ross Goodner made to the policy of relying on their employees' honesty was mandating one intra-year inventory count for each sales office. Management used these inventories, which were taken by the company's two-person internal audit staff, to monitor inventory shrinkage at each sales outlet.

Goodner's inventory shrinkage significantly exceeded the industry norm. The company occasionally purchased large shipments of "seconds" from manufacturers; that is, tires with defects that prevented them from being sold to major retailers. The tires in these lots with major defects were taken to a tire disposal facility. A sales office's accounting records were not adjusted for these "throwaways" until the year-end physical inventory was taken.

Selling Tires on the Sly

Within a few days after Woody hatched his plan to pay off his gambling debts, he visited the remote storage site for the Huntington sales office. Woody rummaged through its dimly lit and cluttered interior searching for individual lots of tires that apparently had been collecting dust for several months. After finding several stacks of tires satisfying that requirement, Woody jotted down their specifications in a small notebook. For each lot, Woody listed customers who could potentially find some use for the given tires.

Later that same day, Woody made his first "sale." A local plumbing supply dealer needed tires for his small fleet of vehicles. Woody convinced the business's owner that Goodner was attempting to "move" some old inventory. That inventory would be sold on a cash basis and at prices significantly below Goodner's cost. The owner agreed to purchase two dozen of the tires. After delivering the tires in his large pickup, Woody received a cash payment of $900 directly from the customer.

Over the next several months, Woody routinely stole inventory and kept the proceeds. Woody concealed the thefts in various ways. In some cases, he would charge merchandise that he had sold for his own benefit to the accounts of large volume customers. Woody preferred this technique since it allowed him to reduce the inventory balance in the Huntington facility's accounting records. When customers complained to him for being charged for merchandise they had not purchased, Woody simply apologized and corrected their account balances. If the customers paid the improper charges, they unknowingly helped Woody sustain his fraudulent scheme.

Goodner's customers frequently returned tires for various reasons. Woody completed credit memos for sales transactions voided by his customers, but instead of returning the tires to Goodner's inventory, he often sold them and kept the proceeds. Goodner occasionally consigned tires to large retailers for promotional sales events. When the consignees returned the unsold tires to Goodner, Woody would sell some of the tires to other customers for cash. Finally, Woody began offering to take throwaways to the tire disposal facility in nearby Shoals, West Virginia, a task typically assigned to a sales outlet's delivery workers. Not surprisingly, most of the tires that Woody carted off for disposal were not defective.

The ease with which he could steal tires made Woody increasingly bold. In late 2006, Woody offered to sell Al Hunt tires he had allegedly purchased from a manufacturer (by this time, Al owned and operated Curcio's Tires). Woody told Al that he had discovered the manufacturer was disposing of its inventory of discontinued tires and decided to buy them himself. When Al asked whether such "self-dealing" violated Goodner company policy, Woody replied, "It's none of their business what I do in my spare time. Why should I let them know about this great deal that I stumbled upon?"

At first reluctant, Al eventually agreed to purchase several dozen tires from Woody. No doubt, the cut-rate prices at which Woody was selling the tires made the decision much easier. At those prices, Al realized he would earn a sizable profit on the tires.

Over the next 12 months, Woody continued to sell "closeout" tires to his friend. After one such purchase, Al called the manufacturer from whom Woody had reportedly purchased the tires. Al had become suspicious of the frequency of the closeout sales and the bargain basement prices at which Woody supposedly purchased the tires. When he called the manufacturer, a sales rep told Al that his company had only one closeout sale each year. The sales rep also informed Al that his company sold closeout merchandise directly to wholesalers, never to individuals or retail establishments.

The next time Al spoke to Woody, he mentioned matter-of-factly that he had contacted Woody's primary supplier of closeout tires. Al then told his friend that a sales rep for the company indicated that such merchandise was only sold to wholesalers.

"So, what's the point, Al?"

"Well, I just found it kind of strange that, uh, that …"

"C'mon, get to the point, Al."

"Well, Woody, I was just wondering where you're getting these tires that you're selling."

"Do you want to know, Al? Do you really want to know, Buddy? I'll tell you if you want to know," Woody replied angrily.

After a lengthy pause, Al shrugged his shoulders and told his friend to "just forget it." Despite his growing uneasiness regarding the source of the cheap tires, Al continued to buy them and never again asked Woody where he was obtaining them.

Internal Auditors Discover Inventory Shortage

On 31 December 2006, the employees of Goodner's Huntington location met to take a physical inventory. The employees treated the annual event as a prelude to their New Year's Eve party. Counting typically began around noon and was finished within three hours. The employees worked in teams of three. Two members of each team climbed and crawled over the large stacks of tires and shouted out their counts to the third member who recorded them on preformatted count sheets.

Woody arranged to work with two delivery workers who were relatively unfamiliar with Goodner's inventory since they had been hired only a few weeks earlier. He made sure that his team was one of the two count teams assigned to the remote storage facility. Most of the inventory he had stolen over the previous six months had been taken from that site. Woody estimated that he had stolen approximately $45,000 of inventory from the remote storage facility, which represented about 10 percent of the site's book inventory. By maintaining the count sheets for his team, Woody could easily inflate the quantities for the tire lots that he and his team members counted.

After the counting was completed at the remote storage facility, Woody offered to take the count sheets for both teams to the sales office where the total inventory would be compiled. On the way to the sales office, he stopped in a vacant parking lot to review the count sheets. Woody quickly determined that the apparent shortage remaining at the remote site was approximately $20,000. He reduced that shortage to less than $10,000 by altering the count sheets prepared by the other count team.

When the year-end inventory was tallied for Goodner's Huntington location, the difference between the physical inventory and the book inventory was $12,000, or 2.1 percent. That percentage exceeded the historical shrinkage rate of approximately 1.6 percent for Goodner's sales offices. But Felix Garcia, the sales manager for the Huntington sales office, did not believe that the 2006 shrinkage was excessive. As it turned out, neither did the accounting personnel and internal auditors at Goodner's corporate headquarters.

Woody continued "ripping off" Goodner throughout 2007. By midyear, Woody was selling most of the tires he stole to Al Hunt. On one occasion, Woody warned Al not to sell the tires too cheaply. Woody had become concerned that Curcio's modest prices and its increasing sales volume might spark the curiosity and envy of other Huntington tire retailers.

In late October 2007, Goodner's internal audit team arrived to count the Huntington location's inventory. Although company policy dictated that the internal auditors count the inventory of each Goodner sales outlet annually, the average interval between the internal audit inventory counts typically ranged from 15 to 20 months. The internal auditors had last counted the Huntington location's inventory in May 2006, two months before Woody Robinson began stealing tires. Woody was unaware that the internal auditors periodically counted the entire inventory of each Goodner operating unit. Instead, he understood that the internal auditors only did a few test counts during their infrequent visits to the Huntington sales office.

After completing their inventory counts, the two internal auditors arrived at an inventory value of $498,000. A quick check of the accounting records revealed a book inventory of $639,000. The auditors had never encountered such a large difference between the physical and book inventory totals. Unsure what to do at this point, the auditors eventually decided to take the matter directly to Felix Garcia, the Huntington sales manager.

The size of the inventory shortage shocked Garcia. He insisted that the auditors must have overlooked some inventory. Garcia, the two internal auditors, and three delivery workers spent the following day recounting the entire inventory. The resulting physical inventory value was $496,000, $2,000 less than the original value arrived at by the auditors.

Following the second physical inventory, the two internal auditors and Garcia met at a local restaurant to review the Huntington unit's inventory records. No glaring trends were evident in those records to either Garcia or the auditors. Garcia admitted to the auditors that the long hours required "just to keep the tires coming and going" left him little time to monitor his unit's accounting records. When pressed by the auditors to provide possible explanations for the inventory shortage, Garcia erupted. "Listen. Like I just said, my job is simple. My job is selling tires. I sell as many tires as I can, as quickly as I can. I let you guys and those other suits up in Youngstown track the numbers."

The following day, the senior internal auditor called his immediate superior, Goodner's chief financial officer (CFO). The size of the inventory shortage alarmed the CFO. Immediately, the CFO suspected that the inventory shortage was linked to the Huntington unit's downward trend in monthly profits over the past two years.

Through 2005, the Huntington sales office had consistently ranked as Goodner's second or third most profitable sales outlet. Over the past 18 months, the unit's slumping profits had caused it to fall to the bottom one-third of the company's sales outlets in terms of profit margin percentage. Tacking on the large inventory shortage would cause the Huntington location to be Goodner's least profitable sales office over the previous year and one-half.

After discussing the matter with T. J. and Ross Goodner, the CFO contacted the company's independent audit firm and arranged for the firm to investigate the inventory shortage. The Goodners agreed with the CFO that Felix Garcia should be suspended with pay until the investigation was concluded. Garcia's lack of a reasonable explanation for the missing inventory and the anger he had directed at the internal auditors caused Goodner's executives to conclude that he was likely responsible for the inventory shortage.

Within a few days, four auditors from Goodner's independent audit firm arrived at the Huntington sales office. Goodner's audit firm was a regional CPA firm with six offices, all in Ohio. Goodner obtained an annual audit of its financial statements because one was demanded by the New York bank that provided the company with a line of credit. Goodner's independent auditors had never paid much attention to the internal controls of the client's sales offices. Instead, they performed a "balance sheet" audit that emphasized corroborating Goodner's year-end assets and liabilities.

During their investigation of the missing inventory, the auditors were appalled by the Huntington unit's lax and often nonexistent controls. The extensive control weaknesses complicated their efforts to identify the source of the inventory shortage. Nevertheless, after several days, the auditors' suspicions began settling on Woody Robinson.

A file of customer complaints that Felix Garcia kept in his desk revealed that over the past year an unusually large number of customer complaints had been filed against Woody. During that time, 14 of his customers had protested charges included on their monthly statements. Only two customers serviced by the other sales rep had filed similar complaints during that time frame.

When questioned by the auditors, Garcia conceded that he had not discussed the customer complaints with Woody or the other sales rep. In fact, Garcia was unaware that a disproportionate number of the complaints had been filed against Woody. When Garcia received a customer complaint, he simply passed it on to the appropriate sales rep and allowed that individual to deal with the matter. He maintained a file of the customer complaints only because he had been told to do so by the previous sales manager whom he had replaced three years earlier.

After the independent auditors collected other incriminating evidence against Woody, they arranged for a meeting with him. Also attending that meeting were Goodner's CFO and Felix Garcia. When the auditors produced the incriminating evidence, Woody disclaimed any knowledge of, or responsibility for, the inventory shortage. Woody's denial provoked an immediate and indignant response from Goodner's CFO. "Listen, Robinson, you may have fooled the people you've been working with, but you're not fooling me. You'd better spill the beans right now, or else." At this point, Woody stood, announced that he was retaining an attorney, and walked out of the meeting.

EPILOGUE

Goodner Brothers filed a criminal complaint against Woody Robinson two weeks after he refused to discuss the inventory shortage at the Huntington sales office. A few weeks later, Woody's attorney reached a plea bargain agreement with the local district attorney. Woody received a five-year sentence for grand larceny, four years of which were suspended. He eventually served seven months of that sentence in a minimum-security prison. A condition of the plea bargain agreement required Woody to provide a full and candid written summary of the fraudulent scheme that he had perpetrated on his employer.

Woody's confession implicated Al Hunt in his theft scheme. Over the 15 months that Woody had stolen from Goodner, he had "fenced" most of the stolen inventory through Curcio's Tires. Although the district attorney questioned Al Hunt extensively, he decided not to file criminal charges against him.[2]

Goodner Brothers filed a $185,000 insurance claim to recoup the losses resulting from Woody's thefts. The company's insurer eventually paid Goodner $130,000, which equaled the theft losses that Goodner could document. After settling the claim, the insurance company sued Curcio's Tires and Al Hunt to recover the $98,000 windfall that Curcio's allegedly realized due to Al Hunt's involvement in the theft ring. The case went to federal district court where a judge ordered Hunt to pay $64,000 to Goodner's insurer. Al Hunt then sued Woody Robinson to recover that judgment. The judge, who had presided over the earlier case, quickly dismissed Al Hunt's lawsuit. According to the judge, Al Hunt's complicity in the fraudulent scheme vacated his right to recover the $64,000 judgment from his former friend.

---

2. Ironically, Woody's confession also implicated his wife, Rachelle. After Woody revealed that Rachelle had typically deposited the large checks written to him by Al Hunt, the district attorney reasoned that Rachelle must have been aware of Woody's fraudulent scheme and was thus an accessory to his crime. However, Woody insisted that he had told his wife the checks were for gambling losses owed to him by Al. After interrogating Rachelle at length, the district attorney decided not to prosecute her.

Questions

1. List what you believe should have been the three to five key internal control objectives of Goodner's Huntington sales office.

2. List the key internal control weaknesses that were evident in the Huntington unit's operations.

3. Develop one or more control policies or procedures to alleviate the control weaknesses you identified in responding to Question 2.

4. Besides Woody Robinson, what other parties were at least partially responsible for the inventory losses Goodner suffered? Defend your answer.

CASE 3.6

Buranello's Ristorante

In 1983, Marta Giordano inherited the restaurant that her grandfather, Alberto Buranello, had established shortly after returning to his hometown of Boston after serving in World War I.[1] For nearly a century, the restaurant, Buranello's Ristorante, has been a landmark and favorite gathering spot for generations of families in Boston's historic North End neighborhood.

Over the years, the large corner restaurant, which has a staff of approximately 40 employees, has been essentially recession-proof. But Giordano's business recently faced two major challenges. Three local, formerly family-owned restaurants that Giordano considers to be her primary competitors were purchased by private investors who then renovated their interiors and facades and refurbished their kitchens. Although Buranello's breakfast and lunchtime traffic were largely unaffected by the competitors' upgrades, its dinner traffic fell by 20 percent. Making matters worse for Giordano during this same time span was another problem that was plaguing the restaurant, namely, abnormally large cash shortages apparently resulting from employee theft. These shortages were typically discovered at the close of business when the daily sales reconciliation worksheet was prepared.

The Suspect

Michael Barnes, Buranello's general manager, was just as frustrated by the cash shortages as his boss, Marta Giordano. Barnes had worked at Buranello's for more than 20 years and was practically a member of the Giordano family. His first position with the restaurant was as a busboy when he was 14 years old. During college he worked as a waiter at the restaurant. When he graduated from Northeastern University with a management degree, Barnes turned down an offer from Giordano to become a member of Buranello's management staff, choosing instead to work for a large, nationally franchised restaurant chain that had an extensive management trainee program. Five years later, though, Barnes returned to Buranello's when Giordano offered him the position of general manager.

Barnes eventually called a meeting of the restaurant's management staff—himself, three shift managers, three assistant managers, and the chef—to address the cash shortages being experienced by Buranello's. At the meeting, which Giordano also attended, Barnes informed his subordinates that the cash shortages were becoming larger and more frequent. He pledged that he would catch the culprit or culprits and prosecute them to the fullest extent of the law. Barnes did not discuss specific measures that he planned to take to determine the source of the cash shortages. Why? Because he suspected that the thief was a member of the management staff. The prime suspect in Barnes' mind was Aaron O'Neil, one of the three shift managers.

Barnes rotates the work assignments for the shift managers so that each of them works the closing shift, which is 3 p.m. to 11 p.m., only twice per week.[2] Buranello's

---

1. This case was developed from a recent legal opinion. The names of the actual parties involved in the case and the location have been changed. In addition, certain of the background details presented in the case are fictionalized accounts of information disclosed in the legal opinion.

2. The opening shift runs from 7 a.m. to 3 p.m. Shift managers supervise four eight-hour shifts each week. During their fifth eight-hour shift each week, they serve as an assistant manager to the shift manager on duty.

311

is closed on Sundays when it often hosts private parties such as family reunions and wedding receptions. One of the responsibilities of the shift manager at closing is to prepare the daily sales reconciliation. To perform this task the shift manager completes one of the standard reconciliation templates used for that purpose within the restaurant industry. The final task of the closing shift manager each night is to prepare the bank deposit for that day's sales. The day's receipts along with the completed deposit slip are left overnight in the restaurant's safe. The following morning, the shift manager who opens the restaurant recounts the receipts, traces the resulting total to the deposit slip, and then takes both to Buranello's bank a few blocks away.

The purpose of the daily sales reconciliation is to reconcile the day's sales reflected by the cash register printout to the total cash and cash items in the cash register at the close of business. The final line item on the reconciliation worksheet is entitled "Variance." A negative variance reflects a cash shortage, while a positive variance indicates a cash overage. Similar to most restaurants and retail businesses, Buranello's typically has a modest cash shortage at the end of each business day.

After Buranello's began experiencing abnormally large cash shortages, Barnes engaged the business's accounting firm to analyze the restaurant's daily sales reconciliations. The accounting firm attempted to correlate the cash shortages with the shifts worked by the management staff and the cashiers but the results of that analysis were inconclusive.[3] The accounting firm also attempted to determine whether the cash shortages were correlated with the presence of a specific shift manager during the closing shifts—Barnes believed that cash was most likely being stolen during the nightly closing procedures. Again, the results were inconclusive. There was no definite trend that linked the shortages to the closing shifts worked by specific shift managers. In Barnes' mind, the results of the accounting firm's analyses suggested that the thief or thieves were sufficiently clever to make it difficult for the cash shortages to be traced directly to them.

The only evidence that linked Aaron O'Neil to the cash shortages was the fact that they began occurring within a few weeks of the date that he began working at Buranello's. But there was another reason that Barnes suspected O'Neil. During the 20 years prior to accepting a position with Buranello's, O'Neil had been employed by seven different restaurants or restaurant chains. That unstable employment history had concerned Barnes when he interviewed him. The reference letters provided by O'Neil's former employers had also posed some degree of concern since they had been lukewarm, at best, in their endorsement of him. Despite the fact that O'Neil was a marginal job candidate, Barnes had hired him because Buranello's management team was chronically understaffed. Similar to most restaurants, management and employee turnover is a constant problem faced by Buranello's.

The Opportunity

The cash shortages infuriated Barnes not only because of the adverse financial impact they had on the restaurant but also because they reflected poorly on his management style and overall performance as the caretaker of the business for the Giordano family. Barnes much prefers "pressing the flesh" with customers and the restaurant's waitstaff rather than taking care of his back-office responsibilities. He often allows his paperwork, which includes health inspection reports, tax reporting schedules, and the daily sales reconciliation worksheets, to pile up on his desk.

---

3. Five individuals have access to Buranello's cash register during each shift: the cashier, the shift manager, the assistant manager, Barnes, and Giordano, who typically spends a few hours each day in the restaurant.

Barnes finds the daily sales reconciliation worksheets particularly wearisome. He would never admit as much to Marta Giordano or any of his subordinates, but even after having completed hundreds of daily sales reconciliations, it is still a challenging task for him on the infrequent occasions when he closes the restaurant.

The objective of a daily sales reconciliation is obvious to Barnes, but the task itself is tedious and frustrating. The process of completing the worksheet at the end of a busy day requires properly analyzing a wide array of nonstandard transactions. These items typically include a variety of coupons redeemed by customers, discounted meals purchased by employees, unpaid meal tickets of "deadbeat" customers who slipped out of the restaurant without paying, duplicate meal tickets issued to replace lost or misplaced tickets, refunds for overcharges, purchases or redemptions of meal cards given as gifts, petty cash expenditures such as modest charitable contributions, discounts or rain checks given to unhappy patrons whose pasta was not cooked to order, and so on and so forth. Each time that he completes a daily sales reconciliation worksheet, Barnes is reminded why he switched his major from accounting to management during his sophomore year of college.

Barnes also finds the task of reviewing completed daily sales reconciliation worksheets unpleasant, which is why he often has a stack of them sitting on his desk. Ironically, despite his accounting "dyslexia," he is the person responsible for the final approval of the reconciliations. The most challenging facet of reviewing the reconciliations is deciphering, comprehending, and then clearing the numerous comments printed or scrawled haphazardly in the margins of the worksheet form. On a typical day, there are six to eight "problem" reconciling items that the closing shift manager must explain in a written comment on the worksheet form—the template used by Buranello's does not have a "comments" section.

The intricate nature of the reconciliation worksheets has convinced Barnes that an unscrupulous shift manager could easily use them as a tool to conceal amounts embezzled from the daily sales receipts. This ever-present opportunity, if not invitation, to steal from the restaurant means that the larger-than-normal cash shortages recently experienced by Buranello's may have been significantly understated.

The Sting

The day following the management meeting in which he addressed Buranello's recurring cash shortages, Barnes met with Marta Giordano. He had developed a plan to address the problem, and he wanted her approval before he went forward with it. Barnes told Giordano that he wanted to carry out a "sting" operation to test the honesty of Aaron O'Neil—Giordano was aware that Barnes considered O'Neil to be the most likely source of the cash shortages.

The plan called for Barnes to replace the closing shift manager on an evening before O'Neil was scheduled to open the restaurant the following day. During the closing procedures, Barnes would prepare a deposit slip that understated the amount of cash receipts by several hundred dollars—Giordano would be present to verify the understatement. Barnes expected, actually hoped, that O'Neil would steal the excess cash prior to making the morning bank deposit. Barnes then planned to contact the police and file theft charges against O'Neil. Giordano reluctantly approved Barnes' plan, although she thought it smacked of entrapment and considered it to be distasteful.

Barnes executed his plan the following week and it seemed to work to perfection. Neither O'Neil nor the bank reported the difference between the cash receipts and the dollar amount reflected on the given deposit slip. In Barnes' mind that meant that O'Neil had stolen the excess cash in the deposit, which amounted to $360.

The following day, Barnes contacted the police and reported the incident. He and Giordano met the police detective assigned to investigate the apparent embezzlement. Barnes told the officer that he believed O'Neil had stolen the $360 and wanted to press charges against him on behalf of Buranello's. Barnes also told the detective that he suspected O'Neil was responsible for the rash of abnormally large cash shortages experienced by the restaurant over the past several months. The detective informed Barnes that it would be necessary for him to provide evidence to support that allegation.

That afternoon, the detective went to O'Neil's apartment with two uniformed officers—O'Neil had not been scheduled to work that day. After the detective explained the circumstances of the alleged embezzlement, O'Neil indicated that he wanted to contact his attorney. The uniformed officers then arrested O'Neil, handcuffed him, and marched him through the large courtyard of his apartment complex on the way to the patrol car.

O'Neil's attorney arrived at the police station to consult with his client later that afternoon. At approximately 5 p.m., the attorney arranged a meeting involving himself, O'Neil, and the detective in charge of the case. During this meeting, the attorney told the detective that O'Neil had not stolen the $360. When counting the cash before making the deposit, O'Neil had discovered that the cash receipts exceeded the amount reported on the deposit slip by $360. O'Neil had then taken that amount and placed it in Buranello's safe in an envelope marked to the attention of Michael Barnes.

The detective telephoned Michael Barnes, passed along the information provided by O'Neil, and asked him to search the safe. Barnes and Giordano went through the safe but could not find the envelope. When the detective told O'Neil that the envelope could not be found, O'Neil asked to be taken to the restaurant to search for it himself. The detective refused to do that.

O'Neil then asked the detective to send a police officer to search the safe. After the detective agreed to send an officer to the restaurant, O'Neil told the detective exactly where the envelope containing the $360 could be found. According to O'Neil, he had placed the letter-sized envelope containing the $360 in a larger envelope that was labeled "Equipment Leases." When the detective asked O'Neil why he had hidden the cash so well, he replied that he believed he was being "set up" by Barnes. O'Neil explained that he had been hoping to "buy some time" to figure out exactly what to do, which also explained why he had not called Barnes immediately and reported the excess cash.

The police officer sent to Buranello's found the hidden cash in a matter of minutes. The charges filed against O'Neil were immediately dropped, and he was released from police custody.

The Lawsuit

Aaron O'Neil never returned to Buranello's, choosing instead to resign immediately, but Michael Barnes and Marta Giordano had not heard the last of him.[4] One month later, O'Neil filed a "malicious prosecution" civil lawsuit that named Buranello's, Barnes, and Giordano as defendants. Following a brief trial, the jury ruled in O'Neil's favor and awarded him a judgment of $66,000. The defendants immediately appealed the jury's ruling. One year later, an appellate court overturned the jury's decision and voided the judgment. The appellate court ruled that because Barnes and Giordano had "probable cause" to file theft charges against O'Neil, they could not be accused of "malicious prosecution."

---

4. The abnormally large cash shortages experienced by Buranello's ended abruptly when O'Neil terminated his employment.

Questions

1. Identify internal control weaknesses evident in Buranello's operations. What risks are posed by these internal control problems?

2. For each internal control weakness you listed in responding to the previous question, identify a measure that Buranello's could implement to remedy that weakness. Indicate whether these measures would be cost-effective.

3. Prepare a list of internal control procedures for a restaurant other than the controls referred to in this case. For each control that you list, identify its underlying objective.

4. Do you believe that Barnes' plan to test Aaron O'Neil's honesty was appropriate? Was it ethical? What ethical responsibilities does a business's senior management or owner have when an employee is suspected of theft?

Foamex International, Inc.

In 1937, Otto Bayer, a research scientist for the large German chemical company IG Farben, discovered a new chemical compound that would become known as polyurethane. During World War II, polyurethane was used principally in the manufacture of military equipment and supplies. Following the war, IG Farben was dismantled by the Allied Forces as punishment for its collaboration with the Nazis. Certain of the company's products had been used by the Nazis to perpetrate unconscionable atrocities on innocent civilians.

During the latter one-half of the twentieth century, polyurethane was used in the manufacture of a wide range of consumer goods, including automotive trims and moldings, batteries, carpet padding, and diapers. Among the most important polyurethane derivatives was a compound initially referred to as "imitation Swiss cheese." Polyurethane foam was "invented" in a research laboratory in the early 1950s when water was accidentally added during the production process for polyurethane.

One of the initial manufacturers of polyurethane foam was the Firestone Tire and Rubber Company. The Firestone division that produced the product would eventually become a freestanding company, Foamex International, Inc. Foamex became the United States' largest producer of polyurethane foam due to an ambitious acquisition program initiated by the company's management during the 1980s. By 2001, Foamex owned and operated more than 50 manufacturing and distributing facilities in the United States, Canada, and Mexico.

An unanticipated by-product of Foamex's acquisition program was a chaotic accounting system. The companies acquired by Foamex continued to use the accounting systems that they had previously employed. As a result, by the year 2000, Foamex's corporate accounting system was an amalgamation of dozens of geographically dispersed "legacy" systems that relied on a haphazard assortment of computer hardware and software components.

Foamex's failure to develop a coherent, integrated corporate accounting system complicated the annual audits of the company. In August 1999, PricewaterhouseCoopers (PwC), Foamex's independent audit firm, notified the company's audit committee that Foamex needed to improve its internal controls. "The auditor reported that Foamex's systems for the preparation of interim financial information did not provide an adequate basis for the auditor to complete, prior to certain filing deadlines, its reviews of Foamex's interim financial statements."[1] In May 2000, following the completion of the 1999 Foamex audit—the company's fiscal year coincided with the calendar year—PwC issued a "Report to Management." This report identified several serious internal control problems or "reportable conditions"[2] and

---

1. This and all subsequent quotes, unless indicated otherwise, were taken from the following source: Securities and Exchange Commission, *Accounting and Auditing Enforcement Release No. 2274*, 11 July 2005.

2. At the time, professional auditing standards defined "reportable conditions" as "matters coming to the auditor's attention that, in his judgment, should be communicated to the audit committee because they represent significant deficiencies in the design or operation of internal control, which could adversely affect the organization's ability to initiate, record, process, and report financial data consistent with the assertions of management in the financial statements" (AU Section 325.02 [superseded]).

recommended that Foamex take the following specific actions to remedy these problems:

(1)   *make significant improvements in the control environment and reporting practices of Foamex's foreign operations;*

(2)   *conduct a comprehensive analysis of financial results on a quarterly basis;*

(3)   *improve inventory reporting; and*

(4)   *develop a comprehensive information technology strategy, including an enterprise-wide security program.*

During the 2000 audit of Foamex, PwC informed the company's audit committee on multiple occasions of reportable conditions similar to those included in the Report to Management issued in May 2000. After completing the 2000 audit, PwC resigned in June 2001. The following month, Foamex retained Deloitte & Touche as its independent audit firm.

Foamex's management informed the SEC in 2002 that the company was in the process of resolving the internal control problems previously identified by PwC. Nevertheless, in early 2003, during its 2002 audit, Deloitte identified five reportable conditions that it communicated to Foamex's audit committee.[3] These conditions involved the following areas of concern:

(1)   *oversight of financial reporting by international subsidiaries;*

(2)   *inventory procedures, processes, and systems;*

(3)   *integration of IT systems;*

(4)   *access and security for IT systems; and,*

(5)   *process for reviewing and approving journal entries.*

In January 2004, Foamex restated the financial statements included in its Form 10-Qs filed with the SEC for the first three quarterly reporting periods of 2003. These restatements were necessary because of a major glitch discovered in the processing of inventory transactions. After completing its 2003 audit of Foamex in March 2004, Deloitte notified the company's audit committee of four reportable conditions. Three of these items involved control issues identified in Deloitte's 2003 report to the audit committee. The fourth reportable condition concerned control weaknesses in Foamex's quarterly financial reporting system.

After receiving Deloitte's internal control report in March 2004, Foamex's audit committee dismissed Deloitte and retained KPMG as the company's new audit firm. Over the following few months, Foamex made several changes in its senior management. One of those changes involved appointing a former Ernst & Young partner to the company's board of directors and audit committee. Foamex's new management team also hired a "special consultant on internal accounting controls" to remedy the company's pervasive internal control problems.

Foamex's efforts in 2004 to improve its internal controls were "too little and too late" to satisfy the SEC. In 2005, Foamex became the first SEC registrant to be sanctioned by the federal agency solely for having inadequate internal controls. In the *Accounting and Auditing Enforcement Release* summarizing its investigation of Foamex, the SEC defended the decision to sanction the company despite its belated attempt to improve its internal controls.

The repeated observations of the auditors and Foamex's history of restating its interim financial reports show that Foamex did not devote the appropriate managerial effort

---

3. The SEC enforcement release for this case did not reveal whether Deloitte discovered reportable conditions in Foamex's internal controls during its 2001 audit.

and other resources to remediate its deficient internal controls, which were identified as reportable conditions in 1999.

The cease and desist order issued to Foamex by the SEC included a road map for the company to follow to improve its internal controls. During the 2005 audit, the SEC ordered Foamex to "cooperate fully" with KPMG's review and evaluation of the company's internal controls pursuant to Section 404 of the Sarbanes–Oxley Act of 2002. Following the 2005 audit, the SEC instructed KPMG to issue a "Section 404 Report" to Foamex's audit committee. That report would document any "significant deficiencies" in Foamex's internal controls. The audit committee would then forward the report to Foamex's special consultant on internal controls.

Within 90 days, the special consultant would issue a report to Foamex's audit committee and the SEC that identified specific recommendations for eliminating the internal control deficiencies. The SEC mandated that Foamex adopt those recommendations or propose alternative measures that would be equally effective. The special consultant was also instructed to issue quarterly reports to Foamex's audit committee and the SEC until all of the reported internal control deficiencies were eliminated.

The SEC's decision to sanction Foamex was interpreted as a "message"[4] being sent by the federal agency to public companies. The intended message was that the SEC would rigorously enforce the new internal control initiatives included in the Sarbanes–Oxley Act. Ironically, absent the SEC's specific directive that required KPMG to perform a Section 404 review and evaluation of Foamex's internal controls, the company would have been exempt from that requirement because it was a "non-accelerated filer."[5] Due to widespread concern that Section 404 audit and internal control remediation costs would be onerous for small public companies, the SEC had delayed the implementation of the principal Section 404 requirements for those registrants. In late 2010, Congress passed a law that permanently exempted non-accelerated filers from being required to obtain Section 404 reports on their internal controls.[6]

Questions

1. Who has the final responsibility for the integrity of an SEC registrant's internal controls: its audit committee, its management team, or its independent auditors? Explain.

2. Under the professional standards currently in effect, what responsibility do auditors have to identify internal control problems within their clients' accounting systems? To whom must auditors communicate such problems? In responding to these questions, indicate how auditors' responsibilities differ, if at all, between public and nonpublic clients.

3. Under what conditions is a public company allowed to dismiss its independent audit firm? Under what conditions is an independent audit firm allowed to resign as the auditor of a public company? What disclosures, if any, does the SEC mandate when a public company experiences a change in its independent auditors?

4. Should the SEC selectively prosecute companies, organizations, or individuals to encourage compliance with legal or professional standards? Defend your answer.

---

4. P. J. Martinek, "SEC Probe into Foamex Internal Controls Won't Be Last," *Compliance Week* (online), 12 April 2006.

5. Non-accelerated filers are generally SEC registrants that have a market capitalization of $75 million or less.

6. The *Wall Street Journal* reported in July 2013 that 5,549 public companies in the United States are exempt from obtaining Section 404 internal control reports. See, E. Chasan, "The Big Number," *Wall Street Journal* (online), 23 July 2013.

The Boeing Company

We say in this nation that we are looking for people with honesty integrity, drive and dedication, and then when we find such people, we take them out and whip them.

Anonymous whistleblower

In January 2007, Matthew Neumann and Nicholas Tides, two Boeing employees, transferred to the company's internal audit department. Neumann, who worked in Boeing's Seattle headquarters, and Tides, who was based in St. Louis, believed that the move would advance their careers with the large aerospace company.

Neumann and Tides were assigned to one of Boeing's two internal audit groups. Their 10-member audit team monitored Boeing's information technology (IT) controls within the company's financial reporting function.[1] The overall mission of their team was to assist company management in its effort to comply with the internal control mandates for public companies included in the Sarbanes–Oxley (SOX) Act of 2002. An important responsibility imposed on corporate executives by SOX is to annually report on the effectiveness of their company's financial reporting controls.

Boeing contracted with PricewaterhouseCoopers (PwC) to obtain the additional manpower needed to help Neumann and Tides' audit team accomplish its mission. Approximately 70 PwC contract auditors worked with the IT SOX internal audit team.

As mandated by SOX, Deloitte, Boeing's independent audit firm, also prepared an annual report on the effectiveness of the company's internal controls over financial reporting. The Deloitte auditors reviewed and relied on the work of Boeing's IT SOX audit team in completing that task each year.

IT Isn't Good

Neumann and Tides quickly found that their new work roles were tension-packed. The source of the tension was management's concern that Deloitte, which at the time was completing its 2006 audit of Boeing's financial statements, would report one or more "material weaknesses" in the company's IT financial reporting controls. Management realized that Boeing would face significant adverse consequences if such weaknesses were reported, including a likely drop in the company's stock price.

By early February 2007, Neumann and Tides had decided, independently of each other, that there were major problems in Boeing's IT financial reporting controls. The two internal auditors, again independently of each other, repeatedly voiced those concerns over the next few months. Collectively, Neumann and Tides notified their superiors of the apparent internal control weaknesses on more than two dozen occasions.

Neumann and Tides identified seven potential problems in Boeing's IT financial reporting controls. Their primary concerns, however, revolved around two of those issues. First, Neumann and Tides believed that the PwC contract auditors were being

---

1. According to Boeing, an IT control "is a policy or procedure implemented by a company to ensure the confidentiality and integrity of its IT functions, such as a procedure requiring the testing and approval of software before installation on a company computer."

given "managerial authority over Boeing employees,"[2] including the company's internal auditors. The SEC's rules for corporate audit committees expressly require that a company's internal auditors be controlled by its audit committee.

Second, and more importantly, Neumann and Tides questioned the overall integrity of Boeing's control environment that had been established by the company's top executives. In particular, they charged that those executives were intentionally undermining the annual SOX-mandated assessment of the company's financial reporting controls. Among specific allegations, the two internal auditors suggested that Boeing management was "potentially misleading the external auditors" by permitting company insiders to "change audit results," was "permitting other tampering with the official internal audit records," and had concealed "failed controls."[3]

Despite the concerns expressed by Neumann and Tides, Boeing management rated the company's internal controls over financial reporting as effective for the company's fiscal years ending 31 December 2006, and 2007. Likewise, for both years, Deloitte issued an unqualified opinion on Boeing's internal controls, meaning that the Deloitte auditors found no indication of one or more material weaknesses in those controls during either of those years.

Paper Tiger

During the spring of 2007, Andrea James, a reporter for the *Seattle Post-Intelligencer*, the city's oldest newspaper, began investigating unpublished reports that Boeing, easily Seattle's largest employer, had serious internal control problems. James contacted numerous Boeing employees, including Matthew Neumann and Nicholas Tides. Neither Neumann nor Tides responded to James' requests for interviews. The two men subsequently reported that, at the time, they had hoped to resolve their concerns regarding Boeing's control problems internally. Both of the internal auditors were also well aware of a Boeing policy that "required employees to refer inquiries of any kind from the news media to the Communications department and also prohibited the release of company information without prior review by that department."

James went to Neumann's home uninvited in May 2007 and asked him to discuss Boeing's internal controls and the company's compliance with SOX. Neumann agreed to speak with James. "[Neumann] described the pressure he felt to render positive audit results and detailed a recent meeting where he and other IT SOX auditors expressed concerns over the role of PricewaterhouseCoopers contractors in audits of Boeing's internal controls." A few days after interviewing Neumann, James e-mailed him an excerpt from the article that she intended to publish in the *Post-Intelligencer*. Neumann responded by noting that the excerpt "looked good." Along with his response to James, Neumann attached an e-mail that he and other IT SOX auditors had been sent by a superior. This e-mail reminded the auditors of Boeing's policy regarding the release of information to the news media.

In July 2007, a week or so prior to James' article being published, Nicholas Tides contacted her. Tides was prompted to contact James by what he believed was an undeserved negative performance evaluation that he had received for the second quarter of 2007. In his e-mail, Tides disclosed the various concerns that he had previously raised with his superiors regarding Boeing's IT-related control weaknesses.

---

2. The following legal opinion is the primary source for this case: *Tides and Neumann v. The Boeing Company*, U.S. Court of Appeals for the Ninth Circuit, 644 F.3d 809; 2011 App. LEXIS 8980. Unless indicated otherwise, the quotations in this case were taken from this source.

3. J. J. Tollefsen, "*Tides and Neumann v. The Boeing Company*, Petition for Writ of Certiorari filed with the U.S. Supreme Court," October 2011.

Tides also forwarded to James copies of various Boeing documents that were relevant to those weaknesses.

The *Post-Intelligencer* published the article coauthored by Andrea James regarding Boeing's internal controls, "Computer Security Faults Put Boeing at Risk,"[4] on 17 July 2007. James and her coauthor described how the company had failed to establish proper controls to protect its "computer systems against manipulation, theft and fraud" and referred to a "threatening company culture" that influenced the work of its internal auditors. In an internal Boeing e-mail that James had obtained, Boeing's chief financial officer (CFO) told certain subordinates that the performance of the company's internal controls was "unacceptable." James also reported that Boeing's external auditor, Deloitte, was aware that "many of Boeing's computer system controls were failing."

James' article revealed that Deloitte had identified a "significant deficiency" in Boeing's internal controls during each of the previous three years. That deficiency involved the company's failure to eliminate "database and software development security holes." This pervasive control weakness created some level of risk that Boeing would suffer significant asset losses due to fraud or theft and increased the likelihood that the company's financial statements would contain material errors. Because Deloitte had concluded that the control problem did not rise to the level of a material weakness, the firm was able to issue an unqualified opinion on Boeing's internal controls during each of those years.

A Boeing spokesperson interviewed by James insisted that the company was working toward remedying the persistent significant deficiency in internal controls identified by Deloitte. The spokesperson also insisted that the company's overall controls were "strong." To demonstrate the company's commitment to improving its internal controls, the spokesperson told James that in 2006 alone the company had spent $55 million in its efforts to comply with the SOX-mandated internal control initiatives.

Termination for Tattling

Prior to the publication of James' article, Boeing's management had come to suspect that one or more employees were communicating with journalists regarding alleged problems in the company's internal controls. That suspicion had caused company officials to initiate an investigation. During that investigation, management began monitoring the computers and e-mail communications of Neumann and Tides and apparently other employees as well.

In September 2007, members of the investigative team interviewed Neumann and Tides. During these separate interviews, both individuals admitted to speaking with James and providing her with company documents. After reviewing the evidence collected during the investigation, including Neumann and Tides' own admissions, an employee review board voted unanimously to terminate them. The following explanation, which accompanied the termination notice delivered to each of them, identified the specific company "PRO" [procedure] policies that they had violated.

> *It has been determined that you created an unacceptable liability for the Company. Specifically, you violated PRO-2227, Information Protection, by disclosing Boeing information[5] to non-Boeing persons without following appropriate procedures, obtaining necessary approvals and putting in place appropriate safeguards. In addition, you*

---

4. A. James and D. Lathrop, "Computer Security Faults Put Boeing at Risk," *Seattle Post-Intelligencer* (online), 17 July 2007.

5. Boeing's corporate policy statement PRO-2227 defined "Boeing information" as "all nonpublic information that is owned by Boeing." Under this corporate policy, "all Boeing information is presumed to have value and be proprietary, confidential, and/or trade secret information."

violated PRO-3439 by not referring inquiries from the news media to Communications, and by releasing information without approval in accordance with the requirements of the said PRO. Your actions are aggravated by the fact that the information had an adverse effect on the Company's reputation and its relations with its employees, customers, shareholders, suppliers and other important constituents, causing significant liability. The company deems your behavior in this incident as unacceptable and in violation of its expectations as defined in PRO-1909.

Fighting Back in the Courts

In late December 2007, three months after they were terminated, Neumann and Tides filed separate "whistleblower" complaints challenging their dismissals. These complaints were filed under SOX Section 806, "Protection for Employees of Publicly Traded Companies Who Provide Evidence of Fraud." In fact, at the time, several federal statutes in addition to SOX provided protection for whistleblowers that subsequently faced some type of retaliation by their employer or another entity. The most prominent of these statutes are the False Claims Act and the Whistleblower Protection Act that deal primarily with whistleblowing incidents involving the federal government or its agencies.

Following the Enron and WorldCom debacles in 2001 and 2002, Congress hurriedly passed the SOX statute in an attempt to strengthen the nation's financial reporting function and reduce the frequency of large-scale corporate frauds that were undermining the credibility of the capital markets. Among the centerpieces of this legislation were the SOX mandates to strengthen public companies' internal controls and to provide more transparency regarding those controls. This enhanced transparency was manifested principally by requiring corporate management teams and independent auditors to annually report on the effectiveness of public companies' financial reporting controls.

Not nearly as well publicized were the whistleblower mandates included in SOX. Section 301 of the statute requires audit committees of public companies to establish procedures for processing "complaints ... regarding accounting, internal accounting controls, or auditing matters." This section also mandates that public company audit committees establish procedures to provide for the "confidential, anonymous submission by employees ... of concerns regarding questionable accounting or auditing matters." In addition, Section 806 of the federal statute provides legal remedies for employees who are fired or otherwise punished after making whistleblower reports.

Two Strikes

In February 2010, a federal district court dismissed Neumann and Tides' whistleblower lawsuits against Boeing. Their attorney immediately appealed that decision to the U.S. Court of Appeals. In May 2011, the appellate court affirmed the lower court's ruling.

The appellate court ruled that the whistleblowing protections included in SOX Section 806 did not apply to the circumstances surrounding Neumann and Tides' dismissals. In particular, the court noted that Section 806 provides for legal remedies for corporate whistleblowers only when they are punished after communicating complaints or other adverse information to one or more of the following three parties: a federal regulatory or law enforcement agency, the U.S. Congress, or a "person with supervisory authority over the employee (or such other person working for the employer who has the authority to investigate, discover, or terminate misconduct)." Because Neumann and Tides had been fired by Boeing for communicating adverse information to a member of the news media, they were not entitled to legal remedies under SOX Section 806.

Neumann and Tides' attorney argued before the appellate court that disclosing Boeing's internal control problems to the news media was equivalent to reporting those problems to the U.S. Congress since one or more members of Congress no doubt became aware of those issues as a result of James' highly publicized article. The attorney also argued that because the overall purpose of the SOX statute is to protect investors and other third parties from self-interested corporate executives, the courts should interpret and apply the protections extended to corporate whistleblowers under the statute as liberally as possible.

The appellate justices seriously considered and analyzed the arguments made by Neumann and Tides' attorney. However, because of the lack of ambivalence in the SOX statute regarding the parties to whom corporate employees may communicate whistleblower complaints, the justices chose not to overturn the lower court's decision to dismiss the lawsuits of Neumann and Tides.

Next, the attorney of the two former Boeing employees filed a petition with the U.S. Supreme Court asking that body to review the decisions handed down by the district and appellate courts. In that petition, the attorney quoted Senator Patrick Leahy, a strong proponent of extending legal remedies for corporate whistleblowers. Senator Leahy contends that the "corporate code of silence" that is pervasive among large public companies damages the integrity of the nation's capital markets and that providing extensive legal remedies for corporate whistleblowers is an effective means to counter that code of silence.

> This 'corporate code of silence' not only hampers investigations, but also creates a climate where ongoing wrongdoing can occur with virtual impunity. The consequences of this corporate code of silence for investors in publicly traded companies, in particular, and the stock market, in general, are serious and adverse, and they must be remedied.[6]

EPILOGUE

In October 2011, the Supreme Court refused to review the prior rulings handed down in Neumann and Tides' whistleblower lawsuits, meaning that those rulings would stand. Several groups that advocate for enhanced transparency on the part of public corporations were dismayed by the Supreme Court's decision. A representative of the National Whistleblowers Center argued that the outcome of the Neumann–Tides case would have a "chilling effect"[7] on corporate whistleblowers in the future. Other critics of the Supreme Court's decision and the earlier rulings in the case pointed out that many large-scale frauds, including the Enron and Madoff Securities scandals, surfaced only after persistent journalists reported allegations communicated to them by corporate insiders or other parties.

Following the Supreme Court's refusal to review Neumann and Tides' case, the prominent business publication *The Economist* suggested that the whistleblowing protections included in the SOX statute are largely ineffective and need to be strengthened. According to that publication, of nearly 1,900 whistleblowing complaints filed under SOX by mid-2012, only 317 had been resolved in favor of the complainants.[8]

6. J. J. Tollefsen, "*Tides and Neumann v. The Boeing Company*, Petition for Writ of Certiorari."

7. National Whistleblowers Center, "9th Circuit Whistleblowers Barred from Talking to the Press," www.whistleblowers.org, 4 May 2011.

8. *The Economist*, "Sacked for Telling Tales," www.economist.com, 7 July 2011.

Similar to many, if not most, corporate whistleblowers, Neumann and Tides had difficulty obtaining jobs after they were dismissed by their employer. In May 2011, their attorney noted on his website that they "both are finally working again, but at significantly reduced salaries."[9]

When asked to comment on the Boeing whistleblowing incident following the dismissal of Neumann and Tides' lawsuit, Andrea James expressed regret that they were fired as a result of her newspaper article. "It is hard for me to talk about because I feel bad. And . . . there's nothing I can do."[10] James also revealed that her article was based upon "discussions with dozens of people"[11] and she was unsure why Neumann and Tides were singled out for punishment by Boeing. "That's always puzzled me. But it's clear that they [Boeing] made an example out of them."[12, 13]

Questions

1. The COSO internal control framework identifies five internal control components. Which of those components is most relevant to the procedures that SOX mandates public companies establish to enable, if not encourage, whistleblowing by corporate employees?

2. Explain the difference between a "significant deficiency" and "material weakness" in internal control. Provide an example of each.

3. Assume that the PwC contract auditors did, in fact, exert "managerial authority" over Boeing employees? What internal control problems or issues would that have posed for Boeing?

4. Would it have been unethical or otherwise inappropriate for Neumann and Tides to have directly communicated their concerns regarding Boeing's IT controls to the company's Deloitte auditors? Explain. Assuming that Neumann and Tides had done just that, how should the Deloitte auditors have responded?

5. Why do you believe that SOX does not provide legal remedies for corporate whistleblowers who are punished by their employers after communicating with members of the news media?

6. Was it ethical for Boeing to monitor the computers and e-mail of Neumann and Tides during the investigation to determine whether one or more employees were communicating with members of the news media? Defend your answer.

---

9. P. Murphy, "Whistleblowers and Sarbanes–Oxley Fallout," www.tollefsenlaw.com, 17 May 2011.

10. *Ibid.*

11. *Ibid.*

12. *Ibid.*

13. The Dodd–Frank Wall Street Reform and Consumer Protection Act was signed into law in July 2010 by President Barack Obama. That statute "allows the SEC to pay financial awards to whistleblowers who provide information that leads to a successful SEC enforcement action with more than $1 million in sanctions" (K. Tysiac, "Hot Tips: SEC Fields 3,000 Whistleblower Complaints in 12 months," www.journalofaccountancy.com, 15 November 2012).

Walmart de Mexico

Sam Walton was born on 29 March 1918, in Kingfisher, Oklahoma, a small town 50 miles northwest of Oklahoma City. Sam's father, a farmer, struggled to support his family during the Great Depression. The Walton family hopscotched around the country before finally settling in Missouri where Sam graduated from high school. After obtaining a degree in economics from the University of Missouri, Sam went to work as a management trainee with J.C. Penney Company at a monthly salary of $75. Following the outbreak of World War II, Sam enlisted in the U.S. Army and served until 1945.

Upon returning to civilian life, Sam Walton borrowed money from his father-in-law to purchase a small retail store in northern Arkansas. Walton purchased additional stores in Arkansas, Kansas, and Missouri over the following years. In 1962, Walton opened the first store branded as a "Wal-Mart" in Rogers, Arkansas, 10 miles from Bentonville, which would become the company's corporate headquarters. Walmart expanded its operations across the continental United States over the next three decades. In 1992, the year Sam Walton died, Walmart surpassed Sears to become the largest retailer in the United States.

By 2012, Walmart employed over two million people, making it the world's largest private employer. In that same year, four members of Sam Walton's family ranked among the top 10 of the *Forbes 400*, the 400 wealthiest individuals in the United States.[1] Those individuals, with a collective wealth of more than $100 billion, included his three surviving children and the widow of his son, John Walton, a former Green Beret who was awarded the Silver Star for heroism during the Vietnam War.

The Lowest Prices Anytime, Anywhere!

Walmart's incredible growth was due to the hypercompetitive business model developed by Sam Walton. The central tenet of Walton's business plan was the motto that he adopted for his company, "The Lowest Prices Anytime, Anywhere!" Walton reasoned that if he undercut the prices charged by his competitors, his company would generate sufficient sales volume to realize significant economies of scale. The most important of those economies of scale would be purchasing merchandise in bulk quantities at discounted wholesale prices that were not available to other retailers.

Walton's simple business plan worked to perfection as Walmart routinely dominated the geographical markets that it entered. The ultimate result of Walmart's alleged "predatory" business model was to drive large numbers of small retailers, including pharmacies, groceries, and general merchandise stores, out of business. In an op-ed piece written for the *New York Times*, Robert Reich, former Secretary of the U.S. Department of Labor, observed that Walmart "Turns main streets into ghost towns by sucking business away from small retailers."[2]

In the early 1990s, Walmart became an international company when it opened retail outlets in Mexico and Canada. After replicating its successful business model in

---

1. From 1982 through 1988, Sam Walton topped the *Forbes 400* as the richest individual in the United States.

2. R. Reich, "Don't Blame Wal-Mart," *New York Times* (online), 28 February 2005.

those countries, Walmart extended its operations outside of North America. Within two decades, approximately one-fourth of the company's sales were produced by its 6,000 retail stores in more than two dozen countries scattered around the globe.

To date, Mexico has easily been Walmart's most successful international venture. Walmart quickly seized control of the retail industry in that country by taking away large chunks of market share previously held by domestic retailers that had operated in the country for decades. By 2012, Walmart's Mexican subsidiary, Walmart de Mexico, was Mexico's largest retailer and that nation's largest private employer.

Bribery Allegations

In April 2012, an article published by the *New York Times*, "Vast Mexico Bribery Case Hushed Up by Wal-Mart After Top-Level Struggle," reported that Walmart had routinely bribed governmental officials to obtain building permits and other business licenses required by Mexican law. A former Walmart de Mexico officer testified that the bribes allowed the Mexican subsidiary "to build hundreds of new stores so fast that competitors would not have time to react."[3] The Pulitzer Prize–winning article in the *New York Times*, which was the culmination of an 18-month long investigation, insisted that the bribes violated the Foreign Corrupt Practices Act of 1977 (FCPA). The article also accused Walmart's senior management of concealing those bribes from U.S. law enforcement authorities.

Walmart's senior executives learned of the bribes being paid by their company's Mexican subsidiary in late 2005 and immediately launched an investigation. "Wal-Mart dispatched investigators to Mexico City, and within days they unearthed evidence of widespread bribery.... They also found documents showing that Wal-Mart de Mexico's top executives not only knew about the payments, but had taken steps to conceal them from Wal-Mart's headquarters in Bentonville, Ark."[4]

Following the discovery of the bribes, Walmart's senior executives disagreed on how to address the problem. The *New York Times* article reported that Walmart's management ultimately decided to resolve the matter quietly and internally. That goal was achieved by placing the Walmart de Mexico executive who had allegedly authorized the bribes in charge of the ongoing investigation of them. The investigation ended shortly thereafter. The subsequent internal report noted that "There is no clear evidence or clear indication of bribes paid to Mexican government authorities with the purpose of wrongfully securing any licenses or permits."[5]

The former FBI agent who served as Walmart's director of corporate investigations found the internal report inadequate. "The report was nonetheless accepted by Wal-Mart's leaders as the last word on the matter."[6] Walmart's senior executives informed the U.S. Department of Justice that their company may have violated the FCPA only after they had learned of the ongoing investigation by the *New York Times*.

The author of the *New York Times* article charged that Walmart's "relentless pursuit of growth" had compromised its commitment to the "highest moral and ethical standards."[7] A follow-up article in the *New York Times* in December 2012, "How Wal-Mart Used Payoffs to Get Its Way in Mexico," described the methods used by

---

3. D. Barstow, "Vast Mexico Bribery Case Hushed Up by Wal-Mart After Top-Level Struggle," *New York Times* (online), 21 April 2012.

4. *Ibid.*

5. *Ibid.*

6. *Ibid.*

7. *Ibid.*

Walmart de Mexico to gain an unfair advantage over its competitors. That article also dismissed the suggestion that Walmart was a "victim" of a corrupt business culture in Mexico that obligated companies to bribe governmental officials.

> The Times' investigation reveals that Wal-Mart de Mexico was not the reluctant victim of a corrupt culture that insisted on bribes as the cost of doing business. Nor did it pay bribes merely to speed up routine approvals. Rather, Wal-Mart de Mexico was an aggressive and creative corrupter, offering large payoffs to get what the law otherwise prohibited. It used bribes to subvert democratic governance—public votes, open debates, transparent procedures. It used bribes to circumvent regulatory safeguards that protect Mexican citizens from unsafe construction. It used bribes to outflank rivals.[8]

After reporting the potential FCPA violations to the U.S. Department of Justice in December 2011, Walmart instructed its audit committee to use "all resources necessary" to "aggressively" investigate the company's "FCPA compliance" not only in Mexico but worldwide.[9] The audit committee hired KPMG and a major law firm to assist in the forensic investigation.[10] Walmart's board also created a network of international "FCPA compliance directors" that would report to a Bentonville-based "Global FCPA Compliance Officer." In an April 2012 press release that addressed the bribery allegations made by the New York Times, Walmart officials declared that, "We will not tolerate noncompliance with the FCPA anywhere or at any level of the company."[11]

Walmart included an interim report of the ongoing FCPA investigation in its Form 10-K for the fiscal year ending 31 January 2013. Company officials reported it was "probable" Walmart would "incur a loss from these matters" but could not "reasonably estimate" the amount of that loss. Nevertheless, they expected that the loss would not have a "material adverse effect on our business." They also disclosed that the company had already spent $157 million on the FCPA investigation. Finally, the interim report revealed that additional "potential FCPA violations" had been uncovered within the company's operations in Brazil, China, and India.

There was widespread speculation in the business press concerning the ultimate outcome of the joint SEC and U.S. Department of Justice investigation of Walmart's alleged FCPA violations. Much of that speculation focused on the magnitude of the monetary fines the federal agencies might levy on Walmart. Many observers believed that those fines could surpass the $450 million in FCPA-related fines imposed on the German engineering and electronics firm Siemens AG in 2008.

The FCPA: From Watergate to Walmartgate

Walmart's widely publicized FCPA problems refocused attention on the origins and nature of that federal statute. The FCPA was a by-product of the scandal-ridden Watergate era of the 1970s. During the Watergate investigations, the Office of the Special Prosecutor uncovered large bribes, kickbacks, and other payments made by U.S. corporations to officials of foreign governments to initiate or maintain business relationships. Widespread public disapproval compelled Congress to pass the FCPA,

---

8. D. Barstow and A. Xanic von Bertrab, "How Wal-Mart Used Payoffs to Get Its Way in Mexico," *New York Times* (online), 17 December 2012.

9. Walmart.com, News release issued 24 April 2012.

10. Ernst & Young was Walmart's audit firm at the time.

11. Walmart.com, News release issued 24 April 2012.

which criminalizes most such payments.[12] The FCPA also requires U.S. companies to maintain internal control systems that provide reasonable assurance of discovering improper foreign payments. In a 1997 *Accounting and Auditing Enforcement Release*, the Securities and Exchange Commission (SEC) highlighted the importance and need for the accounting and internal control requirements embedded in the FCPA.

> *The accounting provisions [of the FCPA] were enacted by Congress along with the antibribery provisions because Congress concluded that almost all bribery of foreign officials by American companies was covered up in the corporations' books and that the requirement for accurate records and adequate internal controls would deter bribery.*[13]

In the two decades following the passage of the FCPA, the SEC seldom charged U.S. companies with violating its provisions. In fact, in 1997 when the SEC filed FCPA-related charges against Triton Energy Ltd., an international oil and gas exploration company, more than 10 years had elapsed since the federal agency's prior FCPA case. At the time, the SEC conceded that the filing of the FCPA charges against Triton Energy was intended to send a "message" to U.S. companies that "it's not O.K. to pay bribes as long as you don't get caught."[14] At the same time, an SEC spokesperson predicted that his agency would be filing considerably more FCPA charges in the future.[15]

The SEC was true to its word. While investigating the suspected FCPA violations by Walmart in 2012, the federal agency reported that it was also investigating potential violations of that federal statute by more than 70 other public companies. Those companies included such prominent firms as Alcoa, Goldman Sachs, Hewlett-Packard, and Pfizer. The World Bank has reinforced the need for the SEC and other global law enforcement agencies to rein in corporate bribery since it estimates that more than $1 trillion in bribes are paid annually to government officials worldwide.[16]

The FCPA is not without its critics. Many corporate executives have complained that the federal statute places U.S. multinational companies at a significant competitive disadvantage to multinational firms based in countries that have do not have a comparable law. Those same executives also find the recent "overzealousness" in prosecuting alleged FCPA violators inappropriate. "We are seeing companies getting scooped up in aggressive enforcement actions and investigations. A culture of overzealousness has grabbed the Justice Department. The last time I checked, we were not living in a police state."[17] In response to that complaint, a representative of the U.S. Department of Justice observed, "This is not the time for the United States to be

---

12. The FCPA was initially unclear regarding whether or not so-called "facilitating payments" qualified as bribes and thus were illegal under that federal statute. Generally, bribes are significant amounts paid to governmental officials, while facilitating or "grease" payments are modest or nominal payments made to lower-ranking governmental officials to expedite or "facilitate" an already authorized or consummated transaction. In 1988, the FCPA was amended to address that issue. As amended, facilitating payments made to encourage "routine governmental action" are not covered by the FCPA.

13. Securities and Exchange Commission, *Accounting and Auditing Enforcement Release No. 889*, 27 February 1997.

14. L. Eaton, "Triton Energy Settles Indonesia Bribery Case for $300,000," *New York Times*, 28 February 1997, D2.

15. *Securities Regulation and Law Report*, "SEC Official Predicts More FCPA Cases in Near Future," Vol. 29, No. 18 (2 May 1997), 607.

16. L. Wayne, "Hits, and Misses, in a War on Bribery," *New York Times* (online), 10 March 2012.

17. *Ibid.*

condoning corruption. We are a world leader and we want to do everything to make sure that business is less corrupt, not more."[18]

To date, the FCPA has not had a significant impact on the auditors of SEC registrants. An audit firm has been named in only one FCPA complaint filed by the SEC. In that case, a representative of KPMG's Indonesian affiliate was charged with paying a bribe to a governmental official to reduce the tax bill of its client. The KPMG affiliate settled the charge by agreeing to a cease and desist order but was not fined.[19] As the FCPA complaint against Walmart unfolded, a reporter for the *Reuters* international news service noted that it was unlikely that Ernst & Young, Walmart's longtime auditor, would become a target of that investigation.[20]

In fact, the FCPA has created a new revenue stream for the major accounting firms that serve as the auditors of most SEC registrants. For example, Deloitte's website lists "Foreign Corrupt Practices Act Consulting" as an ancillary service that it provides to public companies.

> *Our Foreign Corrupt Practices Act (FCPA) Consulting practice helps organizations navigate FCPA risk and respond to potential violations. Utilizing the network of Deloitte member firms and their affiliates including their forensic resources in the United States, Canada, Europe, Russia, Africa, Latin America and Asia, we have worked on a variety of FCPA engagements including investigations, acquisition due diligence, and compliance program implementation and assessments in over fifty countries for some of the world's leading companies.*[21]

Questions

1. Identify control activities that Walmart could have implemented for Walmart de Mexico and its other foreign subsidiaries to minimize the likelihood of illegal payments to government officials. Would these control activities have been cost-effective?

2. What responsibility, if any, does an accountant of a public company have when he or she discovers that the client has violated a law? How does the accountant's position on the company's employment hierarchy affect that responsibility, if at all? What responsibility does an auditor of a public company have if he or she discovers illegal acts by the client? Does the auditor's position on his or her firm's employment hierarchy affect this responsibility?

3. Does an audit firm of an SEC registrant have a responsibility to apply audit procedures intended to determine whether the client has complied with the FCPA? Defend your answer.

4. If the citizens of certain foreign countries believe that the payment of bribes is an acceptable business practice, is it appropriate for U.S. companies to challenge that belief when doing business in those countries? Defend your answer.

---

18. *Ibid.*

19. Securities and Exchange Commission, *Litigation Release No. 17127*, 12 September 2001.

20. N. Byrnes, "Wal-Mart Auditor Unlikely to Suffer in Bribery Case," *Reuters.com*, 4 May 2012.

21. Deloitte, "Foreign Corrupt Practices Act Consulting," www.deloitte.com.

SECTION 4

ETHICAL RESPONSIBILITIES OF ACCOUNTANTS

4

CASE 4.1

Creve Couer Pizza, Inc.

Imagine this scenario. A few years after graduating from the University of Miami, New Mexico State University, or Ohio Wesleyan University with an accounting degree, you find yourself working as an audit senior with an international accounting firm. Your best friend, Rick, whom you have known since kindergarten, is a special agent with the Internal Revenue Service (IRS). Over lunch one day, Rick mentions the IRS's informant program.

"You know, Jess, you could pick up a few hundred dollars here and there working as a controlled informant for us. In fact, if you would feed us information regarding one or two of those large corporate clients of yours, you could make a bundle."

"That's funny, Rick. Real funny. Me, a double agent, spying on my clients for the IRS? Have you ever heard of the confidentiality rule?"

Sound far-fetched? Not really. Since 1939, the IRS has operated an informant program. Most individuals who participate in this program provide information on a one-time basis; however, the IRS also retains hundreds of "controlled informants" who work in tandem with one or more IRS special agents on a continuing basis. Controlled informants provide the IRS with incriminating evidence regarding individuals and businesses suspected of cheating on their taxes. In the early 1990s, the IRS revealed that more than 40 of these controlled informants were CPAs.

Now consider this scenario. You, the audit senior, are again having lunch with your friend Rick, the IRS special agent. Rick knows that the IRS is investigating you for large deductions taken in recent years on your federal income tax returns for a questionable tax shelter scheme. The additional tax assessments and fines you face significantly exceed your net worth. Your legal costs alone will be thousands of dollars. To date, you have been successful in concealing the IRS investigation from your spouse, other family members, and your employer, but that will not be possible much longer.

"Jess, I know this investigation is really worrying you. But I can get you out of this whole mess. I talked to my supervisor. She and three other agents are working on a case involving one of your audit clients. I can't tell you which one right now. If you agree to work with them as a controlled informant and provide them with information that you can easily get your hands on, they will close the case on you. You will be off the hook. No questions. No fines or additional taxes. Case closed ... permanently."

"Rick, come on, I can't do that. What if my firm finds out? I'd lose my job. I would probably lose my certificate."

"Yeah, but face these facts. If the IRS proves its case against you, you are going to lose your job and your certificate ... and probably a whole lot more. Maybe even your marriage. Think about it, Jess. Realistically, the agency is looking at a maximum recovery of $50,000 from you. But if you cooperate with my supervisor, she can probably squeeze several million out of your client."

"You're sure they would let me off ... free and clear?"

"Yes. Free and clear. Come on, Jess, we need you. More important, you need us. Plus, think of it this way. You made one mistake by becoming involved in that phony tax shelter scam. But your client has been ripping off the government, big time, for years. You would be doing a public service by turning in those crooks."

Returning to reality, consider the case of James Checksfield. In 1981, Checksfield, a Missouri CPA, became a controlled informant for the IRS. The IRS special agent who recruited Checksfield had been his close friend for several years and knew that Checksfield was under investigation by the IRS. Reportedly, Checksfield owed back taxes of nearly $30,000 because of his failure to file federal income tax returns from 1974 through 1977.

At the same time the IRS recruited Checksfield, the federal agency was also investigating a Missouri-based company, Creve Couer Pizza, Inc. The IRS believed that the owner of this chain of pizza restaurants was "skimming receipts" from his business—that is, failing to report on his federal income tax returns the total sales revenue of his eight restaurants. Checksfield had served as Creve Couer's CPA for several years, although both the IRS and Checksfield denied that he was recruited specifically to provide information regarding that company.

From 1982 through 1985, Checksfield funneled information to the IRS regarding Creve Couer Pizza. Based upon this information, federal prosecutors filed a six-count criminal indictment against the owner of that business in 1989. This indictment charged the owner with underreporting his taxable income by several hundred thousand dollars. The owner faced fines of nearly $1 million and a prison term of up to 24 years if convicted of the charges. Meanwhile, the IRS dropped its case against Checksfield. Both the IRS and Checksfield maintained that there was no connection between the decision to drop the case against him and his decision to provide the IRS with information regarding Creve Couer Pizza.

Following the indictment filed against the owner of Creve Couer Pizza, the owner's attorneys subpoenaed the information that the IRS had used to build its case against him. As a result, the owner discovered the role played by his longtime friend and accountant in the IRS investigation. Quite naturally, the owner was very upset. "What my accountant did to me was very mean and devious. He sat here in my home with me and my family. He was like a member of the family. On the other hand, he was working against me."[1] Contributing to the owner's anger was the fact that he had paid Checksfield more than $50,000 in fees for accounting and taxation services during the time the CPA was working undercover for the IRS.

The print and electronic media reported the case of the "singing CPA" nationwide, prompting extensive criticism of the IRS. The case also caused many clients of CPAs to doubt whether they could trust their accountants to protect the confidentiality of sensitive financial information. When questioned concerning the matter, the IRS expressed no remorse for using Checksfield to gather incriminating evidence regarding the owner of Creve Couer Pizza. An IRS representative also rejected the contention that communications between accountants and their clients should be "privileged" under federal law similar to the communications between attorneys and their clients. In fact, that representative insisted that accountants had an ethical responsibility to turn over to the IRS any incriminating information that suggests a client has violated federal tax laws.[2]

The accounting profession was appalled by the Checksfield case and tried to minimize the damage it had done to the public's trust in CPAs. In particular, the profession condemned the actions of the IRS and attempted to reassure the public that individual CPAs did not share the IRS's views regarding matters involving client confidentiality.[3]

1. "Accountant Spies on Client for IRS," *Kansas City Star*, 18 March 1992, 2.

2. "The Case of the Singing CPA," *Newsweek*, 17 July 1989, 41.

3. "IRS Oversteps with CPA Stoolies," *Accounting Today*, 6 January 1992, 22.

EPILOGUE

In August 1990, the Missouri State Board of Accountancy revoked James Checksfield's CPA license for violating a state law that prohibits CPAs from disclosing confidential client information without the client's permission. In November 1991, the U.S. Department of Justice suddenly announced that it was dropping the tax evasion charges against the owner of Creve Couer Pizza, although pretrial arguments had already been presented for the case. The Justice Department had little to say regarding its decision. Legal experts speculated that federal prosecutors dropped the charges because the judge hearing the case was expected to disallow the evidence that the IRS had collected with the assistance of Checksfield.

Despite the negative publicity produced by the Creve Couer case, the IRS continues to use accountants both in public practice and private industry as informants. In the late 1990s, *Forbes* magazine reported a case in which a disgruntled controller of a retail electronics chain got even with his boss.[4] Shortly before leaving the firm, the controller copied accounting and tax records documenting a large-scale tax fraud perpetrated by the chain's owner. Thanks to this information, the IRS collected a nearly $7 million fine from the owner and sent him to jail for 10 months. The former controller received a significant but undisclosed "finder's fee" from the IRS for his "cooperation."

In 2007, the IRS Whistleblower Office was established. This office administers a provision of a 2006 federal law that guarantees individuals who report significant tax deficiencies owed by other parties a minimum payment equal to 15 percent of the delinquent taxes collected. Among the largest payments made to date under this program was a $104 million distribution made in 2012 to a former employee of UBS, a large Swiss banking company.[5]

Questions

1. Do CPAs who provide accounting, taxation, and related services to small businesses have a responsibility to serve as the "moral conscience" of those clients? Explain.

2. In a 1984 opinion handed down by the U.S. Supreme Court, Chief Justice Warren Burger noted that "the independent auditor assumes a public responsibility transcending any employment relationship with the client." If this is true, do auditors have a moral or professional responsibility to turn in clients who are cheating on their taxes or violating other laws?

3. Assume that you were Jess in the second hypothetical scenario presented in this case. How would you respond to your friend's suggestion that you become a controlled informant for the IRS? Identify the parties that would be affected by your decision and the obligations you would have to each.

4. J. Novack, "Boomerang," *Forbes*, 7 July 1997, 42–43.

5. L. Saunders and R. Sidel, "Whistleblower Gets $104 Million," *Wall Street Journal* (online), 11 September 2012.

F&C International, Inc.

Alex Fries emigrated to the United States from Germany in the early nineteenth century.[1] The excitement and opportunity promised by the western frontier fascinated thousands of new Americans, including the young German, who followed his dreams and the Ohio River west to Cincinnati. A chemist by training, Fries soon found a job in the booming distillery industry of southern Ohio and northern Kentucky. His background suited him well for an important need of distilleries, namely, developing flavors to make their products more palatable for the public. Alex Fries eventually established his own flavor company. Thanks largely to Fries, Cincinnati became the home of the small but important flavor industry in the United States. By the end of the twentieth century, the flavor industry's annual revenues approached $5 billion.

Alex Fries' success in the flavor industry became a family affair. Two of his grandsons created their own flavor company, Fries & Fries, in the early 1900s. Several decades later, another descendant of Alex Fries, Jon Fries, served as the president and CEO of F&C International, Inc., a flavor company whose common stock traded on the NASDAQ stock exchange. F&C International, also based in Cincinnati, reigned for a time during the 1980s as Ohio's fastest-growing corporation. Sadly, the legacy of the Fries family in the flavor industry came to a distasteful end in the early 1990s.

The Fraud

Jon Fries orchestrated a large-scale financial fraud that led to the downfall of F&C International. At least 10 other F&C executives actively participated in the scam or allowed it to continue unchecked due to their inaction. The methods used by Fries and his cohorts were not unique or even innovative.

Fries realized that the most effective strategy for embellishing his company's periodic operating results was to inflate revenues and overstate period-ending inventories. Throughout the early 1990s, F&C systematically overstated sales revenues by backdating valid sales transactions, shipping customers product they had not ordered, and recording bogus sales transactions. To overstate inventory, F&C personnel filled barrels with water and then labeled those barrels as containing high-concentrate flavor products. The company also neglected to write off defective goods and included waste products from manufacturing processes in inventory. Company officials used F&C's misleading financial statements to sell equity securities and to obtain significant bank financing.

As F&C's fraud progressed, Jon Fries and his top subordinates struggled to develop appropriate sales and inventory management strategies since the company's accounting records were unreliable. To help remedy this problem, F&C created an imaginary warehouse, Warehouse Q.

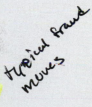

typical fraud moves

---

1. The facts in this case were taken from several SEC enforcement releases and a series of articles that appeared in the *Cincinnati Enquirer*. The key parties in this case neither admitted nor denied the facts reported by the SEC. Those parties include Jon Fries, Catherine Sprauer, Fletcher Anderson, and Craig Schuster.

Warehouse Q became the accounting repository for product returned by customers for being below specification, unusable or nonexistent items, and items that could not be found in the actual warehouses.[2]

Another baffling problem that faced Fries and his confederates was concealing the company's fraudulent activities from F&C's independent auditors. The executives continually plotted to divert their auditors' attention from suspicious transactions and circumstances uncovered during the annual audits. Subversive measures taken by the executives included creating false documents, mislabeling inventory counted by the auditors, and undercutting subordinates' attempts to expose the fraud.

The size and complexity of F&C's fraud eventually caused the scheme to unravel. Allegations that the company's financial statements contained material irregularities triggered an investigation by the Securities and Exchange Commission (SEC). The investigation revealed that F&C had overstated its cumulative pretax earnings during the early 1990s by approximately $8 million. The company understated its pretax net loss for fiscal 1992 alone by nearly 140 percent, or $3.8 million.

The Division Controller

Catherine Sprauer accepted an accounting position with F&C International in July 1992, shortly after the 30 June close of the company's 1992 fiscal year. Sprauer, a CPA, drafted the Management's Discussion and Analysis (MD&A) section of F&C's 1992 Form 10-K registration statement. In October 1992, the 28-year-old Sprauer became the controller of F&C's Flavor Division. Following that promotion, Sprauer continued to help prepare the MD&A sections of F&C's periodic financial reports submitted to the SEC.

In early January 1993, an F&C employee told Sprauer that he saw company employees filling inventory barrels with water in the final few days of June 1992. This individual also advised Sprauer that he had documentation linking two F&C executives to that incident, which was apparently intended to overstate the company's year-end inventory for fiscal 1992. According to the SEC, Sprauer abruptly ended the conversation with this employee and did not discuss his allegations with anyone.

Later that same day, another F&C employee approached Sprauer and confessed that he was involved in the episode recounted to her earlier in the day. This individual told Sprauer that he had acted under the direct instructions of Jon Fries. The employee then attempted to hand Sprauer a listing of inventory items affected by the fraud. Sprauer refused to accept the list. The persistent employee placed the list in Sprauer's correspondence file. The document detailed approximately $350,000 of nonexistent inventory in F&C's accounting records. Sprauer reportedly never showed the list of bogus inventory to her superiors, to other F&C accountants, or to the company's independent auditors. However, she subsequently warned F&C's chief operating officer (COO), Fletcher Anderson, that the company had "significant inventory problems."

The Chief Operating Officer

Fletcher Anderson became the COO of F&C International in September 1992 and joined the company's board of directors a few days later. On 23 March 1993, Anderson succeeded Jon Fries as F&C's president and CEO. During the fall of 1992, Anderson stumbled across several suspicious transactions in F&C's accounting records.

---

2. Securities and Exchange Commission, *Accounting and Auditing Enforcement Release No. 605*, 28 September 1994. All subsequent quotations are taken from this source.

In late September 1992, Anderson discovered sales shipments made before the given customers had placed purchase orders with F&C. He also learned that other sales shipments had been delivered to F&C warehouses rather than to customers. Finally, in early October 1992, Anderson uncovered a forged bill of lading for a customer shipment. The bill of lading had been altered to change the reported month of shipment from October to September. Each of these errors inflated F&C's reported earnings for the first quarter of fiscal 1993, which ended 30 September 1992.

More direct evidence that F&C's financial data were being systematically distorted came to Anderson's attention during the second quarter of 1993. In November, a subordinate told Anderson that some of the company's inventory of flavor concentrate was simply water labeled as concentrate. The following month, Anderson learned of Warehouse Q and that at least $1.5 million of the inventory "stored" in that warehouse could not be located or was defective.

Catherine Sprauer submitted her resignation to Fletcher Anderson in late January 1993. Among the reasons Sprauer gave for her resignation were serious doubts regarding the reliability of the company's inventory records. Anderson insisted that Sprauer not tell him why she believed those records were unreliable because he wanted to avoid testifying regarding her concerns in any subsequent litigation.

In February 1993, shortly before Anderson replaced Jon Fries as F&C's top executive, an F&C cost accountant warned him that the company had an inventory problem "in the magnitude of $3–4 million." Anderson later told the SEC that although the cost accountant had access to F&C's inventory records and its actual inventory, he believed the accountant was overstating the severity of the company's inventory problem.

The Chief Financial Officer

Craig Schuster served as the chief financial officer (CFO) of F&C International during the early 1990s. As F&C's CFO, Schuster oversaw the preparation of and signed the company's registration statements filed with the SEC, including the company's Form 10-K reports for fiscal 1991 and 1992.

Throughout 1992, Schuster became aware of various problems in F&C's accounting records, most notably the existence of Warehouse Q. In March 1992, Schuster learned that his subordinates could not locate many items listed in F&C's perpetual inventory records. A few months later, Schuster discovered that customer shipments were being backdated in an apparent attempt to recognize sales revenue prematurely. In late 1992, Schuster determined that approximately $1 million of F&C's work-in-process inventory was classified as finished goods.

On 17 December 1992, a frustrated Schuster prepared and forwarded to Fletcher Anderson a 23-page list of $1.5 million of inventory allegedly stored in Warehouse Q. The memo indicated that the inventory could not be located or was defective. The SEC's enforcement releases focusing on the F&C fraud did not reveal how or whether Anderson responded to Schuster's memo.

Because he supervised the preparation of F&C's financial reports filed with the SEC, Schuster knew that those reports did not comment on the company's inventory problems. On 1 January 1993, Craig Schuster resigned as the CFO of F&C International. The final F&C registration statement Schuster signed was the company's Form 10-Q for the first quarter of fiscal 1993, which ended 30 September 1993.

The Rest of the Story

In a 28 September 1994, enforcement release, the SEC criticized Catherine Sprauer, Fletcher Anderson, and Craig Schuster for failing to ensure that F&C's financial reports "filed with the Commission and disseminated to the investing public were accurate." The federal agency also chastised the three individuals for not disclosing in F&C's financial reports "significant accounting problems of which they were aware." Finally, the SEC scolded Anderson and Schuster for not establishing adequate internal controls to provide for the proper recognition of revenue and the proper valuation of inventory. In an agreement reached with the SEC to settle the allegations pending against them, the three former F&C executives pledged to "permanently cease and desist" from committing or causing violations of federal securities laws.

A second enforcement release issued by the SEC on 28 September 1994, contained a series of allegations directed at Jon Fries and seven other senior F&C executives. The SEC charged that these executives were primarily responsible for F&C's fraudulent earnings scheme. To settle these charges, each executive pledged not to violate federal securities laws in the future. The settlement agreement permanently banned Jon Fries from serving as an officer or director of a public company. Several of the individuals agreed to forfeit proceeds received from earlier sales of F&C securities. Fries relinquished more than $2 million he had realized from the sale of F&C common stock. Finally, the SEC imposed civil fines on four of the executives that ranged from $11,500 to $20,000.

F&C International filed for bankruptcy in April 1993 shortly after the fraud became public. The following year, a competitor purchased F&C's remaining assets. In March 1995, Jon Fries began serving a 15-month sentence in federal prison for his role in the F&C fraud.

Questions

1. Jon Fries (CEO), Fletcher Anderson (COO), Craig Schuster (CFO), and Catherine Sprauer (division controller) were the four central figures in this case. Identify the key responsibilities associated with the professional roles these individuals occupied. Briefly describe the type and extent of interaction each of these individuals likely had with F&C's independent auditors.

2. Using the scale shown below, evaluate the conduct of the four key individuals discussed in this case. Be prepared to defend your answers.

−100 . . . . 0 100
Highly   Highly
Unethical   Ethical

3. For a moment, step into the shoes of Catherine Sprauer. What would you have done during and following each of the confrontations she had with the two employees who insisted that F&C executives were involved in a fraudulent scheme to misrepresent the company's financial statements?

4. Craig Schuster resigned as F&C's CFO on 1 January 1993. Apparently, Schuster did not reveal to any third parties the concerns he had regarding F&C's accounting records and previous financial statements. In your opinion, did Schuster have a responsibility to inform someone of those concerns following his resignation? Defend your answer.

5. Assume that you, rather than Fletcher Anderson, were F&C's COO in December 1992. What would you have done upon receiving the list of Warehouse Q inventory from Craig Schuster?

Suzette Washington, Accounting Major

Suzette Washington financed her college education by working as an inventory clerk for Bertolini's, a clothing store chain located in the southeastern United States.[1] Bertolini's caters primarily to fashion-conscious young men and women. The company's stores carry a wide range of clothing, including casual wear, business suits, and accessories. The Bertolini's store for which Suzette worked is located a few blocks from the campus of the large state university that she attended. Except for management personnel, most of Bertolini's employees are college students. Suzette's best friend and roommate, Paula Kaye, worked for Bertolini's as a sales clerk. Paula majored in marketing, while Suzette was an accounting major.

During Suzette's senior year in college, Bertolini's began experiencing abnormally high inventory shrinkage in the store's three departments that stocked men's apparel. Suzette's supervisor, an assistant store manager, confided in her that he believed one or more of the sales clerks were stealing merchandise. Over lunch one day in the student union, Suzette casually mentioned the inventory problem to Paula. Paula quickly changed the subject by asking Suzette about her plans for the weekend.

"Paula, rewind for just a second. Do you know something that I don't?"

"Huh? What do you mean?"

"Missing inventory … shrinkage … theft?"

After a few awkward moments, Paula stopped eating and looked squarely into her friend's eyes. "Suzette, I don't know if it's true, but I've heard a rumor that Alex and Matt are stealing a few things each week. Polo shirts, silk ties, jeans. Occasionally, they take something expensive, like a hand-knit sweater or sports jacket."

"How are they doing it?"

"I've heard—and don't repeat any of this now—I've heard that a couple of times per week, Alex stashes one or two items at the bottom of the trash container beneath the number two cash register. Then Matt, you know he empties the trash every night in the dumpster out in the alley, takes the items out and puts them in his car."

"Paula, we can't let them get away with this. We have to tell someone."

"No 'we' don't. Remember, this is just a rumor. I don't know that it's true. If you tell a manager, there will be questions. And more questions. Maybe the police will be brought in. You know that eventually someone's going to find out who told. And then … slashed tires … phone calls in the middle of the night."

"So, don't get involved? Don't do anything? Just let those guys keep stealing?"

"Suze, you work in inventory. You know the markup they put on those clothes. They expect to lose a few things here and there to employees."

"Maybe the markup wouldn't be so high if theft wasn't such a problem."

Now, there was no doubt in Paula's mind that Suzette was going to report the alleged theft scheme to management. "Two months, Suze. Two months till we graduate. Can you wait till then to spill the beans? Then we can move out of state before our cars are spray-painted."

---

1. This case was developed from information provided by a former college student who is now a CPA. The names, location, and certain other background facts have been changed.

One week following Suzette and Paula's conversation, a Bertolini's store manager received an anonymous typed message that revealed the two-person theft ring rumored to be operating within the store. Bertolini's immediately retained a private detective. Over a four-week period, the detective documented $500 of merchandise thefts by Alex and Matt. After Bertolini's notified the police, the local district attorney filed criminal charges against the two young men. A plea bargain agreement arranged by their attorneys resulted in suspended prison sentences for Alex and Matt. The terms of that agreement included making restitution to Bertolini's, completing several hundred hours of community service, and a lengthy period of probation.

Questions

1. What would you do if you found yourself in a situation similar to that faced by Suzette in this case?

2. Do you believe that it was appropriate for Suzette to report the alleged theft ring to a store manager? Would it have been unethical for Suzette *not* to report the rumored theft ring?

3. Accounting majors are preparing to enter a profession recognized as having one of the strongest and most rigorously enforced ethical codes. Given this fact, do you believe that accounting majors have a greater responsibility than other business majors to behave ethically?

4. Briefly discuss internal control activities that might have prevented the theft losses suffered by Bertolini's.

Freescale Semiconductor, Inc.

Who will guard the guardians?

Juvenal

During the summer of 2006, a syndicate of investors led by The Blackstone Group, one of Wall Street's largest private equity investment firms, initiated a secret plan to acquire Freescale Semiconductor. Based in Austin, Texas, Freescale is among the world's largest producers of semiconductors and for decades was a subsidiary of Motorola, Inc., the large electronics company. In July 2004, Motorola spun off Freescale in one of that year's largest initial public offerings.

Blackstone retained Ernst & Young (E&Y) to serve as a consultant for the planned buyout of Freescale. Among other services, Blackstone wanted E&Y to review Freescale's human resource functions and to make recommendations on how to streamline and strengthen those functions following the acquisition. James Gansman, a partner in E&Y's Transaction Advisory Services (TAS) division, was responsible for overseeing that facet of the engagement.

Similar to the other Big Four accounting firms, E&Y became involved in the investment banking industry during the 1990s. In fact, by the late 1990s, the small fraternity of accounting firms could boast of having two of the largest investment banking practices in the world, at least in terms of the annual number of consulting engagements involving merger and acquisition (M&A) deals. In 1998, KPMG consulted on 430 M&A transactions, exactly one more than the number of such engagements that year for PricewaterhouseCoopers (PwC). Despite those impressive numbers, KPMG and PwC had not established themselves as dominant firms in the investment banking industry.

In 1998, the total dollar volume of the M&A engagements on which KPMG and PwC consulted was $1.65 billion and $1.24 billion, respectively. Those numbers paled in comparison to the annual dollar value of M&A transactions for industry giants such as Goldman Sachs, which was involved in M&A deals valued collectively at nearly $400 billion in 1998. At the time, Goldman Sachs, Lehman Brothers, Morgan Stanley, and the other major investment banking firms consulted exclusively on "mega" or multibillion-dollar M&A engagements. By contrast, the "low end" of the M&A market—in which the Big Four firms competed—typically involved transactions measured in a few million dollars.

E&Y's involvement in the huge Freescale M&A deal was a major coup for the Big Four firm. When the transaction was consummated in December 2006, the price paid for the company by the investment syndicate led by The Blackstone Group approached $18 billion. That price tag made it the largest private takeover of a technology company to that point in time as well as one of the 10 largest corporate takeovers in U.S. history.

Not surprisingly, Blackstone demanded strict confidentiality from E&Y and the other financial services firms that it retained to be involved in the planned acquisition of Freescale. James Gansman, for example, was told that Blackstone wanted the transaction to be "super confidential" and was instructed in an internal E&Y e-mail to "not breathe the name of the target [Freescale] outside of the [engagement] team."[1]

---

1. U.S. Department of Justice, "Former Ernst & Young Partner and Investment Banker Charged in Insider Trading Scheme," 29 May 2008 (http://newyork.fbi.gov).

During June and July 2006, while he was working on the Freescale engagement, Gansman passed "inside information about the pending transaction"[2] to Donna Murdoch, a close friend who worked in the investment banking industry. An FBI investigation revealed that Gansman and Murdoch "communicated over 400 times via telephone and text messages"[3] in the weeks leading up to the 11 September 2006, announcement that the Blackstone investment syndicate intended to acquire Freescale. In that time span, Murdoch purchased hundreds of Freescale stock options, which she cashed in on 11–12 September 2006, realizing a windfall profit of $158,000.

The FBI also determined that between May 2006 and December 2007 Gansman provided Murdoch with information regarding six other M&A transactions on which E&Y consulted. In total, Murdoch used that inside information to earn nearly $350,000 in the stock market. Murdoch gave that information to three other individuals, including her father, who also used it to produce significant stock market profits.

Published reports indicate that Murdoch became involved in the insider trading scheme to help make the large monthly payments on a $1.45 million subprime mortgage on her home. The funds she initially used to "play the market" were provided to her by one of the individuals to whom she disclosed the inside information given to her by James Gansman. In addition, Gansman at one point loaned her $25,000.

The Securities and Exchange Commission (SEC) uses sophisticated software programs to detect suspicious trading activity in securities listed on stock exchanges. In early 2007, the SEC placed Murdoch on its "watch list" of individuals potentially involved in insider trading and began scrutinizing her stock market transactions. Information collected by the SEC resulted in criminal charges being filed against Murdoch. In December 2008, she pleaded guilty to 15 counts of securities fraud and two related charges.

In May 2009, Murdoch served as one of the prosecution's principal witnesses against Gansman in a criminal trial held in a New York federal court. During the trial, Gansman testified that he had been unaware that Murdoch was acting on the information he had supplied her. Defense counsel also pointed out that Gansman had not personally profited from any of the inside information that he had been privy to during his tenure with E&Y. Nevertheless, the federal jury convicted Gansman of six counts of securities fraud. A federal judge later sentenced him to a prison term of one year and one day.

EPILOGUE

Personnel at all levels of the Big Four accounting firms routinely gain access to highly confidential inside information, information that can be used to gain an unfair advantage over other stock market investors. Unfortunately for the accounting profession, James Gansman is not the only partner or employee of one of those firms who has been implicated recently in a major insider trading scandal.

In January 2008, the SEC charged two former PwC employees with using confidential client information to earn large profits in the stock market. One of the individuals was on PwC's audit staff, while the other was assigned to PwC's Transaction Services group, the PwC division comparable to E&Y's TAS department.[4] The individual in the Transactions Services group accessed the confidential information

2. *Ibid.*

3. *Ibid.*

4. A. Rappeport, "Ex-PwC Pals Were Inside Traders, SEC Says," *CFO.com*, 15 January 2009.

while working on several M&A consulting engagements for PwC. He then provided that information to his friend on PwC's audit staff, who used it to purchase securities of companies that were acquisition targets. This latter individual's name was recognized by a PwC audit partner when he was reviewing a list of securities transactions for a client that another company was attempting to acquire. The audit partner informed the SEC, which then filed insider trading charges against the two friends.

In November 2010, the U.S. Department of Justice filed insider trading charges against a former Deloitte tax partner and his wife, who had also been employed by that firm.[5] The couple allegedly obtained confidential information regarding seven Deloitte clients that were involved in M&A transactions. According to the SEC, the couple communicated that information to family members living in Europe who then engaged in securities trades involving the companies that were parties to those transactions. The SEC reported that more than $20 million in illicit stock market gains were earned as a result of the scheme.[6] The case was ultimately resolved with the charges being dropped against the tax partner when his wife admitted that she was solely responsible for passing the inside information to relatives. The partner's wife obtained the information by eavesdropping on her husband's telephone conversations. She was subsequently sentenced to 11 months in prison by a federal judge.

In the 38 years that he spent with Deloitte, Thomas Flanagan worked his way up the employment hierarchy of the Big Four accounting firm from staff accountant to vice chairman. In October 2008, Deloitte announced that it was suing Flanagan for trading in the securities of multiple Deloitte audit clients for which he had served as an "advisory"[7] partner.

Deloitte claims that Flanagan held and traded securities of his own clients for the past three years. The firm alleges he bought one of his client's stock one week before it announced an acquisition of a public company. He is also accused of violating the firm's independence and conflict-of-interest policies and hiding his personal securities holdings from Deloitte. In his role as an advisory partner, he attended the audit committee meetings of seven of the twelve clients affected.[8]

The Deloitte clients involved in Flanagan's insider trading scheme included Allstate, Berkshire Hathaway, Best Buy, Sears, and Walgreens.

In August 2010, the SEC announced that it had settled the insider trading charges that it had filed against Flanagan. The terms of the settlement required Flanagan to pay more than $1 million in fines and penalties. Flanagan consented to the settlement without admitting or denying the SEC's allegations. Flanagan's son, who had allegedly made securities trades based upon inside information given to him by his father, reached a similar settlement with the SEC and paid fines and penalties of approximately $120,000. In October 2012, a federal judge sentenced Thomas Flanagan to 21 months in federal prison after he pleaded guilty to insider trading. During the sentencing hearing, Flanagan remarked that his conduct "was stupid, it was arrogant and it was wrong."[9] In addition to the 21-month prison sentence and the SEC fines, Flanagan will reportedly forfeit more than $14 million in pension benefits and

5. P. Lattman, "Couple Accused of Trading Insider Tips," *New York Times* (online), 30 November 2010.

6. E. Stevens, "Pacific Heights Socialites Charged in Elaborate Insider-Trading Scheme," *Bay Citizen* (online), 9 January 2011.

7. A Deloitte "advisory" partner is typically a senior audit partner who has significant industry expertise relevant to a given client. In addition to consulting with members of an audit engagement team on important issues arising during an audit, an advisory partner typically reviews the audit workpapers before the engagement is completed.

8. S. Johnson, "Deloitte Insider Case Sparked Doubts About Audits," *CFO.com*, 10 November 2008.

9. B. Carton, "21-Month Sentence Just One of the Consequences of Former Deloitte Partner's Insider Trading" *www.complianceweek.com*, 30 October 2012.

deferred compensation as a result of settling the civil lawsuit filed against him by Deloitte.

To date, the most publicized case of insider trading by an independent auditor involved Scott London, a longtime and high-profile audit partner with KPMG. In addition to supervising the audit practice of KPMG's large Los Angeles office, London served on Los Angeles' Chamber of Commerce and chaired the Los Angeles Sports Council. In June 2013, London pleaded guilty to insider trading, "admitting he revealed secret information about his company's clients to a friend who used the tips to make more than $1 million from resulting trades."[10] In exchange for the stock tips, which took place over several years, London received gifts and cash payments from his friend.

In a statement issued through his attorney, London indicated that "What I have done was wrong and against everything that I had believed in. I spent nearly 30 years at KPMG and I dedicated my entire life to that firm." During an appearance on CNBC, London's attorney reported that his client had realized that he was violating federal laws when he provided the inside information to his friend. "But he just can't understand why he did it, and it's hard to understand why he did it. It makes no sense.... It made no sense from a dollar-and-cents point of view; it made no sense in terms of his ethics."[11] The attorney added that London's personal and professional lives had been ruined by the scandal. "He's 50 years old, he's lost his career, he'll probably lose his license, he's been disgraced.... It's a very grim reminder of the consequences for anyone who wants to leak insider information."[12] London has yet to be sentenced for his criminal conduct.

Questions

1. Identify the specific circumstances under which auditors are allowed to provide confidential client information to third parties.

2. Suppose that you and a close friend are employed by the same accounting firm. You are assigned to the firm's audit staff, while your friend is a consultant who works on M&A engagements. What would you do under the following circumstances: (1) your friend discloses to you highly confidential "market-moving" information regarding a soon-to-be announced merger; (2) your friend not only discloses such information to you but also informs you that he or she plans to use it to make a "quick" profit in the stock market? In your responses, comment on your ethical responsibilities in each scenario.

3. E&Y was providing a consulting service to The Blackstone Group in connection with its planned acquisition of Freescale Semiconductor. Explain how a CPA's professional responsibilities differ between consulting engagements and audit engagements.

---

10. S. Pfeifer, "Former KPMG Partner Scott London Pleads Guilty to Insider Trading," *Los Angeles Times* (online), 1 July 2013.

11. P. Lattman, "Ex-KPMG Partner Is Charged in Insider Case," *New York Times* (online), 11 April 2013.

12. *Ibid.*

Wiley Jackson, Accounting Major

Wiley Jackson spent three months as an audit intern with a local practice office of a major accounting firm while he was earning an undergraduate accounting degree at the University of Wisconsin–Milwaukee.[1] Wiley thoroughly enjoyed the three-month internship. He made several friends and, more importantly, gained valuable work experience and insight into the nature and work environment of independent auditing. On the final day of his internship, Wiley had an exit interview with the office managing partner (OMP). The OMP told Wiley that he had impressed his superiors and coworkers. Wiley's performance reviews indicated that he had strong technical and interpersonal skills and always conducted himself in a professional and ethical manner. At the end of the exit interview, the OMP offered Wiley a full-time position with the firm once he completed his master's degree in accounting at UWM. Wiley was thrilled by the offer and accepted it immediately.

While working on his graduate degree, Wiley received a packet of documents from his future employer that he was to complete and return. The packet contained standard insurance forms, 401-K elections, a W-4 form, a personal investments worksheet for independence-compliance purposes, and a "Statement of Arrests and Convictions" form. Wiley recalled having completed an earlier version of the latter document before beginning his internship. Among the questions included in this form was the following:

Have you ever been convicted of a misdemeanor (excluding minor traffic violations) or a felony, or driving while intoxicated in this or any other state, or are criminal charges currently pending against you?

The form required a full explanation if this question was answered "Yes." Wiley had previously responded "No" to this question because, at the time, he had a "clean" record, except for a few parking tickets and one speeding violation. But now, as he sat at his desk staring at the form, he was not sure how to respond to the question.

After completing his internship, Wiley had been invited to a graduation party at an off-campus location. Although he was not a "party animal," Wiley had decided to accept the invitation since it would likely be his final opportunity to see many of his friends who were graduating from UWM. When he arrived at the site of the party, Wiley was surprised by the large number of people there. In fact, because the older, two-story home could not accommodate all the partygoers, several dozen of them were congregated in the front yard and on the residential street on which the house was located.

As he made his way through the boisterous crowd, Wiley suddenly came face to face with Sally Jones. Sally, a UWM alumna, had been the audit senior assigned to Wiley's largest client during his internship. While Wiley was talking to Sally, an acquaintance thrust a cold beer into his hand and slapped him on the shoulder. "No talking business here, Dude. It's party time!" As luck would have it, just a few minutes later, the party was "busted" by the local police. Before Wiley realized exactly what

---

1. This case was written by Brian Daugherty, associate professor at the University of Wisconsin–Milwaukee. The facts of this case were developed from an actual series of events. Certain background information has been changed to conceal the identities of the individuals involved in the case.

was happening, a policeman approached him and asked for his I.D. As he handed over his driver's license, Wiley, who was three days short of his 21st birthday, realized that he was in trouble. Moments later, the stone-faced policeman began writing out a minor-in-possession citation. The citation ordered Wiley to appear before a local judge the following month.

Wiley was distraught and had a difficult time sleeping that night. The next morning, he called an attorney and told him what had happened. The attorney informed Wiley that he had dealt with many similar situations involving college students and that Wiley should not be "stressed out" by the incident. For first-time offenders, like Wiley, the attorney had always been successful in persuading a judge to approve "deferred adjudication." As long as Wiley stayed out of trouble over the following two years, the minor-in-possession charge would be expunged from his record, "just like it never happened," according to the attorney.

Questions

1. Place yourself in Wiley's position. How would you respond to the "Arrests and Convictions" question? Before responding, identify the decision alternatives available to you.

2. Suppose that Wiley does not disclose the citation he received. A few weeks after going to work for his new employer, Wiley is called into the OMP's office. The OMP tells Wiley that he recently learned of the minor-in-possession citation that Wiley had been given. The OMP then hands Wiley a copy of the Arrest and Convictions form that he completed after receiving the job offer from the firm. How should the OMP deal with this matter? How, if at all, should Wiley be disciplined? Defend your answer.

3. Assume that Sally Jones was the individual who told the OMP that Wiley had been given a police citation at the graduation party. Do you believe Sally had a moral or ethical responsibility to inform the OMP of that matter? Why or why not?

Arvel Smart, Accounting Major

Arvel Ray Smart was born in Lebanon, Missouri, and grew up in the small town of Bolivar, 40 miles west of Lebanon in southeastern Missouri.[1] Arvel's mother and father graduated from the University of Missouri with accounting degrees in the mid-1970s. The Smarts spent three years working on the tax staff of a Big Eight practice office in Kansas City before deciding to establish their own accounting firm in Bolivar. Arvel helped out in his parents' office during high school, especially when they were facing tax deadlines. He enjoyed the work, which is why he decided to major in accounting when he enrolled at the University of Missouri following graduation from high school. Arvel realized that he would most likely have the opportunity to take over his parents' accounting firm when they retired. His only sibling, an older sister, was a performing arts major at Washington University in St. Louis and had no interest in becoming involved in the family business.

During his junior year at Mizzou, Arvel was admitted into the five-year program in the School of Accountancy. Arvel would receive Bachelor of Science and Master of Accountancy degrees when he completed the 150-hour program. After completing his junior year, Arvel accepted an internship with a Big Four practice office in Kansas City. Because he wanted to gain a better understanding of auditing, Arvel chose to intern on the audit staff of that office. Arvel was surprised by the number of interesting assignments he was given that summer. In fact, by the end of the summer he was reconsidering the decision he had made earlier to choose the tax track of Mizzou's five-year accounting program.

On the final day of Arvel's internship, the office managing partner met with him and offered him an entry-level auditing position. Arvel thanked the partner for the job offer and told him that he would seriously consider accepting it. He explained to the partner that he had not made a final decision about whether to focus on auditing or taxation early in his career. The partner was very understanding and told Arvel that he had plenty of time to make up his mind and then added that the job offer would remain open for 12 months, until the end of the following summer.

Arvel enrolled in the undergraduate auditing course during the spring semester of his fourth year in college. He enjoyed the course so much that he made up his mind to begin his career as an auditor and to accept the job offer from the firm with which he had interned the previous summer. He planned to delay accepting that offer, however, until the end of the summer. Arvel's girlfriend, who was also an accounting major at Mizzou, had accepted an offer for a summer internship with a Big Four practice office in St. Louis. Arvel was hoping to spend the summer in St. Louis, so he had interviewed earlier in the year with two regional accounting firms based in that city. Both of the firms had offered him an internship.

During the final week of the spring semester of his fourth year, Arvel accepted an internship offer from one of the two St. Louis–based accounting firms. Arvel realized that both regional and national accounting firms use internships as a tool to recruit

---

1. This case is based on factual circumstances involving a recent accounting graduate. Key facts, including the individual's name and relevant locations, have been changed to obscure his or her identity.

permanent employees and that they typically offer internships to students who they believe have an interest in eventually accepting a permanent position with them. That realization caused Arvel to experience some degree of guilt when he called and accepted the internship with the St. Louis firm. He quickly cleared his guilty conscience by convincing himself that there was some remote chance he would change his mind and accept a job with the St. Louis accounting firm. In fact, in Arvel's mind, that firm had a responsibility to prove to him that it offered more opportunities than the Big Four accounting firm from which he had already received a job offer.

Questions

1. Before interviewing with the two St. Louis accounting firms, did Arvel have an obligation to inform them that he had an outstanding job offer from a Big Four practice office in Kansas City? Why or why not?

2. Did Arvel Smart behave unethically by accepting the internship with the St. Louis accounting firm when he intended to accept the outstanding job offer from the Big Four accounting firm at the completion of that internship? Defend your answer.

David Quinn, Tax Accountant

We have all had *that* friend, an individual who attaches himself or herself to us without our encouragement—or approval, for that matter.[1] For Debbie Woodruff, *that* friend was David Quinn. Debbie met David in the very first college accounting class that either of them took at the large public university they attended. Shortly before the instructor entered the room, David had rushed in and taken the seat to Debbie's left. Moments later, an out-of-breath David had leaned over and asked Debbie, "Is this Accounting 201?" That question was the beginning of a relationship that would last for decades.

Debbie had little trouble grasping the revenue recognition rule, accrual accounting, straight-line depreciation, and the other fundamental concepts and topics in the introductory financial accounting course. David, on the other hand, struggled to earn a "B" in the course. Debbie never questioned David's intelligence. The problem was that David simply had too many outside interests—campus politics, his social fraternity, and weekend parties—to devote sufficient time to studying for the rigorous departmental exams in ACCT 201.

Before each exam, David would ask Debbie if they could study together. Debbie was not particularly fond of David, but she agreed to tutor him while she prepared for each exam because explaining an accounting concept or principle to someone else made the given item "gel" in her own mind. During two of these tutoring sessions, David asked Debbie for a date. The second time, Debbie told him that she did not mind studying together but that their "chemistry" made dating out of the question. David's outspoken and opinionated manner was the principal source of the chemistry problem between the two accounting majors. On most subjects—politics and economics, in particular—David had an opinion, an expert opinion, which he was more than willing to share with anyone who would listen. Debbie was much more reserved and preferred to spend her time focusing on her studies rather than debating whatever happened to be the front-page issue of the day.

Over the remainder of their college careers, Debbie and David sat side by side in most of their accounting courses and several other business courses, as well. Eventually, Debbie came to accept David's brash personality and considered him a friend—just not a close friend. Debbie maintained a near-perfect 3.9 GPA in her accounting courses, while David finished with a 3.2 GPA in his accounting major. During her final year of college, Debbie accepted an audit staff position with a nearby office of a Big Eight accounting firm. As fate would have it, David accepted a job on the tax staff of that same office.

Debbie wasn't thrilled by the fact that she and David would be working for the same firm. But she expected that they would seldom see each other since she would be working primarily at client locations, while David would likely be "stuck" in the office completing tax returns and doing tax research. Debbie was right. During their first year in public accounting, she saw David only on the rare occasions when she was in the office, which was typically during the wrap-up phase of an audit to which she was assigned.

---

1. The key facts of this case were provided by a former public accountant who is now an accounting professor. The names of all parties and locations have been changed.

Each time she was in the office, David would ask Debbie to go to lunch with him. Debbie always accepted. She didn't like to admit it, but the lunches served a useful purpose, namely, catching up on all the office scuttlebutt. David seemingly made it his business to know everyone else's business. He would joyfully tell Debbie which tax manager had not received a recommendation for promotion, which audit senior was interviewing for a position on a client's accounting staff, and which intra-office relationship was not "working out."

One Friday in early April, Debbie and David met for lunch to celebrate the end of her second busy season. Debbie was in the office tying up loose ends on the soon-to-be-completed audit of her largest client. She was looking forward to the lunch because she hadn't spoken to David since the office Christmas party almost four months earlier.

On their way to a nearby restaurant, David told Debbie that three of his friends on the tax staff of another Big Eight accounting firm would be meeting them for lunch. Debbie realized that the presence of those individuals would likely divert David's attention and deprive her of the latest news from the office grapevine. So, she resigned herself to having a boring lunch. She could not have been more wrong.

During lunch, the four tax professionals swapped war stories regarding the latest returns on which they had worked. Debbie found the topic of the conversation inappropriate. In her mind, it was best to never discuss professional engagements, audit or otherwise, over lunch in a public setting. You just never knew who might be eavesdropping at an adjoining table. Debbie became particularly uncomfortable when David began discussing the tax return of a wealthy local businessman who had previously served several terms on the city council.

"Yeah, you wouldn't believe the investments this guy has," David said to the friend on his left. "The guy is loaded. And I mean ... loaded!" Debbie cringed. Anyone within 20 feet could have heard David's emphatic pronouncement. She attempted to change the subject of the conversation, but David refused to yield the floor.

"No, wait, Debbie, I gotta tell these guys about the latest racket this dude is running." Debbie cringed once more. "You wouldn't believe what he wants us to do. He wants to write off the cost of his daughter's wedding as an entertainment expense. And, you know what? I think we are going to let him do it!"

Debbie couldn't take it anymore. "David, you shouldn't be talking about this at lunch. You don't know who is listening."

"Come on, Debbie. No one's listening."

"David. I'm serious. This is inappropriate."

"What?" David was obviously surprised that his normally meek friend was challenging him. Over the five years that he had known Debbie, she had never behaved in this manner. He was not only surprised but also somewhat miffed that Debbie was running the risk of embarrassing him in front of three fellow tax professionals. "Look around us, Debbie. These people aren't listening to us. Besides, they are all strangers."

"David, that's the point. These people are strangers. And how do you know that they aren't listening? Isn't it possible that one of them might call up your client and tell him what they heard?"

David leaned back in his chair and shook his head. "Oh yeah, I'm sure Grandma over there wrote down every word I just said."

Debbie was flabbergasted at her friend's flippant attitude toward what she considered a very important topic. "David, does the phrase 'client confidentiality' mean anything to you? Surely you tripped across it when studying for the CPA exam?"

"Oh, so you are going to bring up the CPA exam? I guess you *are* trying to embarrass me in front of my friends. Just because you passed that stupid thing the first time and I am still working on it doesn't make you an expert on ethics issues."

"David. You know that's not what I meant," Debbie responded indignantly. "Even if 'Grandma' isn't listening, you are talking about sensitive issues regarding a tax client with three guys from a competing office."

"Oh, I see. My buddies here are going back to their office to report me to the state board, right?" David was no longer miffed; he was angry. "Now, you've gone too far, Debbie. My friends would never do anything to get me into trouble." He then added in a sarcastic tone, "If anyone 'reports me,' it will be you, Miss Self-Righteous."

Debbie reached into her purse and counted out the money for her part of the bill. She then laid the cash on the table in front of her and, without speaking to David or his friends, left the restaurant.

David and Debbie did not speak again until their office's annual Fourth of July golf tournament. To his credit, David approached Debbie and said that he hoped they could put their unpleasant encounter behind them.

"I'm sorry it happened. Why don't we just forget it, Debbie? We've been friends for a long time. There's no reason we can't get over this."

Debbie stepped forward and gave David a light hug and told him that they could be friends once more. Despite the nice overture by David, in the future Debbie made every effort to avoid him when she was working in the office.

EPILOGUE

Debbie sat waiting in the college placement office to meet the managing partner of the practice office where she had worked as a staff accountant and senior auditor. After almost five years in that office, Debbie had decided that public accounting was not for her. Instead, she had decided to pursue a Ph.D.—with the eventual career objective of becoming an accounting professor. Debbie subsequently spent five years earning her doctoral degree, including a stressful 18 months fretting over her dissertation. Ten years later, after accumulating an impressive portfolio of publications, she returned to her alma mater to accept a tenured position in its accounting department. After 15 years at her alma mater, Debbie was a full professor and just a few years away from retirement.

Each fall semester, representatives of the major accounting firms came to Debbie's campus to interview the latest crop of soon-to-be accounting graduates. Today was her former employer's opportunity to attempt to impress her students. Debbie realized that she had a responsibility to interact with the recruiters who came to campus—but she always dreaded meeting with the recruiters from her former employer. She knew that throughout lunch David Quinn, her old friend who was now the managing partner of the office in which she had worked, would tell story after story of their college and coworker days, stories that she had heard repeatedly, stories that became more embellished each year.

In Debbie's mind, the annual lunch with David and his subordinates was a small price to pay to help her students land a job with her former employer. Besides, this year, she had a course to teach immediately after lunch, so she had an excuse to leave early. As she sat waiting for David, she suddenly realized that her course that afternoon was in the same classroom where she had met him for the first time more than 30 years earlier.

Questions

1. Explain the meaning of the phrase "client confidentiality" in the context of a CPA's ethical responsibilities. In your opinion, did David Quinn violate the accounting profession's client confidentiality rule?

2. Assume the role of Debbie Woodruff. How would you have handled the situation that arose in the restaurant?

3. Did Debbie have a responsibility to report David's behavior to a superior in her practice office or to anyone else? Why or why not? Did Debbie have a responsibility to determine whether her firm's tax department was providing appropriate professional advice regarding the deductibility of the entertainment expenses being claimed by David's client?

Dell, Inc.

*Accuracy and completeness are the touchstones of public company
disclosures under the federal securities laws.*

Robert Khuzami,
Director, SEC Division of Enforcement

Like most high school graduates, Michael Dell had a sense of anticipation, if not
exhilaration, when he left home to begin his college career. Because Dell planned
to become a doctor, like his father, he declared premed as his major when he
enrolled in the University of Texas in the fall of 1983. Over the next few months,
Dell's interest in college waned as he began spending most of his time and energy
on a hobby that he had pursued in high school, namely, tinkering with computers.
By the end of his first semester at UT, Dell's dorm room had become a workshop
in which he and a few friends tore apart, reconfigured, and then reassembled personal computers (PCs).

In the spring of 1984, Dell decided to go into business for himself. By the end
of the spring semester, Dell's small business was producing more than $10,000 in
revenues each month from the sale of PCs and PC-related products. The success
of his business convinced him to drop out of college and create Dell Computer
Corporation. Less than a decade later, Michael Dell, at age 27, became the youngest chief executive officer (CEO) of a Fortune 500 company. Dell's company,
which had been renamed Dell, Inc., surpassed Compaq in 2001 as the world's
largest manufacturer of PCs. By 2012, Dell's personal worth was estimated at
nearly $15 billion, which placed him 22nd on the Forbes 400 list of the wealthiest
Americans.

The critical feature of Dell, Inc.'s business model that allowed it to grow so rapidly
was the "Dell Direct" strategy of selling custom-designed PCs. The company's sales
force took purchase orders over the phone or the Internet and then transmitted those
orders to a production facility that assembled the PCs and shipped them in a matter
of days. Unlike competitors, Dell spent only modest amounts on research and development. Instead, Dell focused its operations on delivering state-of-the-art computer
technology developed by other companies at the lowest cost possible by emphasiz-
ing operating efficiencies throughout its supply chain.

Increasing competition that caused profit margins to narrow dramatically on PC
sales began undermining Dell's business model during the late 1990s. In 2002, Dell
faced the unhappy prospect of reporting disappointing earnings to its investors. At
that point, Intel Corporation, which provided the microprocessors for Dell's PCs,
stepped into the breach and offered Dell "exclusivity payments" that would wipe
out its earnings shortfall. Intel made these payments in exchange for a commitment
from Dell that it would not purchase microprocessors from other suppliers, including
Intel's principal competitor, Advanced Micro Devices, Inc. (AMD). Because AMD was
developing microprocessors that were reportedly superior to those of Intel, Intel's
management had become increasingly concerned that Dell would choose AMD as
its primary supplier of microprocessors.

Over the next several years, Dell executives often asked Intel for additional exclusivity payments when it appeared that their company would fall short of its consensus Wall Street earnings forecast for a given quarter. According to the Securities

and Exchange Commission (SEC), Dell management was "quite open with Intel"[1] about the reason it was requesting those payments. Officials of Intel and Dell used the tongue-in-cheek acronym MOAP (mother of all programs) to refer to their mutually beneficial arrangement that resulted in Intel paying Dell more than $4 billion between fiscal 2002 and fiscal 2007.

The exclusivity payments from Intel allowed Dell to meet or surpass its consensus earnings forecasts for 20 consecutive quarterly reporting periods. For fiscal 2003, Intel's exclusivity payments accounted for 10 percent of Dell's reported operating earnings. That figure rose to 38 percent for fiscal 2006 and to 76 percent for the first quarter of fiscal 2007. Dell's impressive earnings trend produced sizable stock market gains for the company's executives. During the time frame that Intel was making exclusivity payments to Dell, Michael Dell earned more than $450 million in compensation, most of which came in the form of gains on stock options granted to him by the company's board.[2]

Dell's management failed to disclose the exclusivity payments and their impact on the company's reported earnings in its periodic earnings news releases and registration statements filed with the SEC. For accounting and financial reporting purposes, Dell netted those payments against its operating expenses without disclosing the payments separately. Instead of disclosing that the exclusivity payments were responsible for the company consistently achieving or surpassing its consensus earnings forecasts, company executives attributed Dell's remarkable earnings record to its "ultra-efficient supply chain and direct-sales strategy."[3] In the company's 2005 annual report, for example, Michael Dell boasted of the company's "best-ever operating results" and alluded to the company's superior business model: "Dell's exceptional performance again demonstrated the ... superb execution of a better way of doing business.... Our business is a model for customer focus, growth, and profitability."

When Dell announced that it would purchase microprocessors from Intel and AMD beginning in the second quarter of 2007, Intel slashed the exclusivity payments, which caused Dell's earnings to drop sharply. Instead of disclosing the true cause of the earnings decline, Dell attributed the decline to evolving competitive issues within its industry. Over the next two years, Dell's stock price drifted downward. An SEC investigation eventually revealed the exclusivity payments made by Intel to Dell and the undisclosed impact those payments had on the company's reported earnings from 2002 through early 2007.

The SEC investigation also revealed that Dell had used so-called "cookie jar reserves" to "smooth" its earnings from 2002 through 2005. Company officials intentionally overstated period-ending reserves for expenses such as warranty-related costs on the products it sold and then "withdrew" those reserves to "cover shortfalls in operating results" for subsequent periods.[4] Dell ultimately issued restated financial statements to properly reflect its operating results for the periods that had been affected by the improper accounting for the Intel exclusivity payments and period-ending reserves.

1. E. Wyatt, "Dell to Pay $100 Million Settlement," *New York Times* (online), 22 July 2010.

2. E. Hess, "Stark Lessons from the Dell Fraud Case," *Forbes.com*, 13 October 2010.

3. A. Jones, "'A Bad Way to Run a Railroad': Dell Pays Big to Settle Fraud Charges," *WSJ.com*, 23 July 2010.

4. Securities and Exchange Commission, *SEC Charges Dell and Senior Executives with Disclosure and Accounting Fraud*, www.sec.gov, 22 July 2010.

In July 2010, the SEC revealed that it had charged Dell and several of its top executives, including Michael Dell, with routinely misleading the investing public by issuing misleading financial statements.

> Dell manipulated its accounting over an extended period to project financial results that the company wished it had achieved, but could not. Dell was only able to meet Wall Street targets consistently during this period by breaking the rules.[5]

Dell agreed to pay a $100 million fine to settle the charges filed against it by the SEC. Several Dell officials also agreed to pay significant fines. Michael Dell paid a $4 million fine for his alleged role in the earnings manipulation scheme, while the company's former chief financial officer paid $3 million. In settling the case and agreeing to the fines, each of the parties, including the company as a whole and Michael Dell, stipulated that they neither "admitted nor denied" those charges.

Revelations of Dell's brazen earnings management schemes angered a wide range of parties and made many critics question how pervasive such schemes are among large public companies. One business professor suggested that their root cause is the pressure on public companies to consistently report impressive quarterly earnings.

> The Dell case illustrates the perverse short-term view prevalent on Wall Street that dictates that growth must occur continuously, smoothly, and linearly every quarter.... Too often, the maniacal focus on creating ever-increasing quarterly earnings drives bad corporate behavior, as it apparently did at Dell. That behavior produces non-authentic earnings that obscure what is really happening in a business. Short-termism can result in a range of corporate and financial games that may enrich management at the expense of market integrity and efficient investor capital allocation.[6]

EPILOGUE

In 2007, a group of Dell, Inc.'s stockholders filed a class-action lawsuit against Michael Dell, other Dell executives, Intel Corporation, and Dell's audit firm PricewaterhouseCoopers (PwC), which had served as Dell's auditor since 1986. The stockholders alleged that the defendants were responsible for the large stock market losses they had suffered as a result of Dell's earnings management schemes.

The class-action lawsuit charged PwC with turning a "blind eye" to the "improper accounting" of Dell and with violating a wide range of "fundamental concepts of GAAS."[7] These alleged violations included failing to maintain a proper attitude of independence during the Dell audits, failing to properly plan those audits, and failing to issue the appropriate audit opinions on Dell's periodic financial statements. In October 2008, a federal judge dismissed the lawsuit after ruling that the plaintiffs' allegations of scienter on the part of the defendants was "too vague."[8]

In February 2013, Michael Dell announced that he and a group of investors planned to purchase the outstanding shares of Dell, Inc. and take the company private. Industry analysts and business journalists speculated that the move was being made to allow Michael Dell and his fellow Dell executives to escape the intense

---

5. *Ibid.*

6. Hess, "Stark Lessons from the Dell Fraud Case."

7. *Amalgamated Bank et al. vs. Dell, Inc. et al.*, U.S. District Court for the Western District of Texas, Civ. Action No. 1: 07-CA-00077-LY, 30 January 2007, 222–223.

8. S. Howard, "Court Flings Dell Shareholder Class Action Aside," *www.law360.com*, 10 October 2008.

scrutiny and regulatory oversight faced by the management teams of public companies. Six months later, in August 2013, billionaire investor and Dell stockholder Carl Icahn filed a lawsuit to thwart Michael Dell's effort to take the company private. Icahn insisted that the per share buyout price being offered to Dell's stockholders by Michael Dell was too low. One month later, however, a majority of Dell's stockholders approved that buyout price, meaning that Michael Dell's plan to take the company private had succeeded.

Questions

1. Define the phrase "earnings management." Under what conditions, if any, is earnings management acceptable? Do auditors' responsibilities include actively searching for instances of earnings management by clients? Defend your answers.

2. Dell recorded the exclusivity payments as an offset or reduction to its operating expenses. What "management assertion" did that accounting treatment violate? What audit procedure or procedures might have resulted in the discovery of that accounting treatment?

3. During the time frame that Intel was making exclusivity payments to Dell, Dell's business model was being adversely affected by the increasingly competitive nature of the PC industry. What responsibility, if any, do auditors have to analyze a client's business model? Do auditors have a responsibility to track and analyze key developments in a client's industry? Defend your answers.

4. What ethical issues do exclusivity agreements such as that between Dell and Intel raise? Are there analogous ethical issues faced by audit firms and their clients? Explain.

Accuhealth, Inc.

One morning in early 1990, William Makadok opened the door to the office occupied by one of his colleagues, a fellow officer of Accuhealth, Inc.[1] Scattered across the individual's desk were large piles of cash and several empty envelopes. Makadok quickly closed the door and returned to his office. Later that day, Makadok observed the officer casually distributing the envelopes, bulging with cash, to executives and senior employees of Accuhealth.

The two scenes just described startled Makadok. Those scenes added to, if not confirmed, Makadok's suspicion that Accuhealth's top executives were embezzling cash from the company. A few weeks earlier, Makadok had discovered a suspicious alteration to a weekly "cash report sheet" prepared for one of Accuhealth's retail drug stores. Each Accuhealth store reported its weekly cash sales to headquarters on this document. On the altered cash report sheet the original cash sales figure had been crossed out and replaced with a lower figure. The difference between the two amounts had been reported on a line item labeled "Office."

William Makadok had been hired in the summer of 1989 to serve as vice president and chief accounting officer of Accuhealth, a New York–based firm that operated a chain of drug stores and a home healthcare business. The fact that his fellow executives were involved in a large-scale and well-organized embezzlement scheme deeply troubled the CPA. In his early 50s at the time, Makadok had more than two decades of professional experience, including several years in public accounting. Never before in his career had he encountered a fraudulent scheme apparently masterminded by a company's top executives. The situation posed a simple question for William Makadok: What would he do?

Accuhealth: A Brief History

Stanley Lepelstat founded Leroy Pharmacies in 1981. Lepelstat, who had more than two decades of work experience with retail drug store chains before he established his own firm, took Leroy Pharmacies public in 1988 and then changed its name to Accuhealth, Inc. two years later. Initially, the company owned and operated a small chain of retail stores that sold prescription drugs, cosmetics, small kitchen appliances, and related merchandise. Lepelstat added a home healthcare line of business to his firm in 1987. In this new line of business, Accuhealth sold and rented home medical equipment and provided in-home infusion (intravenous) therapy for the critically ill. Exhibit 1 summarizes key financial data of Accuhealth for the period 1987–1991.

During the 1980s and early 1990s, Lepelstat, his family, and a few close friends dominated the day-to-day operations of Leroy Pharmacies and its successor, Accuhealth, Inc. Lepelstat served as the firm's president, chief executive officer (CEO), and chairman of the board, while his wife, Sheila, was the company's personnel director and held the titles of vice president, secretary, and treasurer. The Lepelstats' son, Lawrence, joined the firm in 1990 and was placed in charge of its home healthcare

---

1. The facts reported in this case were taken from several enforcement releases issued by the Securities and Exchange Commission, various annual reports of Accuhealth, Inc., and numerous newspaper articles.

	1991	1990	1989	1988	1987
Net Sales	$35,152	$33,797	$32,747	$27,677	$23,207
Gross Profit	10,988	10,350	9,576	7,944	6,756
Net Income	301	(783)	(96)	441	466
Total Assets	12,139	12,033	12,147	8,860	6,892
Total Liabilities	9,349	9,590	8,950	5,720	6,680

Source: Accuhealth's 1987 Form 10-K filed with the Securities and Exchange Commission.

subsidiary. Both Lawrence and his mother sat on Accuhealth's board of directors. Another Lepelstat also served on the company's board of directors in the early 1990s. Mark Lepelstat, Lawrence's brother, was appointed to the board of directors although he was not an employee or otherwise involved with Accuhealth. Other members of the board of directors included several longtime associates of Stanley Lepelstat who held executive positions with the company.

Accuhealth's 1991 annual report disclosed that the company's top executives had modest compensation packages. The average salary of Accuhealth's seven top executives, which included the two senior Lepelstats, averaged only $51,000. Those seven executives easily controlled the bulk of Accuhealth's outstanding common stock. The senior Lepelstats alone owned more than 53 percent of the company's common stock.

In "Accu" rate Financial Statements

In 1993, law enforcement agencies, including the Securities and Exchange Commission (SEC), began investigating rumors that Accuhealth's officers were engaging in a massive fraud. The SEC's investigation revealed that Stanley Lepelstat had directed a systematic cash-skimming operation within his business since its inception in 1981. Lepelstat and his colleagues embezzled funds primarily from cash sales of two of the company's retail drug stores. Each week, a company official called an accounting clerk at one of those two stores to specify the amount of cash to be forwarded to corporate headquarters.

> The store manager segregated the cash and bundled it separately in a paper bag
> for pickup by either Miszke [a senior pharmacist with Accuhealth] or an officer. The
> diverted cash was then taken to the company headquarters where Miszke and/or an
> officer would divide it up and put it into plain white envelopes for distribution.... No
> particular effort was made to conceal the distribution.[2]

A store manager typically recorded the amount of cash embezzled each week from his or her store on the given store's cash report sheet. The manager listed the funds on a line labeled "Office," as William Makadok eventually discovered. At headquarters, the sales and cash receipts recorded for the store was the net figure, that is, the actual weekly sales less the embezzled funds. Accuhealth officials kept meticulous records on an electronic spreadsheet documenting the funds embezzled each week and the weekly cash payments made to individuals within the firm. Stanley Lepelstat reviewed a weekly printout of these cash payments. The company's chief financial officer (CFO) also received a monthly report of the cash receipts stolen from individual stores. Most likely, Accuhealth's officers used the embezzlement data to arrive at compensation adjustments (pay raises) for given employees and to determine the "true" profitability of stores affected by the cash-skimming scheme.

---

2. Securities and Exchange Commission, *Accounting and Auditing Enforcement Release No. 589*, 8 September 1994.

Regulatory authorities estimated that Accuhealth's senior management embezzled between $500,000 and $900,000 annually from 1986 through 1992.[3] The cash-skimming operation negatively impacted Accuhealth's apparent profitability since it reduced the company's reported sales. Beginning in 1989, senior management decided to correct this "problem."

Inflating year-end inventory ranks among the easiest methods to intentionally overstate profits in a retail environment. From 1989 through 1992, Accuhealth executives ordered subordinates to fraudulently increase the company's year-end pharmaceuticals inventory. The employees responsible for counting pharmaceuticals at retail stores simply overstated the quantities of selected items on inventory count sheets for stores where the counting procedures were not observed by the company's independent auditors. Stanley Lepelstat also ordered subordinates to double-count certain high-priced inventory items maintained in Accuhealth's warehouse. One of those subordinates was George Miszke, Accuhealth's senior pharmacist who also participated in the cash-skimming operation.

> After those drugs were counted in the company's warehouse, Miszke, under orders from the CEO [Stanley Lepelstat], transported them at night or over the weekend to drugstores where they were included in inventory and counted again. This surreptitious inventory movement was possible because the physical inventory counts were conducted over several days.[4]

Numerous Accuhealth officers and employees knew of the company's fraudulent schemes and/or participated in them. These individuals apparently had a nonchalant attitude toward the schemes, treating them as just another company policy or procedure. This nonchalant attitude did not prevail when it came to concealing the frauds from the company's independent auditors. Besides the flagrant efforts to conceal the inventory irregularities just described, Accuhealth personnel repeatedly and systematically misled the auditors when they raised questions regarding accounts affected by the fraudulent schemes.

William Makadok Revisited

When we left William Makadok, he faced an unpleasant dilemma: what to do given the nearly irrefutable evidence that his employer was engaging in a large-scale fraud. After considering his options, Makadok decided to avoid the issue.

> Makadok did not take any steps to investigate any of these incidents nor did he bring them to the attention of Accuhealth's independent auditors. He consciously avoided undertaking any effort that would confirm any doubts or concerns caused by his observations.[5]

Makadok made another important decision after stumbling across Accuhealth's embezzlement scam during mid-1990. The chief accountant resolved not to sign off on Accuhealth's 1990 10-K, which would be prepared for the company's fiscal year ending 31 December 1990. True to his conviction, Makadok resigned his position with Accuhealth one month before the company filed its 1990 10-K with the SEC. When Accuhealth's independent auditors learned of Makadok's resignation, they wanted to know why he was leaving the company. Makadok did not reply candidly

---

3. For certain periods, the actual amount of embezzled funds could not be determined because Accuhealth personnel destroyed the relevant documents.

4. Securities and Exchange Commission, *Accounting and Auditing Enforcement Release No. 589*, 8 September 1994.

5. Securities and Exchange Commission, *Accounting and Auditing Enforcement Release No. 588*, 8 September 1994.

to the auditors. Instead, he told them that his decision to leave Accuhealth was motivated purely by another "opportunity."

Although Makadok did not sign off on Accuhealth's 1990 10-K, he did prepare and sign off on the company's financial reports filed with the SEC for the second and third quarters of 1990. Those quarterly financial reports, similar to Accuhealth's annual financial reports, misrepresented the company's operating results and financial condition. The SEC subsequently revealed that company officials stole more than $200,000 of cash receipts during each of those quarters.

An important focus of the SEC's investigation of Accuhealth was the conduct of its key accounting personnel, including William Makadok. In examining Makadok's conduct, a central issue addressed by the SEC was whether he violated Rule 10b-5 of the Securities Exchange Act of 1934. That rule prohibits an individual from making material misstatements in, or omitting material information from, a registration statement filed under the 1934 Act that would cause the document to be misleading to purchasers or sellers of the relevant securities.

In 1984, the U.S. Supreme Court established a major precedent relevant to Rule 10b-5 when it handed down a decision in the *Ernst & Ernst v. Hochfelder et al.* case.[6] Under the Hochfelder ruling, *scienter* must be present for an individual to violate Rule 10b-5—*scienter* being "a mental state embracing intent to deceive, manipulate or defraud." However, the Supreme Court also noted that in some jurisdictions "reckless disregard for the truth" or "recklessness" satisfies the *scienter* requirement. That is, although the individual did not have a conscious intent to deceive third parties, he or she recklessly allowed material representations to be included in a registration statement filed under the 1934 Act without obtaining a reasonable basis for determining whether those representations were true. For purposes of the SEC, an accountant, auditor, or other party associated with an SEC registration statement who engages in "reckless conduct" is subject to severe sanctions by the federal agency.[7]

In deciding if Makadok had breached Rule 10b-5, the SEC first addressed the issue of whether the misrepresentations in Accuhealth's quarterly financial reports that he prepared qualified as "material facts." Earlier court rulings had established the following definition of a material fact in the context of the 1934 Act: "A fact is material if there is a substantial likelihood that a reasonable investor would consider the information to be important."[8] The SEC ruled that the embezzlement scheme Makadok discovered was clearly a material fact that would have been of interest to a "reasonable investor" in Accuhealth's common stock.

The second issue faced by the SEC in deciding if Makadok had violated Rule 10b-5 was whether he had acted recklessly in signing off on Accuhealth's 1990 quarterly financial reports. The SEC correctly observed that Makadok "did not actively participate in the fraud or benefit from it financially." Nevertheless, the federal agency maintained that his conduct qualified as reckless.

> Makadok signed two Form 10-Qs that contained materially false financial information. Makadok signed these reports in reckless disregard of whether the information contained in them was materially misstated. By engaging in such conduct, Makadok directly violated Section 10(b) of the Exchange Act and Rule 10b-5 promulgated thereunder.[9]

---

6. Exhibit 1 in Case 7.6, *First Securities Company of Chicago*, contains Rule 10b-5. That case also includes a discussion of the Supreme Court ruling in the *Ernst & Ernst v. Hochfelder et al.* case.

7. The SEC may also punish individuals who engage in negligent or "highly unreasonable conduct," which is misconduct somewhat less severe than recklessness.

8. *Basic, Inc. v. Levinson*, 485 U.S. 224 (1988), 231–232.

9. Securities and Exchange Commission, *Accounting and Auditing Enforcement Release No. 588*, 8 September 1994.

EPILOGUE

In February 1993, shortly after the SEC publicly announced that it was investigating Accuhealth, Arthur Andersen, Accuhealth's audit firm, withdrew its opinion on the company's most recent financial statements. Trading in Accuhealth's common stock was also suspended following the SEC's announcement and several of the company's directors resigned, including Stanley and Sheila Lepelstat.

The SEC wrapped up its lengthy investigation of Accuhealth's financial affairs in mid-1994 and published the key findings of that investigation in a series of enforcement releases over the next several months. William Makadok received a three-year suspension from practicing before the SEC. Other parties sanctioned included Stanley and Sheila Lepelstat and George Miszke. Several of Accuhealth's former executives, including Stanley Lepelstat, were permanently barred from serving as an officer or director of a public company. The SEC also ordered Stanley Lepelstat to surrender $100,000 of profits that he had realized from selling Accuhealth common stock during the embezzlement scheme. Lepelstat later pleaded guilty to fraud charges filed against him in a U.S. district court.

In October 1994, Accuhealth settled legal claims against several of its former executives that stemmed from the cash-skimming scheme. Stanley Lepelstat agreed to the cancellation of a $600,000 note receivable from Accuhealth. Stanley Lepelstat, Sheila Lepelstat, and several other former Accuhealth executives also agreed to return to the company the Accuhealth common stock they owned. Accuhealth received more than 300,000 shares of common stock as a result of this restitution agreement.

Questions

1. Identify the parties who had a stake in, or would be affected by, the outcome of the ethical dilemma faced by William Makadok in 1990. What obligation, if any, did Makadok have to each of these parties?

2. Place yourself in William Makadok's position. Would you have responded differently than he did to the circumstances he faced? Explain.

3. The SEC did not criticize Accuhealth's independent auditors in the various enforcement releases issued concerning the company's fraudulent schemes. Under what general circumstances should auditors *not* be held at least partially responsible for such schemes? Defend your answer.

4. What specific audit procedures might have led to the detection of Accuhealth's fraudulent cash and inventory schemes?

5. The "control environment" is generally considered the most important component of any organization's internal control process. Defend that generalization. Use examples from this case to support your answer.

CASE 4.10

Wichita Falls

I have had, and may have still, a thousand friends, as they are called in life, who are like one's partners in the waltz of the world/not much remembered when the ball is over.

Lord Byron

In September 1872, several businessmen platted a new town site on a barren stretch of prairie in northwest Texas, just a few miles south of the Red River. The entrepreneurs chose "Wichita Falls" as the name of the new town because of a natural waterfall in the nearby Wichita River. Wichita Falls was strategically located between the Chisholm Trail to its east and the Dodge City Trail to its west. Crews of cowboys headed northward to the railheads of those two trails during the great cattle drives of the 1870s and 1880s created a Wild West atmosphere in the small town. Jesse and Frank James, the leaders of the infamous James-Younger Gang, spent considerable time in the area. Ironically, their sister Susan was one of the founders of the First Baptist Church of Wichita Falls—the father of the three siblings was a Baptist minister. Several decades later, the devil-may-care duo of Bonnie and Clyde hid out from law enforcement authorities in a small, second-story apartment above a popular Wichita Falls grocery store.

The discovery of the nearby Electra oil field in 1911 transformed Wichita Falls from a backwater, frontier-era cow town into an oil boom town. An enterprising accountant recognized that Wichita Falls' rapidly expanding business community needed a wide range of accounting services. The firm that individual organized, which became known as Freemon, Shapard & Story (FSS), lays claim to being the accounting firm that has been registered for the longest period of time with the Texas State Board of Public Accountancy. In addition to its headquarters in Wichita Falls, the firm ultimately opened practice offices in Austin, Dallas, Denton, Marble Falls, and Windthorst over its long history.

By the late 1990s, the ownership interest of FSS was divided equally among three senior partners who had worked together at the firm for more than 25 years. Those gentlemen included two brothers, Mac and Dennis Cannedy, and John Barfield. All three men had obtained their accounting degrees from Midwestern State University in Wichita Falls between 1967 and 1972. The Cannedy brothers chose John Barfield to serve as the managing partner of FSS in 1996.

Originally from the nearby small town of Olney, Barfield was involved in a wide range of civic activities in Wichita Falls, including leadership positions with the local United Way chapter, the Wichita Falls Museum and Art Center, the Wichita General Hospital, and several other community organizations. Unfortunately, Barfield's career ended prematurely when he died of brain cancer on 18 March 2008. His survivors included Ann, his wife of more than 30 years, and their daughter Amber.

The FSS partnership agreement specified that the legal survivor of a partner would receive the "fair value" of his interest in the firm at the date of his death. In October 2009, FSS offered Ann Barfield $602,000 for her late husband's one-third ownership interest in the firm. Ms. Barfield did not believe the offer was reasonable, which prompted her to file a lawsuit six months later against FSS. The lawsuit alleged that

FSS had refused to "negotiate a proper redemption price" and had not acted in "good faith" in resolving Ms. Barfield's claim against the firm.[1]

In a December 2011 trial, a jury in a Texas state court ruled that the fair value of John Barfield's one-third interest in FSS at the time of his death was $4.59 million. "The jury drew its value from a personal financial statement by Mac Cannedy one month before Barfield died that represented his one-third interest in the firm."[2] The market value estimate of Cannedy's ownership interest in FSS had been included in a confidential loan application that he filed in February 2008 with Wells Fargo Bank.[3]

During the trial, the Cannedy brothers retained an appraisal expert to testify regarding the fair value of each partner's ownership interest in FSS at the time of John Barfield's death. That expert established an appraisal value for those ownership interests that was considerably lower than the $4.59 million figure included in Mac Cannedy's February 2008 loan application.[4] Ms. Barfield's attorney suggested that the members of the jury rejected that appraised value because they believed the value included in Cannedy's loan application was more credible. "Giving false information to a federally insured lending institution for the purpose of getting or keeping or guaranteeing a loan is a federal crime, so the jury apparently thought Mr. Cannedy would not falsify his financial statement."[5]

On 21 May 2012, one day before the jury's ruling in the case was to be certified by the presiding judge, FSS filed for Chapter 11 bankruptcy in a federal court. The Chapter 11 bankruptcy filing allowed FSS to continue operating and servicing its clients while it worked toward resolving the dilemma that it faced.

In commenting on the litigation between FSS and Ms. Barfield, her attorney referred to a meeting between her client and the Cannedy brothers following John Barfield's death. "In a conversation with them shortly after John died, one of the Cannedy brothers assured her that they were going to treat her 'just like we'd want our own wives treated.' We are pretty sure that this is not how they would want their own wives treated."[6]

Questions

1. The AICPA's *Code of Professional Conduct* includes six broad ethical principles. Which of those ethical principles are most relevant to this case? Which of the specific "rules" in the *Code of Professional Conduct* are most applicable to this case? Defend your answers.

2. Identify specific factors that may influence the market value of a given accounting firm. Relying on publicly available sources, identify common methods used to assign a market value to an accounting firm or practice.

3. Define what is meant by the phrase "succession planning." How was succession planning relevant to this case?

1. A. Work, "Chapter 11 Filed by Local Business," *TimesRecordNews.com*, 7 June 2012.

2. *Ibid.*

3. The various published reports concerning this case do not reveal how Ms. Barfield's attorney obtained a copy of the confidential loan application or how Cannedy arrived at the $4.59 million value.

4. Published reports did not disclose the specific amount of this appraisal value, although it was apparently in the range of $1 million.

5. Work, "Chapter 11 Filed by Local Business."

6. *Ibid.*

ETHICAL RESPONSIBILITIES OF INDEPENDENT AUDITORS

5

Cardillo Travel Systems, Inc.

*If virtue is not its own reward,
I don't know any other stipend attached to it.*

Lord Byron

Act 1

Russell Smith knew why he had been summoned to the office of A. Walter Rognlien, the 74-year-old chairman of the board and chief executive officer (CEO) of Smith's employer, Cardillo Travel Systems, Inc.[1] Just two days earlier, Cardillo's in-house attorney, Raymond Riley, had requested that Smith, the company's controller, sign an affidavit regarding the nature of a transaction Rognlien had negotiated with United Airlines. The affidavit stated that the transaction involved a $203,000 payment by United Airlines to Cardillo but failed to disclose why the payment was being made or for what specific purpose the funds would be used. The affidavit included a statement indicating that Cardillo's stockholders' equity exceeded $3 million, a statement that Smith knew to be incorrect. Smith also knew that Cardillo was involved in a lawsuit and that a court injunction issued in the case required the company to maintain stockholders' equity of at least $3 million. Because of the blatant misrepresentation in the affidavit concerning Cardillo's stockholders' equity and a sense of uneasiness regarding United Airlines' payment to Cardillo, Smith had refused to sign the affidavit.

When Smith stepped into Rognlien's office on that day in May 1985, he found not only Rognlien but also Riley and two other Cardillo executives. One of the other executives was Esther Lawrence, the firm's energetic 44-year-old president and chief operating officer (COO) and Rognlien's wife and confidante. Lawrence, a long-time employee, had assumed control of Cardillo's day-to-day operations in 1984. Rognlien's two sons by a previous marriage had left the company in the early 1980s following a power struggle with Lawrence and their father.

As Smith sat waiting for the meeting to begin, his apprehension mounted. Although Cardillo had a long and proud history, in recent years the company had begun experiencing serious financial problems. Founded in 1935 and purchased in 1956 by Rognlien, Cardillo ranked as the fourth-largest company in the travel agency industry and was the first to be listed on a national stock exchange. Cardillo's annual revenues had steadily increased after Rognlien acquired the company, approaching $100 million by 1984. Unfortunately, the company's operating expenses had increased more rapidly. Between 1982 and 1984, Cardillo posted collective losses of nearly $1.5 million. These poor operating results were largely due to an aggressive franchising strategy implemented by Rognlien. In 1984 alone that strategy more than doubled the number of travel agency franchises operated by Cardillo.

Shortly after the meeting began, the overbearing and volatile Rognlien demanded that Smith sign the affidavit. When Smith steadfastly refused, Rognlien showed him the first page of an unsigned agreement between United Airlines

---

1. The events discussed in this case were reconstructed principally from information included in Securities and Exchange Commission, *Accounting and Auditing Enforcement Release No. 143*, 4 August 1987. All quotations appearing in this case were taken from that document.

and Cardillo. Rognlien then explained that the $203,000 payment was intended to cover expenses incurred by Cardillo in changing from American Airlines' Sabre computer reservation system to United Airlines' Apollo system. Although the payment was intended to reimburse Cardillo for those expenses and was refundable to United Airlines if not spent, Rognlien wanted Smith to record the payment immediately as revenue.

Not surprisingly, Rognlien's suggested treatment of the United Airlines payment would allow Cardillo to meet the $3 million minimum stockholders' equity threshold established by the court order outstanding against the company. Without hesitation, Smith informed Rognlien that recognizing the United Airlines payment as revenue would be improper. At that point, "Rognlien told Smith that he was incompetent and unprofessional because he refused to book the United payment as income. Rognlien further told Smith that Cardillo did not need a controller like Smith who would not do what was expected of him."

Act 2

In November 1985, Helen Shepherd, the audit partner supervising the 1985 audit of Cardillo by Touche Ross, stumbled across information in the client's files regarding the agreement Rognlien had negotiated with United Airlines earlier that year. When Shepherd asked her subordinates about this agreement, one of them told her of a $203,000 adjusting entry Cardillo had recorded in late June. That entry, which follows, had been approved by Lawrence and was apparently linked to the United Airlines–Cardillo transaction:

Dr Receivables–United Airlines	$203,210	
Cr Travel Commissions and Fees		$203,210

Shepherd's subordinates had discovered the adjusting entry during their second-quarter review of Cardillo's Form 10-Q statement. When asked, Lawrence had told the auditors that the entry involved commissions earned by Cardillo from United Airlines during the second quarter. The auditors had accepted Lawrence's explanation without attempting to corroborate it with other audit evidence.

After discussing the adjusting entry with her subordinates, Shepherd questioned Lawrence. Lawrence insisted that the adjusting entry had been properly recorded. Shepherd then requested that Lawrence ask United Airlines to provide Touche Ross with a confirmation verifying the key stipulations of the agreement with Cardillo. Shepherd's concern regarding the adjusting entry stemmed from information she had reviewed in the client's files that pertained to the United Airlines agreement. That information suggested that the United Airlines payment to Cardillo was refundable under certain conditions and thus not recognizable immediately as revenue.

Shortly after the meeting between Shepherd and Lawrence, Walter Rognlien contacted the audit partner. Like Lawrence, Rognlien maintained that the $203,000 amount had been properly recorded as commission revenue during the second quarter. Rognlien also told Shepherd that the disputed amount, which United Airlines paid to Cardillo during the third quarter of 1985, was not refundable to United Airlines under any circumstances. After some prodding by Shepherd, Rognlien agreed to allow her to request a confirmation from United Airlines concerning certain features of the agreement.

Shepherd received the requested confirmation from United Airlines on 17 December 1985. The confirmation stated that the disputed amount was refundable through 1990 if certain stipulations of the contractual agreement between the two parties were not fulfilled.[2] After receiving the confirmation, Shepherd called Rognlien and asked him to explain the obvious difference of opinion between United Airlines and Cardillo regarding the terms of their agreement. Rognlien told Shepherd that he had a secret arrangement with the chairman of the board of United Airlines. "Rognlien claimed that pursuant to this confidential business arrangement, the $203,210 would never have to be repaid to United. Shepherd asked Rognlien for permission to contact United's chairman to confirm the confidential business arrangement. Rognlien refused. In fact, as Rognlien knew, no such agreement existed."

A few days following Shepherd's conversation with Rognlien, she advised William Kaye, Cardillo's vice president of finance, that the $203,000 amount could not be recognized as revenue until the contractual agreement with United Airlines expired in 1990. Kaye refused to make the appropriate adjusting entry, explaining that Lawrence had insisted that the payment from United Airlines be credited to a revenue account. On 30 December 1985, Rognlien called Shepherd and told her that he was terminating Cardillo's relationship with Touche Ross.

In early February 1986, Cardillo filed a Form 8-K statement with the Securities and Exchange Commission (SEC) notifying that agency of the company's change in auditors. SEC regulations required Cardillo to disclose in the 8-K statement any disagreements involving accounting, auditing, or financial reporting issues with its former auditor. The 8-K, signed by Lawrence, indicated that no such disagreements preceded Cardillo's decision to dismiss Touche Ross. SEC regulations also required Touche Ross to draft a letter commenting on the existence of any disagreements with Cardillo. This letter had to be filed as an exhibit to the 8-K statement. In Touche Ross's exhibit letter, Shepherd discussed the dispute involving the United Airlines payment to Cardillo. Shepherd disclosed that the improper accounting treatment given that transaction had resulted in misrepresented financial statements for Cardillo for the six months ended 30 June 1985, and the nine months ended 30 September 1985.

In late February 1986, Raymond Riley, Cardillo's legal counsel, wrote Shepherd and insisted that she had misinterpreted the United Airlines–Cardillo transaction in the Touche Ross exhibit letter filed with the company's 8-K. Riley also informed Shepherd that Cardillo would not pay the $17,500 invoice that Touche Ross had submitted to his company. This invoice was for professional services Touche Ross had rendered prior to being dismissed by Rognlien.

Act 3

On 21 January 1986, Cardillo retained KMG Main Hurdman (KMG) to replace Touche Ross as its independent audit firm. KMG soon addressed the accounting treatment Cardillo had applied to the United Airlines payment. When KMG personnel discussed the payment with Rognlien, he informed them of the alleged secret arrangement with United Airlines that superseded the written contractual agreement. According to Rognlien, the secret arrangement precluded United Airlines from demanding a refund of the $203,000 payment under any circumstances. KMG refused to accept this explanation. Roger Shlonsky, the KMG audit partner responsible for the Cardillo

---

2. Shepherd apparently never learned that the $203,000 payment was intended to reimburse Cardillo for expenses incurred in switching to United Airlines' reservation system. As a result, she focused almost exclusively on the question of when Cardillo should recognize the United Airlines payment as revenue. If she had been aware of the true nature of the payment, she almost certainly would have been even more adamant regarding the impropriety of the $203,000 adjusting entry.

engagement, told Rognlien that the payment would have to be recognized as revenue on a pro rata basis over the five-year period of the written contractual agreement with United Airlines.[3]

Cardillo began experiencing severe liquidity problems in early 1986. These problems worsened a few months later when a judge imposed a $685,000 judgment on Cardillo to resolve a civil suit filed against the company. Following the judge's ruling, Raymond Riley alerted Rognlien and Lawrence that the adverse judgment qualified as a "material event" and thus had to be reported to the SEC in a Form 8-K filing. In the memorandum he sent to his superiors, Riley discussed the serious implications of not disclosing the settlement to the SEC: "My primary concern by not releasing such report and information is that the officers and directors of Cardillo may be subject to violation of Rule 10b-5 of the SEC rules by failing to disclose information that may be material to a potential investor."

Within 10 days of receiving Riley's memorandum, Rognlien sold 100,000 shares of Cardillo stock in the open market. Two weeks later, Lawrence issued a press release disclosing for the first time the adverse legal settlement. However, Lawrence failed to disclose the amount of the settlement or that Cardillo remained viable only because Rognlien had invested in the company the proceeds from the sale of the 100,000 shares of stock. Additionally, Lawrence's press release underestimated the firm's expected loss for 1985 by approximately 300 percent.

Following Lawrence's press release, Roger Shlonsky met with Rognlien and Lawrence. Shlonsky informed them that the press release grossly understated Cardillo's estimated loss for fiscal 1985. Shortly after that meeting, KMG resigned as Cardillo's independent audit firm.

EPILOGUE

In May 1987, the creditors of Cardillo Travel Systems, Inc., forced the company into involuntary bankruptcy proceedings. Later that same year, the SEC concluded a lengthy investigation of the firm. The SEC found that Rognlien, Lawrence, and Kaye had violated several provisions of the federal securities laws. These violations included making false representations to outside auditors, failing to maintain accurate financial records, and failing to file prompt financial reports with the SEC. In addition, the federal agency charged Rognlien with violating the insider trading provisions of the federal securities laws. As a result of these findings, the SEC imposed permanent injunctions on each of the three individuals that prohibited them from engaging in future violations of federal securities laws. The SEC also attempted to recover from Rognlien the $237,000 he received from selling the 100,000 shares of Cardillo stock in April 1986. In January 1989, the two parties resolved this matter when Rognlien agreed to pay the SEC $60,000.

---

3. Cardillo executives also successfully concealed from the KMG auditors the fact that the United Airlines payment was simply an advance payment to cover installation expenses for the new reservation system.

Questions

1. Identify the accountants in this case who faced ethical dilemmas. Also identify the parties who would be potentially affected by the outcome of each of these dilemmas. What responsibility did each accountant owe to these parties? Did the accountants fulfill these responsibilities?

2. Describe the procedures an auditor should perform during a review of a client's quarterly financial statements. In your opinion, did the Touche Ross auditors who discovered the $203,000 adjusting entry during their 1985 second-quarter review take all appropriate steps to corroborate that entry? Should the auditors have immediately informed the audit partner, Helen Shepherd, of the entry?

3. In reviewing the United Airlines–Cardillo agreement, Shepherd collected evidence that supported the $203,000 adjusting entry as booked and evidence that suggested the entry was recorded improperly. Identify each of these items of evidence. What characteristics of audit evidence do the profession's technical standards suggest auditors should consider? Analyze the audit evidence that Shepherd collected regarding the disputed entry in terms of those characteristics.

4. What are the principal objectives of the SEC rule that requires Form 8-K statements to be filed when public companies change auditors? Did Shepherd violate the client confidentiality rule when she discussed the United Airlines–Cardillo transaction in the exhibit letter she filed with Cardillo's 8-K auditor change statement? In your opinion, did Shepherd have a responsibility to disclose to Cardillo executives the information she intended to include in the exhibit letter?

5. Do the profession's technical standards explicitly require auditors to evaluate the integrity of a prospective client's key executives? Identify the specific measures auditors can use to assess the integrity of a prospective client's executives.

American International Group, Inc.

Cornelius Vander Starr wanted to see the world. In 1918, the 26-year-old Californian emptied his bank account to purchase a one-way ticket to the Far East on a steamship. After "bumming around" Japan for several months, Vander Starr traveled to Shanghai, China, where he landed a job working for an insurance company. Within a short period of time, Vander Starr realized that selling insurance was a low overhead business that was ideally suited for a young entrepreneurial type like himself, so he quit his job and set up his own insurance agency, American Asiatic Underwriters.

Vander Starr's business grew rapidly. By the time of his death in the late 1960s, Starr's one-man firm had become a multibillion-dollar international conglomerate with operating units in Europe, Latin America, the Middle East, and the United States. The Starr Foundation that he created before his death ranks among the world's largest philanthropic organizations.

In 1948, the Chinese civil war forced Vander Starr to relocate his company's headquarters from Shanghai to New York City. As he neared retirement, Vander Starr chose his protégé, Maurice "Hank" Greenberg, to replace him as his company's chief executive officer. During the early 1960s, Greenberg had revamped the company's business model. Instead of focusing on selling life insurance and other insurance products for individuals, Greenberg convinced Starr that the company's principal line of business should be insurance and other financial services products designed for large corporations. In 1969, Greenberg took the company, which had been renamed American International Group, Inc. (AIG), public by listing its stock on the New York Stock Exchange.

Greenberg would serve as AIG's top executive for nearly four decades. Under his leadership, the company became known worldwide for the new and innovative financial services products that it continually developed and the aggressive methods that it used to market those products. These efforts produced impressive financial results for the company. By the turn of the century, AIG was one of the 10 largest companies in the United States and among the 20 largest companies worldwide.

In early 2001, a group of AIG executives came up with an idea for a new financial service that they believed would appeal to a wide range of large corporations. This service would involve AIG creating customized "special purpose entities" or SPEs for such companies. An SPE is typically a limited partnership that two or more companies join together to form. Since an SPE is an unconsolidated subsidiary, a company can download or transfer underperforming assets and related liabilities to that entity to improve its apparent financial condition. This "balance sheet management feature" of SPEs was the principal selling point that AIG intended to rely on in marketing its new service.

In fact, many large corporations were already using SPEs "to perform cosmetic surgery on their balance sheets."[1] Enron Corporation, a large Houston-based energy company, was among the most prolific users of SPEs.[2] Enron had significantly improved its apparent financial condition by "hiding" distressed assets and much of

---

1. J. Kahn, "Off Balance Sheet—And Out of Control," *Fortune*, 18 February 2002, 84.
2. See *Enron Corporation*, Case 1.1.

its outstanding debt in hundreds of SPEs that it had created. AIG's management was convinced that, unlike Enron, most companies did not have the in-house expertise to develop their own SPEs.

AIG's executives realized that their new SPE service, which was effectively an accounting mechanism, would be more credible if one of the major accounting firms was involved in its development and marketing. For that reason, AIG retained Michael Joseph, a partner in the national office of Ernst & Young (E&Y) and a "nationally recognized expert on the accounting for structured financial vehicles and SPEs,"[3] to help develop and market the new service. "To assist AIG in its marketing" of the new SPE service "Joseph caused E&Y to issue reports pursuant to *Statement on Auditing Standards No. 50*, 'Reports on the Application of Accounting Principles.'"[4] These *SAS No. 50* reports indicated that the "nonconsolidation accounting treatment" for the assets and liabilities transferred to an SPE that had been designed by AIG "was an appropriate application of GAAP." In promoting its new SPE service, "AIG referred to E&Y's advice in its marketing materials and referred potential buyers directly to Joseph to answer accounting-related questions."

Among the first companies to express an interest in purchasing AIG's SPE service was PNC Financial Services Group, Inc. (PNC), a large financial services firm that operated the fifth-largest bank in the United States. During the negotiations with AIG, PNC consulted with its independent auditors to determine whether the accounting treatment for AIG's SPE product complied with GAAP. In fact, PNC's audit firm was E&Y, which meant that the company's auditors contacted Joseph to determine whether PNC's proposed SPE would be GAAP-compliant.

Joseph gave the PNC auditors a copy of a *SAS No. 50* report that he had written for AIG. The auditors relied on that report "without performing any meaningful separate analysis" in deciding that the accounting treatment for the proposed SPE was acceptable. Joseph billed the time that he spent interacting with the PNC auditors to the PNC audit engagement.

During July 2001, PNC transferred nearly $100 million of nonperforming loans to an SPE that was created by AIG. A few months later, the company downloaded more than $100 million of additional nonperforming loans to another AIG-created SPE. In an earnings press release in late 2001, PNC reported that it had $361 million of nonperforming loans. That figure did not include more than $200 million of such loans that had been transferred to its SPEs.

Federal Reserve officials contacted PNC in November 2001 and inquired regarding the company's nonperforming loans. When those officials reviewed the transactions that had resulted in $207 million of PNC's nonperforming loans being transferred to SPEs, they questioned whether those transfers were appropriate. At this point, PNC executives asked Michael Joseph to intercede on their behalf with the Federal Reserve. Joseph discussed the matter with the Federal Reserve and defended the accounting and financial reporting treatment for the loans that had been transferred to SPEs. The Federal Reserve disagreed with Joseph and in January 2002 ordered PNC to reverse the SPE transactions and include the $207 million of nonperforming loans in the company's consolidated financial statements.

---

3. Securities and Exchange Commission, *Accounting and Auditing Enforcement Release No. 2523*, 11 December 2006. Unless indicated otherwise, subsequent quotes in this case were taken from this source.

4. Accounting firms typically prepare such reports to provide a third party, other than an audit client, with technical guidance on how to apply existing accounting principles to a new type of transaction. *SAS No. 50* has been integrated into AU Section 625 of the PCAOB's Interim Standards and AU-C Section 915 of the AICPA Professional Standards.

The Federal Reserve's decision to force PNC to reverse its SPE transactions triggered an investigation of the company by the Securities and Exchange Commission (SEC). In reviewing PNC's SPE transactions, the SEC discovered that they were not in compliance with GAAP. For a company to treat an SPE as an unconsolidated subsidiary, an external entity must have a minimum capital investment of 3 percent in the SPE. The external entity that had invested in PNC's SPEs was AIG. However, AIG's investments in the SPEs had not met the required 3 percent threshold, meaning that the financial data for PNC's SPEs should have been included in the company's consolidated financial statements.

EPILOGUE

In July 2002, PNC executives agreed to cease and desist from any future violations of federal securities laws to settle charges pending against the company by the SEC. One year later, PNC agreed to pay $115 million to settle related fraud charges filed against the company by the U.S. Justice Department.

In December 2006, the SEC issued an accounting and auditing enforcement release focusing on Michael Joseph's role in PNC's SPE transactions. In this release, the SEC reported that "Joseph was a cause of PNC's violations" of federal securities laws. The SEC maintained that Joseph should have known that PNC's SPE transactions were not in compliance with GAAP. In this same enforcement release, the SEC alleged that Joseph's dual role with AIG and PNC had been improper and had posed a conflict of interest for him.

> Joseph was involved in the development and marketing of the AIG [SPE] accounting product. He advised AIG on the structure, he prepared several SAS 50 letters used in marketing the product, he participated in conference calls with potential purchasers.... Consequently, Joseph was invested both financially and reputationally in the success of the [SPE] product and therefore had a conflict of interest when he later evaluated the accounting for the product by E&Y's audit client, PNC.

The SEC went on to observe that Joseph's conduct was "highly unreasonable" and undermined the independence of E&Y's PNC audit engagement team. An accounting professor interviewed by the *Los Angeles Times* used an analogy to describe the likely impact that Joseph's conduct had on the PNC audit engagement team. "Did it bias the individual auditors in this particular case? It's like asking whether 40 years of smoking led to someone's lung cancer."[5]

The SEC suspended Joseph for three years from being involved with audits of public companies. In March 2007, the SEC fined E&Y $1.6 million for the firm's independence violations stemming from Joseph's conduct. The following month, E&Y agreed to pay approximately $9 million to settle a class-action lawsuit filed against it for its role in the PNC accounting scandal.

In late 2004, AIG agreed to pay $126 million in fines and restitution for its involvement in PNC's improper SPE accounting. That amount would be dwarfed by the $1.6 billion fine that AIG agreed to pay in late 2005 to settle charges that it had intentionally misrepresented its own accounting records. Among many other allegations, AIG had reportedly recorded bogus sales of insurance policies to inflate its earnings and understated its loss reserves. In addition to the huge fine, Hank Greenberg was forced to resign as AIG's chief executive as a result of the massive accounting fraud.[6]

AIG was front and center in news headlines once more in late 2008 when the largest

---

5. *Los Angeles Times* (online), "Ernst & Young in SEC Probe of PNC's Books," 8 December 2004.

6. In August 2009, Greenberg agreed to pay a $15 million fine to settle civil fraud charges filed against him by the SEC. The settlement also prohibited Greenberg from serving as an officer of a public company for three years.

economic crisis since the Great Depression erupted in the United States and quickly spread around the globe. In September 2008, the federal government seized control of AIG to prevent the company from collapsing. The company had such an extensive role in global credit and insurance markets that financial experts maintained that its collapse would cause a worldwide economic calamity. In exchange for approximately $85 billion of capital, the federal government received an 80 percent equity interest in the company. In the following months, tens of billions of dollars of additional federal "bailout" money was invested in AIG to keep the company afloat. AIG would ultimately receive more federal bailout funds than any other U.S. company during the historic economic crisis of 2008–2009.

Questions

1. Is it ethical for a CPA or CPA firm to help companies "manage" their reported earnings and financial condition? In responding to this question, first assume that the CPA or CPA firm is serving as a consultant, and then assume that the CPA or CPA firm is serving as the given entity's independent auditor. Defend your answers.

2. When a dispute arises between an audit client and its auditor regarding the proper accounting treatment for a transaction or other item, the audit client will sometimes retain another accounting firm to issue a report, previously known as a *SAS No. 50* report, on the proper accounting treatment for the given item [see AU Section 625 and AU-C Section 915]. Identify the potential ethical dilemmas that may result from allowing accounting firms to issue such reports to nonaudit clients.

The North Face, Inc.

Executives of The North Face, Inc., faced a troubling dilemma during the 1990s.[1] For decades, those executives had struggled to develop and maintain an exclusive brand name for their company's extensive line of outdoor apparel and sporting equipment products. By positioning those products for the "high-end" segment of the retail market, North Face's management had consciously chosen to ignore the much larger and more lucrative mainstream market. This decision kept the company's primary customers happy. Those customers, principally small, independent specialty sporting goods stores, did not want North Face to market its merchandise to major discount retailers such as Walmart and Costco.

Economic realities eventually forced North Face's executives to begin selling the company's products to the mainstream market via backdoor marketing channels. Unfortunately, the company's relatively high-priced merchandise did not compete effectively with the mass-market brands sold by the major discount retailers. Making matters worse, as the company's merchandise began appearing on the shelves of discount retailers, those products quickly lost their exclusive brand name appeal, which caused North Face's sales to its principal customers to drop sharply.

North Face's change in marketing strategies, the company's decision to spend millions of dollars to relocate its headquarters from northern California to Colorado, and other gaffes by its management team caused *Chief Executive* magazine to include North Face among the nation's five "worst-managed" corporations. A short time later, North Face's public image and reputation on Wall Street would be damaged even more by public revelations that the company's reported operating results had been embellished with various accounting and marketing gimmicks.

Adventurers, Inc.

Hap Klopp founded North Face in the mid-1960s to provide a ready source of hiking and camping gear that he and his many free-spirited friends and acquaintances needed to pursue their "back to nature" quest. Initially, the business operated from a small retail store in San Francisco's North Beach neighborhood. The company quickly added a mail-order sales operation. In 1970, North Face began designing and manufacturing its own line of products after opening a small factory in nearby Berkeley.

Over the next decade, North Face endeared itself to outdoor enthusiasts by sponsoring mountain-climbing expeditions across the globe, including successful attempts to scale Mount Everest, Mount McKinley, China's K-2, and the highest peaks in South America. The name recognition and goodwill generated by these expeditions allowed North Face to establish itself as the premier supplier of top-quality parkas, tents, backpacking gear, and other apparel and equipment demanded by "professional" mountain climbers. Adding even more credibility to North Face's merchandise was the lifetime warranty that Hal Klopp attached to each item his company sold and the fact that the United States Marine Corps purchased tents and other bivouac supplies from North Face.

1. The development of this case was funded by Glen McLaughlin. I would like to thank Mr. McLaughlin for his generous and continuing support of efforts to integrate ethics into business curricula.

North Face's sterling reputation for rugged and durable hiking, camping, and mountaineering gear prompted company management to begin marketing related lines of apparel and sporting equipment for skiers, whitewater daredevils, and other outdoor types. Among the most popular items marketed by the company were its Mountain Jacket, Snow Leopard Backpack, and Tadpole Tent. The company's expanding product line triggered rapid sales growth during the 1970s and 1980s. Similar to the management teams of many growth companies, North Face's executives confronted several imposing challenges that could undermine their company's financial success. The most critical of those challenges was maintaining quality control in North Face's cramped production facilities.

Company executives prided themselves on producing only the highest-quality outdoor sporting equipment and apparel. To maintain the quality of that merchandise, they insisted on manufacturing all of North Face's products in-house, rather than outsourcing some of the company's manufacturing operations to third parties. By the mid-1980s, North Face's overburdened manufacturing facilities could not satisfy the steadily growing demand for the company's merchandise or maintain the high-quality production standards established by management. North Face's limited production capacity and mounting quality control problems caused the company to routinely deliver merchandise to retail stores after the peak selling seasons for its highly seasonal products. The quality control problems also caused North Face to accumulate a large inventory of "seconds," that is, merchandise items having minor flaws.

In the late 1980s, North Face's management made a decision it would soon regret. The company opened several outlet stores to dispose of obsolete and second-grade merchandise. This decision angered the specialty sporting goods stores that had been North Face's primary customers since the company's inception. To pacify those customers, North Face did a quick about-face and closed the outlet stores.

Over the next several years, North Face continued to struggle with maintaining its image as the leading producer of high-quality outdoor apparel and sporting equipment, while at the same attempting to gradually ease into the mainstream retail market. By this time, Hap Klopp had left the company to become an author—one of his books was entitled *The Complete Idiot's Guide to Business Management*. In fact, the company experienced several changes in company management and ownership during the late 1980s and throughout the 1990s.

In July 1996, a new management team took North Face public, listing the company's common stock on the NASDAQ exchange. Sold initially at $14 per share, the company's stock price peaked at nearly $30 per share in February 1998, fueled by the company's steadily increasing sales and profits. In fiscal 1994, North Face reported total sales of $89 million; four years later in fiscal 1998, the company's sales had nearly tripled, rising to approximately $250 million.

Despite the company's strong operating results, by early 1999 North Face's stock price had plunged from its all-time high. Persistent rumors that North Face's management had enhanced the company's reported revenues and profits by "channel stuffing" and other questionable, if not illegal, practices caused the sharp decline in the stock price. To squelch those rumors, North Face's board of directors attempted to purchase the company in a leveraged buyout underwritten by a large investment banking firm. That effort failed in March 1999 when NASDAQ officials halted public trading of North Face's stock following an announcement that the company would be restating its previously reported operating results due to certain "bad bookkeeping."[2]

---

2. D. Blount, "Shares of Colorado-Based Outdoor Clothing Maker Slump," *Denver Post* (online), 11 May 1999.

In May 1999, North Face officials publicly revealed that their company's audited financial statements for 1997 and the company's preaudited operating results for 1998, which had been released in January 1999, had been distorted by fraudulent accounting schemes. The principal schemes involved violations of the revenue recognition principle. For 1997, North Face's reported revenues of $208.4 million had been overstated by approximately $5 million, while the company's net income of $11.2 million had been overstated by $3.2 million. In January 1999, the company had reported unaudited revenue and net income of $263.3 million and $9.5 million, respectively, for fiscal 1998. The company's actual 1998 revenues were $247.1 million, while the company's actual net income for the year was $3.6 million.

Bartering for Success at North Face

The management team that took over North Face in the mid-1990s established a goal of reaching annual sales of $1 billion by 2003. Many Wall Street analysts believed North Face could reach that goal, given the company's impressive operating results over the previous several years. When the actual revenues and profits of North Face failed to meet management's expectations, the company's chief financial officer (CFO) and vice president of sales took matters into their own hands, literally.

In December 1997, North Face began negotiating a large transaction with a barter company. Under the terms of this transaction, the barter company would purchase $7.8 million of excess inventory North Face had on hand near the end of fiscal 1997. In exchange for that inventory, North Face would receive $7.8 million of trade credits that were redeemable only through the barter company. Historically, companies have used such trade credits to purchase advertising or travel services.

Before North Face finalized the large barter transaction, Christopher Crawford, the company's chief financial officer, asked North Face's independent auditors how to account for the transaction. The auditors referred Crawford to the appropriate authoritative literature for nonmonetary exchanges. That literature generally precludes companies from recognizing revenue on barter transactions when the only consideration received by the seller is trade credits. To circumvent the authoritative literature, Crawford restructured the transaction. The final agreement with the barter company included an oral "side agreement" that was concealed from North Face's independent auditors.

> Crawford, however, structured the transaction to recognize a profit on the trade credits. First, he required the barter company to pay a portion of the trade credits in cash. Crawford agreed that The North Face would guarantee that the barter company would receive at least 60 percent recovery of the total purchase price when it resold the product. In exchange for the guarantee, the barter company agreed to pay approximately 50 percent of the total purchase price in cash and the rest in trade credits. This guarantee took the form of an oral side agreement that was not disclosed to the auditors.[3]

To further obscure the true nature of the large barter transaction, Crawford split it into two parts. On 29 December 1997, two days before the end of North Face's fiscal 1997 fourth quarter, Crawford recorded a $5.15 million sale to the barter company. For this portion of the barter deal, North Face received $3.51 million in cash and trade credits of $1.64 million. Ten days later, during North Face's first quarter of fiscal 1998, the company's accounting staff booked the remaining $2.65 million portion of the barter transaction. North Face received only trade credits from the barter company

---

3. U.S. District Court, Northern District of California, *Securities and Exchange Commission v. Christopher F. Crawford and Todd F. Katz*, February 2003.

for this final portion of the $7.8 million transaction. North Face recognized its normal profit margin on each segment of the barter transaction.

Crawford, who was a CPA, realized that Deloitte & Touche, North Face's auditors, would not challenge the $3.51 million portion of the barter transaction recorded during the fourth quarter of fiscal 1997. There was no reason for the auditors to challenge that component of the transaction since North Face was being paid in cash. Crawford also realized that Deloitte would disagree with the company's decision to recognize revenue for the $1.64 million component of the barter transaction for which North Face would be paid exclusively in trade credits. However, Crawford was aware of the materiality thresholds that Deloitte had established for North Face's key financial statement items during the fiscal 1997 audit. He knew that the gross profit of approximately $800,000 on the $1.64 million component of the barter transaction fell slightly below Deloitte's materiality threshold for North Face's collective gross profit. As a result, he believed that Deloitte would propose an adjustment to reverse the $1.64 million item but ultimately "pass" on that proposed adjustment since it had an immaterial impact on North Face's financial statements. In fact, that is exactly what Deloitte did.

In early January 1998, North Face recorded the remaining $2.65 million portion of the $7.8 million barter transaction. Again, Crawford instructed North Face's accountants to record the full amount of profit margin on this "sale" despite being aware that accounting treatment was not consistent with the authoritative literature. Crawford did not inform the Deloitte auditors of the $2.65 million portion of the barter transaction until after the 1997 audit was completed.

The barter company ultimately sold only a nominal amount of the $7.8 million of excess inventory that it purchased from North Face. As a result, in early 1999, North Face reacquired that inventory from the barter company.

In the third and fourth quarters of fiscal 1998, Todd Katz, North Face's vice president of sales, arranged two large sales to inflate the company's revenues, transactions that were actually consignments rather than consummated sales. The first of these transactions involved $9.3 million of merchandise "sold" to a small apparel wholesaler in Texas. During the previous year, this wholesaler had purchased only $90,000 of merchandise from North Face. The terms of this transaction allowed the wholesaler to return any of the merchandise that he did not resell and required North Face to pay all of the storage and handling costs for that merchandise. In fact, North Face arranged to have the large amount of merchandise stored in a warehouse near the wholesaler's business. Katz negotiated a similar $2.6 million transaction with a small California wholesaler a few months later.

During a subsequent internal investigation, North Face's audit committee questioned the validity of the large transaction with the Texas wholesaler. North Face paid for the Texas customer to fly to North Face's new corporate headquarters in Aspen, Colorado, to discuss that transaction with members of the audit committee and the company's CEO, who were not aware of the true nature of the transaction. The night before the customer met with North Face officials, Katz went to his hotel room and had him sign a fake purchase order for the $9.3 million transaction—a purchase order had not been prepared for the bogus sale when it was originally arranged by Katz.

Several months later, Katz instructed a North Face sales representative to ask the Texas customer to sign an audit confirmation letter sent to him by Deloitte. By signing that letter, the customer falsely confirmed that he owned the $9.3 million of merchandise as of 31 December 1998, North Face's fiscal year-end. The California wholesaler involved in the bogus $2.6 million sale signed a similar confirmation after having been asked to do so by a North Face sales representative. In May 1999, following the completion of North Face's 1998 audit, the Texas customer returned the $9.3 million of merchandise that he had supposedly purchased from North Face.

Erasing the Past

Richard Fiedelman served for several years as the Deloitte "advisory" partner assigned to the North Face audit engagements. Within Deloitte, an advisory partner is typically a senior audit partner who has significant industry expertise relevant to a given audit client. Fiedelman was the advisory partner on the North Face engagement team because he was in charge of Deloitte's "consumer retail group" in the firm's northern California market area. In addition to consulting with members of an audit engagement team on important issues arising during an audit, an advisory partner typically reviews the audit workpapers before the engagement is completed.[4]

Pete Vanstraten was the audit engagement partner for the 1997 North Face audit.[5] Vanstraten proposed the adjusting entry near the end of the 1997 audit to reverse the $1.64 million barter transaction that North Face had booked in the final few days of fiscal 1997. Vanstraten proposed that adjustment because he was aware that the authoritative literature generally precludes companies from recognizing revenue on barter transactions when the only consideration received by the seller is trade credits. Vanstraten was also the individual who "passed" on that adjustment after determining that it did not have a material impact on North Face's 1997 financial statements. Richard Fiedelman reviewed and approved those decisions by Vanstraten.

Shortly after the completion of the 1997 North Face audit, Pete Vanstraten was transferred from the office that serviced North Face. In May 1998, Will Borden was appointed the new audit engagement partner for North Face.[6] In the two months before Borden was appointed the North Face audit engagement partner, Richard Fiedelman functioned in that role.

Fiedelman supervised the review of North Face's financial statements for the first quarter of fiscal 1998, which ended on 31 March 1998. While completing that review, Fiedelman became aware of the $2.65 million portion of the $7.8 million barter transaction that Christopher Crawford had instructed his subordinates to record in early January 1998. Recall that North Face received only trade credits from the barter company for this final portion of the large barter transaction. Despite being familiar with the authoritative literature regarding the proper accounting treatment for barter transactions involving trade credits, Fiedelman did not challenge North Face's decision to record its normal profit margin on the January 1998 "sale" to the barter company. As a result, North Face's gross profit for the first quarter of 1998 was overstated by more than $1.3 million, an amount that was material to the company's first-quarter financial statements. In fact, without the profit margin on the $2.65 million transaction, North Face would have reported a net loss for the first quarter of fiscal 1998 rather than the modest net income it actually reported that period.

In the fall of 1998, Will Borden began planning the 1998 North Face audit. An important element of that planning process was reviewing the 1997 audit workpapers. While reviewing those workpapers, Borden discovered the audit adjustment

---

4. The information regarding the nature and role of a Deloitte advisory partner was obtained from a senior audit manager with that firm.

5. "Pete Vanstraten" is a fictitious name assigned to the 1997 North Face audit engagement partner. The SEC enforcement releases issued in this case and other available sources did not identify that partner's actual name.

6. "Will Borden" is also a fictitious name.

that Pete Vanstraten had proposed during the prior-year audit to reverse the $1.64 million barter transaction. When Borden brought this matter to Fiedelman's attention, Fiedelman maintained that the proposed audit adjustment should not have been included in the prior-year workpapers since the 1997 audit team had *not* concluded that North Face should *not* record the $1.64 million transaction with the barter company. Fiedelman insisted that, despite the proposed audit adjustment in the 1997 audit workpapers, Pete Vanstraten had concluded that it was permissible for North Face to record the transaction as a consummated sale and recognize the $800,000 of profit margin on the transaction in December 1997.

Fiedelman could not offer any viable explanation to Borden as to why the 1997 workpapers included the proposed audit adjustment for the $1.64 million transaction. Borden could have easily addressed that issue by simply contacting Vanstraten; however, he apparently chose not to do so. Nor did he refer to the authoritative literature to determine whether North Face was entitled to record that transaction as a finalized sale. Instead, Borden simply accepted Fiedelman's assertion that North Face was entitled to recognize profit on a "sales" transaction in which the only consideration received by the company was trade credits. Borden also relied on this assertion during the 1998 audit. As a result, Borden and the other members of the 1998 audit team did not propose an adjusting entry to require North Face to reverse the $2.65 million sale recorded by the company in January 1998.

After convincing Borden that the prior-year workpapers misrepresented the decision that Pete Vanstraten had made regarding the $1.64 million barter transaction, Fiedelman "began the process of documenting this revised conclusion in the 1997 working papers."[7] According to a subsequent investigation by the Securities and Exchange Commission (SEC), Deloitte personnel "prepared a new summary memorandum and adjustments schedule reflecting the revised conclusion about profit recognition, and replaced the original 1997 working papers with these newly created working papers." The Deloitte personnel who revised the 1997 workpapers did not document the revisions in those workpapers. "In the end, the 1997 working papers, as revised, did not indicate that the 1997 audit team had originally reached a different conclusion concerning the company's accounting for the 1997 barter transaction."

The SEC requires that a partner not assigned to an engagement team review the audit workpapers for an SEC registrant. The Deloitte "concurring" partner who reviewed the 1998 workpapers questioned Will Borden's decision to allow North Face to recognize revenue on a sales transaction for which it had been paid exclusively in trade credits. The partner then referred to the prior-year workpapers and discovered that the workpapers pertaining to the December 1997 transaction with the barter company had been altered.

Because of concerns raised by the concurring partner, Deloitte investigated the 1997 and 1998 North Face transactions with the barter company. The concurring partner's concerns also prompted North Face's audit committee to retain a second accounting firm to investigate the company's 1997 and 1998 accounting records. These investigations ultimately revealed the true nature of the transactions with the barter company, including the previously undisclosed "side agreement" that Christopher Crawford had made with officials of that company. The investigations also led to the discovery of the two bogus consignment sales that Crawford had arranged during 1998.

---

7. This and all remaining quotes in this case were taken from the following source: Securities and Exchange Commission, *Accounting and Auditing Enforcement Release No. 1884*, 1 October 2003.

EPILOGUE

The SEC sanctioned Richard Fiedelman for failing to document the changes that his subordinates had made in the 1997 North Face workpapers. In commenting on the North Face case, the federal agency stressed the important function of audit workpapers and the need for any ex post changes in those workpapers to be clearly and fully documented.

> *The auditor's working papers provide the principal support for the auditor's report, including his representation regarding the observance of the standards of field work, which is implicit in the reference in his report to generally accepted auditing standards. It therefore follows that any addition, deletion, or modification to the working papers after they had been finalized in connection with the completion of the audit may be made only with appropriate supplemental documentation, including an explanation of the justification for the addition, deletion, or modification.*

The SEC also criticized Fiedelman for failing to exercise due professional care while reviewing North Face's financial statements for the first quarter of 1998. According to the SEC, Fiedelman allowed North Face to record the January 1998 barter transaction "directly contrary to the conclusion reached by Deloitte in its 1997 year-end audit." In October 2003, the SEC imposed a three-year suspension on Fiedelman that prevented him from being involved in the audits of SEC clients.

In February 2003, the SEC suspended Christopher Crawford for five years, which prohibited him from serving as an officer or director of a public company or being associated with any financial statements filed with the federal agency over that time frame. The SEC also fined Crawford $30,000 and required him to disgorge approximately $30,000 of trading profits he had earned on the sale of North Face stock. The SEC also denied Todd Katz, the former vice president of sales who had helped Crawford manipulate North Face's reported operating results, the privilege of serving as an officer of a public company for five years and fined him $40,000. The two former North Face customers involved in the bogus consignment sales arranged by Katz were reprimanded by the SEC.

In May 2000, VF Corporation, the world's largest apparel company, more commonly known as Vanity Fair, made North Face a wholly owned subsidiary by purchasing the company's outstanding common stock for $2 per share. VF immediately installed a new management team to take over North Face's operations. Under the leadership of that new management team, North Face quickly returned to profitability and reestablished itself as one of the nation's premier suppliers of outdoor equipment and apparel.

Questions

1. Should auditors insist that their clients accept all proposed audit adjustments, even those that have an "immaterial" effect on the given financial statements? Defend your answer.

2. Should auditors take explicit measures to prevent their clients from discovering or becoming aware of the materiality thresholds used on individual audit engagements? Would it be feasible for auditors to conceal this information from their audit clients?

3. Identify the general principles or guidelines that dictate when companies are entitled to record revenue. How were these principles or guidelines violated by the $7.8 million barter transaction and the two consignment sales discussed in this case?

4. Identify and briefly explain each of the principal objectives that auditors hope to accomplish by preparing audit workpapers. How were these objectives undermined by Deloitte's decision to alter North Face's 1997 workpapers?

5. North Face's management teams were criticized for strategic blunders that they made over the course of the company's history. Do auditors have a responsibility to assess the quality of the key decisions made by client executives? Defend your answer.

IPOC International Growth Fund, Ltd.

And thus I clothe my naked villainy
With odd old ends stolen out of holy writ;
And seem a saint, when most I play the devil.

William Shakespeare

No doubt, Guy Enright was apprehensive as he talked to the mysterious stranger on the phone. At the time, Enright, a British citizen and Chartered Accountant, was working on an unusual engagement for his employer, KPMG.[1,2] The Big Four accounting firm had been appointed by Bermuda's Minister of Finance to review and report on the financial affairs of a large investment fund, IPOC International Growth Fund, Ltd. (IPOC). Although based in Bermuda, a Danish attorney, Jeffrey Galmond, served as the company's chief executive and was reportedly its principal stockholder.

The individual who had called Enright identified himself as Nick Hamilton. During the phone call, Hamilton told Enright that he needed to speak to him about a matter that had "national security implications for Britain." Hamilton, who had a strong British accent, "led Enright to believe he was a British intelligence officer" and apparently asked Enright not to tell his superiors that he had contacted him.

After considering the strange request for a few moments, Enright agreed to meet with Hamilton in a public place. Hamilton then arranged for the two of them to have lunch a few days later at Little Venice, a popular Bermuda restaurant.

Bermuda Shell Game

A former Merrill Lynch executive organized IPOC in 2000 after the Bermuda government issued a license to the company to operate as a mutual fund. Three years later, after Bermuda regulatory authorities discovered that the company's founder was a convicted felon, he was dismissed and Jeffrey Galmond took control of the company.

Over the next few years, IPOC grew dramatically. The company's principal investments were in Russian telecommunications companies that were a product of the Russian Federation's "privatization programme" during the 1990s. That program converted thousands of state-owned agencies within the former Soviet Union into privately owned companies and was intended to distribute the ownership interests of those new companies to millions of Russian citizens. The majority of those ownership interests, however, were usurped by individuals who had held high-ranking positions in the former Soviet government or who were friends, family members, and business associates of such individuals.

By 2004, the Bermuda government was alarmed by rampant rumors and allegations that IPOC was not operating as a mutual fund but rather was a money-laundering

1. This case was coauthored by Carol A. Knapp and was originally published in the *Journal of Forensic & Investigative Accounting*, Vol. 6, No. 1 (January–June 2014). I would like to thank D. Larry Crumbley, the editor of the *Journal of Forensic & Investigative Accounting*, for granting permission to include this case in this edition of *Contemporary Auditing: Real Issues and Cases*.

2. Much of the background information for this case and the quotes, unless indicated otherwise, were taken from the following source: *Bloomberg Businessweek*, "Spies, Lies & KPMG," *www.businessweek.com*, 25 February 2007.

"criminal" enterprise. Critics of the company insisted that Jeffrey Galmond and other IPOC executives served only as figureheads and that IPOC was actually owned and controlled by Leonid Reiman, Russia's Telecommunications Minister.

Reiman was a longtime friend and close ally of Russian president Vladimir Putin who had appointed him to oversee Russia's emerging telecommunications industry. Allegedly, Reiman had used his position to take control of Russia's key telecommunications companies and place them under the IPOC corporate umbrella. Reiman disputed such claims and insisted that he was not involved with IPOC and that Galmond was the company's principal executive and owner.

To squelch the controversy, IPOC's executives hired Ernst & Young to "audit" their company's business affairs and issue a report on its findings. Copies of the Ernst & Young report obtained by third parties caused even more questions to be raised about IPOC's legitimacy. The E&Y report documented a number of suspicious cash transfers that appeared to have no credible business purpose.

For decades, Bermuda's political leaders have taken strenuous measures to prevent their country, which is technically a British territory, from becoming a headquarters for companies controlled by organized crime syndicates. Several small nations in the nearby Caribbean, on the other hand, have bank secrecy laws that serve as an invitation to such enterprises. Increasing concern regarding the true nature of IPOC's operations goaded Bermuda's Minister of Finance in 2004 to retain KPMG to investigate the company. Two years would pass before the investigation and its findings would be publicly reported. In the meantime, another headline-grabbing controversy involving IPOC erupted.

Cell Phone Mania

In late 2003, IPOC filed a lawsuit against the Alfa Group, a Russian-based company that was attempting to become a major competitor in Russia's mobile phone industry. At the time, IPOC owned, directly or indirectly, a 40 percent interest in one of Russia's largest cell phone companies, MegaFon. Over the previous few years, IPOC had attempted to gain a majority ownership interest in MegaFon by purchasing the 25 percent stake in the company held by Leonid Rozhetskin, a U.S. citizen of Russian descent. IPOC also named Leonid Rozhetskin as a defendant in the lawsuit it filed.

In 1992, Rozhetskin, a 26-year-old Harvard Law School graduate, accepted a job with the Moscow office of a U.S. law firm. Rozhetskin soon left his legal career behind to become a venture capitalist. In 1996, he was involved in registering VimpelCom, a Russian telecommunications company, on the New York Stock Exchange—the first Russian company to be listed on the "Big Board."

Among Rozhetskin's investment partners were George Soros, a billionaire American financier, and Mikhail Fridman, one of Russia's wealthiest businessmen. Both Soros and Fridman were longtime antagonists of Vladimir Putin. In 2000, Putin, a former agent in the Soviet Union's notorious intelligence agency, the KGB, had been elected president of the Russian Federation. Putin succeeded his mentor Boris Yeltsin, the Federation's first president.

Unlike his two wealthy colleagues, Rozhetskin, was openly critical of President Putin and his economic policies. The controversial and ambitious Rozhetskin also maintained a high profile in Russia's nascent investment community. Because of his aggressive persona, the Russian version of *Forbes* magazine placed him on its cover under the caption, "The Most Dangerous Shark in Our Waters."[3]

---

3. *PRNewswire* (online), "Russian Oligarch Fridman, Corporation Sued for Racketeering, Fraud that Used U.S. Banks and Exchanges," 9 June 2006.

IPOC officials sued Alfa Group and Rozhetskin because they insisted that they had negotiated a binding agreement with Rozhetskin that required him to sell his 25 percent ownership interest in MegaFon to their company. Rather than selling his stake in MegaFon to IPOC, Rozhetskin unexpectedly sold it to the Alfa Group in August 2003. Rozhetskin's decision would ultimately trigger the filing of a series of lawsuits and countersuits over the next several years involving IPOC, Alfa Group, and Rozhetskin in British, Russian, Swedish, Swiss, and Russian courts. The bruising legal battle eventually convinced Bermuda's Minister of Finance to hire KPMG to investigate IPOC.

Lunch and Lies

When Guy Enright showed up at the Little Venice restaurant in Bermuda for his luncheon meeting with Nick Hamilton, he was greeted not only by Hamilton but also by an attractive young lady who introduced herself as "Liz from Langley." No doubt, Enright took "Langley" to mean Langley, Virginia, the headquarters of the U.S. Central Intelligence Agency (CIA). Hamilton explained to Enright that he was needed to assist in a "top secret" mission that "involved Britain's national security."

> [Hamilton] … told the accountant he would have to undergo a British government background check to ensure that he was up to the task. [Hamilton] produced an official-looking—but fake—questionnaire with a British government seal at the top and asked for information about Enright's parents, his professional background, any criminal history, and political activities.

A few weeks later, Hamilton and Enright met again at a Bermuda bar. During this meeting, Hamilton told Enright he was being recruited to provide information about KPMG's investigation of IPOC. Hamilton convinced Enright to begin "handing over confidential audit documents, including transcripts of interviews KPMG had conducted in the IPOC investigation." Enright was instructed to place those documents in a plastic container hidden under a large rock in a secluded area on Bermuda. Hamilton would then retrieve those documents.

In fact, Nick Hamilton was not a British intelligent officer, and "Liz" was not a CIA agent as they had led Enright to believe. Instead, Nick Hamilton was actually Nick Day and "Liz" was Gretchen King, one of Day's subordinates. Day was a senior executive of Diligence, Inc., a London-based "business intelligence" firm that he had founded in 2000; King was assigned to Diligence's New York City office. Day did have a background in government intelligence, having served with the United Kingdom Special Forces, a secretive agency of the British government that deals with counter-terrorism and other threats to Britain's national security.[4]

During the legal battle over Leonid Rozhetskin's 25 percent ownership interest in MegaFon, the Alfa Group had hired Barbour Griffith & Rogers (BGR),[5] a Washington, D.C.–based lobbying firm. In turn, BGR had hired Diligence, which maintained an office in Washington, D.C., two blocks from the White House. BGR wanted Diligence to obtain information regarding IPOC that would help Alfa Group retain the 25 percent ownership interest in MegaFon that had been purchased from Rozhetskin.

---

4. Day also served for a time as a special consultant to the popular British TV series *Spooks,* a drama that revolves around the trials and tribulations of a British domestic intelligence organization.

5. BGR was cofounded by the prominent politician Haley Barbour. In 2000, *Fortune Magazine* tabbed BGR as the nation's most powerful lobbying firm.

On its website, Diligence states that it is a "business intelligence firm that helps its clients confront difficult business challenges." The website goes on to note that, "In this role, we provide companies with both the intelligence and analysis to enable them to identify, manage and mitigate risks stemming either from the normal flow of business or from unanticipated contingencies." In laymen's terms, a major focus of Diligence's business model is helping multinational companies deal with threats posed by corporate espionage, real or imagined.

William Webster, the only individual to have served as the head of both the Federal Bureau of Investigation (FBI) and the CIA, was for many years on Diligence's Advisory Board and reportedly helped Nick Day organize the firm in 2000. In 2006, Michael Howard was appointed Diligence's chairman. For several years, Howard had served as the leader of Britain's Conservative Party and would have become the nation's Prime Minister if his party had been successful in defeating the Labour Party headed by Tony Blair.

Unknown to Guy Enright, he had been the focal point of a months-long effort by agents of Diligence to gain inside information regarding IPOC. Diligence's management intended to complete this assignment, which it referred to as Project Yucca, in secrecy to avoid any embarrassment or legal repercussions for itself, Alfa Group, or BGR. An internal memo of Diligence obtained by *Bloomberg Businessweek* noted that, "We are doing it [Project Yucca] in a way which gives [us] plausible deniability, and therefore virtually no chance of discovery."

After being retained by BGR, Diligence went to great lengths to identify one or more individuals who might cooperate in its effort to gain access to IPOC's inner sanctum. When Diligence learned that KPMG was involved in a government-sponsored investigation of IPOC, they contacted staff members of KPMG's Bermuda office. While posing as organizers of a legal conference in Bermuda, two Diligence employees were successful in eliciting from KPMG's secretarial staff the names of the individuals assigned to the IPOC engagement.

Next, Diligence developed psychological profiles to identify the KPMG employees most likely to participate in the agency's covert plan. According to *Bloomberg Businessweek*, the female profile suggested that Diligence should target "a young female who is insecure . . . not honest. Someone who spends money on her looks, clothes, gadgets. Has no boyfriend, and only superficial friends. Has a strong relationship with her mother." The similarly unflattering male profile involved a "male in his mid-20s who is somewhat bored . . . has a propensity to party hard, needs cash, enjoys risk, likes sports, likes women, is disrespectful of his managers, fiddles his expenses, but is patriotic."

After determining that none of the KPMG employees assigned to the IPOC engagement was a good "fit" for the ideal male or female personality profiles that they had developed, the Diligence officials decided to focus their attention on Guy Enright. Throughout the several months required to carry out Project Yucca, the intelligence firm went to great lengths to insure that Enright was not a "double agent" acting on behalf of IPOC. The counter-intelligence measures they employed included tracking Enright as he traveled around Bermuda and searching his garbage.

For its efforts, Diligence was paid $280,000 by BGR and was reimbursed for $30,000 of expenses it incurred. Included in the $280,000 figure was a $60,000 "bonus" paid to Diligence when Nick Day convinced Enright to hand over an early draft of KPMG's report on its IPOC investigation. For his role in the clandestine operation, Enright was given a Rolex watch valued at "thousands of dollars" by Diligence and "was led to believe that it [the watch] was a thank-you gift from the British government."

EPILOGUE

In July 2007, IPOC and Alfa Group announced that they were ending their long-running and costly legal battle. The two companies agreed to "end all court actions and renounce legal claims against each other,"[6] which meant that the Alfa Group would retain the 25 percent ownership interest in MegaFon that it had purchased from Leonid Rozhetskin. By this time, however, IPOC's cover "had been blown." The year before, a Swiss arbitration panel had corroborated one of the key allegations made by Alfa Group against IPOC, namely, that Leonid Reiman, Russia's Telecommunications Minister and Vladimir Putin's close ally, was IPOC's "beneficial owner."[7] A similar conclusion was reached by a law enforcement agency in the British Virgin Islands that also had been investigating IPOC. That agency reported that IPOC "was a front for the laundering of the proceeds of crime of, amongst others, Russian Telecommunications Minister Mr. Leonid Reiman."[8]

In May 2008, after reviewing KPMG's report on IPOC and information culled from other sources, the Bermuda Supreme Court ruled that IPOC had to disband its business operations in Bermuda. In commenting on that ruling, Bermuda's Finance Minister observed that, "We were committed to protecting Bermuda and sending a signal to the world that Bermuda does not trifle with its reputation."[9] The relieved and happy official then added that the "long and complicated case" had "more angles and twists and turns than a James Bond novel."[10]

In late 2005, a bundle of documents that revealed the details of Diligence's "sting operation" involving Guy Enright had been left anonymously at a New Jersey office of KPMG.[11] After reviewing those documents, the Big Four accounting firm filed a civil lawsuit against the British intelligence firm. Although that lawsuit was settled privately between the two parties, numerous sources reported that Diligence paid KPMG $1.7 million to resolve the matter. Despite that settlement, Diligence officials insisted that they had done nothing wrong during the infamous Project Yucca. Those officials reported that they had "obtained information [regarding IPOC] from a whistleblower worried that the inquiry [of IPOC by KPMG] might bury some uncomfortable facts."[12]

The details of Diligence's sting operation were leaked to the press in late 2006 and early 2007. By this time, Guy Enright had left the employment of KPMG and joined the consulting staff of Deloitte & Touche in London.

During the drawn-out legal battle involving himself, Alfa Group, and IPOC, Leonid Rozhetskin continued to be an outspoken critic of the Russian government, particularly Vladimir Putin. In late 2006, a Russian federal prosecutor filed criminal charges against Rozhetskin and issued an arrest warrant for him. The prosecutor alleged that Rozhetskin had engaged in wide-ranging fraudulent activities related to the sale of his 25 percent ownership interest in MegaFon to Alfa Group. After the arrest warrant was issued, "Rozhetskin

---

6. N. Buckley, "Russian Phone Feud Peace Deal," *Financial Times* (online), 30 July 2007.

7. *Ibid.*

8. J. Kent, "The Rise and Fall of IPOC," *The Royal Gazette* (online), 9 May 2008.

9. *Ibid.*

10. *Ibid.*

11. Several parties have speculated that a disgruntled former employee of Diligence, Inc. was the individual who delivered these documents to KPMG.

12. S. Fidler, A. Ostrovsky, and N. Buckley, "MegaFon Diplomacy: A Disputed Stake Pits an Oligarch against a Putin Ally," *Financial Times* (online), 24 April 2006.

maintained that his life was in danger for seeking to expose corruption of President Putin's government."[13]

In March 2008, Rozhetskin disappeared while making a business trip to Latvia. Over the next few years, Russian law enforcement authorities insisted that Rozhetskin had been placed in the federal witness protection program by the U.S. law enforcement authorities and was living under an assumed name in California where he had become involved in the movie industry as a producer. Rozhetskin's mother dismissed that rumor and maintained instead that her son had been abducted by Putin allies. She claimed that he had been abducted because of his public criticism of Putin and because he was planning "a documentary film that would expose government and business corruption in Russia."[14] Four years later, in September 2012, DNA tests revealed that skeletal remains discovered in a remote area of Latvia were those of Leonid Rozhetskin.

Questions

1. Bermuda's Minister of Finance retained KPMG to "audit" the business affairs of IPOC to determine whether the company was a criminal enterprise or a legitimate business operation. What type of professional service was KPMG providing during this engagement? Did the engagement qualify as an assurance, attestation, audit, or consulting engagement? Defend your answer.

2. What moral, ethical, and professional responsibilities did Guy Enright face when he was asked to turn over confidential documents to the individuals who were representing themselves as intelligence agents for the British and the U.S. governments? Which of those responsibilities did he violate and which did he uphold?

3. Compare and contrast the conduct of Guy Enright and Nick Day. Which of these individuals was most ethical (or least unethical)? Defend your answer.

4. How would you respond if you faced a set of circumstances similar to those faced by Guy Enright?

5. KPMG filed a civil lawsuit against Diligence, Inc., in 2005 after learning of the "sting operation" that firm had perpetuated on Guy Enright. What rationale or legal principles would have been the basis for that lawsuit? Do you believe that KPMG would have been successful if it had pursued that lawsuit rather than settling it out of court? Assuming that KPMG believed it would ultimately win a civil judgment against Diligence, why would the accounting firm choose to settle the lawsuit out of court? Explain.

13. B. Gain, "Missing American's Body a DNA Match in Latvia," *www.trutv.com*, 5 September 2012.
14. *Ibid.*

Phillips Petroleum Company

Bill Grant sat in the middle of a large jail cell with 12 other inmates as the long October night dragged on.[1] To pass the time, Grant and several other inmates played cards and talked about their hopes of being reunited with their families. The accommodations of the Tulsa County Jail were not unlike those of most jails: dirty, no lid on the toilet, and 12 beds for 13 inmates. What made this scene unusual was not the less-than-glamorous, overcrowded condition of the jail cell, but rather the presence of Grant, a Big Eight audit partner and graduate of the Harvard Business School. At the time, Grant served as the managing partner of the Tulsa office of Arthur Young & Company, but he was destined to become Arthur Young's comanaging partner in 1988 shortly before that firm merged with Ernst & Whinney to form Ernst & Young.

Earlier that day, Grant had appeared in a Tulsa federal courthouse at a hearing presided over by Judge Allan Barrow. Judge Barrow had ordered Grant to produce certain audit workpapers that had been subpoenaed by a federal grand jury. Those workpapers had been prepared during an audit of the large oil company, Phillips Petroleum Company, a client of Arthur Young's Tulsa office. When Grant respectfully denied the judge's request, he was cited for civil contempt, handcuffed, and led away to jail. Apparently, the judge hoped that an overnight stay in a crowded jail cell would convince Grant to change his mind.

The federal grand jury's interest in the Arthur Young workpapers stemmed from an ongoing investigation of Phillips. That investigation focused on possible tax fraud related to a secret, multimillion-dollar fund that Phillips' executives had established to make political contributions. One contribution made from the secret fund, which was maintained in a Swiss bank account, was an illegal donation of $100,000 to the Committee to Reelect the President (Richard Nixon). Under the terms of an earlier plea bargain agreement with Watergate special prosecutor Archibald Cox, Phillips' chairman of the board had admitted to the $100,000 contribution to President Nixon's 1972 reelection campaign and pleaded guilty to one misdemeanor.[2] Following that plea bargain agreement, federal prosecutors indicted Phillips for filing false federal tax returns that failed to report interest revenue earned on the secret Swiss bank account.

Prior to Bill Grant's appearance before Judge Barrow, Arthur Young had turned over to the federal grand jury approximately 12,000 pages of Phillips audit workpapers. Arthur Young, however, had refused to give the grand jury several workpapers relating to two key items: (1) certain tax accruals made by Phillips and (2) attorneys' letters that Arthur Young had obtained from Phillips' law firms. Among other topics, these attorneys' letters were known to include discussions of "unasserted claims"

---

1. The facts of this case were drawn principally from the following articles: "Arthur Young Aide Cited for Contempt and Jailed in Tulsa," *Wall Street Journal*, 8 October 1975, 10; F. Andrews, "Arthur Young Faces Test on Protecting Client Audit Secrets," *Wall Street Journal*, 14 October 1975, 23; "Arthur Young & Co. Gives Grand Jury Data on Phillips Petroleum," *Wall Street Journal*, 15 October 1975, 28; "Pleas by Phillips Petroleum Filed on U.S. Charges," *Wall Street Journal*, 23 November 1977, 2.

2. Phillips' chairman also revealed that he had delivered $50,000 to Nixon in a New York City apartment during the 1968 presidential campaign in which Nixon eventually defeated Senator Hubert Humphrey.

by Phillips' attorneys. The federal grand jury believed that both sets of workpapers might provide important insight on the tax fraud allegations involving Phillips.

Arthur Young had refused to provide the contested workpapers to the grand jury on the grounds that they contained confidential information that, if disclosed, would be potentially damaging to Phillips. Tax accrual audit workpapers, for example, typically contain an audit firm's analysis of tax-related decisions made by their clients. Access to such workpapers would make it much easier for the Internal Revenue Service (IRS) to "build a case" against a given company.

Bill Grant was released from the Tulsa County Jail on 7 October 1975, but was ordered to make an appearance the following week before Judge Barrow. If Grant again refused to produce the workpapers subpoenaed by the grand jury, he faced the risk of being cited for criminal contempt and receiving a 17-month jail term. During the week between Grant's two court appearances, Arthur Young's attorneys worked out a compromise with Judge Barrow. Under the terms of the agreement, Arthur Young turned over copies of the requested tax accrual workpapers. All matters other than those specifically identified by the subpoena were masked in the copies of the workpapers given to the grand jury. Judge Barrow also granted Arthur Young the right to contest any subsequent court order to provide the original "unmasked" tax accrual workpapers to the grand jury.

Judge Barrow did not relent with respect to the contested attorneys' letters. He ordered Arthur Young to provide copies of those letters to the grand jury. Phillips filed a motion to appeal this order, but that appeal was denied.

EPILOGUE

The Watergate-related problems of Phillips Petroleum continued to plague the company following the resolution of the dispute involving the Arthur Young workpapers. In early 1976, Phillips' executives temporarily turned over control of the company to its outside directors. This decision was spurred by the filing of a large class-action lawsuit against Phillips linked to the charges of illegal campaign contributions. In November 1977, Phillips settled these charges by pleading guilty to engaging in a conspiracy to make illegal campaign contributions, pleading no contest to four related tax evasion charges, and paying a fine of $30,000.

Ironically, Arthur Young's tax accrual workpapers for another audit client, the large oil company Amerada Hess, became the focal point of another major litigation case. The issue in this case was whether the IRS had the right to review copies of auditors' tax accrual workpapers. In 1984, the Supreme Court decided the case by unanimously ruling that the IRS has the right to review tax accrual workpapers prepared during an independent audit.

Questions

1. Do you believe that Bill Grant was justified in refusing to provide the requested workpapers to the grand jury? Explain.

2. What responsibility, if any, does a public accounting firm have to its partners and employees when they are subpoenaed to testify regarding a client?

3. What is the purpose of "attorneys' letters" obtained during the course of an audit? If attorneys are aware that these letters can be routinely subpoenaed, how does this fact likely affect the quality of the audit evidence yielded by the letters?

4. Do you believe the documentation included in tax accrual audit workpapers is likely affected by auditors' knowledge that those workpapers can be obtained by the IRS? Explain.

CASE 5.6

Ryden Trucking, Inc.

Jermell Marshall graduated with an accounting degree from the University of Washington in 1990 and immediately accepted a job with a regional accounting firm based in Seattle.[1] After spending four and one-half years on the auditing staff of that firm, Marshall decided he had worked for someone else long enough and resigned to establish his own accounting practice.

Fifteen years later, Marshall's firm included two other partners, 15 professional employees, and a support staff of 10 paraprofessionals and clerical workers. Marshall served as the managing partner of his firm and supervised most audit, accounting services, and consulting engagements. The firm's audit and accounting services clients were primarily small to moderately sized businesses in the Seattle area that required annual audits or reviews of their financial statements for their banks or other lenders.

In August 2009, Marshall hired Lola Rojas, a 28-year-old accountant who had moved to Seattle from southern California a few weeks earlier to be near her ailing mother. Rojas had earned an accounting degree in 2005 but after several attempts had not passed the CPA exam. Following graduation, Rojas had held three different jobs, two as a staff accountant with small accounting firms and one as an entry-level accountant with a bank. Before hiring Rojas, Marshall asked for letters of recommendation from two of her former employers. Each of those recommendation letters indicated that the cheerful and outgoing Rojas had been a dependable, competent, and hard-working employee.

Marshall assigned Rojas to several audit and accounting services engagements that he supervised during her first six months with the firm. He was very pleased with her performance on those assignments. She was typically the first individual to arrive for work each morning, quickly established friendships with her peers, and was well liked by client personnel. Marshall's impression of Rojas changed abruptly in March 2010 when he received a phone call from Carson Caddell, the principal owner of Ryden Trucking, Inc., a trucking firm that serviced agricultural businesses in Washington and neighboring states. Ryden was easily the largest client of Marshall's firm. Caddell informed Marshall that one of his bookkeepers had discovered compelling evidence that Rojas had embezzled approximately $32,000 during the three weeks she had spent in Ryden's office in early 2010.

Since establishing his firm, Marshall had dealt with several "problem" employees, but a client had never accused one of his employees of theft. Extremely upset, Marshall called Rojas into his office and informed her of the alleged theft reported by Carson Caddell. Within moments, Rojas began weeping and confessed to embezzling the funds. She explained that she needed the cash to pay for the medical expenses incurred over the previous year by her terminally ill mother who had no health insurance. Rojas then pleaded with Marshall to help her. She insisted that she had intended to somehow repay the stolen funds. If Marshall or Caddell reported her to law enforcement authorities, there would be no one to care for her mother.

---

1. This case was developed from an actual legal opinion. The names of the parties involved in the case and the relevant locations have been changed. In addition, certain of the factual circumstances reported in this case are fictionalized accounts of the actual facts disclosed in the legal opinion.

Marshall discussed the situation with his subordinate for more than an hour. Gradually, his anger subsided and he began to feel sorry for the emotionally distraught Rojas. In his mind, here was a young lady who had faced a tragic set of circumstances and made a foolish decision that stood to wreck her personal life and professional career. Finally, Marshall told Rojas that he wanted to discuss the matter with an attorney. In the meantime, he told her that he had no choice but to terminate her employment since he could no longer trust her.

Later that same day, Marshall drove to the law office of Andrew Tao. The two men had been friends since high school and fraternity brothers in college. After explaining the situation to Tao, Marshall asked if there was any way that the matter could be resolved without Rojas facing criminal charges. Tao responded that the decision of whether or not to file charges against Rojas rested with Carson Caddell.

The following morning, Marshall and Tao met with Caddell. During the meeting, Caddell repeatedly insisted that Rojas should be reported to law enforcement authorities. Even after Marshall explained the sad circumstances facing Rojas, Caddell was unmoved. "You can't let something like this slide, Jermell. Come on, she stole more than $30,000 from us. She deserves what she gets."

Marshall made one final attempt to change Caddell's mind. He offered to repay one-half of the stolen funds immediately and sign a promissory note obligating him to repay the remainder within two years if Caddell would agree not to press charges. After several moments, Caddell responded by indicating that he "would think about it."[2]

Three days later, Marshall and Tao met with Rojas. When Marshall told Rojas of his offer to reimburse Ryden for the embezzlement loss, she burst into tears and promised to repay him. After she regained her composure, Marshall reminded Rojas that Caddell had not yet accepted his offer. Before Rojas left Marshall's office a few minutes later, he asked her how she expected to support herself over the coming weeks. Rojas told Marshall that, thanks to a recommendation from a friend, she had found a bookkeeping job with a small manufacturing firm in a nearby Seattle suburb. She was scheduled to begin the job the following Monday.

Marshall telephoned Caddell regarding Lola Rojas each of the next two weeks. During those two conversations, Caddell indicated that he appreciated Marshall's offer but still firmly believed that Rojas should be held accountable for her actions. A few days following the second conversation with Caddell, Marshall was surprised when Rojas walked into his office and told him that she had convinced an uncle to loan her the $32,000 to repay Ryden Trucking. She then handed Marshall an envelope that contained a cashier's check for that amount. Marshall told Rojas that he would give the check to Caddell but warned her that Caddell was still likely to insist on pressing charges. He told her that he would talk with Caddell one more time and try to persuade him to change his mind.

The following day, Marshall, accompanied by Tao, delivered the cashier's check to Caddell. As Marshall had expected, the check did not change Caddell's mind. But, after Marshall made one final, heartfelt plea that Rojas deserved a second chance, Caddell agreed to drop the matter in exchange for Rojas pleading guilty to a misdemeanor.

Two days later, Marshall, Tao, and Rojas met with an assistant district attorney who was a friend of Tao. After reviewing the matter and discussing it with his superiors, the assistant district attorney refused to accept Rojas's misdemeanor plea, explaining that the substantial size of the embezzlement warranted that she be charged with more than a misdemeanor.

---

2. As a point of information, the legal opinion from which this case was developed did not indicate whether Ryden Trucking had insurance that would reimburse the company for the embezzlement loss.

A frazzled and frustrated Marshall reported the decision of the assistant district attorney to Caddell. On hearing the news, an equally frazzled and frustrated Caddell told Marshall, "Let's just forget the whole mess right now. I am sick and tired of this. I just hope that she has learned her lesson."

Less than one month after Caddell decided not to press criminal charges against Lola Rojas, the young accountant was back in court—in handcuffs. Rojas was arrested for embezzling approximately $41,000 from her new employer. Rojas had used the bulk of that amount to repay the funds she had embezzled from Ryden Trucking.

EPILOGUE

The insurance company that reimbursed Rojas's second victim for the $41,000 embezzlement loss filed a lawsuit against Jermell Marshall to recover that payment. The lawsuit included various charges of negligence and gross negligence against Marshall. But, the central premise of the lawsuit was that Marshall had been negligent in failing to warn Rojas's new employer of her prior criminal activity.[3]

The judge who presided over this lawsuit referred to several broad legal principles in reaching his decision, including his jurisdiction's definition of what constitutes negligence: the doing of that which an ordinarily prudent person would not have done under the same or similar circumstances, or the failure to do that which an ordinarily prudent person would have done under the same or similar circumstances. A second legal principle central to the case was the general rule that a person has no legal duty to protect another from the criminal acts of a third party. However, the judge noted that this latter rule is not absolute. For example,

employers who can *reasonably foresee* that an employee *under their control* may commit criminal acts harming third parties generally have a responsibility to warn those parties of the impending criminal behavior.

After a brief trial, the judge ruled, and an appellate court later concurred, that Jermell Marshall had not been negligent in failing to warn Rojas's new employer of her prior criminal conduct. According to the judge, Marshall could not have foreseen or predicted that Lola Rojas would embezzle from future employers. In fact, it was just as likely, reasoned the judge, that Rojas "had learned her lesson" and thus was very unlikely to commit a similar act in the future. Additionally, once Marshall dismissed Rojas as an employee, he had no control over her future conduct. The appellate judge who reviewed the lower court opinion did suggest, however, that despite not having a legal responsibility to warn Rojas's new employer of her prior criminal conduct, Marshall may have been "morally obligated" to do so.

Questions

1. The legal opinion in this case did not indicate how Lola Rojas actually used the funds she embezzled from Ryden Trucking. Suppose that she did use those funds to pay medical expenses of her mother. Given this assumption, would you describe her behavior as "unethical"? Defend your answer.

---

3. This lawsuit also named Lola Rojas and Andrew Tao as codefendants, although the complaints filed against them differed from those filed against Jermell Marshall.

2. What factors may have motivated Jermell Marshall to go to such great lengths to help Rojas? Do you believe that Marshall acted "prudently" in dealing with Rojas?

3. Although not mentioned in this case, the plaintiff that sued Marshall maintained that he had been negligent in supervising Rojas while she was assigned to the Ryden engagement. That negligence, according to the plaintiff, had contributed to Rojas's decision to embezzle funds from Ryden. Briefly describe the supervisory responsibilities that the U.S. auditing standards impose on senior personnel assigned to an audit or accounting services engagement. To what extent does a supervisor on such engagements have a responsibility to prevent his or her subordinates from engaging in criminal activity?

4. The appellate judge who reviewed the lower court opinion in this case observed that Marshall may have been "morally obligated" to warn Rojas's new employer of her prior criminal conduct. Explain the difference between a "moral obligation" and a "legal obligation." If someone fails to honor a moral obligation, has he or she behaved "unethically"?

Richard Grimes, Staff Accountant

Richard Grimes glanced at his wristwatch as he pulled into the nearly deserted parking lot of the corporate headquarters of McCaleb Medical Corporation (MMC).[1] It was 6:25 a.m. on a cold and overcast Friday morning in February. Based in a suburb on the south side of Pittsburgh, Pennsylvania, MMC was a conglomerate whose principal line of business was manufacturing diagnostic instruments used in medical laboratories. The company's common stock traded on one of the major stock exchanges. Richard, a staff accountant with a Big Four accounting firm, was a member of the MMC audit team. He and his colleagues were auditing MMC's financial statements for the company's fiscal year that had ended several weeks earlier on 31 December.

Gwen Tomlinson, the audit senior who was supervising the fieldwork for the MMC audit, had given Richard permission to leave at 4 p.m. that day so that he could attend a family get-together in his hometown of Cumberland, Maryland, a two-hour drive from Pittsburgh. To compensate somewhat for his early departure, Richard had arrived at MMC's headquarters an hour or so before he and his colleagues typically began their workday.

Richard flipped on the lights as he entered a conference room on the third floor of the client's headquarters building that served as the home base for the MMC audit team. One end of the conference room was dominated by a large oval desk where Gwen could typically be found pounding away on her laptop computer, reviewing a file of audit workpapers, or wading through large stacks of client documents. The remaining two-thirds of the conference room was partitioned into cubicle workstations for Richard and the three other staff accountants assigned to the MMC engagement. Two of those staff accountants were "rookies" who had less than three months experience. Similar to Richard, the other staff accountant was beginning her second busy season in public accounting.

After spending a few minutes organizing his workstation for the day, Richard picked up a notepad on which he had jotted down identifying information for six equipment lease contracts that he needed to review. He then headed for a bank of file cabinets in a far corner of the third floor. The file cabinets were tucked in an L-shaped alcove adjacent to the office of MMC's controller, Alva Russell.

As Richard approached Russell's office, he was surprised to see the controller and Daniel Slater, MMC's president and chief operating officer (COO), leaning forward over Russell's desk with their backs to the open door of the office. The two men were having an animated conversation as they studied a large spreadsheet that was unfolded on the desk. Because he didn't want to interrupt them, Richard walked softly past the open door and then made an immediate left into the small alcove containing the file cabinets.

As quietly as possible, Richard opened the file cabinet drawer that contained MMC's equipment lease contracts. As he stood there, he alternately referred to his notepad and then leafed through the open drawer of the file cabinet to retrieve each of the contracts that he intended to review.

---

1. This case is based upon a similar set of circumstances involving a staff accountant of a large audit firm. The names of the individuals involved in the case and other background information have been changed.

While standing there, Richard could clearly hear every word being said by the two MMC executives since they were standing just a few feet away, although he was totally hidden from their view. Slater was informing Russell that the day before he had learned MMC's largest customer would be filing for Chapter 7 bankruptcy sometime within the next several weeks. The receivable from that customer, which was a private company, accounted for 28 percent of MMC's outstanding receivables. Slater told Russell that MMC would be "lucky" to collect a "few pennies on the dollar" from the receivable.

Russell responded to the bad news by telling Slater that the expected loss on the large receivable had to be "addressed somehow" in the company's financial statements to be filed with the SEC in the coming two weeks. Slater quickly replied that MMC was not going to "borrow trouble" by referring to the loss in MMC's upcoming Form 10-K. Besides, he reasoned, the bankruptcy almost certainly would not become "public information" until after the Form 10-K was filed with the SEC.

As the conversation between the two men continued, it was obvious that Russell strongly disagreed with Slater's decision. Near the end of the conversation, an exasperated Russell asked Slater, "What am I supposed to tell the auditors?"

"Don't tell them anything," Slater snapped. "What they don't know, doesn't concern them."

A few moments later, Richard was startled when Daniel Slater strode out of Alva Russell's office and passed within a few feet of him. Richard had anticipated that Slater would turn to the right when he left Russell's office—in which case he would not have walked past the alcove where Richard was standing. As he was walking away, Slater glanced over his shoulder and noticed Richard standing in front of the bank of file cabinets. Slater immediately turned and approached him.

"How long have you been standing there?" Slater snarled. When Richard didn't respond immediately, Slater added, "Aren't you one of the auditors?"

Richard nodded his head affirmatively.

"What's wrong with you? You think you can stand out here and listen to a private conversation?" Slater was angry, very angry. After taking a deep breath, he continued his harangue. "How did you sneak by the office door without us noticing you?" By this time, Alva Russell had stepped out of his office and was standing shoulder to shoulder with Slater.

Richard stood silently before the two men with his mouth slightly ajar, not sure whether he should try to explain his presence or offer an apology or both.

After a long awkward pause, Slater uttered an expletive under his breath and walked away. Russell stood facing Richard for a few additional moments before shrugging his shoulders and returning to his office.

Questions

1. How, if at all, should MMC report the expected loss on the large receivable in its Form 10-K financial statements? Explain.

2. Place yourself in Richard Grimes' position. What decision alternatives does he have after overhearing the conversation between Alva Russell and Daniel Slater? Which of these alternatives should he choose? Why?

3. Did Richard have a responsibility to make the two client executives aware of his presence when he was outside of Russell's office? Why or why not?

4. Do you believe that Daniel Slater would have reacted differently if the auditor in question had been a female rather than a male? Explain.

PROFESSIONAL ROLES

6

Leigh Ann Walker, Staff Accountant

Leigh Ann Walker graduated from a major state university with a bachelor's degree in accounting.[1] During her college career, Walker earned a 3.9 grade point average and participated in several extracurricular activities, including three student business organizations. Her closest friends often teased her about the busy schedule she maintained and the fact that she was, at times, a little too "intense." During her final year of college, Walker interviewed with several public accounting firms and large corporations and received six job offers. After considering those offers, she decided to accept an entry-level position on the auditing staff of a major international accounting firm. Walker was not sure whether she wanted to pursue a partnership position with her new employer. But she believed that the training programs the firm provided and the breadth of experience she would receive from a wide array of client assignments would get her career off to a fast start.

Walker's "start date" was 4 June, exactly one month following her graduation date. She spent the first two weeks on her new job at her firm's regional audit staff training school. On returning to her local office in mid-June, she was assigned to work on the audit of Saint Andrew's Hospital, a large sectarian hospital with a 30 June fiscal year-end. Walker's immediate superior on the Saint Andrew's engagement was Jackie Vaughn, a third-year senior. On her first day on the Saint Andrew's audit, Walker learned that she would audit the hospital's cash accounts and assist with accounts receivable. Walker was excited about her first client assignment and pleased that she would be working for Vaughn. Vaughn had a reputation as a demanding supervisor who typically brought her engagements in under budget. She was also known for having an excellent rapport with her clients, a thorough knowledge of technical standards, and for being fair and straightforward with her subordinates.

Like many newly hired staff auditors, Walker was apprehensive about her new job. She understood the purpose of independent audits and was familiar with the work performed by auditors but doubted that one auditing course and a two-week staff-training seminar had adequately prepared her for her new work role. After being assigned to work under Vaughn's supervision, Walker was relieved. She sensed that although Vaughn was demanding, the senior would be patient and understanding with a new staff auditor. More important, she believed that she could learn a great deal from working closely with Vaughn. Walker resolved that she would work hard to impress Vaughn and had hopes that the senior would mentor her through the first few years of her career.

Early in Walker's second week on the Saint Andrew's engagement, Jackie Vaughn casually asked her over lunch one day whether she had taken the CPA examination in May. After a brief pause, Walker replied that she had not but planned to study intensively for the exam during the next five months and then take it in November.[2]

---

1. This case is based upon a true set of facts; however, the names of the parties involved have been changed. An employee of a job placement firm provided much of the information incorporated in this case. This firm had been retained by the student identified in this case as Leigh Ann Walker.

2. At the time, the CPA examination was offered twice annually, in November and May. In most states, including Leigh Ann's home state, an individual who sat for the exam for the first time was required to take all four parts.

Vaughn indicated that was a good strategy and offered to lend Walker a set of CPA review manuals—an offer Walker declined. In fact, Walker had returned to her home state during the first week of May and sat for the CPA exam, but she was convinced that she had failed it. Fear of failure, or, rather, fear of admitting failure, caused Walker to decide not to tell her coworkers that she had taken the exam. She realized that most of her peers would not pass all sections of the exam on their first attempt. Nevertheless, Leigh Ann wanted to avoid the embarrassment of admitting throughout the remainder of her career that she had not been a "first timer."

Walker continued to work on the Saint Andrew's engagement throughout the summer. She completed the cash audit within budget, thoroughly documenting the results of the audit procedures she applied. Vaughn was pleased with Walker's work and frequently complimented and encouraged her. As the engagement was winding down in early August, Walker received her grades on the CPA exam in the mail one Friday evening. To her surprise, she had passed all parts of the exam. She immediately called Vaughn to let her know of the impressive accomplishment. To Walker's surprise, Vaughn seemed irritated, if not disturbed, by the good news. Walker then recalled having earlier told Vaughn that she had not taken the exam in May. Walker immediately apologized and explained why she had chosen not to disclose that she had taken the exam. Following her explanation, Vaughn still seemed annoyed, so Walker decided to drop the subject and pursue it later in person.

The following week, Vaughn spent Monday through Wednesday with another client, while Walker and the other staff assigned to the Saint Andrew's engagement continued to wrap up the hospital audit. On Wednesday morning, Walker received a call from Don Roberts, the office managing partner and Saint Andrew's audit engagement partner. Roberts asked Walker to meet with him late that afternoon in his office. She assumed that Roberts simply wanted to congratulate her on passing the CPA exam.

The usually upbeat Roberts was somber when Walker stepped into his office that afternoon. After she was seated, Roberts informed her that he had spoken with Jackie Vaughn several times during the past few days and that he had consulted with the three other audit partners in the office regarding a situation involving Walker. Roberts told Walker that Vaughn was very upset by the fact that she (Walker) had lied regarding the CPA exam. Vaughn had indicated that she would not be comfortable having a subordinate on future engagements that she could not trust to be truthful. Vaughn had also suggested that Walker be dismissed from the firm because of the lack of integrity she had demonstrated.

After a brief silence, Roberts told a stunned Walker that he and the other audit partners agreed with Vaughn. He informed Walker that she would be given 60 days to find another job. Roberts also told Walker that he and the other partners would not disclose that she had been "counseled out" of the firm if they were contacted by employers interested in hiring her.

Questions

1. In your opinion, did Vaughn overreact to Walker's admission that she had been untruthful regarding the CPA exam? If so, how would you have dealt with the situation if you had been in Vaughn's position? How would you have dealt with the situation if you had been in Roberts' position?

2. Vaughn obviously questioned Walker's personal integrity. Is it possible that one can fulfill the responsibilities of a professional role while lacking personal integrity? Why or why not?

Bill DeBurger,
In-Charge Accountant

"Bill, will you have that inventory memo done by this afternoon?"[1]

"Yeah, Sam, it's coming along. I should have it done by five, or so."

"Make it three ... or so. Okay, Bub?"

Bill responded with a smile and a nod. He had a good relationship with Sam Hakes, the partner supervising the audit of Marcelle Stores.

Bill DeBurger was an in-charge accountant who had 18 months experience with his employer, a large national accounting firm. Bill's firm used the title "in-charge" for the employment position between staff accountant and audit senior. Other titles used by accounting firms for this position include "advanced staff" and "semi-senior." Typically, Bill's firm promoted individuals to in-charge after one year. An additional one to two years' experience and successful completion of the CPA exam were usually required before promotion to audit senior.

The title "in-charge" was a misnomer, at least in Bill's mind. None of the in-charges he knew had ever been placed in-charge of an audit, even a small audit. Based upon Bill's experience, an in-charge was someone a senior or manager expected to work with little or no supervision. "Here's the audit program for payables. Go spend the next five weeks completing the 12 program steps ... and don't bother me," seemed to be the prevailing attitude in making work assignments to in-charges.

As he turned back to the legal pad in front of him, Bill forced himself to think of Marcelle Stores' inventory—all $50 million of it. Bill's task was to summarize, in a two-page memo, 900 hours of work that he, two staff accountants, and five internal auditors had done over the past two months. Not included in the 900 hours was the time spent on eight inventory observations performed by other offices of Bill's firm.

Marcelle Stores was a regional chain of 112 specialty stores that featured a broad range of products for do-it-yourself interior decorators. The company's most recent fiscal year had been a difficult one. A poor economy, increasing competition, and higher supplier prices had slashed Marcelle's profit to the bone over the past 12 months. The previous year, the company had posted a profit of slightly less than $8 million; for the year just completed, the company's preaudit net income hovered at an anemic $500,000.

Inventory was the focal point of each audit of Marcelle's financial statements. This year, inventory was doubly important. Any material overstatement discovered in the inventory account would convert a poor year profit-wise for Marcelle into a disastrous year in which the company posted its first-ever loss.

Facing Bill on the small table that served as his makeshift desk were two stacks of workpapers, each two feet tall. Those workpapers summarized the results of extensive price tests, inventory observation procedures, year-end cutoff tests, an analysis of the reserve for inventory obsolescence, and various other audit procedures. Bill's task was to assimilate all of this audit evidence into a conclusion regarding Marcelle's inventory. Bill realized that Sam Hakes expected that conclusion to include the

---

1. The source for this case was a former public accountant who is now a college instructor. The names of the parties involved in the case and certain other background facts have been changed.

key catch phrases "present fairly, in all material respects" and "in accordance with accounting principles generally accepted in the United States of America."

As Bill attempted to outline the inventory memo, he gradually admitted to himself that he had no idea whether Marcelle's inventory dollar value was materially accurate. The workpaper summarizing the individual errors discovered in the inventory account reflected a net overstatement of only $72,000. That amount was not material even in reference to Marcelle's unusually small net income. However, Bill realized that the $72,000 figure was little more than a guess.

The client's allowance for inventory obsolescence particularly troubled Bill. He had heard a rumor that Marcelle intended to discontinue 2 of the 14 sales departments in its stores. If that were true, the inventory in those departments would have to be sold at deep discounts. The collective dollar value of those two departments' inventory approached $6 million, while the client's allowance for inventory obsolescence had a year-end balance of only $225,000. Earlier in the audit, Bill had asked Sam about the rumored closing of the two departments. The typically easygoing partner had replied with a terse "Don't worry about it."

Bill always took his work assignments seriously and wanted to do a professional job in completing them. He believed that independent audits served an extremely important role in a free market economy. Bill was often annoyed that not all of his colleagues shared that view. Some of his coworkers seemed to have an attitude of "just get the work done." They stressed form over substance: "Tic and tie, make the workpapers look good, and don't be too concerned with the results. A clean opinion is going to be issued no matter what you find."

Finally, Bill made a decision. He would not sign off on the inventory account regardless of the consequences. He did not know whether the inventory account balance was materially accurate, and he was not going to write a memo indicating otherwise. Moments later, Bill walked into the client office being used by Sam Hakes and closed the door behind him.

"What's up?" Sam asked as he flipped through a workpaper file.

"Sam, I've decided that I can't sign off on the inventory account," Bill blurted out.

"What?" was Sam's stunned, one-word reply.

Bill stalled for a few moments to bolster his courage as he fidgeted with his tie. "Well ... like I said, I'm not signing off on the inventory account."

"Why?" By this point, a disturbing crimson shade had already engulfed Sam's ears and was creeping slowly across his face.

"Sam ... I just don't think I can sign off. I mean, I'm just not sure whether the inventory number is right."

"You're ... *just not sure*?" After a brief pause, Sam continued, this time pronouncing each of his words with a deliberate and sarcastic tone. "You mean to tell me that you spent almost 1,000 hours on that account, and you're just not sure whether the general ledger number is right?"

"Well ... yeah. Ya know, it's just tough to ... to reach a conclusion, ya know, on an account that large."

Sam leaned back in his chair and cleared his throat before speaking. "Mr. DeBurger, I want you to go back into that room of yours and close the door. Then you sit down at that table and write a nice, neat, very precise and to-the-point inventory memo. And hear this: I'm not telling you what to include in that memo. But you're going to write that memo, and you're going to have it on my desk in two hours. Understood?" Sam's face was entirely crimson as he completed his short speech.

"Uh, okay," Bill replied.

Bill returned to the small conference room that had served as his work area for the past two months. He sat in his chair and stared at the pictures of his two-year-old twins, Lesley and Kelly, which he had taped to the wall above the phone. After a few minutes, he picked up his pencil, leaned forward, and began outlining the inventory memo.

Questions

1. What conclusion do you believe Bill DeBurger reached in his inventory memo? Put yourself in his position. What conclusion would you have expressed in the inventory memo? Why?

2. Would you have dealt with your uncertainty regarding the inventory account differently than Bill did? For example, would you have used a different approach to raise the subject with Sam Hakes?

3. Evaluate Sam Hakes' response to Bill's statement that he was unable to sign off on the inventory account. In your view, did Sam deal with the situation appropriately? Was Sam's approach "professional"? Explain.

4. Is it appropriate for relatively inexperienced auditors to be assigned the primary responsibility for such critical accounts as Marcelle Stores' inventory? Explain.

Hamilton Wong, In-Charge Accountant

After spending much of the previous three months working elbow-to-elbow with as many as six colleagues in a cramped and poorly ventilated conference room, Hamilton Wong was looking forward to moving on to his next assignment.[1] Wong was an in-charge accountant on the audit staff of the San Francisco office of a large international accounting firm, the firm that had offered him a job two years earlier as he neared completion of his accounting degree at San Jose State University. His current client, Wille & Lomax, Inc., a public company and the second largest client of Wong's office, owned a chain of retail stores in the western United States that stretched from Seattle to San Diego and as far east as Denver and Albuquerque.

Although Wille & Lomax's stores operated under different names in different cities, each stocked the same general types of merchandise, including briefcases and other leather goods, luggage and travel accessories, and a wide range of gift items, such as costume jewelry imported from Pacific Rim countries. The company also had a wholesale division that marketed similar merchandise to specialty retailers throughout the United States. The wholesale division accounted for approximately 60 percent of the company's annual sales.

A nondescript building in downtown San Francisco, just one block from bustling Market Street, served as Wille & Lomax's corporate headquarters. The company's fiscal year-end fell on the final Saturday of January. With the end of March just a few days away, Hamilton and his fellow "Willies"—the nickname that his office assigned to members of the Wille & Lomax audit engagement team—were quickly running out of time to complete the audit. Wong was well aware that the audit was behind schedule because he collected, coded, and input into an electronic spreadsheet the time worked each week by the individual Willies. He used the spreadsheet package to generate a weekly time and progress report that he submitted to Angela Sun, the senior who supervised the fieldwork on the Wille & Lomax audit.

In addition to Wong and Sun, another in-charge accountant, Lauren Hutchison, and four staff accountants had worked on the Wille & Lomax audit since early January. Wong and Hutchison knew each other well. They shared the same start date with their employer and the past two summers had attended the same weeklong staff and in-charge training sessions at their firm's national education headquarters. Hutchison's primary responsibility on the current year's audit was the receivables account, but she also audited the PP&E (property, plant, and equipment) and leases accounts. Besides his administrative responsibilities, which included serving as the engagement timekeeper and maintaining the correspondence file for the audit, Wong supervised and coordinated the audit procedures for inventory, accounts payable, and a few smaller accounts.

Hamilton was thankful that it was late Friday afternoon. In recent weeks, with the audit deadline looming, Angela Sun had required the Wille & Lomax crew to work

---

1. This case is based upon the experiences of an individual previously employed by one of the major accounting firms. The names of the parties involved in this case and other background information, such as locations, have been changed.

until at least 7 p.m. each weekday except Friday, when she allowed them to leave "early" at 5 p.m. The engagement team had spent three consecutive Saturdays in the client's headquarters and would be spending both Saturday and Sunday of the coming weekend hunched over their workpapers. Wong had just completed collecting and coding the hours worked during the current week by the other members of the engagement team. Now it was time for him to enter in the electronic spreadsheet his chargeable hours, which he dutifully recorded at the end of each work day in his little "black book."

Before entering his own time, Wong decided to walk across the hall and purchase a snack in the employees' break room. In fact, he was stalling, trying to resolve a matter that was bothering him. Less than 30 minutes earlier, Lauren Hutchison had told him that during the current week, which included the previous weekend, she had spent 31 hours on the receivables account, 18 hours on the leases account, and 3 hours on PP&E. What troubled Wong was the fact that he knew Hutchison had worked several additional hours on the Wille & Lomax audit during the current week.

This was not the first time Hutchison had underreported her hours worked. On several occasions, Wong had noticed her secretively slipping workpaper files into her briefcase before leaving for home. The next morning, those files included polished memos or completed schedules that had not existed the previous day. Wong was certain that Hutchison was not reporting the hours she spent working at home on her audit assignments. He was just as certain that each week she consciously chose to shave a few hours off the total number she had spent working at the client's headquarters. Collectively, Wong estimated that Hutchison had failed to report at least 80 hours she had worked on the audit.

"Eating time" was a taboo subject among auditors. Although the subject was not openly discussed, Wong was convinced that many audit partners and audit managers subtly encouraged subordinates to underreport their time. By bringing their jobs in near budget, those partners and managers enhanced their apparent ability to manage engagements. The most avid time-eaters among Wong's peers seemed to be the individuals who had been labeled as "fast-track" superstars in the office.

After Hutchison had reported her time to Wong that afternoon, he had nonchalantly but pointedly remarked, "Lauren, who are you trying to impress by eating so much of your time?" His comment had caused the normally mild-mannered Hutchison to snap back, "Hey, Dude, you are the timekeeper, not the boss. So just mind your own ___ business." Immediately, Wong regretted offending Hutchison, whom he considered his friend. But she stomped away before he could apologize.

Wong knew who Hutchison was trying to impress. Angela Sun would almost certainly be promoted to audit manager in the summer and then become the audit manager on the Wille & Lomax engagement, meaning that there would be a vacancy in the all-important senior position on the engagement team. Both Hutchison and Wong also anticipated being promoted during the summer. The two new seniors would be the most likely candidates to take over the job of overseeing the fieldwork on the Wille & Lomax audit.

The in-charge accountant who handled the administrative responsibilities on the Wille & Lomax engagement was typically the person chosen to take over the senior's role when it came open. But Wong worried that the close friendship that had developed between Lauren Hutchison and Sun might affect his chances of landing the coveted assignment. Almost every day, Hutchison and Sun went to lunch together without extending even a token invitation to Wong or their other colleagues to join them. John Berardo, the audit engagement partner, would choose the new senior for the Wille & Lomax engagement, but Angela Sun would certainly have a major influence on his decision.

There was little doubt in Wong's mind that Hutchison routinely underreported the time she worked on the Wille & Lomax audit to enhance her standing with Sun and Berardo. Not that Hutchison needed to spruce up her image. She had passed the CPA exam shortly after joining the firm, had a charming personality that endeared her to her superiors and client executives, and, like both Sun and Berardo, was a Stanford graduate. Wong, on the other hand, had struggled to pass the CPA exam, was shy by nature, and had graduated from a public university.

What irritated Wong the most about his subtle rivalry with Hutchison was that during the past two weekends he had spent several hours helping her research contentious technical issues for Wille & Lomax's complex lease contracts on its retail store sites. Earlier in the engagement, Hutchison had also asked him to help analyze some tricky journal entries involving the client's allowance for bad debts. In each of those cases, Wong had not charged any time to the given accounts, both of which were Hutchison's responsibility.

Before entering his time for the week, Wong checked once more the total hours that he had charged to date to his major accounts. For both inventory and accounts payable, he was already over budget. By the end of the audit, Wong estimated that he would "bust" the assigned time budgets for those two accounts by 20 to 25 percent each. On the other hand, Hutchison, thanks to her superior "time management" skills, would likely exceed the time budget on her major accounts by only a few hours. In fact, she might even come in under budget on one or more of her accounts, which was almost unheard of, at least on the dozen or so audits to which Wong had been assigned.

After finishing the bag of chips he had purchased in the snack room, Wong reached for the computer keyboard in front of him. In a few moments, he had entered his time for the week and printed the report that he would give to Angela Sun the following morning. After briefly glancing at the report, he slipped it into the appropriate work-paper file, turned off the light in the empty conference room, and locked the door behind him as he resolved to enjoy his brief 16-hour "weekend."

Questions

1. Place yourself in Hamilton Wong's position. Would you report all of your time worked on the Wille & Lomax audit? Why or why not? Do you believe that Lauren Hutchison behaved unethically by underreporting the time she worked on that engagement? Defend your answer.

2. Academic research suggests that underreporting time on audit engagements is a common practice. What are the key objectives of tracking hours worked by individual accounts or assignments on audit engagements? What implications does the underreporting of time have for individual auditors, their colleagues, and the overall quality of independent audits?

3. What measures can accounting firms take to ensure that time budgets do not interfere with the successful completion of an audit or become dysfunctional in other ways?

4. What measures can accounting firms take to reduce the likelihood that personal rivalries among auditors of the same rank will become dysfunctional?

Tommy O'Connell, Audit Senior

Tommy O'Connell had been a senior with one of the major international accounting firms for less than one month when he was assigned to the audit engagement for the Altamesa Manufacturing Company.[1] Tommy worked out of his firm's Fort Worth, Texas, office, while Altamesa was headquartered in Amarillo, the "capital" of the Texas Panhandle. The young senior realized that being assigned to the tough Altamesa engagement signaled that Jack Morrison, the Altamesa audit partner and the office managing partner, regarded his work highly. Serving as the audit senior on the Altamesa job would allow Tommy to become better acquainted with Morrison. Despite the challenges and opportunities posed by his new assignment, Tommy did not look forward to spending three months in Amarillo, a five-hour drive from Fort Worth. This would be his first assignment outside of Fort Worth since his marriage six months earlier. He dreaded breaking the news to his wife, Suzie, who often complained about the long hours his job required.

Altamesa manufactured steel girders used in the construction and renovation of bridges in West Texas, New Mexico, Colorado, and Oklahoma. The company's business was very cyclical and linked closely to the funding available to municipalities in Altamesa's four-state market area. To learn more about the company and its personnel, Tommy arranged to have lunch with Keri Hansel, the audit senior on the Altamesa job the two previous years. According to Keri, Altamesa's management took aggressive positions regarding year-end expense accruals and revenue recognition. The company used the percentage-of-completion method to recognize revenue since its sales contracts extended over two to five years. Keri recounted several disputes with the company's chief accountant regarding the estimated stage of completion of jobs in progress. In an effort to "front-load" as much of the profit on jobs as possible, the chief accountant typically insisted that jobs were further along than they actually were.

Speaking with Keri made Tommy even more apprehensive about tackling the Altamesa engagement. But he realized that the job gave him an excellent chance to strengthen his fast-track image within his office. To reach his goal of being promoted to manager by his fifth year with the firm, Tommy needed to prove himself on difficult assignments such as the Altamesa engagement.

An Unpleasant Surprise for Tommy

It was late May, just two weeks before Tommy would be leaving for Amarillo to begin the Altamesa audit—the company had a 30 June fiscal year-end. Tommy, Jack Morrison, and an audit manager were having lunch at the Cattleman's Restaurant in the Cowtown district of north Fort Worth.

"Tommy, I've decided to send Carl with you out to Amarillo. Is that okay?" asked Jack Morrison.

"Uhh … sure, Jack. Yeah, that'll be fine," Tommy replied.

---

1. This case is based upon an actual series of events. Names and certain background information have been changed to conceal the identities of the individuals involved in the case.

"Of all people," Tommy thought, "he would send Carl Wilmeth to Amarillo with me." Carl was a staff accountant with only a few months' experience, having been hired in the middle of the just-completed busy season. Other than being auditors and approximately the same age, the two young men had little in common. Tommy was from Lockettville, a small town in rural West Texas, while Carl had been raised in the exclusive Highland Park community of north central Dallas. Texas Tech, a large state-supported university, was Tommy's alma mater. Carl had earned his accounting degree from a small private college on the East Coast.

Tommy did not appreciate Carl's cocky attitude, and his lack of experience made him a questionable choice in Tommy's mind for the Altamesa engagement. As he tried to choke down the rest of his prime rib, Tommy recalled the complaints he had heard about Carl's job performance. Over the past three months, Carl had worked on two audits. In both cases, he had performed admirably—too admirably, in fact, coming in well under budget on his assigned tasks.

On one engagement, Carl had completed an assignment in less than 60 hours when the audit budget allotted 100 hours; the previous year, 110 hours had been required to complete that same task. Both seniors who had supervised Carl suspected that he had not completed all of his assigned audit procedures, although he signed off on those procedures on the audit program. The tasks assigned to Carl had been large-scale tests of transactions that involved checking invoices, receiving reports, purchase orders, and other documents for various attributes. Given the nature of the tests, the seniors would have had difficulty confirming their suspicions.

"Boss" Tommy

Six weeks later, in early July, the Altamesa audit was in full swing. Carl had just finished his third assigned task on the job, in record time, of course. "Boss, here's that disbursements file," Carl said as he plopped a large stack of workpapers in front of Tommy. "Anything else you want me to do this afternoon? Since I'm way ahead of schedule, maybe I should take off and work on my tan out on the golf course."

"No, Carl. I think we have plenty to keep you busy right here." Tommy was agitated but he tried not to let it show. "Why don't you pull out the contracts file and then talk to Rachel Simpson in the sales office. Get copies of any new contracts or proposals over the past year and put them in the contracts file."

At this point, Tommy simply did not have time to review Carl's cash disbursements workpapers. He was too busy trying to untangle Altamesa's complex method of allocating overhead costs to jobs in process. Later that afternoon, he had an appointment to meet with the chief accountant and a production superintendent to discuss the status of a large job. Tommy and the chief accountant had already butted heads on two occasions regarding a job's stage of completion. Keri had been right: the chief accountant clearly meant to recognize profit on in-progress jobs as quickly as possible.

With four decades of experience, Scrooge—a nickname Keri had pinned on the chief accountant—obviously considered the young auditors a nuisance and did not appreciate their probing questions. Each time Tommy asked him a question regarding an important issue, the chief accountant registered his disgust by pursing his lips and running his hand through his thinning hair. He then responded with a rambling, convoluted answer intended to confuse rather than inform.

To comprehend Altamesa's accounting decisions for its long-term contracts, Tommy spent several hours of nonchargeable time each night in his motel room flipping through copies of job order worksheets and contracts. Occasionally, he referred to prior-year workpapers, his firm's policy and procedures manual, and even his tattered cost accounting textbook from his college days. Carl, on the other hand, spent most of his evenings in the motel's club being taught the Texas Two-step and Cotton-eyed Joe by several new friends he had acquired.

During July and August, Tommy and Carl worked 50 to 60 hours per week on the Altamesa engagement. Several times, Tommy wondered whether it was worthwhile to work so hard to earn recognition as a "superstar" senior. He was also increasingly concerned about the impact of his fast-track strategy on his marriage. When he tried to explain to Suzie that the long hours and travel would pay off when he made partner, she was unimpressed. "Who cares if you make partner? I just want to spend more time with my husband," was her stock reply.

To Tell or Not to Tell

Finally, late August rolled around and the Altamesa job was almost complete. Jack Morrison had been in Amarillo for the past three days combing through the Altamesa workpapers. Nothing seemed to escape Morrison's eagle eye. Tommy had spent 12 hours per day since Morrison had arrived, tracking down missing invoices, checking on late confirmations, and tying up dozens of other loose ends. Carl was already back in Fort Worth, probably working on his golf swing. Morrison had allowed Carl to leave two days earlier after he had finished clearing the review comments in his workpaper files.

"Tommy, I have to admit that I was a little concerned about sending a light senior out to run this audit. But, by golly, you have done a great job." Morrison did not look up as he signed off on the workpapers spread before him on Altamesa's conference table. "You know, this kid Carl does super work. I've never seen cleaner, more organized workpapers from a staff accountant."

Tommy grimaced as he sat next to Morrison at the conference table. "Yeah, right. They should look clean, since he didn't do half of what he signed off on," Tommy thought. Here was his opportunity. For the past several weeks, Tommy had planned to sit down with Morrison and talk to him regarding Carl's job performance. But now he was reluctant to do so. How do you tell a partner that you suspect much of the work he is reviewing may not have been done? Besides, Tommy realized that as Carl's immediate supervisor, he was responsible for that work. Tommy knew that he was facing a no-win situation. He leaned back in his chair and remained silent, hoping that Morrison would hurry through the last few workpaper files so they could make it back to Fort Worth by midnight.

EPILOGUE

Tommy never informed Jack Morrison of his suspicions regarding Carl's work. Thankfully, no problems—of a legal nature—ever arose on the jobs to which Carl was assigned. After passing the CPA exam on his first attempt, Carl left the accounting firm and enrolled in a prestigious MBA program. Upon graduation,

Carl accepted a job on Wall Street with one of the large investment banking firms. Tommy reached his goal of being promoted to audit manager within five years. One year later, he decided that he was not cut out to be a partner and resigned from the firm to accept a position in private industry.

Questions

1. Compare and contrast the professional roles of an audit senior and a staff accountant. In your analysis, consider the different responsibilities assigned to each role, the job-related stresses that individuals in the two roles face, and how each role contributes to the successful completion of an audit engagement. Which of these two roles is (a) more important and (b) more stressful? Defend your choices.

2. Assume that you are Tommy O'Connell and have learned that Carl Wilmeth will be working for you on the Altamesa audit engagement. Would you handle this situation any differently than Tommy did? Explain.

3. Again, assume that you are Tommy. Carl is badgering you for something to do midway through the Altamesa job. You suspect that he is not completing all of his assigned procedures, but at the time you are wrestling with an important accounting issue facing the client. What would you do at this point? What could you do to confirm your suspicions that Carl is not completing his assignments?

4. Now, assume that Jack Morrison is reviewing the Altamesa workpapers. To date, you (Tommy) have said nothing to Morrison about your suspicions regarding Carl. Do you have a professional responsibility to raise this matter now with Morrison? Explain.

5. Assume that at some point Tommy told Morrison that he suspected Carl was not completing his assigned tasks. The only evidence Tommy had to support his theory was the fact that Carl had come in significantly under budget on every major task assigned to him over a period of several months. If you were Jack Morrison, how would you have handled this matter?

Avis Love, Staff Accountant

"Oh no, not Store 51," Avis Love moaned under her breath. For the third time, Avis compared the dates listed in the cash receipts journal with the corresponding dates on the bank deposit slips. Avis shook her head softly and leaned back in her chair. There was no doubt in her mind now. Mo Rappelle had definitely held open Store 51's cash receipts journal at the end of October.[1]

Avis Love was a staff accountant with the Atlanta office of a large international accounting firm. Several months earlier, Avis had graduated with an accounting degree from the University of Alabama at Birmingham. Although she did not plan to pursue a career in public accounting, Avis had accepted one of the several job offers she received from major accounting firms. The 22-year-old wanted to take a two- or three-year "vacation" from college, while at the same time accumulating a bankroll to finance three years of law school. Avis intended to practice law with a major firm for a few years and then return to her hometown in eastern Alabama and set up her own practice.

For the past few weeks, Avis had been assigned to the audit engagement for Lowell, Inc., a public company that operated nearly 100 retail sporting goods stores scattered across the South. Avis was nearing completion of a year-end cash receipts cutoff test for a sample of 20 Lowell stores. The audit procedures she had performed included preparing a list of the cash receipts reported in each of those stores' accounting records during the last five days of Lowell's fiscal year, which ended 31 October. She had then obtained the relevant bank statements for each of the stores to determine whether the cash receipts had been deposited on a timely basis. For three of the stores in her sample, the deposit dates for the cash receipts ranged from three to seven days following the dates the receipts had been entered in the cash receipts journal. The individual store managers had apparently backdated cash receipts for the first several days of the new fiscal year, making it appear that the receipts had occurred in the fiscal year under audit by Avis's firm.

Avis had quickly realized that the objective of the store managers was not to overstate their units' year-end cash balances. Instead, the managers intended to inflate their recorded sales. Before Avis began the cutoff test, Teddy Tankersley, the senior assigned to the Lowell audit and Avis's immediate superior, had advised her that there was a higher-than-normal risk of cash receipts and sales cutoff errors for Lowell this year. The end of Lowell's fiscal year coincided with the end of a three-month sales promotion. This campaign to boost Lowell's sagging sales included bonuses for store managers who exceeded their quarterly sales quota. This was the first time that Lowell had run such a campaign and it was a modest success. Fourth-quarter sales for the fiscal year just ended topped the corresponding sales for the previous fiscal year by 6 percent.

When Avis uncovered the first instance of backdated cash receipts, she had felt a noticeable surge of excitement. In several months of tracing down invoices and receiving reports, ticking and tying, and performing other mundane tests, the young

---

1. This case was developed from an actual series of events. Names, locations, and certain other background information have been changed to conceal the identities of the individuals involved in the case.

accountant had occasionally found isolated errors in client accounting records. But this was different. This was fraud.

Avis had a much different reaction when she uncovered the second case of backdated cash receipts. She had suddenly realized that the results of her cutoff test would have "real world" implications for several parties, principally the store managers involved in the scheme. During the past few months, Avis had visited six of Lowell's retail stores to perform various interim tests of controls and to observe physical inventory procedures. The typical store manager was in his or her early 30s, married, with one or two small children. Because of Lowell's miserly pay scale, the stores were chronically understaffed, meaning that the store managers worked extremely long hours to earn their modest salaries.

No doubt, the store managers who backdated sales to increase their bonuses would be fired immediately. Clay Shamblin, Lowell's chief executive officer (CEO), was a hard-nosed businessman known for his punctuality, honesty, and work ethic. Shamblin exhibited little patience with subordinates who did not display those same traits.

When Avis came to the last store in her sample, she had hesitated. She realized that Mo Rappelle managed Store 51. Three weeks earlier, Avis had spent a long Saturday afternoon observing the physical inventory at Store 51 on the outskirts of Atlanta. Although the Lowell store managers were generally courteous and accommodating, Mo had gone out of his way to help Avis complete her tasks. Mo allowed Avis to use his own desk in the store's cramped office, shared a pizza with her during an afternoon break, and introduced her to his wife and two small children who dropped by the store during the afternoon.

"Mo, what a stupid thing to do," Avis thought after reviewing the workpapers for the cutoff tests a final time. "And for just a few extra dollars." Mo had apparently backdated cash receipts for only the first two days of the new year. According to Avis's calculations, the backdated sales had increased Mo's year-end bonus by slightly more than $100. From the standpoint of Lowell, Inc., the backdated sales for Mo's store clearly had an immaterial impact on the company's operating results for the year just ended.

After putting away the workpapers for the cutoff test, a thought dawned on Avis. The Lowell audit program required her to perform cash receipts cutoff tests for 20 stores . . . any 20 stores she selected. Why not just drop Store 51 from her sample and replace it with Store 52 or 53 or whatever?

EPILOGUE

Avis brooded over the results of her cutoff test the remainder of that day at work and most of that evening. The following day, she gave the workpaper file to Teddy Tankersley. Avis reluctantly told Teddy about the backdated cash receipts and sales she had discovered in three stores: Store 12, Store 24, and Store 51. Teddy congratulated Avis on her thorough work and told her that Clay Shamblin would be very interested in her findings.

A few days later, Shamblin called Avis into his office and thanked her for uncovering the backdated transactions. The CEO told her that the company's internal auditors had tested the year-end cash receipts and sales cutoff for the remaining 72 stores and identified seven additional store managers who had tampered with their accounting records. As Avis was leaving the CEO's office, he thanked her once more and assured her that the store managers involved in the scam "would soon be looking for a new line of work . . . in another part of the country."

Questions

1. Would it have been appropriate for Avis to substitute another store for Store 51 after she discovered the cutoff errors in that store's accounting records? Defend your answer.

2. Identify the parties potentially affected by the outcome of the ethical dilemma faced by Avis Love. What obligation, if any, did Avis have to each of these parties?

3. Does the AICPA's *Code of Professional Conduct* prohibit auditors from developing friendships with client personnel? If not, what measures can auditors take to prevent such friendships from interfering with the performance of their professional responsibilities?

4. Identify the key audit objectives associated with year-end cash receipts and sales cutoff tests.

5. What method would you have recommended that Avis or her colleagues use in deciding whether the cutoff errors she discovered had a material impact on Lowell's year-end financial statements? Identify the factors or benchmarks that should have been considered in making this decision.

Charles Tollison, Audit Manager

"No, that's okay, Bea. I'll write that memo this weekend and send it to Mr. Fielder. You go on home."[1]

"Are you sure, Chuck? I don't mind staying a while longer."

"Thanks, Bea, but you've already put in too much overtime this week."

After he sent his secretary home, Charles Tollison spent several minutes shuffling through the audit workpapers and correspondence stacked on his desk, trying to decide what work he would take home over the weekend. Finally, only one decision remained. Tollison couldn't decide whether to take the inventory file with him. Compulsive by nature, Tollison knew that if he took the inventory file home, he would have to complete his review of that file, which would increase his weekend workload from 6 hours to more than 12 hours. As he stewed over his decision, Tollison stepped to the window of his office and idly watched the rush-hour traffic on the downtown streets several stories below.

It was nearly 6:30 on a Friday evening in early August. Charles Tollison, an audit manager for a large international accounting firm, had suffered through a tough week. His largest audit client was negotiating to buy a smaller company within its industry. For the past two months, Tollison had supervised the fieldwork on an intensive acquisition audit of the competitor's accounting records. The client's chief executive officer (CEO) suspected that the competitor's executives had embellished their firm's financial data in anticipation of the proposed buyout. Since the client was overextending itself financially to acquire the other firm, the CEO wanted to be sure that its financial data were reliable. The CEO's principal concern was the valuation of the competitor's inventory, which accounted for 45 percent of its total assets.

The client's CEO had requested that Tollison be assigned to the acquisition audit because she respected Tollison and the quality of his work. Normally, an audit manager spends little time "in the trenches" supervising day-to-day audit procedures. Because of the nature of this engagement, however, Tollison had felt it necessary to spend 10 hours per day, six and seven days per week, poring over the accounting records of the takeover candidate with his subordinates.

As Tollison stared at the gridlocked streets below, he was relieved that the acquisition audit was almost complete. After he tied up a few loose ends in the inventory file, he would turn the workpapers over to the audit engagement partner for a final review.

Tollison's tough week had been highlighted by several contentious meetings with client personnel, a missed birthday party for his eight-year-old daughter, and an early breakfast Thursday morning with his office managing partner, Walker Linton. During that breakfast, Linton had notified Tollison that he had been passed over for promotion to partner—for the second year in a row. The news had been difficult for Tollison to accept.

For more than 13 years, Tollison had been a hard-working and dedicated employee of the large accounting firm. He had never turned down a difficult assignment, never

---

1. This case was developed from information obtained from a CPA employed for many years with a large international accounting firm.

complained about the long hours his work required, and made countless personal sacrifices, the most recent being the missed birthday party. After informing Tollison of the bad news, Linton had encouraged him to stay with the firm. Linton promised that the following year he would vigorously campaign for Tollison's promotion and "call in all favors" owed to him by partners in other offices. Despite that promise, Tollison realized that he had only a minimal chance of being promoted to partner. Seldom were two-time "losers" ticketed for promotion.

Although he had been hoping for the best, Tollison had not expected a favorable report from the Partner Selection Committee. In recent weeks, he had gradually admitted to himself that he did not have the profile for which the committee was searching. Tollison was not a rainmaker like his friend and fellow audit manager, Craig Allen, whose name appeared on the roster of new partners to be formally announced the following week. Allen was a member of several important civic organizations and had a network of well-connected friends at the local country club. Those connections had served Allen well, allowing him to steer several new clients to the firm in recent years.

Instead of a rainmaker, Tollison was a technician. If someone in the office had a difficult accounting or auditing issue to resolve, that individual went first to Tollison, not to one of the office's six audit partners. When a new client posed complex technical issues, the audit engagement partner requested that Tollison be assigned to the job. One reason Tollison was a perfect choice for difficult engagements was that he micromanaged his jobs, insisting on being involved in every aspect of them. Tollison's management style often resulted in his "busting" time budgets for audits, although he seldom missed an important deadline. To avoid missing deadlines when a job was nearing completion, Tollison and the subordinates assigned to his engagements would work excessive overtime, including long weekend stints.

Finally, Tollison turned away from his window and slumped into his chair. As he sat there, he tried to drive away the bitterness that he was feeling. "If Meredith hadn't left the firm, maybe I wouldn't be in this predicament," Tollison thought. Three years earlier, Meredith Oliveti, an audit partner and Tollison's closest friend within the firm, had resigned to become the chief financial officer (CFO) of a large client. Following Oliveti's resignation, Tollison had no one within the firm to sponsor him through the tedious and political partner selection process. Instead, Tollison had been "lost in the shuffle" with the dozens of other hard-working, technically inclined audit managers within the firm who aspired to a partnership position.

Near the end of breakfast Thursday morning, Walker Linton had mentioned to Tollison the possibility that he could remain with the firm in a senior manager position. In recent years, Tollison's firm had relaxed its "up or out" promotion policy. But Tollison was not sure he wanted to remain with the firm as a manager with no possibility of being promoted to partner. Granted, there were clearly advantages associated with becoming a permanent senior manager. For example, no equity interest in the firm meant not absorbing any portion of its future litigation losses. On the other hand, in Tollison's mind accepting an appointment as a permanent senior manager seemed equivalent to having "career failure" stenciled on his office door.

Ten minutes till seven, time to leave. Tollison left the inventory file lying on his desk as he closed his bulging briefcase and then stepped toward the door of his office. After flipping off the light switch, Tollison paused momentarily. He then grudgingly turned and stepped back to his desk, picked up the inventory file, and tucked it under his arm.

Questions

1. Do you believe Charles Tollison was qualified for a partnership position with his firm? Explain.

2. Did Tollison's firm treat him "fairly"? Why or why not?

3. Identify the criteria you believe large international accounting firms should use when evaluating individuals for promotion to partner. In your opinion, which of these criteria should be most heavily weighted by these firms? Should smaller accounting firms establish different criteria for evaluating individuals for promotion to partner? Explain.

4. Discuss the advantages and disadvantages of the "up or out" promotion policy followed by many accounting firms.

PROFESSIONAL ISSUES

7

Ligand Pharmaceuticals

In the late 1990s, James Fazio reached what many CPAs consider the pinnacle of success in the accounting profession, namely, partnership in one of the Big Four public accounting firms. For more than a decade, Fazio served as an audit partner with Deloitte & Touche in that firm's San Diego, California, practice office. Similar to his colleagues within Deloitte and the other major accounting firms, Fazio's professional life was disrupted by the Enron and WorldCom debacles. The sudden collapse of those two large companies following the turn of the century prompted a public outcry to impose more rigorous regulatory controls over the financial reporting function for publicly owned companies. The federal government's response to that outcry would further complicate the already complex and stressful nature of James Fazio's professional role as an audit partner with a Big Four accounting firm.

Peek-A-Boo

In the summer of 2002, the U.S. Congress hurriedly passed the Sarbanes–Oxley Act (SOX). The SOX legislation contained the most far-reaching financial reporting reforms at the federal level since the passage of the Securities Act of 1933 and the Securities Exchange Act of 1934. The reforms included a requirement that public companies have their internal controls over financial reporting audited by an independent accounting firm. That requirement, which became effective for most companies in 2004, forced U.S. companies to spend billions of dollars to rethink and, in many cases, completely overhaul their internal control systems.

The SOX legislation was an economic boon for Deloitte and the other Big Four accounting firms since those firms were ideally suited to provide the thousands of internal control audits mandated by SOX. To take full advantage of this large new revenue stream, these firms redesigned their audit processes, retooled their organizational structures, and hired a large number of new employees.

SOX also established a new regulatory structure for the independent audit function that had far-reaching implications for the major accounting firms. The role of the new Public Company Accounting Oversight Board (PCAOB) was to strengthen and improve the independent audit function for public companies and thereby minimize the likelihood of "audit failures." Many parties have alleged that the Enron and WorldCom fiascoes could have been avoided, or at least mitigated, if those companies' financial statements had been audited more rigorously.

Based in Washington, D.C., the PCAOB, commonly referred to as "Peek-a-boo" by auditing practitioners, falls under the regulatory purview of the Securities and Exchange Commission (SEC). The PCAOB's operations are overseen by five board members appointed by the SEC; it has several hundred employees and an annual operating budget exceeding $100 million. The agency's regulatory mandate includes registering and monitoring accounting firms that audit public companies required to file periodic financial statements with the SEC. Other responsibilities of the PCAOB include establishing auditing, ethical, and quality control standards for those firms and carrying out disciplinary investigations.

The years immediately following the passage of SOX presented exciting and profitable opportunities for the Big Four accounting firms but posed enormous challenges for them as well. No one knew exactly how the new regulatory agenda and infrastructure would impact the nature of financial reporting and the independent audit function in the United States. Despite the uncertainty they faced, James Fazio and other Big Four audit partners had more pressing concerns at the time, namely, the everyday "business" of, and professional responsibilities associated with, supervising the audits of their clients.

Deloitte's 2003 Ligand Audit

In early 2004, the 43-year-old Fazio was overseeing the 2003 audit of Ligand Pharmaceuticals, a San Diego–based company whose stock was traded on the NASDAQ exchange. As the audit engagement partner for Ligand, Fazio had a wide range of responsibilities. The following excerpts from Deloitte's *Accounting and Auditing Practice Manual* at the time addressed the role and responsibilities of an audit engagement partner.

> It is the responsibility of the Engagement Partner to form the audit opinion, or to disclaim an opinion, on the financial statements.

> The Engagement Partner has the final responsibility for the planning and performance of the audit engagement, including the assignment, on-the-job training, and audit work of professional staff, and the implementation of the decisions concerning matters that have been the subject of consultation …

> The knowledge and skills of an Engagement Partner should be matched with the needs and characteristics of the engagement.

For several years, James Fazio had been involved in his office's "High Technology Group." Because of his experience with emerging growth companies, Fazio seemed well suited to serve as the audit engagement partner for Ligand, which was still in a developmental stage. In company press releases, Ligand described itself as an "emerging R&D and royalty-driven biotechnology company." The company's principal products included a painkiller and several cancer treatment drugs. The company also had several new products under development. Rising expectations for the company's future prospects had caused its stock price to soar from under $4 per share in early 2003 to nearly $24 per share in early 2004, despite the company never having reported an operating profit.

Deloitte requires each audit engagement team to assess the degree of "engagement risk" posed by a given audit.[1] Fazio and his subordinates concluded that the 2003 Ligand audit posed a "greater than normal" degree of engagement risk due to questions surrounding Ligand's accounting for sales returns. Ligand's distribution channel consisted principally of three large drug wholesalers. These wholesalers purchased Ligand's products and then marketed them to pharmacies and other healthcare facilities throughout the United States. Ligand recorded product shipments made to the three wholesalers as consummated sales transactions although the wholesalers had the right to return any products that they did not "sell through" to their customers. Because of this revenue recognition policy, Ligand was required to record a reserve (allowance) for expected future sales returns at the end of each accounting period.

By early 2004 when Deloitte was auditing Ligand's 2003 financial statements, the company had been marketing its major products for only a short period of time, which meant that Ligand's accountants had limited historical experience on which

---

1. The three levels of engagement risk that can be assigned to a given audit include "normal," "greater than normal," and "much greater than normal."

to base their estimates of future sales returns. Complicating matters was the difficulty Ligand had in obtaining sales and inventory data from its three wholesalers.

Ligand typically shipped product to those wholesalers 12 months before the expiration date of the given product. The wholesalers generally had the right to return product received from Ligand in a 12-month window that extended 6 months on either side of a product's expiration date. To properly assess the quantity of future sales returns, Ligand's accounting staff needed up-to-date "sell-through" data from its wholesalers. However, the three wholesalers frequently failed to provide that data on a timely basis. In fact, Ligand often received large and unexpected shipments of product returns from the three wholesalers.

limited sales return data

The limited sales returns data available to Ligand during 2003 suggested that the company was significantly underestimating its rate of product returns. For example, one product had experienced rates of return ranging from 13 percent to as high as 20 percent on "open lots."[2] Company management was convinced that those return rates were not representative of the overall return rate that product would eventually experience. As a result, management instructed the company's accountants to apply a much more modest 2.5 percent return rate when determining the product's 2003 year-end allowance for future sales returns.

*13-20%
↓ down to
2.5%*

Shortly before Deloitte completed the 2003 Ligand audit in early March 2004, Ligand received additional information from its wholesalers regarding the return rates being experienced by its major products. Although this information was available from the company's accounting staff, the Deloitte auditors did not review it. The updated sales returns data, similar to the earlier data that had been reviewed by the Deloitte auditors, indicated that the 31 December 2003, allowance for future sales returns was inadequate. In some cases, the returns received in early 2004 for products sold in 2003 exceeded those products' total 2003 year-end provision for sales returns.

Fazio was aware of the difficulty Ligand had in estimating its future sales returns and the fact that the projected return rates being applied by the company appeared insufficient given the actual sales returns data available from the company's wholesalers. Despite this knowledge, Fazio authorized the issuance of an unqualified opinion on Ligand's 2003 financial statements on 10 March 2004.

wait, wtf?

The following month, Fazio supervised Deloitte's interim review of Ligand's financial statements for the first quarter of 2004. During that engagement, Fazio and his subordinates obtained Ligand's sales returns data for the first two months of fiscal 2004. Those data alone demonstrated that the year-end allowance for sales returns was significantly understated. However, Ligand's accounting staff also provided forecast data to the auditors indicating that the company would experience a large amount of additional product returns from fiscal 2003 sales during the remaining months of 2004. Despite the considerable evidence that Ligand's 2003 year-end allowance for sales returns was materially understated, Fazio failed to recommend that the company recall and restate its 2003 financial statements.

The Trials and Tribulations of James Fazio

The contentious accounting issues posed by Ligand were not the only challenges that James Fazio faced during the 2003 audit of that company. Several months before that audit began, Fazio's immediate superior, the partner in charge of Deloitte's San

---

2. Ligand used the term "lot" in reference to a given quantity of items of the same product that were manufactured at the same time and had the same expiration date. The term "open lot" referred to a product shipment for which the given wholesaler still had a right to return the unsold inventory from that shipment.

Diego audit practice, asked to meet with him. During that meeting, Fazio was told that concerns were being expressed about his job performance. In fact, members of Deloitte's management had suggested that Fazio no longer be allowed to supervise audits of public companies.

In February 2004, during the course of the 2003 Ligand audit, Fazio's immediate superior met with him once more. During this meeting, Fazio was told that he was perceived as a "quality risk" and was "counseled to resign from the firm."[3] Several of Deloitte's top partners had been involved in the decision to ask for Fazio's resignation. These partners included the director of Deloitte's Risk Management Program, the regional audit managing partner for Deloitte's Pacific Southwest Region, and Deloitte's national audit managing partner.

On 5 March 2004, the San Diego audit managing partner and the regional audit managing partner met with Fazio. Following that meeting, the regional audit managing partner sent an e-mail to the national audit managing partner that summarized the discussions that took place during the meeting. The e-mail documented the reasons why Fazio was being asked to resign from Deloitte.

> Among the reasons given were the views of certain members of Deloitte's management that the Engagement Partner [Fazio] did not have the skills to adequately supervise public company engagements and other engagements with above-average risk profiles and that the Engagement Partner [Fazio] was not suited to handling complex or risky engagements.[4]

Five days later, on 10 March 2004, Fazio signed the unqualified audit opinion issued by Deloitte on Ligand's 2003 financial statements. Fazio remained the audit engagement partner for Ligand following the issuance of that audit report.

On 5 August 2004, Deloitte resigned as Ligand's independent auditor. The price of Ligand's stock declined sharply following Deloitte's abrupt and unexpected resignation. From its high-water mark of nearly $24 per share in April 2004, the stock would eventually fall to under $1.50 per share by late 2008.

EPILOGUE

In May 2005, Ligand's management announced that the company would be restating its financial statements for 2002, 2003, and the first three quarters of 2004. Management reported that a joint investigation by the company's audit committee and new audit firm, BDO Seidman, had revealed material errors in those financial statements. The errors resulted principally from "improperly recognizing revenue on product shipments to distributors."[5] The financial restatement released by Ligand later in 2005 reduced the company's previously reported revenues for 2003 by 52 percent or $59 million in total. The company also increased its reported operating loss for 2003 by 250 percent.

Ligand insisted that the joint investigation by its audit committee and BDO Seidman had "found no evidence of improper or fraudulent actions or practices by any member of management or that management acted in bad faith in adopting and administering the company's historical revenue recognition policies."[6] The

---

3. PCAOB, "Order Instituting Disciplinary Proceedings, Making Findings and Imposing Sanctions: In the Matter of Deloitte & Touche LLP," *PCAOB Release No. 105-2007-005*, 10 December 2007, 7.

4. *Ibid.*

5. J. McEntee, "Ligand to Restate Financials Back to 2002," sandiego.com, 20 May 2005.

6. *Ibid.*

company also reported that it intended to adopt a new revenue recognition model based upon sell-through accounting under which revenue would not be recognized until the company's wholesalers had sold Ligand's products to their customers.

On 10 December 2007, the PCAOB issued joint disciplinary releases announcing sanctions imposed on James Fazio and Deloitte & Touche. These sanctions stemmed from Fazio's involvement in the 2003 Ligand audit.[7] The PCAOB barred James Fazio from being associated with a PCAOB-registered public accounting firm for two years. In a PCAOB press release also issued on 10 December 2007, an agency spokesperson reported that Fazio had violated several professional auditing standards during the 2003 Ligand audit.

> *Mr. Fazio failed to perform appropriate and adequate audit procedures related to Ligand's reported revenue from sales of products for which a right of return existed and failed to supervise others adequately to ensure the performance of such procedures.*

> *Mr. Fazio neither performed nor ensured the performance of procedures that adequately took into account the existence of factors indicating that Ligand's ability to make reasonable estimates of product returns may have been impaired.*

> *Mr. Fazio neither performed nor ensured the performance of procedures that adequately took into account the extent to which Ligand had consistently and substantially underestimated its product returns.*

> *In auditing Ligand's reported revenues, Mr. Fazio failed to [exercise] … the due care and professional skepticism required under the circumstances.*

He also failed to identify and appropriately address issues concerning Ligand's policy of excluding certain types of returns from its estimates of future returns and the adequacy of Ligand's disclosure of this accounting policy.[8]

The PCAOB publicly censured Deloitte and fined the firm $1 million for failing to take "meaningful steps to assure the quality of the audit work"[9] on the 2003 Ligand audit engagement. According to the PCAOB spokesperson, prior to and during the 2003 Ligand audit, "Certain members of Deloitte's management concluded that Mr. Fazio should be removed from public company audits" and that "he should be asked to resign from the firm."[10] The spokesperson went on to note that despite the grave concerns expressed regarding Mr. Fazio's competence, he was allowed to continue as the engagement partner for the 2003 Ligand audit.

The PCAOB's Director of Enforcement and Investigations issued a separate statement on the responsibility of registered accounting firms to ensure that their partners are competent to perform public company audits.

> *Registered public accounting firms must take reasonable steps to assure that their audit partners and other audit professionals are competent to conduct public audits. When concerns about an auditor's competency rise, a firm must act with dispatch to protect audit quality. The firm [Deloitte] failed to meet the Board's auditing standards in the audit led by Mr. Fazio.*[11]

The sanctions imposed on Deloitte were the first levied on a Big Four accounting firm by the PCAOB. A former SEC official noted that the Ligand case was a milestone in the new agency's short regulatory history. "It shows that the PCAOB's Enforcement Division is fully mature and also that we should expect to see within

---

7. Although the PCAOB issued the disciplinary reports in this case, SEC and PCAOB personnel were involved in the related investigations. In 2005, the SEC had announced that it was launching an independent investigation of Ligand. The federal agency apparently completed that investigation without imposing sanctions on Ligand or any Ligand executive or employee.

8. PCAOB, "PCAOB Issues Disciplinary Orders against Deloitte & Touche LLP and a Former Audit Partner," www.pcaobus.org/News_and_Events/2007/12-10.aspx, 10 December 2007.

9. *Ibid.*

10. *Ibid.*

11. *Ibid.*

a short period of time additional cases against not only other Big Four firms, but against the so-called second four firms as well."[12]

Deloitte issued a public statement responding to the sanctions imposed on it by the PCAOB. In that statement, a Deloitte official reported that the firm had "established and implemented changes to its quality-control policies that directly address the PCAOB's concerns."[13] The Deloitte spokesperson went on to insist that the firm was "confident that its audit policies and procedures were among the very best in the profession and that they meet or exceed all applicable standards."[14]

Questions

1. Describe what you believe is implied by the term "engagement risk." What are the key factors likely considered by Deloitte and other audit firms when assessing engagement risk? How, if at all, are auditors' professional responsibilities affected when a client poses a higher-than-normal degree of engagement risk?

2. What quality control mechanisms should major accounting firms have in place to ensure that audit partners have the proper training and experience to supervise audit engagements?

3. Identify the accounting standards and concepts that dictate the proper accounting treatment for sales returns. How were these standards and concepts violated by Ligand?

4. During the review of Ligand's first-quarter financial statements for 2004, the Deloitte auditors learned that the company had significantly underestimated its future sales returns at the end of 2003. What responsibility, if any, did this discovery impose on the Deloitte auditors?

5. Since its inception, the PCAOB has been criticized by many parties. Summarize the principal complaints that have been directed at the PCAOB. Do you believe this criticism is justified? Explain. What measures could the PCAOB take to improve its effectiveness and efficiency as a regulatory body?

---

12. C. Johnson, "Deloitte Settles in Key Case over Faulty Audit," *Washington Post*, 11 December 2007, D01.

13. F. Norris, "Deloitte Agrees to Pay $1 Million Fine," *New York Times* (online), 11 December 2007.

14. *Ibid.*

Sarah Russell, Staff Accountant

Sarah Russell grew up in a small town in the flatlands of western Kansas where she was born.[1] In high school, she was homecoming queen, valedictorian of her graduating class, point guard on her basketball team for two years, and a candy striper (volunteer) at the local hospital. Since her parents had attended the University of Kansas, Sarah was off to Lawrence at age 18.

After spending her freshman year posting straight A's in 30 hours of college courses, Sarah settled on accounting as her major after seriously considering journalism, prelaw, and finance. Although Sarah had yet to take any courses in accounting, she had been impressed by a presentation that a female partner of a large accounting firm had made at a career fair. Sarah was excited by the challenges and opportunities presented by public accounting, as described by the partner. Here was a field in which she could learn a great deal in a short period of time and advance rapidly to a position where she had important responsibilities. Plus, public accounting provided a wide range of career paths. If she really enjoyed public accounting, she could pursue a partnership position with a large accounting firm. Then again, she might "hang out her shingle" in her hometown, see the world on the internal audit staff of a large corporation, or return to college after a couple of years of real-world experience to earn an MBA.

Sarah completed the tough accounting courses at the University of Kansas with only two small blemishes on her transcript—B's in individual and corporate taxation. During the fall semester of her senior year, Sarah accepted a position as a staff accountant with a Big Eight accounting firm. Sarah considered staying in her home state but decided instead to request an assignment in her new employer's Chicago office. She believed that exposure to big-city life would allow her to arrive at a more informed decision when it was time to make a long-term commitment to a career path and a lifestyle.

During her first year on the job, Sarah served on six audit engagements. Her clients included a pipeline company, a religious foundation, and a professional sports team. She worked hard on those assignments and earned impressive performance appraisals from each of her immediate supervisors. Somehow Sarah also squeezed a CPA review course into her hectic schedule that first year. And she was glad she did. She was among the few rookies in her large office to pass each section of the CPA exam on her first attempt. With that barrier out of the way, Sarah focused her energy on being promoted to audit senior as quickly as possible.

Several individuals provided Sarah with much-needed moral support during her first year, including R. J. Bell, an audit partner. Bell was 40 years old and had been a partner for eight years. According to the office grapevine, he was in line to become the new office managing partner within the next year or so. Bell tried to get to know the new staff accountants assigned to the audit staff and to help them adjust to their jobs in any way he could. Several times during the year, Bell invited small groups of staff accountants to his home to have dinner with him and his family. Recognizing

---

1. This case was authored by Carol Knapp, an assistant professor at the University of Oklahoma. This case is based upon experiences related by a young woman previously employed by a large accounting firm. The names of the individuals involved in this case and other background facts, such as locations, have been changed.

that Sarah was new to Chicago, he made a special effort to include her in such social gatherings and to give her complimentary tickets to cultural and sporting events. When Sarah's old car from college died, Bell arranged for her to obtain a loan from a local bank. Sarah appreciated Bell's help and guidance. She considered the firm to be very lucky to have an audit partner so supportive of staff accountants.

Shortly after her first anniversary with the firm, Sarah received a telephone call from Bell at home one Saturday afternoon. At first, Sarah thought there must be a client emergency that required her assistance, but Bell did not bring up any client business during the conversation. Instead, he told Sarah that he had just called to chat. Sarah felt mildly uncomfortable with the situation but spoke with Bell for a few minutes before making up an excuse to get off the phone.

The following day, Sarah, an avid jogger, had just completed a four-mile run on her regular jogging trail in a city park when Bell pulled up as she was walking toward her car. "Hi, Sarah. How was your run?" Bell asked nonchalantly. "I was just driving by and thought you might like to get a Coke after your workout."

As Sarah approached Bell's car she felt awkward but tried to act natural, as if his unexpected appearance was only a coincidence. "Thanks, R. J. But I really need to get back to my apartment. I've got several errands to run and phone calls to make."

"You sure? I'm buying."

"Yeah, I'd better get home."

"Well, okay."

Over the next several weeks, Bell made a concerted effort to develop a personal relationship with Sarah. Eventually, Bell, who was known for working long hours, was calling her nearly every evening from his office just "to chat." Once or twice per week, he invited her to get a drink with him after work. On a couple of occasions, she accepted, hoping that by doing so he would stop asking her. No such luck. Finally, she began avoiding him in the office and stopped answering her home phone when she thought it was him calling. Twice, Bell dropped by her apartment in the evening. Panic-stricken both times, Sarah refused to answer the door, hoping he would quickly decide that she was not home.

Bell's persistence caused Sarah to feel increasing levels of stress and powerlessness. She did not know what to do or to whom she could turn. She was reluctant to discuss the matter with her friends in the office since she did not want to start a rumor mill. Embarrassment prevented her from discussing the matter with her parents or other family members. Worst of all, Sarah began wondering whether she had somehow encouraged Bell's behavior. She racked her brain to recall each time that she had spoken or met with him during her first year on the job. She could not remember saying anything that could have been misconstrued by him. But maybe she had inadvertently said something that had given him the wrong impression. Maybe he had mistaken the sense of respect and admiration she had for him as affection. Maybe she had asked him an inappropriate question. Maybe . . .

EPILOGUE

After more than six weeks of enduring Bell's advances, Sarah summoned the courage to make an appointment with him one Friday afternoon in his office. When Sarah informed Bell that she wanted to keep their relationship on a strictly professional level, he failed to respond for several tense moments. Finally, he remarked that Sarah must have misinterpreted his actions over the past several weeks. He was simply trying to make her feel more comfortable with her job. "I go out of my way to be as friendly and sociable with as many members of the audit staff as I can." Bell then told Sarah that, given the circumstances, he would see to it that she was not assigned to any of his engagements in the future. After another few moments of tense silence, he tersely asked,

"Is there anything else I can do for you, Miss Russell?" Sarah shook her head softly and then got up and left his office.

Sarah had no further contact or conversations with Bell following that Friday afternoon meeting. A few months later, she decided to return to Kansas to be closer to her family. At last report, Sarah was the chief financial officer (CFO) of a charitable organization.

Questions

1. In your opinion, how should Sarah have handled this matter? Identify the factors that Sarah should have considered in dealing with the situation. Also, identify the professional and personal responsibilities of Sarah, R. J. Bell, and other relevant individuals in this matter.

2. What were the costs and potential costs to Sarah's employer in this case? How should accounting firms attempt to prevent these types of situations from occurring? Assume that rather than speaking to Bell, Sarah had told the office managing partner about the problem she faced. How should the office managing partner have dealt with the matter?

3. This case took place several years ago. Do you believe that events similar to those that took place in this case could occur now? Explain.

Bud Carriker, Audit Senior

During childhood, Louis Armstrong Carriker had been tagged with the nickname "Bud" by his paternal grandmother.[1] Bud's father, a New Orleans native, was a life-long fan of the famous blues musician after whom he had named his only son. After graduating from high school, Elliot Carriker joined the military. In April 1951, Elliot, an African-American, married Bud's mother, a Mexican-American, while he was stationed at a military base in Texas. Two years later, Bud arrived. Sadly, Bud's mother died during childbirth. As a result, Bud spent most of his childhood in New Orleans being raised by his grandmother.

When he was a young teenager, Bud was reunited with his father in Dallas, Texas. Bud's new family included a stepmother and one-year old twin sisters. In high school, Bud excelled in both academics and athletics and earned a scholarship to play basketball at a small Division 1 school. Bud realized that his athletic career would end after college, so he dedicated himself to obtaining a degree that would provide him with an opportunity to earn a good livelihood following graduation. After leaving the military, Elliot Carriker had relied on the GI Bill to earn a college degree in finance. Because of his experience in the business world as a senior loan officer for a major metropolitan bank, Elliot encouraged his son to consider majoring in either accounting or finance. After several sessions with his high school career counselor, Bud decided to take his father's advice and pursue an accounting degree in college.

During his senior year in college, Bud interviewed with several of the international accounting firms and with two large Houston-based oil companies. After discussing his job offers with his father, Bud decided to begin his career in the public accounting profession. Bud realized that a few years' experience on the audit staff of a major accounting firm would provide him with a strong background in financial accounting. He intended to use that background to obtain a mid-level position on the accounting staff of a bank with an eventual career goal of becoming either a corporate controller or chief financial officer (CFO) in the financial services industry.

Bud launched his career in public accounting in June 1975 and was promoted to audit senior in the late fall of 1977, just prior to the beginning of his third busy season. By the time his fifth busy season arrived in late 1979, Bud had decided that he would begin searching for a job in the private sector when he was promoted to audit manager, which he expected would be sometime during the following 18 months. Although he enjoyed public accounting, Bud was anxious to get his "real" career started.

In mid-November 1979, Alex Saunders, the managing partner of the practice office that Bud had been assigned to throughout his career, asked Bud to meet with him one afternoon. Saunders informed Bud that the firm had unexpectedly acquired a new client. The new client was a privately owned bank in a midsized city in central Texas. Since accepting a position with his employer, Bud had made it known that he wanted to be assigned to a client in the banking or financial services industries. The acquisition of the new client provided Saunders an opportunity to finally grant Bud's request.

---

1. This case is based upon factual circumstances. Although the key events occurred in the approximate time frame identified in the case, the names of all parties and the locations have been changed.

"Bud, when we picked up this client, I immediately thought of you since you have expressed an interest in gaining some experience in the banking industry. Plus, this is one of those clients where we really need an experienced audit senior to run the engagement."

"Thank you, sir. I am looking forward to this opportunity." Bud's practice office was quite large. As a result, he did not have a close relationship with Alex Saunders. Nevertheless, Bud had considerable respect for Saunders. Saunders, a native of Lubbock, was an imposing man physically, towering well over six feet. He spoke with a distinctive west Texas twang and often wore a bolo tie and cowboy boots to work. Saunders had spent his entire 35-year career in the practice office that he now managed and was well known and respected within the business community. Bud particularly appreciated Saunders' blunt, no-nonsense management style. He had a reputation for candor with his subordinates and with clients. You always knew where you stood with "Big Alex," as he was often referred to by his subordinates.

"Eric Jones will be the audit engagement partner. But I am going to shadow Eric on this job. Just like you, Eric doesn't have any past experience with a bank client. Since I have had a slew of bank clients, he can use me as a sounding board if problems develop. K. T. Wilson will be the audit manager. He's worked on a couple of savings and loan audits."

"Sounds great," Bud commented when Saunders paused. "Of course, I have worked with Eric and K. T. on a couple of audits in the past."

"Let me give you a little background on this client," Saunders continued as he leaned back in his chair and folded his arms across his chest. "This guy, Jim Charles, who owns the bank, is one of those 'self-made' millionaires who is more than happy to tell you his success story. He prides himself on being a 'good ol' boy' from west Texas. Kind of like me, I guess," he added with a smile. "Ya know, he doesn't have a college degree."

"Wow, that is interesting," Bud responded.

"Well, that's what he claims, at least. He got lucky about 15 years ago and brought in a couple of wildcat wells in the Permian Basin. He used that money to buy a small bank in his hometown. In the past few years, the bank has grown by leaps and bounds because of the deregulation of the banking industry. I have reviewed his loan portfolio and it seems to me that he specializes in funding commercial real estate projects and high-risk oil and gas ventures." Bud listened intently as Saunders continued. "That's why I want an experienced audit senior running this engagement. I want you to spend a lot of time in the field. Ya know, in the past, bank clients were always considered extremely low risk. But that has totally changed in the past few years with the new legislation."

"Well, sir, I will do my best."

"I know you will, Bud. What I would like you to do is meet with Eric this afternoon. As luck would have it, the firm has a three-day seminar on bank auditing next week in Houston. I want you and Eric to attend that seminar. K. T.'s schedule won't allow him to make it."

"Okay. Sir, what about the Garrett audit? Will I continue to work on that job?" For the past three years, Bud had spent the majority of the winter months assigned to the audit engagement team for Garrett Manufacturing, a local prefabricated housing company.

"No. You're gonna be too busy with this new client. I have already made arrangements to have Zach Payne take your spot on that job."

When Bud left Saunders' office he felt a surge of excitement. This was just the type of assignment he had been hoping to land. Given the nature of the engagement and his required hands-on role, he would learn a great deal about the banking industry in a short time. Bud realized that this experience would position him well to obtain the type of job he wanted in the banking industry when he left public accounting.

In the two weeks following his meeting with Alex Saunders, Bud attended the banking seminar with Eric Jones and spent several days reviewing copies of the new client's prior-year workpapers that had been obtained from the previous auditor. On a Monday morning in early December, Bud made his first trip to the client's headquarters. He and K. T. Wilson planned to introduce themselves to key client personnel and to do some preliminary internal control work.

The meetings with client personnel went well, at least until they met with Jim Charles, who was not only the principal owner of the bank but also its chief executive officer (CEO). During that meeting, Charles seemed annoyed for some reason. In fact, the meeting lasted no more than a few minutes. Charles told the two auditors that he had several important phone calls to make and rushed them out of his office. Although Charles had been less than cordial, Bud quickly dismissed the episode. He realized that as the audit senior he would have little interaction with Charles.

Bud and K. T. Wilson completed their initial work at the client's headquarters and returned to their firm's office late on Tuesday afternoon. Over the next three days, Bud planned to draft a preliminary copy of the audit program and have it ready for a meeting that he and K.T. had scheduled with Eric Jones and Alex Saunders the following Monday afternoon.

Just as Bud was completing a draft of the audit program on Friday afternoon, Alex Saunders unexpectedly dropped by the cubicle in which he was working. Alex asked Bud to come to his office.

"Do you want me to bring the draft of the audit program? It's almost done."

"No. That won't be necessary," Saunders replied.

As they walked silently down the hall together, Bud suspected that something was wrong. Although he didn't know Saunders well, Bud sensed that the partner was upset. Bud's suspicions were heightened when Saunders turned and closed the door behind them after they entered his office.

"Please sit down, Bud," Saunders said quietly as he motioned to the chair positioned directly in front of his desk. After sitting down himself, Saunders fumbled with a couple of overstuffed workpaper files on his desktop and then spent several moments reviewing a small stack of handwritten telephone messages. Finally, he spoke.

"Bud, I have decided to place you back on the Garrett audit. I have already spoken with Zach Payne. Zach will be taking your place on the bank engagement."

Bud was stunned, too stunned to speak. The sudden and unexpected announcement was both startling and extremely disappointing. Here was the assignment that he had literally coveted and now it was being taken away from him. For several awkward moments, Bud sat facing Saunders, who refused to look at him. Not making eye contact with whomever he was speaking to was uncharacteristic of Saunders.

When Bud realized that Saunders did not intend to provide an explanation for removing him from the bank engagement, he took the initiative. "Sir, I don't understand. I was really looking forward to this assignment. I'm not sure why you believe Zach Payne is more qualified than me to run this job."

Saunders cleared his throat as he turned to the right and gazed out the large plate window that overlooked a busy street several blocks below. Saunders then turned back and faced Bud. "This is not about Zach Payne, Bud. I have decided that you are not the right person for this engagement. I'm sorry, but that's my decision." Saunders paused momentarily and then added, "Thanks for your time, Bud," signaling that the brief meeting had ended.

Still in shock, Bud rose slowly from the chair in which he had been sitting and turned toward the door. After taking a few steps, Bud turned back toward Saunders. "Mr. Saunders, I consider myself a professional. I work hard, I enjoy my work, and I believe I do a good job. I typically don't challenge the decisions of those above me. But I believe that I deserve an explanation for why you are taking me off this job." After speaking, Bud stood his ground, staring directly at Saunders who was once again nervously shuffling papers on his desktop.

After more awkward silence, Saunders rose to his feet and made direct eye contact with Bud as he spoke. "You're right, young man. You deserve an explanation. I'm sorry that I wasn't more to the point. Avoiding issues is not my style." Saunders paused and cleared his throat again before speaking. "Jim Charles called me Wednesday afternoon and told me that he wanted a different senior assigned to the audit. He said that he wouldn't be comfortable working with you." After one final pause, Saunders continued. "That's why we are taking you off the job."

"Comfortable? What does that mean?" Bud blurted out.

Saunders shoved his hands into the pockets of his trousers and shrugged his shoulders in exasperation. "You know what I mean. Charles … Charles wants another … another type of person assigned to the audit."

Now Bud understood. He had a crystal clear understanding of why he was being removed from the bank audit. As he stood there staring at Saunders, Bud felt several emotions, principally anger. He wanted to respond to Saunders, but he wasn't sure exactly what to say. Bud had always been aware that he was different from his colleagues. He was one of a handful of non-Caucasians in his office. In fact, it had been that way throughout his career. But he had never considered his race to be an issue of any kind. At least, not until this moment.

Finally, after an extended period of silence, Saunders turned away from Bud and walked over to his window and stared down at the Friday afternoon traffic. Bud shook his head in disgust, let out a deep breath, and then left Saunders' office. It was the last time that Bud would speak to, or meet with, Alex Saunders.

EPILOGUE

Bud Carriker spent his final busy season with his employer supervising the fieldwork on the Garrett Manufacturing engagement. Shortly after that engagement was completed, he received a brief letter from Alex Saunders congratulating him on his promotion to audit manager that would take effect a few months later on 1 July. However, Bud never officially became an audit manager with the firm.

In June of that year, Bud resigned from the firm and accepted a position as an assistant controller with a large healthcare facility in Dallas.

The banking empire of Jim Charles collapsed suddenly in the early 1980s. Charles' bank was one of hundreds that regulatory authorities closed down during that time period for operating in an "unsafe and unsound" manner. Charles' equity in the bank, along with that of the bank's other investors, was wiped out by huge losses in the bank's loan portfolio.

Questions

1. How do you believe Alex Saunders should have reacted when Jim Charles insisted that Bud be removed from the bank's audit engagement team? What would you have done under similar circumstances if you had been Saunders?

2. In your opinion, did Saunders' decision to comply with Charles' request violate any professional or ethical standards? Defend your answer.

3. How do you believe that Bud should have reacted when Saunders told him why he had been removed from the audit engagement team?

4. The key events in this case transpired during the late 1970s. Do you believe that such a series of events could occur now? Explain.

Hopkins v. Price Waterhouse

In 1978, at the age of 34, Ann Hopkins faced a dilemma that a growing number of professional women are being forced to confront. Hopkins had to make a difficult choice involving her family and her career. Both Hopkins and her husband were employed by Touche Ross & Company. Because of the firm's nepotism rules, she realized that either she or her husband would have to leave the firm. Otherwise, neither would be considered for promotion to partner. Although comfortable with her position, Hopkins chose to make the personal sacrifice. She resigned from Touche Ross and within a few days accepted a position in the consulting division of Price Waterhouse.

Four years later, Hopkins was among the 88 individuals nominated for promotion to partner with Price Waterhouse. Hopkins, a senior manager in the firm's Washington, D.C., office, was the only woman in that group. Hopkins stood out from the other nominees in another respect. She had generated the most business for Price Waterhouse of all the partner candidates. Over the previous four years, clients obtained by Hopkins had produced $40 million of revenues for the firm. Because client development skills generally rank as the most important criterion in partnership promotion decisions, Hopkins appeared to be a shoo-in for promotion.

Strengthening Hopkins' case even more was the unanimous and strong backing her nomination received from the seven partners in the Washington, D.C., office. The extent of home office support for a candidate's nomination was another key factor Price Waterhouse considered in evaluating individuals for promotion to partner.

Much to her surprise, Hopkins was not awarded a partnership position. Instead, the senior manager was told that she would be considered for promotion the following year. A few months later, Hopkins was surprised again when her office managing partner informed her that she was no longer considered a viable candidate for promotion to partner. The firm's top executives did invite her to remain with Price Waterhouse in a nonpartner capacity. Disenchanted and somewhat bitter, Hopkins resigned from Price Waterhouse in January 1984 and accepted a position with the World Bank in Washington, D.C. Eventually, nagging uncertainty regarding her failure to make partner caused Hopkins to file a civil lawsuit against Price Waterhouse.

Prior Criticism of Personnel Practices of Big Eight Firms

The lawsuit Ann Hopkins filed against Price Waterhouse drew attention to an issue simmering within the public accounting profession for years. During a 1976 investigation of the profession by a U.S. Senate subcommittee, several parties charged that Big Eight firms' personnel practices discriminated against females and minorities.[1] At one point during its hearings, the Senate subcommittee requested each of the Big Eight firms to disclose the average compensation of their partners and the number of females and nonwhite males in their partner ranks.

The Senate subcommittee's request evoked uncooperative responses from several of the Big Eight firms. Exhibit 1 presents two of those responses. Exhibit 2 contains

---

1. U.S. Congress, Senate Subcommittee on Reports, Accounting and Management of the Committee on Government Operations, *The Accounting Establishment* (Washington, D.C.: U.S. Government Printing Office, 1977).

a letter that Senator Lee Metcalf, chairman of the investigative subcommittee, wrote to Ernst & Ernst after that firm questioned the Senate's authority to investigate the personnel practices of private partnerships. Six of the Big Eight firms provided the requested information regarding the number of females and minority males among their partners. Collectively, these firms had seven female partners and four partners who were African-American males out of a total of more than 3,500 partners.

EXHIBIT 1

SELECTED RESPONSES TO U.S. SENATE REQUEST FOR INFORMATION REGARDING BIG EIGHT FIRMS' PERSONNEL PRACTICES

June 11, 1976

The Honorable Lee Metcalf, Chairman
Subcommittee on Reports, Accounting, and Management
Committee on Government Operations
United States Senate
Washington, D.C. 20510

Dear Senator Metcalf:

I acknowledge receipt of your letter of June 7, 1976. As you know, this firm has responded and in considerable detail to the Committee's earlier requests. However, we consider the information sought in this letter to exceed the scope of the Committee's investigative authority. Moreover, the information sought includes data proprietary to this firm and its individual members. As a result, we respectfully decline to provide the requested data.

Very truly yours,

Russell E. Palmer
Managing Partner and
Chief Executive Officer
Touche Ross & Company

June 30, 1976

The Honorable Lee Metcalf, Chairman
Subcommittee on Reports, Accounting, and Management
United States Senate
Washington, D.C. 20510

Dear Senator Metcalf:

This will acknowledge your letter of June 7 which was received during the period I was away from my office.

We find it difficult to understand why the compensation of our partners is a matter of valid interest to a subcommittee of the Committee on Government Operations. We are even more perplexed with the suggestion that this could be a matter of importance in an assessment of our professional performance.

Along with these reservations we also confess to a deep-rooted belief that members of a private partnership have a right to maintain privacy over such matters if they wish to do so. Therefore, absent an understanding of its justification, we respectfully decline to furnish the compensation information you have requested.

Two partners (.5% of the total number of our partners) are female. None of our partners are blacks.

Yours very truly,

William S. Kanaga
Arthur Young & Company

EXHIBIT 2

U.S. SENATE
RESPONSE TO ERNST
& ERNST'S
RELUCTANCE TO
PROVIDE REQUESTED
PERSONNEL
INFORMATION

June 28, 1976

Mr. R.T. Baker
Managing Partner
Ernst & Ernst
Union Commerce Building
Cleveland, Ohio 64115

Dear Mr. Baker:

In your letter of June 24, you question the authority of this subcommittee to request information from your firm on various subjects. You note that our authority is primarily directed to the accounting practices of Federal departments and agencies.

Our requests for information from your firm are based on the unusual and substantial relationship which has developed between certain Federal agencies and influential segments of the accounting profession. This relationship has led to official recognition by Federal agencies of judgments on binding standards which have been made entirely within the private sector. The Securities and Exchange Commission has even formalized its acceptance of private decision-making through Accounting Series Release 150. The Moss amendment to the Energy Policy and Conservation Act also contemplates Federal recognition of private decisions on the manner of uniform accounting to be developed for the oil and gas industry.

The substantial reliance by Federal agencies upon decisions made in the private sector represents a significant delegation of the statutory authority vested in those agencies. This arrangement involves important decisions affecting the policies of the Federal government and other segments of our society.

Decisions made by Federal agencies are subject to review by Congress and the public. Much progress has been made both in Congress and the Federal government in opening the processes of decision-making to public scrutiny. The public has a right to know the identity and interests of those who act under the public's authority to determine the directions which this nation shall take.

When public decision-making authority is delegated to the private sector, the public has an even greater interest in knowing who is directing important national policies. As you are well aware, little information is available to Congress or the public concerning the activities of accounting firms. That is why it is necessary for this subcommittee to request information on various activities of accounting firms.

Your firm is substantially involved in the private decision-making process which develops accounting standards that are recognized by Federal agencies. The information which has so far been requested by this subcommittee is only a small fraction of the information that is publicly available regarding the identity and interests of Federal officials, or even major corporate officials. Yet, the decision-making area in which your firm is involved influences public policy as much or more than do many companies for which the requested information is publicly available.

This subcommittee has a responsibility to ensure that Federal accounting practices are responsive to the public interest. We must be informed on matters which are relevant to Federal accounting practices. That is why your firm has been requested to provide information to this subcommittee.

Very truly yours,

Lee Metcalf, Chairman
Subcommittee on Reports,
Accounting, and Management

The criticism of the Big Eight firms' personnel practices spawned by the 1976 Senate investigation spurred academic researchers and the business press to begin monitoring the progress of women and minorities within Big Eight firms. By the late 1980s, when the Hopkins suit against Price Waterhouse was working its way through the courts, neither group had made significant inroads into the top hierarchy of the Big Eight firms. For instance, in 1988, women held approximately 3.5 percent of the partnership positions with Big Eight firms, although those firms had been hiring women in considerable numbers since the mid-1970s.[2]

Continued concern regarding the progress of women and minorities within Big Eight firms focused the accounting profession's attention on Ann Hopkins' civil suit against Price Waterhouse. Although the Hopkins case provides only anecdotal evidence regarding the personnel practices of large international accounting firms, it is noteworthy for several reasons. First, the case yielded revealing insights into the partnership selection process employed by large accounting firms. Second, the case pointed to the need to rid performance appraisal methods of gender-based criteria in all disciplines, including professional fields. Finally, *Hopkins v. Price Waterhouse* stimulated discussion of measures that professional firms could take to facilitate the career success of their female employees.

Price Waterhouse's Consideration of Ann Hopkins for Promotion to Partner

During the 1980s, the partners of Price Waterhouse annually identified and then nominated for promotion to partner those senior managers whom they considered to be partner "material." Price Waterhouse's admissions committee collected these nominations and then provided a list of the nominees to each partner in the firm. The admissions committee invited partners to provide either a "long form" or "short form" evaluation of the individual candidates.

Typically, a partner well acquainted with a nominee provided a long form evaluation. Partners having had little or no contact with a given nominee submitted a short form evaluation or no evaluation at all. Both forms required the partners to assess the partnership potential of the nominees on several scaled dimensions, including client development abilities, interpersonal skills, and technical expertise. After responding to the scaled items, the partners indicated whether the given individual should be promoted, whether he or she should be denied promotion, or whether the promotion decision should be deferred for one or more years. The partners also provided a brief written explanation documenting the key reasons for their overall recommendation for each candidate.

After studying and summarizing the evaluations, the admissions committee prepared three lists of candidates: those recommended for admission to partnership, those not recommended for promotion, and those who had received a "hold" recommendation. These latter candidates typically included individuals having partner potential but also one or more weaknesses that needed to be addressed before they were considered again for promotion. The admissions committee submitted its recommendations to the firm's policy board, which reviewed them and selected the final slate of candidates to be voted on by the entire partnership.[3]

2. E. Berg, "The Big Eight," *New York Times*, 17 December 1977, D1; "Women Comprise Half of 1986–87 Graduates," *Public Accounting Report*, 1 February 1988, 7.

3. This description of Price Waterhouse's partnership selection process was summarized from information presented in the 1985 court opinion *Hopkins v. Price Waterhouse*, 618 F. Supp. 1109 (D.C.D.C. 1985).

The admissions committee received 32 evaluation forms commenting on Ann Hopkins' nomination for partner. Thirteen partners submitted positive recommendations, eight recommended she not be promoted, three suggested she be held over for consideration the following year, and eight did not include a recommendation in their evaluation forms.

The most common criticism of Hopkins by partners who recommended she not be promoted was that she had poor interpersonal skills and an abrasive personality. These individuals criticized her for being too demanding of her subordinates, for using profanity, and for being generally harsh and overly aggressive. Two partners used gender-specific terms when commenting on Hopkins. One partner referred to her as "macho," while another observed that "she may have overcompensated for being a woman."[4]

After reviewing Hopkins' evaluations, the admissions committee recommended that she be held over for consideration, a recommendation accepted by the policy board. The admissions committee decided that her interpersonal skills needed to be strengthened to allow her to function effectively as a partner.

To improve her chances of promotion the following year, Hopkins agreed to undergo a "quality control review" to help her identify specific interpersonal and other job-related skills needing improvement. Subsequent to the quality control review, several partners indicated they would give her opportunities to demonstrate that she was remedying the deficiencies in her interpersonal skills. These partners never followed through on their commitments. Four months after Hopkins completed the quality control review, her office managing partner informed her that she would not be nominated for partner that year. Hopkins was also told that she probably would never be considered again for promotion to partner.

Ann Hopkins' Civil Suit against Price Waterhouse

Ann Hopkins learned of the "hold" recommendation given to her nomination for partner in mid-1983. At that time, her office managing partner discussed with her some of the reservations partners expressed regarding her nomination. In particular, he told Hopkins that several partners believed her appearance and interpersonal manner were overtly masculine and that these traits caused her to be less appealing as a partner candidate.

The office managing partner suggested that she could improve her chances for promotion if she would "walk more femininely, wear makeup, have her hair styled, and wear jewelry." Following her resignation from Price Waterhouse, Hopkins recalled these suggestions and began to question why she had been denied promotion to partner. She began to suspect that Price Waterhouse had denied her promotion not because she was perceived as unqualified to be a partner with the firm but, rather, because she was perceived as unqualified to be a *female* partner with the firm.

Eventually, Hopkins concluded that Price Waterhouse, in fact, did apply different standards for promoting females and males to partner. This issue became the focal point of the civil trial in the *Hopkins v. Price Waterhouse* case. Hopkins included the following four specific allegations in the lawsuit she filed against Price Waterhouse:

1. The criticisms of her interpersonal skills were fabricated by the Price Waterhouse partners.

---

4. This and all subsequent quotations, unless indicated otherwise, were taken from *Hopkins v. Price Waterhouse*, 618 F. Supp. 1109 (D.C.D.C. 1985).

2. Even if the criticisms of her interpersonal skills were valid, Price Waterhouse had promoted male candidates to partner having similar deficiencies in their interpersonal skills.

3. The criticisms of her interpersonal skills resulted from sexual stereotyping by Price Waterhouse partners.

4. Price Waterhouse's partnership selection process did not discount the sexually discriminatory comments made regarding her candidacy.

The judge who presided over the civil trial dismissed Hopkins' first allegation. According to the judge, the defense counsel clearly proved that Hopkins did have poor interpersonal skills, particularly when dealing with subordinates. The judge ruled that Price Waterhouse was well within its rights to deny an individual a partnership position who did not possess adequate interpersonal skills. However, the judge then pointed to court testimony documenting that Price Waterhouse had previously promoted male partner candidates described as "crude, abrasive, and overbearing." These comments were very similar to criticisms of Hopkins' interpersonal skills made during the partner selection process.

A review of the firm's past promotion decisions also revealed that two earlier female partner candidates may have been denied admission to the partnership for reasons identical to those that cost Hopkins her promotion. Evaluation comments made for those candidates criticized them for acting like "Ma Barker" or for trying to be "one of the boys."

An earlier legal case established the precedent that an employer who evaluates a woman with an aggressive or abrasive personality differently than a man with similar personality traits is guilty of sex discrimination. After reviewing all of the evidence presented during the trial, the judge ruled that Price Waterhouse had evaluated Hopkins as a candidate for becoming a female partner rather than simply a partner with the firm.

> [Female] candidates were viewed favorably if partners believed they maintained their femininity while becoming effective professional managers. To be identified as a "women's libber" was regarded as a negative comment. Nothing was done to discourage sexually biased evaluations. One partner repeatedly commented that he could not consider any woman seriously as a partnership candidate and believed that women were not capable of functioning as senior managers—yet the firm took no action to discourage his comments and recorded his vote in the overall summary of the evaluations.

Although Hopkins was found to have been the victim of sex discrimination, the judge deemed that the discrimination was not overt or intentional. In fact, Hopkins freely admitted during the trial that she never perceived she was being discriminated against because of her gender while employed with Price Waterhouse. Instead, sexually discriminatory attitudes latent within the culture of Price Waterhouse victimized Hopkins' candidacy for partner. That is, the partners who made the sexually biased remarks regarding Hopkins were unaware that they were evaluating her unfairly relative to male candidates for partner. Nevertheless, the judge ruled that Price Waterhouse perpetuated an evaluation system that allowed sexual stereotypes to undermine the promotion opportunities of female employees.

> There is no direct evidence of any determined purpose to maliciously discriminate against women, but plaintiff appears to have been a victim of "omissive and subtle" discriminations created by a system that made evaluations based on "outmoded" attitudes. ... Price Waterhouse should have been aware that women being evaluated by male partners might well be victims of discriminatory stereotypes. Yet the firm made no efforts ... to discourage comments tainted by sexism or to determine whether they were influenced by stereotypes.

EPILOGUE

In May 1990, six years after Ann Hopkins filed suit against Price Waterhouse, a federal judge ordered the firm to pay her $400,000 of compensatory damages. More important, the judge ordered the CPA firm to offer Hopkins a partnership position. During a party to celebrate the court's decision, Hopkins maintained that she had no reservations joining a firm that had unfairly rejected her for partnership seven years earlier. She also joked with her male coworkers at the World Bank regarding several less-than-complimentary remarks made regarding her during the trial. In particular, she questioned the assertion of one Price Waterhouse partner that she needed to enroll in charm school. Moments later, Hopkins took a long and noisy slug of champagne—straight from the bottle.

In 1996, five years after rejoining Price Waterhouse, Ann Hopkins documented her difficult road to becoming a partner in a book published by the University of Massachusetts Press that was entitled *So Ordered: Making Partner the Hard Way.* Despite the ordeal that she experienced, Hopkins insists that she has no "hard feelings" toward her fellow partners. In fact, Hopkins' daughter joined PricewaterhouseCoopers (PwC), the successor firm to Price Waterhouse, when she graduated from college in 1998.

Growing numbers of women have obtained partnership positions with the large international accounting firms since the resolution of the *Hopkins* case. But women still remain significantly underrepresented in the partnership ranks of those firms.[5] That fact was a key issue raised by Melissa Page, a former PwC tax manager, when she filed a lawsuit against PwC that was reminiscent of Ann Hopkins' lawsuit two decades earlier. In her complaint, Page alleged that the firm was guilty of "systematically discriminating" against women and suggested that an "old boy network" still pervaded PwC's culture.

> *[Page] claims her career was derailed by a corporate culture that kept women away from the very opportunities that led to partnership—including informal networking events, golf outings, and other activities that would have given her more access to clients and company executives.*[6]

Page's lawsuit prompted other women in the profession to speak out. One of those individuals was Barbara Hufsmith, who reported that she had chosen to establish her own accounting firm after being a victim of gender discrimination in a male-dominated accounting firm.

> *I too have been discriminated against in an old boys CPA firm. It has forced me to start my own firm, for which I am grateful, but it should not have been such a painful and expensive experience. I truly believe that only a couple of partners from my old firm knew what they were doing to me was not fair. The rest of the partners were blind, stupid, and arrogant.*[7]

In 2011, several former female employees of KPMG filed a class-action lawsuit alleging that the firm systematically discriminates against female professional employees. The plaintiffs asked for damages of nearly $400 million. In February 2013, a New York federal judge ruled that the lawsuit could proceed after denying KPMG's request that the case be dismissed.[8]

Among other allegations, the complaint filed by the plaintiffs reported that a KPMG partner justified the firing of a female on the day she returned from maternity leave by suggesting that she "should be fine without a job" because her husband makes "a lot of money."[9]

---

5. A 2012 report indicated that 18.1 percent of Big Four partners are women (D. McClure, "Celebrating Women in the Profession," www.cpapracticeadvisor.com, 5 July 2012).

6. *AccountingWEB.com*, "PricewaterhouseCoopers Faces Discrimination Suit," 29 July 2004.

7. *Ibid.*

8. B. Van Voris, "KPMG Gender-Discrimination Suit Can Proceed, Judge Rules," www.businessweek.com, 7 February 2013.

9. Sanford Heisler, LLP, "KPMG Gender Discrimination Lawsuit," www.sanfordheisler.com, 7 February 2013.

Questions

1. Do public accounting firms have a responsibility to facilitate the career success of female employees? Why or why not? Identify policies accounting firms could implement to increase the retention rate of female employees.

2. In business circles, one frequently hears references to the "old boy network." Many women in professional firms complain that their gender precludes them from becoming a member of the old boy network within their firm. Define, in your own terms, the phrase *old boy network*. Should professional firms attempt to break down these networks?

3. Suppose that an audit client objects to a given auditor because of his or her gender or race. Identify the alternative courses of action the auditor's employer should consider taking in such a case. Which of these alternatives do you believe the accounting firm should take? Defend your answer.

4. The nepotism rules of many professional firms pose a major inconvenience for married couples who work for, or would like to work for, those firms. Discuss the costs and benefits of these rules in a public accounting setting. In practice, do you believe these rules are equally fair (or unfair) to both sexes?

Fred Stern & Company, Inc.
(Ultramares Corporation v. Touche et al.)

In the business world of the Roaring Twenties, the schemes and scams of flim-flam artists and confidence men were legendary. The absence of a strong regulatory system at the federal level to police the securities markets—the Securities and Exchange Commission was not established until 1934—aided, if not encouraged, financial frauds of all types. In all likelihood, the majority of individuals involved in business during the 1920s were scrupulously honest. Nevertheless, the culture of that decade bred a disproportionate number of opportunists who adopted an "anything goes" approach to transacting business. An example of a company in which this self-serving attitude apparently prevailed was Fred Stern & Company, Inc. During the mid-1920s, Stern's executives duped three of the company's creditors out of several hundred thousand dollars.

Based in New York City, Stern imported rubber, a raw material demanded in huge quantities by many industries in the early twentieth century. During the 1920s alone, industrial demand for rubber in the United States more than tripled. The nature of the rubber importation trade required large amounts of working capital. Because Stern was chronically short of funds, the company relied heavily on banks and other lenders to finance its day-to-day operations.

In March 1924, Stern sought a $100,000 loan from Ultramares Corporation, a finance company whose primary line of business was factoring receivables. Before considering the loan request, Ultramares asked Stern's management for an audited balance sheet. Stern had been audited a few months earlier by Touche, Niven & Company, a prominent accounting firm based in London and New York City. Touche had served as Stern's independent auditor since 1920. Exhibit 1 presents the unqualified opinion Touche issued on Stern's 31 December 1923, balance sheet. Stern's management obtained 32 serially numbered copies of that audit report. Touche knew that Stern intended to use the audit reports to obtain external debt financing but was unaware of the specific banks or finance companies that might receive the audit reports.

After reviewing Stern's audited balance sheet, which reported assets of more than $2.5 million and a net worth of approximately $1 million, and the accompanying audit report, Ultramares granted the $100,000 loan requested by the company. Ultramares later extended two more loans to Stern totaling $65,000. During the same time frame, Stern obtained more than $300,000 in loans from two local banks after providing them with copies of the 31 December 1923, balance sheet and accompanying audit report.

Unfortunately for Ultramares and the two banks that extended loans to Stern, the company was declared bankrupt in January 1925. Subsequent courtroom testimony revealed that the company had been hopelessly insolvent at the end of 1923 when its audited balance sheet reported a net worth of $1 million. An accountant with Stern, identified only as Romberg in court records, concealed Stern's bankrupt status from the Touche auditors. Romberg masked Stern's true financial condition by making several false entries in the company's accounting records. The largest of these entries

EXHIBIT 1

TOUCHE, NIVEN &
COMPANY'S AUDIT
OPINION
ON STERN'S
DECEMBER 31,
1923, BALANCE
SHEET

February 26, 1924

**Touche, Niven & Co.
Public Accountants
Eighty Maiden Lane,
New York**

Certificate of Auditors

We have examined the accounts of Fred Stern & Co., Inc., for the year ended December 31, 1923, and hereby certify that the annexed balance sheet is in accordance therewith and with the information and explanations given us. We further certify that, subject to provision for federal taxes on income, the said statement in our opinion, presents a true and correct view of the financial condition of Fred Stern & Co., Inc., as at December 31, 1923.

involved a debit of more than $700,000 to accounts receivable and an offsetting credit to sales.

Following Stern's bankruptcy, Ultramares sued Touche to recover the $165,000 loaned to Stern. Ultramares alleged that the audit firm had been both fraudulent and negligent in auditing Stern's financial records. The *New York Times* noted that the resolution of the negligence claim in the *Ultramares* case would likely establish a legal precedent for future plaintiffs hoping to recover losses from audit firms.[1] The novel aspect of the negligence claim stemmed from the absence of a contractual relationship between Touche and Ultramares. Touche's contract to audit Stern's 31 December 1923, balance sheet was made solely with Stern's management. At the time, a well-entrenched legal doctrine dictated that only a party in privity with another—that is, having an explicit contractual agreement with another—could recover damages resulting from the other party's negligence.

Another interesting facet of the *Ultramares* lawsuit involved the founder of Touche, Niven & Company, Sir George Alexander Touche. George Touche, who served for two years as the sheriff of London during World War I, merged his accounting practice in the early 1900s with that of a young Scottish accountant, John B. Niven, who had immigrated to New York City. The new firm prospered, and George Touche, who was knighted in 1917 by King George V, eventually became one of the most respected leaders of the emerging public accounting profession. John Niven also became influential within the profession. Ironically, Niven was serving as the president of the American Institute of Accountants, the predecessor of the American Institute of Certified Public Accountants, when Fred Stern & Company was declared insolvent. An issue posed by the *Ultramares* lawsuit was whether George Touche and his fellow partners who were not involved in the Stern audit could be held personally liable for any improper conduct on the part of the Touche auditors assigned to the Stern engagement. Ultramares raised that issue by naming each of the Touche partners as codefendants.

Ultramares Corporation v. Touche et al.: A Protracted Legal Battle

The *Ultramares* civil suit against Touche was tried before a jury in a New York state court. Ultramares' principal allegation was that the Touche auditors should have easily discovered the $700,000 overstatement of receivables in Stern's 31 December 1923,

---

1. "Damages Refused for Error in Audit," *New York Times*, 27 June 1929, 50.

balance sheet. That error, if corrected, would have slashed Stern's reported net worth by nearly 70 percent and considerably lessened the likelihood that Ultramares would have extended the company a sizable loan.

A young man by the name of Siess performed most of the fieldwork on the Stern audit. When Siess arrived at Stern's office to begin the audit in early February 1924, he discovered that the company's general ledger had not been posted since the prior April. He spent the next few days posting entries from the client's journals to its general ledger. After Siess completed that task, Stern's accounts receivable totaled approximately $644,000. Stern's accountant, Romberg, obtained the general ledger the day before Siess intended to prepare a trial balance of the company's accounts. After reviewing the ledger, Romberg booked an entry debiting receivables and crediting sales for approximately $706,000. Beside the entry in the receivables account, he entered a number cross-referencing the recorded amount to the company's sales journal.

The following day, Romberg notified Siess of the entry he had recorded in the general ledger. Romberg told Siess that the entry represented Stern's December sales that had been inadvertently omitted from the accounting records. Without questioning Romberg's explanation for the large entry, Siess included the $706,000 in the receivables balance. In fact, the receivables did not exist and the corresponding sales never occurred. To support the entry, Romberg or one of his subordinates hastily prepared 17 bogus sales invoices.

In subsequent testimony, Siess initially reported that he could not recall whether he reviewed any of the 17 invoices allegedly representing Stern's December sales. Plaintiff counsel then demonstrated that "a mere glance" at the invoices would have revealed that they were forged. The invoices lacked shipping numbers, customer order numbers, and other pertinent information. Following this revelation, Siess admitted that he had not examined any of the invoices.[2] Touche's attorneys attempted to justify this oversight by pointing out that audits involve "testing and sampling" rather than an examination of entire accounting populations.[3] Thus, it was not surprising or unusual, the attorneys argued, that none of the fictitious December sales invoices were among the more than 200 invoices examined during the Stern audit.

The court ruled that auditing on a sample basis is appropriate in most cases. But, given the suspicious nature of the large December sales entry recorded by Romberg, the court concluded that Touche should have specifically reviewed the December sales invoices.

> Verification by test and sample was very likely a sufficient audit as to accounts regularly entered upon the books in the usual course of business. ... [However], the defendants were put on their guard by the circumstances touching the December accounts receivable to scrutinize with special care.[4]

Ultramares' attorneys noted during the trial that Touche had even more reason than just the suspicious nature of Romberg's December sales entry to question the integrity of the large year-end increase in receivables. While auditing the company's inventory, Touche auditors discovered several errors that collectively caused the inventory account to be overstated by more than $300,000, an overstatement of 90 percent. The auditors also uncovered large errors in Stern's accounts payable and discovered that the company had improperly pledged the same assets as collateral

2. *Ultramares Corporation v. Touche et al.*, 255 N.Y. 170, 174 N.E. 441 (1930), 449.

3. *Ibid.*

4. *Ibid.*

for several bank loans. Given the extent and nature of the problems revealed by the Touche audit, the court ruled that the accounting firm should have been particularly skeptical of the client's accounting records. This should have been the case, the court observed, even though Touche had not encountered any reason in previous audits to question the integrity of Stern's management.

> *No doubt the extent to which inquiry must be pressed beyond appearances is a question of judgment, as to which opinions will often differ. No doubt the wisdom that is born after the event will engender suspicion and distrust when old acquaintance and good repute may have silenced doubt at the beginning.[5]*

The jury in the *Ultramares* case dismissed the fraud charge against Touche. The jurors ruled that the company's attorneys failed to establish that the audit firm had intentionally deceived Ultramares—intentional deceit being a necessary condition for fraud. Regarding the negligence charge, the jury ruled in favor of Ultramares and ordered Touche to pay the company damages of $186,000.

The judge who presided over the *Ultramares* case overturned the jury's ruling on the negligence charge. In explaining his decision, the judge acknowledged that Ultramares' attorneys had clearly established that Touche had been negligent during its 1923 audit of Stern. Nevertheless, the judge ruled that the jury had overlooked the long-standing legal doctrine that only a party in privity could sue and recover damages resulting from a defendant's negligence.[6]

Ultramares' attorneys quickly appealed the trial judge's decision. The appellate division of the New York Supreme Court reviewed the case. In a 3 to 2 vote, the appellate division decided that the trial judge erred in reversing the jury's verdict on the negligence charge. As appellate Justice McAvoy noted, the key question in the case centered on whether Touche had a duty to Ultramares "in the absence of a direct contractual relation."[7] Justice McAvoy concluded that Touche did have an obligation to Ultramares, and to other parties relying on Stern's financial statements, although the accounting firm's contract was expressly and exclusively with Stern.

> *One cannot issue an unqualified statement [audit opinion] . . . and then disclaim responsibility for his work. Banks and merchants, to the knowledge of these defendants, require certified balance sheets from independent accountants, and upon these audits they make their loans. Thus, the duty arises to these banks and merchants of an exercise of reasonable care in the making and uttering of certified balance sheets.[8]*

Justice McAvoy and two of his colleagues were unwavering in their opinion that Touche had a legal obligation to Ultramares. Nevertheless, the remaining two judges on the appellate panel were just as strongly persuaded that no such obligation existed. In the dissenting opinion, Justice Finch maintained that holding Touche responsible to a third party that subsequently relied upon the Stern financial statements was patently unfair to the accounting firm.

> *If the plaintiff [Ultramares] had inquired of the accountants whether they might rely upon the certificate in making a loan, then the accountants would have had the opportunity to gauge their responsibility and risk, and determine with knowledge how thorough their verification of the account should be before assuming the responsibility of making the certificate run to the plaintiff.[9]*

---

5. *Ibid.*, 444.

6. "Damages Refused for Error."

7. *Ultramares Corporation v. Touche et al.*, 229 App. Div. 581, 243 N.Y.S. 179 (1930), 181.

8. *Ibid.*, 182.

9. *Ibid.*, 186.

Following the appellate division's ruling in the *Ultramares* case, Touche's attorneys appealed the decision to the next highest court in the New York state judicial system, the Court of Appeals. That court ultimately handed down the final ruling in the lengthy judicial history of the case. The chief justice of New York's Court of Appeals, Benjamin Cardozo, was a nationally recognized legal scholar whose opinions were given great weight by other courts.

Justice Cardozo and his six associate justices ruled unanimously that the judge who presided over the *Ultramares* trial had properly reversed the jury's decision on the negligence claim. Justice Cardozo reiterated the arguments made by Justice Finch. He maintained that it would be unfair to hold Touche legally responsible to a third party, unknown to Touche when its audit was performed, that happened to obtain and rely upon Stern's audited balance sheet. However, Justice Cardozo went on to suggest that had Ultramares been clearly designated as a beneficiary of the Stern–Touche contract, his ruling would have been different.

Unfortunately for the accounting profession, Justice Cardozo's opinion did not end with his commentary on the negligence question in the *Ultramares* case. After resolving that issue, he sharply criticized Touche's audit of Stern. The judge implied that Ultramares might have been successful in suing Touche on the basis of gross negligence: "Negligence or blindness, even when not equivalent to fraud, is none the less evidence to sustain an inference of fraud. At least this is so if the negligence is gross. ... [In the *Ultramares* case] a jury might find that ... [the Touche auditors] closed their eyes to the obvious, and blindly gave assent."[10]

The *Ultramares* Decision: Implications for the Accounting Profession

In retrospect, the *Ultramares* decision had two principal implications for the public accounting profession. First, Justice Cardozo's opinion established the precedent that certain direct beneficiaries of an audit, generally referred to as primary beneficiaries, are entitled to recover damages from a negligent auditor. Subsequent to the *Ultramares* ruling, very few plaintiffs were successful in establishing themselves as primary beneficiaries of an audit.[11] Consequently, this "expansion" of the auditor's legal exposure proved to be fairly insignificant.

The second key implication of the *Ultramares* case was that it provided a new strategy for plaintiff counsel to use in suing auditors on behalf of nonprivity parties. Following the *Ultramares* ruling, attorneys representing such plaintiffs began predicating lawsuits against auditors on allegations of gross negligence. Before that ruling, nonprivity third parties faced the heavy burden of proving fraud if they wanted to recover losses resulting from auditor misconduct. Because establishing gross negligence is much easier than proving intent to defraud, the *Ultramares* decision significantly increased auditors' legal exposure to nonprivity third parties.

A secondary issue addressed by Justice Cardozo in the *Ultramares* case was whether Sir George Touche and his fellow partners who had no direct connection with the Stern engagement could be held liable for the deficient Stern audit. This issue was moot regarding the negligence allegation since that charge had already been dismissed. But, the issue was still pertinent to the fraud charge since Justice Cardozo ruled that Ultramares was entitled to a retrial to determine whether Touche's

---

10. *Ultramares Corporation v. Touche et al.*, 255 N.Y. 170, 174 N.E. 441 (1930), 449.

11. Decades later, the *Credit Alliance* case established several restrictive conditions that third parties must satisfy to qualify as primary beneficiaries. See *Credit Alliance Corporation v. Arthur Andersen & Company*, 483 N.E. 2d 110 (N.Y. 1985).

negligence was severe enough to infer fraudulent conduct or gross negligence.[12] Because the auditors assigned to the Stern engagement were acting as agents of the accounting firm's partners, Justice Cardozo ruled that all of Touche's partners were legally responsible for the actions of those individuals.

EPILOGUE

In the years following the *Ultramares* case, the legal exposure of public accountants to third-party financial statement users was gradually extended. The first extension came on the heels of the *Ultramares* case with the passage of the Securities Act of 1933. That federal statute imposed on auditors a very significant legal obligation to initial purchasers of new securities marketed on an interstate basis.

Under the 1933 Act, plaintiffs do not have to prove fraud, gross negligence, or even negligence on the part of auditors. Essentially, plaintiffs must only establish that they suffered investment losses and that the relevant financial statements contain material errors or omissions. If a plaintiff establishes those elements of proof, the defendant accounting firm assumes the burden of proving that its employees were "duly diligent" in performing the audit.[13] To sustain a due diligence defense, an accounting firm must show that, following a "reasonable investigation," it had "reasonable ground to believe and did believe" that the audited financial statements were materially accurate. Federal courts have not been receptive to the due diligence defense if the plaintiffs have clearly established that the financial statements in question contain material errors.[14]

Auditors' legal exposure has also expanded under the common law over the past several decades. In 1965, the American Law Institute issued *Restatement of Torts*, a legal compendium relied on heavily in many jurisdictions. This source suggests that "foreseen" beneficiaries, in addition to primary beneficiaries, should have a right to recover damages from negligent auditors.[15] Foreseen beneficiaries are members of a limited group or class of third-party financial statement users. Auditors are typically aware of this distinct group of potential financial statement users but unaware of the specific individuals or entities who make up that group.

The 1983 *Rosenblum* ruling went beyond the boundary established by the *Restatement of Torts*. That judicial ruling suggested that even "reasonably foreseeable" or "ordinary" third-party financial statement users should be allowed to recover damages from negligent auditors.[16] Reasonably foreseeable third parties include a much larger population of potential financial statement users than "foreseen" third parties. The most liberal definition of "reasonably foreseeable third parties" includes individual investors who happen to obtain a copy of audited financial statements and make a decision based upon them.

---

12. For whatever reason, Ultramares chose not to file an amended lawsuit against Touche that was predicated upon an allegation of gross negligence.

13. Accounting firms have other defenses available to them when sued under the Securities Act of 1933. These defenses include, among others, expiration of the statute of limitations, establishing that the plaintiff knew the relevant financial statements were misleading when he or she purchased the securities, and proving that the plaintiff's damages were not caused by the misleading financial statements.

14. Case 7.6, "First Securities Company of Chicago (*Ernst & Ernst v. Hochfelder et al.*)," examines the legal implications posed for public accounting firms by the Securities Exchange Act of 1934, which is the "sister" statute to the 1933 Act.

15. American Law Institute, *Restatement of the Law, Second: Torts* (Philadelphia: American Law Institute, 1965).

16. *H. Rosenblum, Inc. v. Adler*, 461 A. 2d 138 (N.J. 1983).

Questions

1. Observers of the accounting profession suggest that many courts attempt to "socialize" investment losses by extending auditors' liability to third-party financial statement users. Discuss the benefits and costs of such a policy to public accounting firms, audit clients, and third-party financial statement users, such as investors and creditors. In your view, should the courts have the authority to socialize investment losses? If not, who should determine how investment losses are distributed in our society?

2. Auditors' legal responsibilities differ significantly under the Securities Exchange Act of 1934 and the Securities Act of 1933. Briefly point out these differences and comment on why they exist. Also comment on how auditors' litigation risks differ under the common law and the 1934 Act.

3. The current standard audit report differs significantly from the version issued during the 1920s. Identify the key differences in the two reports and discuss the forces that accounted for the evolution of the audit report into its present form.

4. Why was it common in the 1920s for companies to have only an audited balance sheet prepared for distribution to external third parties? Comment on the factors that, over a period of several decades, resulted in the adoption of the financial statement package that most companies presently provide to external third parties.

5. When assessing audit risk, should auditors consider the type and number of third parties that may ultimately rely on the client's financial statements? Should auditors insist that audit engagement letters identify the third parties to whom the client intends to distribute the audited financial statements? Would this practice eliminate auditors' legal liability to nonprivity parties not mentioned in engagement letters?

First Securities Company of Chicago
(*Ernst & Ernst v. Hochfelder et al.*)

Ladislas Nay immigrated to the United States from Hungary in 1921 at the age of 18. The opportunities offered by his new land excited the industrious young immigrant and he promised himself that he would make the most of them. Shortly after arriving in the United States, Nay made his way to Chicago and landed a job in the booming securities industry with a small brokerage firm. For the next several years, Nay worked long and hard hours learning the brokerage business.

Unfortunately for Nay, the Great Depression hit the securities industry particularly hard. Young stockbrokers like him were the first to be laid off by their firms when personnel cuts were necessary. During the bleak 1930s, Nay, who by this time had Americanized his first name to Leston, endured several job changes and two failed marriages. In 1942, as World War II began to pull the United States out of the Depression, Nay landed a permanent job with the brokerage firm of Ryan-Nichols & Company.

Within two years of joining Ryan-Nichols, Nay was promoted to president. He eventually became the firm's principal stockholder, accumulating more than 90 percent of its outstanding common stock. In 1945, the firm successfully applied for membership to the Midwest Stock Exchange and was renamed First Securities Company of Chicago. Over the next two decades, Nay's career and personal life flourished. Nay and his wife, Elizabeth, participated in a wide range of community affairs, including serving on several prominent civic boards, and eventually purchased a home in the upper-class neighborhood of Hyde Park. Nay made numerous friends among the faculty and staff of nearby University of Chicago. In fact, many of his best customers were associated with the prestigious school.

Nay's personal attention to the financial needs of his customers earned him their respect and admiration. One of his customers described him as a kind and considerate man, much "like an old-fashioned English solicitor who took care of a family's affairs."[1] His conservative investment strategies particularly appealed to his retired clients and those nearing retirement. Nay offered many of these customers an opportunity to invest in a lucrative fund that he personally managed. This fund was not an asset of First Securities, nor were any other First Securities personnel aware it existed. Nay referred to this fund as the "escrow syndicate."

Nay loaned funds invested in the escrow syndicate to blue chip companies that developed sudden and unexpected working capital shortages. These companies paid interest rates well above the prevailing market rates. Individuals who invested in the escrow syndicate earned 7 to 12 percent on their investments, considerably more than the interest rates paid at the time by banks on savings accounts.

One of Nay's closest friends, Arnold Schueren, entrusted him with more than $400,000 over three decades and granted him a power of attorney to make investment decisions regarding those funds. Nay invested a large portion of Schueren's

---

1. J. M. Johnston, "How Broker Worked $1 Million Swindle," *Chicago Daily News*, 13 December 1968, 42, 43.

savings in the escrow syndicate. Another individual who relied heavily on Nay for investment advice was the widow of a close associate of the famed University of Chicago scientist Enrico Fermi. This woman later testified that Nay had managed her family's investments for many years but did not offer her the opportunity to invest in the escrow syndicate until after her husband's death. Nay told her that he only offered this investment opportunity to his "nearest and dearest friends."[2] Following the death of another of his customers, Norman Moyer, Nay convinced Moyer's widow to invest her husband's estate of $90,000 in the escrow syndicate. In total, 17 of Nay's friends and/or their widows invested substantial sums in the escrow syndicate.

Dr. Jekyll and Mr. Hyde: A Tragic Ending

On the morning of 4 June 1968, Leston Nay drove to St. Luke's Hospital in Chicago to pick up his wife, who had fallen and broken her hip the previous week. Earlier that morning, Nay had telephoned his secretary to tell her that he would not be in the office that day because he had a stomach virus. Shortly before noon, as his wife, who was still on crutches, made her way to the kitchen of their apartment, Nay retrieved his 12-gauge shotgun and shot her in the upper back from close range. Nay then laid a suicide note on a dressing table in his bedroom, sat down on his bed, put the muzzle of the gun in his mouth, and pulled the trigger.

News of the murder-suicide shocked the Nays' friends and associates. These same people were shocked again when the Chicago police released the contents of Nay's suicide note. The note revealed that the kindly stockbroker had led a Dr. Jekyll–Mr. Hyde existence for decades. In the note, addressed "To whom it may concern," Nay admitted stealing from his customers for more than 30 years. The escrow syndicate in which his closest friends had invested did not exist—police speculated that Nay had lost the investors' funds in the stock market. Nay had successfully concealed the missing funds for as long as he did because he periodically mailed checks to the investors for interest supposedly earned by the escrow syndicate. These periodic interest payments deterred the victims of the scam from questioning the safety of their investments.

In the suicide note, Nay displayed some remorse when he referred to the 80-year-old Mrs. Moyer, who was penniless as a result of his actions. He also explained why he had decided to take his life. After Arnold Schueren died in 1967, the executor of his estate had demanded that Nay return Schueren's investment in the escrow syndicate. Nay indicated in the suicide note that he had "stalled" as long as he could but that the executor would not be put off any longer. So he took his life. Most likely, Nay murdered his wife to "save" her from the shame she would feel when his fraudulent scheme, of which she was apparently unaware, was disclosed.

Defrauded Customers Sue to Recover Their Investments

The investors in Nay's escrow syndicate filed civil lawsuits against several parties in an effort to recover their collective investments of more than $1 million. Initially, the investors sued the Midwest Stock Exchange. In that suit, the investors alleged that the stock exchange failed to adequately investigate Nay's background before admitting his firm to membership. According to the investors, a more thorough investigation might have revealed that Nay had a history, although well concealed, of unscrupulous business practices. The investors suggested that the discovery of Nay's past unethical conduct would have forced the exchange to deny his firm's membership application and may have prevented him from engaging in the escrow syndicate

---

2. *Ibid.*

fraud. The court hearing the suit quickly dismissed the investors' claims, concluding that the stock exchange had sufficiently investigated Nay's background before approving his firm's membership application.

Nay's 17 escrow participants or their estates also sued First Securities Company of Chicago. The court ruled that the brokerage firm had clearly facilitated Nay's fraudulent activities. But, since the brokerage firm was bankrupt, the escrow investors found themselves thwarted again.

Finally, Nay's former customers filed suit against Ernst & Ernst, the accounting firm that audited First Securities Company for more than two decades. The lawsuit alleged that Ernst & Ernst's negligence had prevented the firm from detecting what became known throughout the lengthy judicial history of the *First Securities* case as Nay's "mail rule." According to the plaintiffs' legal counsel, "Nay had forbidden anyone other than himself to open mail addressed to him, and in his absence all such mail was simply allowed to pile up on his desk, even if it was addressed to First Securities for his attention."[3] Nay's mail rule allowed him to conceal the escrow syndicate scam from his subordinates at First Securities and from the brokerage's independent auditors. Had Ernst & Ernst discovered the mail rule, the plaintiffs alleged, an investigation would have been warranted. Such an investigation would very likely have led to the discovery of Nay's escrow investment scam.

Ernst & Ernst v. Hochfelder et al.

The defrauded investors filed their lawsuit against Ernst & Ernst under the Securities Exchange Act of 1934. That federal statute does not expressly provide civil remedies to stockholders of companies registered with the Securities and Exchange Commission (SEC). However, since the adoption of the 1934 Act, federal courts have allowed stockholders to use the statute as a basis for civil suits against company officers, investment brokers, auditors, and other parties associated with false financial statements filed with the SEC. Most of these suits allege one or more violations of Rule 10b-5 of the 1934 Act, shown in Exhibit 1.

In the *First Securities* case, the plaintiffs charged that Ernst & Ernst's alleged negligence in failing to discover Nay's mail rule constituted a violation of Rule 10b-5.

> The premise [of the investors' suit] was that Ernst & Ernst had failed to utilize "appropriate auditing procedures" in its audits of First Securities. ... Respondents [investors] contended that if Ernst & Ernst had conducted a proper audit, it would have discovered this "mail rule." The existence of the rule then would have been disclosed to the

Employment of manipulative and deceptive devices. It shall be unlawful for any person, directly or indirectly, by the use of any means or instrumentality of interstate commerce, or of the mails or of any facility of any national securities exchange,

(a) To employ any device, scheme, or artifice to defraud,

(b) To make any untrue statement of a material fact or to omit to state a material fact necessary in order to make the statements made, in the light of the circumstances under which they were made, not misleading, or

(c) To engage in any act, practice, or course of business which operates or would operate as a fraud or deceit upon any person, in connection with the purchase or sale of any security.

EXHIBIT 1

RULE 10B-5 OF THE SECURITIES EXCHANGE ACT OF 1934

---

3. *Securities and Exchange Commission v. First Securities Company of Chicago*, 463 F.2d 981 (1972), 985.

Exchange [Midwest Stock Exchange] and to the Commission [SEC] by Ernst & Ernst as an irregular procedure that prevented an effective audit.[4]

To support their claim that the mail rule qualified as a critical internal control weakness having important audit implications, the escrow investors submitted affidavits from three expert witnesses with impressive credentials in the accounting profession. Exhibit 2 lists a portion of one of those affidavits.

The federal district court that initially presided over the *Hochfelder et al. v. Ernst & Ernst* case quickly dismissed the lawsuit.[5] This court deemed that there was no substantive evidence to support the allegation that Ernst & Ernst had negligently audited First Securities. When the investors appealed this decision, the U.S. Court of Appeals reversed the lower court decision and ordered that the case go to trial. In its decision, the appeals court ruled that sufficient doubt existed regarding the negligence claim against Ernst & Ernst to have the case heard. The appeals court also suggested that if the plaintiffs established negligence on the part of Ernst & Ernst, the accounting firm could be held civilly liable to the defrauded investors under Rule 10b-5 of the 1934 Act.

Before the *Hochfelder* case went to trial in a federal district court, Ernst & Ernst appealed the ruling of the U.S. Court of Appeals to the U.S. Supreme Court. Ernst & Ernst argued before the Supreme Court that the negligence allegation of the escrow investors was insufficient, even if proved, to constitute a violation of Rule 10b-5. This issue had surfaced in many previous civil cases filed under the Securities Exchange Act of 1934. In these earlier cases, the federal courts had generally ruled or suggested that negligence constituted a violation of Rule 10b-5. That is, fraud or gross negligence, either of which is much more difficult for a plaintiff to prove than ordinary negligence, did *not* have to be established for a defendant to be held civilly liable to a plaintiff under Rule 10b-5.

Ernst & Ernst contested these earlier rulings by arguing that Rule 10b-5, as worded, could not be construed to encompass negligent behavior. Given the long-standing controversy surrounding this issue, the Supreme Court decided to rule on the issue in the *Hochfelder* case. This ruling would then establish a precedent for future lawsuits filed under Rule 10b-5.

Before the Supreme Court heard Ernst & Ernst's appeal, the SEC filed a legal brief with the Court. This brief supported the defrauded investors' argument that Rule 10b-5 encompassed both fraudulent and negligent conduct. The SEC pointed out that the

EXHIBIT 2

EXCERPT FROM EXPERT WITNESS TESTIMONY REGARDING NAY'S MAIL RULE

Expert Witness No. 3:

If I had discovered in making an audit of a security brokerage business that its president had established an office rule that mail addressed to him at the business address, or to the company for his attention should not be opened by anyone but him, even in his absence; and that whenever he was away from the office such mail would remain unopened and pile up on his desk I would have to raise the question whether such rule or practice could possibly have been instituted for the purpose of preventing discovery of irregularities of whatever nature; would, at a minimum, have to undertake additional audit procedures to independently establish a negative answer to the latter question; also failing such an answer either withdraw from the engagement or decline to express an opinion on the financial statements of the enterprise.

---

4. *Ernst & Ernst v. Hochfelder et al.*, 425 U.S. 185 (1976), 190. (One of the investors defrauded by Nay was Olga Hochfelder.)

5. *Hochfelder et al. v. Ernst & Ernst*, 503 F.2d 1100 (1974).

end result of investors' acting on false financial statements is the same whether the errors in the statements result from fraud or negligence. Because a central purpose of the federal securities laws is to ensure that investors receive reliable information, the SEC argued that the ambiguity in Rule 10b-5 should be resolved in favor of investors.

Surprisingly, the bulk of the Supreme Court's opinion in the *Hochfelder* case responded to the SEC's legal brief rather than the arguments of the defrauded investors or those of Ernst & Ernst. The Court rejected the SEC's largely philosophical argument and instead focused on the question of whether the authors of Rule 10b-5 intended it to encompass both negligent and fraudulent behavior. In addressing this issue, the Court reviewed the legislative history of the 1934 Act and did a painstaking analysis of the semantics of Rule 10b-5.

The Supreme Court eventually concluded that the key signal to the underlying meaning of Rule 10b-5 was the term *manipulative*. As shown in Exhibit 1, the heading of the rule clearly indicates that it pertains to "manipulative and deceptive" devices. According to the Court, negligence on the part of independent auditors or other parties associated with false financial statements could not be construed as manipulative behavior. The Court suggested that, in most cases, for behavior to qualify as manipulative, intent to deceive—the legal term being *scienter*—had to be present.

> When a statute speaks so specifically in terms of manipulation and deception, and of implementing devices and contrivances—the commonly understood terminology of intentional wrongdoing—and when its history reflects no more expansive intent, we are quite unwilling to extend the scope of the statute to negligent conduct.[6]

Two of the nine Supreme Court justices dissented to the *Hochfelder* decision, while one justice abstained. In disagreeing with the majority decision, Justice Harry Blackmun sided with the view expressed by the SEC. He noted that although the decision was probably consistent with the semantics of the Securities Exchange Act of 1934, the decision clashed with the underlying intent of that important federal statute. He wrote: "It seems to me that an investor can be victimized just as much by negligent conduct as by positive deception, and that it is not logical to drive a wedge between the two, saying that Congress clearly intended the one but certainly not the other."[7] Justice Blackmun went on to comment on the "critical importance" of the independent auditor's role and the ultimate responsibility of the auditor to serve the "public interest."[8] Given this societal mandate, Justice Blackmun argued, negligent auditors should be held accountable to investors who rely to their detriment on false financial statements.

An Unresolved Issue

At first reading, the Supreme Court's *Hochfelder* opinion appeared to establish, once and for all, the culpability standard for determining Rule 10b-5 violations. Unfortunately, the opinion is not as precise or definitive as it first appeared. A footnote

---

6. *Ernst & Ernst v. Hochfelder et al.*, 214. A particularly troublesome issue for the Supreme Court to resolve was the underlying meaning of Subsection b of Rule 10b-5. Subsections a and c of that rule refer explicitly to fraud, implying that negligence is not a severe enough form of misconduct to constitute a violation of Rule 10b-5. However, Subsection b contains no explicit reference to fraudulent conduct. The SEC construed this omission to suggest that Subsection b covers both fraudulent and negligent misconduct. The Supreme Court rejected this argument, maintaining instead that the explicit references to fraud in Subsections a and c signaled that fraudulent conduct was the implied, although unstated, culpability standard in Subsection b as well.

7. *Ernst & Ernst v. Hochfelder et al.*, 216.

8. *Ibid.*, 218.

to the opinion suggests that in certain cases, *scienter,* or intent to deceive, may not be a necessary element of proof for a plaintiff to establish in a civil suit alleging a Rule 10b-5 violation. The Court noted that some jurisdictions equate *scienter* with willful or reckless disregard for the truth or, more simply, "recklessness."[9] When engaging in reckless behavior, a party does not possess conscious intent to deceive; that is, *scienter* is not present. For whatever reason, the Court refused to rule on the question of whether reckless behavior would be considered equivalent to *scienter* and thus constitute a violation of Rule 10b-5. This omission caused subsequent plaintiffs to predicate alleged Rule 10b-5 violations by independent auditors on reckless behavior, since that type of professional misconduct is much easier to prove than actual *scienter.*

EPILOGUE

Congressional critics of the Supreme Court's decision in the *Hochfelder* case insisted that the alleged "flaw" in Rule 10b-5 should be corrected legislatively. In late 1978, legislators introduced a bill in the U.S. House of Representatives to hold negligent auditors civilly liable to investors who relied on false financial statements filed with the SEC. Fortunately for independent auditors, Congress rejected that bill.

Questions

1. Under present technical standards, would auditors be required to disclose a company policy similar to Nay's mail rule that they discover during an audit? Explain. Assuming such disclosure had been required at the time this case took place, would that disclosure have resulted in the mail rule being discontinued?

2. Ernst & Ernst argued that the mail rule was not relevant to its audits of First Securities since that rule only involved personal transactions of Nay and the escrow investors. Do you agree? Why or why not?

3. Define *negligence* as that term has been used in legal cases involving independent auditors. What is the key distinction between negligence and fraud? Between recklessness and fraud? For all three types of professional misconduct, provide an example of such behavior in an audit context.

4. Assume that the investors defrauded by Nay could have filed their lawsuit against Ernst & Ernst under the Securities Act of 1933. How, if at all, do you believe the outcome of their suit would have been affected?

5. The *Restatement of Torts* is a legal compendium issued by the American Law Institute. This compendium is relied on by courts in many jurisdictions as the basis for legal rulings. Under the *Restatement of Torts*, courts have ruled that negligent auditors can be held liable to unknown third parties if those parties belonged to a known group of financial statement users who the auditors were aware would likely rely on the audited financial statements. If this legal principle had been invoked in the *Hochfelder* case, would the defrauded investors have been successful in pursuing a negligence claim against Ernst & Ernst under the common law? Why or why not?

---

9. *Ibid.*, 194.

CASE 7.7

Elizabeth Wallace, Audit Senior

Elizabeth Wallace graduated from a large state university with dual undergraduate and graduate accounting degrees.[1] Following graduation, she accepted an entry-level position on the audit staff of a major international accounting firm. Five years later, Elizabeth is a "heavy" senior with hopes of being promoted soon to audit manager. Elizabeth's largest client is Burnham Manufacturing, an auto parts manufacturer that supplies automotive components to factories operated by one of the Big Three domestic auto companies.

Elizabeth is presently supervising the fieldwork on the current year's audit of Burnham. Her subordinates include Anton Nikolov who has two years' experience and was just promoted to audit senior, two staff accountants who each have one year of public accounting experience, and two "rookie" staff accountants who have less than three months' experience. Anton serves as Elizabeth's "first lieutenant" on the Burnham audit. In addition to helping supervise the four staff accountants, Anton is responsible for certain administrative tasks on the engagement, such as preparing the weekly progress reports that are filed each Monday morning with Julius Shen, the Burnham audit engagement partner. Anton is also responsible for Burnham's large inventory account—nearly 35 percent of the time budget for the Burnham audit is allocated to inventory. Two staff accountants and three of Burnham's internal auditors are assisting Anton with the inventory account.

Today is Friday, 19 January, and the Burnham audit should be approximately one-half complete. Unfortunately, the engagement has not gone smoothly and the audit team has fallen well behind schedule. Julius Shen estimates that to complete all of the critical audit procedures by the sign-off date of 14 February, his subordinates on the Burnham audit team will have to work at least 70 hours per week over the next four weeks. Elizabeth, Anton, and Julius each have a somewhat different perspective on the Burnham engagement and why it has become a "problem audit."

Friday Morning, January 19

Anton had looked forward to beginning the Burnham audit because it would be his first as an audit senior. He realized that he would not be "running the job," that would be Elizabeth Wallace's responsibility, but it would be the first assignment on which he had significant supervisory responsibilities.

Prior to beginning the Burnham audit, Anton had not interacted with Elizabeth. Their practice office includes more than 300 professionals, two-thirds of whom are on the audit staff, and the two of them had never been assigned to the same engagement team. Although he had not worked with Elizabeth, several of the individuals from Anton's "start class" with whom he is well acquainted had been assigned to one or more audits that she had supervised. None of those individuals was complimentary of Elizabeth's management style. Terms they used to describe her included "detail-oriented," "stern," and "impetuous."

---

1. This case is based upon a series of events and circumstances disclosed by an audit senior of a major accounting firm who ultimately sought and received treatment for an addiction to prescription drugs. The names of the individuals involved and other background information have been changed.

Despite the generally unpleasant opinions of Elizabeth, Anton had decided to go into the Burnham audit with an open mind. He enjoyed public accounting and realized that if he was to reach his goal of becoming an audit partner, he would occasionally have to deal with "difficult" personalities.

By the end of his first week on the Burnham audit, Anton was wondering why his colleagues who had worked previously with Elizabeth had been so kind in describing her. Instead of "detail-oriented," "stern," and "impetuous," Elizabeth was obsessive-compulsive, insensitive, and perpetually angry. Now that he is several weeks into the Burnham audit, Anton wonders if he can make it to the sign-off date without "blowing up" at Elizabeth. He understands that she is his immediate superior, but he doesn't believe that gives her the right to routinely berate and belittle him, including in the presence of the other members of the audit engagement team. The only saving grace is that he is not being singled out for harsh treatment. Elizabeth treats all of her subordinates on the Burnham audit team with disrespect and contempt.

Making matters worse is the fact that Elizabeth is unreliable. At the beginning of the audit, she made it clear that the standard workweek on the Burnham engagement would be 60 hours. The members of the audit team would work ten-hour days, 8 a.m. to 7 p.m., Monday through Saturday. Despite that mandate, Elizabeth often shows up for work at 10 a.m., and sometimes disappears during the day for several hours without telling Anton how he can reach her. On one occasion, Julius Shen called and asked for Elizabeth when she was nowhere to be found. Shen had been annoyed, if not exasperated, that Elizabeth had not told Anton or her other subordinates how she could be contacted.

Anton has gradually decided over the past few weeks that the source of Elizabeth's unpleasant persona is a serious personal problem, namely, a drug problem. During college, he witnessed firsthand the unraveling of a close friend who had developed an addiction to prescription drugs. He sees in Elizabeth many of the behavioral traits and idiosyncrasies that he observed in that friend.

In addition to her abrasive management style and her habit of disappearing for hours at a time, Elizabeth has random temper tantrums. Any small inconvenience or problem may spark her anger and cause her to suddenly "lose it." During such episodes, Elizabeth typically directs her anger at her nearest subordinate. After her tirade ends, she stomps out of the conference room and disappears for 30 minutes or longer. When she returns, her emotions are under control and she goes back to working as if nothing happened.

Also very telling is Elizabeth's personal appearance. She is a very attractive young woman and wears the latest business fashions, but she sometimes arrives at work disheveled and unkempt. On one occasion, she arrived at the client's conference room wearing shoes that did not match.

Despite her "issues," Elizabeth is somehow able to be civil with client personnel, although it is apparent to Anton that she minimizes her contact with them, especially with client executives. Plus, she is always on her best behavior on Fridays when Julius Shen or Laura Bishop, the audit manager assigned to the Burnham engagement, drops by to check on the status of the audit. Anton is convinced that Elizabeth prepares for those Friday meetings by "over medicating" herself. On Fridays she is often manic, overly effusive, and, most telling, she is almost "human" to Anton and her other subordinates.

Anton is so upset with Elizabeth that he just did something that would have been unthinkable for him a few weeks earlier: he called Julius Shen and asked that they meet and discuss Elizabeth's management style and overall demeanor. To Anton's surprise, the audit partner did not seem the least bit annoyed by his request and arranged for the two of them to have lunch today.

Friday Afternoon, January 19

Elizabeth is livid. She is so distraught that she finds it almost impossible to concentrate on the workpaper file that she is reviewing as she sits at her workstation in the conference room shared by the members of the Burnham audit team. Earlier this morning, Julius Shen came to the conference room. The two of them discussed the Burnham audit for an hour or so. Julius expressed concern over how far behind schedule the audit is and told Elizabeth that she and her team will have to begin working 70-hour weeks to complete the bulk of the audit by the sign-off date.

Elizabeth is not upset by the increased workload. What has upset her is the fact that Julius took Anton Nikolov to lunch without inviting her. It was obvious to Elizabeth that the two of them had made plans to go to lunch together. And, they had obviously planned to exclude her. No doubt, the two of them had discussed her over lunch. In fact, Elizabeth is certain that Anton asked to go to lunch with Julius alone so that they could talk about her privately.

Over the past several weeks, Elizabeth has grown increasingly distrustful of Anton. He is like most of the light seniors or experienced staff accountants who have worked for her on previous engagements. He is self-centered and takes every opportunity to ingratiate himself to the audit engagement partner and audit manager.

A few months ago, Elizabeth was passed over for promotion to audit manager, a decision that had infuriated her. Everyone in her practice office knows that the normal time period for promotion to manager is five years with the firm. She is convinced that she was not promoted because some of her subordinates have complained about her in-your-face management style. Elizabeth realizes that she is demanding of her subordinates, but she is convinced that pushing them to the limit and refusing to coddle them "toughens them up" and makes it more likely that they will succeed in the challenging work environment of public accounting.

Elizabeth also suspects that some of her subordinates are rumormongers. She suspects that they are making up lies about her personal life, which is absolutely none of their business. In college, Elizabeth and a couple of her close friends began taking a stimulant known as Adderall to help them pull "all-nighters" before important exams. At one point, she tried to convince her family doctor to give her a prescription for the drug but he refused. So, she resorted to buying the drug from friends of friends who somehow had access to it.

For the past eight years, she has been taking Adderall off and on … mostly on. But, she is convinced that she doesn't have a "problem" with the drug. Anytime she wants, she can quit taking it. Besides, in her mind, because Adderall is a prescription drug, it has to be safe. Otherwise, doctors wouldn't prescribe it for their patients.

After learning that she was being passed over for promotion this past fall, Elizabeth's anger and frustration caused her to become depressed. One of her longtime friends from her college days offered to give her a few Xanax, a prescription drug used to treat anxiety disorders and depression. Elizabeth took her friend up on the offer. It is amazing to Elizabeth how one of the pills can quickly lift her spirits and help her cope with the day-to-day stress imposed on her by ungrateful and backbiting subordinates such as Anton. Over the past several months, she has become a steady user of Xanax, although she has never bothered to obtain a prescription for it.

Occasionally, Elizabeth worries that the two drugs may somehow interact with each other—quite often, she takes both of the drugs on the same day. But, again, because they are both prescription drugs, she reasons that they must be "safe" even if taken together.

Friday Evening, January 19

It is 7:25 p.m. on Friday evening and Julius Shen is still sitting at his office desk. A few minutes earlier, he called his wife and told her that he would be heading home soon. Julius is troubled. Earlier in the day, he went to lunch with Anton Nikolov, the new audit senior assigned to the Burnham audit. Anton voiced serious complaints about his immediate supervisor on the engagement, Elizabeth Wallace. It is not the first time that Julius has heard such complaints.

Julius is well acquainted with Elizabeth because she serves as the lead senior for the audits of two of his largest clients. In terms of technical competence, Elizabeth is unsurpassed. She has a special knack for identifying, thoroughly documenting, and aggressively investigating "hot spots" in client financial statements. Just as important, Julius never has to worry about Elizabeth giving a client the benefit of the doubt when it comes to a questionable accounting or financial reporting issue. She adamantly refuses to allow clients to "fudge" their numbers or loosely apply accounting standards. In sum, she is an "auditor's auditor," a terrific technician who exudes professional skepticism.

Despite her technical skills, Elizabeth, unfortunately, has a "bedside manner" that leaves much to be desired. Elizabeth is much tougher on her subordinates than she is on her clients. On several occasions, Julius has counseled her during performance appraisal sessions to be more considerate of her subordinates. For whatever reason, though, she always reverts back to her standard "drill instructor" mentality.

Julius had hoped that Elizabeth's failure to be promoted to manager would serve as a wake-up call for her and make her realize that she has to develop a more personable approach to dealing with the individuals that she supervises. But, given the statements of Anton Nikolov, Elizabeth has obviously not changed her management style. If anything, it appears that Elizabeth has become even harsher with her subordinates.

More upsetting to Julius was Anton's suggestion that Elizabeth may have a serious "personal problem." Despite the fact that Anton did not explain what he meant, Julius knew exactly what he was implying. On the previous audit engagement that Elizabeth had served as the audit senior for Julius, one of her subordinates had made a similar insinuation. Plus, in interacting with Elizabeth over the past two years, Julius has personally witnessed several telltale signs typically associated with drug abuse. Most troubling to Julius is the fact that she sometimes disappears for several hours without telling other members of her audit team where she is or how they can reach her.

As an audit partner, Julius has faced many stressful circumstances, nearly all of which have involved complex auditing or accounting issues. The situation he faces now, though, is even more stressful. He isn't sure exactly how he should deal with Elizabeth. Should he confront her directly and speak to her as a "friend"? Julius doesn't relish that option because he and Elizabeth have exclusively a professional relationship. Unlike his other subordinates, Elizabeth has never shown any interest in "letting her guard down" and discussing her career aspirations, private life, or any other non–job related issue with him.

Another option is for Julius to refer the matter to his office's human resources coordinator and take the risk that Elizabeth will be removed from the Burnham engagement, if not dismissed from the firm. That option is also unappealing. Despite her obvious shortcomings, Elizabeth makes his job much easier for him. In sum, Julius' 20 years of experience in public accounting and the countless continuing education seminars that he has taken over that time have not prepared him to deal with this unpleasant and baffling predicament.

Julius glances at his wristwatch one more time. Almost 30 minutes have passed since he spoke with his wife. It's time to go home. Over the weekend, he will decide what to do about Elizabeth.

Questions

1. Do you believe that Anton Nikolov has dealt with his concerns regarding Elizabeth Wallace appropriately? Did he behave ethically in discussing that matter with Julius Shen? Defend your answer.

2. How should Julius respond to the matter involving Elizabeth? Identify the key factors that he should consider in deciding how to proceed.

3. Do public accounting firms have a responsibility to monitor their employees for the purpose of identifying individuals who have substance abuse problems? Do these firms have a responsibility to help their employees address such problems? Defend your answers.

Frank Coleman, Staff Accountant

For the better part of three hours, Frank Coleman pounded away at his calculator as he tried in vain to reconcile his number for the LIFO reserve to the figure recorded by the client.[1] Frustrated and fatigued, Frank finally glanced at his wristwatch. Frank couldn't believe that it was 9:40 p.m. The "official" workday for Frank and the other members of the audit engagement team to which he was assigned was 8 a.m. to 8 p.m. However, it was not unusual for individual team members to remain at work well past 8 p.m. Frank typically chose to leave whenever he reached a suitable stopping point for the given task on which he was working.

After glancing at his wristwatch, Frank stood and began shuffling together the workpapers spread out before him on his desk. He realized that if he hurried, he could make it home by 10 p.m. No doubt, Maggie, his wife of two months, would be upset that he had stayed so late at work, again. Fortunately, Frank and Maggie's home was only a 15-minute drive from his client's corporate headquarters in downtown Dallas.

Frank was assigned to an S-1 audit engagement for a longtime client of his employer that had decided to go public. Because the company's management team had developed an overly optimistic schedule for filing its S-1 registration statement with the SEC, Frank and the other members of his audit team were putting in 70-hour workweeks in the middle of summer, the supposed "slow season" in public accounting.

Since graduating from Texas Christian University a little more than two years earlier and accepting an entry-level position on the audit staff of one of the Big Four accounting firms, Frank had worked on several audit engagements. His clients had included a brokerage firm, a discount retailer, a bank holding company, and a software firm that developed video games for the Xbox generation. Frank enjoyed almost every facet of public accounting, including the challenging assignments, the in-depth exposure to the "real world" of financial accounting and reporting, and the camaraderie of working closely with other professional accountants to achieve a common goal. There was only one aspect of Frank's job that he did not enjoy: the large amount of overtime that he was required to work.

Over the previous two years, Frank's practice office had experienced a steady stream of turnover, most notably among audit staff employees with two or fewer years of experience. Frank was certain that much, if not most, of that turnover was a direct result of the long hours of overtime required in public accounting. The turnover experienced by Frank's office was so relentless that he was surprised when a week passed without someone that he knew leaving the firm. In fact, a group of Frank's coworkers created a "dead pool" to wager on who among them would be the last to leave the firm.

Because of the excellent training and experience they receive in such a short period of time, Big Four auditors are valuable and highly sought-after commodities in the private sector. Overworked auditors suffering from the burnout that is a chronic condition of their jobs are easy targets of corporate headhunters looking to

---

1. This case was developed, in part, from information obtained from a CPA employed for several years with a large international accounting firm.

fill accounting positions in the private sector. Those positions typically come with not only a more reasonable workload but considerably higher salaries and fringe benefits than those offered by Big Four firms.

The long hours required by Frank's job were made somewhat more tolerable by the moral support that he received from his superiors. The audit partner on the S-1 engagement often reminded Frank that, ultimately, he would be rewarded by the firm for his diligence and long overtime hours. But Frank came to seriously question whether the personal sacrifices necessary to make partner were worth the corner office, prestige, and large salary that accompanied the position. Plus, he realized that pursuing and achieving partnership meant an ever-increasing commitment to his firm. Client development activities, entertaining clients, and other "after hours" obligations effectively required one to "live and breathe" the firm. In Frank's mind, being a Big Four partner was not a job, it was an all-consuming lifestyle.

The major international accounting firms recognize that the significant amount of overtime required of their employees is a key factor responsible for the high turnover rates they experience. The accounting profession's leading firms consistently experience turnover rates approaching, if not exceeding, 20 percent each year in their non-management ranks. In recent years, the grueling workload faced by the employees of major accounting firms has become an even more important issue for those firms, but for a different reason.

The U.S. Department of Labor estimates that labor laws entitle 86 percent of U.S. workers to be compensated for the overtime they work, including the majority of white-collar employees.[2] *Business Week* reported in 2007 that there had been an "explosion" in "overtime" lawsuits over the previous few years and that such lawsuits were "the biggest problem" for companies "in the employment area by far."[3] Even corporate defense attorneys, according to *Business Week*, privately admitted that companies and professional firms were routinely violating the state and federal laws that mandate the payment of overtime.

Initially, the primary targets of the plaintiff attorneys who specialize in overtime lawsuits were financial services firms, including the major Wall Street brokerages. Several of those firms paid settlements approaching $100 million to resolve such lawsuits. Plaintiff attorneys next turned their attention to a set of potential defendants from which they could potentially wrest settlements several times that size, namely, the large international accounting firms.

Since 2006, each of the Big Four firms and at least one of the second-tier firms have been named as defendants in class-action lawsuits alleging that they have violated statutory mandates that require them to compensate entry-level employees for the overtime hours they work. In 2008, a federal judge in California "certified" a class-action lawsuit filed against PricewaterhouseCoopers (PwC) by former employees of that firm. This was the first lawsuit in which a federal judge had issued such a certification, which means that the plaintiffs are allowed to collectively pursue their legal claims in court. In 2012, a federal judge certified a similar lawsuit filed against KPMG by former employees of that firm.

Ironically, in 2008, each of the four Big Four–affiliated firms in Canada agreed to begin paying overtime to certain lower-level employees.[4] At the time, overtime

---

2. M. Orey, "Wage Wars," *Business Week* (online), 30 September 2007.

3. *Ibid.*

4. Generally, the Canadian firms pay overtime to staff accountants and seniors who are not Chartered Accountants. Two to three years is typically required for an individual to become a Chartered Accountant after entering public accounting.

lawsuits similar to those filed in the United States were pending against those firms. Reportedly, the Canadian firms chose to change their overtime policies because they feared that they would be forced to pay not only compensatory damages but substantial punitive damages, as well, if the plaintiffs prevailed in those lawsuits.

KPMG Canada implemented an "Overtime Redress Plan" that would retroactively pay qualifying employees for the overtime they had worked since 1 January 2000. When that program was announced, firm officials also issued an apology to the individuals they had slighted. "We very much regret that we did not pay overtime when it was earned by current and former employees. While this was an error of omission, not commission, it should not have happened. The principles of the [Overtime Redress] Plan will be reflected in all KPMG's remuneration in the future."[5]

To date, the Big Four firms in the United States have shown no willingness to settle the overtime lawsuits that have been filed against them. Instead, the Big Four firms have vigorously contested those lawsuits in state and federal courts across the nation. Each of the firms maintains that it was justified in not paying overtime to the former and current employees who are the plaintiffs in those lawsuits because the given individuals were "exempt" employees.

State and federal labor laws do not require employers to compensate employees for the overtime they work if one or more exemptions apply to those individuals. The specific conditions that cause an employee to qualify as exempt from overtime payments vary from jurisdiction to jurisdiction. For professional firms, a common requirement for exempt status for a given employee is the fact that the individual is not closely supervised and, instead, carries out his or her job-related responsibilities with a significant degree of autonomy.

In the state of California where many of the overtime lawsuits have originated, a professional firm is generally not required to pay an employee overtime if that employee routinely exercises "independent discretion and judgment" in carrying out his or her work role.[6] "Professional" employees who require close supervision, on the other hand, are typically considered nonexempt employees and must be paid for overtime.

The large accounting firms that have been sued in California for the nonpayment of overtime maintain that entry-level employees do not require close supervision and, in fact, exercise "independent discretion and judgment" in their work assignments. The plaintiff attorneys counter by insisting that it is common knowledge that audit staff employees below the level of audit senior are required to be closely supervised and are limited in their ability to exercise independent judgment while completing their assigned tasks.

In addition to demanding compensation for prior qualifying overtime worked by the plaintiffs, the overtime lawsuits filed against the major accounting firms typically request that employees be paid for "rest breaks" to which they were entitled as nonexempt employees and call for significant punitive damages. The overtime lawsuits do not specify the total monetary awards being sought by the plaintiffs' legal counsel. That figure will ultimately depend upon two variables: the number of individuals who will agree to be included as plaintiffs in the lawsuits and the number of qualifying overtime hours worked by those individuals.

Once an overtime lawsuit is certified by a judge, the defendant firm is typically ordered to provide the plaintiff attorneys the names and addresses of all potential

5. *Consultant-News.com* (online), "KPMG Canada Implements Unpaid Overtime Compensation Plan," www.consultant-news.com, 20 February 2008.

6. *Public Accounting Report*, "BDO Hit with Overtime Class Action Lawsuit," 30 November 2007, 3–4.

plaintiffs. Plaintiff attorneys have not reported how many current and former Big Four employees may qualify for compensation under those lawsuits. Nor have those attorneys revealed what percentage of those potential plaintiffs they believe will ultimately "join" the overtime lawsuits. Just as difficult to quantify is the number of overtime hours that have been worked by those potential plaintiffs. Not surprisingly, the Big Four firms do not report the average annual number of overtime hours worked by their employees; however, two nationwide surveys collected that information directly from Big Four employees. According to those surveys, "audit staff" of Big Four firms typically average 250 hours of overtime per year, compared to approximately 345 overtime hours worked each year by audit seniors who are exempt from the payment of overtime wages.[7]

One law firm representing plaintiffs in the Big Four overtime lawsuits has released its own "conservative estimate" of the payments to which their clients may be entitled. That estimate is approximately $19,000 for each year of qualifying employment.[8] Another source reports that the total damages sought in a single overtime lawsuit filed in California against Ernst & Young may approach $100 million in total.[9]

EPILOGUE

Within a year of being promoted to audit senior, Frank Coleman left his Big Four employer and accepted a position on the consulting staff of another Big Four firm. His new position came with a large salary increase and a commitment from his new employer that he would have much more reasonable work hours. One month later, Frank was contacted by a plaintiff attorney involved in a class-action overtime lawsuit filed against his former employer. The attorney encouraged Frank to join the lawsuit as a plaintiff. After considering the matter for several days, Frank chose not to become a party to the lawsuit. Among his concerns was that his new employer, which was also a target of multiple overtime lawsuits, would be offended.

Questions

1. As a general rule, do you believe that "professionals" should be compensated for the overtime they work? Defend your answer.

2. At what level within an accounting firm do accountants qualify as "professionals"? Which employment levels (staff accountant—that is, an employee below the rank of audit senior; audit senior; audit manager; audit partner) do you believe should be compensated for overtime that they work? Explain.

---

7. R. Guinn, S. Bhamornsiri, and C. Blanthorne, "Promotion to Partner in Big Firms: Truths and Trends," *The CPA Journal* (online), April 2004.

8. *Public Accounting Report*, "BDO Hit with Overtime Class Action Lawsuit."

9. N. Moody, "North American Big Four Firms Face Lawsuits over Unpaid Overtime," *The Accountant* (online), 15 February 2008.

3. A key issue in the overtime lawsuits is whether audit staff below the position of audit senior require close supervision and have the ability and authority to exercise "independent discretion and judgment." Do professional auditing standards mandate that these employees be closely supervised? Likewise, do those standards prohibit these employees from exercising independent discretion and judgment?

4. Will the overtime policy of prospective employers influence your job choice? Why or why not?

Olivia Thomas, Audit Senior

October 1

"Excuse me, are you Jake Tadlock?"[1]

"No, my name is Eli. Eli Arezzo."

"Hello, Eli. My name is Olivia. Olivia Thomas. I'm sorry. I was told that this was Jake's cubicle."

"No need to be sorry. Jake's cubicle is around the corner," Eli replied as he pointed to his left.

"Thanks," Olivia responded as she extended her right hand. "I'm assuming that you are new to the firm, so welcome aboard."

"Yes, I'm a rookie alright. Thanks for the welcome, Olivia," Eli replied as he shook Olivia's hand before she turned and walked away.

Like most relationships, Eli and Olivia's relationship began with a simple exchange of greetings. They met each other in the "bullpen" of their office. The bullpen was a large room consisting of 20 cubicles. Unassigned staff accountants of the practice office of the Big Four accounting firm that was their employer "hung out" in the bullpen. Eli and Olivia's practice office was located in a large Midwestern city and had more than 400 professional employees.

1 October was Eli's "start" date with the firm. He and a dozen other recent accounting graduates in the bullpen that day were only a few hours into their public accounting careers. Unlike Eli, Olivia was a seasoned professional. She had been with the firm for more than two and one-half years and had been promoted to audit senior three months earlier.

Despite the difference in their employment rank, Olivia and Eli were both 25 years old. Olivia had fast-tracked her way through a five-year joint undergraduate and master's degree program in four years. Eli had initially majored in journalism but had switched his major to accounting during his junior year in college after discovering that a degree from j-school provided limited job opportunities upon graduation. The switch in majors added one and one-half years to his college career.

October 12

"Olivia, I would like you to meet Eli Arezzo."

"Hey, no need to introduce us, Luke. We are old pals, right Eli?"

"Oh yeah, we go way back!"

Olivia and Eli shared a laugh at the expense of Luke Stotts, an audit manager who had attempted to introduce the two of them as all three stood in line at the corner Starbucks near their office. After Olivia explained how she and Eli had met, Luke paid for his drink and excused himself.

"Well, Eli, would you like to join me?" Olivia asked casually as she stepped away from the counter with her latte in hand. "We can kill a little time here while the traffic dies down if you want."

---

1. This case is based upon an actual series of events. Names and background information have been changed to conceal the identities of the individuals involved in the case.

"Sure, why not?" Eli replied.

For more than an hour, Olivia and Eli sat together at a small table discussing topics ranging from the coming weekend's "big" college football game to global warming to their upcoming client assignments.

"Wow, it's after six!" Olivia exclaimed after glancing at her wristwatch. "I guess time flies when you're having fun." Olivia laughed off the awkward but candid statement before adding as she stood to leave, "Eli, I hope to see you around the office soon."

"Uh, sure. I would like that," Eli replied awkwardly as he fidgeted with his necktie.

The parting exchange was awkward for two reasons. First, the two young auditors each realized that there was a mutual attraction between the two of them. Second, they both realized that although intra-office dating was not prohibited by their employer, there was a general understanding within the firm that it was not considered "professional." The firm's formal written policy regarding personal relationships required partners and employees to avoid any and all such relationships that might "impair or influence their judgment" or otherwise pose a "conflict of interests" for them or the firm.

November 2

On a Friday morning, three weeks after Olivia and Eli bumped into each other in Starbucks, Olivia did something that she had pledged to herself she would never do: she invited a coworker on a date. Because she had been in a client's office for most of the previous three weeks, Olivia had not had an opportunity to drop by the bullpen to say "Hi" to Eli. So, that morning, she sent Eli a brief e-mail asking him if he wanted to join her and a couple of her friends from her hometown at a free concert that evening in a local city park.

Olivia was not desperate for a date. She was very attractive and outgoing and had more than her fair share of "ask-outs." But most of the guys who asked her out were either boring, not her type, or, even worse, employees of one of her audit clients. Eli was none of those, but the handsome and articulate young man was a coworker and she was well aware that she was treading on thin ice by asking him to meet her at the concert.

Olivia's apprehension dissipated a few minutes later when Eli replied to her e-mail message. "Sounds great! Should I meet you guys there? Or do you want me to come by your place and pick you up?"

Olivia quickly replied, giving Eli directions to her apartment and letting him know when he could pick her up.

After the concert, Olivia, Eli, and her friends shared a couple of pizzas. Later, when he took her home, she hesitated briefly after opening the car door to leave.

"Would you like to come up and try those chocolate chip cookies I was bragging about?" A few minutes later, the two of them were sitting on Olivia's couch drinking milk and eating cookies. An hour later when there was a lull in their conversation, Eli decided that it was time to excuse himself. He certainly didn't want to overstay his welcome.

"Well, it's getting a little late, I guess I'd better be hitting the road."

"Hey, I had a great time. Thanks for joining us tonight," Olivia said warmly, before adding, "my friends really liked you."

"Yeah, that was a great band and you have some really cool friends. Thanks for inviting me," Eli responded.

As the two of them sat smiling at each other, they both realized it was that uncomfortable point near the end of a first date. Who was going to make a move? Would either of them make a move?

Finally, Olivia leaned over and kissed Eli lightly on his left cheek. "Well, again, thanks, Eli. I really enjoyed the evening."

Eli wasn't sure what to do, but he decided that caution rather than courage was the best choice and so he stood and stepped toward the door. Olivia followed him and then opened the door for him, but before Eli stepped out, she grabbed his left arm lightly.

"We both know this is … a little weird," she said tentatively after Eli turned to face her. "You know, because of, well, the fact that the firm kind of frowns on …" Olivia paused before continuing, "but, I just thought you were a neat guy and that we had a lot in common."

At this point, Eli threw caution to the wind as he wrapped his arms around Olivia's waist, leaned over, and kissed her squarely on the lips.

December 24

Meeting your boyfriend's or girlfriend's parents is always a stressful event, but the tension is compounded when that meeting takes place during a major family gathering. As the Christmas holidays approached, Eli and Olivia were spending the bulk of their weekends together. They realized that it was time to take the next big step in their relationship, namely, meeting each other's family. They decided to spend Christmas Eve with Olivia's family and Christmas Day with Eli's.

As the big day approached, Olivia became increasingly anxious. There was no doubt in her mind that her family would like Eli because he had a charming Italian personality—Eli's parents had emigrated from Italy to the United States shortly before he was born. And, she knew that her mother and younger sister would be awestruck by his stunning good looks. The problem was that her father was also an accountant who had spent several years in public accounting at the beginning of his career. He had once told Olivia that in the "old days" most major accounting firms had a strict policy against "fraternization." He realized that those firms had moved away from that policy and now, at least publicly, had taken a neutral stance on the issue of intra-office dating. Despite that change in policy, he had suggested to Olivia when she accepted a job in public accounting that she keep her personal and professional lives totally separate.

The previous several weeks, Olivia and Eli had played a game of cat and mouse with their coworkers. They had gone to great lengths to avoid restaurants and other public places where they might encounter someone from their firm, which meant that they spent most of their time together at their apartments. Most stressful for Olivia was sidestepping questions from her two best friends in the office who were also audit seniors. As time passed, both of them had become increasingly suspicious why she was typically unavailable when they asked her to go out with them.

The big question was finally popped by Olivia's father 30 minutes after she and Eli stepped through the front door of her parents' home on Christmas Eve morning.

"Eli, Olivia mentioned to her mother a couple of weeks ago that you are also an accountant. Do you work in private accounting?"

Eli took a deep breath as he glanced at Olivia. "No, Sir, I'm in public accounting just like Olivia."

"Oh, that's interesting," Olivia's father replied. "Are you with a Big Four firm or did you sign on with a local or regional firm?"

When Eli paused to clear his throat, Olivia interceded. "Dad, Eli went to work for my office this past October," Olivia paused momentarily to allow her father to process the news bulletin. "He's on the audit staff, but, of course, we don't work on any of the same clients."

After an extended pause, Olivia's father nodded as he tried to maintain a smile on his face. "That is interesting."

January 22

Because of unexpected turnover in her office the previous few months and the new responsibilities that she had to assume as an audit senior, Olivia's busy season proved to be much more demanding than she had anticipated. During the first week of January, Olivia and the four staff accountants she was supervising on the audit of DuClaux Brothers, a manufacturing company in the electronics industry, had begun working 65 hours each week. The only "day off" they had was Sunday afternoon.

Early one Tuesday morning, Sarah Tolbert, the audit manager on the DuClaux engagement, told Olivia that she planned to ask the office's personnel manager to transfer two additional staff accountants to the DuClaux audit. Sarah wanted the staff accountants to help Olivia complete several tedious and time-consuming audit tests for DuClaux's large inventory of electronic components.

Several hours later, Olivia was startled when Sarah walked into the client conference room that served as the workspace for the DuClaux audit team followed by Eli and another staff accountant. "Olivia, I want you to meet Abby Edzards and Eli Arezzo," Sarah announced. "They are going to be helping you knock out those inventory price tests and fill in wherever else you need them over the next few weeks." After gesturing to Abby and Eli, Sarah stepped aside as Olivia rose stiffly from the chair in which she had been seated. Olivia extended her right hand, first to Abby and then to Eli.

After regaining some semblance of composure, Olivia finally spoke. "Well, uh, we certainly can use you guys out here. Welcome to, uh, welcome to the DuClaux job."

Over the next 30 minutes, Olivia sat at the conference room table explaining in detail the nature of the audit procedures that Abby and Eli would be working on jointly. Then, she took them to the office of the assistant controller from whom they would obtain the documents needed to complete those procedures. After introducing them, Olivia turned to head back to the conference room. As she was leaving, Eli followed her.

"Olivia, could I ask you a question real quickly about how Abby and I should charge our hours today?" Eli asked as he rushed to catch up to Olivia as she hurried down the hallway outside the assistant controller's office. When they were safely out of earshot of anyone, Eli leaned forward and whispered," I'm sorry that I couldn't warn you that I was coming. Sarah rode over here with me and so I never had a chance to text you."

Olivia arched her eyebrows nervously as she glanced both directions in the hallway to make sure that no one was near. "Okay, okay," she replied tensely. "We'll just have to make the best of it," she added before instructing Eli to return to the assistant controller's office.

Late that evening, shortly before 7 p.m., Olivia told Eli, Abby, and the four other staff accountants on the DuClaux audit team that they could leave for the night. Eli dawdled while the other staff accountants organized their cubicles and one by one left the conference room. Finally, only he and Olivia remained.

"Whew," Olivia said with a shake of her head. "I think we both deserve an Academy Award nomination for the acting jobs that we did."

"Forget the nomination, you deserve to win the Oscar, hands down," Eli replied sharply.

Taken back by the tone of Eli's voice, Olivia walked to the door of the conference room and closed it and then turned and faced him. "Are you upset about something?"

Eli shrugged his shoulders indifferently as he put on his jacket and prepared to leave.

Olivia stepped forward and placed her hand on Eli's shoulder. "Eli, what's wrong?"

"Nothing, nothing. Just forget it."

"No, I won't 'just forget it.' Now what is this all about?"

"Wait a minute, you may be my supervisor, but you're not my mother," Eli responded. "If I don't want to talk about what's bothering me, I don't have to."

For the first time in their relationship, Olivia and Eli were at odds. Because she was not one to allow a problem to simmer, Olivia decided to make one final attempt to persuade Eli to discuss what was bothering him.

"No, I'm not your mother, but I am your girlfriend. And, I don't like seeing you upset." Olivia paused to make sure that her next words were spoken without any anger. "And, the fact that you're upset, has made me upset. So, can we sit down and discuss this?"

While Olivia was speaking, Eli had refused to face her. After her brief speech, he cleared his throat and turned toward her. "Uh, well, it was just ... just tough to, to, uh, have you treat me so coldly. It was just a little too strange for me, I guess," he added sheepishly.

As she often did, Olivia attempted to defuse a tense moment with humor. "Oh, okay. Tomorrow, each time I ask you to do something, I will give you a big fat kiss and say, 'Honey, would you do this for me?'"

When Eli did not laugh or even smile in response, Olivia quickly added, "Oh, come on, now, I was just teasing you." She then reached up and kissed him on the cheek as she ran her hand through his hair.

Eli finally smiled and reciprocated with a light kiss to Olivia's forehead. "You know what? All of this ticking and tying and tension have made me hungry. What say we head to my apartment and I'll whip us up a big plate of my grandmother's famous rigatoni?" Before Olivia could respond, Eli added in an improvised sarcastic tone, "Boss!"

Olivia and Eli recovered nicely from their squabble. Over the next few weeks, they carried on their charade on the DuClaux Brothers audit without raising the least bit of suspicion on the part of their colleagues.

February 10

As the 15 February deadline for completing all major audit tests on the DuClaux Brothers engagement loomed ever nearer, Olivia began "stressing out." Neither the audit manager nor the audit partner paid much attention to the fact that there were dozens of loose ends that needed to be tied down before the 15th. They seemed to believe that all of the pending issues would be magically resolved somehow by that date. It was also strangely disturbing to Olivia that her two superiors placed total confidence in her ability to wrap up the audit on time despite the fact that the DuClaux engagement was the first major audit on which she had supervised the fieldwork.

As the pressure on Olivia to complete the audit had mounted, the pressure on the staff accountants, including Eli, had subsided. During the hectic last week of a large audit, much of the work that remains is critical wrap-up procedures that must be completed by the audit senior, audit manager, and audit engagement partner. In fact, because Olivia had found it increasingly difficult to keep her subordinates busy, she began sending them home each day at 5 p.m. to get them "out of her hair."

On the evening of 9 February, she had arrived home at her apartment at 9 p.m. expecting Eli to be there. During the previous few weeks, the two of them had met at her apartment after work, but that night her apartment was empty when she got home. When she called and asked where he was, Eli responded that he was "out with some of the guys" from the DuClaux audit. Eli told her that they were celebrating the end of the audit, which was upsetting to Olivia because from her perspective the end of the engagement was still not in sight. Although she didn't raise the issue with Eli, she thought that he should have been more supportive of her given the heavy burden of work and responsibility that she was facing over the next several days.

Even more troubling to Olivia was the fact that one of the "guys" on the DuClaux audit who was likely out partying with Eli was Abby Edzards, the former college cheerleader who had joined the DuClaux audit team on the same day as Eli. Over the previous week, it had become apparent to Olivia that Abby was becoming a little too "chatty" with Eli. On a couple of occasions when she had walked past the cubicle the two of them shared in the client's conference room, she had overheard Abby ask Eli questions that had nothing to do with the audit tests they were completing. One of those questions involved Eli's interest in tennis. Prior to joining the college cheerleading squad, Abby had been a member of the university's tennis team. There was no doubt in Olivia's mind that Abby would soon be challenging Eli, a well-rounded athlete in his own right, to a tennis match—if she hadn't already.

Shortly before 10 a.m. on the morning of 10 February, Olivia told Eli in front of the other members of the audit team that she would like to have lunch with him so they could discuss his performance appraisal for the DuClaux audit. Because she was the immediate supervisor of the staff accountants assigned to the engagement team, Olivia was responsible for completing a performance evaluation report for each of them. She had decided to have lunch individually with her subordinates to discuss their evaluation reports. Eli would be the first to receive his report. In truth, Olivia had less interest in discussing Eli's on-the-job performance than in discussing his off-the-job activities the previous night.

"Okay, Mr. Arezzo, here's your report," Olivia said with a forced smile as she handed Eli his signed performance evaluation report as they sat facing each other at a restaurant a few blocks from DuClaux Brothers' headquarters.

After glancing at the excellent scaled scores that Olivia had given him, Eli responded happily, "Wow, I guess it does help to be buddy-buddy with the boss!"

Olivia was in no mood to be teased so she ignored Eli's lighthearted response. Instead, she decided to subtly raise the issue that was at the forefront of her mind. "You guys must have partied hardy last night. How late did you stay out?"

"Oh, we were out to midnight or so, I guess," Eli replied without looking up from his performance report that he had spread out on the table in front of him.

"Who did 'we' include?" Olivia asked as she picked at her salad.

"Oh, just the guys on the audit team, like I told you last night," Eli responded matter-of-factly without giving much thought to the question.

Olivia reminded herself to stay cool as she tried to come up with an artistic way to get the information she wanted. "You mean Max, Kirk, and Andrew?" she asked as she ticked off the names of the three other male staff accountants assigned to the DuClaux audit team.

"Huh?" Eli replied as he looked up to catch Olivia staring at him.

"Were you out with Max, Kirk, and Andrew?" There was a definite but unintended gritty edge to Olivia's question. The tone of her words immediately caught Eli's attention.

Eli folded the performance report neatly and then laid it aside. He then clasped his hands together and leaned forward before replying. "In other words, was Abby with us last night?"

Olivia realized that she had been exposed. There was no reason to tiptoe around the subject any longer. "Yeah, I guess that's what I'm asking." She paused to choke down a bite of salad before continuing, "I was just wondering if you went out for a late-night tennis match." She immediately regretted the catty remark as soon as the final word left her mouth. Olivia was candid, frank, to-the-point, but being "snide" was not in her repertoire of personality traits.

Eli leaned back in his chair. It was his time to respond in kind, but he thought the better of it. Instead, he chose to respond civilly without a hint of sarcasm or anger in his voice. "Olivia, there were five of us at O'Connell's last night. Myself, Max, Kirk, Andrew, and … Charlotte. Abby had told us the day before that she had other plans and couldn't make it."

EPILOGUE

Olivia and Eli continued to date over the next 12 months. Eventually, their relationship became a "hot ticket" item on the office grapevine. Even after their relationship was no longer a secret, they never acknowledged it publicly and only discussed it with their closest friends within the office.

As the end of Eli's second busy season approached, he decided that public accounting was not for him. A few months later, he was accepted into an MBA program on the East Coast, several hundred miles from the metropolitan area where he and Olivia lived. That August, before he moved away, Eli and Olivia committed to making their long-term relationship work. But, it didn't. The two of them mutually decided to "call it quits" a few months later. After completing one more busy season, Olivia left public accounting and accepted a mid-level accounting position with a major oil firm.

Questions

1. Do you believe that either Olivia or Eli acted "unprofessionally" or "unethically"? Defend your answer.

2. Did Olivia and Eli's relationship likely affect other individuals within their office? Explain.

3. Why do you believe that major accounting firms have become more accepting of intra-office dating over the years? Do you believe that shift in policy is appropriate? Why or why not?

4. Do you agree or disagree with Olivia's father that public accountants should keep their professional and personal lives strictly separate? Explain.

SECTION 8

INTERNATIONAL CASES

Longtop Financial Technologies Limited

In 1996, two friends and business partners, Jia Xiao Gong and Weizhou Lian, founded Longtop Financial Technologies Limited in Beijing. Gong served as Longtop's chairman of the board, while Lian assumed the title of chief executive officer (CEO). The two men developed a business model intended to make Longtop the leading provider of information technology services to the booming banking industry of the People's Republic of China. China's "Big Four" banks dominate the nation's banking industry. In turn, the powerful Ministry of Finance, the government agency that oversees China's economic and fiscal policies, controls the Big Four banks.

By 2010, Longtop had achieved its goal of becoming the leading provider of information technology services to China's banking industry, including three of the nation's Big Four banks. The company's audited financial statements for fiscal 2010 reported a $59 million profit, total revenues of $169 million, and net assets of $600 million. Although modest by U.S. standards, Longtop's profits, revenues, and net assets were growing rapidly and were expected to continue to do so over the years to come. Similar to the previous five years, Deloitte & Touche Shanghai (D & T Shanghai), the Chinese affiliate of U.S.-based Deloitte Touche Tohmatsu, issued an unqualified audit opinion on Longtop's 2010 financial statements.

"Faked" Cash and Red-Faced Auditors

The rapidly expanding Chinese economy has captured the attention of investors worldwide over the past two decades. Companies such as Longtop sought to capitalize on the growing interest in the Chinese economy by listing their securities on international stock exchanges, including the leading exchanges in the United States.

In October 2007, Longtop went public with an initial public offering (IPO) managed by Goldman Sachs and Deutsche Bank. The company's common stock, which was listed on the New York Stock Exchange (NYSE), nearly doubled in price during its first day of trading. By late 2010, Longtop's stock had a total market value of $2.5 billion. Similar to the more than 200 other Chinese companies whose securities have traded on U.S. stock exchanges, Longtop became subject to the regulatory oversight of the Securities and Exchange Commission (SEC) when it listed its common stock on the NYSE.

In the late spring of 2011, Longtop was rocked by allegations that management had recorded bogus revenues to inflate the company's reported operating results and financial condition. Those allegations surfaced just as D & T Shanghai was nearing completion of its Longtop audit for the company's 2011 fiscal year, which ended 31 March 2011.

The source of the claims of fraudulent accounting was a small U.S.-based investment advisory firm that specializes in exposing companies that are "cooking their books." Among other allegations, that firm maintained that much, if not most, of the more than $400 million of cash reported in Longtop's preaudit 2011 financial statements—which accounted for almost 60 percent of the company's total assets—did not exist.

D & T Shanghai responded to the allegations of the investment advisory firm by extending its audit of Longtop's 2011 financial statements. In particular, the audit firm decided to revisit the audit procedures that had been applied to the company's cash accounts. In the past, the principal evidence the auditors had collected to corroborate Longtop's cash balances had been confirmations obtained from local branches of the company's banks.

On 17 May 2011, D & T Shanghai attempted to confirm Longtop's 2011 year-end cash balances by contacting the headquarters offices of the company's banks. Those extended cash confirmation tests were abruptly halted by Longtop officials, as reported by the *New York Times*.

> *"Within hours" of beginning the new round of confirmations on May 17, the confirmation process was stopped ... the result of "intervention by the company's officials, including the chief operating officer." ... Despite the company's efforts, Deloitte learned that Longtop did not have the cash it claimed and that there were "significant bank borrowings" not reflected in the company's books.*[1]

A few days following D & T Shanghai's aborted attempt to reconfirm Longtop's cash balances, Jia Xiao Gong admitted to a partner of that firm that the company had "faked" cash and revenues in its financial statements. That admission prompted D & T Shanghai to resign as Longtop's auditor. Exhibit 1 presents the resignation letter that D & T Shanghai sent to Longtop's audit committee and filed with the SEC on 22 May 2011.

EXHIBIT 1

DELOITTE RESIGNATION LETTER

---

22 May 2011

The Audit Committee
Longtop Financial Technologies Limited
No. 61 Wanghai Road, Xiamen Software Park
Xiamen, Fujian Province
People's Republic of China

Attention: Mr. Thomas Gurnee, Chairman of the Audit Committee

Dear Sirs:

Longtop Financial Technologies Limited (the "Company") and together with its subsidiaries (the "Group") Audit for the Year Ended 31 March 2011

We hereby give you formal notice of our resignation as auditor of the Company.

Background and significant issues encountered by Deloitte Touche Tohmatsu CPA Ltd. (China) ("Deloitte")

As part of the process for auditing the Company's financial statements for the year ended 31 March 2011, we determined that, in regard to bank confirmations, it was appropriate to perform follow-up visits to certain banks. These audit steps were recently performed and identified a number of very serious defects including: statements by bank staff that their bank had no record of certain transactions; confirmation replies previously received were said to be false; significant differences in deposit balances reported by the bank staff compared with the amounts identified in previously received confirmations (and in the books and records of the Group); and significant bank borrowings reported by bank staff not identified in previously received confirmations (and not recorded in the books and records of the Group).

In light of this, a formal second round of bank confirmations was initiated on 17 May. Within hours, however, as a result of intervention by the Company's officials including the Chief

---

1. F. Norris, "The Audacity of Chinese Frauds," *New York Times* (online), 26 May 2011.

EXHIBIT 1—
continued

DELOITTE
RESIGNATION
LETTER

Operating Officer, the confirmation process was stopped amid serious and troubling new developments including: calls to banks by the Company asserting that Deloitte was not their auditor; seizure by the Company's staff of second round bank confirmation documentation on bank premises; threats to stop our staff leaving the Company premises unless they allowed the Company to retain our audit files then on the premises; and then seizure by the Company of certain of our working papers.

In that connection, we must insist that you promptly return our documents.

Then on 20 May the Chairman of the Company, Mr. Jia Xiao Gong, called our Eastern Region Managing Partner, Mr. Paul Sin, and informed him in the course of their conversation "that there was fake revenue in the past so there was fake cash recorded on the books." Mr. Jia did not answer when questioned as to the extent and duration of the discrepancies. When asked who was involved, Mr. Jia answered : "senior management."

We bring these significant issues to your attention in the context of our responsibilities under Statement on Auditing Standards No. 99, "Consideration of Fraud in a Financial Statement Audit" issued by the American Institute of Certified Public Accountants.

Reasons for our Resignation

The reasons for our resignation include: (1) the recently identified falsity of the Group's financial records in relation to cash at bank and loan balances (and also now seemingly in the sales revenue); (2) the deliberate interference by the management in our audit process; and (3) the unlawful detention of our audit files. These recent developments undermine our ability to rely on the representations of management which is an essential element of the audit process; hence our resignation.

Prior periods' financial reports and our reports thereon

We have reached the conclusion that we are no longer able to place reliance on management representations in relation to prior financial reports. Accordingly, we request the Company take immediate steps to make the necessary 8-K filing to state that continuing reliance should no longer be placed on our audit reports on the previous financial statements and moreover that we decline to be associated with any of the Company's financial communications during 2010 and 2011.

Our consent

We hereby consent to a copy of this letter being supplied to the SEC and the succeeding auditor to be appointed.

Section 10A of the Securities Exchange Act of 1934 (U.S.)

In our view, without providing any legal conclusion, the circumstances mentioned above could constitute illegal acts for purposes of Section 10A of the Securities Exchange Act of 1934. Accordingly, we remind the Board of its obligations under Section 10A of the Securities Exchange Act, including the notice requirements to the U.S. Securities and Exchange Commission. You may consider taking legal advice on this.

Yours faithfully,
/s/ Deloitte Touche Tohmatsu CPA Ltd.
c.c.: The Board of Directors

Source: www.sec.gov/Archives/edgar/data/

"The Law on Guarding State Secrets"

Following D & T Shanghai's resignation, published reports from several sources, including the *New York Times*, revealed that employees of Longtop's banks had conspired with company management to conceal the company's fraudulent accounting scheme. For years, those individuals had apparently returned confirmations to D & T Shanghai that vouched for the accuracy of the company's materially overstated cash balances.

In fact, a month before resigning as Longtop's auditor, D & T Shanghai had stepped down as the auditor of China MediaExpress because of concerns regarding the reliability of cash confirmations obtained from that company's banks. A few months earlier, KPMG's Chinese affiliate reported the same concern upon resigning as the auditor of ShengdaTech. Similar to Longtop, both China MediaExpress and ShengdaTech had securities listed on U.S. stock exchanges.

Reports that Chinese banks were complicit in the Longtop accounting fraud stunned the global investment community. An Australian hedge fund official noted that, "Given the centrality of Chinese banks to the global economy ... [this] is a story much bigger than Deloitte or Longtop."[2]

Floyd Norris, a prominent reporter for the *New York Times,* noted that the incidents involving Longtop, China MediaExpress, and ShengdaTech raised the question of whether "defrauding foreign investors is deemed to be a serious crime in China."[3] Norris went on to observe that although accounting frauds and audit failures were a worldwide problem, "the audacity of these frauds, as well as the efforts to intimidate auditors, stand out."[4]

The SEC banned Longtop's securities from U.S. stock exchanges in December 2011. The move was largely symbolic since the company's stock was essentially worthless by that time. *Fraud Magazine* reported that Longtop was among more than two dozen China-based companies whose securities had been banned or suspended from trading on U.S. or European stock markets by late 2011 due to "accounting discrepancies," auditor resignations, or related issues.[5]

In June 2011, the SEC asked D & T Shanghai to turn over the Longtop workpapers that it had in its possession. The SEC believed the workpapers would provide important insights relevant to its ongoing investigation of the Longtop fraud. SEC officials were shocked when D & T Shanghai refused to provide the workpapers. A subsequent subpoena and court order obtained by the SEC failed to persuade D & T Shanghai to comply with the agency's request.

D & T Shanghai reported that it had decided not to give the workpapers to the SEC because doing so would violate an important Chinese law, the Law on Guarding State Secrets, that China's central government had enacted in 1988. According to D & T Shanghai, that law prohibits Chinese citizens and firms from providing documents or other information to foreign entities that relate to "the national economy."[6]

---

2. *Ibid.*

3. *Ibid.*

4. *Ibid.*

5. R. Hurley and T. Harvey, "Chinese Stock Investment Fraud: Separating Fact from Fiction," *Fraud Magazine*, January/February 2012, 59.

6. F. McKenna, "Deloitte Hides From SEC Behind Chinese Wall Over Longtop," *Forbes* (online), 9 September 2011.

Skeptics believed that it was highly unlikely that any "state secrets" were contained in the Longtop audit workpapers. However, an attorney of a major U.S. law firm explained to a *Wall Street Journal* reporter that the Chinese government invokes a "sufficiently broad" definition of "state secret" to routinely blunt the efforts of foreign regulatory bodies to obtain information from Chinese companies and other entities.[7]

Chinese Standoff

The controversy spawned by the Longtop fraud focused greater attention on an issue that the Public Company Accounting and Oversight Board (PCAOB) had been wrestling with for years. The Sarbanes–Oxley Act of 2002 requires the PCAOB to inspect all accounting firms that audit companies that have securities traded on U.S. stock exchanges. This requirement extends to foreign accounting firms that audit such companies, including the foreign affiliates of major international accounting firms based in the United States.

Since the inception of the PCAOB in 2004, nearly 2,400 accounting firms that audit companies having securities traded on U.S. markets have registered with the agency, including more than 900 non-U.S. accounting firms from 85 countries. The latter number includes several dozen Chinese accounting firms. By late 2013, the PCAOB had yet to inspect any of those Chinese accounting firms.

Chinese government officials refused to allow the PCAOB to inspect China-based accounting firms because they insisted that their nation's "own regulatory system was adequate."[8] The failure of China to permit PCAOB inspections of Chinese accounting firms when coupled with the growing list of Chinese accounting scandals caused one U.S. accounting professor to question "whether Chinese companies are auditable in the current regulatory environment."[9]

In November 2011, Senator Charles Schumer slammed the PCAOB for allowing Chinese accounting firms to continue auditing companies with securities traded in the United States. "The board's failure to do what it was created to do—particularly in the face of Chinese corporate accounting scandals that have already cost U.S. investors billions—is deeply troubling."[10]

James Doty, the chairman of the PCAOB, deflected much of the criticism of his agency to the Big Four accounting firms. In particular, Chairman Doty maintained that global accounting firms needed "to improve their quality control over far-flung affiliates" such as D & T Shanghai.[11] Doty observed that "many people are unaware that an audit report signed by a large U.S. firm may be based largely on the work of affiliates in other countries that are completely separate legal entities."[12] He went on to note that in many of those instances the U.S. firms fail to review the work of their foreign affiliates.

---

7. I. Steger, "How Should Auditors Handle China's State Secrets Law?" *Wall Street Journal* (online), 2 November 2011.

8. D. Aubin, "U.S. Auditor Watchdog Hopeful of Access to China," *Reuters* (online), 5 May 2011.

9. P. Gillis, "China Accounting Blog: State Secrets and Auditing," *www.chinaccountingblog.com/weblog/state-secrets-and-auditing.html*, 3 November 2011.

10. M. Rapoport, "Sen. Schumer Urges Audit Watchdog to Act on China," *Wall Street Journal* (online), 22 November 2011.

11. Aubin, "U.S. Auditor Watchdog Hopeful."

12. *Ibid.*

EPILOGUE

In December 2012, the SEC charged the Chinese affiliates of BDO Seidman, Deloitte, Ernst & Young, KPMG, and PricewaterhouseCoopers with violating the Securities Exchange Act of 1934 and the Sarbanes–Oxley Act of 2002. These charges stemmed from the refusal of those firms to comply with the SEC's request to turn over audit workpapers for selected clients that were SEC registrants. The director of the SEC's Division of Enforcement observed that "Only with access to workpapers of foreign public accounting firms can the SEC test the quality of the underlying audits and protect investors from the dangers of accounting fraud."[13] As of December 2013, the charges filed against the five firms were not yet resolved.

In May 2013, the PCAOB signed a "memorandum of understanding" (MOU) with China's Ministry of Finance and another Chinese regulatory agency that established a "cooperative framework between the parties for the production and exchange of audit documents relevant to investigations in both countries' respective jurisdictions."[14, 15] The MOU, however, did not grant the PCAOB the right to inspect Chinese accounting firms that audit companies with securities registered on U.S. stock exchanges.

Questions

1. What are the key conditions or circumstances that must be present for a company to be "auditable"? What uncommon challenges to "auditability" are posed by Chinese companies?

2. Do the major international accounting firms have a responsibility to ensure that their individual national practice units provide independent audit services that are uniform worldwide? Defend your answer.

3. Acme, Inc., a multinational company based in the United States, has a large subsidiary located in Beijing, China. Acme is audited by an international accounting firm headquartered in the United States; its subsidiary is audited by the Chinese affiliate of that firm. Under U.S. auditing standards, what responsibilities, if any, does Acme's U.S. audit firm have to supervise or oversee the audit of the Chinese subsidiary? Would these responsibilities be different under International Standards of Auditing?

4. What alternative strategies or approaches could U.S. regulatory agencies consider invoking to ensure that the audits of non-U.S. companies with securities traded on U.S. markets are adequate?

5. Since ethical and moral values vary from culture to culture and nation to nation, does this mean that a global profession, such as the accounting profession, cannot have a uniform ethical code? Explain.

---

13. U.S. Securities and Exchange Commission, "SEC Charges China Affiliates of Big Four Accounting Firms with Violating U.S. Securities Laws in Refusing to Produce Documents," www.sec.gov, 3 December 2012.

14. M. Cohn, "PCAOB Signs Enforcement Cooperation Agreement with Chinese Regulators," www.accountingtoday.com, 24 May 2013.

15. Although not publicly confirmed by the SEC, Chinese governmental officials reportedly turned over to the SEC certain Longtop audit workpapers in August 2013.

Kaset Thai Sugar Company

The black Toyota minivan made slow but steady progress down the narrow, unpaved road as it approached the village of Takhli in south central Thailand, approximately 150 miles north of Bangkok. On either side of the bumpy road were fields of sugarcane, dense thickets of scrub brush, and an occasional rice paddy. Seated in a rear window seat of the minivan was Michael Wansley, a senior partner with Deloitte Touche Tohmatsu, who was based in that firm's Melbourne, Australia, practice office. The vehicle's four other occupants were Thai nationals and employees of the Kaset Thai Sugar Company. No doubt, the five weary travelers who had spent several hours in the cramped minivan were overjoyed when they finally caught a glimpse of the large sugar mill in the distance that was their final destination. The sugar mill was one of many owned and operated by the Kaset Thai Sugar Company.

For the past several weeks, Michael Wansley had been supervising a debt-restructuring engagement for the company's banks and other lenders. Kaset Thai Sugar had defaulted on nearly $500 million of loans to those lenders. Wansley and the 14 subordinates on his engagement team were to study the company's accounting records and business operations and then make recommendations about how the lenders should proceed in attempting to collect all—or, at least, a significant portion—of the outstanding loans.

Wansley, a well-known debt-restructuring expert, had become all too familiar with remote Thailand communities, such as Takhli, over the previous several months because the services of debt-restructuring specialists were much in demand within Thailand during the late 1990s. In March 1999 when Wansley visited the sugar mill on the outskirts of Takhli, the nation of Thailand was mired in a financial crisis. From 1985 through 1995, Thailand had boasted the highest economic growth rate in the world, averaging almost 9 percent annually over that time span. That trend prompted billions of dollars of foreign direct investment in Thailand companies, the bulk of which was in the form of loans.

Thailand's impressive economic growth came to a jarring halt in 1997, undercut by speculative investments, mismanagement, and extensive fraud on the part of business owners and corporate executives. According to one critic of Thailand's free-wheeling economic system, "cronyism, collusion, corruption, and complacency" had long been the "four modern horsemen of the apocalypse" in that economy.[1] By the late 1990s, hundreds of Thai companies faced bankruptcy, unable to pay back the loans they had secured over the previous decade. In 1999, nearly one-half of the $150 billion in outstanding loans to large Thai companies was classified as "nonperforming"—and it was estimated that $50 billion of that total would never be collected.[2]

As Thailand's financial crisis deepened, the foreign banks and other lenders that had pumped billions of dollars of debt capital into Thai companies began retaining debt-restructuring specialists in Australia, the United States, and other developed countries to help them determine how to deal best with their mounting portfolios

---

1. U. Parpart, "Restructuring East Asia: A Progress Report," *The Milken Institute Review*, Third Quarter 1999, 42.

2. *Ibid.*, 40.

of nonperforming loans. Among the major providers of these debt-restructuring services were the large international accounting firms, including Deloitte, Michael Wansley's firm.

The nature of debt-restructuring services varies significantly, but such engagements often begin with an intense study or "audit" of the given entity's accounting records. This examination is intended to uncover any evidence of embezzlement or other malfeasance by management or other parties. These engagements also commonly include an in-depth analysis of the debtor company's business model to determine whether the entity appears to be economically viable. A debt-restructuring engagement typically concludes with the engagement team developing a series of recommendations intended to help the lenders of the financially troubled company minimize their loan losses. These recommendations may involve replacing the existing management team, having the lender or lenders forgive their outstanding loans in exchange for equity interests in the given company, or liquidating the company to raise funds that can be used to repay or partially repay its outstanding loans.

Not surprisingly given their nature and purpose, debt-restructuring engagements can be rife with tension. *Business Week* noted that Thailand's financial crisis spawned "Debt Wars" in that country that pitted representatives of the large international accounting firms, such as Michael Wansley, against Thai business owners and executives.[3] Thai business owners and executives resented the probing and relentless investigations of the "farangs" (foreigners) who did not appreciate or fully understand the informal and low-key culture of the Thai business community, a culture in which "handshake" contracts were common, disagreements were considered impolite, and face-to-face confrontations were rare. Making matters worse, Thai companies were not accustomed to having their financial records and business operations scrutinized by third parties since the nation's independent audit function was still evolving and was not nearly as rigorous as in developed countries around the world.

The investigative work of debt-restructuring specialists was particularly galling to members of the wealthy Thai families that had long dominated their nation's economy. Until the late 1990s, 15 Thai families controlled networks of businesses that accounted for more than one-half of Thailand's annual gross domestic product.[4] Among these families was the Siriviriyakul family that owned the Kaset Thai Sugar Company. For centuries, these families had operated their business empires with only minimal oversight or regulation from the Thai government or other parties. Suddenly, these prominent families found themselves being forced to respond to embarrassing questions and accusations posed by a small army of foreign accountants.

In January 1999, *Business Week* interviewed the 58-year-old Wansley regarding the difficult and stressful nature of his work in Thailand. Wansley noted that the most frustrating facet of debt-restructuring engagements in Thailand was the belligerent attitude of company owners. "Once you become grossly insolvent you're not supposed to be in a position of great strength, but here they think they are."[5] In a subsequent interview, Wansley also admitted that the hostile nature of the debt-restructuring engagements caused him to sometimes question his and his subordinates' safety. That concern was not unwarranted.

As the black minivan carrying Wansley and the four employees of Kaset Thai Sugar Company rolled to a stop outside the firm's Takhli sugar mill, two men on a

3. F. Balfour, "Fixing Thailand's Debt Mess," *Business Week* (www.businessweek.com), 12 February 2001.

4. Parpart, "Restructuring East Asia," 41.

5. R. Corben, M. Clifford, and B. Einhorn, "Thailand: Bring Your Spreadsheet—and Bulletproof Vest," *Business Week* (www.businessweek.com), 29 March 1999.

motorcycle pulled up beside the vehicle. The man sitting on the rear of the motorcycle leaped off and within a matter of seconds fired eight bullets from an automatic pistol into the interior of the minivan. The bullets struck Michael Wansley in the head, killing him instantly. The four other passengers in the minivan were left unharmed as the gunman and his confederate sped away on the motorcycle.

The murder of Michael Wansley triggered outrage in Australia and the international business community. Australian government officials demanded that Thailand law enforcement authorities vigorously investigate the crime and apprehend those responsible. Eventually, six individuals would face criminal charges for Wansley's murder. These individuals included the gunman, the motorcyclist, the owner of the motorcycle, two employees of Kaset Thai Sugar Company who had allegedly been involved in the conspiracy to kill Wansley, and the owner of the Takhli sugar mill who was a member of the powerful Siriviriyakul family. This latter individual was charged with masterminding Wansley's murder.

The motorcyclist, who was arrested shortly after the incident, was convicted for his role in the crime and given a life sentence. A human resources manager of Kaset Thai Sugar and the owner of the motorcycle, a retired policeman, were convicted of conspiring to murder Wansley and received death sentences. The brother of the human resources manager, who was also a Kaset Thai Sugar employee, was convicted of conspiracy to commit murder but received a life sentence. In July 2008, the individual who allegedly shot Wansley was acquitted of that crime by a Thai court. The only witnesses who identified that individual as the gunman were two of his alleged co-conspirators; however, their testimony was dismissed by the court. The court ruled that the witnesses were not credible since they were convicted felons.

The most controversial outcome in the criminal cases emanating from Wansley's death was the acquittal of the owner of the Takhli sugar mill despite seemingly strong evidence linking him to the crime. During this individual's trial, a witness testified that the defendant had paid him approximately $1,000 to dispose of the motorcycle used in the Wansley murder. Another individual, a senior law enforcement official, revealed that the sugar mill owner had offered him $4 million in exchange for not filing charges against him in the case. Phone records introduced as evidence during the trial documented that prior to the shooting the defendant had frequent telephone conversations with the three individuals convicted of conspiring to kill Wansley.

Court testimony also revealed that shortly before his death, Michael Wansley discovered that approximately $150 million loaned to the Kaset Thai Sugar Company had been secretly transferred to small companies controlled by the sugar mill owner and other members of his family. This testimony established that the defendant had a strong motive to harm Wansley. In fact, a Kaset Thai Sugar employee testified that following Wansley's death, the sugar mill owner had told him, "It's very good the farang is dead; now we can all live comfortably."[6] Despite such evidence, the three-judge tribunal that presided over the trial handed down a "not guilty" verdict, clearing the sugar mill owner of any involvement in Wansley's murder.[7,8]

6. J. Pollard, "Death Penalty for Aussie Auditor's Killers," *The Australian* (www.theaustralian.news.com .au), 6 September 2006.

7. One of the judges initially assigned to the case had been replaced when allegations surfaced that he had been paid a large bribe by the defendant's family.

8. The Siriviriyakul family maintained control of the Kaset Thai Sugar Company following Michael Wansley's death. When the debt-restructuring plan eventually developed by Deloitte was rejected by the company's creditors, a Thai court refused to liquidate the company and instead allowed the Siriviriyakul family to continue operating it.

The six individuals who faced criminal charges stemming from the murder of Michael Wansley were not the only parties blamed for his death. A journalist suggested that Wansley's employer, Deloitte, should shoulder some of the blame for his untimely death. Deloitte officials "should have known that they were sending the locally inexperienced Wansley into a dangerous situation without taking precautions."[9] The journalist pointed out that among the major international accounting firms, Deloitte had established a reputation as a leader in risk assessment and risk management. "These days, expertise in risk assessment—on which D. T. T. [Deloitte Touche Tohmatsu] prides itself—cannot be prudently limited to financial risk."[10]

Deloitte apparently did not respond directly to such criticism. However, several years later, Keith Skinner, the chief operating officer (COO) of Deloitte Touche Tohmatsu and a close friend of Michael Wansley, agreed to be interviewed regarding Wansley's death. In that interview, Skinner indicated that Wansley's murder "has had a lasting impact" on Deloitte's operations in regions of the world that are "culturally different."[11] When asked what specific changes Deloitte had made in response to the incident, Skinner reported that Deloitte was placing a higher priority on "security" issues for professional services engagements in high-risk countries.

During this same interview, Skinner noted that Michael Wansley had not only been a well-respected professional but also an individual who was known for his extraordinary personal integrity and humanitarian efforts. In particular, Wansley had devoted considerable time to working with the International Red Cross.

Questions

1. Suppose in the future you are assigned to an audit engagement that requires you to travel to a foreign country openly hostile to the United States. Because of that hostility, you are uncomfortable with the assignment. What would you do? Before responding, identify the alternatives you have.

2. Do you believe it is appropriate for a professional services firm to ask employees to serve on engagements in which their personal safety is at risk? Defend your answer.

---

9. Parpart, "Restructuring East Asia," 39.

10. *Ibid.*

11. A. Caldwell, "Murdered Accountant's Son Welcomes Sentences," www.abc.net.au, 5 September 2006.

Republic of Somalia

Accounting has a reputation as a fairly unexciting line of work.
That won't be the case in Mogadishu.

Frank James, National Public Radio

The Horn of Africa has long played an important role in world history. Most historians believe that the large triangular peninsula that juts into the Indian Ocean along the east coast of Africa was the home of the legendary Kingdom of Punt, an important trading partner of ancient Egypt during the time of the pharaohs. Centuries later, the tribes that occupied the Horn of Africa played a pivotal role in the development of a strategic trade route linking the East and West. Those tribes patrolled the narrow mouth of the Red Sea that served as a passageway for merchant ships transporting goods to and from the Far East and Eurasia.

In modern times, the Horn of Africa has been home to the Republic of Somalia, a country that gained its independence from Italy and Great Britain in 1960. For most of the past five decades, the arid country with approximately ten million residents has been plagued by a bloody civil war. In 1991, the nation's central government collapsed, resulting in Somalia being carved up into lawless fiefdoms controlled by tribal warlords. In addition to being ravaged by civil war, Somalia has suffered greatly due to frequent military raids launched within its borders by neighboring Ethiopia and Kenya, each of which views the anarchy in Somalia as a threat to its own political and economic stability. Humanitarian organizations estimate that more than one million Somalis have been displaced by the two decades of warfare since Somalia plunged into anarchy. One-third of those Somalis who have not fled their homeland live in abject poverty without access to clean water or the most basic healthcare services.

Somalia has been in the news in recent years because of the gangs of pirates that operate from several camps along its long coastline. Following the turn of the century, these pirates began commandeering commercial ships that must skirt the coast of Somalia on their way to and from the Red Sea. The *New York Times* reported that during 2009 Somali pirates attacked 214 ships and successfully hijacked 47 of them.[1] According to the *Boston Globe*, the pirates received approximately $200 million in ransom payments from private companies and other organizations in a period of less than 15 months in 2008 and 2009. These payments were made in exchange for the release of the cargo and crews of the hijacked ships.[2]

The most pressing international concern posed by the civil unrest in Somalia has been the growing influence of the terrorist organization Al Shabaab within the country. Al Shabaab, which is closely affiliated with Al Qaeda, the terrorist group founded by Osama bin Laden, has established training bases in Somalia and actively recruits large numbers of Somali youths who have few, if any, employment opportunities. Because of Somalia's strategic importance to ocean trade routes and the Middle Eastern oil fields, the United States and other western powers have attempted to blunt the growing influence of Al Shabaab in the country.

---

1. M. McDonald, "Record Number of Somali Pirate Attacks in 2009," *New York Times* (online), 29 December 2009.

2. A. Taylor, "Pirates of Somalia," *Boston Globe* (online), 16 March 2009.

In 2004, the United Nations and the African Union, with the financial support of the United States, organized the Transitional Federal Government (TFG) for Somalia. This new governmental entity was intended to reestablish some degree of civil law and rudimentary social functions, such as an educational system, within Somalia with a long-range objective of mediating the differences among the nation's warring tribes. The bulk of the financial support for the TFG was to be provided by foreign countries and by wealthy Somalis who had fled the country and settled elsewhere, principally in Canada, Great Britain, and the United States. In the first few years following its creation, the TFG received an estimated one billion dollars of foreign aid annually from Somali expatriates and other sources.

Shortly after the TFG was created, it faced a troublesome and largely unanticipated problem. When Somalia's central government disintegrated in 1991, the nation's banking system collapsed. The absence of a banking system made it difficult for the TFG to perform some of the most basic administrative functions necessary to sustain its operations, such as purchasing equipment and supplies and distributing payroll funds. The absence of a banking system when coupled with the TFG's failure to establish reliable accounting and control functions resulted in much of the foreign aid pouring into Somalia each year being embezzled. In turn, the reports of rampant embezzlement made it increasingly difficult for the TFG to raise funds from foreign sources.

To establish financial accountability for the TFG, representatives of a UN agency were stationed in Mogadishu, the country's capital. This UN team was to provide banking and related administrative functions for the TFG. Within a short time, however, the UN withdrew those individuals due to enormous safety concerns posed by the frequent street-to-street fighting, mortar attacks, and suicide bombings within Mogadishu.

In 2009, with the TFG in dire financial straits, the UN brokered a private agreement to have an outside organization manage the TFG's financial affairs. That organization was the world's largest accounting firm, PricewaterhouseCoopers (PwC). In a brief press release issued in July 2009, a PwC spokesperson confirmed that the firm had been "appointed to hold and manage the pledged and allocated funds for institutional capacity building and development [in Somalia]."[3] Citing client confidentiality and security concerns, PwC refused to divulge any more information regarding the unusual engagement or the nature of its contract with the TFG.[4]

Additional details of PwC's contractual agreement with the TFG were eventually leaked to the press. PwC reportedly had made a commitment to station 20 professional accountants and consultants in Nairobi, Kenya, to staff the engagement. (Nairobi is located approximately 600 miles east of Mogadishu—Kenya and Somalia share a long border.) These PwC staffers were charged with developing orderly cash receipts and disbursements functions for the foreign aid funneled to the TFG each year. Before releasing funds requisitioned by a TFG agency, PwC personnel would audit the requisition and establish that the funds were to be used for a legitimate purpose. After funds were disbursed to an agency, PwC would perform postaudit procedures to ascertain whether the funds had been used for their designated purpose.

Since the PwC staff would be stationed in Nairobi, Somali nationals living in the small sector of Mogadishu controlled by the TFG would be hired and trained by the firm to perform day-to-day administrative duties. PwC apparently agreed, however, that members of the Nairobi-based engagement team would occasionally travel to Mogadishu and remain there for short periods of time.

---

3. *BBC* (online), "Somalia Appoints Accountancy Firm," 8 July 2009.
4. *Ibid.*

According to published reports, PwC was to be compensated on a commission basis for its services. The commissions earned by the firm would be equal to 2 to 4 percent of the funds that were ultimately spent for their designated purpose. Although PwC stood to earn tens of millions of dollars annually on the engagement, the firm's compensation was considerably more modest than the 10 to 14 percent commission charged by the UN agency that had previously performed similar services for the TFG.

TFG officials maintained that the services provided by PwC would help them rebuild a social and economic infrastructure for Somalia, as well as strengthen their organization's credibility around the globe. "This is a big step in reconstructing Somalia. In addition, this will enhance transparency and accountability."[5] Despite those expectations, the TFG's decision to hire PwC proved to be very controversial for both parties.

One prominent TFG critic claimed that despite public reports that the UN had brought together PwC and the TFG, the agreement between the two parties had been secretly orchestrated by Kenyan and Ethiopian government officials who were acting in the best interests of their countries, not those of Somalia.[6] This same critic also chided the TFG for choosing PwC rather than one of the other international accounting firms. "Of all the international accounting firms that your government could have hired, PwC should have been the last to be considered for the job. Take a look at how many scandals and lawsuits they have been involved in."[7] This individual then identified 10 high-profile incidents that documented PwC's recent legal troubles, including the firm's role in the Satyam fraud in India.

Several other parties provided less emotional and thus more credible critiques of the TFG's decision to retain PwC. The most common complaint involved the lack of transparency surrounding the decision by the TFG to hire PwC and its failure to publicly disclose the specific nature of PwC's responsibilities. One critic observed that since TFG officials had been involved in previous "illegal agreements," it was inappropriate for them to engage in "confidential" contracts that could provide them an opportunity to once again use foreign donations for their own personal benefit.[8] "The PwC contract will most likely generate windfalls for personal benefit [of TFG officials]. Client confidentiality is a very handy defense for any abuse of power and misappropriation of funds."[9] This same critic noted that Transparency International, a highly regarded organization committed to leading the global fight against corruption, insists that secret contracts such as the TFG–PwC agreement effectively shield corrupt governmental officials from prosecution.[10] (In 2009, Somalia topped Transparency International's list of the most corrupt nations worldwide.)

Certain parties also questioned the judgment of PwC in accepting the Somalia engagement. One concern voiced repeatedly was how the firm could ensure the safety of the individuals assigned to the engagement, particularly when those individuals found it necessary to travel to war-torn Mogadishu. In response to that concern, PwC officials noted that their firm had previously carried out similar but less-publicized engagements in both Afghanistan and Sudan. On its website, PwC disclosed that the individuals who had been assigned to the Sudanese engagement

---

5. *Somalialand Times* (online), "Somalia Hires UK Accountancy Firm," 11 July 2009.

6. *Hiiraan* (online), "There Is No Circular Logic in Honesty," 21 January 2010. (Note: *Hiiraan* is an online Somali news and information service.)

7. *Ibid.*

8. M. M. Uluso, "PwC's Contract Empowers 'The Smartest Guys in the Room,'" *Somaliatalk.com*, 2 August 2009.

9. *Ibid.*

10. *Ibid.*

had been required to participate in a survivalist program known by the acronym THREAT—The Hostile Region Environment Awareness Training. No doubt, the firm required the staff assigned to the Somalia engagement to undergo similar training.[11]

EPILOGUE

Throughout the latter half of 2009 and beyond, Somalia continued to be plagued by violence that often resulted in significant casualties for the TFG militia, Al Shabaab–trained and –financed guerillas, and innocent civilians. Charges of government corruption also continued unabated following the retention of PwC by the TFG. In early 2010, the UN and U.S. government began quarreling over the issue of foreign aid for Somalia. According to the *New York Times*, the UN was upset because U.S. government officials were stymieing the flow of foreign aid into Somalia due to "unfounded allegations" that much of the aid was being "diverted to terrorists."[12] Two weeks later, those U.S. officials referred to a report prepared by the UN's own Security Council to support those "unfounded allegations." This report indicated that as much as one-half of the foreign aid flowing into Somalia was being embezzled by various parties, including corrupt TFG officials and "radical Islamist militants."[13]

In August 2012, with the help of the UN, the TFG was replaced by the Federal Government of Somalia, a new and democratic governmental infrastructure for Somalia. Published reports indicate that PwC continues to play a key role in managing Somalia's financial affairs under the new government regime.

Questions

1. What type of professional services was PwC providing to the TFG? What professional standards apply to such engagements?

2. Do you agree that the client confidentiality rule prohibited PwC from disclosing the contractual details of the TFG engagement? Defend your answer.

3. In addition to client confidentiality, what other ethical issues or challenges did PwC's contractual relationship with TFG present for the accounting firm?

4. Identify the specific risks that the Somalia engagement posed for PwC as a firm. Do you believe that PwC properly considered and mitigated each of those risks? Explain.

---

11. Those parties who criticized PwC for accepting the lucrative Somalia engagement failed to comment on the prominent firm's involvement in important humanitarian activities around the globe. In 2008, the firm committed millions of dollars to a program to help educate Sudanese children living in refugee camps in Chad. Among the many other humanitarian activities supported by PwC is the global initiative of the Save the Children program that provides educational and healthcare services to impoverished children around the globe.

12. J. Gettleman, "U.N. Criticizes U.S. Restrictions on Aid for Somalia," *New York Times* (online), 18 February 2010.

13. J. Gettleman, "Somalia Food Aid Bypasses Needy, U.N. Study Finds," *New York Times* (online), 9 March 2010.

CASE 8.4

Republic of the Sudan

No investor should ever have to wonder whether his or her investments or retirement savings are indirectly subsidizing a terrorist haven or genocidal state.

Christopher Cox, SEC Chairman

In 1956, the Republic of the Sudan obtained its independence from Great Britain. Although unified, Sudan was effectively two countries within one. Northern Sudan, home of the nation's capital, Khartoum, was controlled by Islamic fundamentalists, while southern Sudan was controlled by Christian fundamentalists. In 1989, a military coup led by General Omar Hassan al-Bashir, leader of the National Islamic Front, overthrew Sudan's central government and took control of Khartoum. Almost immediately, the new government imposed Islamic law or *Shari'a* on southern Sudan, triggering widespread violence between the Islamic-controlled Sudanese military and rebel forces organized by Christian leaders in southern Sudan. By the early years of the twenty-first century, the primary battleground in Sudan was the large western region of the country known as Darfur.

Over the past several decades, various organizations, including the United Nations and the International Criminal Court, have documented atrocities on a massive scale that have been inflicted on the citizens of Sudan, principally residents of Darfur and southern Sudan. The *Christian Science Monitor* reported in 2008 that as many as two million Sudanese have died as a result of those atrocities, while four million other Sudanese have been displaced from their homes.[1] In June 2004, United Nations Secretary-General Kofi Annan and United States Secretary of State Colin Powell visited the war-torn country. During that visit, Annan referred to the ongoing civil war in Sudan as the worst humanitarian crisis facing the world, while Powell described the situation as a "humanitarian catastrophe."[2]

Political leaders in numerous Western countries have insisted that the Republic of the Sudan's government is responsible for the war crimes committed in Darfur and southern Sudan. Allegedly, that military dictatorship organized large bands of armed mercenaries or *janjaweed* to attack and wipe out entire villages in those regions of the country. The Sudanese government reportedly used revenues produced by the nation's large oil industry to finance this campaign of terror against its own citizens.

In recent years, governmental authorities and private interest groups across the globe have undertaken initiatives to end the widespread suffering in Sudan. Many of these efforts have involved economic sanctions intended to limit the Sudanese government's ability to finance terrorist attacks on its own citizens. In 1998, President Bill Clinton imposed an economic embargo on Sudan that effectively prevented U.S. companies from engaging in commerce with Sudanese companies or the Sudanese government. During President Clinton's administration, Sudan was also included on the U.S. State Department's list of "state sponsors of terrorism" (SSTs), a list that

---

1. J. Adams, "Renewed Sudan Violence Raises Fears of Return to Civil War," *Christian Science Monitor* (online), 16 May 2008.

2. *CNN.com*, "U.S. Circulates U.N. Resolution on Sudan," 30 June 2004.

includes such countries as Cuba, Iran, and Syria.[3] More recently, several states have passed laws requiring state employee pension funds to divest themselves of investments linked to Sudan.

In 2004, a U.S. House of Representatives committee issued a report calling for the SEC to require companies with securities listed on U.S. stock exchanges to disclose any business operations within, or other relationships with, nations identified as SSTs. The House committee maintained that such information qualified as "material information" under the far-reaching "full and fair disclosure" regulatory mandate of the SEC and thus should be disclosed to investors.

> *A company's association with sponsors of terrorism and human rights abuses, no matter how large or small, can have a material adverse effect on a public company's operations, financial condition, earnings, and stock prices, all of which can affect the value of an investment.*[4]

The SEC responded to this directive by requiring public companies to disclose any and all ties to SST countries. To promote compliance with this new policy, the SEC established the Office of Global Security Risk (OGSR) within its Division of Corporation Finance. The OGSR monitors SEC filings to ensure that SEC registrants make all appropriate SST-related disclosures.

The most controversial measure to date to help investors identify companies with links to SSTs was an Internet search tool created by the SEC in June 2007. This search tool scanned the huge number of documents filed by SEC registrants on the agency's EDGAR (electronic data gathering and retrieval system) website and tagged companies with ties to one or more SSTs. After these companies were identified, they were included on a list that was posted to a webpage on the EDGAR website. The SEC reported that the intent of this new procedure was to provide investors and other parties with direct access to company disclosures involving "past, current or anticipated future business activities in one or more of these [SST] countries."[5] In fact, such disclosures were already available to investors and other parties who wanted to search for them by utilizing the existing search tool on the EDGAR website.

Nearly one hundred companies appeared on the initial SST "blacklist" that was generated by the SEC's Internet search tool. Because of the economic embargo imposed by the U.S. on Sudan, nearly all of these companies were foreign firms that had securities listed on U.S. stock exchanges. Among the more prominent of these companies were Alcatel, Benetton, Cadbury Schweppes, Credit Suisse, Deutsche Bank, HSBC, Nokia, Reuters, Siemens, and Unilever. The SEC reported "exceptional traffic" on the SST webpage. The agency also reported that individuals who visited that webpage typically "clicked" on individual company names to access the relevant financial statement disclosures made by those companies.[6]

Within a matter of days after the SEC initiated its new disclosure policy, the companies affected by that policy began complaining bitterly to the federal agency. Executives of many of these companies insisted that it was unfair for them to be singled out by the SEC since they had only minimal operations in, or some other

---

3. According to the *Encyclopedia Britannica Online*, terrorism is the "systematic use of violence to create a general climate of fear in a population and thereby to bring about a particular political objective."

4. Steptoe & Johnson, "International Law Advisory—SEC Disclosure for Operations in Sensitive Countries," 17 May 2004 (steptoe.com/publications-3091.html).

5. Securities and Exchange Commission, "Concept Release on Mechanisms to Access Disclosures Relating to Business Activities in or with Countries Designated as State Sponsors of Terrorism," *Release Nos. 33-8860 & 34-56803*, 23 November 2007.

6. A. Rappeport, "SEC Removes Terrorism Tool Amid Backlash," *CFO.com*, 23 July 2007.

tenuous connection to, one or more SST countries. For example, a major pharmaceutical company in India, Dr. Reddy's Laboratories, admitted that it marketed several of its products in Sudan. However, the company's CEO maintained that those sales were not "viewed as material to our business or our overall revenue."[7] Despite that point of view, under the SEC's disclosure policy any sales to an SST nation qualified as "material." As a result, when such information was disclosed in an SEC registration statement, the federal agency's search tool ensured that the given company appeared on the webpage listing registrants with SST ties.

Another common complaint voiced by executives of companies appearing on the SEC's SST list was that many firms avoided being included on that list by not disclosing links to terrorist countries in documents filed with the federal agency. One such company was the large U.S.-based investment firm Berkshire Hathaway. In its 2006 annual report, Berkshire Hathaway failed to disclose that it had a large investment in PetroChina, a company with extensive business operations in Sudan. When contacted about this matter, Berkshire Hathaway officials insisted that the PetroChina investment was not material to their company's financial statements and thus did not have to be disclosed as an SST-linked investment in its SEC registration statements. In late 2007, Berkshire Hathaway announced that it had liquidated its PetroChina investment. Warren Buffett, the company's chief executive officer, reported that the PetroChina investment was sold for economic reasons and not because of pressure to do so by parties who had criticized his company for having a Sudan-related investment.[8]

Other critics of the SST disclosure policy suggested that it was inappropriate for the SEC to "single out" registrants involved in one type of questionable business activity while ignoring companies involved in a wide range of other such activities. An officer of the National Foreign Trade Council noted that, "Providing enhanced access … in this particular case is selective and ignores the fact that there are a multitude of other social and political issues that do not receive similar treatment."[9] A similar point of view was expressed by an executive of the American Bankers Association—many large international banks appeared on the SEC's SST webpage. "Some investors feel strongly about activities supporting gambling enterprises, others oppose those businesses generating excessive greenhouse gases, still other investors avoid companies that are not unionized, while others avoid companies that are unionized.… There is simply no basis for the Commission to dedicate special resources to a particular kind of taboo business activity."[10]

Finally, two top executives of the Securities Industry and Financial Markets Association maintained that the SST disclosure policy went beyond the SEC's

7. K. Datta and P. B. Jayakumar, "Dr. Reddy's in SEC List for Terrorist State Links," *Rediff India Abroad* (online), 30 June 2007.

8. In fact, Berkshire Hathaway's board of directors asked the company's shareholders to vote on whether the PetroChina investment should be sold. In presenting that proposal to the stockholders, the board indicated that it did not believe that "Berkshire should automatically divest shares of an investee because it disagrees with a specific activity of that investee" ("Shareholder Proposal Regarding Berkshire's Investment in PetroChina," www.berkshirehathaway.com/sudan.pdf). The stockholders voted not to require the board to sell the PetroChina shares by a margin of 97.5 percent to 2.5 percent.

9. W. A. Reinsch, Letter filed with the SEC in response to SEC *Release Nos. 33-8860 & 34-56803*, "Concept Release on Mechanisms to Access Disclosures Relating to Business Activities in or with Countries Designated as State Sponsors of Terrorism" (www.sec.gov) 18 January 2008.

10. S. Behram, Letter filed with the SEC in response to SEC *Release Nos. 33-8860 & 34-56803*, "Concept Release on Mechanisms to Access Disclosures Relating to Business Activities in or with Countries Designated as State Sponsors of Terrorism" (www.sec.gov) 22 January 2008.

regulatory mandate by involving the federal agency in "foreign policy and national security matters."[11] These individuals went on to raise the issue that became a focal point of the controversy surrounding the SEC's new disclosure policy. That issue was whether the SEC should be allowed to decide what information in registration statements is particularly "material" and thus should be highlighted or otherwise brought specifically to the attention of the investing public.

> *We are not aware of the SEC having previously singled out companies based on disclosures that they have made, unless those disclosures were materially misleading or otherwise violated the law. With any website tool designed to draw attention to disclosures involving activities in countries designated as State Sponsors of Terrorism, however, the SEC in effect would determine what information should concern investors. Though this kind of judgment may be well-intentioned ... it directly conflicts with the SEC's longstanding disclosure-based regulatory scheme, which is designed to elicit material information and then to let investors evaluate the disclosures for themselves.[12]*

EPILOGUE

In July 2007, five weeks after the SEC instituted its new SST disclosure policy, the federal agency yielded to vocal critics of that policy by eliminating the webpage that contained the SST blacklist. At the time, the SEC reported that it would possibly reinstitute the SST disclosure policy or an amended version of it in the future.[13]

Four months later, in November 2007, the SEC issued a "request for comment" release asking for public input regarding the issue of terrorism-linked financial disclosures. The key question raised by the SEC was whether such disclosures in SEC registration statements should be highlighted in some way on the EDGAR website. The large majority of the responses received by the SEC indicated that the federal agency should not bring special attention to such disclosures. To date, the SEC has taken no further action on this matter.

Sudan President al-Bashir bowed to intense pressure in 2005 and accepted a peace agreement brokered by international mediators. The arrangement called for a ceasefire of all hostilities, established a semiautonomous government for southern Sudan, and called for a nationwide referendum on independence for that region of the country. That referendum in January 2011 resulted in nearly 99 percent of the electorate in southern Sudan voting for secession. On 9 July 2011, the Republic of South Sudan became an independent country recognized by the United Nations.

The 2005 peace agreement and the subsequent creation of the Republic of South Sudan did not end the violence between the two dominant Sudanese factions. After South Sudan gained its independence, armed rebels from the Republic of the Sudan began launching organized attacks against military installations in that new country, particularly in South Sudan's large eastern province of Jonglei. By late 2013, this violence had claimed hundreds of lives and

---

11. D. Preston and D. Strongin, Letter filed with the SEC in response to SEC *Release Nos. 33-8860 & 34-56803*, "Concept Release on Mechanisms to Access Disclosures Relating to Business Activities in or with Countries Designated as State Sponsors of Terrorism," (www.sec.gov) 22 January 2008.

12. *Ibid.*

13. Despite closing the webpage that reported companies with links to SSTs, the SEC continues to require public companies to disclose in their SEC registration statements any relationships they have with SSTs.

delayed the planned return of millions of South Sudanese citizens who had been uprooted by the civil warfare.

In March 2009, the International Criminal Court in The Hague, Netherlands, issued an arrest warrant for President al-Bashir. That court, which is recognized by nearly 150 nations worldwide, indicted al-Bashir for a series of war crimes and crimes against humanity. The following year, the court indicted al-Bashir on charges of genocide and issued a second arrest warrant for him. The two arrest warrants were the first ever issued by the court for a national head of state. To date, al-Bashir has ignored the arrest warrants and insisted that the International Criminal Court has no jurisdiction over him.

Questions

1. Do you agree with the assertion that any and all associations that SEC registrants have with SSTs qualify as "material information" for financial reporting purposes and thus should be disclosed in their SEC filings? Are there other "sensitive" or questionable business activities that SEC registrants should be required to disclose? Defend your answers.

2. Should the SEC have the authority to highlight or bring special attention to certain disclosures made by SEC registrants? Why or why not?

3. How does the SEC define "materiality"? How does that definition differ, if at all, from the definitions of materiality included in accounting and auditing standards?

Shari'a

Live together like brothers and do business like strangers.

Arabic proverb

The surging demand for petroleum products in recent decades has produced a windfall of revenues for many oil-rich Islamic countries in the Middle East, including, among others, Kuwait, Saudi Arabia, and the United Arab Emirates. Because Islam limits the types of investments and business ventures in which the world's 1.6 billion Muslims can become involved, the Middle Eastern oil boom has resulted in the emergence of an Islamic economy that is largely distinct from the rest of the global economy.[1] In recognition of this new economy, which is the world's most rapidly growing economic sector, major business publications have established market indices devoted strictly to Islamic business enterprises. These indices include the Dow Jones Islamic Market World Index and the FTSE Global Islamic Index.

Banking ranks among the fastest-growing and most important components of the burgeoning Islamic economy. In the early 1970s, only a few small Middle Eastern banks expressly embraced the restrictive conditions imposed on business transactions and relationships by the Islamic religion and thus qualified as "Islamic" banks. Collectively, the assets of those banks totaled less than $20 million. Four decades later, approximately 300 major banks around the globe cater exclusively or primarily to devout Muslims. Those Islamic banks boast total assets of more than $1.5 trillion dollars.

Although modern Islamic finance is still in its infancy, major Islamic banks have implemented most of the high-tech banking functions and practices used by their Western counterparts. The principal Islamic banking centers are Malaysia, the Middle East, and the United Kingdom, but financial institutions throughout the world have developed aggressive marketing campaigns to attract Muslim clients. By 2013, more than two dozen banks in the United States offered financial services designed exclusively for the estimated six million Muslim-Americans.

Tenets of the Islamic religion dramatically influence the nature of banking practices within the Islamic economy. Easily the biggest difference between Islamic banking and Western banking is the prohibition against interest payments on capital within the Islamic world.

Islamic religious law or *Shari'a*[2] forbids the payment or receipt of *riba* (interest) in personal or business relationships. Islamic banks have been forced to develop unique and elaborate profit and risk-sharing contracts known as *mudarabah* to allow them to provide financial services without paying interest on their depositors' funds or charging interest to their "borrowers." As noted in a special report on Islamic finance published by the London-based *Financial Times*, "Islamic finance tries to replicate the conventional [banking] market, but in a structure that uses profits rather than interest."[3]

---

1. For example, Islam generally prohibits Muslims from being associated with companies whose lines of business involve alcoholic drinks, destructive weapons, gambling, illicit drugs, pornography, pork and pork products, and tobacco.

2. Western publications spell this term in several different ways. The most common spellings include *Shari'a, Sharia, Shari'ah,* and *Shariah.*

3. *Financial Times*, "Islamic Finance: An FT Special Report," ftalphaville.ft.com, 23 May 2007.

The literal interpretation of the term *Shari'a* in Arabic is "path to the water source." Wikipedia defines *Shari'a* as "the legal framework within which the public and private aspects of life are regulated for those living in a legal system based on Islamic principles of jurisprudence." Unlike legal codes in the United States and other Western countries, *Shari'a* is not a compendium of static laws but rather an evolving set of guiding principles and interpretations derived principally from the *Qur'an* and teachings of the Prophet Muhammad. The dynamic nature of *Shari'a* results from numerous religious opinions or *Fatwa* issued periodically by Islamic religious scholars on a wide range of contemporary issues facing Muslims.

Shari'a influences every aspect of day-to-day life in the Islamic world, including politics, family issues, personal hygiene, and business relationships. Within the Islamic economy, the term "*Shari'a* compliant" is used to refer to business practices, economic ventures, and individual transactions that have been sanctioned by Islamic religious scholars. An audit partner of Ernst & Young Global Limited recently observed that "*Shari'a* compliance is the essence of Islamic banking and finance."[4] In fact, only those banks that offer *Shari'a*-compliant financial services and products are considered to be Islamic banks.

The development of *mudarabah* and other *Shari'a*-compliant banking practices have contributed significantly to the growth of Islamic finance in recent years. Islamic banks presently account for less than 3 percent of the worldwide financial services market, but economic experts expect that market share to grow significantly in coming decades if the Islamic banking industry can overcome several major challenges that it faces. A major European financial publication has reported that "Islamic banking's long-term ambition"[5] is to become a dominant force in international financial markets. This same publication noted that among the biggest obstacles to accomplishing that goal is the "lack of uniform and consistent accounting and auditing standards"[6] within the Islamic economy.

The Islamic View of Accounting

Since the inception of the accounting profession, cultural norms have influenced the development of accounting standards within every country, including the United States. Likewise, cultural differences across countries and regions of the world have complicated recent efforts to develop a common set of international accounting standards. Nowhere have cultural nuances had a greater impact on efforts to develop uniform accounting standards than in the Islamic world. Because of its growing size and prominence, the Islamic banking industry has been the principal focus of efforts within Islamic nations to develop domestic accounting standards that cohere with *Shari'a*, or, alternatively, to modify international accounting standards to achieve the same goal.

Similar to every other aspect of Islamic life, accounting principles are considered subordinate to the dictates of *Shari'a*. As one Islamic accounting scholar has noted, "Islam accepts the fact that accounting is a social construction and itself constructs social reality but this social reality which the accounting constructs must conform to the dictates of Islamic belief."[7]

---

4. O. Ansari, "Audit & Shari'a Compliance—Issues in Islamic Banking and Finance," www.icmap.com .pk/ppt/sem_asc_khi.pps, 20 September 2008.

5. N. Dudley, "Islamic Banks Aim for the Mainstream," *Euromoney* 349 (May 1998), 113–116.

6. *Ibid.*

7. B. Maurer, "Anthropological and Accounting Knowledge in Islamic Banking and Finance: Rethinking Critical Accounts," *Journal of Royal Anthropological Institute* 8 (2002), 660.

A more blunt point of view was expressed by another Islamic scholar who suggested that accounting principles can induce behavior inconsistent with fundamental tenets of his religion. "The problem with modern corporate accounting is not a matter of just numbers but a whole philosophy. Accounting can lead to perceptions of reality.... Ultimately, what accounting tells us [is that] what makes more money is the best thing. Over time, people will become mesmerized with this infatuation and act accordingly."[8]

Auditing in the Islamic World

Either because of governmental regulations in their home countries or because of economic necessity brought on by their growing size and involvement in international commerce, most Islamic banks have their annual financial statements audited by an independent accounting firm. In addition to annual financial statement audits, Islamic banks must also have their business activities "audited" each year to determine whether they are in compliance with *Shari'a*. An accounting professor provides the following description of *Shari'a* auditing.

> *We can define Shari'a auditing as a systematic process of objectively obtaining and evaluating evidence regarding assertions about socio-economic, religious and environmental actions and events in order to ascertain the degree of correspondence between those assertions and Shari'a (Islamic law), and communicating the results to users.*[9]

There is a wide divergence in *Shari'a* auditing practices across the nearly 60 Asian and African countries that are predominantly Muslim. This variance results principally from diverse interpretations and applications of *Shari'a* within individual Islamic countries that not only ultimately determine what business practices are acceptable in those nations but also influence how *Shari'a* audits are performed. Similar to Christianity, there are numerous factions or schools of thought within Islam, each of which share certain fundamental beliefs while disagreeing, often significantly, on other facets of their religion. For example, in certain Islamic countries, the *Qur'an* tends to be interpreted literally, while in other Islamic countries the *Qur'an*'s teachings are subject to more expansive or liberal interpretations.

The most common *Shari'a* auditing "model" applied presently is prevalent in the Middle East. Under this audit model, the principal responsibility for determining whether an Islamic bank has complied with *Shari'a* rests with the institution's *Shari'a* Supervisory Board (SSB). An SSB is typically composed of a minimum of three Islamic religious scholars who are independent of the given bank. When an Islamic bank is considering new business ventures, banking practices, or other major operational changes, its SSB will be asked to determine whether the changes are acceptable under *Shari'a*. Under the conventional *Shari'a* audit model, an SSB also reviews the given bank's financial statements and underlying transactions, accounting records, business contracts, and other relationships at the conclusion of each year to determine that the institution has complied with *Shari'a* throughout that period.

Exhibit 1 presents a *Shari'a* audit or compliance report prepared by the SSB of Stehwaz Holding Company, a large Kuwaiti company that has significant investments

---

8. *Ibid.*

9. S. Ibrahim, "The Case for Islamic Auditing," *International Accountant* 41 (2008), 21, 23.

EXHIBIT 1

SHARI'A
COMPLIANCE
AUDIT REPORT
ACCOMPANYING
RECENT FINANCIAL
STATEMENTS OF
STEHWAZ HOLDING
COMPANY

Esteemed Shareholders,

According to our signed contract, we have applied the required auditing for Stehwaz Holding's achieved transactions and concluded contracts to ensure their compliance to Islamic *Shari'ah* principles, as already revealed by our submitted reviews, *Shari'ah* instructions and our decisions during the period ended 31st December, 2008.

The commitment to execute these transactions and contracts in compliance with *Shari'ah* guidelines is Stehwaz's liability, whereas our responsibility is restricted to reviewing the submitted models and agreements.

We hereby certify that all Stehwaz's activities and transactions as well as Zakat calculations were practiced in compliance with the Islamic *Shari'ah* principles and provisions, and no violations have occurred to the best of our knowledge.

Sheikh Dr. Nayef Hajaj Al Ajmi, Board Member
Sheikh Dr. Essam Khalaf Al Inizi, Board Member
Sheikh Dr. Essa Zaki Shaqra, Chairman

Source: 2008 Annual Report of Stehwaz Holding Company

in Islamic financial institutions.[10] Stehwaz's annual report in which this *Shari'a* report was included was very comparable in terms of content and appearance to an annual report of a large U.S. company. For example, Stehwaz's annual report contained a standard set of financial statements—prepared in accordance with International Financial Reporting Standards (IFRS) rather than U.S. GAAP, an accompanying set of detailed financial statement footnotes, and traditional "front matter" including a letter to the company's shareholders from Stehwaz's chairman of the board.

An unqualified audit opinion issued by a Kuwaiti chartered accounting firm preceded Stehwaz's financial statements in the company's annual report. Stehwaz's audit report was comparable to unqualified audit reports issued in the United States with one principal exception—the report indicated that the audit had been performed in accordance with International Standards of Auditing (ISAs). Stehwaz's audit report did not explicitly address the question of whether the company had complied with *Shari'a* during the year under audit. Nevertheless, *Shari'a* compliance is an important issue for independent auditors of Islamic banks and other Islamic entities to consider, whether or not they address that issue explicitly in their audit reports. Because violations of *Shari'a* could have serious financial consequences for an Islamic company, independent auditors in the Islamic economy must consider that possibility in designing and carrying out audit engagements.

A second but less common *Shari'a* audit model results in the financial statement audit report shown in Exhibit 2. That exhibit presents the independent audit report issued by Ernst & Young on recent financial statements of Al Baraka Banking Group, a large international bank based in the Kingdom of Bahrain. Notice in this report that Ernst & Young's audit opinion includes an assertion that the bank's financial statements are in compliance with "*Shari'a* Rules and Principles" as determined by the bank's *Shari'a* Supervisory Board.

---

10. Notice the reference to *zakat* in Exhibit 1. *Zakat* is one of the Five Pillars of Islam, that is, the five specific duties of devout Muslims. Under *Shari'a*, individual Muslims and Muslim businesses are required to contribute a certain percentage of their wealth each year to individuals less fortunate than themselves.

REPORT ON CONSOLIDATED FINANCIAL STATEMENTS

We have audited the accompanying consolidated financial statements of Al Baraka Banking Group B.S.C. ("the Bank") and its subsidiaries ("the Group") which comprise the consolidated statement of financial position as at 31 December 2012 and the consolidated statements of income, cash flows, changes in owners' equity and changes in off-balance sheet equity of investment accountholders for the year then ended, comprising a summary of significant accounting policies and other explanation information.

Board of Directors' and Management's Responsibility for the Consolidated Financial Statements

The Board of Directors and the management are responsible for the preparation and fair presentation of these consolidated financial statements in accordance with the Financial Accounting Standards issued by the Accounting and Auditing Organisation for Islamic Financial Institutions and for such internal control as the Board of Directors and the management determine is necessary to enable the preparation of consolidated financial statements that are free from material misstatement, whether due to fraud or error. In addition, the Board of Directors and the management are responsible for the Group's undertaking to operate in accordance with Islamic Shari'a rules and principles.

Auditor's Responsibility

Our responsibility is to express an opinion on these consolidated financial statements based on our audit. We conducted our audit in accordance with both the Auditing Standards for Islamic Financial Institutions and International Standards of Auditing. Those Standards require that we comply with relevant ethical requirements and plan and perform the audit to obtain reasonable assurance whether the consolidated financial statements are free from material misstatement.

An audit involves performing procedures to obtain audit evidence about the amounts and disclosures in the consolidated financial statements. The procedures selected depend upon our judgment, including the assessment of the risks of material misstatement of the consolidated financial statements, whether due to fraud or error. In making those risk assessments, we consider internal control relevant to the entity's preparation and fair presentation of the consolidated financial statements in order to design audit procedures that are appropriate in the circumstances, but not for the purpose of expressing an opinion on the effectiveness of the entity's internal control. An audit also includes evaluating the appropriateness of accounting policies used and the reasonableness of accounting estimates made by the Board of Directors and management, as well as evaluating the overall presentation of the consolidated financial statements.

We believe that the audit evidence we have obtained is sufficient and appropriate to provide a basis for our audit opinion.

Opinion

In our opinion, the consolidated financial statements present fairly, in all material respects, the financial position of the Group as at 31 December 2012, and its financial performance and cash flows for the year then ended in accordance with Financial Accounting Standards issued by the Accounting and Auditing Organisation for Islamic Financial Institutions.

EXHIBIT 2

ERNST & YOUNG AUDIT REPORT ON 2012 FINANCIAL STATEMENTS OF AL BARAKA BANKING GROUP B.S.C.

(continued)

EXHIBIT 2—
continued

ERNST & YOUNG
AUDIT REPORT ON
RECENT FINANCIAL
STATEMENTS OF AL
BARAKA BANKING
GROUP B.S.C.

REPORT ON OTHER REGULATORY REQUIREMENTS

As required by the Bahrain Commercial Companies Law and the Central Bank of Bahrain (CBB) Rule Book (Volume 2), we report that:

a. the Bank has maintained proper accounting records and the consolidated financial statements are in agreement therewith; and
b. the financial information contained in the Report of the Board of Directors is consistent with the consolidated financial statements.

We are not aware of any violations of the Bahrain Commercial Companies Law, the Central Bank of Bahrain and Financial Institutions Law, the CBB Rule Book (Volume 2 and applicable provisions of Volume 6) and CBB directives, regulations and associated resolutions, rules and procedures of the Bahrain Bourse or the terms of the Bank's memorandum and articles of association during the year ended 31 December 2012 that might have had a material effect on the business of the Bank or on its financial position. Satisfactory explanations and information have been provided to us by management in response to all our requests. The Bank has also complied with the Islamic Shari'a Rules and Principles as determined by the Shari'a Supervisory Board of the Group.

Ernst & Young
20 February 2013
Manama, Kingdom of Bahrain

Source: 2012 Annual Report of Al Baraka Banking Group B.S.C.

In addition to approving new business ventures, banking practices, or other major operational changes, Al Baraka Banking Group's SSB also periodically reviews or "audits" the bank's compliance with *Shari'a*. Under this *Shari'a* audit model, the *Shari'a*-related procedures performed during an entity's independent audit effectively provide a second layer of assurance that the given entity has complied with relevant Islamic religious principles during the year under audit.

The principal *Shari'a*-related procedures integrated into a financial statement audit under this second *Shari'a* audit model are performed by one or more Islamic religious scholars independent of the given audit client. These scholars are retained by the client's accounting firm. If an accounting firm does not have *Shari'a* scholars on its professional staff—which most firms do not—then the firm will retain the services of one or more such scholars on an engagement-by-engagement basis.

Just because an Islamic bank fails to issue a separate *Shari'a* audit report does not mean that the bank's independent auditors will necessarily refer to the issue of *Shari'a* compliance in their audit report on the bank's annual financial statements. Consider Arab National Bank, a large Islamic bank headquartered in Riyadh, Saudi Arabia. Although Arab National Bank has an internal *Shari'a* compliance function, the only reference to *Shari'a* compliance in a recent annual report released by the company was a brief narrative statement included in the letter to stockholders by the bank's chairman. That statement assured the bank's stockholders that all necessary procedures had been taken during the year in question to ensure that the institution complied with *Shari'a*. There was no indication in the bank's annual report of the degree of involvement, if any, of the entity's independent auditors in the *Shari'a* compliance audit.

Enhancing the Uniformity of *Shari'a* Auditing

The wide disparity in *Shari'a* auditing practices has become an increasingly controversial issue within the Islamic economy in recent years. KPMG, a leading supplier of professional accounting and auditing services for Islamic banks, reported in 2009 that there was a need for *Shari'a* compliance audits to be "standardized" since they were highly "subjective" and applied on a "case-by-case basis."[11] Many parties have suggested that the most effective way to accomplish this objective would be to establish a rule-making body that issues authoritative *Shari'a* auditing standards for all Islamic banks and other Islamic businesses. But the lack of consensus in interpreting and applying *Shari'a* across Islamic countries has so far prevented that goal from being accomplished.

To date, the most comprehensive effort to develop a body of consistent standards for *Shari'a* audits has been undertaken by the Accounting and Auditing Organization for Islamic Financial Institutions (AAOIFI). The AAOIFI was founded in 1991 in Bahrain by a cartel of large Islamic banks. By 2013, approximately 200 Islamic banks in 45 countries and other prominent business organizations, including major international accounting firms, were sponsoring members of the AAOIFI.

The AAOIFI employs approximately 20 Islamic religious scholars who review new transactions, contracts, and business structures being considered by Islamic banks. Periodically, the AAOIFI issues "*Shari'a* standards" to be used by SSBs and other parties, such as independent auditors, involved in the *Shari'a* compliance function of Islamic banks. *Shari'a* standards issued by the AAOIFI address a wide range of business transactions and circumstances that are impacted by Islamic religious tenets such as insurance contracting, currency trading, and debt collection. These standards are intended to enhance the consistency of *Shari'a* compliance decisions across the Islamic banking industry. The AAOIFI also has a staff of professional accountants who monitor emerging accounting and independent auditing issues. When deemed appropriate, the AAOIFI releases "best practices" accounting and independent auditing standards for Islamic banks.

By 2013, the AAOIFI had issued 45 *Shari'a* standards, 26 accounting standards, and 5 independent auditing standards. These standards are either mandatory or used as the principal regulatory framework by Islamic banks in Bahrain, Dubai, Jordan, Lebanon, Malaysia, Qatar, Saudi Arabia, Singapore, South Africa, Sudan, and Syria. In other Islamic countries, the AAOIFI's standards are consulted on a regular basis by religious scholars, accountants, and independent auditors of Islamic banks.[12]

Many Islamic academics have suggested that *Shari'a* compliance audits and financial statement audits should be merged. This proposal would leave intact SSBs and

---

11. KPMG.com, "Supporting the Global Islamic Finance Industry's Aspirations," 2009.

12. The AAOIFI is the most prominent standard-setting body for the accounting profession within the Islamic global economy. In 2009, officials of the IASB announced that they would be meeting with the AAOIFI to begin a dialogue regarding the possibility of converging or harmonizing IFRS and AAOIFI accounting standards. Presently, most Islamic countries apply IFRS modified to reflect the unique requirements or features of Islamic business. However, within the banking sector of the Islamic economy, financial institutions domiciled in the same country do not necessarily use the same subset or variation of IFRS. In terms of financial statement auditing, International Standards of Auditing (ISAs) are used extensively in the Islamic world. Many Islamic countries have formally adopted ISAs, while in other Islamic countries the relevant government agency has informally endorsed the use of those standards. In countries that embrace the AAOIFI's auditing standards, such as Bahrain, independent auditors jointly apply the two sets of auditing standards.

other oversight bodies that are charged with making initial decisions on which economic ventures, contracts, transactions, and other business practices are *Shari'a* compliant. However, the responsibility for recurring periodic audits of *Shari'a* compliance by Islamic banks and other Islamic businesses would be delegated to professionally trained *Shari'a* auditors.

An Islamic academic who supports this proposal suggests that the effectiveness of the *Shari'a* compliance function is being undercut by the lack of formal training in auditing concepts and auditing methodologies on the part of the religious scholars principally responsible for that function. "While members of the *Shari'a* Supervisory Boards are preeminently qualified for their role of issuing *Fatwa* on the *Shari'a* permissibility of a financial product, they are not qualified auditors because they are not trained in the collecting and evaluating of evidence."[13, 14]

This problem could be eliminated, according to the Islamic academic, by developing a "new breed" of Islamic accountants and auditors. "What is required is a new breed of Islamic accountants and auditors who would have both a Western accounting qualification and possibly a degree or certification in *Shari'a*."[15] To accomplish this goal, the scholar suggests that intervention by the Organization of Islamic Cooperation (OIC) may be necessary.

The OIC is an organization sponsored by 57 Islamic countries that represents Islamic interests at the United Nations and other global tribunals. Because of its important position in the Islamic world and its financial resources, the OIC may be the only Islamic organization that could eventually persuade differing factions of the Islamic faith to adhere to a common body of *Shari'a* compliance standards, such as those issued by the AAOIFI. The OIC would also likely have the authority and ability to sponsor or oversee a certification program to train accountants capable of performing joint financial statement and *Shari'a* compliance audits.

The Big Four: Gaining Access to the Islamic World

A spokesperson for KPMG recently acknowledged that auditors of Islamic banks require a unique skill set. "It has become evident that the role of the external auditor to Islamic financial institutions requires a different skill set and experience to that possessed by some accounting organizations today."[16] Because of their international credibility and extensive resources, KPMG and the other Big Four accounting firms are well suited to develop accountants who have the skills necessary to perform joint financial statement and *Shari'a* audits.

In recent years, each of the Big Four firms has established an economic beachhead in the Islamic economy. In 2008, KPMG International issued a marketing brochure entitled *Islamic Finance Credentials* that identified the wide range of professional services the firm could offer Islamic banks. According to that brochure, "KPMG was one of the first accountancy organizations to meet the needs of Islamic financial institutions across national boundaries and we continue to be one of the industry's top

---

13. Ibrahim, "The Case for Islamic Auditing," 25.

14. Another complicating factor is the lack of consensus within the Islamic world on exactly who qualifies as a "religious scholar" and is thus qualified to be involved in the *Shari'a* compliance function for Islamic banks and other organizations. Individuals recognized as religious scholars in one Islamic country may not necessarily be recognized as such in other Islamic nations.

15. Ibrahim, "The Case for Islamic Auditing," 25.

16. KPMG International, *Islamic Finance Credentials* (New York: KPMG International, 2008), 2.

international advisors."[17] At approximately the same time, PricewaterhouseCoopers (PwC) made a similar bid to attract clients in the Islamic banking sector.[18]

Both Ernst & Young and Deloitte also claim to be leading providers of professional accounting, auditing, and consulting services to the Islamic finance sector. In late 2007, Deloitte became the first of the Big Four firms to appoint an Islamic religious scholar to its Middle Eastern professional staff. In commenting on this appointment, a Deloitte partner observed that "We hope by this to create a gap big enough to make it difficult [for the other Big Four firms] to compete."[19]

An Ernst & Young partner downplayed the significance of Deloitte's hiring of an Islamic religious scholar. "We have good relationships with a number of scholars and a sound understanding of major *Shari'a* issues. There are variances of opinion among the scholars and, accordingly, the selection of scholars is particular to every organization."[20] In a subsequent press release, Ernst & Young "one-upped" Deloitte by announcing that it was the first of the Big Four firms to actually begin offering *Shari'a* audit services.

> *Ernst & Young was the first professional services firm to establish a dedicated team to service clients in this [Islamic finance] industry and is the only professional services firm to offer Shari'a auditing.... We have an unshakeable belief in the future of Islamic Finance.... As a reflection of the changing needs of the industry, we currently offer more services in more markets and more industry segments in the Islamic financial services industry than any other professional services firm.[21]*

In 2013, Ernst & Young made further inroads into the rapidly developing market for *Shari'a* audit services when it signed an exclusive agreement with the AAOIFI. Under the terms of this agreement, Ernst & Young would be working with the AAOFI to develop new *Shari'a* certification standards for "core banking systems" used by Islamic banks.[22] To exploit this new credential, Ernst & Young announced that it was launching a new advisory service to assist Islamic banks in developing *Shari'a*-compliant core banking systems.

Questions

1. Identify specific financial statement auditing concepts and procedures that could be applied in determining whether an Islamic bank has been *Shari'a* compliant during a given financial reporting period. Would these concepts and procedures be applied differently in *Shari'a* compliance audits compared to conventional financial statement audits? Explain.

2. Do you believe that the proposal to merge *Shari'a* compliance audits with financial statement audits is feasible? Defend your answer.

---

17. *Ibid.*, 4.

18. PricewaterhouseCoopers, "Middle East Region: Industries—Islamic Banking & Takaful," www.pwc.com, September 2008.

19. *Islamic Finance News* (online), "Deloitte 'First' with Shariah Scholar Post: Appoints Mufti Hassan Kaleem," 28 November 2007.

20. *Ibid.*

21. Ernst & Young, "Islamic Financial Services Group," http://www.ey.com/EM/en/Services/Advisory/Advisory_IFSG-Overview, September 2008.

22. L. Murshid, "Ernst & Young Signs Exclusive Agreement with Global Standard Setting Body to Assist in *Shari'a* Certification," www.zawya.com, 5 March 2013.

3. Do you agree with the assertion that "accounting can lead to perceptions of reality"? Why or why not? In deciding whether to adopt a proposed accounting standard, should accounting rule-making bodies consider whether that standard might induce socially irresponsible behavior on the part of economic decision-makers? Defend your answer.

4. Identify the key challenges that the Big Four firms will likely face in their efforts to establish a major presence in the Islamic banking industry.

Mohamed Salem El-Hadad, Internal Auditor

The world is moved along, not only by the mighty shoves of its heroes,
but also by the aggregate of the tiny pushes by each honest worker.

Helen Keller

In 1976, Mohamed El-Hadad earned an undergraduate accounting degree in his native Egypt. Before he began his accounting career, El-Hadad completed his compulsory service in the Egyptian military forces. El-Hadad accepted an entry-level position with a large hotel in Alexandria after being honorably discharged from the military in 1979. Two years later, El-Hadad immigrated to Abu Dhabi, the capital of the United Arab Emirates (UAE), after he learned that there were excellent employment opportunities for accountants in that small Middle Eastern nation.[1]

The determined young accountant soon landed a job with the UAE's Ministry of Education. For 10 years, El-Hadad worked as an auditor with that government agency. Throughout his tenure with the Ministry of Education, El-Hadad regularly received excellent performance appraisals from his superiors.

While on a vacation in the United States in 1992, El-Hadad visited the UAE's embassy in Washington, D.C. During that visit, he became acquainted with the embassy's cultural attaché and the deputy cultural attaché. The cultural attaché was impressed with El-Hadad and his employment history and encouraged him to apply for an open auditing position with the embassy. The position involved "the audit and review of all expenditures and accounting methods of the cultural attaché and the educational expenditures for UAE students in the United States, and reconciliation of all bank accounts."[2] The job would require El-Hadad to supervise eight other accountants. El-Hadad's immediate superior would be the cultural attaché.

El-Hadad was excited by the new job opportunity and the possibility of relocating to the United States. When he returned to the UAE, he informed his superiors in the Ministry of Education of his interest in the Washington, D.C., job. They encouraged him to apply for the position and gave him excellent personal references that were forwarded to the cultural attaché of the UAE's Washington, D.C., embassy. Among other complimentary remarks, the recommendations indicated that El-Hadad "was an exemplary employee who displayed seriousness and integrity."

In January 1993, El-Hadad accepted the supervisory audit position in Washington, D.C. El-Hadad enjoyed his new job and the relationships he developed with his superiors, his subordinates, and the remainder of the embassy staff. He was certain that the increased scope of responsibilities he assumed in the new position would help him develop professionally. El-Hadad also realized that the cultural, educational,

---

1. Approximately 95 percent of UAE's workforce is made up of foreign nationals. For decades, the small, oil-rich country has actively encouraged immigration of foreign nationals to bolster its rapidly growing economy.

2. This and all subsequent quotes were taken from the following source: *Mohamed Salem El-Hadad v. The Embassy of the United Arab Emirates, et al.*, Civil Action No. 96-1943 (RWR), United States District Court for the District of Columbia, 2006. Much of the background information included in this case was drawn from other legal transcripts and news reports.

and recreational opportunities offered by the dynamic Washington, D.C., metropolitan area would be beneficial for himself and his family.

Reluctance and Regret

Unfortunately, within a matter of months, El-Hadad's American "adventure" turned bittersweet. During the performance of routine audit procedures in April 1993, El-Hadad discovered a secret bank account being used by the embassy. Upon further investigation, he determined that his new boss and friend, the embassy's cultural attaché, was maintaining the account with the assistance of the deputy cultural attaché and the embassy's chief accountant. He also determined that the three individuals were diverting UAE government funds into the secret account.

One method used by the conspirators to embezzle funds involved healthcare payments made by embassy employees. The embassy provided healthcare coverage for its employees but not for employee dependents. If an employee elected to have dependents covered by the embassy's healthcare plan, the employee was required to pay the monthly premiums directly to the embassy. The conspirators deposited these payments into the secret bank account and then used UAE government funds to pay the healthcare premiums for employees' dependents. In fact, the monthly amounts that El-Hadad paid to the embassy to provide healthcare coverage for his wife and children were included in the funds diverted into the secret bank account.

Another method used by the conspirators to misappropriate UAE government funds involved tuition refunds that the embassy received from a large number of U.S. universities. The UAE government had established an educational program that paid the college tuition of UAE citizens who chose to attend a U.S. university. The UAE embassy made these tuition payments directly to the given U.S. universities. Not unlike other college students, UAE students frequently dropped courses early in the semester for various reasons. The resulting tuition refunds remitted to the UAE embassy were funneled into the secret bank account discovered by El-Hadad.

Despite harboring feelings of reluctance and regret, El-Hadad knew that he had to "blow the whistle" and report the embezzlement scheme orchestrated by his boss and friend. Instead of informing top officials in the UAE embassy, El-Hadad chose to pass the information to a government official in the Ministry of Education, the agency for which he had worked the past 10 years. This individual in turn notified UAE's Minister of Finance. The Minister of Finance promptly contacted El-Hadad to question him about the scheme and then traveled to the United States to discuss the matter with him in person. The Minister of Finance then sent a team of auditors from his agency to carry out a comprehensive and secret investigation of the fraud. This team of auditors discovered two additional secret bank accounts used by the conspirators and determined that the three individuals had stolen at least $2 million. In early 1994, the cultural attaché, his deputy, and the embassy's chief accountant were fired. Three other embassy employees who were aware of the embezzlement scheme were also dismissed.

Prior to learning that El-Hadad had uncovered his embezzlement scheme, the embassy's cultural attaché completed his annual performance appraisal of El-Hadad for 1993. The cultural attaché indicated that El-Hadad was an "excellent employee" and gave him 99 out of a possible 100 points on the scale used for the performance appraisal. El-Hadad received a similar performance appraisal near the end of 1994 by the embassy's new cultural attaché. The new cultural attaché recommended that he be promoted, receive a salary increase, and a merit bonus for his excellent work. During 1994, El-Hadad also received plaudits from numerous UAE government officials, most notably the Minister of Finance, for his role in uncovering the embezzlement scheme.

Retribution and Recriminations

Not surprisingly, the Minister of Finance, the new cultural attaché, and several other UAE government officials were stunned in late 1995 when the UAE State Audit Division announced that Mohamed El-Hadad had been involved in the embezzlement scheme that he had reported. The State Audit Division, a government agency that provides audit services for other UAE government agencies, reported that El-Hadad had received several improper payments from the conspirators who had maintained the three secret bank accounts. These improper payments included compensation for overtime that he had not worked, expense reimbursements to which he was not entitled, and payment of healthcare premiums for his family.

The State Audit Division investigation that culminated in the charges being filed against El-Hadad had been initiated by another government agency, the Ministry of Higher Education and Scientific Research (HESR). Officials in the latter agency had been embarrassed when the embezzlement scheme at the UAE's Washington, D.C., embassy was publicly revealed in early 1994 since it involved an educational program that fell under the purview of their agency. These same officials also reportedly had an ongoing feud throughout 1994 and beyond with the embassy's new cultural attaché, who was a staunch supporter and ally of El-Hadad. Following the startling announcement that El-Hadad had been involved in the embezzlement scheme, a top official of the HESR Ministry traveled to the Washington, D.C., embassy and personally told several of El-Hadad's coworkers that he was dishonest and a poor employee.

In early 1996, the UAE cultural attaché capitulated to relentless pressure from government officials in Abu Dhabi and fired El-Hadad for his alleged role in the embezzlement scheme. El-Hadad, who had consistently and vehemently insisted that he was innocent of the charges, immediately appealed his dismissal. While his case was being reviewed, El-Hadad secured an entry-level auditing job for the UAE's military attaché in the Washington, D.C., embassy. When the HESR Minister learned of El-Hadad's new job, he notified government officials in Abu Dhabi. Within a matter of days, El-Hadad was fired once more.

In late 1996, El-Hadad's appeal of his dismissal from the supervisory audit position with the UAE embassy was denied. His appeal was denied despite several prominent individuals interceding on his behalf with the appellate tribunal. Among the individuals who wrote letters testifying to El-Hadad's work ethic and integrity were the cultural attaché who had been pressured to fire him, the UAE Minister of Finance, and the U.S. Ambassador to the UAE who was well acquainted with El-Hadad. Despite this impressive show of support for the Egyptian accountant, the appellate tribunal ruled that because El-Hadad's involvement in the fraudulent scheme had been well documented, his dismissal had been justified. The documents used to corroborate his role in the fraud had been provided by the Ministry of HESR.

Throughout the remainder of 1996 and much of 1997, El-Hadad searched for employment as an auditor or accountant in the Washington, D.C., area. Each time that he applied for a job, however, the prospective employer contacted the UAE embassy and learned that El-Hadad had been terminated because of his role in an embezzlement scheme. Economic necessity forced El-Hadad to return with his family to his native Egypt in late 1997 and seek employment there. Similar to his experience in

Washington, D.C., each time that he applied for an accounting or auditing position, the prospective employer learned of his past history and refused to consider him any further.

Frustrated and disheartened, El-Hadad eventually realized that his career in auditing, a career that he had loved and a career to which he had devoted nearly two decades of his life, was over. El-Hadad then decided to pursue a new livelihood. For several years, he sold cosmetics through a small business that he organized. But in 2003 that business failed and El-Hadad was forced to rely on family members for economic support.

Redemption

Prior to leaving the United States in 1997, El-Hadad had retained an attorney to file a lawsuit against the UAE's Washington, D.C., embassy. In this lawsuit, El-Hadad alleged that the embassy had wrongfully terminated him, that he had been defamed, and that his accounting career had been destroyed. Attorneys for the UAE attempted to have El-Hadad's lawsuit dismissed due to the concept of sovereign immunity. This concept generally prohibits criminal or civil lawsuits from being filed in U.S. courts against foreign embassies in the United States. However, the U.S. federal law that dictates the nature and scope of sovereign immunity, the Foreign Sovereign Immunities Act, includes an exception for lawsuits related to "commercial activity." Because the U.S. District Court in which El-Hadad filed his lawsuit ruled that his work as an auditor for the UAE embassy had qualified as "commercial activity," the federal court refused to dismiss the lawsuit.

During El-Hadad's civil trial in July 2001, his attorneys addressed one by one the allegations of dishonesty that had been filed against him by the UAE State Audit Division. The attorneys presented to the court the documents that had been used as the basis for those allegations and easily established that they had been forged. The attorneys also presented other documents and evidence that had been submitted to the State Audit Division during its investigation of El-Hadad, which clearly demonstrated he had not been involved in any way in the embezzlement scheme. For whatever reason, the State Audit Division had ignored that exculpatory evidence. El-Hadad's attorneys went on to prove that not only had he not been involved in the fraud, he had been known for being scrupulously honest while employed by the UAE embassy. For example, evidence presented by his attorneys demonstrated that when filing for expense reimbursements, El-Hadad had understated the amounts to which he was entitled to reimbursement.

The federal judge who presided over El-Hadad's civil trial agreed with his attorneys that he had had been victimized by false and "trumped-up" charges intended to discredit him. The federal judge also ruled that El-Hadad had been defamed by his former employer and that the defamation had ended his career as an accountant and auditor. At the conclusion of the trial, the UAE was ordered to pay El-Hadad $1.25 million for lost wages, $500,000 of damages related to the defamation he had suffered, and accrued interest on both amounts since the date of his termination in 1996.

The UAE's attorneys refused to accept the court's verdict and filed repeated appeals to have it overturned. At each level of the federal court system, the appeals filed by those attorneys regarding major issues central to the case were rejected. In 2007, the verdict was appealed to the U.S. Supreme Court. When the Supreme Court refused to review the case, Mohamed El-Hadad could finally claim victory. At last report, the UAE had yet to pay El-Hadad the more than $2 million that it owes him.

Questions

1. Identify and briefly describe the legal protections that "whistleblowers" have in the United States.

2. Should U.S. companies integrate legal protections for internal whistleblowers into their internal control systems? Defend your answer.

3. Suppose that during your career you discover a fraud similar to that uncovered by Mohamed El-Hadad. List specific measures that you could take to protect yourself from recriminations by your employer or other parties.

4. Did El-Hadad face an ethical or moral dilemma when he discovered the fraud being perpetrated by his superior and friend? Before responding, define "ethical dilemma" and "moral dilemma."

Tae Kwang Vina

During the 1970s, the public accounting profession eliminated its bans on competitive bidding, advertising, direct solicitation, and related practices that the Federal Trade Commission maintained were restraints of trade. The decision to drop those restrictions contributed to the increasingly competitive nature of the market for independent audits over the following decades. That escalating competition was manifested by a rapid increase in the rate of auditor changes by public companies, "lowballing" on the part of certain accounting firms to obtain new clients, and stagnant or declining audit fees.

By the late 1990s, many leading accountants suggested that the independent audit "product" was diminishing in value. The American Institute of Certified Public Accountants (AICPA) concurred with that point of view in an article that appeared in its monthly newsletter. To counter the declining value of independent audits, the AICPA recommended that accounting firms begin developing and marketing other services.

> The audit—the CPA profession's core assurance product—has been declining in value over the past few years, becoming a less marketable product. In fact, revenues from traditional accounting and auditing services have been flat for the past seven years.... Where challenges exist, however, opportunities abound ... [nontraditional] assurance services provide a lucrative opportunity to expand [accounting] practices. CPAs are singularly qualified as independent assurance providers to furnish businesses and their customers with the certainty they need to compete in today's marketplace.[1]

To identify new professional services that accountants could begin providing, the AICPA created the Assurance Services Special Committee that was chaired by Robert Elliott, a senior audit partner with KPMG. Elliott's committee recommended a wide range of new services that accounting practitioners could market. Specific examples of such services included the following: ascertaining the quality of home healthcare providers and assisted living (nursing home) facilities, identifying security breaches of Internet-linked information systems, and helping companies and other organizations identify and manage the economic risks they faced. The AICPA believed that these and other nontraditional services would provide accounting firms an opportunity to significantly increase their revenues while at the same time enhancing their stature and reputation within the business community.

Among the boldest initiatives taken by the AICPA in the late 1990s to expand the product line of services offered by CPAs was a proposal to create a new professional designation for accountants. This new credential would be awarded to individuals who passed a rigorous examination to demonstrate that they qualified as "multidisciplinary business advisers and strategic thinkers."[2] The AICPA believed this new professional designation would help existing CPAs strengthen their credibility as general

---

1. American Institute of Certified Public Accountants, "Assurance Services: Transforming the Quality of Information," *The CPA Letter* (online), May 2001.

2. American Institute of Certified Public Accountants, "Internet Portal, Broad-Based Global Credential Discussed at Regional Council Meetings," *The CPA Letter* (online), May 2000.

business consultants and thereby allow them to gain a larger share of the rapidly expanding market for business consulting services worldwide.

Throughout the 1990s and into the new century, the major international accounting firms began offering an extended product line of nontraditional services. These firms invested heavily in advertising programs and other promotional activities to market these new services. However, as these firms attempted to develop new markets and encroach on existing markets served by other professionals, they encountered unexpected challenges and problems.

Nontraditional professional services marketed by the major accounting firms during the 1990s included "environmental and labor practices audits." These engagements were not financial statement audits but rather examinations intended to determine whether a given company, organization, or specific production facility was complying with state and federal laws, industry rules and regulations, and other predetermined criteria relevant to environmental issues and labor practices.

The accounting profession's dominant firms recognized that there was a growing demand for environmental and labor practices audits and similar engagements during the 1990s. This demand sprang from a social activism movement targeting high-profile companies in the United States that allegedly operated, or purchased goods from, "sweatshops" in foreign countries. Ernst & Young and PricewaterhouseCoopers (PwC) were the most prolific providers of environmental and labor practices audits within the accounting profession. In 1998 alone, PwC performed 1,500 such audits in China's Guangdong province, that nation's industrial epicenter.[3]

Wikipedia defines a sweatshop as a "working environment with very difficult or dangerous conditions, usually where the workers have few rights or ways to address the situation." These conditions may include "exposure to harmful materials, hazardous situations, extreme temperatures, or abuse from employers." Social activists claimed that many large U.S. companies were maximizing their profits by using sweatshops in third-world countries to minimize the production cost of the merchandise they sold.

In 1996, Walmart was blindsided by a firestorm of unfavorable media attention ignited by a social activist organization. This organization revealed that Walmart's popular line of Kathie Lee Gifford apparel was being manufactured under sweatshop conditions in the Central American nation of Honduras. Over the following several years, many other U.S. companies would face similar charges. The company targeted more than any other by the anti-sweatshop activists was Nike, Inc., the world's largest producer of athletic shoes.

Nike's critics insisted that the working conditions in the company's Far Eastern production facilities were harsh, hazardous, and in violation of the given countries' labor laws. Those production facilities were located principally in China, Indonesia, Taiwan, and Vietnam. The company was also berated for paying multimillion-dollar endorsement fees to sports celebrities such as Michael Jordan and Tiger Woods while factory workers in its foreign production facilities received weekly wages of $10 or even less for working upwards of 60 hours.

In early 1997, threats of congressional investigations and consumer boycotts persuaded Nike to hire Andrew Young, a former U.S. Congressman and leading civil rights advocate, to inspect production facilities in countries where the company's products were being manufactured. After visiting several of those factories, Young submitted a written report to Nike's board in which he indicated that the workers in those facilities were being treated well. To garner public support and quell its critics,

---

3. *The Economist*, "Business Ethics: Sweatshop Wars," 27 February 1999, 62.

Nike included favorable comments excerpted from Young's report in full-page ads that it purchased in several major metropolitan newspapers.

Andrew Young's report failed to placate Nike's critics. The company's detractors claimed that Young's visits had been brief and less than rigorous and that he was not qualified to assess the working conditions in the given facilities.

The next measure Nike took to silence its critics was to retain Ernst & Young to perform an environmental and labor practices audit of one of its major Far Eastern production facilities. The facility chosen for that audit was a Vietnamese factory operated by Tae Kwang Vina Industrial Company, Limited, one of Nike's largest manufacturing contractors. That factory, Nike's newest and most modern production facility in the Far East, employed 9,200 workers and produced 400,000 pairs of athletic shoes each month. During the 1990s, U.S. companies that outsourced production operations to Vietnam were responsible for much of that nation's impressive economic growth. In fact, by the late 1990s, Nike's Vietnamese factories accounted for more than 5 percent of that country's gross domestic product.

In the spring of 1997, Ernst & Young submitted a 10-page report to Nike management summarizing the principal findings of its Tae Kwang Vina audit. Only a brief excerpt from that confidential report was released to the press. That brief excerpt suggested that Ernst & Young's overall conclusion regarding the working conditions at the Tae Kwang Vina site was consistent with the conclusion reached by Andrew Young.

The excerpt from the Ernst & Young report provided to the press also indicated that the Tae Kwang Vina facility was complying with Nike's code of conduct. Among many other stipulations, that code required Nike's "business partners" to pay no less than the minimum wage mandated in a given country, to fully compensate workers for overtime hours, and to provide a safe working environment for those workers.

Ernst & Young's conclusion that the Tae Kwang Vina factory was operating in compliance with Nike's code of conduct infuriated the company's critics. In November 1997, several months after Ernst & Young submitted its final report to Nike, one of those critics obtained a copy of the complete report and turned it over to the *New York Times*.

Ernst & Young's 10-page report painted a much different picture of the working conditions at the Tae Kwang Vina facility than the brief excerpt initially provided to the press. The full Ernst & Young report documented numerous abusive labor practices and hazardous working conditions at the site. The *New York Times* disclosed some of the more deplorable working conditions that the accounting firm had found at the factory.

> *Ernst & Young wrote that workers at the factory near Ho Chi Minh City were exposed to carcinogens that exceeded local legal standards by 177 times in parts of the plant and that 77 percent of the employees suffered from respiratory problems. The report also said that employees at the site ... were forced to work 65 hours a week, more than Vietnamese law allows, for $10 per week.[4]*

Other improper practices or incidents reported by Ernst & Young included inadequate ventilation systems, excessive noise levels and temperatures within the factory, insufficient safety equipment, inadequate training for employees required to work with dangerous chemicals, failure to provide workers with sufficient water, refusal to pay wages owed to employees after they were terminated, and mistreatment of workers by supervisors.

---

4. S. Greenhouse, "Nike Shoe Plant in Vietnam is Called Unsafe for Workers," *New York Times* (online), 8 November 1997.

The release of the complete Ernst & Young report to the press provoked an angry public outcry against Nike. In response, the company initially insisted that the problems identified in the report had been largely remedied over the more than six months that had elapsed since Ernst & Young completed its audit of the Tae Kwang Vina facility. That assertion was met with disbelief and ridicule by the company's critics. Several of those critics banded together and filed a lawsuit against Nike that charged the company with intentionally misrepresenting the working conditions within its foreign production facilities.

Ironically, the release of the full Ernst & Young report also resulted in heated criticism of the prominent accounting firm. Although Ernst & Young's report disclosed serious problems at the Tae Kwang Vina factory, a subsequent investigation by Dara O'Rourke, a consultant to the United Nations and a leader of the anti-sweatshop movement, revealed that the facility's working conditions were much worse than reported by Ernst & Young.

O'Rourke suggested that the Ernst & Young personnel involved in the Tae Kwang Vina engagement did not have the necessary qualifications and training to perform environmental and labor practices audits, which had resulted in the engagement being seriously flawed. Alleged deficiencies in Ernst & Young's Tae Kwang Vina engagement included, among others, relying heavily on the factory's management and other secondary sources for the information collected during the engagement, failing to properly test air quality and other working conditions in the factory, and failing to ensure that employees questioned during the engagement were free to respond candidly without any fear of reprisals from management.

Sweatshop activists also challenged Nike's claim that Ernst & Young performed the Tae Kwang Vina engagement as an "independent" third party. A governmental health and compliance officer for the state of California maintained that Nike's hiring of Ernst & Young to complete the Tae Kwang Vina "audit" was equivalent to "putting the fox's paid consultant in charge of the henhouse."[5] Corporate Watch, an international organization that monitors the social responsibility of multinational organizations, pointed out that rather than being independent of Nike, the Ernst & Young auditors had simply followed specific instructions given to them by Nike management in completing the Tae Kwang Vina engagement. To prove this point, the organization quoted the following statement directed to Nike by Ernst & Young it its 10-page report: "The procedures we have performed were those that you [Nike] specifically instructed us to perform. Accordingly, we make no comments as to the sufficiency of these procedures for your purposes."[6]

The Corporate Watch organization went on to suggest that accounting firms were not well suited to perform environmental and labor practices audits. "Indeed, Ernst & Young's incompetence as a social and environmental auditor, combined with Mr. O'Rourke's own findings inside the plant, present a strong argument against using accounting firms to conduct labor and environmental audits."[7] This latter opinion was seconded by the *New York Times*, which called for companies such as Nike to use "truly independent monitors" to complete such engagements.[8]

---

5. D. Rourke, "Vietnam: Smoke from a Hired Gun," November 1997, www.corpwatch.org/article.php?id=966%20.

6. *Ibid.*

7. *Ibid.*

8. *Ibid.*

EPILOGUE

In 2003, the U.S. Supreme Court agreed to hear arguments in the lawsuit filed against Nike that charged the company with falsely denying that it used foreign sweatshops to produce the merchandise that it sold. However, the case was ultimately settled out of court when Nike agreed to pay $1.5 million to help monitor and improve factory working conditions in third-world countries. In 2005, Nike published a self-study of the working conditions in 700 factories scattered around the world that manufactured the merchandise it sold. The report documented that "widespread problems" still existed within those factories.[9] Nike executives pledged to work with social activist groups to resolve those problems.

In a nationwide vote in late 2001, the rank-and-file members of the AICPA rejected the proposal to create a new professional designation to recognize expertise in the field of general business consulting. Several months later, the U.S. Congress passed the Sarbanes–Oxley Act of 2002 in response to the massive losses imposed on investors by the Enron and WorldCom scandals. That statute included a wide range of reforms intended to strengthen independent audits. The Sarbanes–Oxley Act served not only to enhance the perceived importance of the independent audit function in the United States but also refocused the attention of the major accounting firms on the "independent audit product." Thanks largely to the Sarbanes–Oxley reforms, the audit fees charged to public companies by the major accounting firms rose dramatically over the following several years.

Questions

1. Define each of the following types of professional services: consulting services, attestation services, agreed-upon procedures engagements, and assurance services. Explain how, if at all, these services overlap.

2. Visit the websites of the major international accounting firms. Identify nontraditional services currently marketed by these firms. List several of these services and briefly describe their nature. Of the services you identified, are there any that you believe accounting firms should not provide? If so, explain.

3. On what types of engagements must CPAs be "independent"? Identify types of engagements on which CPAs are not required to be independent. What other traits should CPAs possess on professional services engagements?

9. *The Guardian* (online), "Nike Acknowledges Massive Labor Exploitation in its Overseas Markets," 14 April 2005.

INDEX

A

AA Capital Equity Fund, 175, 177–181
AA Capital Partners, Inc., 175–183
  embezzlement scheme, 179–180
  Ernst & Young, 175–182
  generally accepted auditing
    standards, 180–181
  Internal Revenue Service, 177
  John Orecchio, 175, 179–180
  Paul Oliver, 175
  Securities and Exchange Commission
    investigation of, 175–182
ABC News, 143
ABN AMRO, 175
Abu Dhabi, 523
Accountants/accounting. *See also*
  specific accountants
  of Accuhealth, Inc., 361–365
  Arvel Smart, 351–352
  Avis Love, 421–423
  Bill DeBurger, 409–411
  Bud Carriker, 441–445
  Charles Tollison, 425–427
  of Creve Couer Pizza, Inc., 335–337
  David Quinn, 353–356
  of Dell, Inc., 357–360
  Elizabeth Wallace, 469–473
  ethical responsibilities of, 333–368
  of F&C International, Inc., 339–342
  Frank Coleman, 475–479
  of Freescale Semiconductor, Inc.,
    345–348
  Hamilton Wong, 413–415
  Islamic, 512–518
  Leigh Ann Walker, 407–408
  Olivia Thomas, 481–487
  Sarah Russell, 437–439
  Suzette Washington, 343–344
  Tommy O'Connell, 417–420
  of Wichita Falls, 367–368
  Wiley Jackson, 349–350
Accounting and Auditing Enforcement
  Release, 180, 262, 275, 284,
  318, 330
  No. 2238, 51
  No. 3033, 243
Accounting and Auditing Organization
  for Islamic Financial Institutions
  (AAOIFI), 517
Accounting and Auditing Practice
  Manual, 432
Accounting Principles Board (APB), 5
Accounting schemes, 94–97
Accounting Today, 19, 195

ACCT 201, 353
Accuhealth, Inc., 361–365
  financial statements of, 362–363
  history of, 361–362
  Securities and Exchange
    Commission, 362–365
  William Makadok, 363–364
Acosta, Fernando, 95
Adderall, 471
Adelphia Communications, 51, 189
Adidas, 40
Adjustable rate mortgages (ARMs), 149
"Adults Only" game rating, 231
Advanced Micro Devices, Inc. (AMD),
  357–358
Aerosmith, 135
African Union, 502
Akroyd, Dan, 108
Akst, Daniel, 118
Alabama Securities Commission, 44
Al Baraka Banking Group, 514–516
Al-Bashir, Omar Hassan, 505, 508–509
Alberta Securities Commission, 271
Alcatel, 506
Alcoa, 330
Alfa Group, 390–393
Allen, Craig, 426
Allen, Kyle, 265, 267–268
Allen-MacGregor, Jacquelyn, 294
Allenwood Federal Prison Camp, 81
Allied/Federated Department
  Stores, 73
Allied Forces, 317
Allstate, 347
Al Qaeda, 501
Al Shabaab, 501–504
Altamesa Manufacturing Company,
  417–419
Amazon.com, 83–85
Amerada Hess, 396
American Airlines, 372
American Asiatic Underwriters, 377.
  See also American International
  Group, Inc.
American Bankers Association, 507
American Continental Corporation
  (ACC), 93–94, 98–99, 101,
  103–104
American Express, 84, 86
American Family Publishing, 147
American Image Awards, 80
American Institute of Accountants, 456
American Institute of Certified Public
  Accountants (AICPA), 168, 171,
  456, 527, 531

Audit and Accounting Guide—
  Construction Contracts, 227
Code of Professional Conduct, 67
Tae Kwang Vina Industrial
  Company, Limited, 527
American International Group, Inc.
  (AIG), 377–380
  Cornelius Vander Starr, 377
  Ernst & Young, 378–379
  generally accepted accounting
    principles, 378–379
  Maurice "Hank" Greenberg, 377
  PNC Financial Services Group, Inc.,
    378–379
  Securities and Exchange
    Commission investigation of, 379
  special purpose entities used by,
    377–378
American Law Institute, 460
Anarchy, 501
Andersen, Arthur Edward, 3–5, 21
Andersen, Christopher E.,
  190–191, 195
Andersen, Delany & Company, 3
Andersen, John and Mary, 3–5
Anderson, Fletcher, 340–342
Annan, Kofi, 505
Antar, Eddie, 107–115
Antar, Sam E., 109, 114–115
AOL, 83
Aquino, Jennifer, 179
Arab National Bank, 516
Aramony, William, 293–294, 297
Arezzo, Eli, 481–487
"Arnie's Army," 223
Arthur Andersen & Co., 89
  Enron Corporation, 3–5, 8–9, 14–16,
    18–20, 155, 228
  Federal Bureau of Investigation, 98
  Leslie Fay Companies, 77–78
  Lincoln Savings and Loan
    Association, 97–103
  Michael Sullivan, 225–228
  Securities and Exchange
    Commission investigation of, 365
  United Way of America, 296–297
Arthur Young & Company, 97–102,
  104, 395–396
Asics-Tiger, 47
Associated Press, 168
Assurance Services Special
  Committee, 527
Atchison, Jack, 98–100
Athletic Attic, 41
AT&T, 208

SUMMARY OF TOPICS BY CASE

The following index lists the auditing-related topics addressed directly or indirectly in each case included in **Contemporary Auditing: Real Issues and Cases, Tenth Edition**. Those topics followed by the letter "Q" are the subject of a case question.

Enron Corporation, Case 1.1, 3–22

1. "Scope of services" issue facing audit firms (Q)
2. Involvement of auditors in client accounting and financial reporting decisions (Q)
3. Preparation and retention of audit workpapers (Q)
4. Recent "crisis of confidence" facing the public accounting profession (Q)
5. Recommendations to strengthen the independent audit function (Q)
6. Evolution of concept of "professionalism" in public accounting discipline over past several decades (Q)
7. Auditors' responsibilities regarding a client's quarterly financial statements (Q)
8. History of public accounting profession in the United States
9. Roles and responsibilities of key regulatory and rule-making bodies in the public accounting profession
10. Corporate culture as a key determinant of an audit client's control environment
11. Criminal liability faced by auditors and audit firms

Lehman Brothers Holdings, Inc., Case 1.2, 23–38

1. Involvement of auditors in the development of a client's new accounting policy (Q)
2. Responsibility of auditors to approve/review a new client accounting policy (Q)
3. Does "intent matter" in the application and/or development of accounting policies? (Q)
4. Auditors' consideration of whether specific client transactions are "accounting-motivated" (Q)
5. Allocation of responsibility for different facets of a multinational audit (Q)
6. Auditors' responsibility for client financial data external to the audited financial statements (Q)
7. Materiality assessments by auditors (Q)
8. Responsibility of auditors to investigate whistleblower allegations (Q)
9. Factors influencing auditors' legal liability in state vs. federal courts (Q)
10. Auditor consideration of whether a client's application of GAAP resulted in materially misleading financial statements
11. Responsibility of auditors to ascertain which financial statement elements are of primary concern to financial statement users
12. Auditor communications with client audit committee
13. Substance over form concept in financial reporting

Just for FEET, Inc., Case 1.3, 39–52

1. Use of analytical procedures to identify high-risk financial statement items (Q)
2. Identifying internal control risk factors (Q)
3. Impact of control risk factors on audit planning decisions (Q)
4. Identifying inherent risk factors (Q)
5. Impact of inherent risk factors on audit planning decisions (Q)
6. Identifying the most critical audit risk factors for a given audit engagement (Q)
7. Resolution of ethical dilemma faced by a corporate executive (Q)
8. Need to consider economic health of client's industry in audit planning decisions
9. Nature, purpose, and importance of accounts receivable confirmation procedures
10. Role of the SEC in policing financial reporting domain and independent audit function
11. Importance of investigating unusual and/or suspicious client transactions

Health Management, Inc., Case 1.4, 53–70

1. Problems posed by relationships between client personnel and auditors (Q)
2. Audit-related implications of a job offer made by a client to one of its auditors during the course of an audit (Q)
3. Performance of inventory rollback and rollforward procedures (Q)
4. Weighing the cost of an audit procedure against the quantity and quality of audit evidence it yields (Q)
5. Documenting audit test results in audit workpapers (Q)
6. Identifying "red flag" fraud risk factors and determining their impact on each phase of an audit (Q)
7. Auditors' responsibilities for discovering and reporting illegal acts by clients (Q)

8. Historical overview of class-action lawsuits and their impact on public accounting firms
9. Impact of PSLRA of 1995 on auditors' legal exposure under the Securities Exchange Act of 1934
10. Proportionate vs. joint and several liability for auditors
11. Resolution of proposed audit adjustments
12. Nature of GAAS and the responsibilities they impose on auditors
13. Definition of "recklessness" and its implications for auditors' legal exposure under the Securities Exchange Act of 1934

The Leslie Fay Companies, Case 1.5, 71–82

1. Use of analytical procedures to identify high-risk financial statement items (Q)
2. Financial information needed for audit planning decisions (Q)
3. Nonfinancial information needed for audit planning decisions (Q)
4. Control environment issues pertinent to independent audits (Q)
5. Impact on auditor independence when clients and auditors are codefendants (Q)
6. Audit implications of important changes and developing trends in a client's industry
7. Identifying fraud risk factors and determining their impact on each phase of an audit

NextCard, Inc., Case 1.6, 83–92

1. Auditors' consideration of a client's business model (Q)
2. Identifying fraud risk factors (Q)
3. Objectives of audit workpapers (Q)
4. Identifying violations of generally accepted auditing standards (Q)
5. Responsibility of audit partners to serve as mentors for their subordinates (Q)
6. Ethical responsibilities of an auditor who is instructed to violate professional standards by his or her superior (Q)
7. Criminal liability of auditors
8. Impact of Sarbanes–Oxley Act on accounting profession

Lincoln Savings and Loan Association, Case 1.7, 93–106

1. Substance-over-form concept in accounting and its audit implications (Q)
2. Threats to auditor independence (Q)
3. Audit implications of related-party transactions (Q)
4. Assessment of a client's control environment (Q)
5. Determining when gains resulting from the disposition of assets can be recognized (Q)
6. Identification of key management assertions (Q)
7. Audit evidence needed to support management assertions (Q)
8. Identifying appropriate audit procedures to collect desired types of audit evidence (Q)
9. Potential audit impact of personal relationships between auditors and client personnel (Q)
10. Collegial responsibilities of auditors (Q)
11. Auditors' responsibility for detection of fraud (Q)
12. Societal role of independent auditor
13. SEC's oversight role for the independent audit function

Crazy Eddie, Inc., Case 1.8, 107–116

1. Use of financial ratios and other financial measures to identify high-risk financial statement items (Q)
2. Audit procedures used to detect fraudulent misstatements of inventory, accounts payable, and sales (Q)
3. Effect of important changes in a client's industry on audit planning decisions (Q)
4. Potential impact of "lowballing" on the quality of audit services (Q)
5. Objective of year-end inventory cutoff tests (Q)
6. Implications for the independent audit function of audit clients hiring former auditors (Q)
7. Impact of collusion among client executives and employees on auditors' ability to detect fraudulent misrepresentations in a client's accounting records
8. Importance of assessing the integrity of client management
9. Incentive for companies to retain large audit firms when going public

ZZZZ Best Company, Inc., Case 1.9, 117–130

1. Key differences between audits and review engagements (Q)
2. Identification of key management assertions (Q)
3. Audit evidence needed to support management assertions (Q)
4. Identifying appropriate audit procedures to collect desired types of audit evidence (Q)

5. Limitations of audit evidence (Q)
6. Predecessor–successor auditor communications (Q)
7. Auditors' responsibility for a client's earnings press release (Q)
8. Client-imposed restrictions on the scope of an audit (Q)
9. Content of an audit engagement letter
10. SEC's 8-K auditor change disclosure rules

DHB Industries, Inc., Case 1.10, 131–146

1. Identifying material amounts in financial statement data (Q)
2. Identifying fraud risk factors (Q)
3. Auditors' responsibility when client cannot produce critical audit evidence (Q)
4. Auditors' responsibility to search for related-party transactions (Q)
5. Internal control reporting responsibilities of client management and auditors (Q)
6. Impact of auditor changes on audit quality (Q)
7. Professional standards and other rules and regulations relevant to auditor changes (Q)
8. Dealing with hostile audit clients (Q)
9. Responsibility of the SEC and auditors to protect investors (Q)
10. Primary responsibilities of public company audit committees (Q)
11. Disclosure of material internal control weaknesses

New Century Financial Corporation, Case 1.11, 147–164

1. Advantages and disadvantages of having a heavy concentration of audit clients in one industry (Q)
2. Quality control considerations for independent audits (Q)
3. Section 404 of the Sarbanes–Oxley Act (Q)
4. Auditors' responsibility to discover and report significant deficiencies and material weaknesses in internal controls (Q)
5. Auditing accounting estimates (Q)
6. Violations of generally accepted auditing standards (Q)
7. Mark-to-market rule for securities investments (Q)
8. Potential impairment of auditor independence
9. Impact of auditor–client conflicts on audit engagements
10. Audit implications of accounting changes
11. Auditor review of quarterly financial statements
12. Recall of an audit opinion

Madoff Securities, Case 1.12, 165–174

1. Audit procedures applied to client investments (Q)
2. Nature and purpose of peer reviews (Q)
3. Fraud triangle (Q)
4. Common fraud risk factors (Q)
5. Regulatory reforms necessary to improve auditors' fraud detection capabilities (Q)
6. Impairment of auditor independence
7. Criminal liability faced by auditors
8. Civil liability faced by auditors
9. Societal role of independent audit function
10. SEC's regulatory mandate

AA Capital Partners, Inc., Case 1.13, 175–184

1. Factors that contribute to mistakes made by auditors (Q)
2. Quality control measures for audit firms (Q)
3. Circumstances in which auditors may choose not to rely on client internal controls (Q)
4. Responsibility of auditors to search for related parties (Q)
5. Objectives of subsequent period audit tests (Q)
6. Division of responsibilities on an audit engagement team (Q)
7. Auditors' responsibility when client cannot produce critical audit evidence
8. Ensuring proper communication between/among audit team members
9. Planning of audit engagements
10. Reliance on client representations as audit evidence
11. SEC's definition of "reckless" and "negligent" auditor conduct

Navistar International Corporation, Case 1.14, 185–198

1. Advantages and disadvantages of mandatory audit firm rotation (Q)
2. Auditor rotation rules in effect in United States (Q)
3. "Material weaknesses" vs. "significant deficiencies" in internal control (Q)
4. Involvement of auditors in clients' accounting function (Q)
5. Establishment and application of materiality thresholds by auditors (Q)
6. Quality control responsibilities of audit partners and audit firms (Q)
7. Key factors that influence the "culture" of an audit firm (Q)
8. Regulatory role and responsibilities of the PCAOB (Q)
9. Audit firms' legal liability in civil cases

Livent, Inc., Case 1.15, 199–212

1. Identification of inherent risk factors (Q)
2. Role and responsibilities of audit partners (Q)
3. Client attitudes toward auditors (Q)
4. Reports prepared by accounting firms on the application of accounting principles by nonaudit clients (Q)
5. Revenue recognition issues (Q)
6. Responsibility of accountants to investigate potential misrepresentations in their employers' accounting records (Q)
7. Potential conflicts of interest faced by auditors who accept accounting positions with former clients (Q)
8. Accounting firms' responsibilities in due diligence investigations (Q)
9. Forensic investigations by accounting firms
10. Identifying "red flags" indicative of financial statement fraud
11. Audit firms' legal exposure under the Securities Exchange Act of 1934

Jack Greenberg, Inc., Case 2.1, 215–222

1. Audit risk factors commonly posed by family-owned businesses (Q)
2. Key audit objectives for inventory (Q)
3. Quality of audit evidence yielded by internal versus external documents (Q)
4. Nature and purpose of a walk-through audit procedure (Q)
5. Auditors' responsibility to inform client management of significant internal control weaknesses (Q)
6. Whether or not auditors have a responsibility to insist that client management correct significant internal control deficiencies (Q)
7. Segregation of duties concept and its impact on a client's internal controls
8. Need for auditors to thoroughly investigate suspicious transactions and circumstances

Golden Bear Golf, Inc., Case 2.2, 223–230

1. Identifying relevant management assertions for individual financial statement items (Q)
2. Choosing appropriate audit procedures to corroborate specific management assertions (Q)
3. Meaning of the phrase "audit failure" (Q)
4. Auditors' responsibilities on "high-risk" audit engagements (Q)
5. Nature and purpose of AICPA industry accounting and audit guides (Q)
6. Changes in accounting estimates versus changes in accounting principles (Q)
7. Proper application of the percentage-of-completion accounting method
8. Need for auditors to thoroughly investigate suspicious transactions and circumstances
9. Limitations of management representations as audit evidence

Take-Two Interactive Software, Inc., Case 2.3, 231–238

1. Identifying "red flags" in client financial statements (Q)
2. Audit objectives associated with receivables confirmation procedures (Q)
2. Positive vs. negative audit confirmations (Q)
3. Alternative audit procedures for receivables selected for confirmation (Q)
4. Distinguishing between, and among, auditor negligence, recklessness, and fraud (Q)
5. Audit fee decisions (Q)
6. Potential audit impact of personal relationships between auditors and client personnel (Q)
7. Acceptance of "ethically challenged" audit clients (Q)
8. Audit procedures applied to sales returns
9. Role and responsibilities of audit engagement partners

General Motors Company, Case 2.4, 239–244

1. Audit procedures relevant to a client's pension-related financial statement amounts (Q)
2. Circumstances under which auditors should obtain outside experts (Q)
3. Auditors' responsibility to thoroughly investigate questionable accounting decisions made by client (Q)
4. Auditors' materiality assessments (Q)
5. Auditing accounting estimates
6. Auditors' responsibility to consider adequacy of client's footnote disclosures

Lipper Holdings, LLC, Case 2.5, 245–252

1. Identification of fraud risk factors (Q)
2. Auditors' response to identified fraud risk factors (Q)
3. Identification of audit objectives for complex financial instruments and transactions (Q)
4. Factors that contribute to improper audit decisions (Q)
5. Quality control measures for independent audits (Q)
6. Impact of internal control weaknesses on audit planning decisions
7. Auditors' internal control reporting responsibilities
8. Audit confirmation procedures
9. Resolving inconsistencies in audit evidence

CBI Holding Company, Inc., Case 2.6, 253–258

1. Key audit objectives for accounts payable (Q)
2. Search for unrecorded liabilities and reconciliation of year-end payables balances to vendor statements (Q)
3. Differences and similarities in accounts payable and accounts receivable confirmation procedures (Q)
4. Responsibility of auditors when they identify mistakes or other oversights they made in prior-year audits (Q)
5. Client request to remove an auditor from audit engagement team (Q)
6. Considerations relevant to the acceptance of "high-risk" audit clients
7. Need to identify critical audit risk factors and consider those factors in planning an audit engagement
8. Need to thoroughly investigate suspicious transactions and circumstances identified during an audit

Geo Securities, Inc., Case 2.7, 259–264

1. Key management assertions related to contingent liabilities (Q)
2. Nature and purpose of attorneys' letters (Q)
3. Auditors' responsibility for supplemental information accompanying a client's financial statements (Q)
4. Assessing the going-concern status of an audit client (Q)
5. Accounting and financial reporting decisions for loss contingencies
6. Limitations of client representations as a form of audit evidence

Belot Enterprises, Case 2.8, 265–270

1. Negotiating with client regarding proposed audit adjustments (Q)
2. Assessing personal integrity of client personnel and auditors (Q)
3. Potential audit impact of personal relationships between auditors and client personnel (Q)
4. Principal audit objectives for a client's discretionary expense accruals (Q)
5. Conservatism principle in context of accounting estimates (Q)
6. Auditors' responsibilities when reviewing a client's interim financial statements (Q)
7. Career planning for public accountants

Powder River Petroleum International, Inc., Case 2.9, 271–280

1. Identifying audit risk factors posed by a client's business operations (Q)
2. Application of revenue recognition rule (Q)
3. Identification of key management assertions (Q)
4. Distinguishing between, and among, auditor negligence, recklessness, and fraud (Q)
5. Relying on the use of "specialists" during an audit engagement (Q)
6. PCAOB's quality control standards for public company auditors (Q)
7. Reliance on client representations as audit evidence
8. Circumstances requiring the issuance of a going-concern audit opinion
9. Proper staffing of audit engagement teams
10. Undocumented, postaudit changes in audit workpapers

LocatePlus Holdings Corporation, Case 2.10, 281–286

1. Responsibility of auditors to investigate potential client fraud (Q)
2. Purpose and nature of predecessor–successor auditor communications (Q)
3. Primary responsibilities of a "concurring" audit partner (Q)
4. Nature and purpose of a letter of representations (Q)
5. Identification of fraud risk factors during the planning phase of an audit
6. Audit confirmation procedures for receivables
7. SEC oversight of independent audit function

The Trolley Dodgers, Case 3.1, 289–290

1. Tests of controls and substantive tests for the payroll transaction cycle (Q)
2. Identifying internal control weaknesses in the payroll transaction cycle (Q)
3. Audit procedures useful in detecting payroll fraud (Q)
4. Control environment issues

Howard Street Jewelers, Inc., Case 3.2, 291–292

1. Importance of internal controls for small retail businesses (Q)
2. Responsibility of a small business's CPA when alerted to potential control problems facing the client (Q)
3. Meetings with prospective clients (Q)
4. Control environment issues

United Way of America, Case 3.3, 293–298

1. Cost-effective internal controls to limit an organization's exposure to theft losses (Q)
2. Social responsibilities of CPA firms (Q)
3. Client development activities for CPA firms (Q)
4. Audit risk factors commonly posed by not-for-profit organizations (Q)
5. Adoption of Sarbanes–Oxley internal control reforms by not-for-profit organizations

First Keystone Bank, Case 3.4, 299–302

1. Internal control procedures applied to banking operations (Q)
2. General conditions or factors influencing choice of auditing procedures (Q)
3. Auditing procedures applied to cash maintained on a client's premises (Q)
4. Auditing procedures that may uncover client embezzlement schemes (Q)
5. Impact of collusion on integrity of an organization's internal controls

Goodner Brothers, Inc., Case 3.5, 303–310

1. Identifying internal control objectives for a wholesale business (Q)
2. Identifying and remedying internal control weaknesses (Q)
3. Importance of an effective control environment for a business (Q)
4. Impact of management style and operating policies on an entity's internal controls
5. Role of internal auditors in an entity's internal control process
6. Need for auditors and client management to investigate suspicious transactions

Buranello's Ristorante, Case 3.6, 311–316

1. Identifying internal control weaknesses (Q)
2. Identifying remedial measures to eliminate or mitigate internal control weaknesses (Q)
3. Evaluating the cost-effectiveness of internal controls (Q)
4. Identifying internal control procedures for a restaurant (Q)
5. Assessing the ethical quality of management decisions (Q)
6. Integrating ethical considerations into internal control policies and procedures (Q)

Foamex International, Inc., Case 3.7, 317–320

1. Ultimate responsibility for an organization's internal controls (Q)
2. Auditors' responsibility to identify client's internal control weaknesses (Q)
3. Auditors' communication responsibilities for internal control weaknesses (Q)
4. Differences in auditor responsibilities for public versus private clients (Q)
5. Conditions under which public companies can dismiss their auditors (Q)
6. Conditions under which auditors may resign as the auditor of a public company (Q)

7. SEC disclosure requirements for auditor changes (Q)
8. Enforcement policy of SEC (Q)
9. Section 404 assessment of a client's internal controls

The Boeing Company, Case 3.8, 321–326

1. Five components of internal control according to COSO (Q)
2. Integration of whistleblowing provisions into a public company's internal controls (Q)
3. "Material weaknesses" vs. "significant deficiencies" in internal control (Q)
4. Use of "external" internal auditors by public companies (Q)
5. Communication between a company's internal auditors and its independent auditors (Q)
6. Whistleblowing provisions of Sarbanes–Oxley Act (Q)
7. Ethical issues involving the monitoring of employee communications by employers (Q)

Walmart de Mexico, Case 3.9, 327–332

1. Control activities necessary to comply with Foreign Corrupt Practices Act (Q)
2. Determining the cost-effectiveness of control activities (Q)
3. Responsibility of public company accountants when they discover illegal acts perpetrated by their employer (Q)
4. Auditors' responsibility when they discover illegal acts perpetrated by a public company client (Q)
5. Auditors' responsibility to search for violations of the Foreign Corrupt Practices Act (Q)
6. Cultural differences in business practices and ethical issues posed by such differences for accountants and auditors (Q)
7. Regulatory policies and procedures of the SEC
8. Corporate audit committee responsibilities regarding potential violations of the Foreign Corrupt Practices Act
9. Provision of FCPA consulting services by major accounting firms

Creve Couer Pizza, Inc., Case 4.1, 335–338

1. CPAs serving as the moral conscience of small business clients (Q)
2. Conflict between auditors' responsibility to the public interest and the obligations imposed on them by the client confidentiality rule (Q)
3. Resolution of ethical dilemmas by auditors (Q)
4. Privileged communications between auditors and clients (Q)

F&C International, Inc., Case 4.2, 339–342

1. Professional responsibilities of a business's financial executives and high-ranking accountants (Q)
2. Nature of the interaction between client management and independent auditors (Q)
3. Ethical responsibilities of management when they suspect subordinates are engaging in fraud (Q)
4. Need for an entity's executives and financial managers to thoroughly investigate suspicious transactions and events coming to their attention (Q)
5. Common methods used to misrepresent an entity's reported profits
6. SEC's oversight role for the accounting and financial reporting domain

Suzette Washington, Accounting Major, Case 4.3, 343–344

1. Resolution of ethical dilemma faced by an accounting student (Q)
2. Ethical responsibilities of private accountants (Q)
3. Responsibility of accountants to report unethical conduct by their colleagues (Q)
4. Internal controls for a retail business (Q)

Freescale Semiconductor, Inc., Case 4.4, 345–348

1. Exceptions to client confidentiality rule (Q)
2. Analyzing decision contexts involving the client confidentiality rule (Q)
3. Differing professional responsibilities of CPAs on consulting and audit engagements (Q)
4. Ethical challenges posed for CPAs due to their access to confidential client information
5. Negative impact on accounting profession of ethical breaches by individual professionals

Wiley Jackson, Accounting Major, Case 4.5, 349–350

1. Resolution of ethical dilemma by an accounting student (Q)
2. Disciplining of accountants who engage in unethical behavior (Q)
3. Responsibility of accountants to report unethical conduct by their colleagues (Q)

Arvel Smart, Accounting Major, Case 4.6, 351–352

1. Resolution of an ethical dilemma by an accounting student (Q)
2. Ethical issues accounting majors may face when they have multiple job offers outstanding (Q)
3. Internship opportunities available to accounting majors

David Quinn, Tax Accountant, Case 4.7, 353–356

1. Nature and purpose of the client confidentiality rule (Q)
2. Identifying violations of the client confidentiality rule (Q)
3. Resolution of disputes with fellow professionals regarding ethical issues (Q)
4. Responsibility of accountants to report unethical conduct by their colleagues (Q)

Dell, Inc., Case 4.8, 357–360

1. Definition of "earnings management" (Q)
2. Auditors' responsibility to search for instances of earnings management by clients (Q)
3. Identification of key management assertions (Q)
4. Audit procedures effective in uncovering violations of specific management assertions (Q)
5. Auditors' responsibility to monitor developments that impact a client's business model and industry (Q)
6. Ethical issues posed by aggressive client business practices (Q)
7. Full and fair disclosure responsibilities of public companies
8. Use of "cookie jar reserves" by audit clients to "smooth" reported earnings
9. Audit firms' civil legal liability

Accuhealth, Inc., Case 4.9, 361–366

1. Parties potentially affected by ethical dilemmas involving corporate accountants (Q)
2. Ethical responsibilities of corporate accountants who suspect that fraud is impacting their employer's accounting records (Q)
3. Circumstances under which independent auditors are not responsible for detecting fraud affecting a client's financial statements (Q)
4. Audit procedures effective in detecting fraudulent cash and inventory schemes (Q)
5. Critical importance of an entity's control environment (Q)
6. SEC's oversight role for accounting and financial reporting domain

Wichita Falls, Case 4.10, 367–368

1. Ethical "principles" vs. ethical "rules" included in AICPA *Code of Professional Conduct* (Q)
2. Collegial responsibilities of CPAs (Q)
3. Specific factors influencing the economic (market) values of accounting firms (Q)
4. "Succession planning" by accounting firms (Q)

Cardillo Travel Systems, Inc., Case 5.1, 371–376

1. Ethical dilemmas that accountants and auditors must resolve (Q)
2. Parties affected by the resolution of ethical dilemmas facing accountants and auditors (Q)
3. Auditors' responsibilities when reviewing a client's interim financial statements (Q)
4. Importance of communication among members of an audit engagement team (Q)
5. Key characteristics of audit evidence (Q)
6. Evaluation of conflicting audit evidence (Q)
7. SEC's 8-K auditor change disclosure rules (Q)
8. Importance of auditors' assessing the integrity of client management (Q)
9. Methods for assessing integrity of client management (Q)
10. Audit implications of significant auditor–client disputes

American International Group, Inc., Case 5.2, 377–380

1. Ethical issues related to earnings management (Q)
2. Reports on accounting matters by accounting firms to nonaudit clients (Q)
3. Potential ethical issues raised when accounting firms issue reports on accounting matters to nonaudit clients (Q)
4. Threats to auditor independence
5. "Scope of services" issue facing audit firms
6. Involvement of auditors in client accounting and financial reporting decisions

The North Face, Inc., Case 5.3, 381–388

1. Proper treatment of proposed audit adjustments that have an immaterial effect on a client's financial statements (Q)
2. Preventing client from gaining access to materiality thresholds for an audit (Q)
3. Identifying violations of the revenue recognition principle (Q)
4. Principal objectives of audit workpapers (Q)
5. Assessment of client management competence and its impact on the planning and performance of an audit (Q)
6. Role of a concurring audit partner on an SEC engagement

IPOC International Growth Fund, Ltd., Case 5.4, 389–394

1. Distinguishing between/among assurance, attestation, audit, and consulting services (Q)
2. Ethical and moral responsibilities of auditors to clients (Q)
3. Identifying factors or conditions that enhance or diminish the impropriety of specific instances of unethical conduct (Q)
4. Legal actions by accounting firms to protect their self-interests (Q)
5. Business risk posed for accounting firms when they accept high-profile professional services engagements

Phillips Petroleum Company, Case 5.5, 395–398

1. Responsibilities of auditors related to client confidentiality rule (Q)
2. Obligation of CPA firms to provide legal advice and legal support to their employees (Q)
3. Purpose of attorneys' letters (Q)
4. Quality of audit evidence provided by attorneys' letters (Q)
5. Impact on the nature and content of audit workpapers when auditors realize that third parties may gain access to them (Q)

Ryden Trucking, Inc., Case 5.6, 399–402

1. Defining what constitutes "unethical" behavior (Q)
2. Comparing and contrasting "moral" and "legal" obligations (Q)
3. Dealing with unethical behavior by employees (Q)
4. Supervisory responsibilities assumed by senior personnel assigned to auditing and accounting services engagements (Q)
5. Quality control measures relevant to the hiring of entry-level staff accountants by accounting firms

Richard Grimes, Staff Accountant, Case 5.7, 403–404

1. Proper financial statement presentation of material post–balance sheet events (Q)
2. Identifying decision alternatives when facing ethical dilemmas (Q)
3. Protecting the confidentiality of client information vs. other professional responsibilities of auditors (Q)
4. Audit implications of significant auditor–client disputes

Leigh Ann Walker, Staff Accountant, Case 6.1, 407–408

1. Need for auditors to possess personal integrity (Q)
2. Dealing with a lack of personal integrity on the part of staff accountants (Q)
3. Nature of staff accountant's work role and responsibilities

Bill DeBurger, In-Charge Accountant, Case 6.2, 409–412

1. Nature of in-charge accountant's work role and responsibilities (Q)
2. Assimilation of audit evidence to reach an overall audit conclusion (Q)
3. Resolution of conflict between members of an audit engagement team (Q)
4. Performance of major audit assignments by relatively inexperienced auditors (Q)

Hamilton Wong, In-Charge Accountant, Case 6.3, 413–416

1. Ethical issues related to the underreporting of time worked by auditors (Q)
2. Effect of underreporting time worked on quality of independent audits (Q)
3. Measures needed to mitigate the underreporting of time worked (Q)
4. Potentially dysfunctional effects of competitive promotion system within accounting firms on quality of independent audits (Q)
5. Nature of in-charge accountant's work role and responsibilities

Tommy O'Connell, Audit Senior, Case 6.4, 417–420

1. Key differences between the professional roles of audit seniors and staff accountants (Q)
2. Interpersonal conflicts between members of an audit engagement team (Q)
3. Auditor's responsibility when he or she suspects that a colleague is not completing assigned audit procedures (Q)
4. Audit partner's responsibility when a subordinate reports that a member of the audit engagement team is not completing assigned audit procedures (Q)
5. Need for public accountants to achieve a proper balance between their personal and professional lives
6. Impact of a lack of client cooperation on the performance of an audit

Avis Love, Staff Accountant, Case 6.5, 421–424

1. Parties potentially affected by ethical dilemmas facing auditors (Q)
2. Auditors' ethical obligations to third-party financial statement users (Q)
3. Auditors' responsibility to document and investigate financial misstatements revealed by audit procedures (Q)
4. Potential audit impact of personal relationships between auditors and client personnel (Q)
5. Audit objectives of year-end cash receipts and sales cutoff tests (Q)
6. Assessing materiality of financial statement errors (Q)

Charles Tollison, Audit Manager, Case 6.6, 425–428

1. Requisite skills for promotion to partner in a major accounting firm (Q)
2. Partner promotion criteria in large vs. small accounting firms (Q)
3. "Up or out" promotion policy of many accounting firms (Q)
4. Need for public accountants to achieve a proper balance between their personal and professional lives
5. Need for a public accountant to actively plan and manage his or her professional career

Ligand Pharmaceuticals, Case 7.1, 431–436

1. Engagement risk vs. audit risk (Q)
2. Factors influencing engagement risk (Q)
3. Quality control issues for public accounting firms (Q)
4. Application of the revenue recognition principle (Q)
5. Subsequent discovery of material errors in audited financial statements (Q)
6. Nature and purpose of PCAOB's regulatory mandate (Q)
7. Recent criticism of PCAOB (Q)
8. Recommendations for improving effectiveness and efficiency of PCAOB (Q)
9. Impact of Sarbanes–Oxley Act on independent audit function
10. Nature of work role and responsibilities of an audit engagement partner
11. Auditing sales returns
12. Performance appraisal within accounting firms

Sarah Russell, Staff Accountant, Case 7.2, 437–440

1. Interpersonal conflict between an employee and partner of a CPA firm (Q)
2. Responsibility of public accountants to respect personal rights of colleagues (Q)
3. Office managing partner's responsibility to protect the personal rights of his/her subordinates (Q)
4. Nature of staff accountant's work role and responsibilities

Bud Carriker, Audit Senior, Case 7.3, 441–446

1. Client management effort to influence staffing of audit engagement team (Q)
2. Racial discrimination within the auditing discipline (Q)
3. Responsibility of senior members of an audit practice office and/or audit engagement team to protect the civil rights of their subordinates (Q)
4. Resolution of an ethical dilemma by an audit partner (Q)
5. Issues relevant to staffing of audit engagement teams

Hopkins v. Price Waterhouse, Case 7.4, 447–454

1. Responsibility of public accounting firms to facilitate the career success of their female employees (Q)
2. Informal employee networks within public accounting firms and related personnel and professional implications (Q)
3. Nepotism rules of public accounting firms (Q)
4. Acceptance of female and minority public accountants by clients (Q)

6. Necessity and importance of cash confirmation audit procedures
7. Regulatory role and responsibilities of the PCAOB

Kaset Thai Sugar Company, Case 8.2, 497–500

1. Problems faced by accountants when performing independent audits and other professional services in hostile countries (Q)
2. Responsibility of accounting firms to provide for the safety of their employees (Q)
3. Impact of cultural norms and nuances on the performance of professional services engagements

Republic of Somalia, Case 8.3, 501–504

1. Differentiating between/among types of professional services engagements provided by accounting firms (Q)
2. Identifying the professional standards that apply to specific types of professional services engagements (Q)
3. Application of the client confidentiality rule (Q)
4. Ethical issues and challenges posed by high-profile and high-risk professional services engagements (Q)
5. Measures that can be taken to control or mitigate risks posed by high-profile and unusual professional services engagements (Q)
6. Problems faced by accountants when providing professional services in hostile countries
7. Responsibility of accounting firms to provide for the safety of their employees

Republic of the Sudan, Case 8.4, 505–510

1. Regulatory mandate of the SEC (Q)
2. Definition of "material information" for financial reporting purposes (Q)
3. Materiality standard applied by the SEC (Q)
4. Differences in materiality concept in accounting context vs. auditing context (Q)
5. SEC's concept of "full and fair disclosure"

Shari'a, Case 8.5, 511–520

1. Financial statement audits vs. *Shari'a* compliance audits (Q)
2. Application of compliance audit procedures (Q)
3. Merging of financial statement and *Shari'a* compliance audits (Q)
4. Socially responsible accounting standards (Q)
5. Competitive conditions faced by Big Four firms in Islamic economy (Q)
6. Lack of uniformity in *Shari'a* audit practices
7. Promulgation of professional standards in Islamic economy
8. Financial statement audit report in Islamic economy vs. *Shari'a* compliance audit report

Mohamed Salem El-Hadad, Internal Auditor, Case 8.6, 521–526

1. Legal protections afforded whistleblowers in the United States (Q)
2. Integration of whistleblowing measures into internal control systems (Q)
3. Measures that whistleblowers can use to protect themselves from recriminations (Q)
4. Responsibility of organizational insiders to report fraud (Q)
5. Ethical dilemmas vs. moral dilemmas (Q)

Tae Kwang Vina, Case 8.7, 527–532

1. Differences between/among assurance services, attestation services, agreed-upon procedures engagements, and consulting services (Q)
2. Nontraditional accounting services offered by major accounting firms (Q)
3. Professional services requiring CPAs to be independent (Q)
4. Required qualifications of CPAs on various professional services engagements (Q)
5. Commercialism within public accounting profession
6. Provision of environmental and labor practices audits by major accounting firms

SUMMARY OF CASES BY TOPIC

Analytical Procedures: Crazy Eddie, Just for FEET, Leslie Fay.
Assessment of Adequacy of Client Disclosures: AA Capital, Dell, General Motors, Geo Securities, Lehman.
Assessment of Client Management Competence: Crazy Eddie, Lincoln, North Face, ZZZZ Best.
Assessment of Client's Going-Concern Status: Geo Securities, Powder River.
Assurance Services: IPOC, Somalia, Tae Kwang Vina.
Attorney Inquiry Letter: Geo Securities, Phillips.
Audit Committees' Responsibilities: DHB, Walmart.
Audit Committees, Communication with: Foamex, Lehman, Navistar, New Century.
Audit Engagement Letter: Stern, ZZZZ Best.
Audit Evidence—General: AA Capital, Cardillo, DHB, General Motors, Geo Securities, Golden Bear, Health Management, Jack Greenberg, Lehman, Lipper, New Century, Navistar.
Audit Evidence—Limitations: AA Capital, Bill DeBurger, CBI Holding, DHB, Geo Securities, Golden Bear, Health Management, Ligand, Lincoln, Lipper, Phillips, Powder River, ZZZZ Best.
"Audit Failure": Golden Bear.
Audit Fees: Take-Two.
Audit Implications of Control Deficiencies: AA Capital, Crazy Eddie, DHB, First Securities, Goodner, Health Management, Jack Greenberg, Leslie Fay, Navistar, New Century, Take-Two, United Way.
Audit Planning Issues: AA Capital, Crazy Eddie, Dell, First Keystone, Just for FEET, Leslie Fay, Lipper, LocatePlus, Navistar, New Century, ZZZZ Best.
Audit Reports: Geo Securities, LocatePlus, Powder River.
Audit Review Process: North Face, Tommy O'Connell.
Audit Risk (and/or its components): Crazy Eddie, Jack Greenberg, Just for FEET, Leslie Fay, Lincoln, Lipper, Livent, NextCard.
Audit Sampling: Stern.
Audit Specialists, Use of: General Motors, Powder River.
Audit Staffing Issues: AA Capital, Elizabeth Wallace, Frank Coleman, LocatePlus, Navistar, New Century, Olivia Thomas, Powder River.
Audit Time Budgets/Audit Deadlines/Overtime: Charles Tollison, Elizabeth Wallace, Frank Coleman, Hamilton Wong, Olivia Thomas, Tommy O'Connell.
Audit Workpapers: Enron, Health Management, Leslie Fay, New Century, NextCard, North Face, Phillips, Powder River, Tommy O'Connell.
Auditing a Multinational Company: Livent.
Auditing Accounting Estimates: Belot, General Motors, Golden Bear, Health Management, Just for FEET, Ligand, New Century, NextCard.
Auditing Accounts Payable (and other liabilities): CBI, Crazy Eddie.
Auditing Cash: AA Capital, Accuhealth, Avis Love, First Keystone.
Auditing Contingencies: Cardillo, Geo Securities.
Auditing Contracts and Commitments: Cardillo, Creve Couer, Enron, Geo Securities, Golden Bear, Lehman, Lincoln, Powder River, ZZZZ Best.
Auditing Expense Accruals: Belot.
Auditing Investments: Lipper, Madoff.
Auditing Inventory: Accuhealth, Crazy Eddie, DHB, F&C, Goodner, Health Management, Jack Greenberg, Just for FEET, Leslie Fay.
Auditing Payroll-Related Financial Statement Items: Trolley Dodgers.
Auditing Pension-Related Financial Statement Items: General Motors.
Auditing Receivables: Health Management, Just for FEET, NextCard, Take-Two.
Auditing Revenues: Avis Love, Crazy Eddie, Golden Bear, Ligand, Lincoln, Livent, North Face, Powder River, Stern, Take-Two.
Auditor Independence: AIG, Avis Love, Belot, Crazy Eddie, Enron, Health Management, IPOC, Leslie Fay, Lincoln, Madoff, Navistar, New Century, Take-Two.
Auditor Rotation: Navistar.
Auditor–Client Interaction Issues: AA Capital, AIG, Avis Love, Belot, Bud Carriker, Cardillo, CBI, DHB, Enron, F&C, General Motors, Health Management, Howard Street, Jack Greenberg, Kaset Thai, Lincoln, Livent, Locate-Plus, Longtop, Navistar, New Century, North Face, Richard Grimes, Tommy O'Connell.
Auditors, Interaction among Audit Team Members: AA Capital, Belot, Bill DeBurger, Cardillo, Elizabeth Wallace, Hamilton Wong, Health Management, Just for FEET, Navistar, NextCard, North Face, Olivia Thomas, Tommy O'Connell.

Career Development Issues: Arvel Smart, Belot, Bill DeBurger, Bud Carriker, Charles Tollison, David Quinn, Elizabeth Wallace, Frank Coleman, Hamilton Wong, Hopkins, Leigh Ann Walker, Livent, NextCard, Olivia Thomas, Sarah Russell, Tommy O'Connell, Wiley Jackson.

Client Acceptance/Retention Issues: AA Capital, Bud Carriker, CBI, DHB, Jack Greenberg, Kaset Thai, Lincoln, LocatePlus, Longtop, Navistar, Somalia, Take-Two.

Client Confidentiality: Creve Couer, David Quinn, Freescale, IPOC, Longtop, Phillips, Richard Grimes, Somalia.

Client Development Activities: Charles Tollison, Hopkins, Howard Street, Lincoln, Shari'a, United Way.

Client Management Integrity Issues: AA Capital, Belot, Bud Carriker, Cardillo, CBI, Crazy Eddie, DHB, Enron, F&C, First Securities, Foamex, General Motors, Golden Bear, Health Management, IPOC, Jack Greenberg, Kaset Thai, Lehman, Leslie Fay, Lipper, Livent, LocatePlus, Longtop, Madoff, Navistar, New Century, NextCard, North Face, Phillips, Powder River, Richard Grimes, Somalia, Take-Two, Tommy O'Connell, ZZZZ Best.

Client Request to Change Staffing of Audit Engagement Team: Bud Carriker, CBI.

Client-Imposed Audit Scope Limitations: Health Management, Jack Greenberg, Longtop, ZZZZ Best.

Collegial Responsibilities of Auditors: AA Capital, Bill DeBurger, Bud Carriker, Charles Tollison, David Quinn, Elizabeth Wallace, Hamilton Wong, Leigh Ann Walker, Lincoln, LocatePlus, Navistar, NextCard, North Face, Olivia Thomas, Ryden, Sarah Russell, Tommy O'Connell, Wichita Falls, ZZZZ Best.

Comfort Letter/Due Diligence Engagements: Livent.

Commercialism within Public Accounting Profession: AIG, Enron, Navistar, Powder River, Shari'a, Somalia, Tae Kwang Vina.

Competition in U.S. Public Accounting Profession: Lincoln.

Compilation Engagements: Howard Street.

Compliance Audits: IPOC, Shari'a, Tae Kwang Vina.

Concurring Audit Partner: AA Capital, North Face.

Confirmation Procedures: CBI, Just for FEET, Lipper, LocatePlus, Longtop, Take-Two.

Conflict in Auditor and Consultant Roles: AIG, Enron.

Conservatism Principle: Belot, General Motors.

Control Environment: AA Capital, Accuhealth, Belot, Boeing, Cardillo, CBI, Crazy Eddie, Enron, Dell, DHB, F&C, First Securities, Foamex, General Motors, Golden Bear, Goodner, Health Management, Howard Street, IPOC, Jack Greenberg, Lehman, Leslie Fay, Lincoln, Lipper, Livent, LocatePlus, Longtop, Navistar, New Century, NextCard, North Face, Powder River, Richard Grimes, Stern, Take-Two, Trolley Dodgers, United Way, Walmart, ZZZZ Best.

Convergence of International Accounting and/or Auditing Standards: Shari'a.

CPAs in Nonaudit Roles: AIG, Creve Couer, Freescale, Health Management, Howard Street, IPOC, Kaset Thai, Livent, Ryden, Somalia, Tae Kwang Vina.

Detection, Disclosure, and Audit Implications of Illegal Acts: Enron, Health Management, Phillips, Richard Grimes, Walmart.

Disagreements/Conflict between Auditors: Bill DeBurger, Bud Carriker, Elizabeth Wallace, Hamilton Wong, Navistar, NextCard, Tommy O'Connell.

Earnings Management: AIG, Dell.

Engagement Letter: Stern, ZZZZ Best.

Engagement Risk: IPOC, Ligand.

Ethical Conduct vs. Legal Conduct: Buranello's, Lehman, Phillips, Ryden, Wichita Falls.

Ethical Dilemma (definition of): Mohamed Salem El-Hadad.

Ethical Dilemmas vs. Moral Dilemmas: IPOC, Mohamed Salem El-Hadad, Ryden.

Ethical Dilemmas, Resolution of: Accuhealth, Arvel Smart, Avis Love, Belot, Bill DeBurger, Bud Carriker, Buranello's, Cardillo, Creve Couer, David Quinn, Elizabeth Wallace, Hamilton Wong, Health Management, IPOC, Just for FEET, Leigh Ann Walker, Livent, Mohamed Salem El-Hadad, Olivia Thomas, Phillips, Richard Grimes, Ryden, Suzette Washington, Tommy O'Connell, Walmart, Wichita Falls, Wiley Jackson.

Ethical Issues Faced by U.S. Accounting Firms in International Markets: IPOC, Kaset Thai, Shari'a, Somalia, Tae Kwang Vina.

Ethical Issues Involving Accounting Majors: Arvel Smart, Suzette Washington, Wiley Jackson.

Ethical Responsibilities of Accountants in Private Industry: Accuhealth, Belot, Boeing, Cardillo, Dell, Enron, F&C, Golden Bear, Health Management, Jack Greenberg, Leslie Fay, Livent, New Century, Ryden, Suzette Washington, Trolley Dodgers.

Expert Opinions as Audit Evidence: General Motors, Lincoln, Powder River.

Foreign Corrupt Practices Act: Walmart.

Fraud Detection and/or Disclosure: AA Capital, Accuhealth, Cardillo, CBI, Crazy Eddie, DHB, Enron, First Keystone, First Securities, Golden Bear, Health Management, Jack Greenberg, Leslie Fay, Lincoln, Lipper, Livent, LocatePlus, Longtop, Madoff, New Century, NextCard, North Face, Powder River, Stern, Take-Two, United Way, ZZZZ Best.

Fraud Reporting Responsibility (by members of an organization): Cardillo, F&C, First Keystone, Livent, Mohamed Salem El-Hadad, Walmart.

"Full and Fair Disclosure" Doctrine (SEC): General Motors, Sudan.

Hiring of Auditors by Former Clients: Crazy Eddie, Health Management, Lincoln, Livent.

History of Accounting Profession/Audit Function in Nations Other Than U.S.: Shari'a.

History of U.S. Public Accounting Profession: Enron.

Identification of Fraud Risk Factors: AA Capital, DHB, Leslie Fay, Lipper, Livent, LocatePlus, NextCard.

Identification of Inherent Risk Factors: Crazy Eddie, Jack Greenberg, Just for FEET, Leslie Fay, Lipper, Livent, Longtop, Powder River, Take-Two.

Identification of Internal Control Risk Factors: AA Capital, DHB, Just for FEET, Lincoln, Lipper.

Identification of Management Assertions: Dell, Geo Securities, Golden Bear, Lincoln, Powder River, ZZZZ Best.

Impact of Cultural Norms and Values on Independent Audit Function: Longtop, Shari'a.

Internal Auditors: Boeing, First Keystone, Goodner, Mohamed Salem El-Hadad.

Internal Control Deficiencies: AA Capital, Boeing, Buranello's, DHB, First Keystone, First Securities, Foamex, Goodner, Health Management, Howard Street, Jack Greenberg, Leslie Fay, Lipper, Navistar, New Century, NextCard, Take-Two, Trolley Dodgers, United Way, Walmart.

Internal Control Objectives: Goodner, Howard Street, Mohamed Salem El-Hadad, Trolley Dodgers, United Way.

Internal Control Reporting: Boeing, DHB, First Securities, Foamex, Jack Greenberg, Lehman, Lipper, New Century, Walmart.

Internal Control, COSO Framework: Boeing.

Internal Control, Ethical Considerations: Boeing, Buranello's, Walmart.

Internal Controls for Not-for-Profits: Mohamed Salem El-Hadad, United Way.

Internal Controls for Small Businesses: Buranello's, Howard Street, Suzette Washington.

Internal Controls, Cost-Effectiveness: Buranello's, Goodner, Howard Street, United Way, Walmart.

Internal Controls, Remedial Measures: Buranello's, DHB, Foamex, Goodner, United Way, Walmart.

International Accounting Issues: Shari'a.

International Audit Reports: Shari'a.

International Auditing Practices: Longtop, Shari'a.

International Markets, Competitive Issues: Longtop, Shari'a, Tae Kwang Vina.

Issues Related to the Global Accounting Profession: Kaset Thai, Longtop, Shari'a, Somalia, Sudan, Tae Kwang Vina.

Lack of Definitive Guidelines for Client Transactions: Enron, Lehman, Livent.

Legal Liability—Common Law: First Securities, Stern.

Legal Liability—Criminal: Enron, Freescale, Madoff, NextCard, Phillips.

Legal Liability—General: Dell, First Securities, Frank Coleman, Hopkins, IPOC, Lehman, Leslie Fay, Lincoln, Lipper, Madoff, Navistar, New Century, Ryden, Somalia, Stern, Wichita Falls.

Legal Liability—1933 Act: First Securities, Stern.

Legal Liability—1934 Act: First Securities, Health Management, Livent, Stern.

Letter of Representations: Livent, LocatePlus.

"Lowballing" Phenomenon: Crazy Eddie, Tae Kwang Vina.

Materiality Issues: Avis Love, Belot, DHB, General Motors, Lehman, Navistar, New Century, North Face, Sudan.

Need to Follow Up on Suspicious or Unusual Client Transactions: AA Capital, AIG, Avis Love, Cardillo, CBI, DHB, Enron, Golden Bear, Goodner, Health Management, Jack Greenberg, Just for FEET, Lehman, Lincoln, Livent, LocatePlus, Longtop, New Century, NextCard, North Face, Powder River, Stern, ZZZZ Best.

Negligence vs. Gross Negligence: Stern.

Negligence vs. Recklessness: AA Capital, Health Management.

Negligence vs. Recklessness vs. Fraud: First Securities, Powder River, Take-Two.

Nontraditional Professional Services: AIG, Freescale, IPOC, Kaset Thai, Shari'a, Somalia, Tae Kwang Vina.

Opinion Shopping: Cardillo, DHB, Foamex, Lincoln, Livent.

PCAOB, Regulatory Role and Responsibilities: Ligand, Longtop, Navistar, Powder River.

Peer Reviews: Madoff.

Personal Integrity of Auditors: Arvel Smart, Avis Love, Belot, Bill DeBurger, Bud Carriker, Cardillo, David Quinn, Elizabeth Wallace, Enron, Freescale, Hamilton Wong, Health Management, Kaset Thai, Leigh Ann Walker, Madoff, New Century, NextCard, North Face, Phillips, Olivia Thomas, Sarah Russell, Tommy O'Connell, Wiley Jackson.

Personal Lives vs. Professional Work Roles: Avis Love, Belot, Bill DeBurger, Charles Tollison, Elizabeth Wallace, Frank Coleman, Hamilton Wong, Health Management, Hopkins, Leigh Ann Walker, Ligand, Olivia Thomas, Sarah Russell, Tommy O'Connell, Wiley Jackson.

Personnel Issues within Audit Firms: Bill DeBurger, Bud Carriker, Charles Tollison, Elizabeth Wallace, Frank Coleman, Hamilton Wong, Hopkins, Kaset Thai, Leigh Ann Walker, Ligand, New Century, NextCard, Olivia Thomas, Powder River, Sarah Russell, Tommy O'Connell.

Practice Development Issues—International Markets: Kaset Thai, Longtop, Shari'a, Somalia, Tae Kwang Vina.

Predecessor–Successor Auditor Communications: Lincoln, LocatePlus, ZZZZ Best.

Premature Signoff of Audit Procedures: New Century, Tommy O'Connell.

Privileged Communications for Auditors: Creve Couer, Phillips.

Professional Roles of Auditors: Avis Love, Belot, Bill DeBurger, Bud Carriker, Charles Tollison, Elizabeth Wallace, Enron, Frank Coleman, Hamilton Wong, Health Management, Leigh Ann Walker, Ligand, New Century, NextCard, Olivia Thomas, Sarah Russell, Tommy O'Connell.
Professional Services Engagements Requiring Independence: Tae Kwang Vina.
Professional Skepticism: AA Capital, Belot, CBI, DHB, Enron, First Securities, General Motors, Golden Bear, Health Management, Lehman, Ligand, Lipper, LocatePlus, Navistar, New Century, North Face, Powder River, Take-Two.
Professional Standards, Audits vs. Consulting Engagements: Freescale.
Proposed Audit Adjustments (Auditor–Client Negotiations): Belot, Health Management, Livent, North Face.
Quality Control Issues for Audit Firms: AA Capital, Bill DeBurger, Bud Carriker, Cardillo, CBI, Elizabeth Wallace, Freescale, Hamilton Wong, Hopkins, Leigh Ann Walker, Lehman, Ligand, Lincoln, Lipper, LocatePlus, Longtop, Navistar, New Century, NextCard, North Face, Olivia Thomas, Powder River, Ryden, Tae Kwang Vina, Tommy O'Connell.
Recklessness: Health Management.
Regulation of the U.S. Accounting Profession: Enron, Freescale, Ligand, Longtop, NextCard, North Face, Madoff, Navistar, Powder River.
Regulatory Issues Related to Global Accounting Profession: Frank Coleman, Kaset Thai, Livent, Longtop, Shari'a.
Related-Party Transactions: AA Capital, DHB, Enron, Lincoln, Livent.
Review of Client's Tax Returns: Phillips.
Review of Interim Financial Statements: Belot, Cardillo, Enron, Lehman, New Century, North Face, ZZZZ Best.
Rule-Making Processes: Navistar, Shari'a.
Sarbanes–Oxley Act of 2002: Boeing, Ligand, New Century, NextCard, United Way.
Reports on Accounting Matters (formerly SAS No. 50 Reports): AIG, Livent.
Scope of Services Issue (provision of nonaudit services by auditors): AIG, Enron.
Section 404 Engagements: Foamex, New Century.
Securities and Exchange Commission: Accuhealth, AIG, Cardillo, Crazy Eddie, Dell, DHB, Enron, F&C, First Securities, Foamex, Freescale, General Motors, Geo Securities, Health Management, Just for FEET, Leslie Fay, Lincoln, Lipper, Livent, LocatePlus, Longtop, Madoff, Navistar, New Century, NextCard, North Face, Powder River, Sudan, Take-Two, Walmart, ZZZZ Best.
SEC's 8-K Auditor Change Rules: Cardillo, DHB, Foamex, ZZZZ Best.
Societal Role of Audit Function: Enron, First Securities, Lincoln, Madoff, New Century, Stern.
Subsequent Discovery of Errors: Ligand, New Century, North Face.
Subsequent Period Audit Tests: AA Capital, Richard Grimes.
Substance-over-Form Concept: AIG, Enron, Lehman, Lincoln.
Succession Planning, Accounting Firms: Wichita Falls.
Supervision of Staff Accountants: Elizabeth Wallace, Frank Coleman, Leigh Ann Walker, Olivia Thomas, Ryden, Tommy O'Connell.
Supplementary Information Accompanying Audited Financial Statements: General Motors, Geo Securities, Lehman.
Understanding the Client's Industry/Business Model: Crazy Eddie, Enron, Jack Greenberg, Just for FEET, Lehman, Leslie Fay, Lincoln, Lipper, Livent, LocatePlus, New Century, NextCard, North Face, Powder River, ZZZZ Best.
Valuation of Accounting Firms: Wichita Falls.
Walk-through Audit Procedure: Jack Greenberg.
Whistleblowing: Boeing, Enron, Freescale, Lehman, Mohamed Salem El-Hadad.
Withdrawal of an Audit Report: CBI, Health Management, Leslie Fay, Livent, New Century.